Group Benefits

Huebner School Series   *Gary K. Stone, Editor*

Group Health Insurance
Burton T. Beam, Jr.

Readings in Financial Planning
David M. Cordell (ed.)

Fundamentals of Financial Planning
David M. Cordell (ed.)

Readings in Income Taxation
James F. Ivers III (ed.)

McGill's Life Insurance
Edward E. Graves (ed.)

McGill's Legal Aspects of Life Insurance
Edward E. Graves and Burke A. Christensen (eds.)

Group Benefits: Basic Concepts and Alternatives
Burton T. Beam, Jr.

Planning for Retirement Needs
Kenn Beam Tacchino and David A. Littell

Readings in Wealth Accumulation Planning
The American College Faculty (eds.)

Fundamentals of Estate Planning
Constance J. Fontaine (ed.)

Estate Planning Applications
Ted Kurlowicz (ed.)

Planning for Business Owners and Professionals
Ted Kurlowicz, James F. Ivers III, and John J. McFadden

Financial Planning Applications
William J. Ruckstuhl

Financial Decision Making at Retirement
David A. Littell, Kenn Beam Tacchino, and David M. Cordell

The Practitioner's Guide to Advanced Pension Topics
David A. Littell and Kenn Beam Tacchino

Executive Compensation
John J. McFadden (ed.)

Huebner School Series

Group Benefits: Basic Concepts and Alternatives

Seventh Edition

Burton T. Beam, Jr.

The American College/*Bryn Mawr, Pennsylvania*

This publication is designed to provide accurate and authoritative information about the subject covered. While every precaution has been taken in the preparation of this material, the editor and The American College assume no liability for damages resulting from the use of the information contained in this publication. The American College is not engaged in rendering legal, accounting, or other professional advice. If legal or other expert advice is required, the services of an appropriate professional should be sought.

To my mother

About the Author

Burton T. Beam, Jr., CPCU, CLU, ChFC, is director of continuing education and associate professor of insurance at The American College. Mr. Beam did his undergraduate work at the University of Oregon and holds graduate degrees from that institution and the University of Pennsylvania. Prior to joining The American College, Mr. Beam was on the faculties of the University of Florida and the University of Connecticut. He has written extensively in the area of group insurance and has had articles published in several professional journals, including *Benefits Quarterly* and the *Journal of the American Society of CLU & ChFC*. He is also coauthor of *Employee Benefits,* a textbook used at many colleges and universities. Mr. Beam is an assistant editor of the *Journal of the American Society of CLU & ChFC* and is the coauthor of the employee benefits column in that journal. He is a member of the American Risk and Insurance Association and the National Association of Health Underwriters.

Contents

Preface

The first edition of this book in 1982 was prompted by the absence in the marketplace of a single group insurance textbook that totally met the needs of students in The American College's designation programs. In preparing the first edition, several criteria were used. First, it had to be as up-to-date as possible. Second, it had to discuss the products and services for groups of all sizes, from multiple-employer welfare arrangements for the small groups to alternative-funding methods (including self-insurance) for the large groups. Third, it had to be oriented to the broad constituencies served by the designation programs rather than to just agents, home-office employees, or corporate-benefit specialists. Finally, it had to explain the decisions involved in designing an employee benefit plan and not merely describe the products available. These criteria are still being followed in the seventh edition. One change, however, is that the book now serves a broader market since the College now offers the Registered Health Underwriter (RHU) and Registered Employee Benefits Consultant (REBC) designations in addition to the Chartered Life Underwriter (CLU) and Chartered Financial Consultant (ChFC) designations.

The field of group benefits continues to change rapidly. Nowhere have the changes occurred any faster than in the area of medical expense coverage. Employers, still concerned with rising costs, are continuing to turn to self-funding and managed care. Even traditional indemnity plans are adding more elements of managed care with the inclusion of managed maternity programs, the requirement of preapproval of specialists, and the use of carve-out programs for the treatment of mental illness and substance abuse. While calls from some quarters for a complete overhaul of the national health insurance system have been largely ignored, very real reform has recently taken place at the federal level with the passage of the Health Insurance Portability and Accountability Act, the Newborns' and Mothers' Health Protection Act, and the Mental Health Parity Act. Reform also continues on the state level.

Changes are also taking place in other areas of employee benefits. Group universal life insurance and group variable universal life insurance continue to increase in popularity as methods of providing postretirement life insurance coverage. Group term carve-out plans to provide life insurance protection to key employees are also gaining wider acceptance. Voluntary benefit plans, group long-term care insurance, and eldercare benefits continue to become widely accepted.

Changes are also occurring in the administration of employee benefits. Technology is becoming increasingly important for communicating benefits to employees and for enabling them to make benefit changes and elections. Benefits administration is also much more likely than in the past to be outsourced.

These changes are all included in the current edition of the book. In addition, many other revisions have been made to reflect changing practices in the employee benefit arena. Numerous suggestions for improvement from readers of the previous edition have also been incorporated in the book.

The revision of a book such as this one is not the product of only one person. For their help I particularly wish to thank

- The CLU, ChFC, RHU, and REBC students, instructors, and other readers who have offered numerous suggestions for improvement. No book can be properly revised without feedback from those who use it. I hope readers of this edition will continue to give me this needed feedback.
- The many employees of insurance companies and other benefit specialists who have patiently taken the time to answer my questions and provide me with much valuable information.
- My fellow faculty members at The American College, who are always a valuable source of information as well as excellent reviewers of the material.
- The editorial staff of The American College. The book is much more readable because of the editing of Lynn Hayes and Barbara G. Keyser and the proofreading of Rosemary Pagano.
- The production staff of The American College under the direction of Jane Hassinger. Special thanks should be extended to Evelyn Rice. Her task has been more difficult than usual because of the conversion of the books in the Huebner School Series to a new word processing system.
- My assistant, Nancy Cornman, for the pleasant and helpful way she performs all the tasks I ask her to do.

The book is better because of the hard work of all these people.

Group Benefits

1

Introduction to Group Benefits

Chapter Outline

While few would dispute that employee benefits are a major part of the overall compensation for working, even employee benefit specialists disagree over the precise meaning of the term *employee benefits*. However, regardless of the definition used, those in the field agree that the significance of the term has increased in recent years.

The narrowest definition of employee benefits includes only employer-provided benefits for situations involving death, accident, sickness, retirement, or unemployment. Even this narrow interpretation produces disagreement over whether the definition should include benefits that are financed by employer contributions but are provided under social insurance programs, such as workers' compensation insurance, unemployment insurance, and social security.[1]

On the other hand, the broadest definition of employee benefits includes all benefits and services, other than wages for time worked, that employees receive in whole or in part from their employers. This book uses a broad definition and defines employee benefits as including the following five categories:[2]

- legally required payments for government programs. These include employer contributions to such programs as
    social security
    unemployment compensation insurance
    workers' compensation insurance

           temporary disability insurance
- payments for private insurance and retirement plans. These include the cost of establishing such plans, as well as contributions in the form of insurance premiums or payments through alternative funding arrangements. Benefits are provided under these plans for personal loss exposures such as

           old age
           death
           disability
           long-term care expenses
           medical expenses
           dental expenses
           legal expenses
           property and liability losses

- payments for time not worked. These include

           vacations
           holidays
           jury duty
           maternity leave
           National Guard duty

- extra cash payments, other than wages and bonuses based on performance, to employees. Benefits in this category include

           educational assistance
           moving expenses
           suggestion awards
           Christmas bonuses

- cost of services to employees, such as

           subsidized cafeterias
           employee discounts
           wellness programs
           day care
           adoption assistance
           financial planning programs
           retirement counseling
           free parking

The first category is usually referred to as social insurance, and the last four categories are commonly called group benefits. This book covers all five categories of benefits except for the portion of the second category dealing with retirement plans, which is beyond the scope of this text. While all the other topics are covered, the major emphasis is on social insurance and the remaining topics in the second category, which, when grouped together, are referred to as *welfare benefits* (the legal term) or *group insurance* (the term better understood by laypersons). However, the briefer treatment of numerous other types of benefits should not diminish their importance.

GROWTH AND SIGNIFICANCE OF GROUP BENEFITS

In a 1995 study of 864 companies the United States Chamber of Commerce found that the average payment by employers for employee benefits was equal to 42.0 percent of payroll.[3] Of this figure 8.9 percent of payroll went for the employer's share of legally required social insurance payments, 7.5 percent for payments to private retirement and savings plans, and 10.5 percent for medical and medically related benefits, which is the largest single employee benefit expenditure. The remaining 15.1 percent was for all other types of benefits, with paid vacations being the single most costly item in this category. The study showed substantial variations among business firms, with overall percentages ranging from less than 20 percent to more than 65 percent. Large variations were also shown by industry, with transportation equipment having the highest percentage (51.4) and textile products and apparel having the lowest (29.2). Benefit payments generally increased for firms in specific industries as the number of employees increased, and the percentages tended to be highest in the Northeast and lowest in the east north central states. The percentages also tended to be slightly higher for salaried employees than for hourly employees.

The Chamber of Commerce study also estimated that employee benefits for all employees in the United States amounted to slightly over $1.5 trillion in 1995 and that this figure was equal to 41.8 percent of payroll. The reason for the discrepancy between the estimated percentage (41.8) and what was found in the survey mentioned above (42.0) is that the survey was weighted in favor of larger firms. The Chamber of Commerce estimated that the 41.8 percent figure had grown from 3 percent in 1929, 21.5 percent in 1965, 30 percent in 1975, and 36.7 percent in 1988. While the percentages for all categories of employee benefits have increased in recent years, the most rapid increases have occurred in payments for private insurance (because of increasing costs for medical expense benefits) and payments for retirement and savings plans.

In addition to employer costs, employee payroll deductions for benefits amounted to 13.1 percent of payroll in 1995. The majority of this amount was for social security taxes and contributions to retirement and savings plans.

FACTORS IN THE GROWTH OF GROUP BENEFITS

No single factor can be identified as the reason for the substantial growth in group benefits. Rather, this growth has resulted from a combination of elements, many of which are applicable to employee benefits in general. Frequently mentioned factors include (1) industrialization, (2) the influence of organized labor, (3) wage controls, (4) cost advantages, (5) inflation, and (6) legislation.

Industrialization

During the nineteenth century the United States made the transition from an agrarian economy to one characterized by increasing industrialization and urbanization. The economic consequences of death, sickness, accidents, and old age became more significant as individuals began to depend more on monetary wages than on self-reliance and family ties to meet their basic needs. As a result some employers began to provide retirement, death, and medical benefits to their employees. While benevolence may have influenced the decision to provide such benefits, the principal reason was probably the employers' realization that it was in their own best interest to do so. Not only did such benefits improve morale and productivity, they also reduced employee turnover and the expenses associated with it.

While some of the earlier benefits were paid directly by employers, the development of group insurance enabled these benefits to be funded by systematic payments to an insurance company. As group insurance became more common, employers were faced with adopting new or better plans to remain competitive in attracting and keeping employees. This competition in employee benefits continues to exist.

Industrialization has also led to more government benefits, such as social security, unemployment insurance, and workers' compensation insurance.

Organized Labor

Since a Supreme Court ruling in 1949, there has been no question about the right of labor unions to legally negotiate for employee benefits. Although union pressures prior to that time frequently resulted in the establishment or broadening of employee benefit plans, this ruling strengthened the influence of labor unions.

Labor unions have also affected benefits for nonunion employees because some employers provide generous benefit plans in an effort to discourage their employees from unionizing. In addition, employers with both union and nonunion employees often provide the same benefits for the nonunion employees as those stipulated in the union contracts.

Wage Controls

Employee benefit plans grew substantially during World War II and the Korean War. Although wages were frozen, no restrictions were imposed on employee benefits, thus making them an important factor in attracting and retaining employees in labor markets with little unemployment. When wage controls were instituted in the early 1970s, no unusual growth in employee benefit plans took place because the duration of the controls was relatively short and the unemployment rate was higher than in previous years.

Cost Advantages

Because of the economies associated with group underwriting and administration, benefits can usually be obtained at a lower cost through group insurance than through separate policies purchased by individual employees. Similar savings can be realized by directly providing employees with certain services, such as financial planning, day-care centers, and subsidized meals. The Internal Revenue Code also provides favorable tax treatment to employer contributions for certain types of group benefits. The employer may deduct most group insurance contributions as usual business expenses, and employees will often have no taxable income as a result of employer contributions in their behalf. In addition, employees may receive tax-free benefits from certain types of group insurance plans and payments or services from any other types of group benefit programs, even if provided by employer contributions. The extent of the favorable tax treatment applicable to group benefits is discussed in detail in later chapters. Nevertheless, it should be noted here that the types of group benefits with the most favorable tax treatment also tend to be the most prevalent. (See Appendix A for a summary of the federal income tax treatment of group benefits.)

Inflation

Inflation also affects group benefits. When benefit levels are related to employees' wages, the level and cost of these benefits will increase as wages increase; when benefit levels are stated as fixed amounts, inflation results in employee pressure for increases. For most employers the cost of group benefits has been increasing at a rate faster than wages, primarily because of the skyrocketing increase in the cost of providing medical expense benefits.

Legislation

Most states traditionally limited the types of groups that are eligible for group insurance coverage as well as the types, and in some cases the amounts, of coverage that could be written. In recent years the majority of these states have liberalized their laws and allowed more group insurance products to be available to an increasing variety of groups.

Furthermore, the federal government and many states have passed legislation mandating that certain benefits be included in group insurance contracts or that existing benefits be broadened. Examples include legislation requiring benefits for maternity, alcoholism, and drug abuse. These added benefits have also increased the cost of providing group insurance coverage.

Other benefits, such as family leave, must now be provided by many employers.

THE FUTURE

The consensus among employee benefit specialists is that in the absence of adverse economic conditions group benefits will continue to evolve and grow. While there is anything but unanimous agreement about what the specifics of these changes will be, there is reasonable agreement about general trends in the near future:

- Firms with fewer than 50 employees, and especially those with fewer than 10, will continue to be a major market for new benefit plans—particularly group insurance. Over the last few years many insurance companies have developed products for this market, so that small firms can now obtain many of the economies of scale previously available only to large employers.

- Because of increasing benefit costs, employees are more likely to partially or totally finance additional benefits through voluntary plans using payroll deduction.

- The cost of providing medical expense benefits will continue rising faster than will the general rate of inflation. These escalating costs will present a constant challenge to employers and governments seeking to contain them.

- An increasing number of employees will have medical expense coverage provided under managed care plans, such as HMOs, PPOs, and various hybrid arrangements.

- There will be continued interest in providing more secure medical expense benefits, as well as in making coverage available to a greater number of workers. Change will continue to occur at the federal level, but the change will consist of small steps rather than the far-reaching reform that was proposed in the first Clinton administration. Congress will also be more likely to let the states act as laboratories for health care reform.

- More and more employees will have benefits provided under cafeteria plans and will be able to substantially design their own benefit programs.

- Changing demographics will lead to growth in certain benefits, such as day-care centers for children and retirement planning and long-term care for the aging population.

- The efforts to contain medical costs and the generally increasing awareness of the importance of good health bode well for the proliferation and lasting success of wellness and employee-assistance programs.

- Congress will be forced to make tough decisions about reforming the funding of social security and medicare benefits.

IMPORTANCE OF BENEFIT PLANNING

The significant growth in employee benefits has called for increasingly complex decisions. Whether these decisions are by employers providing benefits, unions negotiating for benefits, or employees selecting benefit options, the need for proper benefit planning is crucial. One difficulty in writing a textbook of this nature is determining where to discuss the many issues and decisions that must be faced if proper planning is to take place. A conscious decision to delay a thorough discussion of benefit planning until later chapters was made so that the reader could better understand the issues, products, tax laws, and funding methods that have an impact on planning. While a later chapter of the book is devoted entirely to group benefit plan design and is the only place certain issues are discussed, other planning issues are handled where appropriate throughout the book.

However, a brief treatment of the benefit-planning process is appropriate here to make readers aware that benefit planning is much more than a description of the many types of plans and provisions that are the subject of much of this book.

The Benefit-Planning Process

Employee benefit planning is a dynamic process that must continually be reviewed and modified if an overall benefit plan is to meet the changing needs of a changing environment. The first step in this process is to determine the employer's objectives. Is the benefit package to be in line with the competition? Or is it to be viewed as a leader, better enabling the firm to attract employees?

Once the employer's objectives are determined, a plan should be designed to meet these objectives. This process requires an analysis of plan costs from both a short-term and a long-term standpoint. If the costs are excessive even though the plan has been designed in the most cost-effective manner, the employer's objectives will need revision. A major determinant of a benefit plan's cost is the method of funding. Should it be insured, funded from current revenues, or funded by some combination of the two approaches? Employers are increasingly using alternatives to traditional funding arrangements in an effort to reduce costs.

The third step in the process is to implement the plan. This may be as simple as adding an additional vacation day or as complex as taking competitive proposals for a pension plan from insurance companies, trust departments of banks, and other providers of services.

A crucial step in the employee benefit-planning process is to communicate the plan properly to participating employees. Without good communication it is often difficult for an employer's objectives to be realized effectively. Communication has become more than merely describing benefits; it also involves letting employees know the value of the benefits.

Finally, employers should monitor the plan's performance and make any necessary changes. As new benefits or funding arrangements appear on the scene, should they be considered? Has the character of the work force changed so that a different benefit package would better meet the needs of employees?

Throughout this book the issues and decisions that are part of this process are discussed.

NOTES

1. The Social Security Administration uses a narrow definition in its studies of employee benefit plans. Its definition includes only benefits not underwritten or paid directly by the federal, state, or local governments.
2. These categories are based on those listed in Robert M. McCaffery, *Managing the Employee Benefits Program*, American Management Association, 1972. They are also similar to those used by the United States Chamber of Commerce in its broad definition of employee benefits.
3. United States Chamber of Commerce, *Employee Benefits*, 1996. This study is updated annually.

2

Social Security

Chapter Outline

Social insurance programs in the United States fall into four categories:

- social security
- unemployment insurance
- temporary disability insurance
- workers' compensation insurance

Social security, a totally federal program, is described in this chapter; the remaining three programs are covered in the following chapter.

Social insurance programs are significant for several reasons. First, in the United States nearly one-quarter of the dollars employers spend on benefits for their employees is used to make legally required payments to social insurance programs. For employers with meager benefit plans this proportion will be much higher and may even account for the majority of the total benefit package.

Second, the most significant insurance expense for most individuals is their contribution to social security. For many persons this contribution will exceed the combined cost of all other types of insurance purchased directly by the individual.

Third, these programs form the foundation on which employee benefit programs and individual insurance plans are built. Employers' medical expense, disability income, and retirement plans are often designed in light of the benefits already available to employees under social insurance programs. Some benefit plans apply only to those employees not adequately covered under comparable social insurance programs; other benefit plans may cover all employees but may provide reduced benefits in those areas where similar social insurance benefits are available. In addition, it is impossible to do a proper job of personal insurance planning without taking potential social security benefits into consideration.

Many books have been devoted entirely to social security. Because of space limitations its treatment in this book is rather brief and is devoted primarily to a description of eligibility requirements, financing, and benefits. However, a few words should also be said about the reasons why social security and other social insurance programs exist and the general characteristics of such programs.

REASONS FOR SOCIAL INSURANCE

The existence and scope of social insurance programs are the result of several factors, probably the most significant of which is the need to solve the major social problems that affect a large portion of society. The industrialization of American society and the decreasing self-sufficiency of families have resulted in a greater dependence on monetary income to provide economic security. The widespread lack of such income during the Great Depression led to the passage of the Social Security Act as an attempt to provide economic security by attacking the sources of economic insecurity, including old age and unemployment.

A second reason for the existence of social insurance programs is the difficulty of privately insuring certain types of losses. For example, the inability to predict future unemployment rates and the potential for catastrophic losses make the peril of unemployment virtually uninsurable in the private sector. In addition, broad medical expense coverage for the aged can be marketed commercially only at a price beyond the financial means of many retirees.

Finally, many Americans have come to expect the government to provide at least a degree of economic security against the consequences of premature death, old age, disability, and unemployment. As a result social insurance programs enjoy widespread public acceptance.

CHARACTERISTICS OF SOCIAL INSURANCE

Even though there are variations in social insurance programs, and exceptions to the rule always exist, social insurance programs tend to have the following distinguishing characteristics:

- compulsory employment-related coverage
- partial or total employer financing
- benefits prescribed by law
- benefits as a matter of right
- emphasis on social adequacy

Compulsory Employment-Related Coverage

Most social insurance programs are compulsory and require that the persons covered be attached—either presently or by past service—to the labor force. If a social insurance program is to meet a social need through the redistribution of income, it must have widespread participation.

Partial or Total Employer Financing

While significant variations exist in social insurance programs, most require that the cost of the program be borne fully or at least partially by the employers of the covered persons. This is the basis for including these programs under the broad definition of employee benefits. The remaining cost of most social insurance programs is paid primarily by the persons covered under the programs. With the exception of medicare and certain unemployment benefits, the general revenues of the federal government and state governments finance only a small portion of social insurance benefits.

Benefits Prescribed by Law

Although benefit amounts and the eligibility requirements for social insurance benefits are prescribed by law, benefits are not necessarily uniform for everyone. They may vary by such factors as wage level, length of covered employment, or family status. However, these factors are incorporated into the benefit formulas specified by law, and covered persons are unable to either increase or decrease their prescribed level of benefits.

Benefits as a Matter of Right

Social insurance benefits are paid as a matter of right under the presumption that a need for the benefits exists. This feature distinguishes social insurance programs from public assistance or welfare programs under which applicants, in order to qualify for benefits, must meet a needs test by demonstrating that their income or assets are below some specified level.

Emphasis on Social Adequacy

Benefits under social insurance programs are based more on social adequacy than on individual equity. Under the principle of social adequacy, benefits are designed to provide a minimum floor of income to all beneficiaries under the program regardless of their economic status. Above this floor of benefits persons are expected to provide additional resources from their own savings, employment, or private insurance programs. This emphasis on social adequacy also results in disproportionately large benefits in relation to contributions for some groups of beneficiaries. For some programs high-income persons, single persons or small families, and the young are subsidizing low-income persons, large families, and the retired.

If social insurance programs were based solely on individual equity, benefits would be actuarially related to contributions just as they are under private insurance programs. While this degree of individual equity does not exist, there is some relationship between benefits and income levels (and thus contributions). Within certain maximum and minimum amounts, benefits are a function of a person's covered earnings under social insurance programs. However, the major emphasis is on social adequacy.

SOCIAL SECURITY (OASDHI)

In this book, the broad term *social security* refers to the old-age, survivors, disability, and health insurance (OASDHI) program of the federal government. However, OASDHI is only one of several programs resulting from the Social Security Act of 1935 and its frequent amendments over the years. The act established four programs aimed at providing economic security for the American society:

- old-age insurance
- unemployment insurance
- federal grants for assistance to certain needy groups: the aged, the blind, and children
- federal grants for maternal and child welfare, public health work, and vocational rehabilitation

The old-age insurance program and the benefits that have been added to that program over the years to make it what we now call social security will be discussed here. These additional benefits include survivors insurance (1939), disability insurance (1956), hospital insurance (1965), and supplementary medical insurance (1965). The latter two parts of social security comprise medicare and are often referred to as part A and part B, respectively.

The following discussion of social security begins with a description of the extent of coverage under the program and the way the program is financed. It then focuses on the eligibility requirements and benefits under the various parts of the program. Because of the many differences between medicare and the rest of the program, the discussion treats each part separately beginning with old-age, survivors, and disability insurance, or OASDI. (Note that when the public and the press refer to social security, they are usually referring to OASDI rather than the broader OASDHI program.) Finally, a description of the tax implications of social security benefits and contributions is found at the end of this chapter.

Extent of Coverage

Over 90 percent of the workers in the United States are in covered employment under the social security program. This means that these workers have wages (if they are employees) or self-employment income (if they are self-employed) on which social security taxes must be paid. The following are the major categories of workers who are not covered under the program or who are covered only if they have met specific conditions:

- civilian employees of the federal government who were employed by the government prior to 1984 and who are covered under the Civil Service Retirement System or certain other federal retirement programs. These workers are covered by government plans that provide benefits similar to those available under OASDI. Coverage for new civilian federal employees under the entire program was one of the most significant changes resulting from 1983 amendments to the Social Security Act. It should be noted, however, that *all* federal employees have been covered under social security for purposes of medicare since 1983.

- railroad workers. Under the Railroad Retirement Act employees of railroads have their own benefit system that is similar to OASDI. However, they are covered under social security for purposes of medicare. In addition, there are certain circumstances under which railroad workers receive benefits from the social security program even though their contributions were paid to the railroad program.

- employees of state and local governments unless the state has entered into a voluntary agreement with the Social Security Administration. However, this exemption applies only to those employees who are covered under their employer's retirement plan. Under an agreement with the Social Security Administration the state may either require that employees of local governments also be covered or allow the local governments to decide whether to include their employees. In addition, the state may elect to include all or only certain groups of its employees. Once an agreement is entered into, states and local government units are not allowed to withdraw their employees from social security coverage.

- American citizens working abroad for foreign affiliates of U.S. employers, unless the employer owns at least a 10 percent interest in the foreign affiliate and has made arrangements with the secretary of the treasury for the payment of social security taxes. However, Americans working abroad are covered under social security if they are working directly for U.S. employers rather than for their foreign subsidiaries.

- ministers who elect out of coverage because of conscience or religious principles

- workers in certain jobs such as student nurses, newspaper carriers under age 18, and students working for the school at which they are regularly enrolled or doing domestic work for a local college club, fraternity, or sorority

- certain family employment. This includes the employment of a child under age 18 by a parent. This exclusion, however, does not apply if the employment is for a corporation owned by a family member.

- certain workers who must satisfy special earnings requirements. For example, self-employed persons are not covered unless they have net annual earnings of $400 or more. In addition, certain agricultural workers must have annual cash wages of $150 or more, and domestic workers must earn $1,000 or more in cash wages in a calendar year.

TABLE 2-1			
Changes in Tax Rates and Wage Bases under Social Security			
Year	Wage Base	Tax Rate	Maximum Employee Tax
1950	$ 3,000	1.50%	$ 45.00
1955	4,200	2.00	84.00
1960	4,800	3.00	144.00
1965	4,800	3.65	174.00
1970	7,800	4.80	374.40
1975	14,100	5.85	824.85
1980	25,900	6.13	1,587.67
1985	39,600	7.05	2,791.80
1990	51,300	7.65	3,924.45
1991	first 53,400	7.65	
	next 71,600	1.45	5,123.30
1992	first 55,500	7.65	
	next 74,700	1.45	5,328.90
1993	first 57,600	7.65	
	next 77,400	1.45	5,528.70
1994	first 60,600	7.65	
	additional wages	1.45	***
1995	first 61,200	7.65	
	additional wages	1.45	***
1996	first 62,700	7.65	
	additional wages	1.45	***
1997	first 65,400	7.65	
	additional wages	1.45	***
1998 and after	*	**	

*Subject to automatic adjustment
**Same as 1997
***No determinable maximum due to unlimited wage base for medicare tax

Financing: Tax Rates and Wage Bases

Part B of medicare is financed by a combination of monthly premiums paid by persons eligible for benefits and contributions from the federal government. Part A of medicare and all the benefits of the OASDI program are financed through a system of payroll and self-employment taxes paid by all persons covered under the program. In addition, employers of covered persons are also taxed.

In 1997 an employee and his or her employer pay a tax of 7.65 percent each on the first $65,400 of the employee's wages. Of this tax rate 6.2 percent is for OASDI; 1.45 percent is for the hospital insurance portion of medicare. The medicare tax rate of 1.45 percent is also levied on all wages in excess of $65,400. The tax rates are currently scheduled to remain the same after 1997. However, the wage bases are adjusted annually for changes in the national level of wages. Therefore if wage levels increase by 4 percent in a particular year, the wage base for the following year will also increase by 4 percent. The tax rate for the self-employed is 15.3 percent on the first $65,400 of self-employment income and 2.9 percent on the balance of any self-employment income. This is equal to the combined employee and employer rates.

Over the years both the tax rates and wage bases have been dramatically increased to finance increased benefit levels under social security as well as new benefits that have been added to the program. Table 2-1 shows the magnitude of these increases for selected years.

Adequacy of Financing

The social security program is essentially based on a system of pay-as-you-go financing with limited trust funds. This means that current payroll taxes and other contributions the program receives are used to pay the current benefits of persons who are no longer paying social security taxes because of death, old age, or disability. This is in direct contrast to private insurance or retirement plans, which are based on advance funding, whereby assets are accumulated from current contributions to pay the future benefits of those making the contributions.

All payroll taxes and other sources of funds for social security are deposited into four trust funds: an old-age and survivors fund, a disability fund, and two medicare funds. Benefits and administrative expenses are paid out of the appropriate trust fund from contributions to that fund and any interest earnings on accumulated assets. The social security program does have limited reserves to serve as emergency funds in periods when benefits exceed contributions, such as in times of high unemployment. However, current reserves are relatively small and could pay benefits for only a limited time if contributions to a fund ceased. In addition, the reserves consist primarily of IOUs from the Treasury since the contributions have been "borrowed" to finance the government's deficit.

In the early 1980s considerable concern arose over the potential inability of payroll taxes to pay promised benefits in the future. Through a series of changes, the most significant being the 1983 amendments to the Social Security Act, these problems appeared to have been solved for the OASDI portion of the program—at least in the short run. The changes approached the problem from two directions. On one hand, payroll tax rates were increased; on the other hand, some benefits were eliminated and future increases in other benefits were scaled back. However, the solutions of 1983 have not worked. Without further adjustments, the trust funds will have inadequate resources to pay claims in the foreseeable future.

In times of high unemployment rates and/or downsizing, social security disability claims normally increase in both frequency and duration. Such has been the case for the last few years. As a result the disability trust fund will need additional resources in the very near future. There are plans to strengthen this fund by transferring monies from the old-age and survivors fund.

The trust fund for old-age and survivors benefits will continue to grow and will be quite large by the time the current baby boomers retire. At that time benefits will exceed income, and the fund will begin to decrease as the percentage of retirees grows rapidly. Until recently projections indicated that the size of the fund would stabilize as the baby boomers died and the percentage of elderly returned to a more normal level. However, current projections indicate that the fund will run out of money in about 35 years. Higher interest rates and lower unemployment rates in future years will maintain the solvency of the fund for a longer period.

Because of an increasing number of persons aged 65 or older and medical costs that continue to grow at an alarming rate, there is also concern about the medicare portion of the program. Estimates are that its trust funds will be depleted early in the next century. The urgency of this problem is made clear by the fact that one of the earliest actions of the second Clinton administration was to propose a plan that would maintain the solvency of the medicare trust funds for about 5 additional years, primarily through encouraging additional enrollment in managed care plans and trimming projected payments to HMOs, hospitals, and doctors. The president also called for a bipartisan commission to make recommendations for longer-range financial stability.

It is obvious that changes must be made—either now or later—in the social security program. This demand for change, of course, has significant political implications. While most members of Congress realize the need for reform, neither political party seems willing to take the necessary initiative and risk losing public support. Probably the most important step in finding a solution is to convince the public that changes in a very popular entitlement program must be made.

In the broadest sense the solution lies in doing one or both of the following: increasing revenue into the trust funds or decreasing benefit costs. Possibilities for increasing revenue include the following:

- increasing the social security and/or medicare tax rate
- increasing the wage base on which OASDI taxes are paid
- using more general tax revenue to fund the program
- subjecting a greater portion of income benefits to taxation and depositing the increased tax revenue into the trust funds
- investing all or a portion of trust fund assets in higher-yielding investments than Treasury securities

Suggestions that have been made for decreasing benefit costs include the following:

- raising the normal retirement age beyond the planned increase to age 67
- raising the early retirement age beyond 62
- lowering the benefit formula so that future retirees will get somewhat reduced benefits
- lowering cost-of-living increases
- imposing a means test for benefits
- increasing medicare deductibles and coinsurance
- increasing the medicare part B premium for everyone or possibly only for higher-income retirees
- lowering or slowing the growth of payments to medicare providers
- encouraging or requiring medicare beneficiaries to enroll in managed care plans

Any single change will clearly offend one important group of voters or another. As a result, any ultimate solution will probably involve a combination of several of these changes so that everyone will bear a little of the pain.

Report of Advisory Council on Social Security

A bipartisan advisory council was established in 1994 to make recommendations to solve the long-range financing of OASDI. The 13-member council issued its report in late 1996 but failed to reach consensus on a solution. Instead, the council split into three factions, with each faction offering its own solution. While the options are very different, all the options have some items in common. All three options call for requiring newly hired state and local government workers to be covered under OASDI and increasing income tax on OASDI benefits that exceed lifetime contributions. In addition, the method for investing OASDI revenues would change.

One option largely maintains existing benefits. The payroll tax rate would increase, but not until 2045. This option proposes studying the issue of increasing revenue by investing up to 40 percent of OASDI assets in the stock market.

A second option maintains existing benefits for persons aged 55 or older. A new and radically different OASDI program would be phased in for younger workers. Five percentage points of the payroll tax would be diverted to personal security accounts. A worker would be allowed considerable flexibility in how his or her account was invested and would bear all investment risk. The remaining payroll taxes would be used to finance a minimum guaranteed retirement benefit of $410 per month. The cost to phase in this option would be significant, requiring a 1.52 percentage point increase in the payroll tax rate for 72 years and $1.9 trillion of government borrowing over the next 40 years.

The third option reduces benefits for some middle- and high-income individuals and raises the retirement age. In addition, the payroll tax rate would increase by 1.6 percentage points. These additional funds would be deposited in mandatory savings accounts that would supplement OASDI benefits at retirement. These accounts would be administered by the federal government, and workers could choose from a limited number of investment options.

OASDI: ELIGIBILITY

To be eligible for benefits under OASDI, an individual must have credit for a minimum amount of work under social security. This credit is based on quarters of coverage. For 1997 a worker receives credit for one quarter of coverage for each $670 in annual earnings on which social security taxes are paid. However, credit for no more than 4 quarters of coverage may be earned in any one calendar year, even if all wages are earned within one calendar quarter. Consequently a worker paying social security taxes on as little as $2,680 (that is, $670 x 4) during the year will receive credit for the maximum 4 quarters. As in the case of the wage base, the amount of earnings necessary for a quarter of coverage is adjusted annually for changes in the national level of wages.

Quarters of coverage are the basis for establishing an insured status under OASDI. The three types of insured status are fully insured, currently insured, and disability insured.

Fully Insured

A person is fully insured under OASDI if either of two tests is met. The first test requires credit for 40 quarters of coverage. Once a person acquires such credit, he or she is fully insured for life even if covered employment under social security ceases.

Under the second test a person who has credit for a minimum of 6 quarters of coverage is fully insured if he or she has credit for at least as many quarters of coverage as there are years elapsing *after* 1950 (or *after* the year in which age 21 is reached, if later) and *before* the year in which he or she dies, becomes disabled, or reaches age 62, whichever occurs first. Therefore a worker who reached age 21 in 1985 and who died in 1997 would need credit for only 11 quarters of coverage for his or her family to be eligible for survivors benefits.

Currently Insured

If a worker is fully insured under OASDI, there is no additional significance to being currently insured. However, if a worker is not fully insured, certain survivors benefits are still available if a currently insured status exists. To be currently insured, it is only necessary that a worker have credit for at least 6 quarters of coverage out of the 13-quarter period ending with the quarter in which death occurs.

Disability Insured

In order to receive disability benefits under OASDI, it is necessary to be disability insured. At a minimum a disability-insured status requires that a worker (1) be fully insured and (2) have a minimum amount of work under social security within a recent time period. In connection with the latter requirement, workers aged 31 or older must have credit for at least 20 of the last 40 quarters ending with the quarter in which disability occurs; workers between the ages of 24 and 30, inclusively, must have credit for at least half the quarters of coverage from the time they turned 21 and the quarter in which disability begins; and workers under age 24 must have credit for 6 out of the last 12 quarters, ending with the quarter in which disability begins.

A special rule for the blind states that they are exempt from the recent-work rules and are considered disability insured as long as they are fully insured.

OASDI: TYPES OF BENEFITS

As its name implies, the OASDI portion of social security provides three principal types of benefits:

- retirement (old-age) benefits
- survivors benefits
- disability benefits

Retirement Benefits

A worker who is fully insured under OASDI is eligible to receive monthly retirement benefits as early as age 62. However, the election to receive benefits prior to the normal retirement age of age 65 results in a permanently reduced benefit.

In addition to the retired worker, the following dependents of persons receiving retirement benefits are also eligible for monthly benefits:

- a spouse aged 62 or older. However, benefits are permanently reduced if this benefit is elected prior to the spouse's reaching age 65. This benefit is also available to a divorced spouse under certain circumstances if the marriage lasted at least 10 years.
- a spouse of any age if the spouse is caring for at least one child of the retired worker who is (1) under age 16 or (2) disabled and entitled to a child's benefit as described below. This benefit is commonly referred to as a *mother's or father's benefit.*
- dependent, unmarried children under 18. This child's benefit will continue until age 19 as long as a child is a full-time student in elementary or secondary school. In addition, disabled children of any

age are eligible for benefits as long as they were disabled before reaching age 22.

It is important to note that retirement benefits, as well as all other benefits under social security, are not automatically paid upon eligibility but must be applied for.

Beginning in 2003 the normal retirement age for nonreduced benefits for workers and spouses will gradually increase until it reaches age 67 in 2027. This increase is shown in table 2-2.

TABLE 2-2 Retirement Age for Nonreduced Benefits	
Year of Birth	**Normal Retirement Age**
1937 and before	65 years
1938	65 years, 2 months
1939	65 years, 4 months
1940	65 years, 6 months
1941	65 years, 8 months
1942	65 years, 10 months
1943–54	66 years
1955	66 years, 2 months
1956	66 years, 4 months
1957	66 years, 6 months
1958	66 years, 8 months
1959	66 years, 10 months
1960 and later	67 years

Survivors Benefits

All categories of survivors benefits are payable if a worker is fully insured at the time of death. However, three types of benefits are also payable if a worker is only currently insured. The first is a lump-sum death benefit of $255, payable in the following order of priority:

- to a surviving spouse who was living with the deceased worker at the time of death
- to a surviving spouse (other than a divorced spouse) who was not living with the deceased worker at the time of death if the surviving spouse is eligible for or entitled to benefits based on the deceased wage earner's record for the month of death
- to children who are eligible for or entitled to benefits based on the deceased wage earner's record for the month of death

If none of these categories of survivors exists, the benefit is not paid.

There are two categories of persons who are eligible for income benefits as survivors if a deceased worker was either fully or currently insured at the time of death:

- dependent, unmarried children under the same conditions as previously described for retirement benefits
- a spouse (including a divorced spouse) caring for a child or children under the same conditions as previously described for retirement benefits

The following categories of persons are also eligible for benefits, but only if the deceased worker was fully insured:

- a widow or widower at age 60. However, benefits are reduced if taken prior to age 65. This benefit is also payable to a divorced spouse if the marriage lasted at least 10 years. In addition, the widow's or widower's benefit is payable to a disabled spouse at age 50 as long as the disability commenced no more than 7 years after (1) the worker's death or (2) the end of the year in which entitlement to a mother's or father's benefit ceased.
- a parent aged 62 or over who was a dependent of the deceased worker at the time of death

Disability Benefits

A disabled worker under age 65 is eligible to receive benefits under OASDI as long as he or she is disability insured and meets the definition of disability under the law. The definition of disability is very rigid and requires a mental or physical impairment that prevents the worker from engaging in any substantial gainful employment. The disability must also have lasted (or be expected to last) at least 12 months or be expected to result in death. A more liberal definition of disability applies to blind workers who are aged 55 or older. They are considered disabled if they are unable to perform work that requires skills or abilities comparable to those required by the work they regularly performed before reaching age 55 or becoming blind, if later.

Disability benefits are subject to a waiting period and are payable beginning with the sixth full calendar month of disability. In addition to the benefit paid to a disabled worker, the other categories of benefits available are the same as those described under retirement benefits.

As previously mentioned, certain family members not otherwise eligible for OASDI benefits may be eligible if they are disabled. Disabled children are subject to the same definition of disability as workers. However, disabled widows or widowers must be unable to engage in any gainful (rather than substantial gainful) employment.

Eligibility for Dual Benefits

In many cases a person is eligible for more than one type of OASDI benefit. Probably the most common situation occurs when a person is eligible for both a spouse's benefit and a worker's retirement or disability benefit based on his or her own social security record. In this case and in any other case when a person is eligible for dual benefits, only an amount equal to the highest benefit is paid.

Termination of Benefits

Monthly benefits to any social security recipient cease upon death. When a retired or disabled worker dies, the family members' benefits that are based on the worker's retirement or disability benefits also cease, but the family members are then eligible for survivors benefits.

Disability benefits for a worker technically terminate at age 65 but are then replaced by comparable retirement benefits. In addition, any benefits payable because of disability cease if the definition of disability is no longer satisfied. However, the disability benefits continue during a readjustment period that consists of the month of recovery and 2 additional months.

As long as children are not disabled, benefits will usually terminate at age 18 but may continue until age 19 if the child is a full-time student in elementary or secondary school.

The benefit of a surviving spouse terminates upon remarriage unless remarriage takes place at age 60 or later.

OASDI: BENEFIT AMOUNTS

With the exception of the $255 lump-sum death benefit, the amount of all OASDI benefits is based on a worker's primary insurance amount (PIA). The PIA, in turn, is a function of the worker's average indexed monthly earnings (AIME) on which social security taxes have been paid.

Calculation of AIME

Even though they may initially seem rather complex, the steps in calculating a worker's AIME are relatively simple. These steps are outlined below and will be best understood by referring to table 2-3, which shows the computation of the AIME for a worker who attained age 30 in 1997 and became disabled.

- First, list the earnings on which social security taxes were paid for each year beginning with 1951 (or the year in which age 22 was attained, if later) up to and including the year of death or the year prior to disability or retirement. This list includes all applicable years even if there were no wages subject to social security tax, in which case a zero is included for covered wages. The example in table 2-3 begins with 1989 because that was the year the worker attained age 22.

- Second, index these earnings by multiplying them by an indexing factor that reflects changing wage levels. The only years that are indexed are those prior to the indexing year, which is the year a worker turned 60 for retirement purposes or 2 years preceding the year of death or disability for purposes of survivors or disability benefits. Therefore the indexing

---

TABLE 2-3
Calculation of AIME

Year	Covered Earnings	x	Indexing Factor	=	Indexed Earnings	Earnings for Years to Be Included in Calculation
1989	$15,000	x	1.229164	=	$18,437.56	excluded
1990	16,000	x	1.174894	=	18,798.30	$18,798.30
1991	17,500	x	1.132684	=	19,821.97	19,821.97
1992	19,000	x	1.077183	=	20,466.48	20,466.48
1993	21,000	x	1.067998	=	22,427.96	22,427.96
1994	22,500	x	1.040083	=	23,401.87	23,401.87
1995	24,000	x	1.000000	=	24,000.00	24,000.00
1996	26,500	x	1.000000	=	26,500.00	26,500.00

$$\text{AIME} = \frac{\$173,854.04}{84} = \$2,069 \text{ (rounded to the next lower dollar)}$$

---

factor for the indexing year (1995 in the example) and subsequent years is one. For years prior to the indexing year, the indexing factor for each year is equal to the *average annual covered wages* in the indexing year divided by the average annual covered wages in the year in which earnings are to be indexed. Average annual covered wages are the average wages on which social security taxes were paid. Each year the government makes the figure for the previous year available. In the example the indexing factor for 1989 is 1.229164 because average annual covered wages were $24,705.66 in 1995 and $20,099.55 in 1989.

- Third, determine the number of years to be included in the calculation. For retirement and survivors benefits the number of years is 5 less than the minimum number of quarters necessary to be fully insured. For disability benefits a subtraction may also be made from the minimum number of quarters necessary for fully insured status. This subtraction is five for workers aged 47 or over, four for workers aged 42 through 46, three for workers aged 37 through 41, two for workers aged 32 through 36, one for workers aged 27 through 31, and none for workers under age 27. However, for survivors or disability benefits at least 2 years must remain for purposes of calculating benefits. In the example the worker needs a minimum of 8 quarters to be fully insured, since 8 is the number of years after the worker reached age 21 and prior to the year of disability. Because the worker is aged 30, one year can be subtracted, which leaves 7 years to be included in the calculation. (Note: Up to 3 additional years may be dropped from the calculation if the worker had no income during the year and had a child under the age of 3 living in his or her household during the entire year.)

- Fourth, determine the years to be excluded from the calculation. These will be the years with the lowest indexed earnings. Of course the number of years determined in the previous step must remain. In the example only one year (1989) can be excluded.
- Fifth, add the indexed earnings for the years to be included in the AIME calculation and divide the result by the number of months in these years. In the example the divisor is 84 months, which represents the 7 years of earnings included in the calculation.

As mentioned earlier, the calculation of the AIME for retirement or disability benefits excludes the year in which retirement or disability takes place. However, the indexed earning for that year can be substituted for the lowest year in the calculation if the result will be a larger AIME.

Determination of PIA and Monthly Benefits

Once a worker's AIME has been calculated, his or her PIA is determined by applying a formula to the AIME. The 1997 formula is as follows:

> 90 percent of the first $455 of AIME
> plus 32 percent of the AIME in excess of $455 through $2,741
> plus 15 percent of the AIME in excess of $2,741

The dollar figures in this formula are adjusted annually for changes in the national level of wages. The formula used to determine a worker's retirement benefit is the formula for the year in which the worker turned age 62. Therefore a worker retiring at age 65 in 1997 would use the 1994 formula rather than the 1997 formula. The formula used to determine survivors and disability benefits is the formula in existence for the year in which death or disability occurs, even if application for benefits is made in a later year.

Using the formula for 1997, a disabled worker with an AIME of $2,800 would have a PIA of $1,149.80, calculated as follows:

90 percent of $455	= $ 409.50
plus 32 percent of $2,286	= 731.52
plus 15 percent of $59	= 8.85
	$1,149.87

(rounded to $1,149.80, the next lower $.10)

The PIA is the amount a worker will receive if he or she retires at age 65 or becomes disabled, and it is the amount on which benefits for family members are based. (Note: Initial calculations such as the PIA and family maximum are rounded to the next lower $.10. After all calculations, the benefit paid to any individual is rounded to the next lower dollar.) In 1997 a worker who has had average earnings during his or her lifetime can expect a PIA of about $900. A worker who has continually earned the maximum income subject to social security taxes can expect a PIA of about $1,300 for retirement purposes and a PIA of between $1,300 and $1,450 for purposes of disability and survivors benefits. The higher PIA occurs for workers who are disabled or die at younger ages.

If a worker is retired or disabled, these benefits are paid to family members:

Category	Percentage of Worker's PIA
Spouse aged 65	50%
Spouse caring for disabled child or child under 16	50%
Child under 18 or disabled	50% each

If the worker dies, survivors benefits are as follows:

Category	Percentage of Worker's PIA
Spouse aged 65	100%
Spouse caring for disabled child or child under 16	75%
Child under 18 or disabled	75% each
Dependent parent	82.5% for one, 75% each for two

However, the full benefits described above may not be payable because of a limitation imposed on the total benefits that may be paid to a family. This family maximum will usually be reached if three or more family members (including a retired or disabled worker) are eligible for benefits. The family maximum for purposes of retirement and survivors benefits can be determined for 1997 from the following formula, which, like the PIA formula, is adjusted annually based on changing wage levels:

> 150 percent of the first $581 of PIA
> plus 272 percent of the PIA in excess of $581 through $839
> plus 134 percent of the PIA in excess of $839 through $1,094
> plus 175 percent of the PIA in excess of $1,094

The family maximum for purposes of disability benefits is limited to 85 percent of the worker's AIME or 150 percent of the worker's PIA, whichever is lower. However, in no case can the maximum be reduced below the worker's PIA.

If the total amount of benefits payable to family members exceeds the family maximum, the worker's benefit (in the case of retirement and disability) is not affected, but the benefits of other family members are reduced proportionately. For example, assume a worker dies leaving a spouse under age 65 and three children who are each eligible for 75 percent of his or her PIA of $1,000. Ignoring the family maximum, the benefits will total $3,000 ($750 for each family member). However, the family maximum, using the above formula, is $1,789 (rounded to the next lower $.10). Therefore each family member will have his or her benefit reduced to $447 (rounded to the next lower dollar). When the first child loses benefits at age 18, the other family members will each have benefits increased to $596 (ignoring any automatic increases in benefit amounts, including the family maximum). When a second family member loses eligibility, the remaining two family members will each receive the full benefit of $750 because the total benefits received by the family will now be less than the $1,789 calculated by the formula.

Other Factors Affecting Benefits

Special Minimum PIA

There is a minimum PIA for workers who have been covered under OASDI for at least 10 years but at very low wages. This PIA is used only if it is higher than a worker's PIA based on actual wages, which is usually not the case. The benefit is first determined by multiplying $11.50 times the number of years of coverage less 10, subject to a maximum of 20. This figure is then adjusted for the cumulative change in the consumer price index (CPI) since 1979. In 1997 a worker with 30 or more years of coverage under OASDI will have a minimum PIA at age 65 of $548.30.

Benefits Taken Early

If a worker elects to receive retirement benefits prior to age 65, benefits are permanently reduced by 5/9 of one percent for every month that the early retirement precedes age 65. For example, for a worker who retires at age 62, the monthly benefit will be only 80 percent of that worker's PIA. A spouse who elects retirement benefits prior to age 65 will have benefits reduced by 25/36 of one percent per month, and a widow or widower will have benefits reduced by 19/40 of one percent per month. In the latter case, benefits at age 60 will be 71 1/2 percent of the worker's PIA. If the widow or widower elects benefits at an earlier age because of disability, there is no further reduction.

Delayed Retirement

Workers who delay applying for benefits until after the normal retirement age (currently 65) are eligible for an increased benefit. Benefits are increased for each month of late retirement until age 70. For persons born from 1917 until 1924 the increase is 1/4 of one percent per month, which is equal to 3 percent for delaying application for benefit for one full year. To encourage later retirement, the monthly percent will gradually increase. Table 2-4 shows the percentage for each month of deferral as well as the maximum percentage increase that is available if retirement is postponed until age 70.

TABLE 2-4
Increase for Delayed Retirement

Year of Birth	Monthly Percentage Increase	Maximum Percentage Increase
1917–24	1/4	15.00
1925–26	7/24	17.50
1927–28	1/3	20.00
1929–30	9/24	22.50
1931–32	5/12	25.00
1933–34	11/24	27.50
1935–36	1/2	30.00
1937	13/24	32.50
1938	13/24	31.42
1939	7/12	32.67
1940	7/12	31.50
1941	15/24	32.50
1942	15/24	31.25
1943–54	2/3	32.00
1955	2/3	30.67
1956	2/3	29.33
1957	2/3	28.00
1958	2/3	26.67
1959	2/3	25.33
1960 and later	2/3	24.00

It should be pointed out that these increases apply to a worker's PIA as determined at the time a worker applies for retirement benefits. If a person continues to work during the period of delayed retirement and covered wages are sufficiently high, it is possible for a worker's PIA to be higher than it would have been at normal retirement age. Therefore the increased monthly retirement benefit from working past normal retirement age may be greater than the percentages in the table.

Earnings Test

Benefits are reduced for social security beneficiaries under the age of 70 if they have work wages that exceed a specified level. The rationale behind having such a reduction tied to wages, referred to as an earnings test, is that social security benefits are intended to replace lost wages but not other income such as dividends or interest. In 1997 social security beneficiaries aged 65 through 69 are allowed annual wages of $13,500 without any reduction in their benefits. This amount is scheduled to increase to $14,500 in 1998, $15,500 in 1999, $17,000 in 2000, $25,000 in 2001, and $30,000 in 2002. Beneficiaries under age 65 are allowed earnings of $8,640. This figure is adjusted annually on the basis of national wage levels. If a beneficiary earns in excess of the allowable amount, his or her social security benefit is reduced. For persons aged 65 through 69 the reduction is $1 for every $3 of excess earnings; for persons under age 65 the reduction is $1 for every $2 of excess earnings. Social security beneficiaries aged 70 or older can earn any amount of wages without a reduction of benefits.

The reduction in a retired worker's benefits resulting from excess earnings is charged against the entire benefits that are paid to a family and based on the worker's social security record. If large enough, this reduction may totally eliminate all benefits otherwise payable to the worker and family members. In contrast, excess earnings of family members are charged against their individual benefits only. For example, a widowed mother who holds a job outside the home may lose her mother's benefit, but any benefits received by her children will be unaffected.

Cost-of-living Adjustments

OASDI benefits are increased automatically each January as long as there has been an increase in the CPI for the one-year period ending in the third quarter of the prior year. The increase is the same as the increase in the CPI since the last cost-of-living adjustment, rounded to the nearest 0.1 percent.

There is one exception to this adjustment. In any year that the combined reserves of the OASDI trust funds drop below 20 percent of expected benefits, the cost-of-living adjustment will be limited to the lesser of the increase in the CPI or the increase in national wages used to adjust the wage base for social security taxes. When benefit increases have been based on wage levels, future cost-of-living increases can be larger than changes in the CPI to make up for the lower benefit increases in those years when the CPI was not used. However, this extra cost-of-living increase can be made only in years when the reserve is equal to at least 32 percent of expected benefits.

Offset for Other Benefits

Disabled workers under age 65 who are also receiving workers' compensation benefits or disability benefits from certain other federal, state, or local disability programs will have their OASDI benefits reduced to the extent that the total benefits received (including family benefits) exceed 80 percent of their average current earnings at the time of disability. In addition, the monthly benefit of a spouse or surviving spouse is reduced by two-thirds of any federal, state, or local government pension that is based on earnings not covered under OASDI on the last day of employment.

OASDI: REQUESTING BENEFIT INFORMATION

In 1995 the Social Security Administration began sending an annual Earnings and Benefit Estimate Statement to each worker aged 60 and older. By the year 2000, this statement will be provided annually to all workers over age 25. In the meantime these persons should periodically check their records with the Social Security Administration by filing Form SSA-7004 (Request for Earnings and Benefit Estimate Statement). The form is quite brief, and the statement received enables an employee to verify his or her contributions to the OASDI program and medicare. It also contains an estimate of benefits that will be available upon retirement, disability, or death.

Employers can encourage this prudence on the part of employees by requesting bulk copies of the form and distributing them periodically. The results will help employees to understand their total benefit package as well as enable any errors in earnings records to be corrected while information is readily available.

MEDICARE: ELIGIBILITY

Part A, the hospital portion of medicare, is available to any person aged 65 or older as long as the person is entitled to monthly retirement benefits under social security or the railroad retirement program. Civilian employees of the federal government aged 65 or older are also eligible. It is not necessary for these workers to actually be receiving retirement benefits, but they must be fully insured for purposes of retirement benefits. The following persons are also eligible for part A of medicare at no monthly cost:

- persons aged 65 or older who are dependents of fully insured workers aged 62 or older

- survivors aged 65 or older who are eligible for OASDI survivors benefits
- disabled persons at any age who have been eligible to receive OASDI benefits for 2 years because of their disability. This includes workers under age 65, disabled widows and widowers aged 50 or over, and children 18 or older who were disabled prior to age 22.
- workers who are either fully or currently insured and their spouses and dependent children with end-stage renal (kidney) disease who require renal dialysis or kidney transplants. Coverage begins either the first day of the third month after dialysis begins or earlier for admission to a hospital for kidney-transplant surgery.

Most persons aged 65 or over who do not meet the previously discussed eligibility requirements may voluntarily enroll in medicare. However, they must pay a monthly part A premium and also enroll in part B. The part A premium may be as high as $311 in 1997, depending on the quarters of coverage a person earned under social security. The premium is adjusted annually to reflect the full cost of the benefits provided.

Any person eligible for part A of medicare is also eligible for part B. However, a monthly premium must be paid for part B. This premium, $43.80 in 1997, is adjusted annually and represents only about 25 percent of the cost of the benefits provided. The remaining cost of the program is financed from the general revenues of the federal government.

Persons receiving social security or railroad retirement benefits are automatically enrolled in medicare if they are eligible. If they do not want part B, they must reject it in writing. Other persons eligible for medicare must apply for benefits. As a general rule, anyone who rejects part B or who does not enroll when initially eligible may later apply for benefits during a general enrollment period that occurs between January 1 and March 31 of each year. However, the monthly premium will be increased by 10 percent for each 12-month period during which the person was eligible but failed to enroll.

Medicare secondary rules, which are covered in detail in chapter 12, make employer-provided medical expense coverage primary to medicare for certain classes of individuals who are over 65, who are disabled, or who are suffering end-stage renal disease. These persons (and any other medicare-eligible persons still covered as active employees under their employer's plans) may not wish to elect medicare because it largely constitutes duplicate coverage. When their employer-provided coverage ends, these persons have 8 months to enroll in part B, and the late enrollment penalty is waived.

MEDICARE: PART A BENEFITS

Part A of medicare provides benefits for expenses incurred in hospitals, skilled-nursing facilities, and hospices. Home health care benefits are also covered. In order for benefits to be paid, the facility or agency providing benefits must participate in the medicare program. Virtually all hospitals are participants, as are most other facilities or agencies that meet the requirements of medicare.

Part A of medicare, along with part B, provides a high level of benefits for medical expenses. However, as will be described in the next few pages, deductibles and copayments may be higher than in prior group or individual coverage. In addition, certain benefits that were previously provided may be excluded or limited. For this reason, persons without supplemental retiree coverage from prior employment may wish to consider the purchase of a medigap policy in the individual marketplace.

Hospital Benefits

Part A pays for inpatient hospital services for up to 90 days in each benefit period (also referred to as a *spell of illness*). A benefit period begins the first time a medicare recipient is hospitalized and ends only after the recipient has been out of a hospital or skilled-nursing facility for 60 consecutive days. A subsequent hospitalization then begins a new benefit period.

In each benefit period, covered hospital expenses are paid in full for 60 days, subject to an initial deductible of $760 in 1997. This deductible is adjusted annually to reflect increasing hospital costs. Benefits for an additional 30 days of hospitalization are also provided in each benefit period, but the patient must pay a daily coinsurance charge ($190 in 1997) equal to 25 percent of the initial deductible amount. Each recipient also has a lifetime reserve of 60 additional days that may be used if the regular 90 days of benefits have been exhausted. However, once a reserve day is used, it cannot be restored for use in future benefit periods. When using reserve days, patients must pay a daily coinsurance charge ($380 in 1997) equal to 50 percent of the initial deductible amount.

There is no limit on the number of benefit periods a person may have during his or her lifetime. However, there is a lifetime limit of 190 days of benefits for treatment in psychiatric hospitals.

Covered inpatient expenses include the following:

- room and board in semiprivate accommodations. Private rooms are covered only if required for medical reasons.
- nursing services (except private-duty nurses)
- use of regular hospital equipment, such as oxygen tents or wheelchairs
- drugs and biologicals ordinarily furnished by the hospital
- diagnostic or therapeutic items or services
- operating room costs
- blood transfusions after the first three pints of blood. Patients must pay for the first three pints of blood unless they get donors to replace the blood.

There is no coverage under part A for the services of physicians or surgeons.

Skilled-Nursing Facility Benefits

In many cases a patient may no longer require continuous hospital care but may not be well enough to go home. Consequently part A provides benefits for care in a skilled-nursing facility if a physician certifies that skilled-nursing care or rehabilitative services are needed for a condition that was treated in a hospital within the last 30 days. In addition, the prior hospitalization must have lasted at least 3 days. Benefits are paid in full for 20 days in each benefit period and for an additional 80 days with a daily coinsurance charge ($95 in 1997) that is equal to 12.5 percent of the initial hospital deductible. Covered expenses are the same as those described for hospital benefits.

A skilled-nursing facility may be a separate facility for providing such care or a separate section of a hospital or nursing home. The facility must have at least one full-time registered nurse, and nursing services must be provided at all times. Every patient must be under the supervision of a physician, and a physician must always be available for emergency care.

One very important point should be made about skilled-nursing facility benefits. Custodial care is not provided under any part of the medicare program unless skilled-nursing or rehabilitative services are also needed.

Home Health Care Benefits

If a patient can be treated at home for a medical condition, part A will pay the full cost for an unlimited number of home visits by a home health agency. Such agencies specialize in providing nursing services and other therapeutic services. To receive these benefits, a person must be confined at home and be treated under a home health plan set up by a physician. No prior hospitalization is required. The care needed must include skilled-nursing services, physical therapy, or speech therapy. In addition to these services, medicare will also pay for the cost of part-time home health aides, medical social services, occupational therapy, and medical supplies and equipment provided by the home health agency. There is no charge for these benefits other than a required 20 percent copayment for the cost of durable medical equipment such as iron lungs, oxygen tanks, and hospital beds. Medicare does not cover home services furnished primarily to assist people in activities of daily living such as housecleaning, preparing meals, shopping, dressing, or bathing.

Hospice Benefits

Hospice benefits are available under part A of medicare for terminally ill persons who have a life expectancy of 6 months or less. While a hospice is thought of as a facility for treating the terminally ill, medicare benefits are available primarily for hospice-type benefits provided to patients in their own homes. However, up to 20 percent of the days of hospice treatment may be as an inpatient in a facility of the organization providing home treatment or in a hospital or other facility with which it cooperates. In addition to including the types of benefits described for home health care, hospice benefits also include drugs, bereavement counseling, and inpatient respite care when family members need a break from caring for the ill person.

In order to qualify for hospice benefits, a medicare recipient must elect such coverage in lieu of other medicare benefits, except for the services of the attending physician or services and benefits that do not pertain to the terminal condition. There are modest copayments for some services.

Once hospice benefits are elected, there are 210 days of benefits—two 90-day periods and one 30-day period. These three periods can be used consecutively. A beneficiary may cancel the hospice coverage at any time (for example, to pursue chemotherapy treatments) and return to regular medicare coverage. Any remaining days of the current hospice benefit period are lost forever, but the beneficiary can elect hospice benefits again if there are any remaining benefit periods available. The 210 days of benefits can be extended if the beneficiary is recertified as terminally ill.

Exclusions

There are some circumstances under which part A of medicare will not pay benefits. In addition, there are times when medicare will act as the secondary payer of benefits. Exclusions under part A include the following:

- services outside the United States and its territories or possessions. However, there are a few exceptions to this rule for qualified Mexican and Canadian hospitals. Benefits will be paid if an emergency occurs in the United States and the closest hospital is in one of these countries. However, persons living closer to a hospital in one of these countries than to a hospital in the United States may use the foreign hospital even if an emergency does not exist. Finally, there is coverage for Canadian hospitals if a person needs hospitalization while traveling the most direct route between Alaska and another state in the United States. However, this latter provision does not apply to persons vacationing in Canada.
- elective luxury services, such as private rooms or televisions
- hospitalization for services not necessary for the treatment of an illness or injury, such as custodial care or elective cosmetic surgery
- services performed in a federal facility, such as a veterans' hospital
- services covered under workers' compensation

Under the following circumstances, medicare is the secondary payer of benefits:

- when primary coverage under an employer-provided medical expense plan is elected by (1) an employee or spouse aged 65 or older or (2) a disabled beneficiary
- when medical care can be paid under any liability policy, including policies providing automobile no-fault benefits
- in the first 18 months for end-stage renal disease when an employer-provided medical expense plan provides coverage. By law employer plans cannot specifically exclude this coverage during this 18-month period.

Medicare pays only if complete coverage is not available from these sources and then only to the extent that benefits are less than would otherwise be payable under medicare. These medicare secondary rules are covered in more detail in chapter 12.

MEDICARE: PART B BENEFITS

Benefits

Part B of medicare provides benefits for the following medical expenses not covered under part A:

- physicians' and surgeons' fees. These fees may result from house calls, office visits, or services provided in a hospital or other institution. Under certain circumstances benefits are also provided for the services of chiropractors, podiatrists, and optometrists.
- diagnostic tests in a hospital or in a physician's office
- physical therapy in a physician's office, or as an outpatient of a hospital, skilled-nursing facility, or other approved clinic, rehabilitative agency, or public-health agency
- drugs and biologicals that cannot be self-administered
- radiation therapy
- medical supplies, such as surgical dressings, splints, and casts
- rental of medical equipment, such as oxygen tents, hospital beds, and wheelchairs
- prosthetic devices, such as artificial heart valves or lenses after a cataract operation
- ambulance service if a patient's condition does not permit the use of other methods of transportation
- mammograms
- pneumococcal vaccine and its administration
- home health services as described for part A when a person does not have part A coverage

Exclusions

Although the preceding list may appear to be comprehensive, there are numerous medical products and services not covered by part B, some of which represent significant expenses for the elderly. They include the following:

- drugs and biologicals that can be self-administered except drugs for osteoporosis
- routine physical, eye, and hearing examinations except mammograms
- routine foot care
- immunizations, except pneumococcal vaccinations or immunization required because of an injury or immediate risk of infection
- cosmetic surgery unless it is needed because of an accidental injury or to improve the function of a malformed part of the body
- dental care unless it involves jaw or facial bone surgery or the setting of fractures
- custodial care
- eyeglasses, hearing aids, or orthopedic shoes

In addition, benefits are not provided to persons eligible for workers' compensation or to those treated in government hospitals. Benefits are provided only for services received in the United States, except for physicians' services and ambulance services rendered for a hospitalization that is covered in Mexico or Canada under part A. Part B is also a secondary payer of benefits under the same circumstances described for part A.

Amount of Benefits

With some exceptions part B pays 80 percent of the approved charges for covered medical expenses after the satisfaction of a $100 annual deductible. Annual maximums apply to outpatient psychiatric benefits ($450) and physical therapy in a therapist's office or at the patient's home ($400). A few charges are paid in full without any cost sharing. These include (1) home health services, (2) pneumococcal vaccine and its administration, (3) certain surgical procedures that are performed on an outpatient basis in lieu of hospitalization, and (4) diagnostic preadmission tests performed on an outpatient basis within 7 days prior to hospitalization.

Beginning in 1992 the approved charge for doctor's services covered by medicare is based on a fee schedule issued by the Health Care Financing Administration. A patient will be reimbursed for only 80 percent of the approved charges above the deductible—regardless of the doctor's actual charge. Most doctors and other suppliers of medical services accept an assignment of medicare benefits and therefore are prohibited from charging a patient in excess of the fee schedule. They can, however, bill the patient for any portion of the approved charges that were not paid by medicare because of the annual deductible and/or coinsurance. They can also bill for any services that are not covered by medicare.

Since 1993 doctors who do not accept assignment of medicare benefits have not been permitted to charge a medicare patient more than 115 percent of the approved fee for nonparticipating doctors. Because the approved fee for nonparticipating doctors is set at 95 percent of the fee paid for participating doctors, a doctor who does not accept an assignment of medicare benefits can charge a fee that is only 9.25 percent greater than if an assignment had been accepted (115 percent x 95 percent = 109.25 percent). As a result, some doctors either do not see medicare participants, or they limit the number of such patients that they treat.

The previous limitation on charges does not apply to providers of medical services other than doctors. Although a provider who does not accept assignment can charge any fee, medicare will pay only 80 percent of what the fee schedule shows has been approved. For example, assume the approved charge for medical equipment is $100 and the actual charge is $190. Medicare will reimburse $80 (.80 x $100), and the balance must be borne by the medicare recipient.

MANAGED CARE COVERAGE UNDER MEDICARE

Medicare participants may elect to have covered services provided through a managed care plan offered by a health maintenance organization (HMO) or an insurance company, and a growing number (currently about 10 percent) of medicare participants are electing this option. HMOs and other forms of managed care are covered in detail later in this book. For many persons a managed care option is a viable alternative to a medigap policy for obtaining broader coverage than is available under medicare.

It is important to note that a medicare participant can terminate coverage under a managed care plan and return to the regular medicare program, effective the first day of the following month.

HMO Coverage

In order for an HMO to enroll medicare participants, the HMO must enter into a contract with the Department of Health and Human Services. Approval requires that the HMO offer benefits at least as broad as those that are available under medicare. As a general rule, approval also requires the HMO to have been in existence for at least 2 years and to have an enrollment comprising at least 25,000 persons. Furthermore, no more than 50 percent of the HMO's enrollment can consist of medicare participants. The HMO is then reimbursed by medicare for the services it provides to participants who elect coverage. In effect, the HMO is acting as a subcontractor in providing benefits for medicare.

If an HMO is approved to participate, a medicare participant can elect coverage during a specified 30-day open enrollment period. Under the first two HMO arrangements described below, all eligible applicants must be accepted, subject to certain maximum limits; under the third arrangement, an HMO can reject unhealthy applicants. In order to be eligible, a medicare participant must meet the following requirements:

- be enrolled in part B of medicare and continue to pay the part B premium
- live in the service area of the HMO
- not be receiving care in a medicare-certified hospice
- not have permanent kidney failure

In addition, the person must pay any periodic premium charged by the HMO. This premium is set in a manner that takes into account the contribution that will be made by medicare, which is 95 percent of what medicare would have paid in benefits for the same class of employees if they had remained under medicare. Because of economies associated with the HMO arrangement, most medicare HMOs are able to provide coverage without an additional premium while also increasing benefits. Such benefits include eliminating deductibles, lowering copayments, and providing expanded coverage for such benefits as prescription drugs, eyeglasses, hearing aids, and routine physical examinations. However, some HMOs do charge a small premium when these additional benefits are provided, particularly if the additional benefits are substantial.

As discussed later in this book, there may be some drawbacks to HMO participation. Probably the most significant one is that participants may have negative attitudes toward the concept of managed care. For example, participants must use the HMO's network of doctors and hospitals and will have less choice in selecting providers than under the regular medicare program. However, this drawback will concern fewer persons as more employees have coverage under managed care plans at the time of retirement.

One issue that persons electing a medicare HMO must address is whether there is any need to purchase a medigap policy or maintain a policy already in force. There is little need for such a policy because it will only duplicate (and therefore not pay) benefits provided by the medicare HMO. However, if a medicare HMO participant later leaves the HMO and wants a medigap policy to supplement regular medicare benefits, he or she may be unable to buy the policy of choice, particularly if health problems exist. (The Clinton administration has proposed a change in medigap rules so that a person who drops a medigap policy after joining a medicare managed care plan can obtain a new policy without evidence of insurability if the person leaves the managed care plan.)

There are three types of arrangements for providing HMO benefits to medicare participants. It is unlikely that any individual HMO will make more than one of these arrangements available. These three arrangements are listed in order of their prevalence.

Medicare Risk Plan

The medicare risk plan is by far the most common HMO arrangement for medicare beneficiaries. Under a medicare risk plan, the HMO provides all medicare services and normally also provides additional benefits to the participant. Once HMO coverage is elected, the participant has effectively rejected the regular medicare program and must look to the HMO coverage.

A problem may arise if a medicare risk plan participant lives part of the year in another location or travels extensively. While medicare and a medigap policy would provide coverage at these locations (at least in the United States), it might be difficult to obtain HMO benefits in nonemergency situations. However, some medicare risk plans affiliate with one another to provide coverage when a participant travels from one HMO's service area to another's service area.

Medicare Cost Plan

Under a medicare cost plan, a participant can receive all medical care from the HMO or go outside the HMO network for services as desired. Medicare reimburses the HMO for the actual cost of providing care to participants. When care is received outside the HMO network, medicare pays its usual benefits, which means that participants are responsible for the usual medicare deductibles and coinsurance.

Medicare Health Care Prepayment Plan

This is a more limited version of the previous plans in that medicare reimburses the HMO to provide limited services, usually those available under part B. Participants must go outside of the HMO network for other services, for which they receive regular medicare benefits.

Medicare Select Policies

Medicare select policies are available through a trial program. Under this program, participants may purchase a private insurance contract that is similar to a medigap policy. However, the policy must also provide part A benefits and possibly part B benefits. In order to receive benefits provided under the policy, a participant must receive care from a designated network of medical providers. However, the subscriber can receive services outside the network and receive regular medicare benefits. This is a form of point-of-service plan, which is discussed in a subsequent chapter on managed care.

If a participant decides to terminate a medicare select policy and return to regular medicare coverage, he or she must be given the option to purchase any medigap policy sold by the company that issues the medicare select policy.

The medicare select program, originally available in only 15 states, was expanded to all states in 1995. The trial phase of the program now extends to June 30, 1998, at which time the program will become permanent unless the

Department of Health and Human Services concludes that it should be discontinued. In making its decision, the department will evaluate cost, quality, and accessibility of medicare select policies.

TAXATION OF SOCIAL INSURANCE BENEFITS

Deductibility of Premiums

Employer contributions to the social insurance programs described in this chapter are tax deductible for federal income tax purposes. Any employee contributions must be paid with aftertax dollars. Since 1990, however, self-employed persons have been able to deduct one-half of their social security tax as a business expense.

Taxation of Income Benefits

Until 1984 all social security benefits were received free of federal income taxation. Since that time, benefits received in the form of monthly income under OASDI have been partially subject to income taxation for some social security recipients. To determine the amount of social security benefits subject to taxation, it is necessary to calculate modified adjusted gross income, which is the sum of the following:

- the taxpayer's adjusted gross income (disregarding any foreign income and savings bond exclusions)
- the taxpayer's tax-exempt interest received or accrued during the year
- one-half of the social security benefits for the year

If the modified adjusted gross income is $25,000 or less for a single taxpayer ($32,000 or less for a married taxpayer filing jointly), social security benefits are not taxable. If the modified adjusted gross income is between the base amount and $34,000 ($44,000 for a married taxpayer filing jointly), up to 50 percent of the social security benefit will be includible in taxable income. If the modified adjusted gross income exceeds $34,000 ($44,000 for a married taxpayer filing jointly), up to 85 percent of the social security benefit will be includible in taxable income. The exact amount of the taxable social security benefit is determined by complex formulas that are beyond the scope of this discussion. (Note: Prior to the election of President Clinton, 50 percent was the maximum amount of social security benefits that could be included in taxable income, regardless of a taxpayer's income. Now that the Republicans have gained control of Congress, there is considerable support to roll back the newer 85 percent amount to the previous level.)

3

Other Social Insurance Programs

Chapter Outline

This chapter focuses on the three major social insurance programs other than social security—unemployment insurance, workers' compensation insurance, and temporary disability laws. Unemployment insurance is a joint federal and state program, and workers' compensation insurance and temporary disability laws are solely under state control. Because the programs of each state are unique, the discussion in this chapter is general in nature. Readers should familiarize themselves with the programs in their own state and not assume that these programs will always conform to the generalizations that follow.

UNEMPLOYMENT INSURANCE

Prior to the passage of the Social Security Act in 1935, relatively few employees had any type of protection for income lost during periods of unemployment. The act stipulated that a payroll tax was to be levied on covered employers for the purpose of financing unemployment insurance programs that were to be established by the states under guidelines issued by the federal government. Essentially the federal law levied a federal tax on certain employers in all states. If a state established an acceptable program of unemployment insurance, the taxes used to finance its program could be offset against up to 90 percent of the federal tax. If a state failed to establish a program, the federal tax would still be levied, but no monies collected from the employers in that state would be returned for purposes of providing benefits to the unemployed there. Needless to say, all states quickly established unemployment insurance programs. These programs (along with a federal program for railroad workers) now cover over 95 percent of all working persons, but major gaps in coverage exist for domestic workers, agricultural workers, and the self-employed.

There are several objectives to the current unemployment insurance program. The primary objective is to provide periodic cash income to workers during periods of involuntary unemployment. Benefits are generally paid as a matter of right, with no demonstration of need required. While federal legislation has extended benefits during times of high unemployment, the unemployment insurance program is basically designed for workers whose periods of unemployment are short-term; the long-term and hard-core unemployed must rely on other measures, such as public assistance and job-retraining programs, when unemployment insurance benefits are exhausted.

A second major objective of unemployment insurance is to help the unemployed find jobs. Workers must register at local unemployment offices, and unemployment benefits are received through these offices. Another important objective is to encourage employers to stabilize employment. As will be described later, this is accomplished through the use of experience rating in determining an employer's tax rate. Finally, unemployment insurance contributes to a stable labor supply by providing benefits so that skilled and experienced workers are not forced to seek other jobs during short-term layoffs, thereby remaining available to return to work when called back.

Financing of Benefits

Unemployment insurance programs are financed primarily by unemployment taxes levied by both the federal and state governments. The federal tax is equal to 6.2 percent of the first $7,000 of wages for each worker, but this tax is reduced by up to 5.4 percentage points for taxes paid to state programs. The practical effect of this offset is that the federal tax is actually equal to 0.8 percent of covered payroll. A few states levy an unemployment payroll tax equal to only the maximum offset (5.4 percent on the first $7,000 of wages), but most states have a higher tax rate and/or levy their tax on a higher amount of earnings.

No state levies the same tax on all employers. Rather they use a method of experience rating whereby all employers, except those that have been in business for a short time or those with a small number of employees, pay a tax rate that reflects their actual experience within limits. Thus an employer who has laid off a large percentage of employees will have a higher tax rate than an employer whose employment record has been stable.

An employer who has good experience will often have to pay a state tax of less than one percent of payroll and possibly even as little as 0.1 percent. On the other hand, some employers may pay a state tax as high as 9 or 10 percent. Regardless of the amount of actual state tax paid, the employer will still pay the 0.8 percent federal tax.

The major argument for experience rating is that it will provide a financial incentive for employers to stabilize employment. However, those who are opposed to its use contend that many employers have little control over economic trends that affect employment. In addition, they argue that tax rates will tend to escalate in bad economic times and thus may actually serve as an obstacle to economic recovery.

The entire unemployment insurance tax is collected by the individual states and deposited in the Federal Unemployment Insurance Trust Fund, which is administered by the secretary of the Treasury. Each state has a separate account that is credited with its taxes and its share of investment earnings on assets in the fund. Unemployment benefits in the state are paid from this account. The federal share of the taxes received by the fund is deposited into separate accounts and is used for administering the federal portion of the program and for giving grants to the states to administer their individual programs. In addition, the federal funds are available for loans to states whose accounts have been depleted during times of high unemployment.

Eligibility for Benefits

In order to receive unemployment benefits a worker must meet the following eligibility requirements:

- have a prior attachment to the labor force
- be able to work and be available for work
- be actively seeking work
- have satisfied any prescribed waiting period
- be free of disqualification

Prior Attachment to the Labor Force

The right to benefits depends on the worker's attachment to the labor force within a prior *base period*. In most states this base period is the 52 weeks or 4 quarters prior to the time of unemployment. During this base period the worker must have earned a minimum amount of wages or worked a minimum period of time, or both.

Able to Work and Available for Work

The right to benefits is also contingent on an unemployed worker's being both physically and mentally capable of working. The worker must also be available for work. Benefits may be denied if suitable work is refused or if substantial restrictions are placed on the type of work that will be accepted.

Actively Seeking Work

In addition to registering with a local unemployment office, most states require a worker to make a reasonable effort to seek work.

Waiting Period

Most unemployment programs have a one-week waiting period before benefits commence. Benefits are not paid retroactively for that time of unemployment.

Free of Disqualification

All states have provisions in their laws under which a worker may be disqualified from receiving benefits. This disqualification may take the form of (1) a total cancellation of benefit rights, (2) the postponement of benefits, or (3) a reduction in benefits. Common reasons for disqualification are

- voluntarily leaving a job without good cause
- discharge for misconduct
- refusal to accept suitable work
- involvement in a labor dispute
- receipt of disqualifying income. This includes dismissal wages, workers' compensation benefits, benefits from an employer's pension plan, or primary insurance benefits under OASDI.

Benefits

The majority of states pay "regular" unemployment insurance benefits for a maximum of 26 weeks; the remaining states pay benefits for slightly longer periods. In most states the amount of the weekly benefit is equal to a specified fraction of a worker's average wages during the highest calendar quarter of the base period. The typical fraction is 1/26, which yields a benefit equal to 50 percent of earnings. Other states determine benefits as a percentage of average weekly wages or annual wages during the base period. Some states also modify their benefit formulas to provide relatively higher benefits (as a percentage of past earnings) to lower-paid workers. Benefits in all states are subject to minimum and maximum amounts. Minimum weekly benefits typically fall within the range of $20 to $70, maximum benefits in the range of $180 to $350, and the average benefit in the range of $140 to $215. In addition, a few states currently provide additional benefits if there are dependents who receive regular support from the worker.

States also provide reduced benefits for partial unemployment. Such a condition occurs if a worker is employed less than full-time and has a weekly income less than his or her weekly benefit amount for total unemployment.

Since 1970 there has been a permanent federal-state program of "extended" unemployment benefits for workers whose regular benefits are exhausted during periods of high unemployment. These benefits are financed equally by the federal government and the states involved and can be paid for up to 13 weeks, as long as the total of regular and extended benefits does not exceed 39 weeks. This program is operable when the *insured unemployment rate* in a state exceeds a specified level. The insured unemployment rate is the percentage of workers covered by unemployment insurance who are receiving regular benefits. Benefits can also be triggered if a state's *total unemployment rate* exceeds specified criteria. In this case an additional 20 weeks of benefits can be paid.

In periods of severe unemployment, the federal government often enacts legislation to provide additional benefits that are financed with federal revenue. The last such program expired in 1994.

Problems and Issues

The current system of unemployment insurance has increasingly become subject to criticism, especially regarding the level of benefits. At current levels the majority of employees receive benefits that are less than half of their former wages. Because of maximum limits on the amounts of benefits, higher-income employees will receive proportionately smaller benefits than lower-paid employees if they are unemployed.

In addition to the level of benefits, the percentage of persons receiving benefits at any point in time has dropped over the last two decades. Typically fewer than 40 percent of the unemployed are receiving benefits. Some persons have benefits denied because of more stringent rules, particularly those dealing with initial benefit disqualification. Other persons exhaust the benefits that are available. Of course there are those who argue that without disqualifications and limits on benefits, there would be little incentive for many of the unemployed to seek work.

Few employers provide any type of supplemental unemployment benefits. The plans that do exist are in highly unionized industries and result from collective bargaining. These plans are briefly discussed in the chapter on other group benefits.

There seems to be a feeling among economists that unemployment insurance programs are less effective in dealing with unemployment issues than in the past. In theory, unemployment compensation insurance should be a counterbalance against recessions. In practice this is often not the case, perhaps because of the low percentage of persons receiving benefits. In addition, the degree of experience rating has declined over time, reducing the incentive for employers to retain employees in bad times rather than laying them off. It also shifts an increasing burden for financing the program to employers in industries with stable employment.

TEMPORARY DISABILITY LAWS

At their inception state unemployment insurance programs were usually designed to cover only unemployed persons who were both willing and able to work. Benefits were denied to anyone who was unable to work for any reason, including disability. Some states amended their unemployment insurance laws to provide coverage to the unemployed who subsequently became disabled. However, five states—California, Hawaii, New Jersey, New York, and Rhode Island—and Puerto Rico went one step further by enacting temporary disability laws under which employees can collect disability income benefits regardless of whether their disability begins while they are employed or unemployed. While variations exist among the states, these laws (often referred to as nonoccupational disability laws since benefits are not provided for disabilities covered under workers' compensation laws) are generally patterned after the state unemployment insurance law and provide similar benefits.

In the six jurisdictions with temporary disability laws, most employers are required to provide coverage for their employees. In most jurisdictions except Rhode Island, which has a monopolistic state fund, coverage may be obtained from either a competitive state fund or private insurance companies. Private coverage must provide at least the benefits prescribed under the law, but it may be more comprehensive. As with workers' compensation insurance, self-insurance is generally permitted. Depending on the jurisdiction, the cost of an employer's program may be borne entirely by employee contributions, entirely by employer contributions, or by contributions from both parties.

Eligibility

Before an employee is eligible for benefits under a temporary disability law, the employee must satisfy (1) an earnings or employment requirement, (2) the definition of disability, and (3) a waiting period.

Earnings or Employment Requirement

Every jurisdiction requires that an employee must have worked for a specified time and/or have received a minimum amount of wages within some specific period prior to disability in order to qualify for benefits.

Definition of Disability

Most laws define disability as the inability of the worker to perform his or her regular or customary work because of a nonoccupational injury or illness. New Jersey has the most stringent definition of disability, which requires that an employee be unable to perform any work for remuneration. As with workers' compensation laws, certain types of disabilities are not covered. In most jurisdictions these include disabilities caused by self-inflicted injuries or by illegal acts.

Waiting Period

The usual waiting period for benefits is 7 days. However, in some jurisdictions the waiting period is waived if the employee is hospitalized.

Benefits

Benefits are a percentage, ranging from 50 percent to 66 2/3 percent, of the employee's average weekly wage for some period prior to disability, subject to maximum and minimum amounts. Benefits are generally paid up to 26 weeks if the employee remains disabled that long.

WORKERS' COMPENSATION LAWS

Prior to the passage of workers' compensation laws, it was difficult for employees to receive compensation for their work-related injuries or diseases. Group benefits were meager and the social security program had not yet been enacted. The only recourse for employees was to sue their employer for damages. In addition to the time and expense of such actions (as well as the possibility of being fired), the probability of a worker's winning such a suit was small because of the three common-law defenses available to employers. Under the contributory negligence doctrine, a worker could not collect if his or her negligence had contributed in any way to the injury. Under the fellow-servant doctrine, the worker could not collect if the injury had resulted from the negligence of a fellow worker. And finally, under the assumption-of-risk doctrine, a worker could not recover if he or she had knowingly assumed the risks inherent in the trade.

To help solve the problem of uncompensated injuries, workers' compensation laws were enacted to require employers to provide benefits to employees for losses resulting from work-related accidents or diseases. These laws are based on the principle of liability without fault. Essentially an employer is absolutely liable for providing the benefits prescribed by the workers' compensation laws, regardless of whether the employer would be considered legally liable in the absence of these laws. However, benefits, with the possible exception of medical expense benefits, are subject to statutory maximums.

All states have workers' compensation laws. In addition, the federal government has enacted several similar laws. The Federal Employees Compensation Act provides benefits for the employees of the federal government and the District of Columbia. Railroad employees and workers aboard ships are covered under the Federal Employer's Liability Act, and stevedores, longshoremen, and workers who repair ships are covered under the United States Longshoremen's and Harbor Workers' Act.

Type of Law

Most workers' compensation laws are compulsory for all employers covered under the law. A few states have elective laws, but the majority of employers do elect coverage. If they do not, their employees are not entitled to workers' compensation benefits and must sue for damages resulting from occupational accidents or diseases. However, the employer loses the right to the three common-law defenses previously described.

Financing of Benefits

Most states allow employers to comply with the workers' compensation law by purchasing coverage from insurance companies. Several of these states also have competitive state funds from which coverage may be obtained, but these funds usually provide benefits for fewer employers than insurance companies. Six states have monopolistic state funds that are the only source for obtaining coverage under the law.

Almost all states, including some with monopolistic state funds, allow employers to self-insure their workers' compensation exposure. These employers must generally post a bond or other security and receive the approval of the agency administering the law. While the number of firms using self-insurance for workers' compensation is small, these firms account for approximately one-half the employees covered under such laws.

In virtually all cases, the full cost of providing workers' compensation benefits must be borne by the employer. Obviously if an employer self-insures benefits, the ultimate cost will include the benefits paid plus any administrative expenses.

Employers who purchase coverage pay a premium that is calculated as a rate per $100 of payroll, based on the occupations of their workers. For example, rates for office workers may be as low as $.10, and rates for workers in a few hazardous occupations may exceed $50. Most states also require that employers with total workers' compensation premiums above a specified amount be subject to experience rating. That is, the employer's premium is a function of benefits paid for past injuries to the employer's workers. To the extent that safety costs are offset or eliminated by savings in workers' compensation premiums, experience-rating laws encourage employers to take an active role in correcting conditions that may cause injuries.

Covered Occupations

Although it is estimated that about 90 percent of the workers in the United States are covered by workers' compensation laws, the percentage varies among the states from less than 70 percent to more than 95 percent. Many laws exclude certain agricultural, domestic, and casual employees. Some laws also exclude employers with a small number of employees. Furthermore, coverage for employees of state and local governments is not universal.

Eligibility

Before an employee can be eligible for benefits under a workers' compensation law, he or she must work in an occupation covered by that law and be disabled or killed by a covered injury or illness. The typical workers' compensation law provides coverage for *accidental occupational injuries (including death) arising out of and in the course of employment.* In all states this includes injuries arising out of accidents, which are generally defined as sudden and unexpected events that are definite in time and place. Most workers' compensation laws exclude self-inflicted injuries and accidents resulting from an employee's intoxication or willful disregard of safety rules.

Every state has some coverage for illnesses resulting from occupational diseases. While the trend is toward full coverage for occupational diseases, some states cover only those diseases that are specifically listed in the law.

Benefits

Workers' compensation laws typically provide four types of benefits:

- medical care
- disability income
- death benefits
- rehabilitative services

Medical Care

Benefits for medical expenses are usually provided without any limitations on time or amount. In addition, they are not subject to a waiting period.

Disability Income

For an employee to collect disability income benefits under workers' compensation laws, his or her injuries must result in one of the following four categories of disability:

- temporary total. The employee cannot perform any of the duties of his or her regular job. However, full recovery is expected. Most workers' compensation claims involve this type of disability.
- permanent total. The employee will never be able to perform any of the duties of his or her regular job or any other job. Several states also list in their laws certain disabilities (such as loss of both eyes or both arms) that result in an employee's automatically being considered permanently and totally disabled even though future employment might be possible.
- temporary partial. The employee can perform only some of the duties of his or her regular job but is neither totally nor permanently disabled. For example, an employee with a sprained back might be able to work part-time.
- permanent partial. The employee has a permanent injury, such as the loss of an eye, but may be able to perform his or her regular job or may be retrained for another job.

Most workers' compensation laws have a waiting period for disability income benefits that varies from 2 to 7 days. However, benefits are frequently paid retroactively to the date of the injury if an employee is disabled for a specified period of time or is confined to a hospital.

Disability income benefits under workers' compensation laws are a function of an employee's average weekly wage over some time period, commonly the 13 weeks immediately preceding the disability. For total disabilities, benefits are a percentage (usually 66 2/3 percent) of the employee's average weekly wage, subject to maximum and minimum amounts that vary substantially by state. Benefits for temporary total disabilities continue until an employee returns to work; benefits for permanent total disabilities usually continue for life but have a limited duration (such as 10 years) in a few states.

Benefits for partial disabilities are calculated as a percentage of the difference between the employee's wages before and after the disability. In most states the duration of these benefits is subject to a statutory maximum. Several states also provide lump-sum payments to employees whose permanent partial disabilities involve the loss (or loss of use) of an eye, an arm, or other body member. These benefits, which are determined by a schedule in the law, may be in lieu of or in addition to periodic disability income benefits.

Death Benefits

Most workers' compensation laws provide two types of death benefits: burial allowances and cash income payments to survivors.

Burial allowances are a flat amount in each state and vary from $300 to $5,000 with benefits of $1,000 and $1,500 common.

Cash income payments to survivors, like disability income benefits, are a function of the worker's average wage prior to the injury resulting in death. Benefits are usually paid only to a surviving spouse and children under 18. In some states benefits are paid until the spouse dies or remarries and all children have reached 18. In other states, benefits are paid for a maximum time, such as 10 years, or until a maximum dollar amount has been paid, such as $50,000.

Rehabilitation Benefits

All states have provisions in their workers' compensation laws for rehabilitative services for disabled workers. Benefits are included for medical rehabilitation as well as for vocational rehabilitation, including training, counseling, and job placement.

A difficulty faced in providing vocational rehabilitation is that employers are reluctant to hire workers with a permanent physical impairment because a subsequent work-related injury may result in their total disability and thus an increased workers' compensation premium. For example, a worker who lost an arm in a previous work-related accident would probably be totally and permanently disabled if the other arm was lost in a later accident. Consequently most states have established second-injury funds. If a worker is disabled by a second injury, the employer is responsible only for providing benefits equal to those that would have been provided to a worker who had not suffered the first injury. Any remaining benefits are provided by the second-injury fund.

Problems and Issues

As with unemployment insurance, there are problems and issues associated with workers' compensation insurance. These involve the extent of coverage, the size of benefit payments, and increasing costs. One often-discussed issue is whether a system of 24-hour coverage would be an improvement.

Extent of Coverage

Labor unions have been particularly critical of workers' compensation insurance because of its incomplete coverage of workers. State laws do not cover all workers because of elective laws, numerical exemptions, and exclusions or less-than-full coverage for certain groups, such as agricultural, domestic, and casual workers. It is estimated that nationally between 10 and 15 percent of workers are without coverage and that this figure is as high as 30 percent in some states.

Adequacy of Benefits

Benefits have been criticized as inadequate because they seldom exceed two-thirds of a worker's earnings prior to injury, and most states do not adjust income benefits for inflation. However, some lower-paid workers may have little incentive to return to work because benefits may actually exceed their prior take-home pay. This results from relatively high minimum benefits and the fact that workers' compensation benefits are not subject to social security tax and personal income tax. In terms of the replacement of lost income, the situation is worst for higher-paid employees because of the maximum dollar limits on benefits.

Increasing Costs

A major concern of employers is the soaring cost of workers' compensation coverage. Estimates are that these costs have tripled over the past decade. This increase is the result of a combination of several factors, including the following:

- soaring increases in the cost of medical care
- increased benefits. Most states have increased benefits faster than average wages have increased. One interesting result of higher benefit levels is that they tend to result in an increased number of claims filed and an increase in the duration of claims.
- expansion of coverage to additional workplace injuries and diseases, such as mental stress
- increased litigation. Estimates are that approximately one-quarter of workers' compensation costs are associated with attorneys' fees and other legal costs.

These increasing costs have resulted in large underwriting losses for many insurance companies, leading in turn to higher premiums and more stringent underwriting. As underwriting has tightened, more employers have been forced into the substandard insurance market, where costs are even higher. These higher costs are ultimately passed on to consumers and increase inflationary pressures. Some firms, particularly small ones, are also finding their financial survival threatened by these high costs.

At the state level, there always seems to be talk of workers' compensation reform. However, labor sees reform as increased benefits, and employers see it as lower costs. As a result fundamental changes usually do not occur.

24-Hour Coverage

When workers' compensation laws were first passed, most employees did not have employer-provided benefits for medical expenses or disability income. Today both types of benefits are common. As a result there are suggestions that the old systems are obsolete, and the concept of 24-hour coverage should be adopted. Under this concept employees would have a single benefit plan that would respond to injuries whether they occurred on or off the job. This concept could be applied to medical expense coverage only or to medical expense coverage and some or all types of disability income coverage. Arguments in favor of 24-hour coverage include the following:

- The financial needs of employees are the same regardless of whether an injury or illness is work-related.
- It is often impossible to determine whether an injury or illness is work-related.
- Twenty-four-hour coverage would be better at controlling medical costs because cost-containment techniques used in group insurance could also be used for work-related claims.
- The current system is fragmented and may have both gaps and overlapping benefits. A single comprehensive system may be able to provide better benefits at a lower cost.

Naturally there are also arguments against 24-hour coverage:

- The principle of liability without fault would be violated if employees were required to assume deductibles and coinsurance for work-related claims.
- Smaller firms that have few employee benefits could not afford 24-hour coverage and might be forced out of business.
- The strong emphasis on loss control that is associated with workers' compensation insurance might be jeopardized if the program were merged with traditional group insurance programs.

The concept of 24-hour coverage continues to receive a considerable amount of attention. It is an integral part of some proposals for reforms to the nation's health care system. In addition, at least one state now allows 24-hour coverage to be written for medical expenses, with the employer purchasing a workers' compensation policy to provide benefits other than medical expenses.

FEDERAL TAXATION

Unemployment insurance benefits are included in a recipient's gross income. However, workers' compensation benefits are received free of income taxation.

Benefits received under temporary disability laws must be included in gross income. However, disabled persons with gross incomes below a specified level may be eligible for a federal tax credit. In those jurisdictions where benefits can also be received by unemployed persons, any benefits paid to unemployed persons are considered unemployment insurance benefits and are taxed accordingly.

4

Basic Concepts of Group Insurance

Chapter Outline

This first chapter on group insurance is devoted to an introduction of its basic characteristics, with particular emphasis on underwriting. The chapter also briefly discusses the reasons for the increasing use of alternatives to the traditional fully insured group insurance contract. The chapter concludes with a few significant statistics about the major categories of group insurance.

GROUP INSURANCE CHARACTERISTICS

Group insurance is characterized by a group contract, experience rating of larger groups, and group underwriting. Perhaps the best way to define group insurance is to compare its characteristics with those of individual insurance, which is underwritten on an individual basis.

The Group Contract

In contrast to most individual insurance contracts the group insurance contract provides coverage to a number of persons under a single contract issued to someone other than the persons insured. The contract, referred to as a *master contract*, provides benefits to a group of individuals who have a specific relationship to the policyowner. Group contracts usually cover individuals who are full-time employees, and the policyowner is either their employer or a trust established to provide benefits for the employees. Although the employees are not actual parties to the master contract, they can legally enforce their rights. Consequently employees are often referred to as third-party beneficiaries of the insurance contract.

Employees covered under the contract receive *certificates of insurance* as evidence of their coverage. A certificate is merely a description of the coverage provided and is not part of the master contract. In general, a certificate of insurance is not even considered to be a contract and usually contains a disclaimer to that effect. However, some courts have held the contrary to be true when the provisions of the certificate or even the explanatory booklet of a group insurance plan varies materially from the master contract.

In individual insurance the coverage of the insured normally begins with the inception of the insurance contract and ceases with its termination. However, in group insurance individual members of the group may become eligible for coverage long after the inception of the group contract, or they may lose their eligibility status long before the contract terminates.

Experience Rating

A second distinguishing characteristic of group insurance is the use of experience rating. If a group is sufficiently large, the actual experience of that particular group will be a factor in determining the premium the policyowner will be charged. The experience of an insurance company will also be reflected in the dividends and future premiums associated with individual insurance. However, such experience will be determined on a class basis and will apply to all insureds in that class. This is also true for group insurance contracts when the group's membership is small. The use of experience rating is discussed in the chapter on group insurance pricing.

Group Underwriting

The applicant for individual insurance must generally show evidence of insurability. For group insurance, on the other hand, individual members of the group are usually not required to show any evidence of insurability when initially eligible for coverage. This is not to say that there is no underwriting, but rather that underwriting is focused on the characteristics of the group instead of on the insurability of individual members of the group. As with individual insurance, the underwriter must appraise the risk, decide on the conditions of the group's acceptability, and establish a rating basis.

The purpose of group insurance underwriting is twofold: (1) to minimize the problem of *adverse selection* (meaning that those who are likely to have claims are also those who are most likely to seek insurance) and (2) to minimize the administrative costs associated with group insurance. Because of group underwriting, coverage can be provided through group insurance at a lower cost than through individual insurance.

Underwriting considerations peculiar to specific types of group insurance are discussed in the chapter on group insurance pricing. However, there are certain general underwriting considerations applicable to all or most types of group insurance that affect the contractual provisions in group insurance contracts as well as insurance company practices pertaining to group insurance. These general underwriting considerations include

- the reason for the group's existence
- the stability of the group
- the persistency of the group
- the method of determining benefits
- the provisions for determining eligibility
- the source and method of premium payments
- the administrative aspects of the group insurance plan
- the prior experience of the plan
- the size of the group
- the composition of the group
- the industry represented by the group
- the geographic location of the group

Reason for Existence

Probably the most fundamental group underwriting principle is that a group must have been formed for some purpose other than to obtain insurance for its members. Such a rule protects the group insurance company against the adverse selection that would likely exist if poor risks were to form a group just to obtain insurance. Groups based on an employer-employee relationship present little difficulty with respect to this rule.

Stability

Ideally an underwriter would like to see a reasonable but steady flow of persons through a group. A higher-than-average turnover rate will result in increased administrative costs for the insurance company as well as for the employer. If turnover exists among recently hired employees, the resulting costs can be minimized by requiring employees to wait a certain period of time before becoming eligible for coverage. However, such a *probationary period* does leave newly hired employees without protection if their previous group insurance coverage has terminated.

A lower-than-average turnover rate often results in an increasing average age for the members of a group. To the extent that a plan's premium is a function of the mortality (death rates) and the morbidity (sickness and disability rates) of the group, such an increase in average age will result in an increasing premium rate for that group insurance plan. This high rate may cause the better risks to drop out of a plan, if they are required to contribute to its cost, and may ultimately force the employer to terminate the plan because of its increasing cost.

Persistency

An underwriter is concerned with the length of time a group insurance contract will remain on the insurance company's books. Initial acquisition expenses, often including higher first-year commissions, frequently cause an insurance company to lose money during the first year the group insurance contract is in force. Only through the renewal of the contract for a period of time, often 3 or 4 years, can these acquisition expenses be recovered. For this reason firms with a history of frequently changing insurance companies or those with financial difficulty are often avoided.

Determination of Benefits

In most types of group insurance the underwriter will require that benefit levels for individual members of the group be determined in some manner that precludes individual selection by either the employees or the employer. If employees could choose their own benefit levels, there would be a tendency for the poorer risks to select greater amounts of coverage than the better risks would select. Adverse selection could also exist if the employer could choose a separate benefit level for each individual member of the group. As a result this underwriting rule has led to benefit levels that are either identical for all employees or determined by a benefit formula that bases benefit levels on some specific criterion, such as salary or position.

Benefits based on salary or position may still lead to adverse selection because disproportionately larger benefits will be provided to the owner or top executives, who may have been involved in determining the benefit formula. Consequently most insurance companies have rules for determining the maximum benefit that may be provided for any individual employee without evidence of insurability. Additional amounts of coverage either will not be provided or will be subject to individual evidence of insurability.

The general level of benefits for all employees is also of interest to the underwriter. For example, benefit levels that are too high may encourage overutilization and malingering, while benefit levels that are unusually low may lead to low participation if a plan is voluntary.

Determination of Eligibility

The underwriter is also concerned with the eligibility provisions in a group insurance plan. As previously mentioned, many group insurance plans contain probationary periods that must be satisfied before an employee is eligible for coverage. In addition to minimizing administrative costs, a probationary period will also discourage persons with known medical conditions from seeking employment primarily because of a firm's group insurance benefits. This latter problem is also addressed by the requirement that an employee be actively at work before coverage commences or by limiting coverage for preexisting conditions, particularly with major medical coverage.

Most group insurance plans normally limit eligibility to full-time employees since the coverage of part-time employees may not be desirable from an underwriting standpoint. In addition to having a high turnover rate, part-time employees are more likely to seek employment primarily to obtain the group insurance benefits that are available. Similar problems exist with seasonal and temporary employees, and consequently eligibility is often restricted to permanent employees.

Premium Payments

Group insurance plans may be contributory or noncontributory. Members of *contributory plans* pay a portion, or possibly all, of the cost of their own coverage. When employees pay the entire portion, these plans are often referred to as fully contributory or employee-pay-all plans. Under *noncontributory plans* the policyowner pays the entire cost. Since all eligible employees are usually covered, this type of plan is desirable from an underwriting standpoint because adverse selection is minimized. In fact, most insurance companies and the laws of many states require 100 percent participation of eligible employees under noncontributory plans. In addition, the absence of employee solicitation, payroll deductions, and underwriting of late entrants into the plan results in administrative savings to both the policyowner and the insurance company.

Most state laws prohibit an employer from requiring an employee to participate in a contributory plan. The insurance company is therefore faced with the possibility of adverse selection since those who elect coverage will tend to be the poorer risks. From a practical standpoint 100 percent participation in a contributory plan would be unrealistic since for many reasons some employees neither desire nor need the coverage provided under the plan. However, insurance companies will require that a minimum percentage of the eligible members of a group elect to participate before the contract will be issued. The common requirement is 75 percent, although a lower percentage is often acceptable for large groups and a higher percentage may be required for small groups. A 75 percent minimum requirement is also often a statutory requirement for group life insurance and sometimes for group health insurance.

A key issue in contributory plans is how to treat employees who did not elect to participate when first eligible but who later desire coverage, or who dropped coverage and want it reinstated. Unfortunately this desire for coverage may arise when these employees or their dependents have medical conditions that will lead to claims once coverage is provided. To control this adverse selection, insurance companies commonly require individual evidence of insurability by these employees or their dependents before coverage will be made available. However, there is one exception. Some plans have short periodic open enrollment periods during which the evidence-of-insurability requirement is lessened or waived.

Insurance companies frequently require that the employer pay a portion of the premium under a group insurance plan. This is also a statutory requirement for group life insurance in most states and occasionally for group health insurance. Many group insurance plans set an average contribution rate for all employees, which in turn leads to the subsidizing of some employees by other employees, particularly in those types of insurance where the frequency of claims increases with age. Without a requirement for employer contributions, younger employees might actually find coverage at a lower cost in the individual market, thereby leaving the group with only the older risks. Even when group insurance already has a cost advantage over individual insurance, its attractiveness to employees is enhanced by employer contributions. With constantly increasing health-care costs, employer contributions help cushion rate increases to employees and thus minimize participation problems as contributions are raised. In addition, underwriters feel that the absence of employer contributions may lead to a lack of employer interest in the plan and consequently poor cooperation with the insurance company and poor plan administration.

Administration

To minimize the expenses associated with group insurance, the underwriter will often require that the employer carry out certain administrative functions. These commonly include communicating the plan to the employees, handling enrollment procedures, collecting employee contributions on a payroll-deduction basis, and keeping certain types of records. In addition, employers are often involved in the claims process. Underwriters are concerned not only with the employer's ability to carry out these functions but also with the employer's willingness to cooperate with the insurance company.

Prior Experience

For most insurance companies a large portion of newly written group insurance consists of business that was previously written by other insurance companies. Therefore it is important for the underwriter to ascertain the reason for the transfer. If the transferred business is a result of dissatisfaction with the service provided by the prior insurance company, the underwriter must determine whether his or her insurance company can provide the type and level of service desired. Since an employer is most likely to shop for new coverage when faced with a rate increase, the underwriter must evaluate whether the rate increase was due to excessive claims experience. Often, particularly with larger groups, poor claims experience in the past is an indication that there might be poor experience in the future. Occasionally, however, the prior experience may be due to circumstances that will not continue in the future, such as a catastrophe or large medical bills for an employee who died, totally recovered, or terminated employment.

Excessive past claims experience may not result in coverage denial for a new applicant, but it will probably result in a higher rate. As an alternative, changes in the benefit or eligibility provisions of the plan might eliminate a previous source of adverse claims experience.

The underwriter must determine the new insurance company's responsibility for existing claims. Some states prohibit a new insurance company from using a preexisting-conditions clause to deny the continuing claims of persons that were covered under a prior group insurance plan if these claims would otherwise be covered under the new contract. The rationale for this "no-loss no-gain" legislation is that claims should be paid neither more liberally nor less liberally than if no transfer had taken place. Even in states that have no such regulation, an employer may still wish to provide employees with continuing protection. In either case the underwriter must evaluate these continuing claims as well as any liability of the previous insurance company for their payment.

Finally, the underwriter must be reasonably certain that the employer will not present a persistency problem by changing insurance companies again in the near future.

Size

The size of a group is a significant factor in the underwriting process. With large groups there is usually prior group insurance experience that can be used as a factor in determining the premium, and considerable flexibility also exists with respect to both rating and plan design. In addition, adjustments for adverse claims experience can be made at future renewal dates under the experience-rating process.

The situation is different for small groups. In many cases coverage is being written for the first time. Administrative expenses tend to be high in relation to the premium. There is also an increased possibility that the owner or major stockholder might be interested in coverage primarily because he or she or a family member has a medical problem that will result in large immediate claims. As a result contractual provisions and the benefits available tend to be quite standardized in order to control administrative costs. Furthermore, because past experience for small groups is not necessarily a realistic indicator of future experience, most insurance companies use pooled rates under which a uniform rate is applied to all groups that have a specific coverage. Since poor claims experience for a particular group is not charged to that group at renewal, more restrictive underwriting practices relating to adverse selection are used. These include less liberal contractual provisions and in some cases individual underwriting for group members.

Composition

The age, sex, and income of employees in a group will affect the experience of the group. As employees age, the mortality rate increases. Excluding maternity claims, both the frequency and the duration of medical and disability claims also increase with age.

At all ages the death rate is lower for females than for males. However, the opposite is true for medical expenses and disability claims. Even if maternity claims are disregarded, women as a group tend to be hospitalized and disabled more frequently and to obtain medical and surgical treatment more often than men, except at extremely advanced ages.

Employees at high income levels tend to incur higher-than-average medical and dental expenses. This is partly because practitioners sometimes base charges on a patient's ability to pay. (Since a high percentage of individuals now have health insurance, this practice is less common than in the past.) In addition, higher-income persons are more likely to seek specialized care or care in more affluent areas, where the charges of practitioners are generally higher. On the other hand, low-income employees can also pose problems. Turnover rates tend to be higher, and there is often difficulty in getting and retaining proper levels of participation in contributory plans.

Adjustments can often be made for all these factors when determining the proper rate to charge the policyowner. Some states, however, require the use of unisex rates, in which case the mix of employees by sex becomes an underwriting consideration. A major problem can arise in contributory insurance plans. To the extent that higher costs for a group with a less-than-average mix of employees are passed on to these employees, a lower participation rate may result.

Industry

The nature of the industry represented by a group is also a significant factor in the underwriting process. In addition to different occupational hazards among industries, employees in some industries have higher-than-average health insurance claims that cannot be directly attributed to their jobs. Therefore insurance companies commonly make adjustments in their life and health insurance rates based on the occupations of the employees covered as well as on the industries in which they work.

In addition to occupational hazards the underwriter must weigh other factors as well. Certain industries are characterized by a lack of stability and persistency and thus may be considered undesirable risks. The underwriter must also be concerned with the impact that changes in the economy will have on a particular industry.

Geographic Location

The size and frequency of health insurance claims vary considerably among geographic regions and must be considered in determining a group insurance rate. For example, medical expenses tend to be higher in the Northeast than in the South and higher in large urban areas than in rural areas. Certain geographic regions also tend to have a higher frequency of disability claims.

A group with geographically scattered employees will also pose more administrative problems and probably result in greater administrative expense than a group at a single location. In addition, the underwriter must determine whether the insurance company has the proper facilities to service policyowners at their locations.

ALTERNATIVE FUNDING METHODS

As the cost of providing insurance benefits to employees has risen, employers have increasingly turned from fully insured plans to alternative funding methods to minimize this cost. In some cases these alternative methods consist of variations in group insurance contracts, such as premium-payment delays and reserve-reduction arrangements. At the opposite end of the spectrum are totally self-funded (self-insured) plans, in which no insurance is purchased and benefits are paid from either current revenue or a trust to which periodic payments have been made. Between these two extremes are programs such as minimum-premium plans, stop-loss arrangements, and big-deductible plans that combine various aspects of traditionally insured plans with those of self-funding. Even when self-funding is used, employers often contract with an insurance company or other organization for administrative services.

These alternative funding methods are discussed in detail in a later chapter. At this point, however, it should be noted that the use of alternative funding methods does not eliminate the need for making decisions regarding such factors as eligibility, benefit levels, and claims handling. In most cases provisions for these factors will be similar, if not identical, to the provisions found in the types of group insurance contracts that are discussed throughout this book.

THE SIGNIFICANCE OF GROUP INSURANCE

In the first chapter overall employee benefit statistics were presented to emphasize the magnitude of group benefits. Specific statistics (as of 1995) can also be given for the major categories of group insurance.[1]

Group Life Insurance

- Coverage amounting to $4.7 trillion is in force under approximately 1 million master contracts and 145 million certificates of insurance. This amount represents a doubling of the amount of insurance in force since 1984.

- Over 90 percent of the coverage in force is term insurance.
- Employer-employee groups account for approximately 90 percent of coverage in force.
- Group insurance amounts to almost 40 percent of total life insurance coverage in force, up from 20 percent in 1950.
- The amount of coverage under the average-size group life insurance certificate covering persons in employer-employee groups is approximately $33,000, compared to about $50,000 under the average-size ordinary life insurance policy in force.
- Nearly 700,000 beneficiaries each year receive a total of over $12 billion in benefits.

Group Disability Income Insurance

- Over three-quarters of persons in the workforce have some type of short-term protection provided through group arrangements. More than half of these persons have some or all of their coverage under formal plans using self-funding. This approach continues to provide an increasing portion of coverage in force.
- Approximately one-fourth of persons in the workforce have some form of long-term protection through group insurance arrangements.

Group Medical Expense Insurance

- Since 1980 premiums for medical expense coverage have risen from approximately $85 billion to over $300 billion. In 1980 this amount represented 9.2 percent of the gross national product; in 1995 it represented almost 14 percent. Almost 90 percent of these premiums represent the cost of coverage under group insurance arrangements, as opposed to individual insurance.
- In recent years the percentage of persons with medical expense protection under group arrangements with insurance companies, Blue Cross and Blue Shield, and independent plans (including health maintenance organizations and preferred-provider organizations) has increased, while the percentage of persons having individual coverage has decreased. During the last 10 years the number of persons with coverage from group contracts of insurance companies has dropped from about 100 million to just over 75 million. The number covered by Blue Cross and Blue Shield plans has decreased somewhat to about 65 million, while the number covered by HMOs and self-funded plans has doubled to over 110 million. Note that some persons have coverage

from more than one type of provider, and the total number of persons represented by these statistics is about 185 million.

- During the last 10 years the percentage of the civilian population under age 65 having some form of hospital and surgical benefits from nongovernmental sources has remained relatively stable at about 70 percent. The remaining 30 percent is about evenly split among those covered under government programs and the uninsured.

Group Dental Insurance

- During the last 15 years, the percentage of persons under age 65 with dental coverage grew from less than 25 percent to over 60 percent.

NOTE

1. Sources: American Council of Life Insurance, *Life Insurance Fact Book*; and Health Insurance Institute of America, *Source Book of Health Insurance Data*. Both sources are updated annually.

5

The Governmental Environment
for Group Insurance

Chapter Outline

The character of group insurance has been greatly influenced by the numerous laws and regulations that both the state and federal governments have imposed. The major impact of state regulation has been felt through the insurance laws governing insurance companies and the products they sell. Traditionally these laws have affected only those benefit plans funded with insurance contracts. However, as a growing number of employers are turning toward self-funding of benefits, there has been an increasing interest on the part of state regulatory officials to extend these laws to plans using alternative funding methods. The federal laws affecting group insurance, on the other hand, have generally been directed toward any benefit plans that employers establish for their employees, regardless of the funding method used.

STATE REGULATION

Even though the United States Supreme Court has declared insurance to be commerce and thus subject to federal regulation when conducted on an interstate basis, Congress gave the states substantial regulatory authority by the passage of the McCarran-Ferguson Act (Public Law 15) in 1945. The act exempts insurance from certain federal regulations to the extent that individual states actually regulate insurance. In addition, it provides that most other federal laws are not applicable to insurance unless they are specifically directed at the business of insurance.

As a result of the McCarran-Ferguson Act a substantial body of laws and regulations has been enacted in every state. While no two states have identical laws and regulations, there have been attempts to encourage uniformity among the states. The most significant influence in this regard has been the National Association of Insurance Commissioners (NAIC), which is composed of state regulatory officials. Since the NAIC has as one of its goals the promotion of uniformity in legislation and administrative rules affecting insurance, it has developed numerous model laws. Although states are not bound to adopt these model laws, numerous states have enacted many of them.

Some of the more significant state laws and regulations affecting group insurance include those pertaining to the types of groups eligible for coverage, benefit limitations, contractual provisions, and taxation. Moreover, since many employers have employees in several states, the extent of the regulatory jurisdiction of each state is a matter of some concern.

Eligible Groups

Most states do not allow group insurance contracts to be written unless a minimum number of persons are insured under the contract. This requirement, which may vary by type of coverage and type of group, is most common in group life insurance, where the minimum number required for plans established by individual employers is generally 10 persons. A few states have either a lower minimum or no such requirement. A higher minimum, often 100 persons, may be imposed on other plans, such as those established by trusts, labor unions, or creditors. Only about half the states impose any minimum number requirement on group health insurance contracts—it is usually either 5 or 10 persons.

Most states also have insurance laws concerning the types of groups for which insurance companies may write group insurance. Most of these laws specify that a group insurance contract cannot be delivered to a policyowner in the state unless the group meets certain statutory eligibility requirements for its type of group. In some states these eligibility requirements even vary by type of coverage. While the categories of eligible groups may vary, at least five types of groups are acceptable in virtually all states: individual employer groups, negotiated trusteeships, trade associations, creditor-debtor groups, and labor union groups. Other types of groups, including multiple-employer welfare arrangements, are also acceptable in some states. Some states have no insurance laws regarding the types or sizes of groups for which insurance companies may write group insurance. Rather, eligibility is determined by the underwriting standards of insurance companies.

Individual Employer Groups

The most common type of eligible group is the individual employer group in which the employer may be a corporation, a partnership, or a sole proprietorship. Many state laws are very specific about what constitutes an employee for group insurance purposes. In addition to those usually considered to be employees of a firm, coverage can generally be written for retired employees and employees of subsidiary and affiliated firms. Furthermore, individual proprietors or partners are usually eligible for coverage as long as they are actively engaged in and devote a substantial part of their time to the conduct of the organization. Similarly, directors of a corporation may be eligible for coverage if they are also employees of the corporation.

Negotiated Trusteeships (Taft-Hartley Trusts)

Negotiated trusteeships are formed as a result of collective bargaining over benefits between a union and the employers of the union members. Generally the union employees are in the same industry or a related one. For the most part these industries, such as trucking or construction, are characterized by frequent movement of union members among employers. The Taft-Hartley Act prohibits employers from paying funds directly to a labor union for the purpose of providing group insurance coverage to members. Payments must be made to a trust fund established for the purpose of providing benefits to employees. The trustees of the fund, who must consist of equal numbers of representatives from both the employers and the union, can elect either to self-fund benefits or to purchase insurance contracts with themselves as the policyowners. Since eligible employees include only members of the collective-bargaining unit (which may include some nonunion members), benefits for other employees must be provided in some other manner.

Negotiated trusteeships differ from other types of groups in the way benefits are financed and the way eligibility for benefits is determined. Employers often make contributions based on the number of hours worked by the employees covered under the collective-bargaining agreement, regardless of whether these employees are eligible for benefits. Eligibility for benefits during a given period is usually based only on some minimum number of hours worked during a previous period. For example, a union member might receive coverage during a calendar quarter (even while unemployed) if he or she worked at least 300 hours in the previous calendar quarter. This situation, where the employees for whom contributions are made may differ from those who are eligible for benefits, presents a unique problem for the underwriter. Rates must be adequate to build up the contingency reserves necessary to pay benefits in periods of heavy layoffs, during which a large portion of contributions ceases but eligibility for benefits continues.

While negotiated trusteeships normally provide benefits for the employees of several employers, they can also be established for the employees of a single employer. However, situations involving collective bargaining with a single employer will usually result in the employer's being required to provide benefits for the employees under a group insurance contract purchased by the employer. Although benefits and eligibility are specified in the bargaining agreement, the employer is the policyowner and the group is an individual employer group rather than a negotiated trusteeship. This approach also enables the employer to provide benefits for nonunion employees under the same contract.

Trade Associations

For eligibility purposes a trade association is an association of employers that has been formed for reasons other than obtaining insurance. In most cases these employers are in the same industry or type of business. Many such associations frequently have a large number of employers without the minimum number of employees necessary to qualify for an individual employer group insurance contract. While in some states the master contract is issued directly to the trade association, most states require that a trust be established. Through payment of premiums to the association or the trust, individual employers may provide coverage for their employees.

Both adverse selection and administrative costs tend to be greater in trade association groups than in many other types of groups. Therefore most underwriters and state laws require that a minimum percentage of the employers belonging to the association, such as 50 percent, participate in the plan and that a minimum number of employees, possibly as high as 500, be covered. In addition, individual underwriting or strict provisions regarding preexisting conditions may be used, and employer contributions are usually required. To ensure adequate enrollment the underwriter must determine whether the association has the resources as well as the desire to promote the plan enthusiastically and to administer it properly.

Labor Union Groups

Labor unions may establish group insurance plans to provide benefits for their members, with the master contract issued to the union. In addition to the prohibition by the Taft-Hartley Act of employer payments to labor unions for insurance premiums, state laws generally prohibit plans in which union members pay the entire cost from their own pockets. Consequently the premiums come solely from union funds or partially from union funds and partially from members' contributions. Labor union groups account for a relatively small amount of group insurance, most of which is life insurance.

Multiple-Employer Welfare Arrangements

The final type of eligible group designed to provide benefits for employees is the multiple-employer welfare arrangement (MEWA). MEWAs are a common but often controversial method of marketing group benefits to employers who have a small number of employees. MEWAs are legal entities (1) sponsored by an insurance company, an independent administrator, or some other person or organization and (2) organized to provide group benefits to the employees of more than one employer. Each MEWA must have an administrator who is either an insurance company or a professional administrator. MEWAs may be organized as trusts, in which case there must be a trustee that may be an individual but is usually a corporate trustee, such as a commercial bank.

MEWAs are generally established to provide group benefits to employers within a specific industry, such as construction, agriculture, or banking. However, employers are not required to belong to an association. MEWAs may provide either a single type of insurance (such as life insurance) or a wide range of coverages (for example, life, medical expense, and disability income insurance). In some cases alternative forms of the same coverage (such as comprehensive health insurance or basic health insurance) are available.

An employer desiring to obtain insurance coverage for its employees from a MEWA must subscribe and become a member of the MEWA. The employer is issued a joinder agreement, which spells out the relationship between the MEWA and the employer and specifies the coverages to which the employer has subscribed. It is not necessary for an employer to subscribe to all coverages offered by a MEWA.

A MEWA may either provide benefits on a self-funded basis or fund benefits with a contract purchased from an insurance company. In the latter case the MEWA, rather than the subscribing employers, is the master insurance contract holder. In either case the employees of subscribing employers receive benefit descriptions (certificates of insurance in insured MEWAs) in a manner similar to the usual group insurance arrangement.

In addition to alternative methods of funding benefits, MEWAs can also be categorized according to how they are administered, that is, whether by an insurance company or by a third-party administrator. It is generally agreed that there are three types of MEWAs. Unfortunately the terminology used to describe the three types is not uniform and is often misleading. In this text the following terminology and definitions will be used:

- fully insured multiple-employer trust (MET). Benefits are insured and the MET is administered by an insurance company. (All MEWAs were once referred to as METs. In 1982, however, ERISA was amended to clarify the regulation of such arrangements. The act used the term *multiple-employer welfare arrangement* rather than the term *multiple-employer trust*. Over time, MEWA has become the accepted overall terminology, but most insurance companies continue to use the term *MET* to describe fully insured MEWAs as a way to distinguish them from the more controversial self-funded MEWAs.)
- insured third-party-administered MEWA. Benefits are insured and the MEWA is administered by a third party.

- self-funded MEWA. Benefits are self-funded and the MEWA is administered by a third party.

Fully Insured METs. Fully insured METs are established and administered by insurance companies, with a commercial bank usually acting as trustee. Coverage under such METs is normally marketed by the sales force of the insurer involved and may be made available to other licensed producers. It should be noted that a trust purchases coverage from the insurance company, and what is being marketed to employers is the availability of insurance through participation in the trust, not an insurance contract from the insurance company.

Fully insured METs were developed to provide group insurance to small employer groups. A single insurance company may have one MET or several, with each designed for a different industry (such as construction or manufacturing). Through METs, insurance companies have provided group insurance at a cost lower than the cost of a direct sale to the employer or to individual employees. Regulatory restrictions regarding minimum group size are overcome since the employees of many small employers are insured under a single group contract issued to the trust. Costs are also minimized because each type of coverage offered by the trust tends to be standardized for all employers using the trust.

In addition, underwriting standards have been developed to minimize the problems of adverse selection and the higher administrative costs associated with providing coverage to small groups of employees. While these standards vary among companies, the following are some common examples:

- more stringent participation requirements, such as 100 percent, for employers with fewer than five employees
- a requirement that life insurance coverage be purchased. This tends to be a profitable and stable form of coverage for insurance companies. In some cases the more life insurance coverage that is purchased, the more comprehensive the medical expense benefits that are made available.
- limitations on the period of time for which rates are guaranteed, rarely more than 6 months
- probationary periods, often 2 or 3 months, for new employees
- restrictive provisions for preexisting conditions
- limitations on the amounts of life insurance coverage available on a simplified or guaranteed-issue basis (for example, $20,000 for four or fewer employees; $40,000 for five or more). Additional coverage may be available but individual evidence of insurability will be required.
- limitations on the amount of long-term disability insurance coverage that will be issued, such as 50 percent or 60 percent of income, subject to a $1,500 monthly maximum
- ineligible groups. Most METs have a lengthy list of ineligible groups, including those characterized by poor loss experience or high turnover rates.

Since it has generally been accepted under insurance regulatory law that an insurance contract is subject to regulation by the state in which the contract was delivered, many insurers have established METs where they consider the regulatory climate to be favorable. This has allowed an insurance company, in effect, to offer a nationally standardized contract to small employers (through subscribing to the trust) rather than different contracts to comply with the regulatory requirements in each subscriber's state. However, some states require METs to make their coverage conform to applicable state law when an employer from that state becomes a subscriber.

During the 1980s the importance of METs (and insured, third-party-administered MEWAs) decreased somewhat. Some insurers, primarily because of difficulties in providing medical expense coverage to small employers, left the group insurance business. HMOs increasingly and successfully sought business from smaller employers. In addition, many employers—particularly those with 25 to 100 employees—are more likely to use self-funding. However, in many parts of the country METs remain a major source of group insurance coverage for small employers.

Insured Third-Party-Administered MEWAs. Insured third-party-administered MEWAs are similar to fully insured METs in that benefits are provided through an insurance contract issued to a trust. However, these MEWAs are administered by some person or organization other than an insurance company.

The impetus for the establishment of an insured third-party-administered MEWA may come from either the insurance company or the administrator. An insurance company desiring to enter the MEWA field may feel it lacks the expertise or resources to administer MEWAs properly at a competitive cost. Consequently a number of insurance companies have sought out third-party administrators to provide many of the necessary administrative functions. The third-party administrators under such arrangements are normally organizations specializing in either the administration of various types of insurance programs or solely the management of MEWAs. In addition to general administrative duties, the third-party administrator (subject to the insurance company's rules) may be involved in any or all of the following functions associated with MEWAs: underwriting, claims administration, benefit design, or marketing.

Third-party administrators desiring to enter the MEWA field or hoping to increase their share of MEWA business might seek out insurance companies to provide the insurance coverages for the MEWAs they wish to establish. Some of these administrators specialize in the administration of insurance programs; others are insurance agents or brokers who desire a product over which they can have marketing control.

Unfortunately the experience of insured third-party-administered MEWAs was not always satisfactory. There were several instances of mismanagement that caused some of these MEWAs to cease operations. In some cases eagerness to enter the field resulted in inadequate rates or lax underwriting; in other situations administrators were more interested in management fees and sales commissions than in making a profit for the insurance company. While such occurrences have tarnished the image of insured third-party-administered MEWAs in the past, many did operate successfully and were managed by capable administrators. Two factors have minimized these difficulties in recent years. First, insurance companies, aware of past experiences, are cautious as they enter the field, giving particular regard to the selection of their administrators. Second, some states have passed legislation aimed at regulating administrators of MEWAs and other insurance arrangements.

Self-Funded MEWAs. Self-funded MEWAs are normally established and marketed by the persons or organizations who will administer them. The MEWA does not purchase an insurance contract, except possibly for stop-loss coverage; instead benefits are self-funded with premiums paid by subscribing employers. While many self-funded MEWAs have operated successfully and have been well administered, others have gone bankrupt and left participants with unpaid claims. (Under an insured MEWA the insurer would be responsible for paying claims even if the MEWA failed.) Again administrators often did not charge enough to establish proper reserves for future benefits, or they were more concerned with generating management fees and sales commissions than in properly managing the MEWA. In some cases outright fraud was involved.

In 1982 Congress enacted legislation that provides for state regulation of self-funded MEWAs. For several years state insurance departments had tried to obtain the power to shut down mismanaged MEWAs, but the administrators of these plans argued that ERISA exempted them from state regulation. The legislation, however, made clear that insured MEWAs were subject to state regulation. Self-funded MEWAs can apply for ERISA certification, but even if it is granted, the MEWA will still be subject to state rules governing reserves and contributions. In addition, while ERISA certification is pending, a MEWA will have to meet all state insurance regulations, or the state can force it to cease operations. State regulation also applies if a MEWA either fails to apply for certification or is denied certification.

Initially the overall effect of the 1982 legislation was to greatly reduce the number of self-funded MEWAs. However, two major factors caused an increase in the numbers of MEWAs. First, many insurers abandoned the small-group market or became increasingly strict in their underwriting. As a result self-funded MEWAs became the only alternative for some employers. Second, MEWAs frequently wrote coverage at a cost significantly below the cost of alternative coverage, often because of inadequate actuarial calculations regarding the size of future claims and the need for establishing adequate reserves.

Unfortunately the resurgence of self-funded MEWAs was accompanied by many bankruptcies and unpaid claims. The General Accounting Office estimates that between 1988 and 1991 almost 200 self-funded MEWAs failed and left nearly 400,000 employees with $132 million of unpaid claims. There seems to be little doubt that many states have been unsuccessful in adequately regulating MEWAs. Even when appropriate laws exist, many MEWAs simply ignore them.

The insurance department finds out about a MEWA only when a complaint is received, and by then the MEWA may be in serious financial difficulty or out of business.

Creditor-Debtor Groups

Creditor-debtor relationships give rise to groups that are eligible for group term life insurance and group disability income insurance. While the types of creditors and debtors may vary, coverage is normally made available for organizations such as banks, finance companies, and retailers with respect to time-payment purchases, personal loans, or charge accounts. A unique feature of group credit insurance is that the creditor must be the beneficiary of the coverage in addition to being the policyowner even though the debtors are the insured. In group credit life insurance, any payments to the creditor must be used to cancel the insured portion of the debt; in group credit disability income insurance, any payments must be used to relieve the debtor of making periodic payments during the insured period of disability. Premiums for group creditor insurance may be shared by the creditor and the debtor or may be totally paid by either party.

The following traditional restrictions imposed by eligibility statutes also reflect insurance company underwriting practices:

- maximum amount of coverage. Many states limit the maximum amount of coverage that may be written on a single debtor. In addition, since the amount of coverage can never exceed the amount of the indebtedness, coverage decreases as the debt is paid.
- maximum loan duration. It is common for states to limit the loan duration under contributory plans to maximum periods, such as 5 or 10 years. There is usually no maximum loan duration if the creditor pays the cost of the coverage.
- minimum participation percentage. Many states require that all eligible debtors be insured when the creditor pays the entire premium and that at least 75 percent of eligible debtors be insured under contributory plans.
- minimum number of entrants into the plan. In many cases this number is 100 for each policy year.

Because of the abuses associated with such factors as coercion, excessive premium rates, and lack of disclosure, many states have additional regulations pertaining to group credit insurance. Common provisions are

- proper disclosure to the debtor, including a description of the coverage and the charge for the coverage
- an option for the debtor to provide coverage through existing insurance or the purchase of a policy from another source
- a requirement that the charge by a creditor to a debtor for coverage may not exceed the premium charged by the insurance company

- a refund of any unearned premium paid by the debtor if the indebtedness is paid prior to its scheduled maturity
- limitations on the maximum rates that may be charged by insurance companies

While this book will concentrate on the use of group insurance as an employee benefit, it should be noted that group creditor insurance, particularly creditor life insurance, is a significant form of group insurance. According to the American Council of Life Insurance, $230 billion of credit life insurance was in force at the end of 1995, under approximately 65 million individual policies or certificates of group insurance. Detailed statistics are not available, but it is estimated that between 80 and 90 percent of this amount is group insurance.

Other Groups

Numerous other types of groups, such as alumni associations, professional associations, veterans' groups, savings account depositors, and credit card holders, may be eligible for group insurance under the regulations of many states. Insurance company underwriting practices and state regulation may impose more stringent requirements on these types of groups than on those involving an employer-employee relationship. Individual evidence of insurability is frequently required for other than small amounts of coverage. In addition, a larger minimum size is generally imposed upon the group.

Contractual Provisions

Through its insurance laws every state provides for the regulation of contractual provisions. In many instances certain contractual provisions must be included in group insurance policies. These mandatory provisions may be altered only if they result in more favorable treatment of the policyowner. Such provisions tend to be most uniform from state to state in the area of group life insurance, primarily because of the widespread adoption of the NAIC model bill pertaining to group life insurance standard provisions. As a result of state regulation, coupled with industry practices, the provisions of most group life and health insurance policies are relatively uniform from company to company. Although an insurance company's policy forms can usually be used in all states, riders may be necessary to bring certain provisions into compliance with the regulations of some states.

Traditionally the regulation of contractual provisions has focused on provisions pertaining to such factors as the grace period, conversion, and incontestability rather than on those pertaining to the types or levels of benefits. These latter provisions have been a matter between the policyowner and the insurance company, but in recent years this situation has changed in many states. In some states certain benefits, such as well-baby care and treatment for alcoholism or drug abuse, must be included in any group insurance contract; in other states they must be offered to group policyowners but are optional. Still other state laws and regulations specify minimum levels for certain benefits if those benefits are included.

It is interesting to note that with few exceptions the regulation of contractual provisions affects only those employee benefit plans funded with insurance contracts because provisions of ERISA seem to exempt employee benefit plans from most types of state regulation. However, there are exceptions to this exemption, including insurance regulation and therefore the provisions in insurance contracts. As a result of ERISA exemption, states have few laws and regulations applying to the provisions of uninsured benefit plans. However, ERISA does not exempt uninsured plans from state regulation in such areas as age and sex discrimination, and laws pertaining to these areas commonly apply to all benefit plans. A few states are also trying to mandate other types of benefits for uninsured plans, and ultimately the issue will probably have to be settled by Congress or the Supreme Court.

Benefit Limitations

Statutory limitations may be imposed on the level of benefits that can be provided under group insurance contracts issued to certain types of eligible groups. With the exception of group life insurance, these limitations rarely apply in situations involving an employer-employee relationship. In the past most states limited the amount of group life insurance that could be provided by an employer to an employee, but only Texas still has such a restriction. However, several states limit the amount of coverage that can be provided under contracts issued to groups other than individual employer groups. In addition, some states limit the amount of life insurance coverage that may be provided for dependents.

Taxation

Every state levies a premium tax on foreign (out-of-state) insurance companies licensed to do business in its state, and most states tax the premiums of insurance companies domiciled in their state. These taxes, which are applicable to premiums written within a state, average about 2 percent.

The imposition of the premium tax has placed insurance companies at a competitive disadvantage with alternative methods of providing benefits. Premiums paid to health maintenance organizations are not subject to the tax, nor are premiums paid to Blue Cross–Blue Shield plans in many states. In addition, the elimination of this tax is one cost saving under self-funded plans. Because the trend toward self-funding of benefits by large corporations has resulted in the loss of substantial premium tax revenue to the states, there have been suggestions that all premiums paid to any type of organization or fund for the purpose of providing insurance benefits to employees be subject to the premium tax.

Where state income taxation exists, the tax implications of group insurance premiums and benefits to both employers and employees are generally similar to those of the federal government. Employers may deduct any premiums paid as business expenses, and employees have certain exemptions from taxation with respect to both premiums paid on their behalf and benefits attributable to employer-paid premiums.

Regulatory Jurisdiction

A group insurance contract will often insure individuals living in more than one state—a situation that raises the question of which state or states have regulatory jurisdiction over the contract. This issue is a crucial one since factors such as minimum enrollment percentages, maximum amounts of life insurance, and required contract provisions vary among the states.

Few problems arise if the insured group qualifies as an eligible group in all the states where insured individuals reside. Individual employer groups, negotiated trusteeships, labor union groups, and creditor-debtor groups fall into this category. Under the *doctrine of comity*, by which states recognize within their own territory the laws of other states, it is generally accepted that the state in which the group insurance contract is delivered to the policyowner has governing jurisdiction. Therefore the contract must conform only to the laws and regulations of this one state, even though certificates of insurance may be delivered in other states. However, a few states have statutes that prohibit insurance issued in other states from covering residents of their state unless the contract conforms with their laws and regulations. While these statutes are effective with respect to insurance companies licensed within the state (that is, admitted companies), their effectiveness with respect to nonadmitted companies is questionable, since states lack regulatory jurisdiction over these companies.

This does not mean that the policyowner may arbitrarily seek out a situs (place of delivery) that is most desirable from a regulatory standpoint. Unless the state of delivery has a significant relationship to the insurance transaction, other states may seek to exercise their regulatory authority. Therefore it has become common practice that an acceptable situs must be at least one of the following:

- the state where the policyowner is incorporated (or the trust is created if the policyowner is a trust)
- the state where the policyowner's principal office is located
- the state where the greatest number of insured individuals are employed
- any state where an employer or labor union that is a party to a trust is located

While a policyowner may have a choice of situs if these locations differ, most insurers are reluctant to issue a group contract in any state unless a corporate officer or trustee who can execute acceptance of the contract is located in that state and unless the principal functions related to the administration of the group contract will be performed there.

The issue of regulatory jurisdiction is more complex for those types of groups that are not considered to be eligible groups in all states. Multiple-employer welfare arrangements are a typical example. If a state has no regulation to the contrary and if the insured group would be eligible for group insurance in other states, the situation is the same as previously described. In addition, most other states will accept the doctrine of comity and will not interfere with the regulatory jurisdiction of the state where the contract is delivered. However, some states either prohibit coverage from being issued or require that it conform with the state's laws and regulations other than those pertaining to eligible groups.

FEDERAL REGULATION

Many aspects of federal regulation have affected the establishment and character of group insurance, especially the following, which are covered in some detail in this book:

- the Age Discrimination in Employment Act
- the Civil Rights Act
- the Employee Retirement Income Security Act
- the Americans with Disabilities Act
- the Social Security Act
- the Internal Revenue Code
- the Health Maintenance Organization Act
- the Consolidated Omnibus Budget Reconciliation Act (COBRA)
- the Health Insurance Portability and Accountability Act
- the Newborns' and Mothers' Health Protection Act
- the Mental Health Parity Act
- the Family and Medical Leave Act

This chapter focuses on the first four acts listed, since these have had a similar influence on most types of group insurance, and on nondiscrimination rules.

The Social Security Act was discussed in detail in an earlier chapter, and discussions in later chapters consider the integration of group disability income and group medical expense benefits with the benefits provided under the act.

The income tax implications of the Internal Revenue Code, which may vary for different types of group insurance coverage, are described in those chapters pertaining to each type of coverage.

The next five acts affect medical expense coverage and are described at various places in the four later chapters on group medical expense coverage.

Finally, the Family and Medical Leave Act is covered along with the discussion of family leave in the chapter on other group benefits.

The Age Discrimination in Employment Act

The Age Discrimination in Employment Act applies to employers with 20 or more employees and affects employees aged 40 and older. With some exceptions, such as individuals in executive or high policymaking positions, compulsory retirement is no longer allowed. Employee benefits, which traditionally ceased or were severely limited at age 65, must be continued for older workers. However, some reductions in benefits are allowed. While the *federal* act does not prohibit such discrimination in benefits for employees under age 40 or for all employees of firms that employ fewer than 20 persons, some *states* may prohibit such discrimination under their own laws or regulations.

The act permits a reduction in the level of some benefits for older workers so that the cost of providing benefits for older workers is no greater than the cost of providing them for younger workers. However, the most expensive benefit—medical expense coverage—cannot be reduced. The following discussion is limited to reductions after age 65—probably the most common age for reducing benefits, even though reductions can start at an earlier age if they are justified on a cost basis. It should be emphasized that these restrictions apply to benefits for active employees only; there are no requirements under the act that any benefits be continued for retired workers.

When participation in an employee benefit plan is voluntary, an employer can generally require larger employee contributions instead of reducing benefits for older employees, as long as the proportion of the premiums paid by older employees does not increase with age. Thus if an employer pays 50 percent of the cost of benefits for younger employees, it must pay at least 50 percent of the cost for older employees. If employees pay the entire cost of a benefit, older employees may be required to pay the full cost of their coverage to the extent that this is a condition of participation in the plan. However, this provision is not applicable to medical expense benefits—employees over age 65 cannot be required to pay more for their coverage than is paid by employees under age 65.

In cases where benefits are reduced, two approaches are permitted: a benefit-by-benefit approach or a benefit-package approach. Under the *benefit-by-benefit approach* each employee benefit may be reduced to a lesser amount as long as each reduction can be justified on a cost basis. Under a *benefit-package approach* the overall benefit package may be altered. Some benefits may be eliminated or reduced to a lesser amount than can be justified on a cost basis, as long other existing benefits are not reduced or the benefit package is increased by adding new benefits for older workers. The only cost restriction is that the cost of the revised benefit package may be no less than if a benefit-by-benefit reduction had been used. The act also places two other restrictions on the benefit-package approach by prohibiting any reduction in medical expense benefits or retirement benefits.

In reducing a benefit, an employer must use data that approximately reflect the actual cost of the benefit to the employer over a reasonable period of years. Unfortunately such data either have not been kept by employers or are not statistically valid. Consequently reductions have been based on estimates provided by insurance companies and consulting actuaries. This approach appears to be satisfactory to the Equal Employment Opportunity Commission, which enforces the act's provisions. The act allows reductions to take place on a yearly basis or to be based on age brackets of up to 5 years. Any cost comparisons must be made with the preceding age bracket. For example, if 5-year age brackets are used, the cost of providing benefits to employees between 65 and 69 must be compared with the cost of providing the same benefits to employees between 60 and 64.

While reductions in group insurance benefits for older employees are permissible, they are not required. Some employers make no reductions for older employees, but most employers reduce life insurance benefits at age 65 and long-term disability benefits at age 60 or 65.

Group Term Life Insurance Benefits

Basing their conclusions on mortality statistics, most insurance companies feel that group term life insurance benefits can be reduced to certain percentages (shown in table 5-1) of the amount of coverage provided immediately prior to age 65.

TABLE 5-1	
Age	**Percentage**
65–69	65
70–74	45
75–79	30
over 79	20

Therefore if employees normally receive $40,000 of group term life insurance, employees between the ages of 65 and 69 can receive only $26,000; employees between the ages of 70 and 74 can receive $18,000, and so forth. Similarly if employees normally receive coverage equal to 200 percent of salary, this coverage may be reduced by 35 percent to 130 percent of salary at age 65, with additional reductions at later ages.

Reductions may also be made on an annual basis. If an annual reduction is used, it appears that a reduction of up to 11 percent of the previous year's coverage can be actuarially justified, starting at age 65 and continuing through age 69. Starting at age 70, the percent should be 9 percent.

In a plan with employee contributions the employer may either reduce benefits as described above and charge the employee the same premium as those employees in the previous age bracket, or continue full coverage and require the employee to pay an actuarially increased contribution.

Group Disability Income Benefits

The act allows reductions in insured short-term disability income plans. However, no reductions are allowed in uninsured salary continuation plans. While disability statistics for those aged 65 and older are limited, some insurance companies feel a benefit reduction of approximately 20 percent is appropriate for employees between 65 and 69, with additional decreases of 20 percent of the previous benefit for each consecutive 5-year period. However, the laws of the few states that require short-term disability income benefits to be provided allow neither a reduction in benefits nor an increase in any contribution rate for older employees.

Under the act, two methods are allowed for reducing long-term disability income benefits for those employees who become disabled at older ages. Either the level of benefits may be reduced without altering benefit eligibility or duration, or the benefit duration may be reduced without altering the level of benefits. Again these reductions must be justified on a cost basis. Unfortunately no rough guidelines can be given since any possible reductions will vary considerably, depending upon the eligibility requirements and the duration of benefits under a long-term disability plan. For example, one insurance company suggests that if a plan previously provided full benefits until age 70, then the duration of the benefits could be reduced to 12 months for disabilities occurring between the ages of 70 and 74 and 6 months for disabilities occurring after age 74.

Group Medical Expense Benefits

The Age Discrimination in Employment Act requires employers to offer *all* employees over age 65 (and any employees' spouses who are also over age 65) the same medical coverage they provide for younger employees (and their spouses). The employer's plan is the primary payer of benefits, with medicare assuming the secondary-payer role. However, employees may reject the employer's plan and elect medicare as the primary payer of benefits, but regulations prevent an employer from offering a health plan or option designed to induce such a rejection. This effectively prohibits an employer from offering any type of supplemental plan to employees who have elected medicare as primary. (However, supplemental and carve-out plans can be used for retirees.) Therefore most employees will elect to remain with the employer's plan unless it requires large employee contributions. When medicare is secondary, the employer may pay the part B premium for those employees who are also eligible for medicare, but the employer has no legal responsibility to do so.

Unlike the provisions applying to other types of benefits under the Age Discrimination in Employment Act, the provisions under the act require that equal health care benefits be provided. Consequently benefits cannot be reduced for older employees because of increasing cost to the employer. In addition, older employees cannot be required to contribute more than younger employees.

When the employer's plan is primary, medicare payments will be made for medical expenses that are covered by medicare but not by the employer's plan. For purposes of these payments, medicare deductibles and coinsurance will generally not apply. However, medicare benefits are limited to what medicare would have paid in the absence of the employer's plan.

The Civil Rights Act

Traditionally pregnancy has been treated differently from other medical conditions under both individual and group insurance policies. However, the 1978 amendment to the Civil Rights Act requires that women affected by pregnancy, childbirth, or related medical conditions be treated the same for employment-related purposes (including receipt of benefits under an employee benefit plan) as other persons who are not so affected but who are similar in their ability to work. The amendment (also referred to as the Pregnancy Discrimination Act) applies only to the benefit plans (both insured and self-funded) of employers who have 15 or more employees. While employers with fewer employees are not subject to the provisions of the amendment, they may be subject to comparable state laws. Similarly since the amendment applies only to employee benefit plans, pregnancy may be treated differently from other medical conditions under insurance policies that are not part of an employee benefit plan.

While the amendment itself is brief, enforcement falls under the jurisdiction of the Equal Employment Opportunity Commission, which has issued a lengthy set of guidelines containing its interpretation of the amendment. The highlights of these guidelines are as follows:

- If an employer provides any type of disability income or sick-leave plan for employees, the employer must provide coverage for pregnancy and its related medical conditions on the same basis as other disabilities. For example, maternity cannot be treated as a named exclusion in a disability income plan. Similarly an employer cannot limit disability income benefits for pregnancies to a shorter period than that applicable to other disabilities.
- If an employer provides medical expense benefits for employees, the employer must provide coverage for the pregnancy-related conditions of female employees (regardless of marital status) on the same basis as for all other medical conditions. For example, an employer cannot limit hospitalization coverage to $1,500 for pregnancy-related conditions while paying up to 80 percent of expenses for other medical conditions, nor can the employer have a preexisting-conditions clause applying to

pregnancy unless the clause also applies to other preexisting conditions in the same manner.

- If an employer provides medical expense benefits for dependents, the employer must provide equal coverage for the medical expenses (including those arising from pregnancy-related conditions) of spouses of both male and female employees. The guidelines do allow a lower level of benefits for the pregnancy-related conditions of spouses of male employees than for female employees but only if all benefits for spouses are lower than those for employees. The guidelines also allow an employer to exclude pregnancy-related benefits for female dependents other than spouses as long as such an exclusion applies equally to the nonspouse dependents of both male and female employees.
- Extended medical expense benefits after termination of employment must apply equally to pregnancy-related medical conditions and other medical conditions. Thus if pregnancy commencing during employment is covered until delivery, even if the employee is not disabled, a similar nondisability extension of benefits must apply to all other medical conditions. However, no extension is required under the guidelines as long as all medical conditions are treated in the same manner.
- Medical expense benefits relating to abortions may be excluded from coverage except when the life of the woman is endangered. However, complications from an abortion must be covered. In addition, abortions must be treated like any other medical condition with respect to sick leave and other fringe benefit plans.

The Employee Retirement Income Security Act

The Employee Retirement Income Security Act (ERISA) was enacted to protect the interests of participants in employee benefit plans as well as the interests of participants' beneficiaries. While all sections of the act (sometimes referred to as the Pension Reform Act) generally apply to pension plans, certain sections also apply to employee welfare benefit plans, including most traditional group insurance plans. The most significant sections dealing with employee welfare benefit plans are those pertaining to (1) fiduciary responsibility and (2) reporting and disclosure. Since the act and its accompanying regulations are lengthy and extremely complex, only the highlights of ERISA and its effect on employee welfare benefit plans will be discussed below.

Administration of ERISA

While the responsibility for carrying out the provisions of ERISA is shared by the Department of Labor, the Treasury Department, and the Pension Benefit Guaranty Corporation, the Department of Labor bears the main responsibility for those aspects of ERISA affecting group benefit plans. The Department of Labor has been given responsibility for issuing regulations and enforcing the reporting, disclosure, and fiduciary provisions of the act. The Labor-Management Services Administration, a branch of the Department of Labor, is responsible for the field operations of ERISA, and since it has offices in most major cities, it is a source of information regarding ERISA. Many insurance companies have information for agents and insureds to guide them in complying with the act.

Employee Welfare Benefit Plans

The employee welfare benefit plans to which ERISA applies are defined as including any plan, fund, or program established or maintained by an employer (or an employee organization) for the purpose of providing for its participants or their beneficiaries, through the purchase of insurance or otherwise, any of the following benefits:

- medical, surgical, or hospital care or benefits
- benefits in the event of sickness, accident, disability, death, or unemployment
- vacation benefits
- apprenticeship or other training programs
- day-care centers
- scholarship funds
- prepaid legal services
- any benefit described in section 302(c) of the Labor Management Relations Act of 1947 (such as holiday pay and severance pay)

However, certain types of employee welfare benefit plans are specifically exempt from regulation under ERISA. Among these are

- government plans
- church plans (unless they elect to be covered)
- plans maintained solely to comply with workers' compensation, unemployment compensation, or disability insurance laws

In addition, through regulations issued by the secretary of labor, certain types of plans have been declared not to be employee welfare benefit plans and are thus exempt from the regulations of ERISA. Among these are

- compensation for work performed under other than normal circumstances (including overtime pay and shift, holiday, and weekend premiums)
- compensation for absences from work because of sickness, vacation, holidays, military duty, jury duty, or sabbatical leave and training programs to the extent that such compensation is paid out of the general assets of the employer

- group insurance programs under which (1) no contributions are made by the employer; (2) participation is completely voluntary for employees; (3) the sole function served by the employer, without endorsing the program, is to collect premiums through payroll deduction and remit the amount collected to the insurer; and (4) no consideration is paid to the employer in excess of reasonable compensation for administrative services actually performed. Most of the voluntary benefit plans described in later chapters fall into this category.

The Requirement of a Written Instrument

One of the requirements of ERISA is that every employee welfare benefit plan that is subject to the act's regulations be established and maintained pursuant to a written instrument. This instrument must provide for one or more named fiduciaries who have the authority to control and manage the plan's operation and administration. In the case of an insured plan, the fiduciary (or fiduciaries) will have the responsibility for selecting the insurance carrier. In addition, a plan administrator is usually named. The plan administrator, who has the responsibility for complying with the reporting and disclosure requirements under ERISA, may be the employer (that is, the corporation, partnership, or sole proprietorship) but is usually a benefits committee or a specific person, such as the benefits manager or, in the case of a small firm, the owner. If no plan administrator is named, the plan sponsor is considered to be the plan administrator. In the case of an employee welfare benefit plan established or maintained by a single employer (including those situations where coverage is arranged through a multiple-employer welfare arrangement), the employer is considered to be the plan's sponsor. It should be pointed out that there is not a prohibition against the administrator of a plan also being its named fiduciary.

In addition to naming a fiduciary, the plan instrument must accomplish the following:

- provide a procedure for establishing and carrying out a funding policy and method consistent with the plan's objectives
- provide a procedure for amending the plan and for identifying the persons who have the authority to amend it
- specify the basis on which payments are made to and from the plan

A common misconception leading to noncompliance with ERISA is that no plan instrument is required if a plan is insured. The method of funding a plan may affect the details in the plan instrument, but a plan instrument is required for every employee welfare benefit plan (except those specifically excluded from ERISA regulations), regardless of whether it is insured.

Establishment of a Trust

Unless the assets of an employee welfare benefit plan consist of insurance contracts or are held by an insurance company, ERISA requires that all assets of an employee welfare benefit plan be held in trust by one or more trustees. The trustee (or trustees) may be named in either the trust instrument or in the written plan instrument or may be appointed by the named fiduciary. The trustee has the exclusive authority and discretion to manage and control the plan's assets except where the trustee is subject to the direction of the named fiduciary or where the authority to manage, acquire, or dispose of plan assets is delegated to one or more investment managers.

Fiduciary Responsibility

ERISA prescribes very detailed standards for fiduciaries and other parties-in-interest of employee welfare benefit plans. In addition to the named fiduciary (or fiduciaries) in a plan instrument, a fiduciary is defined as any person who

- exercises discretionary authority or control over plan management or assets
- provides investment advice to a plan for a fee or other compensation
- has discretionary authority or responsibility in the administration of a plan

ERISA requires that a fiduciary discharge his or her duties regarding a plan solely in the interest of the participants and their beneficiaries and that the fiduciary do so

- for the exclusive purpose of (1) providing benefits to participants and their beneficiaries and (2) defraying reasonable expenses of administering the plan
- with the same care, skill, prudence, and diligence under the given circumstances that a prudent person acting in a like capacity and familiar with such matters would use in a similar situation
- by diversifying the investments of the plan to minimize the risk of large losses, unless under the circumstances it is clearly prudent not to do so
- in accordance with the documents and instruments governing the plan insofar as such documents and instruments are consistent with the fiduciary provisions of ERISA

Any fiduciary who breaches any of these duties is personally liable for the full amount of any loss resulting from such actions. Furthermore, a fiduciary will also be personally liable for similar breaches by another fiduciary to the extent that his or her actions contributed to the other fiduciary's breach. A breach of fiduciary responsibilities can also result in civil penalties and, if the breach is willful, in criminal penalties as well.

ERISA also contains a list of prohibited transactions for parties-in-interest to an employee welfare benefit plan. In addition to fiduciaries a party-in-interest is defined as including

- any counsel or employee of the plan
- any person providing services to the plan
- an employer of any covered employees of the plan
- an employee organization, any of whose members are covered under the plan
- any owner, direct or indirect, of 50 percent or more of the firm sponsoring the plan
- any relative of a party-in-interest
- certain other related corporations, employees, officers, directors, partners, and joint venturers

The results of the prohibited-transactions provision are that a party-in-interest may not

- cause the plan to engage in any transaction with a party-in-interest that constitutes a direct or indirect (1) sale, exchange, or leasing of property; (2) lending of money; (3) extension of credit; (4) furnishing of goods, services, or facilities; or (5) transfer of any plan assets to a party-in-interest or use of any plan assets by or for the benefit of a party-in-interest
- acquire or hold more than 10 percent of the plan assets in employer securities or real estate
- deal with the assets of the plan in his or her own interest or for his or her own account
- act in any capacity in any transaction involving the plan on behalf of a party whose interests are adverse to the interests of the plan, its participants, or its beneficiaries
- receive any consideration for his or her own personal account from any party dealing with the plan in connection with a transaction involving plan assets
- be paid for his or her services, if already receiving full-time pay from an employer whose employees are participants in the plan, except for reimbursement of expenses incurred

Several specific exemptions to these prohibited transactions are provided under ERISA. Two of these exemptions are

- any loans made by the plan to parties-in-interest who are participants of the plan, if such loans are available on a nondiscriminatory basis, are made in accordance with plan rules regarding loans, have a reasonable rate of interest, and are adequately secured
- reasonable arrangements made with a party-in-interest for office space or legal, accounting, or other services necessary for the plan

The secretary of labor may grant additional exemptions from prohibited transactions as long as such exemptions are administratively feasible, in the best interests of the plan and its participants, and protective of the rights of plan participants. One of these exemptions applies to agents and brokers who receive fees and/or commissions from an employee welfare benefit plan. Without this exemption agents and brokers who are also parties-in-interest are ineligible to receive such compensation. Essentially the exemption applies as long as the agent or broker is not a trustee, administrator, named fiduciary, or fiduciary with specific written discretionary authority over plan assets.

Reporting and Disclosure—General Requirements

ERISA requires that certain information concerning any employee welfare benefit plan be made available by the plan administrator to some or all of the following: (1) plan participants (including beneficiaries of plan participants who are receiving benefits), (2) the Department of Labor, and (3) the Internal Revenue Service. This information must consist of

- a summary plan description
- a summary of material modification
- an annual return/report—Form 5500 (or one of its variations)
- a summary annual report
- any terminal report
- certain underlying documents

ERISA imposes significant monetary penalties for failure to comply with the reporting and disclosure requirements within the prescribed time periods. For example, a fine of up to $1,000 per day can be imposed from the date of failure or refusal to file Form 5500, and a fine of up to $100 per day can be imposed for failure to provide certain requested information to plan participants within 30 days of request. In addition, civil and criminal action can be taken against any plan administrator who willfully violates any of the requirements or who knowingly falsifies or conceals ERISA disclosure information.

Summary Plan Description. The summary plan description must be automatically provided to each plan participant and the Department of Labor within 120 days after the adoption of an employee welfare benefit plan. Copies must be provided to new participants within 90 days of first becoming eligible to participate, and an updated summary plan description must be provided once every 5 years if a plan has been materially modified, otherwise once every 10 years. (However, employers must notify employees that they may request a summary of any plan changes in the interim.) The summary plan description must contain the following information:

- name of the plan
- name, address, and telephone number of the plan administrator
- name and address of the plan's sponsor
- name and address of the agent for service of legal process
- name and address of any trustee(s)
- employer identification number assigned to the plan sponsor by the IRS and the plan number assigned by the plan sponsor
- type of employee welfare benefit plan (such as medical expense or disability income)
- type of administration (self-administered or administered by another party)
- sources of contribution to the plan and the method by which these contributions are calculated
- identity of funding medium (not applicable to a fully insured plan unless a separate fund is established apart from the insurance contract)
- ending date of the plan's fiscal year (which may or may not coincide with the renewal date of any insurance contract used to fund the plan's benefits)
- eligibility requirements
- if applicable, a statement that the plan is maintained pursuant to a collective-bargaining agreement and that copies are available upon request from the plan administrator
- circumstances that may result in disqualification; ineligibility; or denial, loss, forfeiture, or suspension of benefits
- procedure for filing claims and the remedies available under the plan for the redress of denied claims. Participants must be informed that they will be provided with a written notice specifying the reasons for denial of any claim and that they may request in writing a review of any denied claim by the party who processed it. If the claim is again denied, the participant may make a written request for a review by the plan administrator.
- statement of ERISA rights. Plan participants must be informed that they have the right to (1) examine, without charge, at the plan administrator's office and at other specified locations all plan documents and copies of all documents filed by the plan with the Department of Labor; (2) obtain copies of all plan documents and other plan information upon written request from the plan administrator, who may charge the participant a

reasonable fee for the request; and (3) receive a summary of the plan's annual financial report.

ERISA does not require that a summary plan description be provided on a specific form, only that certain information be provided. Some employers use a single document; other employers incorporate much of the required information into the employee benefits handbook provided to their employees.

Summary of Material Modification. For most welfare benefit plans, the summary of material modification must be automatically provided to each plan participant and the Department of Labor within 210 days after the end of a plan year (that is, the plan's fiscal year) in which a material change has been made in the plan. This summary covers the same information contained in the summary plan description and is essentially an annual update of any information that has been changed.

The Health Insurance Portability and Accountability Act significantly changed this requirement for group health plans (see the definition in chapter 9). If there is a material change in covered services or benefits under such a plan, the summary of material modification must be furnished to participants and beneficiaries no later than 60 days after the change. As an alternative, employers can provide the notification at regular intervals of no longer than 90 days. The summary plan description must identify any health insurance issuer (for example, an insurance company or HMO) that is responsible for the financing or administration of the plan and provide its address.

Annual Return/Report (Form 5500). The annual return/report must be filed with the Internal Revenue Service within 210 days after the end of a plan year. This form, which includes financial information about the plan, must be furnished to any plan participant upon written request to the plan administrator. Form 5500-C is used by employers with fewer than 100 employees.

Summary Annual Report. A summary annual report must be automatically provided to each plan participant within 9 months after the end of a plan year. The information provided in this form is a relatively brief summary of some of the information in the annual return/report and consists of a list of the plan's assets and liabilities (or a description of the insurance contract used) and a schedule of the plan's receipts and disbursements.

Terminal Report. A terminal report must be filed with the Internal Revenue Service for a plan that has been terminated. The requirements for a terminal report may be satisfied by the filing of the annual return/report for the final plan year. This report must be furnished to plan participants upon request.

Underlying Documents. Underlying documents consist of those under which the plan was established or is operated, such as a trust agreement or a collective-bargaining agreement. The plan administrator must file these documents with the Department of Labor only if so requested. In addition, certain other records must be provided if requested by the Department of Labor. These documents and records must also be made available to plan participants under certain circumstances.

Reporting and Disclosure—Small Groups

Employee welfare benefit plans that cover fewer than 100 participants at the beginning of a plan year are exempt from certain reporting and disclosure requirements if either of the following conditions is met:

- Benefits are paid as needed solely from the general assets of the employer or employee organization maintaining the plan.
- Benefits are provided exclusively through insurance contracts or policies. The employer (or employee organization) must pay premiums directly from its general assets or partly from its general assets and partly from participants' contributions (provided that the employer forwards participants' contributions to the insurance company within 3 months of receipt). Upon entering the plan, contributing participants must be informed of the provisions for the allocation of refunds.

If these requirements are met, the plan administration does not have to furnish a summary annual report to participants or furnish an annual report or terminal report upon request. However, the annual report must be available for examination in the plan administrator's office.

Form 5500 (the annual return/report) must be filed for plans that provide educational assistance and cafeteria benefits. When the IRS issues further guidelines, Form 5500 will also be required for group term life, accident and health, and dependent-care plans.

It should be noted, however, that a plan administrator must still furnish a summary plan description and a summary of material modification to plan participants. In addition, certain underlying documents must be furnished upon a participant's request.

The Americans with Disabilities Act

The Americans with Disabilities Act (ADA), which deals with employment, public services, public accommodations, and telecommunications, is the most far-reaching legislation ever enacted in this country to make it possible for disabled persons to join the mainstream of everyday life.

At the time of the act's passage in 1990 it was estimated that almost 45 million Americans were disabled, and nearly $300 billion of government resources was devoted annually to this group. Fifteen million of the disabled were of working age, but only about 30 percent of these were in the workforce, compared to 80 percent of the nondisabled.

As with any social legislation, the act provides benefits, including a better quality of life, for many disabled persons and annual savings in the form of decreased government payments to the disabled. However, there are also costs, many of which are borne by employers and some of which take the form of increased expenditures for employee benefits.

Title I of ADA, which pertains to employment, makes it unlawful for employers with 15 or more employees to discriminate on the basis of disability against a qualified individual with respect to any term, condition, or privilege of employment. This includes

- payments for private insurance and retirement plans
- legally required payments for government programs, such as social security
- payments for time not worked, such as vacations
- extra cash payments to employees, such as educational assistance
- the cost of services to employees, such as wellness programs and retirement counseling

Congress gave the responsibility for enforcing Title I to the Equal Employment Opportunity Commission (EEOC), which has a lengthy Technical Assistance Manual to help qualified individuals understand their rights and to facilitate and encourage employer compliance.

While the act has resulted in significant improvements in public accommodations and the availability of telecommunications for the disabled, the percentage of disabled in the workforce has increased only slightly. However, it should be noted that many employers hired the disabled before ADA. Although intuition might suggest that the disabled would be more likely than other employees to have conditions requiring ongoing medical care, many employers who have made an effort to hire the disabled have not found this to be the case. In fact, some employers feel that the disabled make excellent workers and actually save them money. With jobs more difficult to obtain for the disabled, there is the feeling that the disabled are less likely to switch employers (thus minimizing costs to train new employees) and may actually work harder to keep the jobs they have. Whether this situation will continue as more severely disabled persons enter the workforce and have more opportunities to change jobs is an unanswered question.

Effect on Employment Practices

The ADA defines a disabled person as one who has a physical or mental impairment that substantially limits one or more major life activities, such as caring for oneself, performing manual tasks, walking, seeing, hearing, speaking, breathing, and learning. The EEOC specifically mentions the following as being disabilities: epilepsy, cancer, diabetes, arthritis, hearing and vision loss, AIDS, and emotional illness. A person is impaired even if the condition is corrected, as in the case of a person who is hearing-impaired and wears a hearing aid. The ADA does exclude from the definition of disability persons who are currently engaging in the illegal use of drugs. However, anyone who has successfully completed a supervised rehabilitation program or is currently in such a program is subject to the act's protection as long as he or she is not currently engaging in drug use.

The act does not set quotas or require that the disabled be hired. It does, however, provide that a person cannot be discriminated against if he or she is able to perform the essential functions of a job with or without *reasonable accommodation,* which includes making existing facilities that employees use readily accessible and usable by individuals with disabilities. Reasonable accommodation may be as simple as rearranging furniture or changing the height of a work space to accommodate a wheelchair. (There are estimates that a significant percentage of the disabled can be accommodated with expenditures of $100 or less for each disabled person.) Reasonable accommodations do not include changes that would cause undue hardship to an employer. The act defines *undue hardship* as a significant difficulty or expense by the employer in light of such factors as the cost of the accommodation, the employer's financial resources, and the impact on other employees. With one exception reasonable accommodation is for specific individuals for an individual job; it need not be made just because a disabled person may someday apply for work. The exception is that an employer must make facilities for *applying* for a job accessible to the handicapped and provide employment information that is usable by persons who are hearing- or vision-impaired.

The portion of ADA pertaining to employment practices has been a source of many lawsuits and complaints to the EEOC. The vast majority of these lawsuits and complaints pertain to issues of hiring, termination of employment, and the failure to make reasonable accommodations. Employee benefits, on the other hand, have been a relatively minor issue.

Effect on Employee Benefits

The ADA was less precise with respect to employee benefits, and the original Technical Assistance Manual was vague. However, the situation was significantly clarified in June 1993, when the EEOC issued interim enforcement guidance for EEOC investigators to use when investigating ADA claims pertaining to health insurance. Some questions remain unanswered, however, and additional regulations are still needed.

The ADA specifically allows the development and administration of benefit plans in accordance with accepted principles of risk assessment. The EEOC guidelines state that the purpose of the act is not to disrupt the current regulatory climate for self-insured employers or the current nature of insurance underwriting. Furthermore, its purpose is not to alter current industry practices in sales, underwriting, pricing, administrative and other services, claims, and related activities. The act allows these activities based on classification of risks as regulated by the states, unless these activities are being used as a subterfuge to evade the purpose of the act.

The EEOC guidelines stipulate that employees with disabilities be accorded equal access to whatever health insurance coverage the employer provides to other employees. Coverage for dependents is also subject to ADA rules, but the scope of coverage for dependents can be different from the scope of coverage that applies to employees.

The EEOC guidelines recognize that certain coverage limitations are acceptable. For example, a lower level of benefits is permissible for mental and nervous conditions than is provided for physical conditions. Even though such a limitation may have a greater impact on certain persons with disabilities, the limitation is not considered discriminatory because it applies to the treatment of many dissimilar conditions and affects individuals both with and without disabilities. Similarly a lower level of benefits for eye care is singled out as acceptable.

The guidelines allow blanket preexisting-conditions clauses that exclude from coverage the treatment of conditions that predate an individual's eligibility for benefits under a plan. The exclusion of experimental drugs or treatment and elective surgery is also permissible. The guidelines allow coverage limits for procedures that are not exclusively, or nearly exclusively, utilized for the treatment of a specific disability. This category includes, for example, limits on the number of blood transfusions or X rays, even though such limits may adversely affect persons with certain disabilities.

However, "disability-based" provisions are not allowed. These include the exclusion or limitation of benefits for (1) a specific disability, such as deafness, AIDS, or schizophrenia; (2) a discrete group of disabilities, such as cancer, muscular dystrophy, or kidney disease; and (3) disability in general.

If the EEOC determines that a health plan violates the ADA, the burden of proving otherwise is on the employer. To do this an employer must show that

- the plan is bona fide in that it exists and pays benefits, and its terms have been adequately communicated to employees
- the plan's terms are not inconsistent with applicable state law as determined by the appropriate state authorities
- the challenged portion of the plan is not a subterfuge to evade the purpose of the ADA

The guidelines contain the following "noninclusive list of potential business/insurance justifications" that an employer can use to prove that a plan provision that has been challenged by the EEOC is not a violation of the ADA. Note that the italicized words are taken directly from the guidelines. While examples used in the guidelines answer some questions about the exact meaning of the words, their precise meaning is open to interpretation until clarified by regulation or the courts.

- The employer may prove that *it has not engaged in the disability-based disparate treatment alleged.* For example, if it is alleged that a benefit cap for a particular catastrophic disability is discriminatory, the employer may prove that its health insurance plan actually treats all similarly catastrophic conditions in the same way.

- The employer may prove that *the disparate treatment is justified by legitimate actuarial data, or by actual or reasonably anticipated experience, and that conditions with comparable actuarial data and/or experience are treated in the same fashion.* In other words, the employer may prove that the disability-based disparate treatment is attributable to the application of legitimate risk classification and underwriting procedures to the increased risks (and thus increased cost) of the disability, and not to the disability per se.

- The employer may prove that *the disparate treatment is necessary to ensure that the challenged health insurance plan satisfies the commonly accepted or legally required standards for the fiscal soundness of such an insurance plan.* For example, the employer may prove that it limited coverage for the treatment of a discrete group of disabilities because continued unlimited coverage would have been so expensive as to cause the health insurance plan to become financially insolvent, and there was no nondisability-based health insurance plan alternative that would have avoided insolvency.

- The employer may prove that *the challenged insurance practice or activity is necessary to prevent the occurrence of an unacceptable change either in the coverage of the health insurance plan, or in the premiums charged for the health insurance plan.* An unacceptable change is a drastic increase in premium payments (or in copayments or deductibles), or a drastic alteration to the scope of coverage or level of benefits provided that would (1) make the health insurance plan effectively unavailable to a significant number of other employees, (2) make the health insurance plan so unattractive as to result in significant adverse selection, or (3) make the health insurance plan so unattractive that the employer could not compete in recruiting and maintaining qualified workers due to the superiority of health insurance plans offered by other employers in the community.

- *If coverage for a disability-specific treatment is denied, the employer may prove by reliable scientific evidence that the disability-specific treatment does not cure the condition; slow the degeneration, deterioration, or harm attributable to the condition; alleviate the symptoms of the condition; or maintain the current health status of disabled individuals who receive the treatment.*

Nondiscrimination Rules

For many years nondiscrimination rules have applied to employee benefit plans that provided retirement benefits. The purpose of these rules is to deny favorable tax treatment to plans that do not provide equitable benefits to a large cross section of employees. In effect, the owners and executives of a business cannot receive tax-favored benefits if a plan is designed primarily for them. Nondiscrimination rules in recent years have slowly been applied to various other types of employee benefit plans, but these rules, each of which is complex, have not been uniform. Congress attempted to eliminate this lack of uniformity by adding Sec. 89 to the Internal Revenue Code as part of the Tax Reform Act of 1986. This code section was extremely far-reaching and complex, and it would have been very costly both for the government to implement and for employers to comply with. As a result Sec. 89 was repealed in 1989, and all the old nondiscrimination rules it replaced were reinstated. These rules are discussed where appropriate throughout this book.

6

Group Life Insurance: Term Coverage

Chapter Outline

Traditionally most group life insurance plans were designed to provide coverage during an employee's working years, with coverage usually ceasing upon termination of employment for any reason. Today the majority of employees are provided with coverage that will continue, often at a reduced amount, when termination is a result of retirement. Group term insurance is described in this chapter. The methods and contracts used to provide coverage after retirement are discussed in the following chapter.

The oldest and most common form of group life insurance is group term insurance. Coverage virtually always consists of yearly renewable term insurance that provides death benefits only, with no buildup of cash values. The group insurance marketplace with its widespread use of yearly renewable term contrasts with the individual marketplace, in which until recently such coverage has accounted for only a small percentage of the life insurance in force. This is primarily due to increasing annual premiums, which become prohibitive for many insureds at older ages. In group life insurance plans, the overall premium, in addition to other factors, is a function of the age distribution of the group's members. While the premium for any individual employee increases with age, the flow of younger workers into the plan and the retirement of older workers tend to result in a relatively stable age distribution and thus an average group insurance rate that remains constant or rises only slightly.

The following discussion of group term insurance focuses largely on common contract provisions, other coverages that are often added to the basic contract, and relevant federal tax laws.

CONTRACT PROVISIONS

The provisions contained in group term insurance contracts are more uniform than those found in other types of group insurance. Much of this uniformity is a result of the adoption by most states of the NAIC Group Life Insurance Standard Provisions Model Bill. This bill, coupled with the insurance industry's attempts at uniformity, has resulted in provisions that are virtually identical among insurance companies. While the following contract provisions represent the norm and are consistent with the practices of most insurance companies, some states may require slightly different provisions, and some companies may vary their contract provisions. In addition, negotiations between a policyowner and an insurance company may result in the modification of contract provisions.

Benefit Schedules

The purpose of the benefit schedule is twofold. It classifies the employees who are eligible for coverage, and it specifies the amount of life insurance that will be provided to the members of each class, thus minimizing adverse selection because the amount of coverage for individual employees is predetermined. A benefit schedule can be as simple as providing a single amount of life insurance for all employees or as complex as providing different amounts of insurance for different classes of employees. For individual employer groups, the most common benefit schedules are those in which the amount of life insurance is based on either earnings or position.

Earnings Schedules

Most group term life insurance plans use an earnings schedule under which the amount of life insurance is determined as a multiple (or percentage) of each employee's earnings. For example, the amount of life insurance for each employee may be twice (200 percent of) the employee's annual earnings. Most plans use a multiple between one and two, but higher and lower multiples are occasionally used. The amount of insurance is often rounded to the next higher $1,000 and for underwriting purposes may be subject to a maximum benefit, such as $100,000. For purposes of the benefit schedule, an employee's earnings usually consist of base salary only and do not include additional compensation like overtime pay or bonuses.

An alternative to using a flat percentage of earnings is to use an actual schedule of earnings such as the one in table 6-1.

TABLE 6-1	
Annual Earnings	**Amount of Life Insurance**
Less than $20,000	$ 20,000
$20,000 to $29,999	40,000
$30,000 to $39,999	75,000
$40,000 to $49,999	100,000
$50,000 and over	150,000

This type of schedule may be designed so that all employees receive an amount of coverage that is approximately equal to the same multiple of annual earnings or, as in this example, larger multiples with higher earnings. Benefit schedules usually provide for a change in the amount of an employee's coverage when the employee moves into a different classification, even if this does not occur on the policy anniversary date. For example, the schedule in table 6-1 indicates that the amount of coverage for an employee earning $28,000 would increase from $40,000 to $75,000 if the employee received a $4,000 raise. Some schedules, however, specify that adjustments in amounts of coverage will only be made annually or on monthly premium due dates.

Position Schedules

Position schedules are similar to earnings schedules except that, as table 6-2 shows, the amount of life insurance is based on an employee's position within the firm rather than on the employee's annual earnings.

Because individuals in high positions are often involved in designing the benefit schedule, underwriters are concerned that the benefits for these individuals be reasonable in relation to the overall plan benefits. Position schedules may also pose problems in meeting nondiscrimination rules if excessively large amounts of coverage are provided to persons in high positions.

TABLE 6-2	
Position	**Amount of Life Insurance**
President	$200,000
Vice presidents	100,000
Managers	60,000
Salespersons	40,000
Other employees	20,000

Even though position schedules are often used when annual earnings can be easily determined, they are particularly useful when it is difficult to determine an employee's annual income. This is the situation when income is materially affected by such factors as commissions earned, number of hours worked, or bonuses that are based on either the employee's performance or the firm's profits.

Flat-Benefit Schedules

Under flat-benefit schedules the same amount of life insurance is provided for all employees regardless of salary or position. This type of benefit schedule is commonly used in group insurance plans covering hourly paid employees, particularly when benefits are negotiated with a union. In most cases the amount of life insurance under a flat-benefit schedule is relatively small, such as $5,000 or $10,000. When an employer desires to provide only a minimum amount of life insurance for all employees, a flat-benefit schedule is often used.

Length-of-Service Schedules

In the early days of group life insurance, length-of-service schedules were relatively common and viewed as a method for rewarding longtime employees. However, because of the current view that the primary purpose of group life insurance is to replace income, such schedules are not extensively used. These schedules may also be considered discriminatory if a disproportionate number of the persons with longer service records are also the most highly paid employees. Table 6-3 is an example of a length-of-service schedule.

Pension Schedules

Under pension schedules the amount of life insurance is a function of an employee's projected pension at retirement. For example, under an employer's plan the amount of life insurance for each employee might be 100 times the monthly pension that will be payable to the employee at normal retirement age. The amount of life insurance may also be subject to a maximum benefit.

TABLE 6-3	
Length of Service	**Amount of Life Insurance**
Less than 2 years	$ 4,000
2 years but less than 5 years	8,000
5 years but less than 10 years	12,000
10 years but less than 15 years	16,000
15 years but less than 20 years	20,000
20 years or more	25,000

Combination Benefit Schedules

It is not unusual for employers to have benefit schedules that incorporate elements from several of the various types previously discussed. While there are numerous possible combinations, a common benefit schedule of this type provides salaried employees with an amount of insurance that is determined by a multiple of their annual earnings and provides hourly employees with a flat amount of life insurance.

Reduction in Benefits

It is common for a group life insurance plan to provide for a reduction in benefits for active employees who reach a certain age, commonly 65 to 70. Such a reduction, which is due to the high cost of providing benefits for older employees, will be specified in the benefit schedule of a plan. Any reduction in the amount of life insurance for active employees is subject to the provisions of the Age Discrimination in Employment Act, which are discussed in the chapter on the governmental environment for group insurance.

Benefit reductions fall into three categories: (1) a reduction to a flat amount of insurance; (2) a percentage reduction, such as to 65 percent of the amount of insurance that was previously provided; or (3) a gradual reduction over a period of years (for example, a 10 percent reduction in coverage each year until a minimum benefit amount is reached).

Eligibility

Group insurance contracts are very precise in their definition of what constitutes an eligible person for coverage purposes. In general, an employee must be in a covered classification, work full-time, and be actively at work. In addition, any requirements concerning probationary periods, insurability, or premium contributions must be satisfied.

Covered Classifications

All group insurance contracts specify that an employee must fall into one of the classifications contained in the benefit schedule. While these classifications may be broad enough to include all employees of the organization, they may also be so limited as to exclude many employees from coverage. In some cases these excluded employees may have coverage through a negotiated trusteeship or under other group insurance contracts provided by the employer; in other cases they may have no coverage because the employer wishes to limit benefits to certain groups of employees. No employee may be in more than one classification, and the responsibility for determining the appropriate classification for each employee falls on the policyowner.

Full-time Employment

Most group insurance contracts limit eligibility to full-time employees. A full-time employee is generally defined as one who works no fewer than the number of hours in the normal work week established by the employer, which must be at least 30 hours. Subject to insurance company underwriting practices, an employer can provide coverage for part-time employees. When this is done, part-time is generally defined as less than full-time but more than some minimum number of hours per week. Part-time employees may be subject to more stringent eligibility requirements. For example, full-time hourly paid employees may be provided with $20,000 of life insurance immediately upon employment, while part-time employees may be provided with only $10,000 of life insurance and may be subject to a probationary period.

Actively-at-Work Provision

Most group insurance contracts contain an actively-at-work provision, whereby an employee is not eligible for coverage if absent from work because of sickness, injury, or other reasons on the otherwise effective date of coverage under the contract. Coverage will commence when the employee returns to work. This provision is often waived for employers with a large number of employees when coverage is transferred from one insurance company to another and the employees involved have been insured under the previous insurance company's contract.

Probationary Periods

Group insurance contracts may contain probationary periods that must be satisfied before an employee is eligible for coverage. When a probationary period exists, it rarely exceeds 6 months, and an employee will be eligible for coverage on either the first day after the probationary period or on the first day of the month following the end of the probationary period.

Insurability

While most group insurance contracts are issued without individual evidence of insurability, in some instances underwriting practices will require evidence of insurability. This commonly occurs when an employee fails to elect coverage under a contributory plan and later wants coverage or when an employee is eligible for a large amount of coverage. In these cases an employee will not be eligible for coverage until he or she has submitted the proper evidence of insurability and the insurance company has determined that the evidence is satisfactory.

Premium Contribution

If a group insurance plan is contributory, an employee will not be eligible for coverage until the policyowner has been given the proper authorization for payroll deductions. If this is done before the employee otherwise becomes eligible, coverage will commence on the eligibility date. During the next 31 days, coverage will begin when the policyowner receives the employee's authorization. If the authorization is not received within 31 days, the employee must furnish evidence of insurability at his or her own expense to obtain coverage. Evidence of insurability will also be required if an employee drops coverage under a contributory plan and wishes to regain coverage at a future date.

Beneficiary Designation

With few exceptions an insured person has the right to name the beneficiary under his or her group life insurance coverage. These exceptions include credit life insurance, where the creditor is the beneficiary, and dependent life insurance, where the employee is the beneficiary. In addition, the laws and regulations of some states prohibit naming the employer as beneficiary. Unless a beneficiary designation has been made irrevocable, an employee has the right to change the designated beneficiary at any time. While all insurance contracts require that the insurance company be notified of any beneficiary change in writing, the effective date of the change may vary, depending on contract provisions. Some contracts specify that a change will be effective on the date it is received by the insurance company; others make it effective on the date the change was requested by the employee.

Under individual life insurance policies, death benefits are paid to an insured person's estate if no beneficiary has been named or if all beneficiaries have died before the insured. Some group term insurance contracts contain an identical provision; others stipulate that the death benefits will be paid through a *successive beneficiary provision.* Under the successive beneficiary provision the proceeds will be paid, at the option of the insurance company, to any one or more of the following survivors of the insured person: spouse, children, parents, brothers and sisters, or executor of the employee's estate. In most cases insurance companies will pay the proceeds to the person or persons in the first category that includes eligible survivors.

Two other provisions, each of which is often called a *facility-of-payment provision,* are sometimes found in group term insurance contracts. The first of these provides that a specified amount, generally $500 or less, may be paid to any person who appears to be entitled to such a sum by reason of having incurred funeral or other expenses relating to the last illness or death of the person insured. The other provision applies to any beneficiary who is a minor or who is physically, mentally, or otherwise incapable of giving a valid release for any payment received. Under this provision the insurance company has the option, until a claim is made by the beneficiary's guardian, of paying the proceeds to any person or institution that appears to have assumed responsibility for the care, custody, or support of the beneficiary. These payments will be made in installments in the amount specified under any optional method of settlement that the insured selected or, in the absence of such a selection, in installments not to exceed some specified amount, such as $100 per month.

Settlement Options

With the exception of survivor income benefit insurance plans (discussed later in this chapter), group term insurance contracts covering employees provide that death benefits will be payable in a lump sum unless an optional mode of settlement has been selected. Each employee insured under the contract has the right to select and change any available mode of settlement during his or her lifetime. If no optional mode of settlement is in force at the employee's death, the beneficiary generally has the right to elect any of the available options. The most common provision in group term insurance contracts is that the available modes of settlement are those customarily offered by the insurance company at the time the selection is made. The available options are not generally specified in the contract, but information about them is usually given to the group policyowner. In addition, many insurance companies have brochures that describe either all or the most common options available to employees. Any guarantees associated with these options will be those that are in effect when the option is selected.

In addition to a lump-sum option, most insurance companies offer all the following options and possibly other options as well:

- an interest option. The proceeds are left on deposit with the insurance company, and the interest on the proceeds is paid to the beneficiary. The beneficiary can usually withdraw the proceeds at any time. The amount of any periodic installment is a function of the interest rate paid by the insurance company.
- an installment option for a fixed period. The proceeds are paid in equal installments for a specified period of time. The amount of any periodic installment is a function of the time period and the amount of the death proceeds.
- an installment option for a fixed amount. The proceeds are paid in equal installments of a specified amount until the proceeds plus any interest earnings are exhausted.
- a life income option. The proceeds are payable in installments during the lifetime of the beneficiary. A choice of guarantee periods is usually available during which a secondary beneficiary or the beneficiary's estate will continue to receive benefits even if the beneficiary dies. The amount of any periodic installment will be a function of the age and sex of the beneficiary, the period for which payments are guaranteed, and the amount of the death proceeds.

Premiums

Group insurance contracts stipulate that it is the responsibility of the policyowner to pay all premiums to the insurance company, even if the group insurance plan is contributory. Any required contributions from employees will be incorporated into the employer's group insurance plan, but they are not part of the insurance contract and therefore do not constitute an obligation to the insurance company by the employees. Rather, these contributions represent an obligation to the employer by the employees and are commonly paid by payroll deduction. Subject to certain limitations, any employee contributions are determined by the employer or as a result of labor negotiations. Most states require the employer to pay at least a portion of the premium for group term insurance (but not for other group insurance coverage), and a few states impose limitations on the amounts that may be paid by any employee. The most common restriction limits the contribution of any employee to the greater of 60 cents per month per $1,000 of coverage or 75 percent of the premium rate for that employee. This limitation is adhered to by companies licensed to do business in the state of New York and is often incorporated into their contracts. However, for some hazardous industries a higher contribution than 60 cents per month is permitted.

Premiums are payable in advance to the insurance company or any authorized agent for the time period specified in the contract. In most cases premiums are payable monthly but may be paid less frequently. The rates used to determine the premium for any policyowner are guaranteed for a certain length of time, usually one year. The periodic premium is determined by applying these rates to the amount of life insurance in force. Consequently the premium actually payable will change each month as the total amount of life insurance in force under the group insurance plan varies. A detailed explanation of premium computations is contained in the chapter on group insurance pricing.

Group insurance contracts state that any dividends or experience refunds are payable to the policyowner in cash or may be used at the policyowner's option to reduce any premium due. To the extent that these exceed the policyowner's share of the premium, they must be used for the employees' benefit. This is usually accomplished by reducing employee contributions or increasing benefits.

Claims

The provision concerning death claims under group life insurance policies is very simple. It states that the amount of insurance under the contract is payable when the insurance company receives written proof of death. No time period is specified in which a claim must be filed. However, most companies require that the policyowner and the beneficiary complete a brief form before a claim is processed.

Assignment

For many years the owners of individual life insurance policies have been able to transfer any or all of their rights under the insurance contract to another party. Such assignments have been commonly used to avoid federal estate tax by removing the proceeds of an insurance contract from the insured's estate at death. Historically assignments have not been permitted under group life insurance contracts, often because of state laws and regulations prohibiting them. In recent years most states have eliminated such prohibitions, and many insurance companies have modified their contracts to permit assignments, or they will waive the prohibition upon request. Essentially an assignment will be valid as long as it is permitted by and conforms with state law and the group insurance contract. Generally insurance companies require any assignment to be in writing and to be filed with the company.

Grace Period

Group life insurance contracts allow for a grace period (almost always 31 days) during which a policyowner may pay any overdue premium without interest. If the premium is not paid, the contract will lapse at the end of the grace period unless the policyowner has notified the insurance company that an earlier termination should take place. Even if the policy is allowed to lapse or is terminated during the grace period, the policyowner is legally liable for the payment of any premium due during the portion of the grace period when the contract was still in force.

Entire Contract

The entire contract clause states that the insurance policy, the policyowner's application that is attached to the policy, and any individual (unattached) applications of any insured persons constitute the entire insurance contract. All statements made in these applications are considered to be representations rather than warranties, and no other statements made by the policyowner or by any insureds can be used by the insurance company as the basis for contesting coverage. When compared with the application for individual life insurance, the policyowner's application that is attached to a group insurance contract may be relatively short. Often most of the information the insurance company needs is contained in a preliminary application that is not part of the insurance contract. On the delivery of many group insurance contracts the policyowner signs a final "acceptance application," which in effect states that the coverage as applied for has been delivered. Consequently a greater burden is placed on the insurance company to verify the statements the policyowner made in the preliminary application.

The entire contract clause also stipulates that no agent has any authority to waive or amend any provisions of the insurance contract and that a waiver of or amendment to the contract will be valid only if certain specified corporate officers of the insurance company have signed it.

Incontestability

Like individual life insurance contracts, group insurance contracts contain an incontestability provision. Except for the nonpayment of premiums the validity of the contract cannot be contested after it has been in force for a specified period, generally either one or 2 years. During this time the insurance company can contest the contract on the basis of policyowner statements in the application attached to the contract that are considered to be material misrepresentations. Statements by any insured person can be used as the basis for denying claims during the first 2 years that coverage is in force on the insured but only if such statements relate to the individual's insurability. In addition, the statements must have been made in a written application signed by the individual, and a copy of the application must have been furnished to either the individual or his or her beneficiary. It should be pointed out that the incontestability clause will not concern most covered persons, since evidence of insurability is not usually required and thus no statements about individual insurability will be made.

Misstatement of Age

If the age of any person covered under a group term insurance policy is misstated, the benefit payable will be the amount that is specified under the benefit schedule. However, the premium will be adjusted to reflect the true age of the individual. This is in contrast to individual life insurance contracts, where benefits are adjusted to the amount that the premium paid would have purchased at the true age of the individual. Under a group insurance contract the responsibility for paying any additional premium or the right to receive a refund belongs to the policyowner and not to the individual employee whose age is misstated, even if the plan is contributory. If the misstated age would have affected the employee's contribution, this is a matter to be resolved between the employer and the employee.

Termination

All group insurance contracts stipulate the conditions under which the insurance company or the policyowner may terminate the contract and under which the coverage for a particular insured person will terminate.

A group term insurance contract can be terminated for nonpayment of premium at the end of the grace period. Insurance companies may also terminate coverage for an individual employer group on any premium due date if certain conditions exist and notice of termination has been given to the policyowner at least 31 days in advance. These conditions include the failure to maintain a stated minimum number of participants in the plan and in contributory plans the failure to maintain a stated minimum percentage participation. The policyowner may also terminate the contract at any time by giving the insurance company 31 days' advance written notice. Moreover, the policyowner has the right to request the amendment of the contract at any time by notifying the insurance company.

The coverage for any insured person will terminate automatically (subject to any provisions for a continuation or conversion of coverage) when

- the employee terminates employment
- the employee ceases to be eligible (for example, if the employee no longer satisfies the full-time work requirement or no longer falls into a covered classification)
- the policyowner or insurance company terminates the master contract
- any required contribution by the employee has not been made (generally because the employee has notified the policyowner to cease the required payroll deduction)

Temporary Interruption of Employment

Most group term insurance contracts provide that the employer may elect to continue coverage on employees during temporary interruptions of active full-time employment arising from leaves of absence, layoffs, or inability to work because of illness or injury. The employer must continue paying the premium, and the coverage may be continued only for a relatively short period of time, such as 3 months, unless the time period is extended by mutual agreement between the employer and the insurance company. Also in electing to continue coverage, the policyowner must act in a way that precludes individual selection.

Continuation of Coverage for Disabled Employees

Most group term insurance contracts make some provision for the continuation of coverage on employees whose active employment has terminated due to disability. By far the most common provision in use today is the *waiver-of-premium provision*. Under this provision life insurance coverage is continued without the payment of premium as long as the employee is totally disabled, even if the master contract is terminated. However, certain requirements must be met:

- The disability must commence while the employee is insured under the master contract.
- The disability must begin prior to a specified age, commonly age 60.
- The employee must be totally disabled. Total disability is normally defined as the employee's complete inability to engage in any gainful occupation for which he or she is or becomes qualified by reason of education, training, or experience.
- The employee must file a claim within a prescribed period (normally 12 months) and must submit annual evidence of continuing disability.

If an employee no longer meets the definition of disability and returns to work, the employee may again be insured under the group insurance contract on a premium-paying basis as long as the employee meets the contract's eligibility requirements. If for any reason the employee is not eligible for insurance under the group insurance contract, he or she can exercise the conversion privilege.

A few insurance companies refer to their waiver-of-premium provision as an extended death benefit. This terminology is somewhat confusing since historically an extended-death-benefit provision has allowed coverage to continue on a disabled employee for a maximum of only one year. After that time coverage ceases. This type of provision, once quite common, is still used occasionally but has generally been replaced by a waiver-of-premium provision.

Another provision relating to disabled employees is a maturity-value benefit. Under this type of provision the face amount of a totally disabled employee's group life insurance will be paid to the employee in a lump sum or in monthly installments. Like the extended-death-benefit provision, a maturity-value-benefit provision was once widely used but is no longer common.

A small but growing trend is for disabled employees to be continued as eligible employees under a group insurance contract, with the employer paying the periodic cost of their coverage just as if they were active employees. At the termination of the contract the insurance company has no responsibility to continue coverage unless a disabled employee is eligible, elects to convert coverage, and pays any required premiums. However, depending on the provisions of the group insurance plan, the employer may have a legal responsibility to continue coverage on disabled employees in some manner.

Conversion

All group term insurance contracts covering employees contain a conversion privilege that gives any employee whose coverage ceases the right to convert to an individual insurance policy. The terms of the conversion privilege vary, depending upon the reason for the termination of coverage under the group contract. The most generous conversion rights are available to those employees who either have terminated employment or no longer fall into one of the eligible classifications still covered by the master contract. These employees have the right to purchase an individual life insurance policy from the insurance company without evidence of insurability, but it is usually one without disability or other supplementary benefits. However, this right is subject to the following conditions:

- The employee must apply for conversion within 31 days after the termination of employment or membership in an eligible classification. During this 31-day period the employee's death benefit is equal to the amount of life insurance that is available under the conversion privilege, even if the employee does not apply for conversion. Disability and supplementary benefits are not extended during this period unless they are also subject to conversion. The premium for the individual policy must accompany the conversion application, and coverage will be effective at the end of the conversion period.
- The individual policy the employee selects may generally be any form, except term insurance, the insurance company customarily issues at the age and amount applied for. Some insurance companies also make term insurance coverage available, and a few states require that employees be allowed to purchase term insurance coverage for a limited time (such as one year) after which an employee must convert to a cash value form of coverage.
- The face amount of the individual policy may not exceed the amount of life insurance that terminated under the group insurance contract.
- The premium for the individual policy will be determined using the insurance company's current rate applicable to the type and amount of the individual policy for the employee's attained age on the date of conversion and for the class of risk to which the employee belongs. Although no extra premium may be charged for reasons of health, an

extra premium may be charged for any other hazards considered in an insurance company's rate structure, such as occupation or avocation.

It is estimated that only one or two percent of eligible employees actually take advantage of the conversion privilege. Several reasons account for this. Many employees will obtain coverage with new employers; others are discouraged by the high cost of the permanent insurance to which they must convert. Still others, if they are insurable at standard rates, may find coverage at a lower cost with other insurers and be able to purchase supplementary coverage (such as disability benefits) that are not available under conversion policies. In addition, insurance companies have not actively encouraged group conversions because those who convert tend to be the poorer risks. Finally, since some employers are faced with conversion charges as a result of experience rating (see the chapter on group insurance pricing), they are also unlikely to encourage conversion.

There is a more restrictive conversion privilege if an employee's coverage is terminated because the master contract is terminated for all employees or is amended to eliminate eligible classifications. Under these circumstances the employee is given a conversion right only if he or she was insured under the contract for a period of time (generally 5 years) immediately preceding the date on which coverage was terminated. In addition, the amount of insurance that can be converted is limited to the lesser of (1) $2,000 or (2) the amount of the employee's life insurance under the contract at the date of termination, reduced by any amount of life insurance for which the employee becomes eligible under any group life insurance policy that the same or another insurance company issues or reinstates within 31 days after such termination.

Accelerated Benefits

Over the last several years many insurers have introduced an accelerated benefits provision in their individual life insurance products. Under such a provision an insured is entitled to receive a portion of his or her death benefit while still living if one or more of the following events occur: (1) a terminal illness that is expected to result in death within 6 or 12 months; (2) a specified catastrophic illness, such as AIDS, a stroke, or Alzheimer's disease; and (3) the incurring of nursing home and possibly other long-term-care expenses. The categories of triggering events and the specific definitions of each vary among insurers.

Often what becomes popular in the individual marketplace starts to show up in the group insurance marketplace. Such is the case with accelerated benefits, which are now offered by most group insurers. In fact, many group insurers make accelerated death benefits a part of their standard group term coverage unless an employer does not want the benefit provided.

Most group insurers allow accelerated benefits for terminal illnesses only. Some insurers use a life expectancy of 6 months or less; most use a life expectancy of 12 months or less. In either case a doctor must certify the life expectancy.

The amount of the accelerated benefit is expressed as a percentage of the basic life insurance coverage and may range from 25 percent to 100 percent. In addition, most insurers limit the maximum benefit to a specified dollar amount that may vary from $25,000 to $250,000. Any amount not accelerated is paid to the beneficiary upon the insured's death.

There are no limitations on how the accelerated benefit can be used. It might be used to pay medical expenses and nursing home care not covered by other insurance, or it could even be used to prepay funeral expenses.

Although some insurers make no charge for the inclusion of an accelerated death benefit, most do levy some type of charge. In some cases, this may be a higher premium levied the policyowner. In other cases, any accelerated death benefit paid will be reduced by an amount equal to the interest that could have been earned on the money over the next 6 to 12 months. Finally, a few insurers levy a modest transaction charge when an accelerated death benefit is taken.

ADDED COVERAGES

Group term insurance contracts often provide additional insurance benefits through the use of riders. These benefits are also forms of group term insurance and consist of (1) supplemental life insurance, (2) accidental death and dismemberment insurance, (3) survivor income benefit insurance, and (4) dependent life insurance. These added benefits may be provided for all employees insured under the basic group term contract or may be limited to certain classes of employees. With the exception of dependent life insurance these coverages may also be written as separate contracts.

Supplemental Life Insurance

The majority of group life insurance plans enable all or certain classes of employees to purchase additional amounts of life insurance. Generally the employer will provide a basic amount of life insurance to all eligible employees on a noncontributory basis. This is commonly a flat amount of coverage or a multiple of annual earnings. The supplemental coverage is contributory and may be either incorporated into the basic group life insurance contract or contained in a separate contract. The latter method tends to be more common when the supplemental coverage is available to only a select group of employees. Although the employee may pay the entire cost of the supplemental coverage, either state laws that require employer contributions or insurance company underwriting practices will often result in the employer's paying a portion of the cost. It is not unusual for there to be two sets of rates—one for smokers and another for nonsmokers.

The amount of supplemental coverage available will be specified in a benefit schedule. Under some plans an employee must purchase the full amount of coverage; under other plans an employee may purchase a portion of the coverage. Tables 6-4 and 6-5 are two examples of benefit schedules for a basic-plus-supplemental life insurance plan.

TABLE 6-4	
Type of Coverage	**Amount of Life Insurance**
Basic insurance Supplemental insurance	$25,000 50,000

TABLE 6-5	
Type of Coverage	**Amount of Life Insurance**
Basic insurance Supplemental insurance	1 times salary 1/2, 1, 1 1/2, or 2 times salary, subject to a maximum (including basic insurance) of $200,000

Since giving employees the right to choose their benefit amounts leads to adverse selection, stringent underwriting requirements usually accompany supplemental coverage. These often include requiring individual evidence of insurability, except possibly when the additional coverage is modest. Higher rates may be charged for the supplemental insurance than for the basic coverage.

Accidental Death and Dismemberment Insurance

Many group life insurance contracts contain an accidental death and dismemberment provision that gives additional benefits if an employee dies accidentally or suffers certain types of injuries. Traditionally this group coverage was available only as a rider to a group life insurance contract. Now, however, it is common to find these benefits in separate group insurance contracts in which coverage is usually contributory on the part of employees. Such contracts are referred to as voluntary accidental death and dismemberment insurance.

Traditional Coverage

Under the usual traditional form of accidental death and dismemberment insurance, an employee eligible for group life insurance coverage (and electing the life insurance coverage if it is contributory) will automatically have the accidental death and dismemberment coverage if the employer has added it. A few plans impose a probationary period, such as 6 months, before coverage begins. Under the typical accidental death and dismemberment rider, the insurance company will pay an additional amount of insurance that is equal to the amount of coverage under the basic group life insurance contract (referred to as the principal sum) if an employee dies as a result of accidental bodily injuries while he or she is covered under the policy. It is specified that death must occur within a certain time, often 90 days, following the date that injuries are sustained, but some courts have ruled this time period to be invalid and have required insurance companies to pay claims when longer periods have been involved. In addition to an accidental death benefit, the benefit schedule shown in table 6-6 is provided for certain specific types of injuries.

TABLE 6-6	
Type of Injury	**Benefit Amount**

Loss of (including loss of use of):
  Both hands or both feet
  The sight of both eyes
  One hand and sight of one eye
  One foot and sight of one eye
  One foot and one hand
  One hand
  One foot
  The sight of one eye
	
	The principal sum
	The principal sum
	The principal sum
	The principal sum
	The principal sum
	One-half the principal sum
	One-half the principal sum
	One-half the principal sum

In some cases the accidental death and dismemberment rider is written to provide the same benefits for any accident covered under the contract. However, it is not unusual to have a higher level of benefits for accidents that occur while the employee is traveling on business for the employer. These larger travel benefits may apply to death benefits only. They may also be limited to accidents that occur while the employee is occupying (or entering, alighting from, or struck by) a public conveyance and possibly a company-owned or personally owned vehicle. Table 6-7 is an example of a benefit schedule reflecting some of these variations.

TABLE 6-7	
Type of Loss	**Benefit Amount**
Death while traveling on business when occupying, boarding, alighting from, or struck by any motor vehicle, airplane, or other conveyance, including company-owned or personally owned vehicles	3 times the principal sum
Death at all other times	2 times the principal sum
Dismemberment	Up to the principal sum (as shown in the previous schedule)

Death benefits are paid in accordance with the beneficiary provision of the group life insurance contract, and dismemberment benefits are paid to the employee. Coverage is usually written to cover both occupational and nonoccupational accidents. However, when employees are in hazardous occupations, coverage may apply only to nonoccupational accidents, in which case employees would still have workers' compensation coverage for any occupational accidents.

Coverage is generally not subject to a conversion privilege. When life insurance coverage is continued after retirement, accidental death and dismemberment benefits are normally no longer available. As with the life insurance coverage, however, this coverage may be continued during temporary periods of unemployment. In contrast to the group term insurance policy to which it is attached, group accidental death and dismemberment insurance does contain some exclusions. These exclusions include losses resulting from the following:

- suicide at any time (It is interesting to note that, except for a few multiple-employer trusts, group term insurance does not contain a suicide provision.)
- disease or bodily or mental infirmity, or medical or surgical treatment thereof
- ptomaines or any infection other than one occurring simultaneously with and through an accidental cut or wound
- war
- travel or flight in any type of aircraft either as a pilot, as a student pilot, or as an officer or member of the crew. (However, there is a trend toward eliminating this exclusion, particularly when coverage is written on large groups.)

Voluntary Coverage

The provisions of voluntary group accidental death and dismemberment insurance are practically identical to those in a group life insurance contract with an accidental death and dismemberment insurance rider. However, there are a few differences. Voluntary plans usually require the employee to pay the entire cost of coverage, and they virtually always provide both occupational and nonoccupational coverage. Subject to limitations, the employee may select the amount of coverage desired, and the maximum amount of coverage available tends to be larger than when coverage is provided through a rider. For example, one plan allows coverage to be purchased at the following levels: $25,000, $50,000, $75,000, $100,000, $200,000, or $300,000 as long as the amount selected does not exceed 10 times annual salary. The amount of coverage often decreases after age 65 or 70, just as the amount of traditional coverage decreases when it is a function of a life insurance benefit that is lowered at older ages.

Another difference is the frequent use in voluntary plans of a common accident provision, whereby the amount payable by the insurance company is limited to a stipulated maximum for all employees killed or injured in any single accident. If this exceeds the sum of the benefits otherwise payable for each employee, benefits are prorated. A final difference is that some plans allow an employee to purchase coverage on dependents. For example, under one plan the coverage on a spouse is equal to 40 percent of the coverage on the employee, and coverage on each child is 10 percent of the employee's coverage.

Survivor Income Benefit Insurance

Survivor income benefit insurance represents an attempt to more closely relate life insurance benefits to the actual needs of each employee's survivors. Instead of paying death benefits in a lump sum to a named beneficiary, benefits are paid in the form of periodic income to specified dependents who survive the employee. No death benefits are paid unless an employee has qualified survivors, and benefit payments will cease when survivors are no longer eligible. Like regular group term insurance, a survivor income benefit insurance plan may be contributory or noncontributory.

Survivor income benefit insurance plans, which have been available since the 1960s, have never gained widespread acceptance, but new cases continue to be written. Employees without qualified survivors often view such plans as discriminatory since these employees have no life insurance coverage. Consequently survivor income benefit insurance is normally written in conjunction with a group term insurance plan that will provide a basic amount of life insurance for all eligible employees. This basic amount of life insurance will serve as a means of providing for the burial and other last expenses associated with the death of any employee. In addition, there is a feeling among employers that employees are not as appreciative of a benefit expressed as a certain amount of dollars per month as they are of one expressed as a larger lump-sum amount. Also the final decision about what type of group life insurance coverage to buy is frequently made by an older executive. Such a person may not view survivor income benefit plans with enthusiasm since they generally offer potentially greater benefits to younger workers who tend to have younger survivors.

Eligible survivors under survivor income benefit insurance coverage generally include only the employee's spouse and any dependent children. The spouse is typically defined as a person who has been lawfully married to the employee for at least 90 days and who is not legally separated from the employee. A spouse's eligibility to receive benefits usually ceases if the spouse remarries or reaches a certain age, such as 65. At this age it is assumed that the spouse will be eligible for benefits under social security. Some plans also make a payment of one or two years' benefits to spouses who remarry. The purpose of this "dowry payment" is to encourage the spouse to report the remarriage.

Dependent children are defined as unmarried dependent children of the employee, including stepchildren and children the employee has legally adopted. Benefits to dependent children will cease upon marriage or reaching a certain age, such as 19. Benefits may be paid longer for unmarried children who are in school.

Under some survivor income benefit insurance plans, the benefit amount is determined by the number of eligible survivors even though the entire benefit will be paid to the surviving spouse. Only if there is no surviving spouse or if the spouse later dies will the benefits be paid directly to the children. Under other plans separate benefits are made available to the surviving spouse and the dependent children. These benefits may be based on specified dollar amounts or they may be a function of the deceased employee's salary.

Some survivor income benefit insurance plans pay a monthly benefit (either a flat amount or a percentage of salary) regardless of the number and types of survivors. In some instances a larger benefit is paid for a certain period of time following the employee's death. This transitional benefit will give the survivors a better opportunity to adjust their standard of living to a level consistent with the regular survivor income benefits. Survivor income benefits are generally substantially less than the employee's former income and are viewed as a supplement to any social security benefits for which the survivors will be eligible. In those few instances in which benefits are more generous, they are likely to be reduced by any social security benefits that survivors receive. Tables 6-8 and 6-9 are two examples of benefit schedules under group life insurance plans that have been supplemented with survivor income benefit insurance.

For regulatory purposes most states treat survivor income benefit insurance the same as group term insurance, including the requirement for a conversion provision. The amount eligible for conversion by an employee is the commuted value of the benefit payments that eligible survivors would receive if the employee died at the time of conversion. This amount is determined by calculating the present value of potential benefits, using the mortality table and the interest rates employed by the insurance company. The present value of these benefits, which is a function of the number and ages of eligible survivors, can be substantial for an employee with young survivors.

TABLE 6-8	
Benefit	**Amount of Benefit**
Basic life insurance for each employee	$25,000
Surviving spouse benefit*	10% of the employee's average monthly salary during the year prior to death
Surviving child benefit*	5% of the employee's average monthly salary during the year prior to death for each child
*Subject to a maximum family benefit of $400 per month	

TABLE 6-9	
Benefit	**Amount of Benefit**
Basic life insurance for each employee	$10,000
Transition survivor benefit for 24 months	$1,000 per month
Survivor benefit after the transition period	$500 per month

Because of the adverse selection accompanying conversion, insurance companies have been concerned about the size of the conversion benefit. Some states allow the conversion amount to be expressed as a multiple of the potential monthly benefit. On the average this results in a lower conversion amount than if the commuted value is used. A few states also allow insurance companies to market their survivor income benefit product as an "annuity with contingencies." One advantage to having the product considered an annuity is that no conversion provision is required.

Dependent Life Insurance

Some group life insurance contracts provide insurance coverage on the lives of employees' dependents. Dependent life insurance has been viewed as a method of giving the employee resources to meet the funeral and burial expenses associated with a dependent's death. Consequently the employee is automatically the beneficiary. The employee also elects and pays for this coverage if it is contributory. Coverage for dependents is almost always limited to employees who are themselves covered under the group contract. Thus if an employee's coverage is contributory, the employee must elect coverage for himself or herself in order to be eligible to elect dependent coverage.

For purposes of dependent life insurance coverage, dependents are usually defined as an employee's spouse who is not legally separated from the employee and an employee's unmarried dependent children (including stepchildren and adopted children) who are over 14 days of age but under some specified age, commonly 19 or 21. To prevent adverse selection an employee usually cannot select coverage on individual dependents. A few policies do allow an employee to elect coverage for the spouse only or for children only. If dependent coverage is selected, all dependents fitting the definition are insured. When dependent coverage is in effect for an employee, any new eligible dependents are automatically insured.

The amount of coverage for each dependent is usually quite modest. Some states limit the maximum amount of life insurance that can be written, and a few states actually prohibit writing any coverage on dependents. Employer contributions used to purchase more than $2,000 of coverage on each dependent will result in income to the employee for purposes of federal taxation. However, amounts in excess of $2,000 may be purchased with employee contributions without adverse tax consequences. In some cases the same amount of coverage will be provided for all dependents; in other cases a larger amount will be provided for the spouse than for the children. It is also not unusual for the amount of coverage on children to be less until the children attain some specified age, such as 6 months. Tables 6-10 and 6-11 are examples of benefit schedules under dependent coverage.

TABLE 6-10

Class	Amount of Insurance
Each dependent	$2,000

TABLE 6-11

Class	Amount of Insurance
Spouse	50% of the employee's insured amount, subject to a maximum of $5,000
Dependent children: at least 14 days old but less than 6 months 6 months or older	$ 500 $1,000

A single premium applies to the dependent coverage for each employee and is unrelated to the number of dependents. In some cases the premium may vary, depending on the age of the employee (but not the dependents), but more commonly it is the same amount for all employees regardless of age. Dependent coverage usually contains a conversion privilege that applies only to the coverage on the spouse. However, some states require that the conversion privilege apply to the coverage on all dependents. Assignment is almost never permitted, and no waiver of premium is available if a dependent becomes disabled. However, if the basic life insurance contract contains a waiver-of-premium provision applicable to the employee, the employee's disability will sometimes result in a waiver of premium for the dependent coverage. A provision similar to the actively-at-work provision pertaining to employees is often included for dependents. It specifies that dependents will not be covered when otherwise eligible if they are confined in a hospital (except for newborn children, who are covered after 14 days). Coverage will commence when the dependent is discharged from the hospital.

TAXATION

A discussion of group term insurance is incomplete without an explanation of the tax laws affecting its use. While discussions of these laws are often limited to federal income and estate taxation, federal gift taxation and taxation by the states should also be considered.

Federal Taxation

The growth of group term insurance has been greatly influenced by the favorable tax treatment afforded it under federal tax laws. This section is devoted to the effects of these tax laws on basic group term insurance and on coverages that may be added to a basic group term insurance contract. A complete explanation of the federal tax laws pertaining to group term insurance and their interpretation by the Internal Revenue Service would be lengthy and is beyond the scope of this book. Consequently this discussion and subsequent discussions of federal tax laws will only highlight these laws. The Appendix contains a summary of the relevant tax laws, as well as references to the Internal Revenue Code for those who wish to investigate the subject further.

Deductibility of Premiums

In general, employer contributions for an employee's group term insurance coverage are fully deductible to the employer as an ordinary and necessary business expense as long as the employee's overall compensation is reasonable. The reasonableness of compensation (which includes wages, salary, and other fringe benefits) is usually only a potential issue for the owners of small businesses or the stockholder-employees of closely held corporations. For income tax purposes a firm may not deduct any compensation that the Internal Revenue Service determines to be unreasonable. In addition, the Internal Revenue Code does not allow a firm to take an income tax deduction for contributions (1) that are made in behalf of sole proprietors or partners under any circumstances or (2) that are made in behalf of stockholders unless they are providing substantive services to the corporation. Finally, no deduction is allowed if the employer is named as beneficiary.

Contributions by any individual employee are considered payments for personal life insurance and are not deductible for income tax purposes by that employee. Thus the amount of any payroll deductions authorized by an employee for group term insurance purposes will be included in the employee's taxable income.

Employees' Income Tax Liability

In the absence of tax laws to the contrary, the amount of any compensation for which an employer receives an income tax deduction (including the payment of group insurance premiums) represents taxable income to the employee. However, Sec. 79 of the Internal Revenue Code gives favorable tax treatment to employer contributions for life insurance that qualifies as group term insurance.

Sec. 79 Requirements. In order to qualify as group term insurance under Sec. 79, life insurance must meet the following conditions:

- It must provide a death benefit excludible from federal income tax.
- It must be given to a group of employees, defined to include all employees of an employer. If all employees are not covered, membership must be determined on the basis of age, marital status, or factors relating to employment.
- It must be provided under a policy carried directly or indirectly by the employer. This includes (1) any policy for which the employer pays any part of the cost or (2) if the employer pays no part of the cost, any policy arranged by the employer if at least one employee is charged less than his or her cost (under Table I) and at least one other employee is charged more than his or her cost. If no employee is charged more than the Table I cost, a policy is not group term insurance for purposes of Sec. 79.

  A policy is defined to include a master contract or a group of individual policies. The term *carried indirectly* refers to those situations when the employer is not the policyowner but rather provides coverage to employees through master contracts issued to organizations such as negotiated trusteeships or multiple-employer welfare arrangements.
- The plan must be arranged to preclude individual selection of coverage amounts. However, it is acceptable to have alternative benefit schedules based on the amount an employee elects to contribute. Supplemental

plans that give an employee a choice, such as either 1, 1 1/2, or 2 times salary, are considered to fall within this category. An employee can be allowed to reject coverage in excess of $50,000 if he or she does not want any imputed income.

All life insurance that qualifies under Sec. 79 as group term insurance is considered to be a single plan of insurance, regardless of the number of insurance contracts used. For example, an employer might provide coverage for union employees under a negotiated trusteeship, coverage for other employees under an individual employer group insurance contract, and additional coverage for top executives under a group of individual life insurance policies. Under Sec. 79 these all constitute a single plan. This plan must be provided for at least 10 full-time employees at some time during the calendar year. For purposes of meeting the 10-life requirement, employees who have not satisfied any required waiting periods may be counted as participants. Employees who have elected not to participate are also counted as participants—but only if they would not have been required to contribute to the cost of other benefits besides group term insurance if they had participated. As is described later, a plan with fewer than 10 full-time employees may still qualify for favorable tax treatment under Sec. 79 if it meets more restrictive requirements.

Exceptions to Sec. 79. Even when all the previous requirements are met, there are some situations in which Sec. 79 does not apply. In some cases different sections of the Internal Revenue Code provide alternative tax treatment. For example, when group term insurance is issued to the trustees of a qualified pension plan and is used to provide a death benefit under the plan, the full amount of any life insurance paid for by employer contributions will result in taxable income to the employee.

There are three situations in which employer contributions for group term insurance will not result in taxable income to an employee, regardless of the amount of insurance: (1) if an employee has terminated employment because of disability, (2) if a qualified charity (as determined by the Internal Revenue Code) has been named as beneficiary for the entire year, or (3) if the employer has been named as beneficiary for the entire year.

Coverage on retired employees is subject to Sec. 79, and these persons are treated in the same manner as active employees. Thus they will have taxable income in any year in which the amount of coverage received exceeds $50,000. However, a grandfather clause to this rule stipulates that it does not apply to group term life insurance plans (or to comparable successor plans or plans of successor employers) in existence on January 1, 1984, for covered employees who (1) retired before 1984 or (2) were at least 55 years of age before 1984 and were employed by the employer any time during 1983. There is one exception to this grandfather clause; it does not apply to persons (either key or nonkey employees) retiring after 1986 if a plan is discriminatory. The factors that make a plan discriminatory are discussed later.

General Tax Rules. Under Sec. 79 the cost of the first $50,000 of coverage is not taxed to the employee. Since all group term insurance provided by an employer that qualifies under Sec. 79 is considered to be one plan, this exclusion applies only once to each employee. For example, an employee who has $10,000 of coverage that is provided to all employees under one policy and $75,000 of coverage provided to executives under a separate insurance policy would have a single $50,000 exclusion. The cost of coverage in excess of $50,000, less any employee contributions for the entire amount of coverage, represents taxable income to the employee. For purposes of Sec. 79 the cost of this excess coverage is determined by a government table called the Uniform Premium Table I (see table 6-12). This table will often result in a lower cost than would be calculated using the actual premium paid by the employer for the coverage.

TABLE 6-12	
Uniform Premium Table I	
Age	**Cost per Month per $1,000 of Coverage**
29 and under	$ .08
30–34	.09
35–39	.11
40–44	.17
45–49	.29
50–54	.48
55–59	.75
60–64	1.17
65–69	2.10
70 and over	3.76

To calculate the cost of an employee's coverage for one month of protection under a group term insurance plan, the Uniform Premium Table I cost shown for the employee's age bracket (based on the employee's attained age at the end of the tax year) is multiplied by the number of thousands in excess of 50 of group term insurance on the employee. For example, if an employee aged 57 (whose Table I monthly cost is $.75 per $1,000 of coverage) is provided with $150,000 of group term insurance, the employee's monthly cost (assuming no employee contributions) is calculated as follows:

Coverage provided	$150,000
Less Sec. 79 exclusion	50,000
Amount subject to taxation	$100,000

Monthly cost = $.75/$1,000 x $100,000 = $75

The monthly costs are then totaled to obtain an annual cost. Assuming no change in the amount of coverage during the year, the annual cost is $900. Any employee contributions for the entire amount of coverage are deducted from the annual cost to determine the taxable income that an employee must report. If an employee contributes $.30 per month ($3.60 per year) per $1,000 of coverage, the employee's total annual contribution for $150,000 of coverage is $540. This reduces the amount reportable as taxable income from $900 to $360.

One final point is worthy of attention. When the Uniform Premium Table I was incorporated into the IRS regulations for Sec. 79, it resulted in favorable tax treatment for the cost of group term insurance, because the monthly costs in the table were always lower than the actual cost of coverage in the marketplace. Today group term insurance coverage can often be purchased at a lower cost than Table I rates. There are some who argue that in these instances the actual cost of coverage can be used in place of the Table I cost for determining an employee's taxable income. From the standpoint of logic and consistency with the tax laws this view makes sense. However, the regulations for Sec. 79 are very specific: only Table I costs are to be used.

Nondiscrimination Rules. Any plan that qualifies as group term insurance under Sec. 79 is subject to nondiscrimination rules, and the $50,000 exclusion will not be available to key employees if a plan is discriminatory. Such a plan favors key employees in either eligibility or benefits. In addition, the value of the full amount of coverage for key employees, less their own contribution, will be considered taxable income, based on the greater of actual or Table I costs. (The actual cost of discriminatory coverage is determined by a complex process that is not covered in this book. See IRC Reg. 1.79-4T.)

A key employee of a firm is defined as any person who at any time during the current plan year or the preceding 4 plan years is any of the following:

- an officer of the firm who earns from the firm more than 50 percent of the Internal Revenue Code limit on the amount of benefits payable by a defined-benefit plan. This amount (50 percent of $125,000, or $62,500, for 1997) is indexed annually. For purposes of this rule the number of employees treated as officers is the greater of 3 employees or 10 percent of the firm's employees, subject to a maximum of 50. In applying the rule the following employees can be excluded: persons who are part-time, persons who are under 21, and persons with less than 6 months of service with the firm.
- one of the 10 employees owning the largest interests in the firm and having an annual compensation from the firm of more than $30,000
- a 5 percent owner of the firm. For a corporation, this is a person who owns (1) more than 5 percent of the firm's outstanding stock or (2) stock that has more than 5 percent of the combined voting power of all

the firm's stock. For a noncorporate entity, it is any person who owns more than 5 percent of the firm's capital or profits.

- a 1 percent owner of the firm who earns over $150,000 a year. The definition of a 1 percent owner is the same as that of a 5 percent owner with 1 percent substituted for 5 percent.

Note that the definition of key employee includes not only active employees but also retired employees who were key employees at the time of retirement or separation from service.

Eligibility requirements are not discriminatory if (1) at least 70 percent of all employees are eligible, (2) at least 85 percent of all employees who are participants are not key employees, (3) participants comprise a classification that the IRS determines is nondiscriminatory, or (4) the group term insurance plan is part of a cafeteria plan and Sec. 125 requirements are satisfied. For purposes of the 70 percent test employees with less than 3 years' service, part-time employees, and seasonal employees may be excluded. Employees covered by collective-bargaining agreements may also be excluded if plan benefits were the subject of good-faith bargaining.

Benefits are not discriminatory if neither the type nor amount of benefits discriminates in favor of key employees. It is permissible to base benefits on a uniform percentage of salary.

One issue that arose after the passage of the nondiscrimination rules in 1984 was whether they applied separately to active and to retired employees. A technical correction in the Tax Reform Act of 1986 clarified the issue by stating that the rules do apply separately to the extent provided in IRS regulations. However, such regulations have yet to be issued.

Groups with Fewer than 10 Full-time Employees. A group insurance plan that covers fewer than 10 employees must satisfy an additional set of requirements before it is eligible for favorable tax treatment under Sec. 79. These rules predate the general nondiscrimination rules previously described, and it was assumed that the under-10 rules would be abolished when the new rules were adopted. However, that was not done, so smaller groups are subject to two separate and somewhat overlapping sets of rules. Again, note that Sec. 79 applies to an employer's overall plan of group insurance, not to separate group insurance contracts. For example, an employer providing group insurance coverage for its 50 hourly employees under one group insurance contract and for its six executives under a separate contract is considered to have a single plan covering 56 employees and thus is exempt from the under-10 requirements. While the stated purpose of the under-10 requirements is to preclude individual selection, their effect is to prevent the group insurance plan from discriminating in favor of the owners or stockholder-employees of small businesses.

With some exceptions plans covering fewer than 10 employees must provide coverage for all full-time employees. For purposes of this requirement employees who are not customarily employed for more than 20 hours in any one week or 5 months in any calendar year are considered part-time employees. It is permissible to exclude full-time employees from coverage under the following circumstances:

- The employee has reached 65.
- The employee has not satisfied the waiting period under the plan, which may not exceed 6 months.
- The employee has elected not to participate in the plan, but only if the employee would not have been required to contribute to the cost of other benefits besides group term life insurance if he or she had participated.
- The employee has not satisfied the evidence of insurability required under the plan. An employee's eligibility for insurance (or the amount of insurance on the employee's life) may be subject to evidence of insurability. However, this evidence of insurability must be determined solely on the basis of a medical questionnaire completed by the employee and not by a medical examination.

The amount of coverage must be a flat amount, a uniform percentage of compensation, or an amount based on different employee classifications. These employee classifications, which are referred to as coverage brackets in Sec. 79, may be determined in the manner described earlier in this chapter in the section on benefit schedules. The amount of coverage for each employee in any classification may be no greater than 2 1/2 times the amount of coverage provided to each employee in the next lower classification. In addition, each employee in the lowest classification must be provided with an amount of coverage that is equal to at least 10 percent of the amount for each employee in the highest classification. There must also be a reasonable expectation that there will be at least one employee in each classification. The benefit schedule shown in table 6-13 would be unacceptable for two reasons. First, the amount of coverage provided for the hourly employees is only 5 percent of the amount of coverage provided for the president. Second, the amount of coverage on the supervisor is more than 2 1/2 times the amount of coverage provided for the hourly employees. The benefit schedule in table 6-14, however, would be acceptable.

TABLE 6-13	
Classification	**Amount of Coverage**
President	$100,000
Supervisor	40,000
Hourly employees	5,000

TABLE 6-14	
Classification	Amount of Coverage
President	$100,000
Supervisor	40,000
Hourly employees	20,000

If a group insurance plan that covers fewer than 10 employees does not qualify for favorable tax treatment under Sec. 79, any premiums paid by the employer for such coverage will represent taxable income to the employees. The employer, however, will still receive an income tax deduction for any premiums paid in behalf of the employees as long as overall compensation is reasonable.

Taxation of Proceeds

In most instances the death proceeds under a group term insurance contract do not result in any taxable income to the beneficiary if they are paid in a lump sum. If the proceeds are payable in installments over more than one taxable year, only the interest earnings attributable to the proceeds will be included in the beneficiary's income for tax purposes.

Under certain circumstances the proceeds are not exempt from income taxation if the coverage was transferred (either in whole or in part) for a valuable consideration. Such a situation will arise when the stockholder-employees of a corporation name each other as beneficiaries under their group term insurance coverage as a method of funding a buy-sell agreement. The mutual agreement to name each other as beneficiaries is the valuable consideration. Under these circumstances any proceeds paid to a beneficiary constitute ordinary income to the extent that the proceeds exceed the beneficiary's tax basis, as determined by the Internal Revenue Code.

In many cases benefits paid by an employer to employees or their beneficiaries from the firm's assets receive the same tax treatment as benefits provided under an insurance contract. This is not true for death benefits. If they are provided other than through an insurance contract, the amount of the proceeds will represent taxable income to the beneficiary. (Until late 1996, up to $5,000 of benefits could be provided from the firm's assets on a tax-free basis.) For this reason employers are less likely to use alternative funding arrangements for death benefits than for disability and medical expense benefits.

Proceeds of a group term insurance contract, even if paid to a named beneficiary, are included in an employee's gross estate for federal estate tax purposes as long as the employee possessed incidents of ownership in the coverage at the time of death. However, no estate tax is levied on any amounts, including life insurance proceeds, left to a surviving spouse. In addition, taxable estates of $600,000 or less are generally free of estate taxation regardless of the beneficiary.

When an estate would otherwise be subject to estate taxation, an employee may remove the proceeds of group term insurance from his or her taxable estate by absolutely assigning all incidents of ownership to another person, usually the beneficiary of the coverage. Incidents of ownership include the right to change the beneficiary, to terminate coverage, to assign coverage, or to exercise the conversion privilege. For this favorable treatment, however, the Internal Revenue Code requires that such an assignment be permissible under both the group term insurance master contract and the laws of the state having jurisdiction. The absolute assignment is usually in the form of a gift, which is not without its own tax implications. The amount of insurance is considered a gift made each year by the employee to the person to whom the absolute assignment was granted. Consequently if the value of the gift is of sufficient size, federal gift taxes will be payable. Since the Internal Revenue Code and the Internal Revenue Service regulations are silent on the specific gift tax consequences of assigned group term insurance, there is disagreement about whether the gift should be valued at Table I costs or at the actual premium for the coverage.

The assignment of group term life insurance also results in the inclusion of some values in the employee's estate. If the employee dies within 3 years of making the assignment, the full amount of the proceeds will be included in the employee's estate. If death occurs more than 3 years after the assignment is made, only the premiums paid within the 3 years prior to death will be included in the employee's taxable estate. In the past a problem arose if the employer changed group insurance carriers, thus requiring the employee to make a new assignment and again be subject to the 3-year time limit. However, the Internal Revenue Service now considers this type of situation to be a continuation of the original assignment as long as the amount and provisions of the new coverage are essentially the same as those of the old coverage.

As of 1997, the tax treatment of accelerated death benefits was added to the Internal Revenue Code. If certain requirements are satisfied, benefits paid to persons who are either terminally or chronically ill will receive favorable tax treatment. Benefits received because of a terminal illness are treated as income-tax-free death benefits as long as a physician has certified that the insured has an illness or physical condition that can reasonably be expected to result in death within 24 months or less after the date of certification. If a group contract provides accelerated death benefits to other categories of individuals, benefits can also be received with favorable tax treatment if a person is chronically ill and the coverage qualifies as a long-term care insurance contract. The definition of *chronically ill* and the conditions to qualify as a long-term care insurance contract are discussed when group long-term care insurance is covered in a later chapter.

Treatment of Added Coverages

Supplemental life insurance can be written as either a separate contract or as part of the contract providing basic group term life insurance coverage. If it is a separate contract and if the supplemental group life insurance meets the conditions of qualifying as group term insurance under Sec. 79, the amount of coverage provided is added to all other group term insurance for purposes of calculating the Uniform Premium Table I cost. Any premiums the employee pays for the supplemental coverage are included in the deduction used to determine the final taxable income. In all other ways supplemental life insurance is treated the same as group term insurance.

Many separate supplemental contracts are noncontributory, and the cost for each employee's coverage does not exceed the Table I cost. In this case the supplemental contract does not qualify as group term life insurance under Sec. 79. As a result the value of the coverage is not included in an employee's income.

When supplemental life insurance coverage is written in conjunction with a basic group life insurance plan, employers have the option of treating the supplemental coverage as a separate policy of insurance as long as the premiums are properly allocated among the two portions of the coverage. There is no advantage in treating the supplemental coverage as a separate policy if it would still qualify by itself as group term insurance under Sec. 79. However, this election will minimize taxable income to employees if the cost of the supplemental coverage is paid totally by the employees and all employees are charged rates at or below Table I rates.

Premiums paid for accidental death and dismemberment insurance are considered to be health insurance premiums rather than group term insurance premiums. However, these are also deductible to the employer as an ordinary and necessary business expense the same as for group term insurance. Benefits paid to an employee under the dismemberment portion of the coverage are treated as benefits received under a health insurance contract and are income tax free. Death benefits received under the coverage are treated like death benefits received under group term life insurance.

For federal tax purposes, survivor income benefit insurance is considered to be a group term insurance coverage. Under Sec. 79 the amount of the benefit is considered to be the commuted value of benefit payments that eligible survivors would have received if the employee had died during the year. This amount normally is provided annually by the insurance company. A commuted value is also used for estate tax purposes. In all other respects survivor income benefit insurance is treated the same as group term insurance.

Employer contributions for dependent life insurance coverage are fully deductible by the employer as an ordinary and necessary business expense if the employee's overall compensation is reasonable. Employer contributions do not result in taxable income to an employee as long as the value of the benefit is *de minimis.* This means that the value is so small that it is administratively impractical for the employer to account for the cost on a per-person basis. Dependent coverage of $2,000 or less on any person falls into this category. The Internal Revenue Service considers amounts of coverage in excess of $2,000 on any dependent to be more than *de minimis*. If more than $2,000 of coverage is provided for any dependent from employer contributions, the cost of the entire amount of coverage for that dependent (as determined by Uniform Premium Table I rates) will be considered taxable income to the employee.

Death benefits will be free of income taxation and will not be included in the dependent's taxable estate for estate tax purposes.

State Taxation

In most instances state tax laws affecting group term insurance are similar to the federal laws. However, two major differences do exist. In most states the payment of group term insurance premiums by the employer will not result in any taxable income to the employee, even if the amount of coverage exceeds $50,000. In addition, death proceeds receive favorable tax treatment under the estate and inheritance tax laws of most states. Generally the proceeds are at least partially, if not totally, exempt from such taxation.

7

Group Life Insurance: Postretirement Coverage

Chapter Outline

Group term insurance plans were traditionally designed to provide employees with preretirement life insurance coverage. At retirement an employee was faced with the decision of whether to let coverage terminate or to convert to an individual policy at an extremely high premium rate. In recent years, however, an increasing number of group life insurance plans have been designed to provide postretirement as well as preretirement life insurance coverage. In some cases this has been accomplished by continuing group term insurance coverage, often at a reduced amount, after retirement. In other cases it has been done through life insurance that provides permanent benefits funded during employees' working years.

The popularity of various approaches for providing postretirement life insurance coverage has changed over time, primarily because of changes in tax laws. Older and once popular products such as group paid-up insurance and group ordinary insurance are no longer written. Newer products like group universal life insurance have come on the scene and grown in popularity. This chapter discusses five approaches that are currently used:

- current funding to continue group term insurance
- retired lives reserve to continue group term insurance
- group universal life insurance
- group variable universal life insurance
- group term carve-outs

CURRENT FUNDING TO CONTINUE GROUP TERM

Most postretirement life insurance coverage consists of the continuation of group term insurance. This requires the employer to make two important decisions: the amount of coverage to be continued and the method of paying for the continued coverage. Although the full amount of coverage prior to retirement may be continued, the high cost of group term insurance coverage for older employees frequently results in a reduction in the amount of coverage. In some cases employees are given a flat amount of coverage (such as $2,000 or $5,000); in other cases employees are given a percentage (such as 50 percent) of the amount of coverage they had on the date of retirement.

The cost of providing postretirement life insurance is usually paid from current revenue, with each periodic premium the insurance company receives based on the lives of all employees covered, both active and retired. Since retired employees have no salary or wages from which payroll deductions can be made, most postretirement life insurance coverage is noncontributory.

The tax implications of providing postretirement group term insurance on a current-revenue basis are the same for both the employer and the employee as those discussed in the previous chapter.

RETIRED LIVES RESERVE TO CONTINUE GROUP TERM

In the late 1970s and early 1980s increasing interest was shown in prefunding the cost of postretirement group term insurance coverage through retired-lives-reserve arrangements. Much of this interest stemmed from Internal Revenue Service Sec. 79 regulations that made previously popular products less attractive. The concept was not new; retired lives reserves, while not extensively used prior to that time, had been in existence for many years, primarily for very large employers. However, the trend in the 1970s was to establish them for smaller employers since the tax laws allowed the plans to be designed so that they often provided significant benefits to the firm's owners or key employees. Because the Tax Reform Act of 1984 imposed more stringent requirements on retired lives reserves and because of the availability of newer products for postretirement coverage, there is little interest in establishing new plans. Nevertheless, plans still exist, primarily in heavily unionized industries and usually for employers with 2,000 to 5,000 employees.

A retired lives reserve is best defined as a fund established during employees' working years to pay all or a part of the cost of their group term insurance after retirement. The fund may be established and maintained through a trust or with an insurance company. If properly designed, a retired lives reserve (1) will enable an employer to make currently tax-deductible contributions to the fund during employees' working years and (2) will not result in any taxable income to employees before retirement.

At retirement, the assets of the fund can be used to pay the cost of maintaining the postretirement coverage. If assets are withdrawn from a trust, there is the possibility of the fund's being inadequate in the long run because of higher premiums and/or shorter life expectancies than anticipated. However, insurance company products typically assume the adverse mortality risk and guarantee that the fund will be adequate to maintain the promised benefits as long as the prescribed contributions have been deposited with the insurer.

Tax Deductibility of Employer Contributions

An employer's contributions to a retired lives reserve are currently deductible for federal income tax purposes as long as certain conditions are met:

- The contributions must be an ordinary and necessary business expense.
- The balance in the reserve must be held solely for the purpose of providing life insurance coverage for currently retired employees or for active employees when they retire.
- The amount added annually to the reserve must be no greater than an amount that would be required to fairly allocate (on an actuarially level basis) the unfunded cost of the postretirement life insurance coverage over the remaining working lives of the employees involved. (There is no requirement that the entire permissible annual contribution be made. Any missed contributions may be made at a later date on an actuarially level basis only and not in a lump sum.)
- The employer must not have a right to recapture any portion of the assets in the reserve as long as any employees (either active or retired) covered under the plan are still alive. The effect of this condition is extremely significant and is often the reason that a retired lives reserve

is not established. Even if a retired lives reserve plan is discontinued, assets must be used to provide the promised postretirement benefits to active and retired employees previously covered under the plan, as long as such employees are living and the reserve has any assets. (Of course, this condition may be popular with unions because it makes future benefits highly secure.)

Current deductions may be taken only for prefunding coverage that will be received tax free by retired employees under Sec. 79. This amount is generally $50,000 but may be higher for certain employees, subject to a grandfather clause. In addition, contributions on behalf of key employees cannot be deducted if the plan is discriminatory under Sec. 79.

Taxation to Employees

As long as an employee has no rights in a retired lives reserve except to receive postretirement group term insurance coverage until his or her death, the Internal Revenue Service has ruled that the employee will incur no income taxation as a result of either employer contributions to the reserve or investment earnings on the reserve. In addition, up to $50,000 can be received income tax free by beneficiaries.

In those instances where death benefits are paid directly from trust assets, the tax consequences to the employee are the same as if death benefits were provided through group term insurance contracts, except that death proceeds will represent taxable income to the beneficiary.

GROUP UNIVERSAL LIFE INSURANCE

Beginning in the mid-1980s many of the large writers of group insurance started to sell group universal life insurance, a trend that has been greeted with much interest by insurers, employers, and even employees. This interest seems to stem primarily from five factors:

- the phenomenal success of universal life in the individual marketplace. Introduced in the 1970s, universal life insurance now accounts for about 25 percent of newly written individual life insurance premiums.
- tax legislation that resulted in employer-provided term life insurance in excess of $50,000 becoming taxable after retirement
- the clarification of the tax treatment of universal life insurance. For the first few years after the introduction of universal life insurance, there was concern that the IRS would not grant it the same favorable tax treatment that was granted to traditional cash value life insurance policies. There was speculation that the interest paid on the cash value might become subject to taxation and also that the death benefit would

be considered taxable income to the beneficiary. For the most part these fears have been laid to rest by tax legislation as long as a universal life insurance policy meets certain prescribed guidelines. Therefore the cash value of a universal life insurance policy accumulates tax free, and death benefits are free of income taxation.

- the interest of employers to contain employee benefit costs. Little needs to be said about the attempts of employers to minimize the costs of their employee benefit plans. Group universal life insurance plans can make life insurance available to employees with little cost to the employer.
- less favorable tax treatment for two formerly popular products for prefunding postretirement life insurance—group ordinary life insurance (also called Sec. 79 plans) and retired lives reserves

Group universal life insurance products are being marketed primarily as supplemental life insurance plans—either to replace existing supplemental group term life insurance plans or as additional supplemental plans. Some insurers are selling them as a way of providing the basic life insurance plan of the employee as well. Marketing efforts tout group universal life insurance as having the following advantages to the employer:

- no direct cost other than those associated with payroll deductions and possibly enrollment, since the entire premium cost is borne by the employee. In this sense group universal life insurance plans are much like payroll deduction plans described later in this book.
- no ERISA filing and reporting requirement as long as the master contract is issued to a trust and as long as there are no employer contributions for the cost of coverage. The current products are marketed through multiple-employer trusts, with the trust being the policyowner.
- the ability of employees to continue coverage into retirement, alleviating pressure for the employer to provide postretirement life insurance benefits

The following advantages are being claimed for employees:

- the availability of a popular life insurance product at group rates
- the opportunity to continue insurance coverage after retirement, possibly without any postretirement contributions
- flexibility in designing coverage to best meet the needs of the individual employee

The current plans being marketed are still evolving, and differences do exist among the plans being offered by competing insurance companies. Because of the flexibility given policyholders, the administrative aspects of a group universal plan are formidable, and most insurers originally designed their plans only for employers with a large number of employees, usually at least 1,000. However, some insurers that write the product now make it available for as few as 50 lives or less.

Skeptics, including employees of some insurance companies offering group universal life, wonder if the administrative aspects can be accomplished in such a manner that it can be offered at a cost significantly lower than coverage in the individual marketplace. In raising this question, skeptics point out the administrative problems and costs that have arisen when universal life insurance has been included in payroll deduction individual insurance plans, as well as the highly competitive market for individual universal life insurance that has resulted in rates with extremely low margins for contributions to surplus. These drawbacks, coupled with the lack of employer contributions, make the potential for savings to employees through the group insurance approach less than for many other types of insurance. Other critics point out that the popularity of universal life insurance in general has decreased as interest rates have dropped over the last few years, and they wonder how successful universal life will be if interest rates drop further. However, plans that are installed are usually well received by employees, and participation generally meets or exceeds expectations.

In 1995, universal life accounted for about 2 percent of group life insurance certificates in force.

General Nature

Group universal life insurance is a flexible-premium policy that, unlike traditional cash value life insurance, divides the pure insurance protection and the cash value accumulation into separate and distinct components. The employee is required to pay a specified initial premium, from which a charge is subtracted for one month's mortality. This mortality charge in effect is used to purchase the required amount of pure or term insurance (often referred to as the *amount at risk)* at a cost based on the insured's current age. Under some policies an additional deduction is made for expenses. The balance of the initial premium becomes the initial cash value of the policy, which, when credited with interest, becomes the cash value at the end of the period. The process continues in succeeding periods. New premiums are added to the cash value, charges are made for expenses and mortality, and interest is credited to the remaining cash value. Employees receive periodic disclosure statements showing all charges made for the period, as well as any interest earnings.

Group universal life insurance offers an employee considerable flexibility to meet several life-cycle financial needs with a single type of insurance coverage. The death benefit can be increased because of marriage, the birth of a child, or an increase in income. The death benefit can be reduced later when the need for life insurance decreases. Cash withdrawals can be made for the down payment on a home or to pay college tuition. Premium payments can be reduced during those periods when a young family has pressing financial needs. As financial circumstances improve, premiums can be increased so that an adequate retirement fund can be accumulated. The usual settlement options found in traditional cash value life insurance are available, so an employee can periodically elect to liquidate the cash accumulation as a source of retirement income.

Types of Group Universal Products

Two approaches have been used in designing group universal life insurance products. Under the first approach there is a single group insurance plan. An employee who wants only term insurance can pay a premium equal to the mortality and expense charges so that there is no accumulation of cash values. Naturally an employee who wants to accumulate cash values must pay a larger premium.

Under the second approach there are actually two group insurance plans—a term insurance plan and a universal life insurance plan. An employee who wants only term insurance contributes to the term insurance plan, and an employee who wants only universal life insurance contributes to the universal life insurance plan. With this approach an employee purchasing universal life insurance must make premium payments that are sufficient to generate a cash value accumulation. Initially the employee may be required to make minimum premium payments, such as two or three times the cost of the pure insurance. If an employee who has only the term insurance coverage later wants to switch to universal life insurance coverage, the group term insurance certificate is cancelled, and the employee is issued a new certificate under the universal life insurance plan. An employee can also withdraw his or her cash accumulation under the universal life insurance plan and switch to the term insurance plan or can even have coverage under both plans. Typically an employee is eligible to purchase a maximum aggregate amount of coverage under the two plans. For example, if this amount is three times annual salary, the employee can purchase term insurance equal to two times salary and universal life insurance that has a pure insurance amount equal to one times salary.

Underwriting

Insurance companies that write group universal life insurance have underwriting standards concerning group size, the amounts of coverage available, and insurability.

Currently most group universal life insurance products are being limited primarily to employers who have at least 100 or 200 employees. However, a few insurers write coverage for even smaller groups. Some insurance companies also have an employee percentage-participation requirement, such as 20 or 25 percent, that must be satisfied before a group can be installed. Other insurance companies feel their marketing approach is designed so that adequate participation will result and therefore have no participation requirements.

Employees can generally elect amounts of pure insurance equal to varying multiples of their salaries, which typically start at one-half or one and range as high as three or five. There may be a minimum amount of coverage that must be purchased, such as $10,000. The maximum multiple an insurance company will offer is influenced by factors such as the size of the group, the amount of insurance provided under the employer's basic employer-pay-all group term insurance plan, and the percentage participation in the plan. In general the rules regarding the amounts of coverage are the same as those that have been traditionally applied to supplemental group term life insurance plans. The initial premium, which is a function of an employee's age and death benefit, is frequently designed to accumulate a cash value at age 65 equal to approximately 20 percent of the total death benefit.

Other approaches for determining the death benefit may be used, depending on insurance company practices and employer desires. Under some plans employees may elect specific amounts of insurance, such as $25,000, $50,000, or $100,000. Again an employee's age and the death benefit selected determine the premium. Some plans allow an employee to select the premium he or she wants to pay. The amount of the premium and the employee's age then automatically determine the amount of the death benefit.

The extent to which evidence of insurability is required of individual employees is also similar to that found under most supplemental group term life insurance plans. When an employee is initially eligible, coverage is usually issued on a guaranteed basis up to specified limits, which again are influenced by the size of the group, the amount of coverage provided under the employer's basic group term insurance plan, and the degree of participation in the plan. If an employee chooses a larger death benefit, simplified underwriting is used up to a second amount, after which regular underwriting is used. Guaranteed issue is often unavailable for small groups, in which case underwriting on the basis of a simplified questionnaire is used up to a specific amount of death benefit, after which regular underwriting is used.

With some exceptions future increases in the amount of pure insurance are subject to evidence of insurability. These exceptions include additional amounts resulting from salary increases as long as the total amount of coverage remains within the guaranteed issue limit. A few insurance companies also allow additional purchases without evidence of insurability when certain events occur, such as marriage or the birth of a child.

The Death Benefit

The policyowner under an individual group universal life insurance policy typically has a choice of two death benefit options. Option A provides a level death benefit in the early policy years. As the cash value increases, the amount of pure insurance decreases so that the total amount paid to a beneficiary upon the insured's death remains constant. Without any provision to the contrary, the cash value would eventually approach the amount of the total death benefit. To prevent this from occurring, and also to keep the policy from failing to qualify as a life insurance policy under existing tax regulations, the amount of pure insurance does not decrease further once the cash value reaches a predetermined level. Thereafter the total death benefit will increase unless the cash value decreases. Figure 7-1 graphically demonstrates option A. Note that this and the following figure are for illustrative purposes only. The actual death benefit for a particular individual will vary by such factors as the amount of interest credited, premiums paid, loans, and withdrawals.

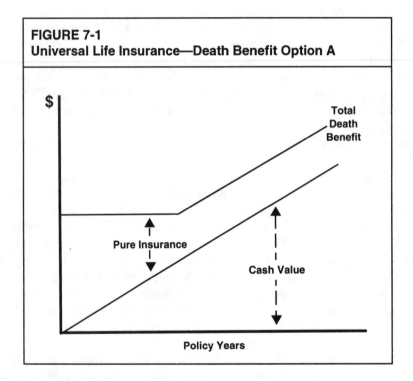

FIGURE 7-1
Universal Life Insurance—Death Benefit Option A

Under option B the amount of pure insurance is constant, and the death benefit increases each period by the change in the policy cash value. This is shown graphically in figure 7-2.

With group universal life insurance products, an employee usually has only one death benefit option available, and whether it is option A or option B depends on which one the employer has selected. In general there seems to be a feeling that the availability of both options makes a plan more difficult to explain to employees and more costly to administer. Most employers have selected option B, which is usually more easily marketed to employees since the increasing total death benefit is a visible sign of any increase in their cash value or "investment." As a result several insurers now make only option B available with their group products.

Universal life insurance products give the insured the right to increase or decrease the death benefit from the level originally selected as circumstances change. For example, the policyowner might have initially selected a pure death benefit of $100,000 under option B. Because of the birth of a child, this amount might be increased to $150,000. Increases, but not decreases, typically require that the insured provide evidence of insurability.

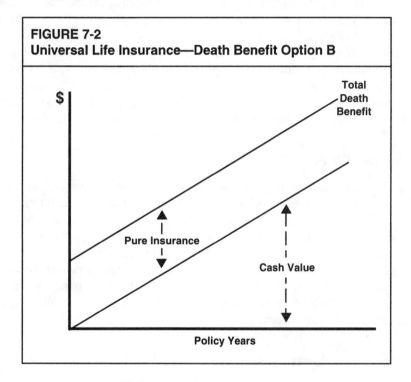

FIGURE 7-2
Universal Life Insurance—Death Benefit Option B

Mortality Charges

Most products have a guaranteed mortality charge for 3 years, after which the mortality charge will be based on the experience of each particular group. As with experience rating in general, the credibility given to a group's actual experience will be greater for larger groups. Most insurance companies guarantee that any future increases in the mortality charge will not exceed a stated maximum.

The products designed for small groups typically use pooled rates that apply to all groups insured through a particular trust. Therefore the mortality charge for any employer will vary, not with the employer's overall experience but rather with the overall experience of the trust.

Expense Charges

Probably the greatest variations among group life insurance products occur in the expense charges that are levied. Typically a percentage of each premium, such as 2 percent, is deducted for expenses. In addition, there is a flat monthly charge, normally ranging from $1 to $3, to maintain the accumulation account. Some insurance companies levy this charge against all certificate holders, even those who are contributing only enough to have the pure insurance coverage. Other insurance companies levy the charge only against those accounts that have a positive cash value accumulation. A few insurance companies also load their mortality charges for expenses. Finally many companies levy a transaction charge, such as $25, that often applies to withdrawals in early policy years. A transaction charge may also apply to policy loans and additional lump-sum contributions. In evaluating the expense charges of different insurers, one should remember that an insurer with a lower-than-average charge may be subtly compensating for this charge by having a higher mortality charge or crediting a lower interest rate to cash value accumulations than would otherwise be paid.

Interest Rates

Most insurance companies guarantee that the initial interest rate credited to cash value accumulations will be in effect for one year. After that time the rate is typically adjusted quarterly or semiannually but cannot be below some contractual minimum such as 4 or 4.5 percent. The interest rate credited is usually determined on a discretionary basis but is influenced by the insurance company's investment income and competitive factors. However, some insurers stipulate that it will be linked to some money market instrument, such as 3-month Treasury bills. In general the same interest is credited to all groups that an insurance company has underwritten.

Premium Adjustments

Employees are allowed considerable flexibility in the amount and timing of premium payments. Premiums can be raised or lowered and even suspended. In the latter case the contract will terminate if an employee's cash value accumulation is inadequate to pay current mortality and expense charges. Of course, premium payments could be reinstated to prevent this from happening. Additional lump-sum contributions may also be made to the accumulation account.

Two restrictions are placed on premium adjustments. First, the premium payment cannot be such that the size of the cash value accumulation becomes so large in relationship to the pure protection that an employee's coverage fails to qualify as a policy of insurance under IRS regulations. Second, since changes in premium payments through payroll deductions are costly to administer, many employers limit the frequency with which adjustments are allowed.

Loans and Withdrawals

Employees are allowed to make loans and withdrawals from their accumulated cash values, but for administrative reasons the frequency of loans and withdrawals may be limited. There are also minimum loan and withdrawal amounts, such as $250 or $500. In addition, an employee is usually required to leave a minimum balance in the cash value account sufficient to pay mortality and expense charges for some time period, possibly as long as one year. If an option A death benefit is in effect, the amount of the pure insurance is increased by the amount of the loan or withdrawal so that the total death benefit remains the same. With an option B death benefit the amount of the total death benefit is decreased.

The interest rate charged on policy loans is usually pegged to some index, such as Moody's composite bond yield. In addition, the interest rate credited to an amount of the cash value equal to the policy loan is reduced. This reduced interest rate may be the guaranteed policy minimum or may also be based on some index, such as 2 percent less than Moody's composite bond yield.

An employee can withdraw his or her entire cash value accumulation and terminate coverage. Total withdrawals are subject to a surrender charge during early policy years. The charge decreases with policy duration and is usually in addition to any transaction charge that might also be levied.

Dependent Coverage

Most products allow an employee to purchase a rider that provides term insurance coverage on his or her spouse and children. For example, one insurance company allows an employee to elect spousal coverage of $10,000 to $50,000 in $10,000 increments and coverage on children in the amount of either $5,000 or $10,000. Other insurers make varying amounts available.

Some insurance companies allow separate universal life insurance coverage to be elected, but usually only for the spouse. In such cases the coverage is provided under a separate group insurance certificate rather than a rider.

Accidental Death and Waiver of Premium

A group universal life insurance plan may provide accidental death benefits and a disability waiver of premium. These benefits are not optional for each employee; rather they are part of the coverage only if the employer has elected to include them in the plan. When a waiver of premium is included, all that is waived in case of disability is the portion of the premium necessary to pay the cost of the pure insurance protection for the employee and any dependents.

Employee Options at Retirement and Termination

Several situations may arise in which an employee is no longer actively working, or a group universal plan might be terminated by the employer.

Several options are available to the retiring employee. First, the employee can continue the group insurance coverage like an active employee. However, if premium payments are continued, the employee will be billed by the insurance company, probably on a quarterly basis. Because of the direct billing, the employee may also be subject to a higher monthly expense charge. Second, the employee can terminate the coverage and completely withdraw his or her accumulated cash value. Third, the employee can elect one of the policy settlement options for the liquidation of the cash value in the form of annuity income. Finally, some insurers allow the retiring employee to decrease the amount of pure insurance so that the cash value will be adequate to keep the policy in force without any more premium payments. In effect the employee then has a paid-up policy.

The same options are generally available to an employee who terminates employment prior to retirement. In contrast to most other types of group insurance arrangements, the continuation of coverage does not involve a conversion and the accompanying conversion charge; rather the employee usually remains in the same group. This ability to continue group coverage after termination of employment is commonly referred to as *portability*. If former employees who continue coverage have higher mortality rates, this will be reflected in the mortality charge for the entire group. However, at least one insurer places terminated employees into a separate group consisting of terminated employees from all plans. These persons will be subject to a mortality charge based solely on the experience of this group. Thus any higher mortality due to adverse selection will not be shared by the actively working employees.

If the employer terminates the group insurance arrangement, some insurance companies keep the group in force on a direct-bill basis, even if the coverage has been replaced with another insurer. Other insurance companies continue the group coverage only if the employer has not replaced the plan. If replacement occurs, the insurance company terminates the pure insurance amount and either gives the cash value to participants or transfers it to the trustee of the new plan.

Enrollment and Administration

Variations exist in the method by which employees are enrolled in group universal life insurance plans. Some early plans used agents who were compensated in the form of commissions or fees, but several insurance companies have dropped this practice. The actual enrollment is typically done by the employer with materials the insurance company provides. However, salaried or commissioned representatives of the insurer usually meet with the employees in group meetings to explain the plan.

The employer's main administrative function is to process the payroll deductions associated with a plan. As previously mentioned, employee flexibility may be somewhat limited to minimize the costs of numerous changes in payroll deductions.

The insurance company or a third-party administrator performs other administrative functions, including providing employees with annual statements about their transactions and cash value accumulation under the plan. Toll-free telephone lines are often maintained to provide information and advice to employees.

Taxation

Group universal life insurance products are not designed to be policies of insurance under Sec. 79. In addition, each employee pays the full cost of his or her coverage. Therefore the tax treatment is the same to employees as if they had purchased a universal life insurance policy in the individual insurance marketplace.

GROUP VARIABLE UNIVERSAL LIFE INSURANCE

In the mid-1990s, most major insurers that wrote group universal life insurance introduced a variable product, which has the same basic characteristics that were previously described for group universal life with one major difference—employees have a series of investment accounts to which they may allocate their net premiums. Once an employee elects the initial allocation, all future net premiums are allocated in the same proportion unless the employee makes a written request for a change. With the one exception described below, there are no minimum guarantees, and the full investment risk rests solely with the employee.

Most group variable universal life insurance plans offer between eight and fifteen differing types of investment funds. These typically include at least one and possibly more of the following: growth funds, bond funds, money market funds, index funds, international stock funds, mortgage securities funds, and small company stock funds. Employers can choose the investment options that will be made available to employees. For ease of administration and communication, this number is often in the range of four to six.

Many group variable universal life insurance products also have an account that has a minimum interest-rate guarantee. An employee who is selecting a 100 percent allocation to this account in effect has the equivalent of coverage under a group universal life insurance contract rather than a variable contract. This feature leads some observers to predict that if the variable product should gain widespread acceptance, there will be little need for insurers to maintain both a group universal life product and a group variable universal life product.

GROUP TERM CARVE-OUTS

Prior to 1984 employees had no taxable income if they were provided with postretirement coverage under a group term life insurance plan. At that time coverage in excess of $50,000 became subject to the imputed income rules of Sec. 79, based on Table I costs. In 1989 Table I was revised, and these costs were raised significantly for persons aged 65 and older. As a result employers have increasingly turned to group term carve-outs. While carve-outs can be used for any employee with more than $50,000 of group term coverage, they typically apply only to shareholders and key executives.

Bonus Plans

In the simplest sense a carve-out works like this: The employer decides which employees will be covered under the carve-out plan and limits coverage for these employees under its group term plan to the $50,000 that can be received tax free. The employer then gives any premium savings to each "carved-out" employee in the form of a bonus, which is fully deductible to the employer as long as the employee's overall compensation is reasonable. The bonus amounts will be either paid directly to an insurance company for individual coverage on the lives of the participants in the carve-out plan or in some cases provided to the employees as compensation to pay life insurance premiums. In most cases the coverage purchased under the carve-out plan will be some form of permanent life insurance protection that will provide paid-up coverage at retirement. Traditional whole life insurance, universal life insurance, and variable life insurance are all viable alternatives. At retirement the employee can either keep the coverage in force (possibly at a reduced paid-up amount) or surrender the policy for its cash value.

The popularity of carve-out plans lies in the fact that a comparable or greater amount of life insurance coverage can often be provided to participants at a lower cost than if the participants had received all their coverage under the group term life insurance plan. Since the carve-out plan does not qualify as a plan of insurance under Sec. 79, each participant will have taxable income in the amount of the bonus. However, this income will be offset by the absence of any imputed income from Table I.

In reality carve-out plans are more complex. In many cases the cost of permanent coverage for an employee may actually be greater than the cost of group term coverage during the working years. However, this high cost is often more than compensated for by the cash value at retirement and the absence of imputed income after retirement. Under some carve-out plans, participants must pay this increased premium cost with aftertax dollars. Under other plans the employer increases the bonus amount. In effect the employer is now paying more than if the carve-out plan did not exist, but this arrangement is often acceptable to the employer as a way of providing shareholders and key executives with a benefit that is not available to other employees. In many plans the bonus is also increased to compensate the employee for any additional income taxes that must be paid because of the carve-out plan. Such an arrangement is commonly referred to as a zero-tax approach.

A carve-out plan can pose a potential problem if there are rated or uninsurable employees, but the problem is ameliorated if the plan has enough participants that the insurance company will use simplified underwriting or grant concessions on impaired risks. Any employee who is still uninsurable can be continued in the group term plan.

Other Types of Carve-Out Plans

While a bonus arrangement is the most common type of carve-out plan, other alternatives are available. Some carve-out plans are designed as death-benefit-only plans, under which the employer agrees only to pay a death benefit to the employee's beneficiary out of corporate assets. The employer often funds the plan with corporate-owned life insurance on the employee's life. With this approach the employee has no taxable income, but death benefits will result in taxable income to the beneficiary. In addition, the employer is unable to deduct the premiums as a business expense but does receive the death proceeds tax free.

Some firms also use split-dollar life insurance in carve-out plans. The most common approach is to use a collateral assignment arrangement under which the employer pays most of the premium, and the employee collaterally assigns a portion of the cash value and death benefit to the employer equal to the employer's premium payments. At retirement (or any other predetermined time) the employee withdraws the cash value necessary to repay the employer, who then removes the collateral assignment. At that time the employee has full control of the policy, and the remaining cash value can be used to keep coverage in force. Many split-dollar arrangements are also used to provide nonqualified retirement benefits to key employees as a supplement to the benefits under the employer's qualified retirement plan.

Determining the Best Plan

In many instances carve-out plans are the most cost-effective approach for providing benefits to key employees. The best plan depends on the overall benefit objectives of the employer. A proper analysis of alternatives involves a complex consideration of many factors, including the employer's tax bracket, the effect on the employer's financial statements, the employee's tax bracket, premium costs, and the time value of money.

8

Group Disability Income Insurance

Chapter Outline

The purpose of disability income insurance is to partially (and sometimes totally) replace the income of employees who are unable to work because of sickness or accident. While an employee may miss a few days of work from time to time, there is often a tendency to underestimate both the frequency and severity of disabilities that last for longer periods. At all working ages the probability of being disabled for at least 90 consecutive days is much greater than the chance of dying. One out of every three employees will have a disability that lasts at least 90 days during his or her working years, and one out of every ten employees can expect to be permanently disabled prior to age 65.

In terms of its financial impact on the family, long-term disability is more severe than death. In both cases income ceases. In the case of long-term disability, however, family expenses—instead of decreasing because of one less family member—may actually increase because of the cost of providing care for the disabled person.

Employers are less likely to provide employees with disability income benefits than with either life insurance or medical expense benefits. It is difficult to estimate the exact extent of disability coverage because often benefits are not insured and workers are sometimes covered under overlapping plans. However, a reasonable estimate would be that at least three-quarters of all employees have some form of short-term employer-provided protection, and only about one-third have protection for long-term disabilities. This does not mean that almost all employees have some sort of disability income coverage, because many employees have both short-term and long-term protection and thus are included in both estimates. These estimates are also somewhat misleading because most employees have long-term disability income coverage under social security as well as coverage for certain types of disabilities under other government programs.

Group disability income protection consists of two distinct products:

- short-term disability income plans, which provide benefits for a limited period of time, usually 6 months or less. Benefits may be provided under uninsured salary continuation plans or under insured plans, often referred to as accident and sickness insurance or weekly indemnity benefits.
- long-term disability income insurance, which provides extended benefits (possibly for life) after an employee has been disabled for a period of time, frequently 6 months

Two important tasks in designing and underwriting insured group disability income plans are to coordinate them with each other (if both a short-term and a long-term plan are provided for employees) and to coordinate them with other benefits to which employees might be entitled under social insurance programs or uninsured salary continuation plans. A lack of coordination can lead to such a generous level of benefits for employees that absences from work because of disability might be either falsified or unnecessarily prolonged.

SALARY CONTINUATION PLANS

Employers use two approaches to provide short-term disability benefits to employees: salary continuation plans and short-term disability income insurance plans. Salary continuation plans (often called sick-leave plans) are uninsured and generally fully replace lost income for a limited period of time, starting on the first day of disability. In contrast, short-term disability income insurance plans (which are covered in the next section of this chapter) usually provide benefits that replace only a portion of an employee's lost income and often contain a waiting period before benefits start, particularly for sickness. While it is impossible to obtain precise statistics, surveys indicate that about half the employees with short-term coverage obtain benefits under salary continuation plans, about one-quarter under insured plans, and about one-quarter under plans that combine the two approaches.

Traditionally many salary continuation plans were informal, with the availability, amount, and duration of benefits for an employee being discretionary on the part of the employer. Although some plans used by small firms or for a limited number of executives still operate this way, informal plans are generally inappropriate. There is a possibility that the IRS will consider benefit payments to be either a gift or a dividend and therefore not tax deductible by the employer. In addition, an informal plan increases the likelihood of suits brought by persons who do not receive benefits. As a result, the vast majority of salary continuation plans are now formalized and have specific written rules concerning eligibility and benefits.

Eligibility

Almost all salary continuation plans are limited to permanent full-time employees, but benefits may also be provided for permanent part-time employees. Most plans also require an employee to satisfy a short probationary period (commonly 1 to 3 months) before being eligible for benefits. Salary continuation plans may also be limited to certain classes of employees, such as top management or nonunion employees. The latter is common when the union employees are covered under a collectively bargained, but insured, plan.

Benefits

Most salary continuation plans are designed to provide benefits equal to 100 percent of an employee's regular pay. Some plans, however, provide a reduced level of benefits after an initial period of full pay.

Several approaches are used in determining the duration of benefits. The most traditional approach credits eligible employees with a certain amount of sick leave each year, such as 10 days. The majority of plans using this approach allow employees to accumulate unused sick leave up to some maximum amount, which rarely exceeds 6 months (sometimes specified as 130 days or 26 weeks). A variation of this approach is to credit employees with an amount of sick leave, such as one day, for each month of service. Table 8-1 is an example of a benefit schedule that uses this variation.

TABLE 8-1	
Length of Service	**Amount of Sick Leave***
Less than 3 months	None
3 or more months	1 day at full pay for each month of service (retroactive to date of employment)
*Maximum unused sick leave: 130 days	

Another approach, illustrated in table 8-2, bases the duration of benefits on an employee's length of service.

An alternative to this approach provides benefits for a uniform length of time to all employees, except possibly those with short periods of service. However, benefits are reduced to a level less than full pay after some period of time that is related to an employee's length of service. Table 8-3 is an illustration of this increasingly common approach.

TABLE 8-2

Length of Service	Maximum Days of Sick Leave per Year
Less than 3 months	0
3 months to 1 year	5
2 years	10
3 years	15
5 years	20
7 years	25
10 years ·	30

TABLE 8-3

	Weeks of Sick Leave per Disability		
Length of Service	100% of Pay	50% of Pay	Total Weeks
Less than 6 months	0	0	0
6 months to 1 year	2	0	2
1 year	4	22	26
2 years	8	18	26
3 years	12	14	26
4 years	16	10	26
5 years	20	6	26
6 years or more	26	0	26

In some instances an employee is not eligible for salary continuation benefits if he or she is eligible for benefits under social insurance plans, such as workers' compensation. However, most salary continuation plans are coordinated with social insurance programs. For example, if an employee is entitled to 100 percent of pay and receives 60 percent of pay as a workers' compensation benefit, the salary continuation plan will pay the remaining 40 percent.

A problem for the employer is how to verify an employee's disability. In general, the employee's word is accepted for disabilities that last a week or less. Most salary continuation plans have a provision that benefits for longer periods will be paid only if the employee is under the care of a physician, who certifies that the employee is unable to work.

INSURED DISABILITY INCOME PLANS

As mentioned, insured disability income plans consist of two distinct products: short-term coverage and long-term coverage. In many respects the contractual provisions of both short-term and long-term disability income contracts are the same or very similar. In other respects—notably, the eligibility requirements, the definition of disability, and the amount and duration of benefits—there are significant differences.

Eligibility

The eligibility requirements in group disability income insurance contracts are similar to those found in group term insurance contracts. In addition to being in a covered classification, an employee must usually work full-time and be actively at work before coverage will commence. Any requirements concerning probationary periods, insurability, and premium contributions must also be satisfied.

Short-term and long-term disability income insurance plans frequently differ in both the classes of employees who are eligible for coverage and the length of the probationary period. Employers are more likely to provide short-term benefits to a wider range of employees, and it is not unusual for short-term plans to cover all full-time employees. However, these plans may be a result of collective bargaining and apply only to union employees. In this situation other employees frequently have short-term disability benefits under uninsured salary continuation plans.

Long-term disability plans often limit benefits to salaried employees. Claims experience has traditionally been less favorable for hourly paid employees for a number of reasons. Claims of hourly paid employees tend to be more frequent, particularly in recessionary times when the possibility of temporary layoffs or terminations increases. Such claims also tend to be of longer duration, possibly because of the likelihood that these employees hold repetitive and nonchallenging jobs. Some long-term plans also exclude employees below a certain salary level since this category of employees, like hourly paid employees, is considered to have a reasonable level of benefits under social security.

Long-term disability income plans tend to have longer probationary periods than short-term disability income plans. While the majority of short-term disability plans (as well as group term insurance plans and medical expense plans) either have no probationary period or have a probationary period of 3 months or less, it is common for long-term disability plans to have probationary periods ranging from 3 months to 1 year. While short-term plans only require that an employee be actively at work on the date he or she is otherwise eligible for coverage, long-term plans sometimes require that the employee be on the job for an extended period (such as 30 days) without illness or injury before coverage will become effective.

Definition of Disability

Benefits are paid under disability income insurance contracts only if the employee meets the definition of disability as specified in the contract. Virtually all short-term disability income insurance contracts define disability as *the total and continuous inability of the employee to perform each and every duty of his or her regular occupation*. A small minority of contracts use a more restrictive definition, requiring that an employee be unable to engage in any occupation for compensation. Partial disabilities are usually not covered, but a few newer plans do provide benefits. In addition, the majority of short-term contracts limit coverage to nonoccupational disabilities, since employees have workers' compensation benefits for occupational disabilities. This limitation tends to be most common when benefits under the short-term contract are comparable to or lesser in amount than those under the workers' compensation law. In those cases where workers' compensation benefits are relatively low and the employer desires to provide additional benefits, coverage may be written for both occupational and nonoccupational disabilities.

A few long-term disability income contracts use the same liberal definition of disability that is commonly used in short-term contracts. However, the term *material duties* often replaces the term *each and every duty*. A few other contracts define disability as *the total and continuous inability of the employee to engage in any and every gainful occupation for which he or she is qualified or shall reasonably become qualified by reason of training, education, or experience*. However, the majority of long-term disability contracts use a dual definition that combines these two. Under a dual definition, benefits will be paid for some period of time (usually 24 or 36 months) as long as an employee is unable to perform his or her regular occupation. After that time, benefits will be paid only if the employee is unable to engage in any occupation for which he or she is qualified by reason of training, education, or experience. The purpose of this combined definition is to require and encourage a disabled employee who becomes able after a period of time to adjust his or her lifestyle and earn a livelihood in another occupation.

A more recent definition of disability found in some long-term contracts contains an occupation test and an earnings test. Under the occupation test a person is totally disabled if he or she meets the definition of disability as described in the previous paragraph. However, if the occupation test is not satisfied, a person will still be considered disabled as long as an earnings test is satisfied. This means that the person's income has dropped by a stated percentage, such as 50 percent, because of injury or sickness. This newer definition makes a group insurance contract similar to an individual disability income policy that provides residual benefits.

The definition of disability in long-term contracts may differ from that found in short-term contracts in several other respects. Long-term contracts are somewhat more likely to provide benefits for partial disabilities. Generally these benefits are provided in a manner similar to that described in an earlier chapter for workers' compensation insurance. However, the amount and duration of such benefits may be limited when compared with those for total disabilities, and the receipt of benefits is usually contingent upon a prior period of disability. In addition, most long-term contracts provide coverage for both occupational and nonoccupational disabilities. Finally, short-term contracts usually have the same definition of disability for all classes of employees. Some long-term contracts use different definitions for different classes of employees—one for most employees and a more liberal definition for executives or salaried employees.

Exclusions

Under certain circumstances disability income benefits will not be paid even if an employee satisfies the definition of disability. Common exclusions under both short-term and long-term disability income contracts specify that no benefits will be paid

- for any period during which the employee is not under the care of a physician
- for any disability caused by an intentionally self-inflicted injury
- unless the period of disability commenced while the employee was covered under the contract. For example, an employee who previously elected not to participate under a contributory plan cannot obtain coverage for an existing disability by deciding to pay the required premium.
- if the employee is engaged in any occupation for remuneration. This exclusion applies in those situations when an employee is totally disabled with respect to his or her regular job but is engaged in other employment that can be performed despite the employee's condition.

Until the 1978 amendment to the Civil Rights Act it was common for disabilities resulting from pregnancy to be excluded. Such an exclusion is now illegal under federal law if an employer has 15 or more employees. Employers with fewer than 15 employees may still exclude pregnancy disabilities unless they are subject to state laws to the contrary.

Additional exclusions are often found in long-term contracts. These commonly deny benefits for disabilities resulting from

- war, whether declared or undeclared
- participation in an assault or felony
- mental disease, alcoholism, or drug addiction. However, some contracts provide benefits for an employee who is confined in a hospital or institution that specializes in the care and treatment of such disorders; other contracts provide employees with benefits but limit their duration (such as for 24 months).
- preexisting conditions

The exclusion for preexisting conditions is designed to counter the adverse selection and potentially large claims that could occur if an employer established a group disability income plan or if an employee elected to participate in the plan because of some known condition that is likely to result in disability. While variations exist, a common provision for preexisting conditions excludes coverage for any disability that commences during the first 12 months an employee is covered under the contract if the employee received treatment or medical advice for the disabling condition both (1) prior to the date the employee became eligible for coverage and (2) within 90 consecutive days prior to the commencement of the disability.

When coverage is transferred from one insurance company to another, it is not unusual, particularly in the case of large employers, for the new insurance company to waive the limitation for preexisting conditions for those employees who were insured under the previous contract. This situation is often referred to as prior coverage credit. In some instances the provision is modified so that benefits are limited to those that would have been provided under the previous contract, possibly for a specified period of time, such as one year. Note that a transfer of coverage has no effect on the responsibility of the prior insurance company to continue paying benefits for claims that have already occurred, except in rare instances in which some arrangement is made for the new contract to provide benefits.

Benefits

A discussion of the benefits under disability income contracts is more complex than a discussion of the benefits under group life insurance contracts. A similarity exists in that there are benefit schedules that classify employees and specify the amount of disability income to be provided. However, the relationship between an employee's earnings and the employee's potential benefits is more important in disability income insurance than in group life insurance. In addition, disability benefits are subject to several provisions not found in group life insurance contracts. These pertain to the length of time that benefits will be paid and the coordination of benefits with other available types of disability income.

Benefit Schedules

As in group life insurance, there is a variety of benefit schedules found in group disability income contracts. Benefits may be available to all employees or limited to specific groups of employees. In addition, benefits may be expressed as either flat-dollar amounts, varying dollar amounts by classification, or a percentage of earnings.

A major difficulty in disability insurance is determining the appropriate level of benefits to provide. Absenteeism is encouraged and the incentive to return to work is diminished if a disabled employee is given a level of income that is comparable to his or her regular earnings. In general, disability income plans are designed to provide a level of benefits that replaces between 50 and 70 percent of an employee's gross income. While this may appear to represent a substantial reduction of regular earnings, it should be remembered that a disabled employee does not have the usual expenses associated with working, such as transportation costs. In addition, disability income benefits are not subject to social security taxation after a period of time and, depending on the source and amount, may be free of income taxation. Despite the logic in providing a reduced level of income, some short-term disability income plans provide employees with 100 percent of their predisability earnings. In most cases this level of benefits is either a result of collective bargaining or an effort by employers to provide nonunion employees with a level of benefits that is comparable to that of union employees.

Many short-term disability income plans and the majority of long-term plans base benefits on a single percentage of regular earnings (excluding bonuses and overtime). This percentage varies widely for short-term plans, and benefits as low as 50 percent or as high as 100 percent are not unusual. However, many insurers are reluctant to underwrite plans that provide benefits higher than 70 percent of earnings. In some instances short-term plans, like salary continuation plans, may use different percentages, such as 100 percent of earnings for 4 weeks and 70 percent of earnings for the remaining benefit period. The length of time for which the higher level of benefits will be provided may also be a function of the length of an employee's service.

Long-term plans typically provide benefits that range from 50 to 70 percent of earnings, with 60 and 66 2/3 being the most prevalent percentages. Some plans also use a sliding scale, such as 66 2/3 percent of the first $4,000 of monthly earnings and 40 percent of earnings in excess of $4,000.

It is common for plans that determine benefits as a percentage of earnings to also place a maximum dollar amount on the benefit that will be provided, regardless of earnings. For example, a short-term plan covering hourly employees may have a benefit equal to 70 percent of earnings that might be subject to a maximum of $250 per week. Similarly a long-term plan may provide benefits equal to 66 2/3 percent of earnings, but might be subject to a monthly maximum that varies from $1,000 for some small groups to $4,000 or $5,000 (and sometimes higher) for large groups. The purpose of such a maximum is to prevent the absolute benefit from being so high that an employee, by adjusting his or her lifestyle, could live comfortably on the disability income benefit and thus have no financial incentive to return to work.

Other types of benefit schedules are found in short-term disability income plans, particularly when these plans are designed for hourly paid employees. If the weekly earnings of most employees fall within a narrow range, the benefit might be expressed as a flat-dollar amount. For example, if all employees earn between $300 and $400 per week, a benefit of $225 per week might be used. If earnings vary widely, a benefit schedule such as the one shown in table 8-4 might be used.

TABLE 8-4	
Weekly Earnings	**Weekly Benefit**
$221 to $260	$170
$261 to $300	200
$301 to $340	220
$341 to $380	250
Over $380	280

A similar approach is occasionally used in long-term disability income plans, as shown in the table 8-5 benefit schedule for salaried employees earning in excess of $18,000 per year.

TABLE 8-5	
Monthly Earnings	**Monthly Benefit**
$1,500 to $2,500	$1,200
$2,501 to $3,500	1,800
$3,501 to $4,500	2,400
Over $4,500	3,000

Period of Benefits

To determine the period for which disability income benefits will be paid, it is necessary to determine when benefits will begin and how long they will be paid. In both respects there are differences between short-term and long-term plans.

Short-term Plans. Short-term disability income contracts commonly contain a waiting period (referred to in such contracts as an *elimination period*). The waiting period is the length of time for which an employee covered under the contract must be disabled before benefits begin. In the typical short-term contract there is no waiting period for disabilities resulting from accidents, but a waiting period of 1 to 7 days is used for disabilities resulting from sicknesses. However, some plans have a single waiting period that applies to disabilities from either accidents or sicknesses; a few plans have no waiting periods for either. Waiting periods longer than 7 days are occasionally used, particularly when there is a salary continuation plan to provide benefits during the initial portion of a disability. Besides lowering the cost of a disability income plan, the waiting period discourages unwarranted absences from work due to sickness. In a few cases benefits are paid retroactively to the date of disability if the disability lasts for a predetermined period of time, but it is generally felt that retroactive benefits cause employees to prolong their return to work in order to receive benefits for the full period of their disability.

Once an employee begins receiving benefit payments under a short-term disability contract, the benefits continue until the end of the benefit period specified in the contract, if the employee remains disabled for that long. Although short-term contracts may provide benefits up to 2 years (with long-term contracts providing benefits for periods over 2 years), benefits rarely continue for more than a year. In fact, the majority of short-term contracts stipulate that benefits will be paid for either 13 or 26 weeks, with the latter period being most prevalent. Short-term plans are often described in terms of their elimination period and their duration of benefits. For example, a "1-8-26" plan pays benefits for a maximum of 26 weeks beginning with the first day of disability in the case of an accident and with the eighth day of disability in the case of sickness.

In a few cases the maximum period of benefits applies to a specified duration of time (such as any consecutive 12 months) regardless of the number of separate disabilities. However, in most plans both the maximum benefit period and the elimination period apply to each separate disability. Moreover, successive periods of disability caused by the same accident or the same or related sickness are generally considered to be a single disability unless they are separated by a period (normally 2 weeks) of continuous resumption of active employment. This provision prevents an employee from briefly returning to work in order to obtain a second maximum period of benefits for the same disability.

Although reducing short-term disability income benefits for older employees may be justifiable on a cost basis, few plans have done so.

Long-term Plans. While waiting periods in long-term disability income plans may be as short as 30 days or as long as a year or more, most plans have elimination periods of from 3 to 6 months, with 6 months most common. The length of the waiting period will often correspond to the length of time benefits will be paid under a firm's short-term disability income plan or salary continuation plan. Unlike short-term plans, the waiting periods for sicknesses and accidents are the same.

Long-term disability income benefits may be paid for as short a period as 2 years or as long as the lifetime of the disabled employee. In a few cases the length of the benefit period may differ, depending on whether the disability was a result of an accident or a sickness. At one time it was common for long-term disability income benefits to stop at age 65, but this is no longer permissible under the Age Discrimination in Employment Act. Several different approaches are now used for older employees. In a few cases benefits are paid until age 70 for any disability that occurred before that age. For disabilities occurring at age 70 or later, benefits are paid for a reduced duration. A more common approach is to use a graded benefit period and give benefits to age 65 for employees who are disabled before a specified age. Employees disabled after the specified age get benefits for a limited duration, as shown in table 8-6.

TABLE 8-6

Age at Commencement of Disability	Benefit Duration
59 and younger	To age 65
60–64	5 years
65–69	To age 70
70–74	1 year
75 and older	6 months

A similar approach uses a sliding level of benefit durations after a certain age. For example, a plan may provide that employees disabled prior to age 60 will receive benefits until age 65. The schedule shown in table 8-7 might then be used for employees who are disabled at age 60 or older.

TABLE 8-7

Age at Commencement of Disability	Benefit Duration (in Years)
60	5
61	4
62	3½
63	3
64	2½
65	2
66	2
67	1
68	1
69	1

As in short-term disability income plans, provisions are made in long-term plans for successive disabilities. The majority of contracts stipulate that successive periods of disability that are separated by less than some period (usually varying from 3 to 6 months) of continuous, active full-time employment will be considered a single disability, unless the subsequent disability (1) arises from an unrelated cause and (2) begins after the employee has returned to work.

Coordination with Other Benefits

To minimize the possibility that an employee will receive total benefits higher than his or her predisability earnings, disability income plans commonly stipulate that benefits will be integrated with other sources of disability income. The effect of this integration is to reduce (either totally or partially) the benefits payable under the disability income contract to the extent that certain other benefits are available. In general, the insurance laws or regulations of most states allow such reductions to be made as a result of benefits from social insurance programs and group insurance or retirement plans provided by the employer, but not as a result of benefits from individual disability income contracts unless they were purchased by the employer. Employers and employees often resent the fact that disability income benefits that they have "paid for" may be reduced. However, such reductions are considered in determining the rates charged for disability income insurance. In effect, the employer is purchasing a contract that is only a supplement to these other available sources of disability income rather than being penalized because these resources are available.

For various reasons, including the limited duration of benefits and the desire for simplified operating procedures, integration with other benefits is less likely to exist in short-term plans than in long-term plans. If a short-term plan covers only nonoccupational disabilities, there is no need for integration with workers' compensation benefits; and unless benefits are provided for disabilities lasting longer than 5 months, there is no need to integrate benefits with social security. In general, benefits under short-term plans are integrated with (1) workers' compensation benefits, if the plan covers occupational disabilities; (2) temporary disability laws, if they are applicable; and (3) social security benefits, if the maximum benefit period is longer than 5 months.

Some insurance companies will sell long-term disability income coverage without any provision for coordination with other disability income benefits. However, the availability and potential magnitude of other benefits will be an underwriting factor in determining the maximum amount of coverage that will be written. Long-term disability income benefits, however, are usually integrated with benefits provided under the following:

- social security
- workers' compensation laws
- temporary disability laws

- other insurance plans for which the employer makes a contribution or payroll deduction
- pension plans for which the employer has made a contribution or payroll deduction to the extent that the employee elects to receive retirement benefits because of disability
- salary continuation plans
- earnings from employment, either with the employer or from other sources

The integration with social security may be based solely on the benefit a disabled worker receives for himself or herself (referred to as the employee's primary insurance amount). It may also be based on the employee's total family benefit if the employee has eligible dependents.

Two basic approaches to integration are used: a full-integration approach and a dual-percentage approach. Under the *full-integration approach,* long-term disability income benefits are reduced to the extent that any benefits subject to integration are received. For example, assume that an employee earning $2,500 per month is entitled to a disability income benefit of 60 percent, or $1,500 per month. In addition, suppose the employee is entitled to a disability benefit of $900 under social security, as well as additional family benefits of $450 (a total of $1,350). If the long-term disability income benefit plan provides for integration with total family benefits, the employee will receive $1,500 ($1,350 from social security and the remaining $150 from the long-term plan). However, if full integration is provided only with respect to the primary insurance amount (in other words, the $450 of family benefits is not considered), the employee will receive $1,950 ($1,350 from social security and $600 from the long-term disability plan).

Under the *dual-percentage approach* two percentages are used: one that is applicable to benefits that will be provided under the long-term plan when there are no other benefits subject to integration, and another higher percentage that is applicable to total benefits payable from the long-term plan and other sources subject to integration. For example, an insured plan might provide benefits equal to 60 percent of earnings in the absence of other benefits subject to integration. If there are benefits subject to integration, benefits under the insured plan will be reduced to the extent that the sum of the benefits under the long-term disability plan and the benefits subject to integration exceed another percentage, such as 70 percent. Using these percentages and the previous example, 70 percent of earnings will be $1,750. Since the long-term disability benefit and all the social security benefits total $2,850, the long-term disability benefit will be reduced by $1,100 if the plan provides for integration with total family benefits. Therefore the employee will receive a total benefit of $1,750 ($1,350 from social security and $400 from the long-term plan).

It is possible for the integration with other benefits to totally eliminate a long-term disability benefit. To prevent this from happening, many plans provide (and some states require) that a minimum benefit, such as $25 or $50 per month, be paid. Most plans also contain a provision freezing the amount of any social security reduction at the initial level that was established when the claim began. For example, assume an employee is entitled to receive $1,000 per month in disability income benefits under a long-term plan that contains a provision for full integration with social security. If the employee initially receives $400 from the long-term plan and $600 from social security, the $400 will continue to be paid under a provision that freezes the offset even if social security benefits are increased. If a 5 percent increase is later granted in social security benefits, the employee will receive a total benefit of $1,030. Without such a provision the intended effect of increases in social security benefits would be erased by equivalent reductions in other disability income benefits provided to the employee. This is seen by some regulators as being contrary to public policy and thus a reason for requiring insured plans to contain a freeze in the amount of the social security offset.

As a general rule, both the insured and the insurer will benefit if the insured is able to collect social security benefits for a disability. The insured will have an increased overall benefit, and the insurer will have a substantially lower claim to pay. Consequently insurers are often willing to provide assistance to claimants by helping them with the filing of social security claims and the appealing of decisions denying claims.

Supplemental Benefits

It is becoming increasingly common to find group long-term disability income plans that provide employees with a base of employer-paid benefits and that allow each covered employee to purchase additional coverage at his or her own expense. For example, a plan may provide basic benefits of 50 percent of earnings and an option for an employee to increase this amount to 55, 66 2/3, or 70 percent of earnings. These supplemental or "buy-up" plans are becoming more popular because employers feel the need to control the costs of benefits by shifting a greater burden of the cost to employees.

Some plans are also designed to "carve out" benefits for certain employees, frequently key executives. For example, an employer might design one plan to cover most of its employees, but top executives might be covered with another group plan that provides enhanced benefits in the form of a larger percentage of earnings and a more liberal definition of disability. Another variation of a carve-out plan would provide the executives with a lower benefit percentage than other employees receive, but it could provide supplemental benefits in the form of individual disability income policies. In addition to more favorable policy provisions, a carve-out plan might offer better rate guarantees and an overall higher benefit than a group plan could offer. Furthermore, the portability of the individual policy might be attractive to executives but might not necessarily appeal to the employer.

Other Contract Provisions

Many provisions in group disability income contracts are similar to those in group term insurance contracts and will not be discussed further in this chapter. These provisions pertain to incontestability, a grace period, the entire contract, and the payment of premiums. The provisions that will be discussed either are unique to group disability income benefit contracts or differ in certain respects from similar provisions found in group term insurance contracts.

Claims

The provisions concerning claims under both short-term and long-term disability income contracts are essentially the same. The insurance company must be notified within a relatively short time period—20 or 30 days (or as soon as is reasonably possible)—after the disability for which benefits are being claimed begins. A formal proof of loss must then be filed with the insurance company, usually within 90 days after the commencement of the disability or after the end of the week, month, or other time period for which benefits are payable. The proof of loss normally consists of a statement by the employee concerning the disability, a statement by the attending physician, and a statement by the employer indicating the date and reason that active employment ceased. Provisions also require periodic reports from the attending physician or permit the insurance company to request such reports at reasonable intervals. The insurance company also has the right to have the employee examined by a physician of its own choice (and at its own expense) at reasonable time periods during the duration of the claim.

Payment of Benefits

The insurance company is not obligated to make benefit payments until a proof of loss has been filed. Although benefits are usually payable to the employee, a facility-of-payment provision is included to allow payments to a guardian if the employee is physically, mentally, or otherwise incapable of giving a valid release for any payment received. Benefits may be assigned to another party if such an assignment is permissible under state law and the insurance contract.

Rehabilitation

As an incentive to encourage disabled employees to return to active employment as soon as possible, but perhaps at a lower-paying job, most insurance companies include a rehabilitation provision in their long-term disability income contracts. This provision permits the employee to enter a trial work period of 1 or 2 years in rehabilitative employment. During this time disability benefits will continue but will be reduced by some percentage (varying from 50 to 80 percent) of the earnings from rehabilitative employment. For example, with a 50 percent reduction, an employee who is otherwise entitled to a disability benefit of $1,500 per month will have this benefit reduced by only $600 if he or she can earn $1,200 in the new job. If the trial work period indicates that the employee is unable to perform the rehabilitative employment, the original long-term benefits will be continued and the employee will not be required to satisfy a new waiting period.

While there are seldom other provisions in long-term disability income contracts that require the insurance company to aid in the rehabilitation of disabled employees, it has become increasingly common for insurance companies to provide benefits for rehabilitation when it is felt that the cost of these benefits will be offset by shortening an employee's disability period. These benefits may be in the form of physical therapy, job training, adaptive aids to enable a disabled person to perform job functions, or even the financing of a business venture.

The rehabilitation of disabled workers is continuing to grow in importance among companies. In fact, the rehabilitative services provided are often used as a selling feature for an insurance company's product. More and more companies are taking a proactive role in managing disability claims by employing more skilled professionals and by intervening earlier in the claims process. Since early intervention is undoubtedly a key factor in getting disabled employees back to work sooner, many benefit consultants see an advantage in an employer's using the same company for a firm's short-term and long-term disability income plans. This approach enables the insurer's rehabilitation staff to become involved when a claim is filed under the short-term plan rather than waiting until the elimination period for long-term benefits has been met.

In addition to providing rehabilitation benefits, insurance companies are monitoring claims data more closely so that they can better advise employers of areas where action can be taken to reduce the number of future claims.

Termination

For the most part the provisions in disability income contracts concerning either the termination of the master contract or an employee's coverage are the same as those found in group life insurance. However, there is one notable exception: a conversion privilege is rarely included, based on the theory that the termination of employment will also terminate an employee's income and thus the need for disability income protection. If a conversion privilege is available, an extra charge is made for the coverage.

One other situation should be mentioned. When an employee meets the definition of total disability under a disability income contract, the employee is considered to have terminated employment by reason of ceasing to be an active, full-time employee. Without some provision to the contrary, an employee who resumes work is then required to resatisfy any eligibility requirements, including a new probationary period. However, most group disability income contracts allow the employer to consider disabled employees as not having terminated employment for insurance purposes. The employer may continue coverage as long as it is done on a nondiscriminatory basis and as long as the required premiums are paid. In short-term contracts, coverage is generally continued by the payment of premiums on the same basis as for active employees. However, it is common for long-term contracts to contain a waiver-of-premium provision.

It should be noted that the only practical effect of continuing coverage on a disabled employee is to guarantee that the employee will again be eligible for disability income benefits after he or she has returned to active employment. The continuation of coverage (or termination of coverage) has no effect on the future disability income benefits to an employee who is currently disabled and therefore entitled to receive benefits.

Additional Benefits

Several types of additional benefits are occasionally found under long-term disability income contracts. The most common are a cost-of-living adjustment (COLA), a pension supplement, and a survivors' benefit.

Some disability income plans have cost-of-living adjustments so that inflation does not erode the purchasing power of disability income benefits being received. Under the typical COLA formula, benefits increase annually along with changes in the consumer price index.

Many firms make provisions in their pension plan for treating disabled employees as if they were still working and accruing pension benefits. Such a provision requires that contributions on behalf of disabled employees be made to the pension plan, usually from the employer's current revenues. However, some disability income contracts stipulate that the contributions necessary to fund a disabled employee's accruing pension benefits will be paid from the disability income contract.

It should also be noted that some pension plans provide disability income benefits by allowing disabled employees to begin receiving retirement benefits when they are totally and permanently disabled. It is common, however, to limit these early retirement benefits to employees who have satisfied some minimum period of service or who have reached some minimum age. In recent years the feeling among employee benefit consultants seems to be that it is preferable to have separate retirement and disability income plans.

Some long-term contracts provide a benefit to survivors in the form of continued payments after the death of a disabled employee. In effect the disability income payments will be continued, possibly at a reduced amount, for periods ranging up to 24 months. Payments are generally made only to eligible survivors, who commonly are the spouse and unmarried children under age 21.

While even less common, other types of additional benefits may also be found. Examples include child-care payments for disabled employees who can work on a part-time basis, spousal disability benefits payable to the employee, and benefits to pay premiums for medical expense coverage.

FEDERAL TAXATION

As with group life insurance, employer contributions for an employee's disability income insurance are fully deductible to the employer as an ordinary and necessary business expense if the employee's overall compensation is reasonable. Salary continuation payments are similarly tax deductible. Contributions by an individual employee are considered payments for personal disability income insurance and are not tax deductible.

Income Tax Liability of Employees

In contrast to group life insurance, for which employer contributions may result in some taxable income to an employee, employer contributions for disability income insurance result in no taxable income to an employee. However, the payment of benefits under an insured plan or salary continuation plan may or may not result in the receipt of taxable income. In order to make this determination, it is necessary to look at whether the plan is fully contributory, noncontributory, or partially contributory.

Fully Contributory Plan

Under a fully contributory plan the entire cost is paid by employee contributions and benefits are received free of income taxation.

Noncontributory Plan

Under a noncontributory plan the entire cost is paid by the employer and benefits are included in an employee's gross income. However, the Internal Revenue Code provides a tax credit to persons who are permanently and totally disabled. A tax credit is subtracted from an individual's federal income tax liability, not deducted from gross income. For purposes of this tax credit the IRS uses the social security definition of disability; that is, an employee must be unable to engage in any kind of gainful work because of a medically determinable physical condition that has lasted or is expected to last at least 12 months or to result in death.

The maximum credit is $750 for a single person, $1,125 for a married person filing jointly, and $562.50 for a married person filing separately. The credit cannot exceed the taxable disability benefit actually received. The maximum credit is reduced if a single individual has an adjusted gross income (including the disability benefit) over $7,500, if a married person filing jointly has an adjusted gross income over $10,000, or if a married person filing separately has an adjusted gross income over $5,000. The reduction is equal to 7 1/2 percent of any income over the limit. In addition, the credit is reduced by 15 percent of any tax-free income received as a pension, an annuity, or a disability benefit from certain government programs, including benefits from social security. Since disability income plans are usually integrated with social security, the tax credit available to most individuals who receive disability benefits from employer plans will be substantially reduced or may be eliminated altogether.

Partially Contributory Plan

Under a partially contributory plan, benefits attributable to employee contributions are received free of income taxation. Benefits attributable to employer contributions are includible in gross income, but employees are eligible for the tax credit described previously.

The portion of the benefits attributable to employer contributions (and thus subject to income taxation) is based on the ratio of the employer's contributions to the total employer-employee contributions for an employee who has been under the plan for some period of time. For example, if the employer paid 75 percent of the cost of the plan, 75 percent of the benefits would be considered attributable to employer contributions and 25 percent to employee contributions. The time period used to calculate this percentage varies, depending upon the type of disability income plan and the length of time that the plan has been in existence. Under group insurance policies the time period used is the 3 policy years ending prior to the beginning of the calendar year in which the employee is disabled. If coverage has been in effect for a shorter time, IRS regulations specify the appropriate time period that should be used. Similar provisions pertain to contributory salary continuation plans. There is one major exception however, that stipulates that the time period is based on calendar years rather than policy years. If benefits are provided under individual disability income insurance policies, the proportion is determined on the basis of the premiums paid for the current policy year.

Tax Withholding and Social Security Taxes

Benefits paid directly to an employee by an employer under a salary continuation plan are treated like any other wages for purposes of tax withholding. Disability income benefits paid by a third party (for instance, an insurance company or a trust) are subject to the withholding tax rules and regulations only if the employee requests that taxes be withheld. In both cases, benefits that are attributable to employer contributions are subject to social security taxes. However, social security taxes are payable only during the last calendar month in which the employee worked and during the 6 months that follow.

STATE TAXATION

For income tax purposes, some states consider an individual's taxable income to be the figure shown on the individual's federal income tax return, and those states treat disability income and salary continuation benefits as the federal government does. While considerable variations exist in other states, disability income and salary continuation benefits are generally treated more favorably than under the federal tax laws and are often totally exempt from state income taxation.

9

Group Medical Expense Benefits: The Changing Environment

Chapter Outline

Medical expense insurance is the most significant type of group insurance in terms of both the number of persons covered and the dollar outlay. With the exception of employers with a very small number of employees, virtually all employers offer some type of medical expense plan. In almost all cases coverage identical to that offered for employees is also available for eligible dependents. In the absence of employee contributions, the cost of providing medical coverage for employees will be several times greater for most employers than the combined cost of providing life insurance and disability income insurance.

Group medical expense contracts are not as standardized as group life insurance and group disability income insurance. Coverage may be provided through Blue Cross and Blue Shield plans, health maintenance organizations (HMOs), and preferred-provider organizations (PPOs) as well as insurance companies. In addition, a large and increasing percentage of the benefits is provided under plans that are partially or totally self-funded (self-insured). An overall medical expense plan may be limited to specific types of medical expenses, or it may be broad enough to cover almost all medical expenses. Even when broad coverage is available, benefits may be provided either under a single contract or under a combination of contracts. Furthermore, in contrast to other types of group insurance, benefits may be in the form of services rather than cash payments. Finally, the skyrocketing cost of providing medical expense benefits over a long period of time has led to changes in coverage and plan design aimed at controlling these costs. Many of these changes have resulted in more similarities among the providers of medical expense coverage than existed in the past.

Over the last decade two major issues—affordability and accessibility of medical care—have led to profound changes in the health care industry. Not only has there been a continued shift to managed care plans, but the entire character of the health care industry has changed. Where once there was a distinction between the providers of care (such as doctors and hospitals) and the organizations that financed the care (such as insurers, the Blues, and HMOs), this distinction is becoming blurred. Physicians and hospitals are establishing HMOs and PPOs. Physicians may be employees of managed care plans. Some Blue Cross Associations are merging with hospitals. There are those who feel that in the not-too-distant future most Americans will receive their medical expense coverage from one of a small number of large organizations that both provide medical care and finance the cost of the medical care.

The issues surrounding medical care have also become a concern of government. Many states have enacted programs to make coverage available to the uninsured, including those who work for employers with a small number of employees. At the federal level lively debate over health care has occurred and is likely to continue.

This chapter, the first of four chapters devoted to group medical expense coverage, discusses the following topics:

- a brief history of the development of medical expense coverage
- an overview of the trend toward cost containment and managed care
- state initiatives to make medical expense coverage more available
- a discussion of national health insurance—the extent to which it already exists and proposals to expand its scope

Chapter 10 is devoted to traditional medical expense plans, while managed care approaches are discussed in chapter 11. Common provisions of medical expense plans and the tax treatment of medical expense premiums and benefits are covered in chapter 12.

DEVELOPMENT OF MEDICAL EXPENSE COVERAGE

In order to understand the wide array of medical expense plans available today, it is appropriate to understand their historic development. There is further discussion of each type of plan in later chapters.

Until the 1930s, medical expenses were borne primarily by ill or injured persons or their families. It was not unusual, however, for hospitals and physicians to provide care on a charity basis if the patient lacked the resources to pay. What have been described as the earliest "health insurance" plans were in reality disability income coverage. However, at that time medical costs were relatively low, and the continuation of income was often the difference between a person's ability to pay medical bills and the need to rely on charity.

The Birth of the Blues

The Great Depression saw the development of the first organizations that would later be called Blue Cross. These organizations, which were initially controlled by hospitals, were designed to provide first-dollar coverage for hospital expenses, but with a limited duration of benefits. In the late 1930s, physicians followed the hospitals' approach and established Blue Shield plans. Through the 1940s the Blues were the predominant providers of medical expense coverage.

Early HMOs

Although it is often thought that health maintenance organizations were a product of the 1970s, some HMOs were among the earliest providers of medical expense coverage. What is usually considered to be the first HMO, the Ross-Loos Clinic, was founded in Los Angeles in 1929. Other HMOs, such as the Kaiser Plans, had their beginnings in the 1930s. However, HMOs remained only a small player in the marketplace for medical expense coverage until the last two decades.

Early Efforts of Insurance Companies

Insurance companies, seeing the success of Blue Cross, entered the market for hospital insurance in the 1930s and later added coverage for surgical expenses and physicians' expenses. However, insurance companies were only modestly successful in competing with the Blues until a new product was introduced in 1949—major medical insurance. As a result by the mid-1950s insurance companies surpassed the Blues in premium volume and number of persons covered.

The 1960s—An Era of Government Involvement

The number of persons covered by medical expense insurance plans grew rapidly during the 1950s and 1960s. Much of this growth was in employer-sponsored plans as a result of a 1949 Supreme Court ruling that employee benefits were subject to collective bargaining.

While the types of products available underwent little change during this period, there were two major developments in the mid-1960s. For the first time the federal government became a major player in providing medical expense coverage by creating national health insurance programs for the elderly and the poor. Medicare provides benefits for persons aged 65 and older. The financing of the benefits under this program comes from three sources: government revenue, premiums of medicare beneficiaries, and the FICA taxes paid by most working persons and their employers.

The second program—medicaid—provides medical benefits for certain classes of low income individuals and families. There is little doubt that medicare and medicaid both provide benefits to major segments of the population with large numbers of persons who would otherwise be unable to receive adequate medical care. However, the effect of so many additional persons with coverage beginning at the same time created shortages of medical facilities and professionals. This increased demand for medical care is one reason for the high rate of inflation for health care costs that soon developed.

The 1970s—The First Reactions to Spiraling Costs

In 1950, expenditures for health care equaled 4.4 percent of GNP and increased to 5.4 percent in 1960 and 7.3 percent in 1970. When these spiraling costs received the attention of employers and the federal government, large employers started turning to the self-funding of medical expense benefits. In addition to improved cash flow, savings were achieved by the avoidance of state-mandated benefits and state premium taxes. The passage of ERISA in 1974 thwarted initial state attempts to bring self-funded plans under their insurance regulations. This federal legislation freed self-funded plans from state regulation and hastened the growth of this financing technique.

The 1970s also saw the first large-scale debate over national insurance. As in the mid-1990s, the majority of the members of Congress supported one of the many plans that were introduced, but opinions were diverse and little common ground was found. However, one significant piece of legislation was passed— the Health Maintenance Organization Act of 1973. This legislation sought to encourage the growth of HMOs by providing funding for their development costs and mandating that certain employers make these plans available to employees. There is little doubt that the growth of HMOs is a result of this legislation.

The 1980s and 1990s—Continued Change

Attempts to rein in the cost of medical care in the 1970s seemed to have little effect. By 1980, expenditures for health care reached 9.2 percent of GNP. This figure was 12.2 percent by 1990, and estimates are that it will top 15 percent by the end of the 1990s. In addition, about 14 percent of the population, including many employed persons and their families, is uninsured.

Reactions to these statistics have come from many sources. Many state governments have adopted programs to make coverage more available and affordable to the uninsured. At the federal level there have been suggestions that the entire health care system needs an overhaul. While the initial national health insurance proposal by the Clinton administration is dead, there is still continued support by members of Congress for changes in the nation's approach to providing and financing health care. Significant federal legislation was enacted in 1996, and further changes are likely.

The many efforts by employers to contain costs include the following:

- growth in the self-funding of benefits. Much of this growth comes from small and medium-sized employers.
- cost-shifting to employees. It is becoming increasingly common for employers to raise deductibles and require employees to pay a larger portion of their medical expense coverage.
- increased use of managed care plans that are alternatives to HMOs, such as PPOs and point-of-service plans. These approaches will often overcome the reluctance of some employees to participate in managed care plans.
- requiring or encouraging managed care plans. Some employers have dropped traditional medical expense plans and offer managed care alternatives only. However, a more prevalent approach is to offer employees a financial incentive to join managed care plans.

Many of these reactions are reflected in changing statistics about the extent of varying types of medical expense coverage, although unfortunately precise statistics are difficult to obtain. For example, many Blue Cross and Blue Shield associations and health maintenance organizations report only the total number of persons covered and make no distinction between individual coverage and group coverage. Many persons receive portions of their coverage from different types of providers, such as hospital coverage from a Blue Cross plan and other medical expense coverages from an insurance company under a supplemental major medical contract. In addition, self-funded plans may operate as HMOs, purchase stop-loss coverage, and/or utilize preferred-provider organizations.

Even though precise statistics cannot be obtained, there is no doubt that a significant change has taken place over the last decade. In 1980 approximately 90 percent of all insured workers were covered under "traditional" medical expense plans, and 5 percent were covered under health maintenance organizations. *Traditional* means that if a worker or family member was sick, he or she had complete freedom in choosing a doctor or a hospital. Medical bills were paid by the plan, and no attempts were made to control costs or the utilization of services. It is estimated that between 10 and 15 percent of the employees under these traditional plans were in plans that were totally self-funded by the employer; the remainder of the employees were split fairly evenly between plans written by insurance companies and the Blues.

By the mid-1990s the figures had changed dramatically, with the majority of employees now covered under plans that control costs and the access to medical care. It is now estimated that close to 75 percent of employees are enrolled in managed care plans—either HMOs, PPOs, or point-of-service plans often owned by insurance companies or the Blues. Of the remaining employees, few are in traditional plans. Many are still with insurance companies and the Blues, but under traditional plans that have been redesigned to incorporate varying degrees of managed care.

One important change is hidden in these statistics—the increasing trend toward self-funding of medical expenses by employers. It is estimated that over 50 percent of all workers are covered under plans that are totally or substantially self-funded. Self-funding is more prevalent as the number of employees increases, with between 80 and 90 percent of persons who work for employers with more than 20,000 employees being covered under self-funded plans. However, employers with as few as 25 to 50 employees also use self-funding. It should be noted that the way benefits are provided under a self-funded plan can vary—the employer may design the plan to provide benefits on an indemnity basis or as an HMO or PPO.

Despite the difficulty in obtaining precise statistics, the data collected by one consulting firm in its surveys is in line with most estimates of what is actually happening. These statistics show that the percentage of employers' primary medical expense plans (defined as the plan covering the most employees) that can be characterized as traditional indemnity plans has dropped from over 70 percent to 24 percent since 1990. During the same time period, the number of plans that use preferred-provider organizations has increased fivefold to 32 percent. Point-of-service plans and HMOs have grown more slowly and now account for about 21 percent and 23 percent, respectively, of the number of plans.

COST CONTAINMENT AND MANAGED CARE

Between 1970 and the early 1990s, the average annual increases in the cost of medical care were approximately twice the average annual increases in the consumer price index. No single factor accounts for these increases. Rather, it was a combination of the following reasons:

- technological advances. In the last few years many exciting technological advances have taken place. Numerous lives are now being saved by such techniques as CAT scans, MRIs, fetal monitoring, and organ transplants. As miraculous as many of these techniques are, they are also very expensive. Technological advances can also prolong the life of the terminally ill and increase associated medical expenses.
- increasing malpractice suits. The providers of care are much more likely to be sued than in the past, and malpractice awards have outpaced the general rate of inflation. This development has resulted in higher malpractice premiums, which are ultimately passed on to consumers. The increase in malpractice suits has also led to an increase in defensive medicine, with routine tests likely to be performed more often.
- increases in third-party payments. A growing portion of the country's health care expenditures is now paid by private health insurers or the government. Patients and providers of health care often have no financial incentives to economize on the use of health care service.
- undercapacity of medical facilities. Currently the United States has an overabundance of hospital beds, and a surplus of physicians is also beginning to develop. Empty hospital beds are expensive to maintain, and an oversupply of physicians tends to drive up the average costs of medical procedures so that physicians' average income does not drop.
- design of medical expense plans. Many medical expense plans now provide first-dollar coverage for many health care costs. There is often little incentive for patients to avoid the most expensive forms of treatment.
- AIDS. The continuing increase in the number of AIDS cases over the last 10 years has resulted in increasing costs to employers. Costs in excess of $100,000 for an employee with AIDS are not unusual.
- an aging population. The incidence of illness increases with age. Current demographics indicate that this trend will be a source of cost increases for several years to come.

During the period from 1994 to 1996, several factors caused the cost of medical expense coverage to remain uncharacteristically stable, particularly for managed care plans. Many providers of medical services and medical expense plans were reluctant to raise costs while the Clinton health care proposal was being debated. In addition, managed care plans were holding down premiums while actively increasing enrollments.

However, most benefit consultants feel that increases in excess of the inflation rate, but not of the magnitude of the 1980s and 1990s, are likely to return soon. There is a feeling that expanding managed care plans have saturated the market to the point that savings resulting from additional employees moving to managed care plans will be modest. There is also an interesting trend occurring among medical providers. The large number of mergers of hospitals and other providers of medical services in many parts of the country may in fact shift the balance of bargaining power to these providers from managed care plans and other buyers of medical services. In addition, costs will increase somewhat because of federal and state legislation that continues to mandate benefits.

Increasing health care costs have become the concern of almost everyone—government, labor, employers, and consumers. In this introduction to cost containment many of the measures employers use are enumerated. Some of the following measures will be discussed in more detail throughout the next three chapters; others will be discussed later in the book:

- benefit plan design
- alternative providers
- alternative funding methods
- claims review
- health education and preventive care
- encouragement of external cost-control systems
- managed care

Benefit Plan Design

Numerous design features of a medical expense plan can control costs. These have traditionally been in the form of contractual provisions that shift costs to employees. Examples are

- deductibles
- coinsurance
- exclusions and limitations
- maximum benefits

In recent years design features have been aimed at reducing costs rather than shifting them. In fact, benefit plans are often designed to provide a higher level of benefits if less costly alternatives are used. Examples of these cost-containment features are

- permission testing
- second surgical opinions
- coordination of benefits
- the use of alternatives to hospitals—such as skilled-nursing facilities, home health care, hospice care, birthing centers, and ambulatory care centers

- the use of medical savings accounts

Alternative Providers

The use of HMOs and PPOs has been popular for some years as a cost-containment method. These methods have now been joined by point-of-service plans. Each is described in more detail in the chapter on managed care plans.

Alternative Funding Methods

Employers are increasingly turning to funding methods that are alternatives to the traditional insurance company plan or Blue Cross–Blue Shield plan. Chapter 15 is devoted to a discussion of these techniques.

Claims Review

There is no doubt that claims review can generate substantial cost savings. In general this review is done not by the employer but by the provider of medical expense benefits, a third-party administrator, or some independent outside organization. At a minimum claims should be reviewed for patient eligibility, eligibility of the services provided, duplicate policies, and charges that are in excess of usual, customary, and reasonable amounts. Many medical expense plans routinely audit hospital bills, particularly those that exceed some amount, such as $5,000 or $10,000. They check for errors in such items as length of stay, services performed, and billed charges. Many insurance companies have found that each dollar spent on this type of review results in two or three dollars of savings.

A newer trend in claims review is utilization review or case management, which may be done on a prospective basis, a concurrent basis, a retrospective basis, or a combination of the three. A prospective review involves analyzing a case to see what type of treatment is necessary. Hospital preadmission authorization, second surgical opinions, and predetermination of dental benefits fall into this category. However, when a patient is hospitalized, concurrent review can lead to shorter stays and the use of less expensive facilities. Concurrent review is normally carried out by a registered nurse and typically begins with precertification of a hospital stay for an initial specified length of time. The nurse then works with the patient's physician to monitor the length of stay and to determine whether other alternatives to hospitalization—such as hospices or home health care—can be used. Many providers of medical expense benefits will pay for these alternative forms of treatment even if they are not specifically covered under the medical expense plan as long as their cost is lower than the cost of continued hospitalization.

A retrospective review involves an analysis of care after the fact to determine if it was appropriate. Such a review may lead to a denial of claims, but its purpose is often to monitor trends so that future actions can be taken in high-cost areas. For example, a retrospective review may lead to the establishment of a concurrent review program for a hospital with excessive lengths of stay.

Health Education and Preventive Care

There is little doubt that persons who lead healthy lifestyles will tend to have fewer medical bills, particularly at younger ages. It is also evident that healthier employees save an employer money by taking fewer sick days and having fewer disability claims. For these reasons employers are increasingly establishing wellness programs and employee-assistance plans, both of which are discussed in chapter 17. With increasing health awareness among the general population the existence of these programs has a positive side effect—the improvement of employee morale.

The Encouragement of External Cost-Control Systems

While a certain degree of cost containment is within the control of employers, the proper control of costs is an ongoing process that requires participation by consumers (both employers and individuals), government, and the providers of health care services. The National Council on Health Planning and Development, an advisory body to the secretary of health and human services, identifies needs, monitors resources, establishes priorities, recommends courses of action, and oversees laws pertaining to health care. The council, which was created by the National Health Planning and Resources Development Act of 1974, oversees state and local activities that are carried out by state health planning and development agencies and local health system agencies (HSAs). Many employers encourage and are actively involved with these agencies.

At the state and local level many employers are active in coalitions whose purpose is to control costs and improve the quality of health care. These groups—which may also involve unions, providers of health care, insurance companies, and regulators—are often the catalyst for legislation, such as laws authorizing PPOs and establishing hospital budget-review programs. Some coalitions act as purchasing groups to negotiate lower-cost coverage for members. For example, one midwestern coalition consists of several large corporations and offers a uniform health plan to the 50,000 employees of its members. The plan is self-funded by the coalition and utilizes the services of about 1,000 primary care physicians and 4,000 specialists. Another coalition, an example of a different approach, represents over 10,000 companies with fewer than 150 employees each. The coalition negotiates with providers of medical expense coverage and offers its members a choice of about a dozen different group plans. The annual increase in cost to coalition members has been significantly less than the annual increase in cost for other companies in the area that do not belong to the coalition.

Managed Care

The current buzzword with respect to cost containment is *managed care*. In a general sense the term can be defined to include any medical expense plan that attempts to contain costs by controlling the behavior of participants. However, in practice the term is used by many persons to mean different things. At one extreme are traditional indemnity plans that require second opinions and/or hospital precertification. At the other extreme are HMOs and PPOs that limit a participant's choice of medical providers, negotiate provider fees, and use case management.

Managed care plans have evolved over the last few years. Today it is generally felt that a true managed care plan should have five basic characteristics:

- *controlled access of providers.* It is difficult to control costs if participants have unrestricted access to physicians and hospitals. Managed care plans attempt to encourage or force participants to use predetermined providers. Because a major portion of medical expenses results from referrals to specialists, managed care plans tend to use primary care physicians as gatekeepers to determine the necessity and appropriateness of specialty care. By limiting the number of providers, managed care plans are better able to control costs by negotiating provider fees.
- *comprehensive case management.* Successful managed care plans perform utilization review at all levels.
- *preventive care.* Managed care plans encourage preventive care and the attainment of healthier lifestyles.
- *risk sharing.* Managed care plans are most successful if providers share in the financial consequences of medical decisions. Newer managed care plans have contractual guarantees to encourage cost-effective care. For example, a physician who minimizes diagnostic tests may receive a bonus. Ideally such an arrangement will eliminate unnecessary tests, not discourage tests that should be performed.
- *high-quality care.* A managed care plan will not be well received and selected by participants if there is a perception of inferior or inconvenient medical care. In the past too little attention was paid to this aspect of cost containment. Newer managed care plans not only select providers more carefully but also monitor the quality of care on a continuing basis.

There seems to be a reasonable consensus among employers and benefit specialists that there is a negative correlation between benefit costs and the degree of managed care. That is, the greater the degree of managed care, the lower the cost. For example, studies generally rank benefit plans in the following order (from highest to lowest) with respect to annual benefit costs:

- traditional insurance company and Blue Cross and Blue Shield plans without case management
- traditional insurance company and Blue Cross and Blue Shield plans with case management
- preferred-provider organizations
- point-of-service plans
- independent practice association HMOs
- closed-panel HMOs

It is interesting to note that the degree of managed care increases as one goes down the list. There also seems to be a high correlation between annual benefit costs and the rate of cost increases. For example, the cost of traditional benefit plans has been increasing recently at an annual rate of approximately double the annual increase in cost for closed-panel HMOs.

STATE REFORMS

Often overlooked in the debate over national health insurance is the role of the states in health care reform. Since 1989, almost all states have passed some type of legislation to make medical expense coverage more available and less costly to certain segments of the population. Some of this legislation was passed before the initial national health insurance proposal of the Clinton administration, and it is interesting to note that some of the administration's ideas reflected practices already instituted in some states. Other states continued to pass their own reforms as the debate over national health insurance continued at the national level during most of the first Clinton administration. The potential importance of state actions should not be overlooked. There has been and continues to be considerable support in Congress for having the states, rather than the federal government, take the initiative in health care reform.

State reforms fall into two categories. One category is laws and regulations aimed at uninsured individuals other than employees. These are not discussed in this book. The other category is those laws and regulations that comprise what is commonly referred to as "small-group reform." It is in these groups of fewer than 25 or 50 employees that the majority of employees without employer-sponsored coverage is found. Most states have passed NAIC model legislation, and a few states have gone even further with other types of legislation. With much of the state legislation being relatively recent, it is still too early to see its effect on significantly reducing the number of uninsured. However, early results do seem to be somewhat mixed. On one hand, some states report modest results, but on the other hand, several insurers no longer choose to write business for small groups.

The NAIC Model

The most common approach to state reform has been the adoption of one of the versions of the NAIC Small Employer Health Insurance Availability Model Act. The stated purpose and intent of the model act are "to promote the availability of health insurance to small employers regardless of their health status or claims experience, to prevent abusive rating practices, to require disclosure of rating practices to purchasers, to establish rules regarding renewability of coverage, to establish limitations on the use of preexisting-conditions exclusions, to provide for development of basic and standard health benefit plans to be offered to all small employers, to provide for establishment of a reinsurance program, and to improve the overall fairness and efficiency of the small-group health insurance market." While some provisions of the model act may result in lower costs for certain employers, the main emphasis of the model act is on the availability of coverage, not on the employer's or employees' ability to afford the coverage.

Although the following discussion focuses on the provisions of the NAIC model act, it is important to remember that states often adopt model acts with variations. Some of the more significant variations are described. Note that some states will need to modify certain provisions of the model act that conflict with the new federal Health Insurance Portability and Accountability Act.

Plans Subject to the Act

The model act defines a small employer as one who had 25 or fewer employees working on at least 50 percent of the days during the previous calendar quarter. Several states extend their legislation to employers with as many as 50 employees and/or exclude groups of one or two employees.

The model act applies to most medical expense products provided by insurance companies, HMOs, and prepaid service plans. Certain types of coverage are specifically excluded from the act's provisions—specifically dental insurance, vision insurance, medicare supplements, long-term care insurance, and disability income insurance. In addition, payroll deduction plans of individual medical expense insurance under which the employer pays no portion of the cost may or may not be subject to a specific state's legislation.

The small-group legislation does not force the providers of medical expense coverage to operate in the small-employer market. However, if a provider of coverage does sell medical expense coverage to small employers, the provisions of the legislation must be followed.

Benefit Provisions

The model act establishes a committee representing providers of medical expense coverage, employers, employees, health care practitioners, and agents to recommend the form and level of coverage to be made available to small employers. The committee must recommend a basic plan and a more comprehensive standard plan and make decisions regarding benefit levels, cost-sharing levels, exclusions, and limitations. In designing the basic plan, the committee can ignore any state mandates for benefits unless the small-group legislation specifically requires them.

Preexisting-conditions provisions are allowed but with limitations. A medical condition can be treated as preexisting if it was treated (or if a prudent person would have sought treatment) within a specified prior period, which cannot exceed 6 months. Coverage for preexisting conditions cannot be excluded for more than 12 months following the effective date of coverage. Preexisting conditions must be covered as any other medical conditions if a person had benefits for the medical condition under a prior medical expense plan for at least 90 continuous days prior to the effective date of the new coverage.

One unfortunate and probably unintended side effect of the small-group legislation is that the policies that must be made available in many states are very precisely prescribed, making it impossible for insurance companies to use the same policies in multiple states. The expense of designing and refiling policies for many states, coupled with rate controls and the inability to underwrite for medical conditions, has resulted in several insurers leaving the small-group market.

Underwriting

With few exceptions coverage must be written for all small employers. An insurance company or other provider of medical expense coverage is permitted to have requirements for minimum participation and minimum employer contributions as long as these requirements are the same for all similarly sized groups. These requirements cannot be increased after an employer has been accepted for coverage.

Coverage must be made available to all employees and their dependents. However, persons who did not enroll when initially eligible can be denied coverage for up to 18 months or have coverage excluded for preexisting conditions for up to 18 months.

Rates and Renewability

The model act prescribes a procedure for determining an "index rate" to be charged by each provider of medical expense coverage. Under certain circumstances, such as the use of more than one type of marketing system, the provider can use different rates for different classes of business to reflect substantial differences in expected claims experience or administrative costs. However, the index rate for any class of business cannot be more than 20 percent higher than the index rate for any other class of business.

Although the act allows rate differences among groups because of variations in age, sex, industry, geographic area, family composition, and group size, far fewer refinements are allowed than would be the case without this legislation. Some states have adopted more restrictive legislation and require community rating.

At annual renewals, rates can be changed because of changes in the index rate, changes in the mix of employees, and possibly group experience. In the latter case, the size of the adjustment is limited to a modest amount. The provider of medical expense coverage must renew all policies subject to certain exceptions, such as nonpayment of premium or the failure to meet any minimum participation requirement. The provider may also elect not to renew all policies for small employers in a state. However, proper notification (usually 180 days) must be given to the insurance commissioner and all employers.

Relation to New Federal Legislation

The Health Insurance Portability and Accountability Act contains provisions that are similar to many provisions of the NAIC model act. State law will continue to apply to insured medical expense plans unless it interferes with the new federal legislation. Provisions of the state law will supersede the federal legislation if they are more generous toward insured individuals. For example, the maximum allowable length of preexisting-conditions periods may be shorter in some states than under the federal legislation.

Other State Reforms

Other reforms passed by the states are

- tort reform. Several states have passed legislation to control medical malpractice suits. This legislation ranges from limiting recovery for noneconomic loss to mandatory arbitration.
- claim administration reform. A few states now require the use of standardized claim forms, including a uniform system of coding diagnoses and procedures.
- the establishment of health insurance purchasing cooperatives (HIPCs). Several states have laws that establish HIPCs, entities that act as brokers between the purchasers and providers of medical expense coverage. They negotiate alternative plans of coverage on the basis of price and quality. Those eligible to use the HIPC, which may vary from all purchasers to small employers only, may elect one of the available plans directly from the HIPC. With some HIPCs, an employer deals directly with the cooperative without using agents or brokers. In one state, however, an employer can purchase coverage through an agent or broker or deal directly with the cooperative and receive a discount equal to the commission that would be paid to an agent or broker. An unexpected result of this arrangement is that almost 70 percent of the employers have elected to use an agent or broker. Clearly these

employers feel that the services agents and brokers provided are worth the extra cost. Because of concern that many HIPCs will need exemptions from federal antitrust legislation to operate effectively, some states have either not implemented or only partially implemented the legislation that has been passed.

A few states are considering the adoption of even more radical reforms to the health care market, such as the adoption of single-payer plans, which are discussed in the next section of this chapter.

NATIONAL HEALTH INSURANCE

Few issues in recent years have gotten as much attention as the debate over national health insurance. With health care expenditures taking nearly one out of every six dollars spent in this country and 15 percent of the population without adequate coverage for medical expenses, the magnitude of the problem cannot be overemphasized. There are no easy solutions to the problems of increasing costs and the lack of coverage for everyone. Health care is an emotional issue, and any reform will be complex and affect almost all Americans to varying degrees.

The following discussion of national health insurance does not give any precise answers or solutions. Rather it addresses many aspects of the issue, describes some approaches suggested for solving current problems, and attempts to predict what seems most feasible in the short term. The major goal of this discussion is to provide readers with a better framework for following—and perhaps participating in—the debate that will undoubtedly continue for some time.

Some Basic Questions

The issue of national health insurance is best addressed by having an understanding of its many dimensions. This discussion is organized around several questions, not all of which have precise or easy answers.

Don't We Already Have National Health Insurance?

The answer is yes for many Americans. Unlike most other industrialized countries, however, the United States does not have a system of national health insurance that covers everyone. Although national health insurance does exist in the form of medicare, medicaid, certain veterans' benefits, and coverage of military personnel and their families, each of these programs attempts to address the issue of health insurance for a specific group and takes a different approach.

Some people would say that most other Americans are also covered under a national health insurance program. While the role of the federal government is probably not extensive enough for most persons to agree with this observation, the federal government does in fact have an influence on the design of employer-provided medical expense plans of almost all but the smallest employers. This influence comes from numerous pieces of federal legislation, such as ERISA, COBRA, the Family and Medical Leave Act, the Age Discrimination in Employment Act, the Americans with Disabilities Act, and the Health Insurance Portability and Accountability Act.

Many Americans have a tendency to feel that the federal government should have no role in health care reform. But approximately 50 percent of all medical care expenditures are for persons who are either employees of the federal government or covered under the national health insurance programs previously mentioned. Therefore the government and the taxpayers who fund its activities have a direct stake in controlling the cost of medical care. However, it is easy for many observers to become a bit cynical when they compare their own medical expense plan with the generous plan available to members of Congress.

What Is the Objective of National Health Insurance?

It is difficult to determine exactly what a national health insurance program should accomplish. Alternative proposals either have different objectives or place varying degrees of emphasis on a combination of objectives. There are two primary concerns with the current health care system—rapidly increasing costs and the lack of coverage for a large segment of the population. Some programs are essentially a proposed solution to only one of these concerns; other proposals address both concerns in varying degrees. It would be much easier to find a solution if there was consensus on the scope of the actual problem.

Unfortunately the two problems are not independent, and solving one problem may actually exacerbate the other. For example, making broad coverage available to everyone might so increase the demand for medical treatment that costs would go up because of a shortage of medical providers. This situation occurred after the passage of medicare. In addition, efforts to control costs could lead to rationing of medical care so that some types of care would be available only to the more affluent segment of the population who could afford some type of supplemental insurance protection.

Do Americans Want Reform?

This is a difficult question to answer. During the health care debate over the last few years, numerous polls were taken. There seemed to be overwhelming agreement among the American people that the health care system is broken and needs fixing. Some proponents of national health insurance inferred from this opinion that there was support for radical reform.

As the debate continued and more polls about the underlying mood of the public were conducted, a different picture began to emerge. Most Americans were happy with their own medical expense coverage. They were also aware of rapidly rising costs, but those in managed care plans had been less significantly affected by them. In fact, as many employees elected managed care options, they actually saw their out-of-pocket medical expenses decrease. Although the public was not in favor of changes that would affect their relationships with providers of medical care, a surprisingly large percentage of the public was aware that reform carried a financial cost, and within limits many Americans were willing to foot the bill.

These further surveys also indicated that the major concern of Americans was the lack of security surrounding their own medical expense coverage, particularly if they became unemployed or changed jobs. There was fear that the loss of employment would put them in the category of uninsured. Even if coverage could be continued under COBRA, its high cost would make it unaffordable. Considerable concern was also expressed over the lack of coverage when changing jobs because of preexisting-conditions provisions in the new employer's coverage. While Congress is often considered out of touch with the electorate, these, in fact, were significant issues addressed by major health insurance legislation in 1996.

One final observation about these surveys: they showed that the majority of Americans do not want another program as bureaucratic as they view medicare to be.

Is the Goal Universal Coverage or Universal Access?

Some national health insurance programs call for universal coverage, which means that all Americans would be covered. Unfortunately the cost of universal coverage would be very expensive, and it is questionable whether such a program could be accomplished voluntarily. As long as some people are in a position of voluntarily electing coverage, there are those who would be unwilling to pay the price, even if it was subsidized. Therefore universal coverage probably requires a program similar to medicare and accompanying tax revenue to support the program. With the majority of the public wanting a nongovernment program of health insurance, many other national health insurance proposals focus on universal access and realize that a goal of slightly less than universal coverage is all that is realistically attainable. But even this goal will require subsidies for some segments of the population.

Who Should Pay the Cost?

A majority of the uninsured have inadequate resources to pay the cost of voluntary coverage, even if it was suddenly available. As a result there will be some need to subsidize the cost of coverage if the number of uninsured is going to be reduced substantially. Who pays? The alternatives are many, but they can largely be summed up in one word—taxes. There have been numerous suggestions about the form of these taxes, but in all cases they will fall on some or all taxpayers. These alternatives include general tax revenue, additional social security taxes, and taxes on cigarettes because smoking is the source of many medical problems.

Sometimes overlooked is the fact that many of the uninsured do receive medical treatment. Even though uninsured persons may be unable to pay, treatment by hospitals and physicians will usually not be denied for serious illnesses or injuries. However, when the hospital or physician writes off a large portion of these bills as uncollectible, the cost is in effect being passed on to those who do pay their bills (usually through insurance) in the form of higher charges than would otherwise be made. In theory the cost to many individuals or employers will decrease if a larger portion of the population has the resources to pay their own expenses. This is used as the rationale for taxing employers or individuals to pay the cost of providing protection for the uninsured.

What Benefits Should Be Available?

One of the major debates in designing a national health insurance program involves the scope of the benefits that will be included. At one extreme in the debate are those who feel the government should guarantee only a minimum level of health care. Private medical expense insurance or personal resources would be necessary to obtain broader benefits. At the other extreme are those who feel that a comprehensive level of health care should be available to all Americans. This group views complete health care protection as a basic right that belongs to everyone regardless of income.

The current system of health insurance falls somewhere between these two extremes, and this is probably where any ultimate solution will be found. Most Americans do not have coverage for long-term care, and many have limitations on benefits such as mental health and substance abuse. Some medical expense plans limit coverage for prescription drugs. Such limitations exist not because employers see no value in these benefits; rather realistic cost constraints dictate the benefits that are provided. Employers cannot afford a medical expense plan that will do everything for everyone, and it is questionable whether Americans are willing to pay the cost of a national health insurance program that has such a lofty goal.

Another issue is whether a uniform package of benefits should be available nationwide. Under some proposals, benefits would be determined on a state-by-state basis, while under other proposals, a national benefit standard would be established. These proposals typically call for the abolishment of state benefit mandates.

Does Cost Containment Harm Quality?

While there are undoubtedly inefficiencies in the health care system, many of these inefficiencies have been addressed in recent years. For example, hospitals, faced with limits on medicare and medicaid reimbursements, have been forced to operate in a more cost-effective manner. However, future efforts to control costs will probably need to be more severe and may come with a high price. Americans arguably have the best and most innovative health care system in the world. Can this quality be continued if prices are controlled? Or will it continue only for those who have additional resources to pay? Control of costs, if taken beyond a certain point, will lead to the situation that exists in most countries with national health insurance programs—rationing of medical care. Questions such as the following will then need to be answered: Should organ transplants be limited to persons under age 50? Should very expensive health care continue to be provided to premature babies who have a less than 25 percent chance of survival? To what extent should medical treatment be provided to persons with AIDS and other terminal illnesses? Will controls on the cost of prescription drugs eliminate the resources needed to develop the next generation of medicines?

Are Employer Mandates the Proper Approach?

National health care proposals differ with respect to the employer's role in making coverage available to its employees. Some proposals would require virtually all employers to make coverage available to employees (including part-time employees) and their dependents and to pay a portion of the cost. Under all such proposals, there are additional programs for the unemployed and subsidies to some employers for whom the cost exceeds a certain limit. However, small employers would be hit hard by most of these proposals and have lobbied against employer mandates. There is considerable support for the argument that the cost of employer mandates would force some small employers out of business.

One major argument for employer mandates is that the alternative is a government-run program with its accompanying bureaucracy.

What Is the Role of Medicare and Medicaid?

Many differences exist over the role of medicare and medicaid in health care reform. Although some argue for a single system to cover all Americans, opponents argue that the medicare and medicaid programs serve specific groups and are working reasonably well. Why alter the part of the system that is already closest to the concept of universal coverage?

It is interesting to note that national health insurance proposals are much more likely to fold medicaid recipients into a new program than they are to include medicare recipients. This fact reflects the reality that tinkering with medicare can have grave consequences because of the high voter turnout of the elderly.

What Are the Political Realities?

The possibility of any national health insurance program depends on whether Congress can design a program that receives broad-based support.

Republicans are unlikely to offer solutions that are as far-reaching as the initial Clinton administration's proposal and that will offend as many segments of society. However, public clamor for change will undoubtedly lead to some reform, modest though it may be. Clearly any change will be designed to appeal to a different class of constituents. While the initial Clinton administration's proposal appealed to such groups as organized labor, the Republicans are much more likely to be influenced by the concerns of small businesses. However, no program will be successful and politically palatable unless it receives support from many diverse groups, including employers, insurers, hospitals, physicians, drug companies, and the general public.

Possible Approaches

One difficulty for the author of any textbook is the extent to which current proposals should be covered in detail. In a debate such as the one occurring over health insurance, new proposals are continually replacing old ones, and those that are around for any length of time undergo revision. For this reason, the discussion is general and describes the following generic approaches that are being discussed:

- managed competition plans
- single-payer plans
- medical savings accounts
- reform on a state-by-state basis
- modest reform of the current system

It is important to remember that the use of any one of these approaches does not dictate a specific national health insurance plan. Within each approach there is wide latitude to address many of the issues discussed in the previous pages.

Managed Competition Plans

The term *managed competition* received considerable attention because it was the approach taken by the Clinton administration in designing its initial national health insurance proposal. However, the term and the concept have been discussed since the 1970s. The basic philosophy behind the idea of managed competition is that competition for medical expense insurance should be based on price rather than on the risk characteristics of those needing coverage. A managed competition plan would create a new type of organization—often referred to as a HIPC or health insurance purchasing cooperative. A HIPC would act as a purchasing agent and negotiate with insurance companies, HMOs, and other providers of medical expense coverage to offer a menu of different insurance plans to employers and individuals who subscribe to the HIPC. In addition to price, subscribers would be given information on each plan's quality of care.

Under most managed care proposals, HIPCs would be established under state regulation, would operate in a specified geographic region, and would not compete with each other. Some proposals require all employers to be subscribers to the HIPC in their area, which would be the only source for providing coverage to employees. To varying degrees, however, most managed competition proposals allow larger employers to establish their own HIPCs for self-funding benefits.

Most managed care proposals also establish standards for what are often called approved or accountable health plans (AHPs). These AHPs are the only medical providers that can deal with a HIPC, which would require each AHP to offer a standard set of benefit packages. HMOs are in a position to do this, but other providers would need to form alliances, such as an insurance company forming an AHP with a network of hospitals and physicians.

All employers (and also unemployed and self-employed persons) would be eligible for coverage from the HIPC, and there would be no preexisting-conditions provisions for employees. Some proposals use community rating, which would establish a set price per covered person for the plan selected. Other proposals would adjust rates by factors such as age or sex.

While individual proposals for national health insurance may vary, there is nothing in the basic idea of managed competition that dictates any specific benefit package, level of employer contribution to the cost of the coverage for employees, or government price controls.

The critics of managed competition are many. It involves a fundamental change in the delivery of health care and has been opposed by many physicians who fear that their ability to treat patients will come under government control. Insurance agents have been particularly vocal because their role would be virtually eliminated. However, there would still be a modest role for benefit consultants to advise employers on the selection of alternative plans under the HIPC. HIPCs are also unappealing to persons who are not already in managed care plans and wish to retain control over their choice of medical practitioners. Employers that operate in many regions would also be required to deal with several HIPCs.

Managed competition has also been criticized for creating another level of health care bureaucracy by the formation of HIPCs and the additional regulation that would be needed. It has been suggested that this might also negate the effect of any cost-saving features of the approach.

Single-Payer Plans

Several proposals for national health insurance can be categorized as single-payer plans, which is the approach taken in Canada and many European countries. Under a single-payer plan, everyone is automatically covered by a single program run by the government, and the same benefit package is provided to everyone. Some proposals have a totally federal program; other proposals call for each state to administer the program for its residents, but under specific federal guidelines.

Single-payer plans eliminate the employer's role in providing medical expense benefits to employees. The agent's role is also eliminated unless the plan benefits are at a level where there is a market for supplemental insurance. However, most proposals call for very comprehensive coverage with few if any copayments.

Most proposals for a single-payer plan call for the financing of the program through taxes rather than premiums. While the taxes could take a variety of forms, a social security type of payroll tax on both employers and employees is most commonly mentioned.

In some respects a single-payer plan can be viewed as a medicare-type program that covers everyone. However, the single-payer approach goes further and calls for more government control of medical care. A national health care budget would be established, and reimbursement schedules to providers would be determined at the state or federal level within the constraints of this budget. In addition, the budget would result in the government's exercising controls over the types of treatment available for specific conditions and the extent to which monies would be spent on new technology and medical facilities. In effect, a single-payer plan rejects market forces as the allocator of medical resources and implies that there would be some rationing of medical care under government guidelines.

Although the broad nature of a single-payer plan would result in additional costs because of increased demand for health care, these costs would be offset by efficiencies associated with the approach. For example, the claim process would be dramatically streamlined, and marketing costs would be virtually eliminated. Furthermore, the widespread availability of medical care would probably lead to more preventive care, which would minimize the need for more expensive treatments in the future.

Much of the support for a single-payer approach to the health care problem arises from the perception that Americans have of the Canadian health care system. There is no doubt that Canadians overwhelmingly believe they have a good system, but just as in the United States the system is becoming a subject of national debate. Costs are lower than in the United States, but they are increasing at a rapid rate. Moreover, there is rationing of care, which can lead to lengthy waits to schedule surgeries. As a result some Canadians come to the United States for treatment that privately insured Americans can receive upon demand. These facts, coupled with the American public's concern over bigger government and its bureaucracy, make the adoption of a single-payer approach unlikely.

Medical Savings Accounts

Unlike the two previous approaches to national health insurance, the use of medical savings accounts is seldom proposed as the sole method of providing medical expense coverage. Instead, their use is an option that would be available to employers. Depending on the proposal, employers might use this approach for all employees or let employees choose a medical savings account in lieu of another form of medical expense coverage.

A medical savings account (MSA) is an alternative to a medical expense plan and it has few copayments. Instead an employee gets a comprehensive medical plan with virtually total coverage for medical expenses to the extent that they exceed a high deductible, such as $2,000. The employer then contributes part of the savings in premium to an MSA, which is often an interest-bearing account. An employee can draw from the account to pay medical expenses not covered by the medical expense plan, such as charges for routine office visits or the cost of eyeglasses. At the end of the year any monies in the MSA might be left in the MSA to pay future unreimbursed medical expenses or be paid to the employee.

The rationale for a medical savings account is that significant cost savings can occur for two primary reasons. First, the expensive cost of administering small claims is largely eliminated, as demonstrated by the fact that a major medical policy with a $2,500 deductible can often be purchased for about one-half the cost of a policy with a $250 deductible. Second, employees now have a direct financial incentive to avoid unnecessary care and to seek out the most cost-effective form of treatment.

A few employers have used medical savings accounts for some time with positive results. Costs have in fact been lowered or risen less rapidly than would otherwise be expected. Reactions of employees have generally been favorable, but there has been one major drawback—contributions to an MSA have constituted taxable income to employees. However, as described later in chapter 10, this issue has been addressed by recent legislation.

As with almost any approach to cost containment, medical savings accounts have their critics. It is argued that MSAs may make sense when used with traditional indemnity plans, but long-term health care reform should focus on managed care. However, proponents counter that the concept could also work with HMOs or PPOs. Another argument against MSAs is that employees will minimize treatment for minor medical expenses and preventive care that would have been covered under a plan without an MSA. This avoidance of medical care, contend the critics, may lead to major expenses that could have been avoided or minimized with earlier treatment. A final criticism of MSAs is that they do not focus on the uninsured's problem. However, proponents argue that any technique that lowers costs for employers will encourage some additional small employers to provide coverage that would have previously been unaffordable.

State Reform

There is increasing support in Congress for the idea that national health insurance should take the form of a series of state programs rather than a single federal program. This support comes from many new members of Congress who are more amenable to having the states rather than the federal government solve some of the nation's problems. Support also comes from some state governors. Some other members of Congress, who might otherwise prefer a federal solution, feel that reform at the state level is preferable to partisan debate at the national level with little chance of any real reform.

In order to give the states flexibility in health care reform, it will be necessary for the states to be free of constraints such as ERISA. Without an ERISA preemption, states will be unable to apply reform to employees who are in self-funded plans, Employers who self-fund benefits, particularly those who have been successful with cost containment, will be reluctant to support such a change in federal law because it may ultimately result in increased costs, particularly if a state adopts some type of community rating. Self-funded employers that operate in many states would also be burdened by having to comply with each state's mandates.

An interesting paradox has developed in Congress. While Republican control has increased interest in letting the states solve problems, there is also increased sympathy for the wishes of business. As a result support for an ERISA preemption seems less likely than in the past.

Reform of the Current System

The 1994 elections, which resulted in a more conservative Congress, effectively ended any hopes of the Clinton administration for a major comprehensive restructuring of the nation's health care system. However, despite very divergent views in Washington, 1996 saw the most far-reaching federal legislation to affect medical expense insurance in many years. It was clear to all sides that the public strongly supported certain changes, and these changes were enacted with bipartisan support. In addition, each side seemed willing to give the other side a little bit of what it wanted. While the overall result is not a basic restructuring of the health care system, it clearly represents significant reform and change.

The primary piece of health care legislation in 1996 was the Health Insurance Portability and Accountability Act. Although a detailed discussion of many of the act's provisions appears in the appropriate sections of later chapters, these provisions can be summarized as follows:

- increased availability of medical expense coverage, discussed in the next section of this chapter
- a trial program of tax-favored medical savings accounts, discussed in chapter 10

- increased portability of medical expense coverage, discussed in chapter 12
- expansion of eligibility for COBRA benefits, discussed in chapter 12
- increased tax deductibility of medical expense premiums for the self-employed, discussed in chapter 12
- favorable income tax treatment for long-term care insurance, discussed in chapter 13

The Health Insurance Portability and Accountability Act was not the only 1996 legislation to affect group medical expense coverage. The Mental Health Parity Act will require many employers to provide increased benefits for mental illnesses. In addition, the Newborns' and Mothers' Health Protection Act may increase the length of inpatient benefits for childbirth in many cases. The effect of each act on medical expense plans is discussed in chapter 10.

For the foreseeable future, it appears that changes to the health care system will continue on a piecemeal approach to address specific issues and problems. For example, at the time this book is being revised, the Clinton administration is proposing legislation to make medical expense benefits available to more children.

Increased Availability of Medical Expense Coverage

The Health Insurance Portability and Accountability Act contains several provisions designed to help both employees and employers obtain coverage more easily. Portions of the act that deal with preexisting conditions are covered in a later chapter when the issue of eligibility is discussed. The discussion in this chapter focuses on the plans covered by the act and portions of the act that address nondiscrimination rules, special enrollment periods, renewability, and small groups.

The provisions discussed here generally become effective for plan years beginning after June 30, 1997. The effective date for plans established under collective-bargaining agreements will vary, depending on the dates a collective-bargaining agreement was ratified and expires.

Covered Plans

The act applies to *group health plans* that cover two or more employees, whether insured or self-funded. However, there is a long list of *excepted benefits,* to which the act does not apply. These include the following:

- coverage for accident or disability insurance, liability insurance or coverage issued as a supplement to liability insurance, workers' compensation insurance, automobile medical payments insurance, coverage for on-site medical clinics, and other similar insurance specified in regulations, under which benefits for medical care are secondary or incidental to other insurance benefits

- limited vision or dental benefits, long-term care insurance, nursing home insurance, home health care insurance, and insurance for community-based care if these benefits are offered separately rather than as an integral part of a medical expense plan
- coverage for a specific disease or illness, or hospital or other fixed indemnity insurance if the benefits are not coordinated with other coverage under a medical expense plan
- medicare supplement insurance or other similar supplemental coverage if the policy is offered as a separate insurance policy

With one exception, all employers—including the federal government—must comply with the act's provisions. Nonfederal government plans can elect to be excluded for a specific plan year.

Nondiscrimination Rules

The act prohibits the use of any of the following health-related factors as a reason to exclude an employee or dependent from coverage under a group health plan or to charge the individual or dependent a higher premium:

- health status
- medical condition, including both physical and mental condition
- claims experience
- receipt of health care
- medical history
- genetic information
- evidence of insurability, including conditions caused by domestic violence
- disability

It is important to note that these factors relate to coverage for specific individuals under a plan. The overall plan itself (except for plans in the small-group market, as explained later) can still be subject to traditional underwriting standards. In addition, group health plans are not required to offer any specific benefits and can limit benefit levels as long as they do not discriminate on the basis of these health-related factors. The act does not restrict the amount an insurance company or other provider of health care coverage can charge an employer for coverage. The act does allow an employer or provider of medical expense coverage to establish premium discounts or rebates or to modify copayments or deductibles for persons who adhere to programs of health promotion or disease prevention. For example, a lower premium can be given to nonsmokers.

Special Enrollment Periods

For various reasons, employees and their dependents may elect not to enroll in an employer's plan when they are initially eligible for coverage. For example, a new employee may have coverage under a spouse's plan. The act requires employers to allow these employees and dependents to enroll in the employer's plan under any one of several specified circumstances as long as the employee had previously stated in writing that the original declination was because there was other coverage. However, the requirement of a written declination does not apply unless the employer requires it and notifies the employee that it is a requirement for future coverage. The following are the circumstances for special enrollment:

- The other coverage was lost because of loss of eligibility under the other plan. This loss of eligibility can result from circumstances such as divorce, the spouse's termination of employment, or death.
- The other coverage was lost because employer contributions for the coverage terminated.
- The other coverage was COBRA coverage that is exhausted.

The employee has 30 days following the loss of coverage to request enrollment in the employer's plan.

In addition, new dependents (including children placed for adoption) are also eligible for coverage under special enrollment rules. The employee must enroll the dependent within 30 days of his or her gaining dependent status. Coverage for a new spouse must become effective no later than the first month beginning after the employee's request. However, coverage for children must go into effect as of the date of birth, adoption, or placement for adoption.

Guaranteed Renewability

All group health insurers must renew existing health insurance coverage unless one of the following circumstances exists:

- The plan sponsor failed to pay premiums or the issuer of health insurance coverage failed to receive timely premiums.
- The plan sponsor performed an act of fraud or made an intentional misrepresentation of material fact under the terms of the coverage.
- The plan sponsor failed to comply with a material plan provision relating to employer contribution or group participation rules as long as these rules are permitted under applicable state or federal law. For example, an employer might fail to maintain a minimum required percentage of participation under a plan.
- There is no covered employee who lives or works in the service area of a network plan such as an HMO.

- The employer is no longer a member of the association that sponsors a plan.
- The issuer of coverage ceases to offer coverage in a particular market. The issuer must notify each plan sponsor, participant, and beneficiary at least 90 days prior to the discontinuation of coverage, and the issuer must offer each plan sponsor the option to purchase other health insurance coverage currently being offered by the issuer to a group health plan in the market. If the issuer exits the market entirely, the period of notice is 180 days, and the issuer cannot reenter the market and sell health insurance coverage for at least 5 years.

Similar rules require multiemployer plans and multiple-employer welfare arrangements to renew coverage for employers. It also establishes guaranteed-issue rules for the individual marketplace.

Guaranteed Issue for Small-Group Plans

With some exceptions, the act requires insurers, HMOs, and other providers of health care coverage that operate in the small-group market to accept all small employers—defined as employers with two to 50 employees—that apply for coverage. In addition, all employees of small employers and their dependents must be accepted for coverage as long as they enroll during the period in which they are first eligible. This rule is in line with the small-group legislation of many states. However, some states have similar rules for groups as small as one employee or have an upper limit of 25, above which the small-group legislation does not apply.

Exceptions to this guaranteed-issue requirement are allowed if a provider of coverage in the small-group market has inadequate network or financial capacity or if applicants are not in a plan's service area.

Minimum participation or employer contribution requirements are acceptable as long as they are permitted under applicable state law.

Interrelationship of State and Federal Legislation

For the most part, the new federal legislation does not preempt state laws pertaining to group health insurance except in those situations where any state standard or requirement would prevent the application of the federal law. To prevent any preemption, most states will need to make some modifications to their laws and regulations. (As explained in a later chapter, the situation is different for the rules pertaining to preexisting conditions.)

The act permits a state to enforce its provisions with respect to insurance companies and other medical expense providers. However, the federal government can take over enforcement if a state does not perform its duties. In that case, enforcement will be by the secretary of health and human services. The secretary of labor has enforcement power for the act's provisions as they apply to group health plans themselves. When there is federal enforcement, the penalty for noncompliance can be up to $100 per day for each individual with respect to whom a plan or issuer is in noncompliance.

Group Medical Expense Benefits: Traditional Plans

Chapter Outline

Prior to the mid 1970s, most employees were covered by what are commonly referred to as traditional, or indemnity, plans. Medical expenses were incurred, patients had considerable freedom in choosing the providers of medical care, and claims were paid with virtually no attempts to control costs. As was pointed out in the previous chapter, many employees are still covered under plans that are largely traditional in nature. However, these plans have evolved.

While they are still far from what might be called managed care plans, these plans increasingly contain provisions designed to control costs and influence the behavior of persons needing medical care.

This chapter begins with a brief discussion of the providers of traditional medical expense coverage. It continues by first analyzing plans that provide basic coverage and then discussing major medical coverage. The chapter next reviews some managed care techniques that might be found in traditional plans. Other techniques are described where appropriate throughout the chapter.

The chapter concludes with a discussion of medical savings accounts. The rationale for including their coverage in this chapter is that almost all medical savings accounts being established are used in conjunction with traditional major medical plans that have a high deductible.

PROVIDERS OF TRADITIONAL COVERAGE

Providers of traditional coverage include Blue Cross–Blue Shield plans, insurance companies, and employers using self-funded arrangements, which are discussed in more detail in the chapter on alternative funding methods. While the plans described in this chapter are characteristic of those offered by the Blues and insurance companies, self-funded plans must be properly designed to be effective. Such plans have "borrowed" liberally from insured plans and contain similar—if not identical—provisions.

Blue Cross–Blue Shield Plans

Prior to the Great Depression "health" insurance contracts provided by insurance companies were primarily designed to give income benefits to persons who were disabled by accidents and, to a limited degree, illnesses. However, it was generally accepted that individuals should pay their own medical expenses from their savings. During the depression the savings of many individuals disappeared, unemployment was severe, and most insurance companies ceased writing disability income contracts. Faced with financial difficulties arising from the inability of many patients to pay their bills, many hospitals established plans for the prepayment of hospital expenses. By paying a monthly fee to the hospital, a subscriber (the term used to describe persons covered by such plans) was entitled to a limited number of days of hospitalization per year. The early plans were limited to a single hospital, but by the mid-1930s many plans had become communitywide or statewide operations, offering subscribers the choice of using any participating hospital. Much of this expansion resulted from actions by the American Hospital Association to promote and control this type of plan. In the late 1930s the American Hospital Association adopted the Blue Cross name and emblem and permitted them to be used only by plans that met standards established by the association. As a general rule only one plan within a geographic area was allowed to use the Blue Cross name. Eventually the Blue

Cross activities of the American Hospital Association were transferred to a separate national organization, the Blue Cross Association.

The success of the early Blue Cross plans and the inability of physicians to collect bills for their services during the depression resulted in the development of Blue Shield plans, established by local medical associations to prepay physicians' charges. The evolution of Blue Shield plans has paralleled that of Blue Cross plans, with the American Medical Association acting similarly to the American Hospital Association. Eventually the role of the American Medical Association was transferred to the National Association of Blue Shield Plans, which then became the national coordinating body.

To a large extent the persons covered by Blue Shield plans were the same ones whose hospital charges were covered by Blue Cross plans, and in many geographic regions this overlapping led to a close working relationship between the two. For many years in some areas of the country, one plan administered the other. However, this administration was typically on a fee-for-administration basis, with the two plans being separate legal entities. In recent years there has been a consolidation of most Blue Cross and Blue Shield plans. Usually this consolidation has taken the form of a complete merger; in a few cases the consolidation has only been partial. These partial consolidations have resulted in Blue Cross–Blue Shield plans that operate under a single staff but with separate governing boards.

There has been consolidation at the national level also. In 1978 the staffs of the two national organizations were merged, and a new organization—the Blue Cross and Blue Shield Associations—was formed to act on matters of mutual interest to both Blue Cross plans and Blue Shield plans. It was governed by members of the boards from both the Blue Cross Association and the National Association of Blue Shield Plans. In 1982 a complete merger took place with the resulting organization called the Blue Cross and Blue Shield Association.

As of mid-1997 there were 49 plans in existence that jointly wrote Blue Cross and Blue Shield coverage. In addition, there were six separate Blue Cross plans and four separate Blue Shield plans. Although most states are served by a single Blue Cross–Blue Shield plan, in a few states there is more than one plan, each operating within a specific geographic region. In a few instances plans may cover more than one state. Only in rare cases is there any overlapping of the geographic areas served by individual plans.

Each local Blue Cross, Blue Shield, or Blue Cross–Blue Shield plan is a legally separate entity operated by a governing board, which establishes specific practices for the plan in accordance with the broad standards of the national Blue Cross and Blue Shield Association. Consequently individual plans may differ substantially from one another. The boards of these plans used to be dominated by the providers of coverage, but now the boards of most plans are dominated by "nonproviders," including representatives of consumer organizations, foundations, labor unions, businesses, and the general public.

Traditionally Blue Cross and Blue Shield plans have been nonprofit corporations and acted as insurers of last resort in most states. This meant that they wrote coverage on almost anyone at competitive rates. For this, the Blues tended to receive favorable tax treatment. However, as insurance companies and HMOs expanded market share, they tended to take the better business and leave the Blues with books of business that had an increasing number of unhealthy lives. As a result, the Blues have become more restrictive in their underwriting practices. In addition, a few of the Blues have changed to for-profit status in order to raise the capital necessary to compete more effectively with other types of providers of medical expense coverage. Many of the Blues also own subsidiaries that are run to make a profit.

Insurance Companies

For many years, Blue Cross and Blue Shield plans were the predominant providers of medical expense coverage; insurance companies were much slower to enter the market and took a different approach. Rather than emphasizing basic first-dollar coverage for hospital or physicians' charges, most insurers chose to write major medical coverage with deductibles and coinsurance. By the mid-1950s insurance companies surpassed the Blues in premium volume for medical expense coverage.

Like other types of insurance, medical expense coverage is written by both stock and mutual insurance companies. While some coverage is written by insurers that specialize in the medical expense market, the majority of the premium volume for group coverage is written by large life insurance companies. It is interesting to note that medical expense coverage is also a line of insurance sometimes written by property-casualty insurance companies.

A Comparison of the Blues and Insurance Companies

Perhaps the best way to describe the characteristics of Blue Cross–Blue Shield plans and insurance company plans is to compare their characteristics. Traditionally the similarities between the Blues and insurance companies were overshadowed by their differences. Over time, however, intense competition has often caused one type of provider to adopt the more popular but differing practices of the other. As a result insurance companies and the Blues are becoming increasingly similar, in spite of their many distinctly different characteristics.

Regulation and Taxation

In a few states, Blue Cross–Blue Shield plans are regulated under the same laws that apply to insurance companies. However, in most states the Blues are nonprofit organizations and are regulated under special legislation. Typically this regulation is carried out by the same body that regulates insurance companies. However, in some respects the Blues receive preferential treatment over insurance companies, probably the most significant example being their exemption from premium taxation and income taxation by the majority of states. Since premium taxes (usually about 2 percent of premiums) are passed on to consumers, this gives the Blues a cost advantage. In many other respects, however, the Blues are subject to more stringent regulation than insurance companies. For example, in most states their rates are subject to regulatory approval. With recent trends toward consumerism, this approval has become more burdensome and expensive.

In addition, the Blues are also accorded favorable tax treatment under the federal income tax laws. Prior to the Tax Reform Act of 1986 the Blues (except for the few plans that were incorporated as insurance companies) were exempt from federal income taxation. The tax act eliminated this complete exemption. Because of various deductions that can be taken, however, the average effective tax rate for the Blues is significantly below the average tax rate for insurance companies.

Form of Benefits

Traditionally the Blues have offered benefits in the form of services, while insurance companies have offered benefits on an indemnity (or reimbursement) basis. Under the service-benefit concept, benefits are expressed in terms of the services that will be provided by the hospitals or physicians participating in the plan rather than in terms of dollar maximums. For example, a Blue Cross plan might provide up to 90 days of hospitalization per year in semiprivate accommodations. In contrast, an insurance company might provide reimbursement for hospital charges subject to both dollar and duration limits, such as $400 per day for 90 days. In both cases, however, any charges in excess of the benefits must be borne by the covered person.

Blue Cross–Blue Shield plans involve two separate types of contractual relationships: a plan promises to provide specified services to a subscriber for whom a premium has been paid, and it has contracts with providers of services whereby the providers are reimbursed for the cost of services rendered to subscribers. In general subscribers are not billed for the cost of covered services or required to file claim forms. Rather, this cost is negotiated between the plan and the providers. This type of arrangement generally requires that subscribers receive their services from providers participating in the plan; however, most hospitals and physicians are participants. If nonparticipating providers can be used (such as for emergencies), benefits are usually paid on an indemnity basis, as is done by insurance companies.

In contrast, an insurance company agrees only to reimburse a covered person for medical expenses up to the limits specified in the insurance contract. There is no contractual relationship between the providers of medical services and the insurance company. Thus covered persons must file the appropriate claim forms. While covered persons have a legal obligation to pay their medical bills, the insurance company's obligation (unless benefits are assigned) is only to reimburse the covered person, not to actually pay the providers. However, most hospitals and many other providers require that any potential insurance benefits be assigned to them by a patient before they will render services. In effect, such an assignment requires the insurance company to pay benefits directly to the provider on behalf of the covered person.

In the past insurance companies incorporated maximum daily room and board limits into their contracts that did not cover medical expenses in full. However, to compete with the Blues, many insurance companies now frequently write contracts that provide full reimbursement for certain medical expenses. Even though a covered person may see little difference in the benefits received from either type of provider, the traditional distinction still exists: the Blues are providing services while insurance companies are providing reimbursement for the cost of services.

Types of Benefits

Over the years the Blues have specialized in providing basic medical benefits, with Blue Cross providing coverage for hospital expenses and Blue Shield providing coverage for surgical expenses and physicians' visits. Major medical benefits were rarely available. However, competition from insurance companies and increased cooperation between Blue Cross and Blue Shield have resulted in the Blues' now offering virtually the same coverages as insurance companies. It is interesting to note that as the Blues have expanded the scope of benefits offered, they have frequently included deductible and coinsurance provisions similar to those used by insurance companies. When there is a deductible, a covered person is required to pay expenses up to some limit (such as $100 per year or per illness) out of his or her own pocket before benefits will be paid. When coinsurance is used, a covered person is required to pay a percentage (such as 20 percent) of some or all expenses, the remaining portion being covered under the medical expense plan.

The advantage many insurance companies have had over the Blues has been their ability to offer a wide variety of group benefits, including life insurance coverage and disability income coverage. Until a few years ago most states had laws and regulations that prevented the Blues from offering any coverage other than medical expense benefits. However, because of changes in these laws and regulations, the Blues can now offer a wider range of group benefits to their subscribers. While competition between the Blues and insurance companies over writing these other benefits is increasing, the Blues currently write relatively little coverage other than medical expense benefits.

Reimbursement of Providers

The method by which the Blues reimburse the providers often results in their having a competitive advantage over insurance companies. Most Blue Cross plans pay participating hospitals on a per diem basis for each day a subscriber is hospitalized. Periodic negotiations with Blue Cross determine the amount of this payment (which includes room-and-board charges as well as other covered charges) for each hospital. For example, if the per diem amount is $600, the hospital will receive $600 for each day a subscriber is hospitalized, regardless of what the actual charges might be. While this per diem amount will be adequate on the average, the hospital will "lose money" on some patients but "make money" on others.

In addition to the administrative simplicity of this method of reimbursement, the per diem amount is often less than the average daily hospital charges. Frequently it is determined by excluding such hospital costs as bad debts, charity care, and nursing school costs. These costs, however, are used in determining charges for patients who are not Blue Cross subscribers. Therefore Blue Cross subscribers in effect receive a discount on the charges made to other patients, including those whose benefits are provided by insurance companies. This discount (except to the extent that it results from administrative savings) has not been allowed in some states and has come under increasing criticism where it is the normal practice. In general its size has been reduced in recent years, often due to legislation or regulation. There have been some experimental attempts by insurance companies to lower their cost of claims handling by using a similar reimbursement procedure with hospitals.

Under some Blue Shield plans physicians may also be reimbursed at less than their actual charges, as will be discussed later in this chapter.

National Coverage

While Blue Cross–Blue Shield plans operate in precise geographic regions, many insurance companies operate on a national basis. Therefore the Blues have had a more difficult time competing with insurance companies for the group insurance business of employers whose employees are located in areas served by various Blue Cross–Blue Shield plans. Even though the Blues have developed procedures for providing coverage to these "national accounts," most benefits specialists seem to feel that insurance companies have the competitive advantage in this regard.

Flexibility

There also seems to be a feeling among benefit consultants that insurance companies have a greater degree of flexibility in modifying their group contracts to meet employers' needs and desires. Blue Cross–Blue Shield contracts have traditionally been quite standardized, with few, if any, variations allowed. One major reason for this rigidity is that changes in the benefits promised to subscribers also have an effect on the contracts between the Blues and the providers. However, with employers increasingly wanting new approaches to medical expense benefits, often for cost-containment reasons, many Blue Cross–Blue Shield plans have taken a more flexible approach. Many variations exist among plans, and some have been very innovative in meeting the demands of the marketplace, even going as far as to administer benefit plans that are self-funded by employers.

Rating

In their early years the Blues used only a "community-rating" approach in determining what premium rates to charge. Under this approach each plan uses the same rate structure for all subscribers, regardless of their past or potential loss experience and regardless of whether coverage is written on an individual or a group basis. Usually the only variations in the rate structure result from variations in coverage: whether it is for an individual, a couple without children, or a family. The philosophy behind the community-rating approach is that coverage should be available to the widest range of persons possible at an affordable cost. Charging lower premium rates to segments of the community with better-than-average loss experience is thought to result in higher and possibly unaffordable premium rates for other segments of the community.

Community rating placed Blue Cross and Blue Shield at a competitive disadvantage when insurance companies began to aggressively market group medical expense insurance and use experience rating, which allowed them to charge certain employer groups much lower premiums than those charged by the Blues. As a result by the mid-1950s insurance companies surpassed the Blues in the number of persons covered. Faced with the growing dilemma that rate increases necessary to compensate for the loss of better-than-average business tended to drive even more business to the insurance companies, the Blues initiated the use of experience rating for groups. Today there is little difference in this regard between these two major providers with respect to group business. However, the Blues still use community rating in pricing products for smaller employers and for the individual marketplace.

Marketing

The Blues tend to have lower acquisition expenses than insurance companies, and most coverage is marketed by salaried employees. However, more than half of the plans also market coverage through agents and/or brokers in addition to their own sales forces. In general the commissions paid to agents or brokers are below the commissions paid by insurance companies.

BASIC MEDICAL EXPENSE COVERAGES

Historically medical expense coverage consisted of separate benefits for hospital expenses, surgical expenses, and physicians' visits. Coverage was limited, and many types of medical expenses were not covered. In this environment two developments took place: basic coverages for other types of medical expenses were developed, and a vast majority of employers began to provide more extensive benefits to employees than had previously been available through the commonly written basic coverages. While this broader coverage is often provided through a single comprehensive contract, many employees are still covered under medical expense plans that consist of selected basic coverages supplemented by a major medical contract. This is particularly true for large employers, while small employers are much more likely to use a single major medical contract. Basic coverages consist of the three traditional coverages for

- hospital expense benefits
- surgical expense benefits
- physicians' visits expense benefits

as well as the following newer coverages for

- extended care facilities
- home health care
- hospice care
- ambulatory care
- birthing centers
- diagnostic X-ray and laboratory services
- radiation therapy
- supplemental accident benefits
- prescription drugs
- vision care

While many of these coverages can be written separately, it is not unusual for them to be incorporated into a single contract. Many of the medical expenses for which basic benefit coverage is either limited or excluded would be covered under a supplemental major medical contract.

Hospital Expense Benefits

Hospital expense coverage provides benefits for charges incurred in a hospital by a covered person (that is, the employee or his or her dependents) who is an inpatient or, in some circumstances, an outpatient. Every medical expense contract defines what is meant by a hospital. While the actual wording may vary among insurance companies and in some states, the following definition is typical:

The term *hospital* means (1) an institution that is accredited as a hospital under the hospital accreditation program of the Joint Commission on Accreditation of Healthcare Organizations or (2) any other institution that is legally operated under the supervision of a staff of physicians and with 24-hour-a-day nursing service. In no event should the term *hospital* include a convalescent nursing home or include any institution or part thereof that (1) is used principally as a convalescent facility, rest facility, nursing facility, or facility for the aged; or (2) furnishes primarily domiciliary or custodial care, including training in the routines of daily living; or (3) is operated primarily as a school.

Inpatient Benefits

Hospital inpatient benefits fall into two categories: coverage for room-and-board charges and coverage for "other charges."

Room and Board. Coverage for room-and-board charges includes the cost of the hospital room, meals, and the services normally provided to all inpatients, including routine nursing care. Separate charges for such items as telephones and televisions are usually not covered. Benefits are normally provided for a specific number of days for each separate hospital confinement, a time period that may vary from 31 days to 365 days. Some contracts provide coverage for an unlimited number of days. For purposes of this time period as well as for other benefits, most contracts stipulate that successive periods of hospital confinement will be treated as a single hospital confinement unless they (1) arise from entirely unrelated causes or (2) are separated by the employee's return to continuous full-time active employment for some period of time, such as 2 weeks. For dependents this latter requirement is replaced by one specifying that they must completely recover or remain out of the hospital for some period of time, such as 3 months.

The amount of the daily room-and-board benefit may be expressed in one of two ways: either a flat-dollar maximum or the cost of semiprivate accommodations. Under the first approach benefits are provided for actual room-and-board charges up to a maximum daily amount, such as $500. Employers using this approach may have different maximum benefits for employees in different locations to reflect geographic variations in hospital costs.

The majority of hospital expense contracts cover actual room-and-board charges up to the cost of semiprivate accommodations (that is, two-person rooms) in the hospital in which the covered person is confined. This is the traditional approach used by Blue Cross plans and increasingly used by insurance companies. The cost of a private room may be covered in full if it is medically necessary. If not, covered persons electing such accommodations must usually pay any charges above the normal semiprivate room rate. However, a few insurance plans provide additional coverage, usually a fixed daily dollar amount, for elective private room occupancy.

Many hospital expense contracts include additional room-and-board benefits for confinement in an intensive care unit. In some cases, particularly when normal room-and-board benefits are subject to a dollar maximum, intensive care benefits are expressed as some multiple (commonly two) of the normal room-and-board benefit. In those cases where benefits are provided for the cost of semiprivate accommodations, intensive care charges are frequently covered in full. However, in both cases intensive care benefits may be subject to either a time limit or an overall dollar maximum.

Other Charges. Coverage for "other charges" (often referred to as miscellaneous charges, ancillary charges, or hospital extras) provides benefits for certain services and supplies ordered by a physician during a covered person's hospital confinement, such as drugs, operating room charges, laboratory services, and X rays. However, with a few exceptions only the hospital portion of these charges is covered; any associated charges for professional services such as physicians' fees are not covered. The exceptions often include charges for anesthesia and ambulance services. Traditionally anesthesia and its administration were provided and billed by the hospital and considered a covered expense. As anesthesia came to be administered and separately billed by physicians not employed by the hospital, many hospital expense benefit contracts were altered to cover anesthesia if it was administered in a hospital, whether the patient was billed by the hospital or by a physician. Recently, however, the trend has been toward covering anesthesia as a surgical expense benefit instead of a hospital expense benefit.

The amount of the benefit for other charges is usually expressed in one of the following three ways:

- full coverage up to a dollar maximum. This approach is most commonly found in contracts when the daily room-and-board benefit is also subject to a dollar limit. In most cases this maximum is some multiple (often 20) of the daily room-and-board benefit. For example, a contract with a daily room-and-board benefit of $500 might have a $10,000 maximum for other charges.
- full coverage up to a dollar maximum (again, often expressed as a multiple of the room-and-board benefit) and partial coverage for a limited amount of additional expenses. For example, a contract might cover the first $2,000 of charges in full and 75 percent of the next $3,000 in charges.
- full payment subject only to the duration for which room-and-board benefits are payable. While this approach is normally associated with contracts that provide room-and-board benefits equal to the cost of semiprivate accommodations, it may also be used when room-and-board benefits are subject to a daily maximum.

When coverage for ambulance services is provided, it is common to limit the benefit to a dollar maximum, such as $50 per hospital confinement. A few plans have a mileage limit in lieu of a dollar limit.

Preadmission Certification. As a method of controlling costs medical expense plans are increasingly adopting utilization review programs. One aspect of these programs, discussed in the previous chapter, is preadmission certification. Such a program requires that a covered person or his or her physician obtain prior authorization for any nonemergency hospitalization. Authorization usually must also be obtained within 24 to 48 hours of admissions for emergencies.

The initial reviewer, typically a registered nurse, determines whether hospitalization or some type of alternative care is most appropriate and what the appropriate length of stay for the medical condition should be. If the preapproved length of stay is insufficient, the patient's physician must obtain prior approval for any extension.

Most plans reduce benefits if the preadmission certification procedure is not followed. Probably the most common reduction is to pay only 50 percent of the benefit that would otherwise be paid. If a patient enters the hospital after a preadmission certification has been denied, many plans will not pay for any hospital expenses, whereas other plans will provide a reduced level of benefits.

Outpatient Benefits

Although hospital expense contracts did not originally cover outpatient expenses, today it is common to find coverage for such expenses arising from the following:

- surgery. When the coverage for surgery performed on inpatients is broader than the coverage for surgery on outpatients, there is no question that unnecessary hospitalization is encouraged. The purpose of this benefit is to provide comparable coverage and thus lower hospital utilization (when surgical procedures can be performed on an outpatient basis). It should be noted that this benefit covers only hospital charges (such as the use of operating facilities), not the surgeon's fee.
- preadmission testing. The first day or two of hospital confinement, particularly for surgical procedures, were historically devoted to necessary diagnostic tests and X rays. This benefit encourages the performance of these procedures on an outpatient basis prior to hospitalization by covering the costs as if the person was an inpatient. For benefits to be paid, these procedures must generally be (1) performed after a hospital confinement for surgery has been scheduled, (2) ordered by the same physician who ordered the hospital confinement, (3) performed in the hospital where the confinement will take place, and (4) accepted by the hospital in lieu of the same tests that would normally be performed during confinement. Benefits are paid even if the preadmission testing leads to a cancellation of the scheduled confinement.
- emergency room treatment. Hospital expense contracts commonly provide coverage for emergency room treatment of accidental injuries within some specified time period (varying from 24 to 72 hours) after an

accident. In a few cases similar benefits are also provided for sudden and serious illnesses. It should be noted that any emergency room charges incurred immediately prior to hospitalization are considered inpatient expenses.

In most cases these outpatient expenses are treated like other charges, but in some hospital expense plans, separate benefits may apply to outpatient surgery and emergency room treatment.

Exclusions

While variations exist among the providers of hospital coverage (some of which result from state legislation), most hospital expense contracts do not usually cover expenses resulting from the following:

- occupational injury or disease to the extent that benefits are provided by workers' compensation laws or similar legislation. Many contracts exclude coverage for benefits available through workers' compensation laws. Thus work-related hospital expenses are excluded even if the employer has not purchased workers' compensation coverage.
- cosmetic surgery unless such surgery is to correct a condition resulting from an accidental injury incurred while the covered person is insured under the contract
- physical examinations (including diagnostic tests and X rays) unless such examinations are necessary for the treatment of an injury or illness
- convalescent, custodial, or rest care
- private-duty nursing
- services furnished by or on behalf of government agencies unless there is a requirement for either the patient or the patient's medical expense plan to pay for the services. Prior to the passage of the Consolidated Omnibus Budget Reconciliation Act of 1985, it was common for employee benefit plans to exclude payment for medical services received in a Veterans' Administration or military hospital since the patient had no legal obligation to pay. Under provisions of the act medical expense plans must generally pay benefits to the government on the same basis as they would have paid if care had been received elsewhere. However, if a plan does not pay charges in full because of deductibles, coinsurance, or plan limitations, the patient is not responsible for the balance. With respect to VA hospitals the provisions of the act apply only to non-service-connected disabilities. The rules for military hospitals apply to retired (but not active) members of the armed services and most spouses and dependent children of active or retired military persons.

Mental Illness, Alcoholism, and Drug Addiction. In the absence of state mandates to the contrary, some hospital expense contracts either exclude (or provide limited benefits for) expenses arising from mental illness, alcoholism, and/or drug addiction. Benefit plans that cover more than 50 employees and that have benefit limitations pertaining to mental illness must be in compliance with the Mental Health Parity Act for plan years beginning on or after January 1, 1998. This act is discussed in more detail later in this chapter under the section on major medical coverage. It should be noted that most limitations in hospital expense contracts are probably consistent with the new legislation.

Maternity. Until the amendment in the Civil Rights Act in 1978 it was not unusual to exclude maternity-related expenses from hospital expense contracts. However, the act now requires that benefit plans of employers with 15 or more employees treat pregnancy, childbirth, and related conditions the same as any other illness. (See the discussion in the chapter on the governmental environment for group insurance.)

In the absence of state laws to the contrary, pregnancy may be and is sometimes excluded under group insurance contracts written for employers with fewer than 15 employees. If these employers wish to provide such coverage, it can usually be added as an optional benefit. In some cases pregnancy is treated like any other illness covered under the contract. In other cases benefits are determined in accordance with a schedule that most commonly provides an all-inclusive benefit for hospital, surgical, and certain other expenses associated with delivery. Regular physician visits and diagnostic tests may or may not be covered. Table 10-1 is an example of a maternity schedule.

TABLE 10-1	
Type of Pregnancy	**Benefit**
Normal Delivery	$1,500
Cesarean	3,000
Miscarriage	750

A variation of this schedule that is often used by Blue Cross–Blue Shield plans provides a surgical benefit (possibly including visits prior to delivery) but covers hospital expenses on a semiprivate room basis.

An expense associated with maternity is the nursery charge for a newborn infant, which in most cases will be equal to at least 50 percent of a hospital's normal room-and-board charge. This expense is not covered as part of a maternity benefit and is not covered under many hospital expense contracts if the infant is healthy (since the contract covers only expenses associated with accidents and illnesses). However, some contracts do cover nursery charges, and a number of states require that they be covered.

Beginning with plan years on or after January 1, 1998, group health plans are subject to the provisions of the Newborns' and Mothers' Health Protection Act. This federal act is very broad and, with one exception, applies to all employers regardless of size and to self-funded plans as well as those written by health insurers and managed care plans. The exception is for plans subject to similar state legislation, which exist in over half the states. The impetus for such legislation at both the state and federal level arose over consumer backlash from the practice of an increasing number of HMOs and insurance companies limiting maternity benefits to 24 hours after a normal vaginal birth and 48 hours after a cesarean section. The act affects maternity benefits if they are provided. It does not mandate that such benefits be included in benefit plans. Of course, many employers are subject to other state and federal laws that do mandate maternity benefits.

The act prohibits a group health plan or insurer from restricting hospital benefits to less than 48 hours for both the mother and the newborn following a normal vaginal delivery and 96 hours following a cesarean section. In addition, a plan cannot require a provider to obtain authorization from the plan or insurer for a stay that is within these minimums. While a new mother, in consultation with her physician, might agree to a shorter stay, a plan or insurer cannot offer a monetary incentive to the mother for this purpose. In addition, the plan or insurer cannot limit provider reimbursement because care was provided within the minimum limits or make incentives available to providers to render care inconsistent with the minimum requirements.

If a plan has deductibles, coinsurance, or other cost-sharing requirements, these cannot be greater than those imposed on any preceding portion of the hospital stay.

The Newborns' and Mothers' Health Protection Act treats the imposition of the minimum-stay requirement as a material modification for purposes of ERISA and requires each plan sponsor to provide a summary of material modification to plan participants and the Department of Labor within 60 days after the start of the plan year (rather than the usual 210 days after the end of the plan year) for which the requirements apply.

Deductibles and Coinsurance

It is common for deductibles and coinsurance to apply to major medical expense coverages. In contrast, hospital expenses under basic hospital expense coverage (and benefits under other basic medical expense coverages as well) are usually not subject to deductibles or coinsurance. Rather, any limitations that exist are most likely to be in the form of maximum amounts that will be paid. It should be noted, however, that deductibles and coinsurance are more likely to be used for basic coverages than was once the case.

Surgical Expense Benefits

Surgical expense coverage provides benefits for physicians' charges associated with surgical procedures. While one tends to think of a surgical procedure as involving cutting, insurance contracts typically define the term broadly to include such procedures as suturing, electrocauterization, removal of a stone or foreign body by endoscopic means, and the treatment of fractures or dislocations.

Even though surgical expense coverage is frequently sold in connection with hospital expense coverage, surgical expense coverage normally provides benefits for surgery performed not only in the hospital (either as an inpatient or an outpatient), but also as an outpatient in a free-standing (that is, separate from a hospital) ambulatory surgical center and in a physician's office. To discourage unnecessary hospitalization, some surgical expense benefit contracts actually provide larger benefits if a procedure is performed as outpatient surgery.

Outpatient surgery also results in charges for medical supplies, nurses, and the use of facilities. As mentioned, these charges are often covered if surgery is performed on an outpatient basis in a hospital. However, typically neither hospital expense coverage nor surgical expense coverage provides such benefits if the surgery is performed in a physician's office or in an ambulatory surgical center. Even though not specifically covered, costs of alternate facilities are paid by some insurance companies (and required by some states) when their use has clearly prevented hospital expenses from being incurred. As will be discussed later in this chapter, benefits for ambulatory care centers are sometimes included as an additional basic coverage.

Benefits

Surgical expense coverage traditionally provided benefits only for the fee of the primary surgeon. However, newer contracts often provide separate benefits for assistant surgeons and anesthesiologists as well. Since both hospital expense coverage and surgical expense coverage often cover anesthesia, it is important that an overall medical expense plan be properly designed to make sure this benefit is neither omitted nor overlapping. The major difficulty in this regard occurs when different providers are used for the hospital and surgical benefits.

Benefit amounts may be expressed in several ways, ranging from a schedule of fees to the full payment of actual charges.

Fee Schedule. In providing basic surgical expense benefits, some insurance companies and some Blue Shield plans use either a fee schedule or a relative value schedule in which charges are paid up to the maximum amounts specified in the schedule of surgical procedures in the master contract. It is common to refer to a fee schedule by the maximum amount that will be paid for the most expensive procedure, even though for the vast majority of procedures the benefits that will be paid are less, reflecting the relatively lower costs for such procedures. Table 10-2 is an excerpt from a $2,000 schedule.

TABLE 10-2	
Surgical Procedure	**Maximum Benefit**
Cardiovascular system	
Aortic valve replacement	$2,000
Pericardiectomy	1,200
Digestive system	
Adenoidectomy	100
Appendectomy	400
Tonsillectomy, under age 18 years	150
Tonsillectomy, over age 18 years	200
Respiratory system	
Pneumonectomy	1,000
Tracheotomy	200

The benefit specified in the schedule of surgical procedures is the maximum amount that will be paid to the primary surgeon for all charges, including follow-up visits. To the extent that the charges of the primary surgeon are below this amount, the balance can generally be applied to charges of assistant surgeons and possibly anesthesiologists. If separate benefits are provided for an assistant surgeon, they are usually a percentage, commonly 20 percent, of this amount. If benefits are provided for an anesthesiologist, a separate dollar maximum also varying by procedure will usually be specified. The typical fee schedule contains between 100 and 200 of the more common surgical procedures. When other surgical procedures are performed, payment is based on an amount determined by the insurance company but consistent with the fee schedule. For example, if the charge for an unlisted procedure is typically the same as for an appendectomy, the benefit maximum for that procedure will most likely be used. If more than one surgical procedure is performed at the same time, the total benefit is normally limited to the maximum benefit payable for the most expensive procedure plus 50 percent of the maximum benefit payable for any other procedures. However, usually no additional amounts will be paid for the second procedure if it is considered incidental and is performed through the same incision.

Relative-Value Schedule. A variation of the fee schedule is the relative-value schedule in which the value of each surgical procedure is expressed in unit values that are relative to each other. For example, a surgical procedure with the unit value of 50 is considered to be twice as expensive as one with a unit value of 25. These relative values are based on statistics from insurance companies or state medical associations and may vary depending on the source of the statistics. Table 10-3 is an excerpt from a relative-value schedule.

TABLE 10-3	
Surgical Procedure	**Relative-Value Units**
Skin	
Biopsy	3
Excision of pilonidal cyst	30
Stomach	
Excision of ulcer or tumor	60
Total gastrectomy	100

To determine the actual maximum benefit that will be paid, it is necessary to multiply the relative value by a dollar-conversion factor selected by the policyowner and specified in the master contract. For example, with a $20 conversion factor $60 would be paid for a skin biopsy and $1,200 for the removal of a stomach ulcer. Providers using relative-value schedules usually have the same schedule in all contracts but vary the levels of benefits for different policyowners by using different dollar-conversion factors. Employers can also take geographic variations in surgical costs into consideration by using different dollar-conversion factors for employees in different locations.

Reasonable-and-Customary Charges. The majority of surgical expense plans follow the approach used in major medical contracts and provide benefits to the extent that surgical charges are reasonable and customary. Unfortunately the precise meaning of these terms in insurance contracts is vague, and each company determines what it considers reasonable and customary. In general, reasonable-and-customary charges (sometimes referred to as usual, customary, and reasonable charges or prevailing charges) are considered to be those that fall within the range of fees normally charged for a given procedure by physicians of similar training and experience within a geographic region.

The usual practice of insurance companies is to pay charges in full as long as they do not exceed some percentile (usually ranging from the 85th to the 95th) of the range of charges for a specific surgical procedure within a certain geographic region. For example, if an insurance company uses the 90th percentile and if for a certain procedure 90 percent of the charges are $300 or less, this is the maximum amount that will be paid. The covered person will be required to absorb any additional charges if he or she uses a more expensive physician. Through the use of computers insurance companies now have statistics that categorize expenses by geographic regions that are as small as the zip codes of medical-care providers. Thus while $300 may be the maximum reasonable-and-customary amount in one part of a metropolitan area, $350 may be considered reasonable and customary in another part of the same metropolitan area.

Blue Shield plans often use a somewhat modified approach in determining the maximum amount that will be paid. Each year physicians file their charges for the coming year with the Blue Shield plan, and during that year the plan will pay charges in full up to some percentile of these filed charges. Under some plans the physicians agree not to charge Blue Shield patients amounts in excess of their filed fees. Participating physicians in other Blue Shield plans agree to accept any Blue Shield payment as payment in full, particularly for employees with an income level below a certain amount, such as $10,000 for an individual and $15,000 for a family.

Second Surgical Opinions

In an attempt to control medical costs by eliminating unnecessary surgery, many medical expense plans, both basic and major medical, now provide benefits for second surgical opinions. While such opinions undoubtedly cause some patients to decide against surgery, it is still unclear whether the cost savings of second surgical opinions are illusory. For example, surgery may still be required at a later date, or long-term costs for alternative treatment may be incurred.

A voluntary approach for obtaining second surgical opinions is often used. If a physician or surgeon recommends surgery, a covered person can seek a second opinion and the cost will be borne by the medical expense plan. In some instances the benefit is limited to a specific maximum, but in most cases the costs of the second opinion, including X rays and diagnostic tests, are paid in full. Some plans will also pay for a third opinion if the first two opinions disagree. When there are divergent opinions, the final choice is up to the patient, and the plan's regular benefits will usually be paid for any resulting surgery. As an incentive to encourage second opinions, some plans actually provide larger benefits for a covered person who has obtained a second opinion, even if it does not agree with the first opinion.

In the last few years it has become increasingly common for medical expense plans to require mandatory second opinions, which may apply to any elective and nonemergency surgery but frequently apply only to a specified list of procedures. In most cases a surgeon selected by the insurance company or other provider of benefits must give the second opinion. If conflicting opinions arise, a third opinion may be obtained. The costs of the second and third opinions are paid in full. In contrast to voluntary provisions, mandatory provisions generally specify that benefits will be paid at a reduced level if surgery is performed either without a second opinion or contrary to the final opinion.

The trend toward mandatory second opinions has had an interesting result. Since many employers felt money was being saved under their voluntary programs, wouldn't it be logical to save more money by making the program mandatory? Unfortunately the opposite situation has often been the case: people who voluntarily seek a second opinion are frequently looking for an alternative to surgery, while those who obtain a second opinion only because it is required are more likely to accept surgery as the best alternative. Employers have also found that a second opinion by a surgeon is still likely to call for surgery. As a result there seems to be a growing feeling that the cost of mandatory second opinions may exceed any decrease in surgical benefits paid. Consequently some employers have returned to voluntary programs or stopped providing coverage for second opinions altogether.

Exclusions

As with hospital expense coverage and virtually all other types of medical expense coverage, exclusions exist under basic surgical expense contracts for occupational injuries or disease, certain services provided by government agencies, and cosmetic surgery. All surgical expense contracts have an exclusion for certain types of dental surgery. However, the extent of the exclusion varies and care must be taken in properly integrating any dental coverage with other basic coverages. At one extreme some contracts exclude virtually any procedures associated with the teeth or disease of the surrounding tissue or bone structure. At the other extreme a more common exclusion eliminates coverage for most dental procedures but does provide surgical benefits if a covered person is hospitalized for the removal of impacted teeth or for surgery of the gums or bone structure surrounding the teeth. It is interesting to note that although benefits for oral surgery may not be paid even if a covered person is hospitalized, the hospital expenses are often covered under hospital expense contracts.

Physicians' Visits Expense Benefits

Physicians' visits expense coverage (often referred to as medical expense coverage or regular medical expense coverage) provides benefits for fees of attending physicians other than surgeons (since the charges of the latter are paid under surgical expense benefits coverage). Benefits are usually provided only for physicians' visits while a covered person is hospitalized. However, coverage may also include office and home visits.

In-Hospital Coverage

In-hospital coverage is designed to provide benefits for physicians' charges when a covered person is hospitalized as an inpatient. Three general approaches determine the amount and duration of benefits. Under one approach physicians' fees are paid on a reasonable-and-customary basis, up to a specific number of visits per hospitalization. In most cases this will correspond to the period of time for which hospital expense benefits are provided. Under the second approach benefits are limited to a daily maximum, again up to a specified period of time.

The daily maximum may be expressed as a dollar amount (such as $50) or as a relative value (such as 1.5) that is generally multiplied by the same dollar conversion factor applicable to surgical expense benefits. However, a separate conversion factor might be used. A difficulty with this approach is that physicians often charge more for initial hospital visits, so the daily maximum in some contracts is increased for the first day (or for 2 or 3 days) of hospitalization. The third approach expresses the total benefit as a lump-sum amount equal to the daily benefit times the number of days hospitalized. For example, if the daily benefit is $40 and the covered person is hospitalized for 10 days, physicians' charges would be paid in full up to $400, regardless of the charges incurred on any specific day or the number of visits made by the physician.

Three additional types of benefits are sometimes included when in-hospital coverage is provided:

- coverage for physicians' visits when a covered person is in an intensive care unit. If benefits are paid on a reasonable-and-customary basis, these charges will be covered in the same manner. Under plans with a daily maximum the maximum may be increased to reflect the more expensive charges normally associated with intensive care.
- coverage for consultation services. Although most plans cover only the charges of attending physicians, some plans provide benefits for the consultation services of other physicians. This benefit may be subject to a dollar maximum or paid on a reasonable-and-customary basis.
- coverage for physicians' visits in other types of medical care facilities, such as extended care centers. This benefit is most commonly provided when room-and-board charges for these alternative facilities are also covered.

In-Hospital and Out-of-Hospital Coverage

In addition to the benefits previously described, coverage for physicians' visits may also include physicians' charges incurred in a physician's office or in a covered person's home. This broader coverage is usually not written as a separate and distinct benefit but rather as a single overall coverage for all types of physicians' visits. Benefits may be paid on a reasonable-and-customary basis or be subject to a dollar maximum per visit. In the latter case it is not unusual to have two different dollar maximums: one for hospital visits and home visits and a lesser one for office visits. Benefits will be subject to some overall maximum limit, which may be expressed as either a dollar amount (such as $1,000) or a specified number of visits (such as 60). This limit may be applied on an annual basis or for any single illness or injury. Most plans contain a waiting period, commonly ranging from one to five visits, before benefits for home and office visits will be paid. However, this waiting period is often waived in the case of an accident.

Some plans also provide coverage for well-baby care, which includes benefits for inoculations and physicians' examinations (both in and out of the hospital) of healthy infants for a limited period of time, such as 3 months after birth. In addition, coverage sometimes includes benefits for hospital nursery charges. Some states require that medical expense contracts cover these benefits for newborns only until the infant is discharged from the hospital.

Exclusions

Most of the exclusions mentioned previously in connection with surgical expense coverage also apply to physicians' visits expense coverage. In addition to these exclusions, there are usually no benefits for physical examinations, eye examinations, or dentistry. Fees charged when a physician did not actually see a patient (such as for a telephone consultation) are often excluded. Finally, charges made by a physician who is a salaried staff member of a hospital are frequently not covered.

Other Benefits

When medical expense plans consist of basic coverages supplemented by major medical insurance, it is not unusual for the basic benefits to cover only hospital expenses, surgical expenses, and sometimes physicians' visits. Other types of basic benefits might also be provided, which in most cases cover expenses that either are included or may be included in a supplemental major medical contract. However, providing such coverage in the form of separate basic benefits may result in a greater reimbursement to an employee since deductibles and coinsurance often do not apply.

Extended Care Facility Benefits

Many hospital patients recover to a point where they no longer require the full level of medical care provided by a hospital, but they cannot be discharged because they still require a period of convalescence under supervised medical care. Extended care facilities (often called convalescent nursing homes or skilled-nursing facilities) have been established in many areas to provide this type of care. To the extent that patients can be treated in these facilities (which are often adjacent to hospitals), daily room-and-board charges can be reduced— often substantially. Obviously this type of care is discouraged if it is not covered on a comparable basis with confinement in a hospital. However, even when comparable coverage is provided, there seems to be a reluctance on the part of both patients and physicians to use such facilities. It becomes an additional facility for physicians to visit, and patients often express concern about the quality of care provided.

Extended care facility coverage provides benefits to the person who is an inpatient in an extended care facility, which is typically defined as an institution that furnishes room and board and 24-hour-a-day skilled-nursing care under the supervision of a physician or a registered professional nurse. It does not include facilities that are designed as a place for rest or domiciliary care for the aged. In addition, facilities for the treatment of drug abuse and alcoholism are often excluded from the definition.

To receive benefits the following conditions must usually be satisfied:

- The confinement must be recommended by a physician.
- Twenty-four-hour-a-day nursing care must be needed.
- The confinement must commence within (1) 14 days after termination of a specified period of hospital confinement (generally 3 days) for which room-and-board benefits were payable or (2) 14 days of a previous confinement in an extended care facility for which benefits were payable. A few but an increasing number of contracts include benefits for situations where extended care facilities are used in lieu of hospitalization.
- The confinement must be for the same or a related condition for which the covered person was hospitalized.

Benefits are provided in much the same manner as under hospital expense coverage. If hospital expense benefits are on a semiprivate accommodation basis, extended care facility benefits are generally paid on the same basis. If hospital expense benefits are subject to a daily dollar maximum, extended care facility benefits are usually likewise subject to a daily dollar maximum, most typically equal to 50 percent of the daily hospital benefit. The maximum length of time for which extended care benefits will be paid may be independent of the period of time for which a person is hospitalized, in which case a maximum of 60 days' coverage is fairly common. Alternatively the benefit period may be related to the number of unused hospital days. The most common approach in this instance is to allow 2 days in an extended care facility for each unused hospital day. For example, if a hospital expense plan provides benefits for a maximum period of 90 days and if a covered person is hospitalized for 50 days, the 40 unused hospital days can be exchanged for 80 days of benefits in an extended care facility. Other charges incurred in an extended care facility may be treated in one of several ways. They may be covered in full, subject to a separate dollar limit, or treated as part of the maximum benefit payable for other charges under hospital expense coverage.

Home Health Care Benefits

Home health care coverage is similar to extended care facility benefits but designed for those situations when the necessary part-time nursing care ordered by a physician following hospitalization can be provided in the patient's home. Coverage is for (1) nursing care (usually limited to a maximum of 2 hours per day) under the supervision of a registered nurse; (2) physical, occupational, and speech therapy; and (3) medical supplies and equipment, such as wheelchairs and hospital beds.

In most cases the benefits payable are equal to a percentage, frequently 80 percent, of reasonable-and-customary charges. Benefit payments are limited to either a maximum number of visits (such as 60 per calendar year) or to a period of time (such as 90 days after benefits commence). In the latter case the time period may be a function of the unused hospital days, such as 3 days of home visits for each unused hospital day.

Hospice Benefits

Hospices for the treatment of terminally ill persons are a recent development in the area of medical care. Hospice care does not attempt to cure medical conditions but rather is devoted to easing the physical and psychological pain associated with death. In addition to providing services for the dying patient, a hospice may also offer counseling to family members. While a hospice is usually thought of as a separate facility, this type of care can also be provided on an outpatient basis in the dying person's home. Where hospice care is available, the cost of treating terminally ill patients is usually much less than the cost of traditional hospitalization. Currently few benefit plans provide hospice coverage, but considerable interest in such coverage has been generated among employers as a means of controlling medical costs.

Ambulatory Care Expense Benefits

Recent years have seen the development of ambulatory care centers, often called surgicenters. These centers, designed for outpatient surgery, are separate from hospitals. Since such facilities fail to meet the definition of a hospital, benefits for their use are not included under hospital expense coverage. Consequently some basic medical expense plans provide benefits for ambulatory care expenses. Ambulatory care centers are generally defined as permanent facilities that (1) are operated primarily for the purpose of performing surgical procedures, (2) have continuous physician services and professional nursing services, and (3) do not provide services or other accommodations for patients to stay overnight. In most cases benefits are paid as if the covered person was an inpatient in a hospital. However, to encourage the use of such facilities as a less expensive alternative to hospitals, benefits may be paid at a higher level or even in full. Benefits cover any charges for use of the facility as well as other charges, such as medical supplies, X rays, and diagnostic tests.

Birthing Centers

Another recent development in medical care is birthing centers, which are designed to provide a homelike facility for the delivery of babies. Like ambulatory care centers, they are separate from hospitals.

The cost of using birthing centers is considerably less than using hospitals. Deliveries are performed by nurse-midwives, and mothers and babies are released shortly after birth. Benefits may be paid as if the mother had used a hospital and obstetrician but are frequently paid in full as an incentive to use these lower-cost facilities.

Diagnostic X-ray and Laboratory Expense Benefits

In recent years the use of diagnostic X rays (including CAT scans and MRIs) and laboratory services has increased substantially (often because of defensive medicine practiced by physicians). Under the previous coverages mentioned, benefits include the cost of these services if a covered person is an inpatient. However, outpatient benefits cover only costs connected with surgery at a hospital or ambulatory care center or preadmission testing. Diagnostic X-ray and laboratory coverage provides benefits for the cost of these services (including physicians' charges) when performed on an outpatient basis and when not otherwise covered under other portions of a basic medical expense plan. While benefits are usually provided for both illnesses and injuries, they may be provided only for illnesses if a medical expense plan contains a separate supplemental accident expense benefit (as is described later in this chapter).

Several approaches are used to provide diagnostic X-ray and laboratory coverage. One approach includes a schedule of procedures (similar to a surgical schedule) with maximum benefits specified for each procedure. Plans taking this approach usually contain a single overall maximum benefit or possibly separate overall maximum benefits for X rays and laboratory services. This maximum benefit may apply on a per-illness or per-injury basis or on an annual basis. A second approach covers all charges in full up to a specified maximum amount per procedure. A third approach pays benefits as if the X rays and laboratory examinations had been performed while the covered person was an inpatient in a hospital. In this situation the maximum benefit specified for other charges under hospital expense coverage applies to the aggregate of these outpatient charges and any other miscellaneous charges (associated with the same illness or injury) that are incurred while the covered person is hospitalized.

Since diagnostic X-ray and laboratory expense coverage is designed to complement other basic coverages, benefits that might be provided under these other coverages are generally excluded from diagnostic X-ray and laboratory expense coverage. In addition, exclusions generally exist for routine physical examinations and dentistry.

Radiation Therapy Expense Benefits

The use of radiation therapy is a common form of treatment for some illnesses, particularly cancer. Under the traditional basic coverages, benefits are provided under hospital expense coverage only as long as a covered person is hospitalized, so the primary purpose of radiation therapy expense benefits is to cover the cost of these treatments when performed on an outpatient basis. However, coverage may also be written to supplement any such benefits under hospital expense coverage. The use of radiation for diagnostic purposes is not covered because such coverage is provided by diagnostic X-ray and laboratory expense benefits. Coverage is often provided for the treatment of both malignant and benign conditions, but sometimes it is limited to cancerous conditions only.

Benefits are generally provided for the administration of the therapy, the use of facilities, and any materials and their preparation. Some insurance companies treat radiation therapy as a single category of benefits, while others divide it into two categories: treatments involving the use of X-ray machines and treatments involving the use of radioactive isotopes, radioactive iodine, or other radioactive substances that are applied to the body or taken internally. Benefits may be paid on a reasonable-and-customary basis or in accordance with a fee or relative-value schedule. An overall maximum limit (or limits if two categories of benefits are used) may also apply. This limit may be based on some time period, such as 12 months, or it may apply to the entire course of treatment for a condition, regardless of duration.

Prescription Drug Expense Benefits

With the exception of drugs administered in a hospital or in an extended care facility, the cost of prescription drugs is covered as a basic benefit only if prescription drug expense coverage is purchased. Although the cost of prescription drugs has typically been covered under major medical insurance, for a long time separate prescription drug plans have often been a result of collective bargaining even when there is a major medical plan. This benefit is highly visible to employees who periodically have prescriptions that must be filled either for themselves or for members of their family. Many benefit consultants also feel that a separate prescription drug plan may result in cost savings since the large number of relatively small claims lends itself to more economical methods of administration and processing of claims. As a result, many major medical plans carve out prescription drugs and provide them under a separate plan. However, this may also lead to a higher number of claims because of the elimination of the "shoe box effect." If a person must complete a claim form each time a prescription is filled, claims are often put aside (in a shoe box or elsewhere) and never filed. In a prescription drug plan without claim forms or with electronic filing, all claims are paid. However, the economies of a drug plan should more than offset any increase in the number of claims.

The cost of prescription drugs is over 10 percent of all medical expense claims and growing on a percentage basis. This increase results from several factors. One is the availability and prescribing of high-priced new pharmaceutical products. Another factor is increased use arising from several sources: the aging population, which uses more prescription drugs, and the shift from inpatient to outpatient treatment, resulting in more intensive pharmaceutical treatments. Finally, new drugs have been found for many previously untreatable conditions. As a result, managed care techniques have been applied to prescription drug plans in an attempt to control costs. It is common for prescription drug plans to have formal utilization review programs. Some plans do the review at the time a prescription is filled; others do the review retrospectively or use a combination of both approaches. As managed care has become more common, there is an increasing feeling that all medical treatment, including the use of prescription drugs, should be subject to a single system of management. As a result a few employers have backed away from separate carve-out plans, but incentives may still exist to encourage employees to use generic drugs and pharmacies that charge lower costs.

Pharmacy Benefit Managers. While separate prescription drug plans have existed for many years, the initial focus was on obtaining lower costs through discounts with participating pharmacies and mail-order suppliers of drugs. However, the situation changed significantly in the early 1980s when pharmacy benefit managers (PBMs) appeared in the marketplace. It has been estimated that by the mid-1990s more than 50 percent of prescription drugs were provided through PBMs, and that fewer than 10 large PBMs covered over 80 percent of the health plan participants who received drugs in this manner. PBMs may be affiliated with pharmaceutical companies or health care providers, such as insurance companies. They may also be independently owned.

PBMs administer prescription drug plans on behalf of self-funded employers, HMOs, PPOs, insurance companies, Blue Cross–Blue Shield plans, and third-party administrators. The on-line capabilities of PBMs enable them to offer considerable flexibility in designing a prescription drug program for a specific employer.

In addition to developing networks for the dispensing of prescription drugs, PBMs typically also do the following:

- drug utilization review. This practice compares information gathered from a patient's medical and prescription drug records to determine such factors as overutilization, underutilization, drug-to-drug interactions, improper drugs for pregnant patients, early refills, and therapeutic duplication.
- physician profiling and education. For example, physicians whose prescribing patterns lie outside acceptable variations from established benchmarks can be identified and counseled.
- pharmacy profiling and education. For example, pharmacies that recommend large amounts of brand-name drugs might be contacted about making more use of generic substitutions.
- patient profiling and education. For example, patients treated for hypertension can be identified and sent educational materials on their condition. This material focuses on the risks associated with the condition, safety issues associated with drug treatment, and the

importance of complying with prescribed drug regimens. Patients who fail to refill needed medication can also be identified and contacted.

PBMs are also increasingly developing disease management programs that focus on diagnostic aids identification, treatment guidelines, education, and outcomes measurement for specific diseases. PBMs may also be involved in the overall case management of a patient.

PBMs have been leaders in the integration of formularies into prescription drug plans. A formulary is a list, developed by a committee of pharmacists and physicians, of preferred medications for a specific medical condition. This list is provided to physicians with the hopes that it will positively affect their prescribing behavior. A formulary, for example, will let physicians know of approved uses of new drugs on the market, appropriate uses for existing drugs, and appropriate times to use generic and therapeutic substitutions. A therapeutic substitution is a drug with a similar therapeutic effect as the prescribed drug. Unlike generic substitution, which can often be made by patients or pharmacists, a physician's permission is needed for a therapeutic substitution.

Most prescription drug plans do not have a price differential for a patient if formulary drugs are not prescribed. However, PBMs will offer plans that either cover formulary drugs only or provide a financial incentive for patients to use them.

Nature of Plans. The typical prescription drug plan covers the cost of drugs (except those dispensed in a hospital or in an extended care facility) that are required by either state or federal law to be dispensed by prescription. Drugs for which prescriptions are not required by law are usually not covered even if a physician orders them on a prescription form. One frequent exception to this general rule is injectable insulin, which is generally covered despite the fact that in many states it is a nonprescription drug. No coverage is provided for charges to administer drugs or the cost of the therapeutic devices or appliances, such as bandages or hypodermic needles. It is also common to exclude benefits for a quantity of drugs in excess of a specified amount. In some plans this quantity is expressed as the amount normally prescribed by physicians; in other plans it is expressed as a supply for a certain time period, often 34 days. However, refills are considered new prescriptions.

Some plans cover maintenance drugs, such as medicine for the treatment of high blood pressure; other plans exclude them. Excluding these drugs, however, may be a false economy. Although the current cost of a prescription drug plan will be lower, medical conditions may remain untreated, and preventable surgical and hospital expenses may result. Contraceptive drugs may also be covered or excluded. Some prescription drug plans take a middle approach by covering these drugs only when they are prescribed for treating some medical condition rather than for preventing conception.

Most prescription drug plans have a deductible (often referred to as a copayment) that must be paid by a covered person for any prescriptions filled. In most cases this is a flat amount varying from $3 to $5 per prescription. Some plans have two copayments—one for generic drugs and a higher one for brand-name drugs. Some plans also provide financial incentives for prescriptions to be filled by mail-order pharmacies. A few plans have quarterly, semiannual, or annual spending caps. For example, benefits might be limited to $500 per person per quarter or $3,000 per year per family.

Two basic methods are used to provide prescription drug coverage: a reimbursement approach and a service approach. Under plans using a reimbursement approach, a covered individual personally pays the cost of prescription drugs. The person may be able to use any pharmacy he or she chooses or may be required to use a participating pharmacy. A claim for reimbursement is then filed with the provider of benefits, either by the employee or electronically by the pharmacy. Reimbursement (subject to any copayments) is made to the covered person on the basis of either billed charges or reasonable-and-customary charges.

While coverage for prescription drugs under major medical plans is often on a reimbursement basis, the majority of prescription drug plans use a service approach. Under this approach drugs are provided to covered persons by participating pharmacies upon receipt of a prescription, proper identification (usually a card issued by the plan), and any required copayments. The pharmacy then bills the provider of coverage (usually electronically) for the remaining cost of any prescription filled. This provider may be a PBM, a Blue Cross–Blue Shield association, an HMO, an insurance company, or a third-party administrator acting on behalf of either an insurance company or an employer with a self-insured plan. Because of the specialization that can be used in handling many small claims and the need to establish a system of participating pharmacies, most insurance companies, except for a few large ones, use PBMs for their prescription drug plans.

Under virtually all service plans the provider of coverage or the third-party administrator negotiates a contract with participating pharmacies to provide the drugs at a reduced cost, usually equal to the wholesale cost of the drug plus a flat dispensing fee, such as $3 for each prescription. Prescriptions filled at nonparticipating pharmacies are often covered but handled on a reimbursement basis. In addition, reimbursement in these cases is typically less than the cost of the prescription. In some cases the plan will pay up to the amount that would have been paid to a participating pharmacy. In other cases benefits may be limited to some percentage (for example, 75 percent) of the cost of a prescription purchased at a nonparticipating pharmacy, less any copayment.

Vision Care Expense Benefits

Because the previous coverages discussed do not provide benefits for the cost of eyeglasses and only rarely cover the cost of routine eye examinations, vision care expense coverage is designed to provide benefits for these expenses. Coverage may be provided by insurance companies, Blue Cross–Blue Shield plans, plans of state optometric associations patterned after Blue Shield, closed-panel HMO-type plans established by local providers of vision services, vision care PPOs, or third-party administrators.

Benefits are occasionally provided on a reasonable-and-customary basis or are subject to a flat benefit per year that may be applied to any covered expenses. Normally, however, a benefit schedule will be used that specifies the type and amounts of benefits and the frequency with which they will be provided. Table 10-4 is an example of one such schedule. If the plan is written by a provider of vision services, it is common for a discount, such as 20 percent, to be available for costs incurred with the provider that are not covered by the schedule of benefits. Under some plans most benefits are provided on a service basis rather than being subject to a maximum benefit. However, these plans usually cover only the cost of basic frames, which the covered persons can upgrade at an additional expense.

TABLE 10-4	
Type of Benefit	**Maximum Amount**
Any 12-month period	
Eye examination	$ 45
Lenses, pair	
single vision	45
bifocal	75
trifocal	125
lenticular	200
contact (when medically necessary)	300
contact (when not medically necessary)	125
Any 24-month period	
Frames	60

Exclusions commonly exist for any extra charge for plastic lenses or the cost of safety lenses or prescription sunglasses. Benefits are generally provided for eye examinations by either an optometrist or an ophthalmologist, and larger benefits are sometimes provided if the latter is used. Vision care plans do not pay benefits for eye surgery or treatment of eye diseases since these are covered under other basic coverages or major medical coverage.

Supplemental Accident Expense Benefits

Some basic medical expense plans (as well as an occasional major medical plan) include a supplemental accident expense benefit whose purpose is to cover expenses associated with accidents to the extent that they are not provided under other medical expense coverages. There would probably be little need for this type of coverage if a basic medical expense plan included all the coverages previously described. Most basic medical expense plans consist only of hospital, surgical, and physicians' visits coverage, however, with little coverage for treating accidental injuries except on an inpatient basis.

Benefits usually apply to expenses incurred within 90 days after an accident and pay for such items as professional fees, diagnostic X rays, laboratory examinations, and physical therapy. In addition, benefits are subject to a maximum limit, with $300 and $500 limits most commonly used.

Supplemental accident coverage has been the subject of controversy, since there seems to be no logical reason for providing different benefits for accidental injuries than for illnesses. However, the benefit is popular among employees and its cost is relatively small.

MAJOR MEDICAL COVERAGE

Most employees have some type of major medical expense coverage that protects against catastrophic medical expenses, with few exclusions or limitations. However, employees must often pay part of the cost of these medical expenses in the form of a deductible and/or coinsurance.

Types of Major Medical Coverage

There are two general types of plans for providing major medical coverage—supplemental (or superimposed) plans and comprehensive plans. Supplemental plans coordinate major medical coverage with various basic medical expense coverages. Figure 10-1 shows one example of such a plan.

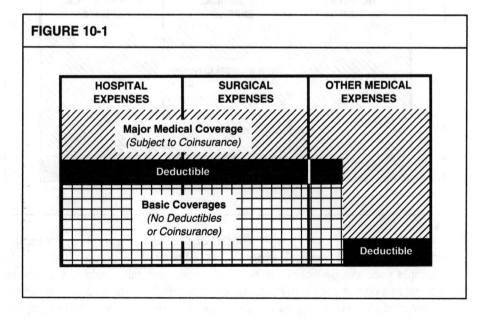

FIGURE 10-1

| HOSPITAL EXPENSES | SURGICAL EXPENSES | OTHER MEDICAL EXPENSES |

Major Medical Coverage (Subject to Coinsurance)

Deductible

Basic Coverages (No Deductibles or Coinsurance)

Deductible

Subject to its own limitations and exclusions, a supplemental major medical plan covers the following expenses:

- expenses not within the scope of the basic coverages. For example, benefits for office visits to a physician may be included if the basic coverages only provide benefits for in-hospital visits.
- expenses no longer covered under the basic coverages because those benefits have been exhausted. For example, if the basic coverages provide room-and-board benefits in full, but only for a maximum of 60 days, the major medical plan will cover the cost of room and board beginning on the 61st day.
- expenses in excess of the dollar maximum provided under the basic coverages. For example, if the basic coverages list a maximum benefit of $500 for a specific surgical procedure, and the cost of the procedure is $700, the major medical plan will cover the remaining $200.
- expenses specifically excluded under the basic coverages. For example, if the basic coverages exclude hospital charges for the treatment of alcoholism, the major medical coverage may provide benefits. However, expenses that are excluded under the basic coverages are often excluded under the major medical plan.

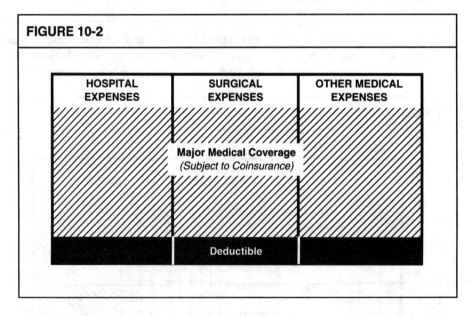

FIGURE 10-2

In the comprehensive type of major medical coverage a single major medical contract covers all medical expenses, as illustrated in figure 10-2. In this example once the deductible is satisfied, most medical expenses are covered subject to a coinsurance provision. Although figure 10-2 shows a comprehensive major medical plan in its purest form, most comprehensive medical expense contracts contain modifications that either eliminate or reduce the deductible or coinsurance provision for certain expenses. These variations will be discussed later in this chapter.

Supplemental versus Comprehensive

At first glance it might appear that the simplicity of a comprehensive major medical plan makes it preferable to a supplemental plan. However, supplemental plans continue to cover a large number of employees, even though most newly written plans are of the comprehensive type. In a few instances the continued use of supplemental plans has been based on tradition. When some firms with basic medical plans found it necessary to expand that coverage, they added a supplemental plan instead of redesigning the entire medical expense plan itself. In most cases, however, there have been a number of more valid reasons for choosing separate coverages, such as the employer's desire to (1) use more than one provider of coverage, (2) offer first-dollar coverage, or (3) use different contribution rates for the basic and supplemental coverages. However, there are also disadvantages to using supplemental plans, including more difficult administration and communication.

More than One Provider of Coverage

Frequently the provider of a supplemental major medical plan is different from the provider of the underlying basic coverages. Usually Blue Cross or Blue Shield provides the basic coverages and an insurance company provides the supplemental coverage. In the past only a few of the Blues offered major medical coverage because (1) some of them felt such coverage was not within the scope of their traditional benefit structure, (2) some states legally prohibited it, and (3) some Blues experienced administrative difficulties over the effective and efficient coordinating of these broader benefits. Although most Blue Cross–Blue Shield plans now offer major medical coverage (often referred to as extended benefits), insurance companies are still by far the largest providers of major medical benefits.

The most common type of supplemental plan is the one shown in figure 10-1, but occasionally a major medical plan is designed to supplement only a basic Blue Cross plan, as shown in figure 10-3. This type of plan is most common in those geographic areas where the Blues do not operate jointly and thus cannot offer a single coordinated basic plan.

First-Dollar Coverage

Under the traditional comprehensive major medical plan, a deductible and coinsurance apply to all covered expenses. However, because of competition or labor negotiations, employers frequently offer their employees *first-dollar coverage* for certain medical expenses. With first-dollar coverage there is no deductible and usually no coinsurance, and the basic medical expense plan will consist only of those benefits provided on a first-dollar basis. Because first-dollar coverage has been characteristic of the Blues, they are frequently used as the providers of basic coverages. Therefore in order to compete with them, most insurance companies now offer comprehensive major medical plans that are modified to provide similar first-dollar coverage.

FIGURE 10-3

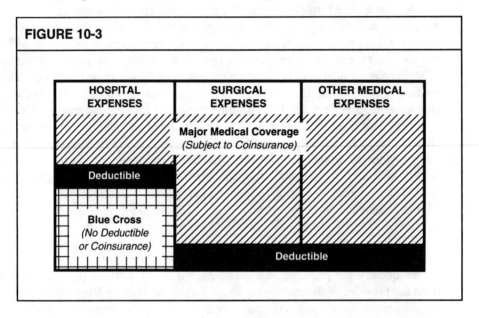

It should be emphasized that, all other things being equal, first-dollar coverage will increase the cost of a medical expense plan. Employers have become increasingly concerned with the cost of providing medical expense coverage and are less likely than in the past to provide first-dollar coverage.

Different Contribution Rates

Some employers still maintain separate basic medical and major medical expense plans, since different employer contributions are made for each plan. The most common arrangement under these circumstances has the employer paying the entire cost of the basic coverages for the employee (and possibly his or her dependents) and the employee paying a portion, if not all, of the costs of the major medical coverage. The current trend, however, is to have a single plan even when the contribution rates for the basic and major medical coverages differ.

Administration and Communication

Most employers want to have benefit plans that minimize administrative problems and that can be easily communicated to employees. In both respects comprehensive plans have the advantage. With supplemental plans the employer must often deal with two providers of coverage, so two plans must be properly coordinated so that no undesired gaps in coverage exist. In addition, the processing of claims becomes more burdensome for both the employer and the employees. The complexity of medical expense plans in general makes them difficult to communicate to employees, and the task becomes even more challenging when two plans are used.

Even when a single provider supplies both the basic medical expense plan and a supplemental major medical plan, the same problems may exist. The employer must often negotiate the plans with separate divisions of the provider's organization, and separate claims forms and claims departments are frequently used.

Characteristics of Major Medical Coverage

The distinguishing features of major medical expense plans—either supplemental or comprehensive—include a broad range of covered expenses, deductibles, coinsurance, and high overall maximum benefits.

Covered Expenses

Major medical plans give broad coverage for necessary expenses incurred for medical services and supplies that a physician has ordered or prescribed. These services and supplies, which are specified in the contract, generally include

- hospital room and board. Traditionally coverage has not been provided either for confinements in extended care facilities or for home health care. However, major medical plans now often include such coverage. Some plans also provide benefits for room and board in alternative facilities such as birthing centers.
- other hospital charges
- charges of outpatient surgical centers
- anesthetics and their administration
- services of doctors of medicine or osteopathy. Coverage for the services of other medical practitioners (such as chiropractors or podiatrists) may also be included.
- private-duty nursing by a registered nurse. The services of a licensed practical nurse may also be covered.
- prescription drugs
- physical and speech therapy
- diagnostic X-ray and laboratory services
- radiation therapy
- blood and blood plasma

- artificial limbs and organs
- pacemakers
- casts, splints, trusses, braces, and crutches
- rental of wheelchairs, hospital beds, and iron lungs
- ambulance services

The expenses of dental care may also be included as a major medical benefit. However, dental benefits (discussed in a later chapter) are usually provided under a separate dental expense plan.

Even though coverage is broad, major medical contracts contain certain exclusions and limitations.

Exclusions. Common exclusions found in major medical contracts include charges arising from the following:

- occupational injuries or diseases to the extent that benefits are provided by workers' compensation laws or similar legislation
- services furnished by or on behalf of government agencies, unless there is a requirement for the patient or the patient's medical expense plan to pay
- cosmetic surgery, unless such surgery is to correct a condition resulting from either an accidental injury or a birth defect (if the parent has dependent coverage when the child is born)
- physical examinations, unless such examinations are necessary for the treatment of an injury or illness. While most major medical plans contain this exclusion, it should be noted that some employers provide coverage for physical examinations. In most cases, however, benefits will be provided under a separate, and often self-funded, plan and not as part of the major medical coverage.
- convalescent, custodial, or rest care
- dental care except for (1) treatment required because of injury to natural teeth and (2) hospital and surgical charges associated with hospital confinement for dental surgery. This exclusion will not be included if dental coverage is provided under the major medical contract.
- eye refraction, or the purchase or fitting of eyeglasses or hearing aids. Like the dental care exclusion, this exclusion will not be included if the major medical coverage provides benefits for vision and hearing care. These benefits, however, are most likely to be provided under a separate plan.
- expenses either paid or eligible for payment under medicare or other federal, state, or local medical expense programs
- benefits provided by any other benefit program to which the employer makes a contribution. This includes any benefits provided under basic medical expense plans if a supplementary major medical plan is used.

To minimize the problem of adverse selection, most major medical plans also contain an exclusion for preexisting conditions. However, this exclusion applies only for a limited time, after which the condition will no longer be considered preexisting and will be covered in full, subject to any other contract limitations or exclusions. It is interesting to note that a preexisting-conditions clause is common in major medical contracts, but it is rarely found in basic medical expense contracts.

A *preexisting condition* is typically defined as any illness or injury for which a covered person received medical care during the 3-month period prior to the person's effective date of coverage. Usually the condition is no longer considered preexisting after the earlier of (1) a period of 3 consecutive months during which no medical care is received for the condition or (2) 12 months of coverage under the contract by the individual.

The use of preexisting-conditions provisions in group medical expense plans was affected by the passage of the Health Insurance Portability and Accountability Act, but the traditional time periods that apply to such conditions are within the act's guidelines. However, the act does limit the use of preexisting-conditions provisions with respect to newborn or adopted children. In addition, preexisting-conditions provisions cannot apply to pregnancy. The topic of preexisting conditions is discussed in more detail in chapter 12.

Some insurance companies provide limited coverage rather than exclude coverage for preexisting conditions. During the time a condition is considered preexisting, benefits may be paid subject to limitations, such as a 50 percent coinsurance provision or a calendar-year maximum of $1,000. It is also not unusual, particularly with large employers, for the preexisting-conditions clause to be waived for persons who are eligible for coverage on the date a master contract becomes effective. However, future employees will be subject to the provision.

Limitations. Major medical plans also contain "internal limits" for certain types of medical expenses. Although the expenses are covered, the amounts that will be paid under the contract are limited. Benefits are very rarely paid for charges that exceed what is reasonable and customary. In addition, limitations are often placed on the following expenses:

- hospital room and board. Benefits are generally limited to the charge for semiprivate accommodations unless other accommodations are medically necessary. However, in some cases a flat-dollar maximum is placed on the daily semiprivate accommodation rate.
- extended care facilities, home health care benefits, and hospice benefits (if provided). Benefits for extended care facilities are often subject to a dollar limit per day for room-and-board charges as well as a time limit on the number of days that coverage will be provided. Similarly home health care benefits are often subject to a maximum daily benefit and limited to a certain number of visits within a specific time period.

Hospice benefits are usually limited to a specified maximum amount, such as $5,000.

- surgery. Although most major medical contracts pay surgical expenses on a reasonable-and-customary basis, some use a surgical schedule as was described earlier in this chapter.
- dental care, vision and hearing care, and physical examinations. When these are covered under major medical contracts, benefits are frequently subject to schedules and annual limitations.

Teatment of Mental Illness, Alcoholism, and Drug Addiction. It is common for major medical plans to provide limited benefits for treatment for mental and nervous disorders, alcoholism, and drug addiction. Unless state laws require that such conditions be treated like any other medical condition, inpatient coverage is often limited to a specific number of days each year (commonly 30 or 60). Outpatient benefits, which are even more limited, are usually subject to 50 percent coinsurance and to a specific dollar limit per visit. One unfortunate effect of more stringent limitations on outpatient care is that it encourages many persons to seek inpatient treatment, which is significantly more expensive but no more effective in the eyes of many medical experts. As a result some plans have started to carve out coverage from the major medical plan. Benefits are then coordinated by a managed care plan that specializes in mental health and/or substance abuse problems. These plans provide more generous benefits but control costs by emphasizing outpatient treatment. In addition, case management has been successful in encouraging more people to actually begin prescribed treatment and finish treatment once it has started. This type of carve-out approach is being tried not only by indemnity plans but also by HMOs and PPOs.

It has been common for major medical plans to impose an annual maximum (such as $1,000) and/or an overall maximum lifetime limit (such as $25,000) on benefits for mental and nervous disorders, alcoholism, and drug addiction. Under recent federal legislation, such limitations will no longer be allowed for mental health benefits in many employee benefit plans.

At the time of the 1996 debate over the Health Insurance Portability and Accountability Act, there was considerable disagreement over the issue of requiring mental illness to be treated as any other illness for purposes of medical expense coverage. With estimates that complete parity would raise the cost of providing medical expense benefits by 4 to 10 percent (depending on whose estimate one believed), Congress left the issue unresolved. The debate continued after the passage of the previously mentioned act and resulted in the passage of another act the following month—the Mental Health Parity Act. However, because of cost considerations, its provisions are limited and the use of the term *parity* is probably a misnomer.

The provisions of the act are effective for plan years beginning on or after January 1, 1998, and apply only to employers that have more than 50 employees. The act prohibits a group health plan, insurance company, or HMO from setting annual or lifetime *dollar* limits on mental health benefits that are less than the limits applying to other medical and surgical benefits. If there are no such dollar limitations for substantially all other (meaning two-thirds or more) medical and surgical benefits under a plan, there can be none for mental health benefits. If substantially all benefits are subject to an annual or lifetime limit, the parity requirements can be satisfied by either having separate dollar limits that are equal for mental health benefits and other medical and surgical benefits or applying a uniform dollar limit to all benefits in the aggregate. If a plan has different limits for different categories of benefits, the act calls for the use of a weighted average of all the limits to be used for the mental health limitations.

Besides imposing no limitations on benefits for alcoholism or drug addiction, the act is noteworthy for other things it does not do. It does not require employers to make any benefits available for mental illness, and it does not impose any other restrictions on mental health benefits. Employers can still impose limitations such as an annual maximum on number of visits or days of coverage and different cost-sharing provisions for mental health benefits than those that apply to other medical and surgical benefits.

Congressional advocates of the act estimate that overall medical costs to employers should not increase by more than .4 percent. Any employer who can prove that the act's provisions will increase its costs by more than 1 percent is exempt from the act.

The act is subject to a sunset provision of September 30, 2001. As of that date, any benefits required by the act can be eliminated unless Congress extends the date or removes the sunset provision prior to that time.

Deductibles

A deductible is the initial amount of covered medical expenses an individual must pay before he or she will receive benefits under a major medical plan. For example, if a plan has an annual deductible of $200, the covered person is responsible for the first $200 of medical expenses incurred each year. Covered expenses in excess of $200 are then paid by the major medical plan, subject to any limitations or coinsurance. In addition to the different types of deductibles there are variations in (1) the amounts of the deductible, (2) the frequency with which it must be satisfied, and (3) the expenses to which it applies.

Types of Deductibles. Probably the simplest form of deductible is the *initial deductible* commonly used in comprehensive major medical plans (see figure 10-2). Essentially a covered person must satisfy this deductible before the plan will pay any insurance benefits.

Most supplemental medical expense plans use a *corridor deductible* (see figure 10-1), under which no benefits are paid by the major medical plan until an individual has incurred a specific amount of covered expenses above those paid under his or her basic coverages. For example, assume an individual incurs $4,000 of covered medical expenses, $2,500 of which are paid by the basic coverages. If the supplemental major medical plan has a $200 corridor deductible, the plan will pay $1,300 of the expenses, subject to any limitations or coinsurance. This is determined as follows:

Covered expenses	$4,000
Less expenses covered under basic protection	2,500
	$1,500
Less deductible	200
	$1,300

In those situations when no benefits are paid under the basic coverages, the corridor deductible operates as if it was an initial deductible.

Some supplemental major medical expense plans contain an *integrated deductible*, which tends to be large (at least $500), but any amounts paid under the basic coverages can be used to satisfy it. For example, assume the specified deductible is $1,000 per year. If an individual incurs $1,000 or more of covered expenses under the basic coverages, the annual deductible is satisfied. As another example, assume a person incurs $1,500 of medical expenses, $800 of which is for hospital charges that are covered in full under the individual's basic coverages and $700 of which consists of noncovered outpatient expenses. The $800 for hospital charges can be used toward satisfying the deductible. However, the individual must pay the next $200 of medical expenses out of his or her own pocket in order to satisfy the remaining deductible amount. Therefore in this case only $500 of the $700 of outpatient charges would be paid, subject to any other limitations and coinsurance, under the major medical coverage.

Although the integrated deductible was once quite common, its complexity has precluded its being as popular as the corridor deductible. Currently it is found in only a few supplemental major medical expense plans.

Deductible Amounts. With the exception of the integrated deductible, deductible amounts for any covered person tend to be relatively small. Most deductibles are fixed-dollar amounts that apply separately to each person and usually fall within the range of $100 to $250. A few major medical expense plans contain deductibles that are based on a percentage of an employee's salary (such as 1 or 2 percent), possibly subject to a maximum annual limit (such as $250).

In most major medical expense plans the deductible must be satisfied only once during any given time period (usually a calendar year), regardless of the number of causes from which medical expenses arise. This type of deductible is often referred to as an *all-causes deductible*. However, a few plans have *per-cause deductibles* (also referred to as *per-disability deductibles*) under which the deductible amount must be satisfied for each separate accident or illness before major medical benefits will be paid.

Deductibles apply to each covered individual, including the dependents of an employee. However, to minimize the family's burden of satisfying several deductibles, most major medical expense plans also contain a *family deductible*. Once the family deductible is satisfied, future covered medical expenses of all family members will be paid just as if every member of the family had satisfied his or her individual deductible.

Two basic types of family deductibles are found in major medical expense plans. The most common type waives any deductible requirements for other family members once a certain number of family members (generally two or three) have satisfied their individual deductibles. However, two important points should be noted. First, major medical benefits will be paid for each individual family member once his or her individual deductible is satisfied, even though the family deductible has not been met. Second, the waiver of any deductible requirements that results from the satisfaction of the family deductible does not apply to medical expenses incurred prior to the date the deductible is satisfied. For example, assume a family deductible is satisfied when each of three family members incurs $200 in covered medical expenses. If a fourth family member has had $60 in medical expenses up to that point, future medical expenses for that person will be paid under the major medical coverage. The $60, however, will not be covered. In effect the satisfaction of the family deductible freezes the deductible for each family member at the lesser of the individual deductible or the amount of medical expenses incurred up to that time.

Another approach taken in some major medical plans is to have a fixed-dollar amount for the family deductible (such as $500). In addition, each family member has to meet an individual deductible (such as $200). Major medical benefits will be paid for any given family member once his or her deductible is satisfied, and future deductible requirements for all family members will be waived once the family maximum has been reached. Although the same expenses can satisfy both the family deductible and an individual deductible, any amount that is applied toward the family deductible cannot exceed the individual deductible. For example, if a family has deductibles of $200 for an individual and $500 for the family and if one family member incurs $1,000 in covered medical expenses, the $800 exceeding the individual deductible will be paid under the major medical plan, subject to any limitations and coinsurance. The $200 used to satisfy the individual deductible, but no more, can also be applied to the family deductible. However, the family deductible will not be completely satisfied until other family members incur another $300 in covered expenses (but no more than $200 from any one family member).

Most major medical expense contracts contain a *common accident provision*, whereby if two or more members of the same family are injured in the same accident, the covered medical expenses for all family members will at most be subject to a single deductible, usually equal to the individual deductible amount. This deductible establishes the maximum amount of medical expenses an employee must bear for his or her family before major medical benefits will be paid. Sometimes the employee may actually bear a smaller portion of the medical expenses if the amount satisfies the family or individual deductibles. For example, if each of three family members incurs $300 of medical expenses in an accident under a plan that contains a $200 deductible, at least $700 of these expenses will be covered under the major medical coverage. However, if due to previous medical expenses only $40 is needed to satisfy the family deductible, then $860 of these expenses will be covered under the major medical plan.

Deductible Frequency. An all-causes deductible usually applies to medical expenses incurred within a 12-month period, typically a calendar year (January 1 to December 31). Under such a *calendar-year deductible* expenses incurred from January 1 apply toward the deductible. Once it has been satisfied, the balance of any covered expenses incurred during the year are then paid by the major medical plan, subject to limitations and coinsurance.

Many plans with a calendar-year deductible also have a carryover provision that allows any expenses (1) applied to the deductible and (2) incurred during the last 3 months of the year to also be applied to the deductible for the following year. For example, assume an individual satisfies only $150 of a $200 deductible prior to October 1. If less than $50 of covered expenses are incurred in the last 3 months of the year, the deductible will not be totally satisfied for the year, but this amount can be applied to the deductible for the following year. If $50 or more of covered expenses are incurred in this 3-month period, not only will the deductible be satisfied for the year but this amount ($50) can also be applied to the deductible for the following year. No carryover is allowed if the deductible for the year is satisfied prior to the last 3 months of the year.

A rarely used variation of the calendar-year deductible allows expenses incurred during any 12-month period to satisfy the deductible. Once an individual incurs covered medical expenses equal to the deductible in any consecutive 12-month period, major medical benefits will be paid for the remainder of the period. Table 10-5 illustrates these two types of deductibles.

TABLE 10-5	
Year 1	
January 15	$40.00
March 9	40.00
August 20	40.00
December 1	60.00
Year 2	
May 5	$100.00
May 20	40.00
July 11	60.00
September 8	80.00
October 15	120.00

Assume an individual incurs the covered medical expenses that are shown in the table. If the person has a $200 calendar-year deductible, the deductible will not be satisfied during the first year, because only $180 of expenses have been incurred. However, if the individual's plan contains a carryover provision, the deductible for the second year will be satisfied on May 20, since $60 of expenses can be carried over from the first year. Consequently the expenses in July, September, and October will be paid subject to any limitations and coinsurance. If, however, the plan does not contain a carryover provision, the deductible will not be satisfied until July 11, and only the September and October expenses will be covered.

If this same individual has a deductible based on any consecutive 12-month period, it will be satisfied on May 5 of the second year (the date on which $200 of expenses will have been incurred within a consecutive 12-month period). Since the first expense included in the period occurred on August 20 of year one, any expenses between May 5 and August 19 of year two will be paid (that is, the May 20 and July 11 expenses totaling $100). After August 19 the individual must incur covered expenses of $200 or more within another consecutive 12-month period before a deductible will again be satisfied. In this example a second deductible will be satisfied with the October 15 expense. Since the first expense toward the satisfaction of this second deductible occurred on September 8, major medical benefits will be paid from October 16 of year two to September 7 of year three. Because this type of deductible is more difficult to explain to employees and more burdensome administratively than a calendar-year deductible, it is rarely used.

With a per-cause deductible, a different approach is normally taken. Medical expenses used to satisfy the deductible for each illness or accident must be incurred within a specified *accumulation* period. Although the accumulation period can be a calendar-year or some other 12-month period, most accumulation periods consist of any consecutive 2-month, 3-month, or 6-month periods. Once the deductible for an accumulation period has been met, benefits will be paid for a *benefit period,* which usually begins when the deductible is satisfied, but sometimes begins on the date the first expense toward the deductible is incurred. (In the latter case, expenses used to satisfy the deductible are not paid by the major medical plan.) The benefit period typically lasts until the earlier of (1) 2 years or (2) the end of some time period (usually 60 or 90 days) in which covered medical expenses from that cause are less than a small but specified dollar amount (such as $25 or $50). Once the benefit period ends, an individual must again satisfy the deductible before a new benefit period will begin.

Expenses to Which the Deductible Applies. Most major medical plans have a single deductible that applies to all medical expenses. However, some plans have two (or more) deductibles that apply separately to different categories of medical expenses. While many variations exist, the most common plan of this type has a small deductible (such as $50) that applies to those expenses over which individuals have the least control (for example, hospital charges, surgical charges, and charges resulting from accidents). A larger deductible (such as $100) applies to all other medical expenses.

In some major medical plans the deductible does not apply to certain expenses, in effect giving the covered person first-dollar coverage for these charges. Insurance companies sometimes write comprehensive major medical expense plans without any deductible for hospital and/or surgical expenses as their way of competing with the first-dollar coverage offered by the Blues. In addition, often these expenses are not subject to a coinsurance provision, but a dollar maximum may be placed on the amount of benefits that will be paid in full. Above this maximum, coinsurance will apply.

Coinsurance

Major medical expense plans contain a coinsurance provision, whereby the plan will pay only a specified percentage (in most cases 80 percent) of the covered expenses that exceed the deductible. The term *coinsurance* as used in this book refers to the percentage of covered expenses paid by a medical expense plan. Thus a plan with 80 percent coinsurance, sometimes referred to as an 80/20 plan, will pay 80 percent of covered expenses while a person who receives benefits under the plan must pay the remaining 20 percent. In some plans the term *coinsurance* is not used, but rather a percentage participation, such as 20 percent, is specified. As commonly used, a percentage participation (sometimes also referred to as a copayment) refers to the percentage of covered medical expenses that will not be paid by a medical expense plan and that must be paid by a person receiving benefits.

If a comprehensive major medical expense plan has a $200 calendar-year deductible and an 80 percent coinsurance provision that applies to all expenses, an individual who incurs $1,200 of covered medical expenses during the year (assuming no limitations) will receive an $800 reimbursement, calculated as follows:

Covered expenses	$1,200
Less deductible	200
	$1,000
Times coinsurance percentage	.80
	$ 800

The individual will have to pay the remaining $400 from his or her own pocket (that is, the deductible plus 20 percent of those expenses exceeding the deductible). It has been argued that having such provisions is a financial incentive for employees to control their use of medical care, since they must bear a portion of the cost of any expenses incurred.

Just as deductibles vary, so do coinsurance provisions. Sometimes different coinsurance percentages apply to different categories of medical expenses. For example, outpatient psychiatric charges may be subject to 50 percent coinsurance, while other covered medical expenses are subject to 80 percent coinsurance. In addition, certain medical expenses may be subject to 100 percent coinsurance (and usually no deductible), which in effect means that the expenses are paid in full, subject to any limitations. Such full coverage is most likely to exist (1) for those expenses over which an individual has little control, (2) when there is a desire to provide first-dollar coverage for certain expenses, or (3) when there is a desire to encourage the use of the most cost-effective treatment (such as outpatient surgery, preadmission testing, or birthing centers).

Figures 10-4 through 10-7 illustrate some possible modifications that could be made in both the deductible and coinsurance provisions of a comprehensive major medical expense plan.

Figure 10-4 illustrates a medical expense plan that has both the deductible and the coinsurance provision waived for hospital expenses, surgical expenses, and certain other expenses up to specified limits. This type of modification results in a plan similar to a Blue Cross–Blue Shield plan that has supplemental major medical coverage but no corridor deductible. Figure 10-5 shows a comprehensive major medical expense plan that is designed to provide first-dollar coverage for hospital expenses only. Notice the similarity between this plan and a Blue Cross plan that has supplemental major medical coverage (figure 10-3). Figures 10-6 and 10-7 illustrate two other possible variations. In figure 10-6 the deductible and the coinsurance provision are completely waived for certain medical expenses. In figure 10-7 only the coinsurance provision—and not the deductible—is waived.

FIGURE 10-4

FIGURE 10-5

FIGURE 10-6

FIGURE 10-7

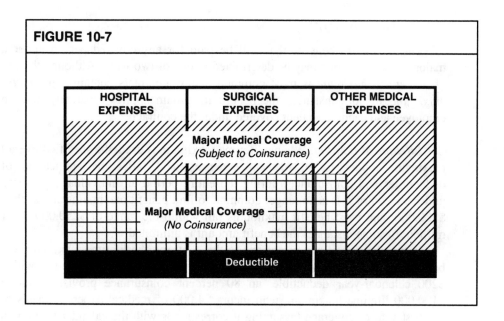

In the case of catastrophic medical expenses the coinsurance provision could result in an individual's having to assume a large dollar amount of his or her own medical expenses. Consequently many major medical expense plans place a limit (often called a *stop-loss* or *coinsurance limit* or *cap*) on the amount of out-of-pocket expenses that a covered person must bear during any time period. It is sometimes specified that the coinsurance provision only applies to a limited amount of expenses and that expenses over this limit will be paid in full. For example, the plan may have a $200 deductible, an 80 percent coinsurance provision that applies to the next $3,000 of covered expenses, and full coverage for any remaining covered expenses. Therefore the most an individual will have to pay out of pocket in any year is the $200 deductible and 20 percent of $3,000 (for a total of $800). Occasionally this type of plan is modified to allow a gradual increase in the coinsurance percentage, such as 80 percent of the first $2,000 of covered expenses above the deductible, 90 percent of the next $2,000, and 100 percent of the remainder.

Another way of limiting coinsurance is to state the maximum dollar amount of expenses that any individual (or a family) must bear during a specific period. Once this limit is reached, by paying either deductibles or a percentage of medical expenses, additional expenses will be paid in full. For example, under a plan with a $200 deductible and an 80 percent coinsurance provision, a limit of $1,000 will be met if total medical expenses reach $4,200. Of this amount the individual will be responsible for the $200 deductible and 20 percent of the remaining $4,000 (for a total of $1,000). Any medical expenses in excess of $4,200 will be paid in full.

Maximum Benefits

The maximum benefits that will be paid for any covered person under a major medical contract may be determined in one of two ways. Although the use of a *lifetime maximum* is most common, a few contracts contain a *per-cause maximum*. In both instances the benefit maximum applies separately to each employee and each dependent covered under the contract.

Lifetime Maximum. When a lifetime maximum is used, the specified overall maximum applies to all medical expenses paid (after the application of deductibles and coinsurance) during the entire period an individual is covered under the contract. It is no longer common to find benefit maximums of less than $100,000, and most benefit maximums fall within the range of $250,000 to $1 million. In some instances the benefit amount is unlimited.

In the absence of any provisions to the contrary, the lifetime maximum will be reduced by the amount of any benefits paid. For example, an individual with a $200 calendar-year deductible, an 80 percent coinsurance provision, and a $100,000 lifetime maximum, who incurs $4,000 of medical expenses in his or her first year of coverage (assuming it corresponds with the calendar year), will receive benefits of $3,040 (that is, 80 percent of $3,800). This will reduce the remaining lifetime benefit to $96,960.

Major medical contracts commonly contain provisions for restoring (either partially or totally) the lifetime maximum to its original level. Most contracts stipulate that on some date each year (often January 1) the entire deficit in the lifetime maximum will be automatically restored, subject to a maximum annual restoration that may vary from $1,000 to $5,000. However, the overall maximum cannot be increased above its original limit. If the plan in the previous example has a $1,000 automatic annual restoration, the amount of the remaining benefit will initially be increased to $97,960. Ignoring any future reductions for benefits paid, this limit will continue to increase by $1,000 each year until the original $100,000 maximum is restored.

Most contracts also state that after a covered person has used up a specified amount (often $1,000 or $2,000), he or she may have the maximum benefit restored to its original level upon supplying satisfactory evidence of insurability to the insurance company. Although insurance contracts are silent on what constitutes evidence of insurability, most insurance companies use the same standards and procedures that apply to applicants for individual medical expense insurance.

In addition to the overall lifetime maximum, *internal maximums* are sometimes found in major medical contracts. For example, a plan may have a $1 million overall lifetime maximum, but a $10,000 lifetime maximum for benefits relating to alcoholism and drug addiction. In other words only $10,000 of the $1 million will be paid for expenses relating to these conditions. Such a limitation has also been common for mental and nervous disorders, but the provisions of the Mental Health Parity Act prohibit this type of maximum for many employee benefit plans, effective for plan years beginning on or after January 1, 1998. A few plans do contain calendar-year or per-disability maximums. The provision for restoring benefits does not apply to the calendar-year or per-disability maximums and may or may not apply to internal maximums.

Per-Cause Maximum. A few plans contain maximum limits for each cause of medical expenses, but in general this type of maximum limit is used only when the deductible is also applied on a per-cause basis. Most plans of this type do not have an automatic restoration-of-benefits provision but do allow benefits to be reinstated upon satisfactory evidence of insurability. If this evidence is not (or cannot be) provided, coverage will terminate for any cause for which the maximum benefits have been paid. However, coverage will remain in force for expenses arising from other causes.

MANAGED CARE PROVISIONS IN TRADITIONAL PLANS

Traditional medical expense plans have contained few provisions aimed at managing the care of covered persons, but this situation continues to change. Some of these changes have already been discussed. Requirements for hospital certification and second surgical opinions have existed for several years, but the carve-out of benefits for mental illness and substance abuse is much newer. Other recent changes include maternity management and the preapproval of visits to specialists. These programs are distinct from standard precertification and utilization review.

Maternity Management

The identification of high-risk pregnancies and proper medical treatment can result in significant cost savings to a benefit plan. For example, the expenses associated with premature birth can amount to several hundred thousand dollars. As a result many plans have begun to incorporate maternity management, which focuses on low-frequency, high-cost claims in contrast to many cost-containment efforts. While there is a charge for this coverage, its cost will usually be more than offset if only one large claim is avoided.

A maternity-management provision requires an employee to notify the organization providing utilization management within some prescribed time period after confirmation of pregnancy. Failure to obtain this *precertification* may result in a reduction of benefits. A case manager, usually a registered nurse, works closely with the expectant mother and her physician throughout the pregnancy to see that a complete assessment of the mother's health is made so that unfavorable risk factors can be monitored. Individualized maternity education is provided through brochures and telephone contact. This education focuses on such aspects of prenatal care as nutrition, alcohol use, and smoking.

Preapproval of Visits to Specialists

Many persons elect to bypass primary-care physicians, such as family physicians and pediatricians, and use specialists and the emergency room as their primary access to medical care, which results in additional costs but does not improve medical outcomes in the opinion of much of the medical community. To counter this practice, some medical expense plans require that a visit to a specialist be preceded by a visit to a primary-care physician. It is not necessary for the primary-care physician to actually certify that a trip to a specialist is necessary, only that he or she has been told that the patient plans to make such a visit. The rationale for this procedure is that the primary-care physician may convince the patient that he or she is able to treat the condition and that a specialist is unnecessary, at least at that time. If a specialist is needed, the primary-care physician is also in a better position to recommend the right type of specialist and to coordinate health care for persons seeing multiple specialists.

Failure to use the primary-care physician as a quasi gatekeeper will result in a reduction in benefits. Usually benefits will still be paid but at a lower level.

MEDICAL SAVINGS ACCOUNTS

The concept of medical savings accounts (MSAs) as a method of reforming the nation's health care system was discussed in chapter 9. The use of MSAs will undoubtedly increase as a result of the Health Insurance Portability and Accountability Act. The act provides favorable tax treatment for MSAs established under a pilot project that began on January 1, 1997, as long as prescribed rules are satisfied. The project, which runs through the end of 2000, allows the establishment of up to approximately 750,000 MSAs. At the end of the 4-year trial period, no more tax-favored MSAs can be established unless Congress expands the program. However, existing MSAs can generally continue in force after that time under the current rules. During this 4-year period, the act calls for two studies to assist Congress in making its decision regarding MSAs. First, the Treasury Department will assess MSA participation and its effect on tax revenue. Second, the General Accounting Office will assess the effect of MSAs on the small-group market by looking at factors such as the effect of MSAs on health care costs and the use of preventive care.

It should be noted that MSAs, which existed on a non-tax-favored basis prior to 1997, will probably need to be revised to meet the act's requirements and receive favorable tax status.

General Nature

An MSA is a personal savings account from which unreimbursed medical expenses, including deductibles and copayments, can be paid. Coverage can be limited to an individual or include dependents. The MSA must be in the form of a tax-exempt trust or custodial account established in conjunction with a high-deductible health (that is, medical expense) plan. An MSA is established with a qualified trustee or custodian in much the same way that an IRA is established. Any insurance company or bank (as well as certain other financial institutions) can be a trustee or custodian, as can any other person or entity already approved by the IRS as a trustee or custodian for IRAs. While there are some similarities between MSAs and IRAs, there are also differences. As a result, an IRA cannot be used as an MSA, and an IRA and MSA cannot be combined into a single account.

Even though employers can sponsor MSAs, these accounts are established for the benefit of individuals and are portable. If an employee changes employers or leaves the workforce, the MSA remains with the individual.

Eligibility for an MSA

Two types of individuals are eligible to establish MSAs:

- an employee (or spouse) of a *small employer* that maintains an individual or family *high-deductible health plan* covering that individual. These persons will establish their MSAs under an employer-sponsored plan.
- a self-employed person (or spouse) maintaining an individual or family high-deductible health plan covering that individual. These persons will need to seek out a custodian or trustee for their MSAs.

A *small employer* is defined as an employer who has an average of 50 or fewer employees (including employees of controlled group members and predecessor employers) on business days during either of the two preceding calendar years. In the case of a new employer, the number of employees is based on an estimate of the reasonably expected employment for the current year. After the initial qualification as a small employer is satisfied, an employer can continue to make contributions to employees' MSAs, and employees can continue to establish MSAs until the first year following the year in which the employer has more than 200 employees. At that time participating employees may take over contributions to their accounts, but no employer contributions can be made and nonparticipating employees may not start new accounts.

A *high-deductible health plan,* for purposes of MSA participation, is a plan that has the following deductibles and annual out-of-pocket limitations, all of which will be adjusted for inflation after 1998:

- In the case of individual coverage, the deductible must be at least $1,500 and cannot exceed $2,500. The maximum annual out-of-pocket expenses cannot exceed $3,000.

- In the case of family coverage, the deductible must be at least $3,000 and cannot exceed $4,500. The maximum annual out-of-pocket expenses cannot exceed $5,500.

A high-deductible plan can be written by an insurance company or a managed care organization, such as an HMO. At the time this book was being revised, the early high-deductible plans were being written primarily by insurance companies in the form of traditional major medical products but possibly with the requirement that covered persons use preferred-provider networks. No HMOs had established high-deductible plans.

A high-deductible plan can be part of a cafeteria plan, but the MSA must be established outside the cafeteria plan.

With some exceptions, a person who is covered under a high-deductible health plan is denied eligibility for an MSA if he or she is covered under another health plan that does not meet the definition of a high-deductible plan but that provides any benefits that are covered under the high-deductible health plan. The exceptions include coverage for accident, disability, dental care, vision care, and long-term care as well as medicare supplement insurance, liability insurance, insurance for a specific disease or illness, and insurance paying a fixed amount per period of hospitalization.

The intent of Congress was that the number of MSAs be limited to approximately 750,000. There are lower statutory limits that, if reached at various specified cutoff dates, will close off individuals' ability to establish MSAs unless they are covered under an employer's high-deductible plan that existed prior to the cutoff date.

Contributions

Either the account holder of an MSA or the account holder's employer, but not both, may make a contribution to an MSA. If the employer makes a contribution, even one below the allowable limit, the account holder may not make a contribution. Contributions must be in the form of cash.

Contributions by an employer are tax deductible to the employer and are not included in an employee's gross income or subject to social security and other employment taxes. Employee contributions are deductible in computing adjusted gross income. As with IRAs, individuals' contributions must generally be made by April 15 of the year following the year for which the contributions are made.

The amount of the annual deductible contribution to an employee's account is limited to 65 percent of the deductible for the health coverage if the MSA is for an individual. The figure is 75 percent if an MSA covers a family. If each person in a married couple has an MSA and if one or both of the MSAs provide family coverage, the aggregate deductible contribution is equal to 75 percent of the deductible for the family coverage with the lowest deductible. The deductible contribution is split equally between the two persons in the couple unless they agree to a different division.

The actual MSA contribution that can be deducted is limited to 1/12 of the annual amount, as described in the previous paragraph, times the number of months that an individual is eligible for MSA participation. For example, assume that the deductible under an individual's health plan is $1,800. The maximum annual contribution to the MSA is then 65 percent of this amount, which is $1,170, and the monthly amount is $97.50. If the individual is covered under a high-deductible plan only for the first 8 months of the year, then the annual deductible contribution is eight times $97.50, or $780. Note, however, that there are no requirements that contributions be made on a monthly basis or at any particular time. In this example, the full $1,170 could have been made early in the year. The excess over $780 would then be an excess contribution.

An excess contribution occurs to the extent that contributions to an MSA exceed the deductible limits or are made for an ineligible person. Any excess contribution made by the employer is included in the employee's gross income. In addition, account holders are subject to a 6 percent excise tax on excess contributions for each year these contributions are in an account. This excise tax can be avoided if the excess amount and any net income attributable to the excess amount are removed from the MSA prior to the last day prescribed by law, including extensions, for filing the account holder's income tax return. The net income attributable to the excess contributions is included in the account holder's gross income for the tax year in which the distribution is made.

An employer that makes contributions to MSAs is subject to a comparability rule that requires the employer to make comparable contributions for all employees who have MSAs. However, full-time employees and part-time employees (those working fewer than 30 hours per week) are treated separately. The comparability rule requires that the employer contribute either the same dollar amount for each employee or the same percentage of each employee's deductible under the health plan. Failure to comply with this rule subjects the employer to an excise tax equal to 35 percent of the aggregate amount contributed to MSAs during the period when the comparability rule was not satisfied.

Growth of MSA Accounts

Unused MSA balances carry over from year to year, and there is no prescribed period in which they must be withdrawn. Earnings on amounts in an MSA are not subject to taxation as they accrue.

Distributions

An individual can take distributions from an MSA at any time. The amount of the distribution can be any part or all of the account balance. Subject to some exceptions, distributions of both contributions and earnings are excludible from an account holder's gross income if used to pay medical expenses of the account holder and the account holder's family as long as these expenses are not paid by other sources of insurance. For the most part, the eligible medical expenses are the same ones that would be deductible, ignoring the 7.5 percent of adjusted gross income limitation, if the account holder itemized his or her tax deductions. However, tax-free withdrawals are not permitted for the purchase of insurance other than long-term care insurance, COBRA continuation coverage, or premiums for health coverage while an individual receives unemployment compensation. In addition, in any year a contribution is made to an MSA, tax-free withdrawals can be made to pay the medical expenses of only those persons who were eligible for coverage under an MSA at the time the expenses were incurred. For example, MSA contributions could not be withdrawn tax free to pay the unreimbursed medical expenses of an account holder's spouse who was covered under a health plan of his or her employer that was not a high-deductible plan.

Distributions for reasons other than paying eligible medical expenses are included in an account holder's gross income and are subject to a 15 percent penalty tax unless certain circumstances exist. The penalty tax is not levied if the distribution is made after the account holder turns 65 or because of the account holder's death or disability. In addition, the penalty tax does not apply to funds rolled over to a new MSA as long as the rollover is done within 60 days. Transfers of MSA accounts as a result of divorce are also tax free.

Estate Tax Treatment

Upon death, the remaining balance in an MSA is includible in the account holder's gross estate for estate tax purposes. If the beneficiary of the account is a surviving spouse, the MSA belongs to the spouse and he or she can deduct the account balance in determining the account holder's gross estate. The surviving spouse can then use the MSA for his or her medical expenses. If the beneficiary is anyone else, or if no beneficiary is named, the MSA ceases to exist.

11

Group Medical Expense Benefits:
Managed Care Plans

Chapter Outline

The concept of managed care was introduced in the first chapter on group medical expense benefits. This chapter is devoted primarily to an analysis of the types of managed care plans that are available—health maintenance organizations, preferred-provider organizations, and point-of-service plans. The chapter begins with a discussion of some of the differences between traditional medical expense plans and managed care plans.

DIFFERENCES FROM TRADITIONAL PLANS

One of the major characteristics of managed care plans that differentiates them from traditional medical expense plans is the limitations on the choice of medical care providers that may be used. Then, the question arises as to whether these choice limitations lead to a different quality of care. Despite these apparent or perceived differences, about three-quarters of the population is now in some type of managed care plan, and most seem satisfied with the arrangement. In the last few years much of this growth in managed care has come from employers with fewer than 50 employees. Unlike larger employers, who usually give employees a choice between one or more managed care plans and a traditional indemnity plan, small employers are more likely to offer a single managed care plan rather than any options.

Limited Choice of Medical Providers

Managed care plans attempt to eliminate the unrestricted use of medical care providers by either requiring or encouraging participants to use preapproved providers. The earliest managed care plans usually provided no coverage for treatment outside the managed care network, discouraging enrollment because many Americans valued the choice that had traditionally been available when medical treatment was needed. Today, many managed care plans do allow treatment outside the managed care network, but they may include financial penalties for pursuing this option. However, the availability of this choice has resulted in an increasing number of persons electing managed care plans.

Managed care plans also typically allow a wide variety of choice within the managed care network. Patients can usually choose from a lengthy list of primary-care physicians, but there is more limited choice for treatment by a specialist.

Reasons for Use

There are many reasons why an employee would elect coverage under a managed care plan. First, it may be the only plan the employer provides. However, most employers allow a choice of benefit plans. In those situations, the following factors have been identified as reasons why a managed care plan might be selected:

- the reputation of the managed care plan. To some extent this is a function of the managed care plan's experience. In areas where managed care plans have been established for many years, a larger percentage of employees participate.
- the extent to which employees have established relationships with physicians. Employees are reluctant to elect a managed care option if it requires them to give up a physician with whom they are satisfied. However, in some cases this physician may also participate in the managed care plan. In general new employees are more likely to elect a managed care option if they are new residents of the area or are just entering the labor force.

- the attitude of the employer. Employees are more likely to elect a managed care plan if their employer effectively and enthusiastically communicates the option.
- costs. Managed care plans are obviously more attractive to employers when they offer a less expensive alternative to coverage under insurance company plans. However, in some cases a managed care option will be more expensive to an employee, but the expense may be more than offset by broader coverage and the lack of deductibles and coinsurance. If employees view a managed care alternative as being less expensive in the long run, their participation will be greater.

Quality of Care

A difficult question to answer is whether persons covered by managed care plans receive the same quality of care as persons covered under traditional medical expense plans. If the sole objective of a managed care plan is to offer coverage at the lowest possible cost, there may be a decline in the quality of care. However, some type of quality assurance program is one aspect of any managed care plan. If properly administered, this type of program can weed out providers who give substandard and unnecessary care. In this regard, managed care plans may be more progressive than the medical field as a whole.

The results of numerous surveys and studies on the quality of medical care plans have been mixed. Some studies show that persons in managed care plans are less likely than persons in traditional medical expense plans to receive treatment for a serious medical condition from specialists, and they are also likely to have fewer diagnostic tests. There are those who argue that family physicians can treat a wide variety of illnesses and avoid unnecessary diagnostic tests and referrals to specialists. On the other hand, an opposing argument contends that the decline in the use of tests and frequency of diagnostic tests is also a clear indication that there is a decline in the level of medical care. Other studies show that persons in managed care plans are much more likely than the rest of the population to receive preventive care and early diagnosis and treatment of potentially serious conditions such as high blood pressure and diabetes. In addition, managed care plans are viewed as having been successful in coordinating care when it is necessary for a person to see several different types of specialists. There is no doubt that there are some small provider networks with a limited choice of specialists, but most networks are relatively large or allow persons to select treatment outside the network. There are also many managed care plans that do refer patients to highly regarded physicians and hospitals or have these providers as part of their network.

In evaluating the quality of medical care, it is also interesting to look at surveys of participants in the various types of medical expense plans. Most persons in traditional medical expense plans are convinced they receive better care because of their unlimited ability to choose providers of medical care as needed. However, surveys of participants in managed care plans usually show a high degree of satisfaction with the medical care received and little concern about whether the care is inferior to that received by persons in traditional medical expense plans.

Recent Developments

Two recent developments relate to the quality of care provided by managed care organizations—an increased interest in accreditation and the introduction or passage of laws in many states aimed at solving consumer and provider concerns about access to care, quality of care, and choice.

Accreditation

As managed care matures and becomes more widespread, there is an increasing focus by some employers on quality. This has led many employers, particularly large employers, to require that managed care organizations for their employees meet some type of accreditation standards.

The leading organization for accrediting managed care organizations appears to be the National Committee for Quality Assurance (NCQA). Founded by two trade organizations that represented HMOs and PPOs, it has been an independent, nonprofit organization since 1990. The NCQA accredits managed care organizations by evaluating six areas of performance: quality improvement, physicians' credentials, members' rights and responsibilities, preventive health services, utilization management, and medical records.

The NCQA has also developed a set of performance measures to serve employers as purchasers of managed care services. These measures are commonly referred to as the Health Plan Employer Data and Information Set, or HEDIS. The current version has 75 measures that fall into eight categories: effectiveness of care, member satisfaction, descriptive information, health plan stability, access to and availability of care, informed health care choice, cost of care, and use of services.

Just as there is competition among managed care organizations, there is competition among accrediting bodies. The Joint Commission on Accreditation of Healthcare Organizations (JCAHO) has for many years accredited hospitals and currently accredits over 5,000. In the last few years, JCAHO has expanded to accredit numerous other types of organizations, such as nursing homes, long-term care facilities, and home health care agencies. In 1994, it began to accredit health care networks, including HMOs and PPOs.

Still another source of accreditation is the American Accreditation HealthCare Commission, Inc. (formerly the Utilization Review Accreditation Commission). It began as a body to accredit external organizations that perform utilization reviews for all types of organizations, including HMOs, PPOs, and third-party administrators. In 1995, the commission expanded the scope of its operations by beginning to accredit various types of managed care organizations.

Legislation to Address Consumer and Provider Concerns

Until recently legislatures have paid little attention to the actual practices of managed care organizations. However, as enrollment has grown, there has been a consumer and provider backlash over some of these practices, which are often a result of intense competition to control costs within the managed care industry, causing legislators to take notice. As a result several types of legislation have been introduced and often passed by state legislatures and even the federal government. The following discussion highlights some of the forms this legislation has taken.

"Any Willing Provider" Laws. There has been some concern, particularly by physicians, that managed care organizations exclude or expel doctors for providing care and/or tests that the doctor, but not the managed care organization, feels is necessary. As a result several states have passed "any willing provider" laws. These laws require HMOs and other networks of medical care providers to accept any provider who is willing to accept the plan's basic terms and fees. This legislation has been opposed by managed care plans on the basis that it will prevent them from negotiating for the best possible terms with highly qualified and efficient providers. In effect, it eliminates quality guidelines as the sole source for recruiting providers. Estimates are that this type of legislation could result in an increase of 15 to 30 percent in managed care premiums.

Postpartum Stays. About half the states have passed legislation providing minimum stays of at least 48 hours for mothers and newborns following delivery. Similar legislation has also been passed at the federal level.

Emergency Care. Managed care organizations have been criticized for often refusing to pay for emergency room care, claiming that emergency room treatment was unnecessary. For example, some plans will not pay if a person who goes to an emergency room with chest pains is found to have indigestion rather than a heart attack. Several states now require a plan to pay emergency room charges whenever a prudent lay person considers a situation to be an emergency. In addition, care cannot be delayed to get plan authorization for treatment.

No Gag Rules. Several states have passed legislation preventing managed care organizations from including provisions in their contracts that prevent doctors from discussing with patients treatment options that may not be covered under their health plans or from referring very ill patients for specialized care by providers outside the plan.

Other Legislation. Other types of legislation have been introduced in several states, but the number of states adopting the legislation has been small to date. Examples include

- requiring that patients and/or state regulators be informed of financial incentives offered to providers
- requiring that patients have the option of going outside the managed care network if they are willing to pay a higher fee. In effect, this would make any managed care plan a point-of-service plan.
- granting patients access to all prescription drugs approved by the government for sale
- making health care plans disclose their policies for covering experimental treatments
- improving state monitoring of managed care plans by requiring these plans to report the status of patient grievances to the states

It should be noted that some of these changes would bring managed care plans closer to traditional indemnity plans in terms of both coverage and cost.

HEALTH MAINTENANCE ORGANIZATIONS

Since the early 1970s the concept of health maintenance organizations (HMOs) has received considerable attention. Because the nature of these organizations varies, a precise definition is difficult. However, HMOs are generally regarded as organized systems of health care that provide a comprehensive array of medical services on a prepaid basis to voluntarily enrolled persons living within a specified geographic region. HMOs act like insurance companies and the Blues in that they finance health care. However, unlike insurance companies and the Blues, they also deliver medical services.

Even though the term *health maintenance organization* is relatively new, the concept of the HMO is not. For many years prepaid group practice plans (as they were called) have operated successfully in many parts of the country. However, growth was relatively slow until the passage of the Health Maintenance Organization Act of 1973. This act resulted from a belief on the part of the federal government that HMOs were a viable alternative method of financing and delivering health care and thus should be encouraged. In fact, the act also resulted in many employers' formerly being required to offer their employees the option of coverage by an HMO instead of by a more traditional medical expense plan. As of 1996 there were almost 600 HMOs in existence. During the last decade, the number of persons enrolled in HMOs has more than doubled, but the number of HMOs has decreased by about 20 percent, for the most part because of plan mergers. Currently the 25 largest plans enroll one-third of the HMO participants. In addition, almost 85 percent of HMO subscribers are in plans that belong to one of about 50 chains of HMOs.

Characteristics of HMOs

HMOs have several characteristics that distinguish them from insurance companies and the Blues.

Comprehensive Care

HMOs offer their subscribers a comprehensive package of health care services, generally including benefits for outpatient services as well as for hospitalization. Subscribers usually get these services at no cost except the periodically required premium (referred to as a capitation payment). However, in some cases a modest copayment, such as $5 per physician's visit or $3 per drug prescription, may be imposed. HMOs emphasize preventive care and provide such services as routine physicals and immunizations. The cost of such preventive care is usually not covered under the contracts of insurance companies or the Blues, even when major medical coverage is provided. (A comparison of two HMO plans with a major medical plan of an insurance company is presented later in this chapter.)

Delivery of Medical Services

HMOs provide for the delivery of medical services, which in many cases are performed by salaried physicians and other personnel employed by the HMO. Although this approach is in contrast to the usual fee-for-service delivery system of medical care, some HMOs do contract with providers on a fee-for-services basis.

Subscribers are required to obtain their care from providers of medical services who are affiliated with the HMO. Since HMOs may operate in a geographic region no larger than a single metropolitan area, this requirement may result in limited coverage for subscribers if treatment is received elsewhere. Most HMOs do have "out-of-area coverage" but only in the case of medical emergencies.

HMOs emphasize treatment by primary-care physicians to the greatest extent possible. These practitioners provide a gatekeeper function and historically have controlled access to specialists. The traditional HMO covers benefits provided by a specialist only if the primary-care physician recommends the specialist. This specialist may be a fellow employee in a group-practice plan or a physician who has a contract with the HMO. The subscriber has little or no say regarding the specialist selected, which has been one of the more controversial aspects of HMOs and one that has discouraged larger enrollment. In response to consumer concerns, many HMOs now make the process of seeing a specialist easier. Referrals can often be made by nurses in physicians' offices or by staff members of the HMO whom subscribers can contact by telephone. Some HMOs, referred to as direct-access or self-referral HMOs, allow subscribers to see network specialists without going through a gatekeeper. However, the specialist may have to contact the HMO for authorization before proceeding with tests or treatment. Other forms of HMOs (called *point-of-service plans*) allow even more freedom of choice. These plans are discussed later.

Cost Control

A major emphasis of HMOs is the control of medical expenses. By providing and encouraging preventive care, HMOs attempt to detect and treat medical conditions at an early stage, thereby avoiding expensive medical treatment in the future. HMOs have also attempted to provide treatment on an outpatient basis whenever possible. Because insurance companies and the Blues have provided more comprehensive coverage for a hospitalized person in the past, less expensive outpatient treatments were often not performed. This emphasis on outpatient treatment and preventive medicine has resulted in a much lower hospitalization rate for HMO subscribers than for the population as a whole. However, some of this decreased hospitalization rate appears to be a result of younger and healthier employees' being more likely to elect HMO coverage.

The use of salaried employees by many HMOs may also result in lower costs since the physician or other care provider has no financial incentive to prescribe additional, and possibly unnecessary, treatment. In fact, the physicians and other medical professionals in some HMOs may receive bonuses if the HMO operates efficiently and has a surplus.

Sponsorship of HMOs

Traditionally most HMOs operated as nonprofit organizations and had the majority of subscribers until recently. However, the majority of new HMOs are profit making. While many subscribers are covered by HMOs that have been sponsored by consumer groups, a sizable and increasing portion is covered by plans sponsored by insurance companies or the Blues. Sponsorship may also come from physicians, hospitals, labor unions, or private investors. Many recently established HMOs have been formed by physician-hospital organizations (PHOs). A PHO is a legal entity that is formed by one or more physicians' groups and hospitals. It negotiates, contracts, and markets the services of the physicians and the hospitals. PHOs may form their own HMOs, or they may contract with existing HMOs or other types of managed care organizations.

The issue of whether insurance companies should be involved with HMOs was once a source of disagreement within the industry. Some insurance companies viewed HMOs as competitors with the potential of putting them out of the health insurance business. Other insurance companies viewed them as a viable alternative method of financing and delivering health care that can be offered to employers as one of the products in their portfolio.

Over time the latter viewpoint prevailed. In addition to actually sponsoring and owning HMOs, some insurance companies are actively involved with them in a variety of ways. These include

- consulting on such matters as plan design and administration
- administrative services, such as actuarial advice, claims monitoring, accounting, and computer services
- marketing assistance, such as designing sales literature. In a few cases the agents of insurance companies have been used to market HMOs. This has been done in conjunction with the marketing of the insurance company's hospitalization plan when the HMO does not provide hospitalization coverage to its subscribers.
- providing hospitalization coverage. HMOs that do not control their own hospital facilities may provide this benefit by purchasing coverage for their subscribers.
- providing emergency out-of-area coverage. An insurance company operating on a national basis may be better equipped to administer these claims than an HMO.
- providing financial support in a variety of ways, including reinsurance if an HMO experiences greater-than-expected demand for services and agreements to bail out financially troubled HMOs

Types of HMOs

There are several types of HMOs. The earliest plans can best be described as closed-panel plans under which subscribers must use physicians employed by the plan or by an organization with which it contracts. With most closed-panel plans having several general practitioners, subscribers can usually select their physician from among those accepting new patients and make medical appointments just as if the physician was in private practice. However, there is frequently little choice among specialists since a plan may have a contract with only one physician or a limited number of physicians in a given specialty.

The number of closed-panel plans is relatively small, but they account for about 30 percent of all HMO subscribers. The three different types of closed-panel plans—staff-model HMOs, group-model HMOs, and network-model HMOs—are discussed in more detail below.

Many newer HMOs have been formed as individual practice associations, which can be described as open-panel plans. This type of plan has more flexibility with respect to subscribers choosing physicians and the ability of physicians to participate in the plan. About 40 percent of HMO subscribers are in individual practice associations.

Most of the remaining subscribers to HMOs receive their coverage in a variety of ways under mixed-model plans. Some subscribers are also in open-ended HMOs, which are discussed later in this chapter as point-of-service plans.

Staff-Model HMO

Under a staff-model HMO, the HMO owns its own facilities and hires its own physicians. It may own hospitals, laboratories, or pharmacies, or it may contract for these services. The HMO may also have contracts with specialists to treat subscribers if it is not large enough to justify hiring its own specialists in a given medical field.

Employees of staff-model HMOs are paid a salary and possibly an incentive bonus. A staff-model HMO offers a great degree of control over costs since it controls the salaries of the physicians who might find themselves unemployed if the HMO is unprofitable or if they do not provide care within the cost and utilization parameters of the HMO.

Despite the potential for cost savings in staff-model HMOs, few have actually been established, primarily because of high start-up costs and high fixed costs once they are operating.

Group-Model HMO

The most common type of closed-panel plan is the group-model HMO. Under this arrangement, physicians (and other medical personnel) are employees of another legal entity that has a contractual relationship with the HMO to provide medical services for its subscribers. In most cases, this is an exclusive arrangement and the provider's physicians only treat subscribers of the HMO. These physicians also typically operate out of one or more common facilities.

Under a group-model plan, the HMO may contract with a single provider of medical services or with different providers for different types of services (for example, one contract for physicians' services and another for hospital services). The HMO usually pays for services on a capitation basis, which means that the provider of services gets a predetermined fee per year for each subscriber and must provide any and all covered services for this capitation fee. The fee is independent of how the provider compensates its own employees. Under this arrangement the provider shares the risk in that it will lose money if utilization is higher than expected or increase its profit if utilization is lower than expected. Therefore the provider has a very real incentive to control costs.

Network-Model HMO

A network-model HMO differs from a group-model HMO in that it contracts with two or more independent groups of physicians to provide medical services to its subscribers. Physician groups that enter into this type of arrangement often treat non-HMO patients on a fee-for-service basis.

Individual Practice Associations

In individual practice associations (IPAs), participating physicians practice individually or in small groups at their own offices. In most cases these physicians accept both non-HMO patients, on a traditional fee-for-service basis, and HMO subscribers. IPAs are often referred to as open-panel plans since subscribers choose from a list of participating physicians. The number of physicians participating in this type of HMO is frequently larger than the number participating in group practice plans and may include several physicians within a given specialty. In some geographic areas most physicians may participate; in other geographic areas only a relatively small percentage of physicians may participate. Since most of the newer HMOs are IPAs, the percentage of HMO subscribers served by these plans is growing.

Several methods may be used to compensate physicians participating in an IPA. The most common is a fee schedule based on the services provided to subscribers. To encourage physicians to be cost effective, it is common for plans to have a provision for reducing payments to physicians if the experience of the plan is worse than expected. On the other hand, the physicians may receive a bonus if the experience of the plan is better than expected. Particularly with respect to general practitioners, some individual practice association plans pay each physician a flat annual amount for each subscriber who has elected to use him or her. For this annual payment the physician must see these subscribers as often as necessary during the year.

It is unusual for IPAs to own their own hospitals. Rather, they enter into contracts with local hospitals to provide the necessary services for their subscribers.

Mixed-Model HMOs

An increasing number of HMOs are now operating as mixed-model plans, which means that the organization of the plan is a combination of two or more of the approaches previously described. Such a combination generally occurs as a plan continues to grow. For example, a plan might have been established as a staff-model HMO, and at a later time the HMO decided to expand its capacity or geographic region by adding additional physicians under an IPA arrangement. Some mixed models have also resulted from the merger of two plans that each used a different organizational form.

Extent of HMO Use

It is estimated that approximately 50 million employees and dependents are covered under health maintenance organizations, with the enrollment varying considerably by geographic region. For example, a few states (California, Massachusetts, and Oregon) have more than 30 percent of their population enrolled in HMOs, while several other states have enrollments of 5 percent or less. There are also significant variations by metropolitan area, with approximately two-thirds of all enrollees living in 30 metropolitan areas. In a few metropolitan areas, such as Oakland and Sacramento, California, and Rochester, New York, the majority of persons are covered by HMOs.

Except in rare instances employees covered by HMO plans have elected this form of coverage as an alternative to their employer's insurance company plan or Blue Cross–Blue Shield plan. Although state law may require certain employers to offer an HMO option, other employers voluntarily offer it. The administrative details of such an option may be burdensome and expensive for small employers, but they seem to pose few problems for large employers with specialized employee benefit staffs. In many cases the financial consequences to the employer of such an option are insignificant since the employer will make the same contribution on an employee's behalf regardless of which plan is selected. Until recently the general attitude of employers toward HMOs seems to have been somewhat ambivalent: some employers have been in favor of them, others against, and the majority indifferent. However, according to several recent studies, most employers feel that HMOs have been a very effective technique for controlling benefit costs.

On the other hand, some employers feel that HMOs may actually increase the cost of providing medical care because they have tended to attract the younger, healthier employees. In fact, many HMOs have designed their plans to appeal most to this group by providing benefits popular to the group, such as well-baby care. When these younger, healthier persons leave the insurance company plan or Blue Cross plan, its average cost per remaining employee will increase if the plan is experience rated. Unless the employer's cost for the HMO coverage drops correspondingly, the employer's aggregate medical expense premiums will increase.

Where there is a choice of medical expense plans, most employees do not elect an HMO option unless there is a financial incentive to do so. However, studies have revealed that employees who have elected HMOs are for the most part satisfied with their choice and are unlikely to switch back to an insurance company plan or Blue Cross–Blue Shield plan as long as the HMO option remains available.

The Health Maintenance Organization Act of 1973

The Health Maintenance Organization Act of 1973 has had a significant influence on both the interest in and the growth of HMOs. The act introduced the concept of the *federally qualified* HMO. For several years after the acts' passage, most HMOs were formed to take advantage of this federal qualification, which entitled them to federal grants for feasibility studies and development (including grants to solicit subscribers) and federal loans (or loan guarantees) to assist them in covering initial operating deficits. In addition, many employers were required to make federally qualified HMOs available to their employees until late 1995. Federal qualification also exempted federally qualified HMOs from restrictive laws in many states that effectively prevented them from being established. Such state laws have now essentially disappeared.

The need now for a federal HMO law is debatable. Most states have similar legislation. While newer HMOs often forgo federal qualification, the majority of older HMOs still retain that status. It is felt that this grants them a "seal of approval" from the federal government. In addition, many employers will deal only with federally qualified HMOs. However, this practice is changing as employers are increasingly requiring some type of accreditation (either solely or as an alternative to federal qualification) as their measure of quality. Finally, federal qualification continues to be one way that HMOs can satisfy certain qualifications necessary to provide coverage for medicare recipients.

It should be pointed out that an HMO may have more than one line of business, with some lines being federally qualified and other lines not being federally qualified.

Requirements for Federal Qualification

To become federally qualified an HMO must meet certain requirements (set forth in the act) to the satisfaction of the secretary of health and human services. In return for a periodic prepaid fee an HMO must provide the following basic benefits to its subscribers at no cost or with nominal copayments:

- physicians' services, including consultant and referral services, up to 10 percent of which may be provided by physicians who are not affiliated with the HMO
- inpatient and outpatient hospital services
- medically necessary emergency health services
- short-term (up to 20 visits) outpatient mental health services
- medical treatment and referral services for alcohol or drug abuse or addiction
- diagnostic laboratory services and diagnostic and therapeutic radiologic services
- home health services
- preventive health services, such as immunizations, well-baby care, periodic physical examinations, and family-planning services
- medical social services, including education in methods of personal health maintenance and in the use of health services

The HMO may also provide the following supplemental benefits either as part of its standard benefit package or as optional benefits for which an additional fee may be charged:

- services of intermediate and long-term care facilities

- vision care
- dental care
- additional mental health services
- rehabilitative services
- prescription drugs

In addition to the benefits that either are required or may be included, an HMO must meet the following other requirements with respect to its operations:

- a fiscally sound operation, including provisions against the risk of insolvency
- annual open enrollment periods
- an ongoing quality assurance program

Prior to 1988 the HMO Act required HMOs to determine their rates on the basis of community rating for all employer groups. This provision of the act decreased the attractiveness of HMOs to employers whose employees had lower-than-average benefit claims. A 1988 amendment to the act permits HMOs to establish advance rates based on an employer's past and projected claims experience if a group has 100 or more employees. Experience rating can also be used for groups of fewer than 100 employees, but the advance rate cannot be more than 10 percent higher than the HMO's community rates. In contrast to the usual practice of experience rating (see the chapter on group insurance pricing), HMOs are *not* allowed to make retrospective rate adjustments if claims turn out to be higher or lower than expected.

Open Enrollment Periods

Once an HMO option is made available, an employer must provide for a group enrollment period of at least 10 working days each year in which eligible employees may transfer between any available health insurance plans without the application of waiting periods, exclusions, or limitations based on health status. During this open enrollment period and at least 30 days prior to it, an employer must allow any participating HMOs to have fair and reasonable access to eligible employees for purposes of presenting and explaining their programs.

A problem may arise if an HMO ceases operations because of financial difficulties. Unfortunately this has occurred in some cases, even among HMOs that have met the standards for federal qualification. Unless the cessation of HMO coverage coincides with an open enrollment period, these employees may not be able to join or rejoin their employer's insurance company plan or Blue Cross–Blue Shield plan without showing evidence of insurability. However, under these circumstances many insurance companies and Blue Cross–Blue Shield plans will include provisions in their contracts for coverage without evidence of insurability for these employees. In fact, many HMOs also have a similar provision in case other plans available to employees cease operations for any reason.

Contributions

Employers who voluntarily offer federally qualified HMOs are required to make nondiscriminatory contributions to the HMOs. Under regulations issued in 1996 by the Health Care Financing Administration, the following five employer contribution practices are considered nondiscriminatory:

- The employer may contribute the same amount it contributes to non-HMO alternatives.
- The employer's contributions may vary by class of enrollee on the basis of attributes, such as age, sex, and family status, that are reasonable predictors of utilization, experience, costs, or risks. For each enrollee in a class, the employer would contribute the same amount, regardless of the plan that an employee chooses.
- If the employer requires employee contributions, the employee contribution rate to the HMO plan cannot be greater than 50 percent of the contribution rate to the most popular non-HMO plan.
- The employer may pay the same percentage of the cost of all available health plans.
- The employer and an HMO may negotiate a payment schedule that is mutually acceptable as long as it meets the basic criteria for nondiscrimination against employees who enroll in HMOs.

State Regulation

HMOs are heavily regulated by the states. All states have numerous laws that are enforced by various state officials, often including both the insurance and public health commissioners. In many cases, the state legislation largely duplicates the federal HMO act.

Almost all states have adopted the NAIC Health Maintenance Organization Model Act, which focuses substantially on issues relating to licensing of HMOs and the maintenance of their financial solvency. However, it also addresses numerous other issues, such as the types of activities in which HMOs can engage, the requirement of a quality assurance program, standards for materials given to subscribers, grievance procedures, enrollment periods, and coordination-of-benefits provisions.

HMO Coverage as an Alternative to Major Medical

Most health maintenance organizations provide broad protection for medical expenses. In fact, federally qualified HMOs often give more comprehensive protection than most major medical plans, since in addition to covering such items as routine examinations and immunizations, they tend to require fewer out-of-pocket expenses by the members. HMOs that meet the requirements for federal qualification are allowed to use copayments for services (1) if the copayment for any single service does not exceed 50 percent of the cost for that service and (2) if the total of all copayments does not exceed more than 20 percent of the cost of supplying all basic health services. In practice, copayments (if used at all) are usually substantially below these permissible limits. In addition, no subscriber is required to copay more than 50 percent of the annual subscriber fee that would have been charged if coverage had been written without any copayments.

Table 11-1 on the following pages compares the major medical plan and two HMOs that are offered to the employees of one organization. All three plans are reasonably representative of their respective plan type.

PREFERRED-PROVIDER ORGANIZATIONS

A concept that continues to receive considerable attention from employers and insurance companies is the preferred-provider organization (PPO). A few PPOs have existed on a small scale for many years, but since the early 1980s PPOs have grown in number and are being viewed as a new weapon to control increased medical care costs. By 1997 approximately 2,500 PPOs were in existence, and an estimated 120 million employees and dependents had the option of using them for medical care.

While many variations exist, PPOs can basically be described as groups of health care providers that contract with employers, insurance companies, union trust funds, third-party administrators, or others to provide medical care services at a reduced fee. PPOs may be organized by the providers themselves or by other organizations such as insurance companies, the Blues, or groups of employers. Like HMOs they may take the form of group practices or separate individual practices. They may provide a broad array of medical services, including physicians' services, hospital care, laboratory costs, and home health care, or they may be limited only to hospitalization or physicians' services. Some PPOs are very specialized and provide specific services such as dental care, mental health benefits, substance abuse services, maternity care, or prescription drugs.

PPOs typically differ from HMOs in two major respects. First, they rarely provide benefits on a prepaid basis. The participants in the PPO are generally paid on a fee-for-service basis as their services are used. However, fees are usually subject to a schedule that is the same for all participants in the PPO, and participants may have an incentive to control utilization through bonus arrangements. Second, employees are not required to use the practitioners or facilities of PPOs that contract with their group insurance company, Blue

(Text continues on page 272.)

TABLE 11-1

A Comparison: Insured Plan versus HMOs

	Insured Comprehensive Major Medical Expense Plan	Group-Model HMO	Individual Practice Association HMO
Choice of Physician	Member may select any licensed physician or surgeon.	Member selects a personal physician from the medical group, who coordinates and directs all health care needs, including referrals to specialists.	Members select a personal primary-care physician from among the health plan physicians.
Where Primary Care and Specialty Care Are Available	Care is provided in physician's office or outpatient facility.	Care is provided at four multispecialty centers.	Care is provided in participating private physicians' offices.
Choice of Hospitals	Member may select any accredited hospital—choice depends on where physician has admitting privileges.	Selection is from participating hospitals.	Selection is from participating hospitals.
Annual Deductible and Coinsurance	There is a $200 deductible. The plan has no coinsurance for hospitalization, but it does have 80% coinsurance for other covered services. There is no coinsurance on covered services after $3,000 in benefits is paid.	There is no deductible and no coinsurance (except small copayments for home visits and outpatient mental health).	There is no deductible and no coinsurance (except small copayments for home visits, outpatient mental health, and a deductible for prescription drugs).

TABLE 11-1 (Cont.)

A Comparison: Insured Plan versus HMOs

	Insured Comprehensive Major Medical Expense Plan	Group-Model HMO	Individual Practice Association HMO
Maximum Benefit	$1 million lifetime maximum	No overall maximum limit	No overall maximum limit
Preventive Care			
Routine physicals	Not covered	Covered in full	Covered in full
Well-baby care	Not covered	Covered in full	Covered in full
Pap smears	Routine exams not covered	Covered in full	Covered in full
Immunizations	Not covered	Covered in full	Covered in full
Eye exam	Not covered	Covered in full, including written prescriptions for lenses	Paid in full for children up to age 18
Hearing exam	Not covered	Covered in full	Covered in full
Health education	Available through some physicians' offices	Periodic classes held on diet, prenatal care, physical fitness, etc.	Covered in full through participating hospital programs
Physician Care			
Surgery	Covered at 80% after satisfying deductible	Covered in full	Covered in full
Inpatient visits	Covered at 80% after deductible	Covered in full	Covered in full
Office and home	Covered at 80% after deductible	Office visits covered in full, home visits covered in full, charge of $3 per allied health professional home visit	Office visits covered in full; charge of $5 per doctor's home visit
X rays and lab	Covered at 80% after deductible	Covered in full	Covered in full

Hospital Services		
Room and board	Covered in full for unlimited days in semiprivate room after satisfying deductible	Covered in full for unlimited days in semiprivate room	Covered in full for unlimited days in semiprivate room
Supplies, tests, medication, etc.	Covered in full for covered benefit days	Covered in full	Covered in full
Private-duty nurse	Covered in full while hospitalized (outpatient licensed practical nurse services covered at 50% up to $250 per year)	Covered in full	Covered in full
Emergency Care	Covered in full for care received in hospital outpatient department within 24 hours of an accident	Covered in full for around-the-clock emergency care by plan physicians and in participating hospitals. Emergency care by nonplan physicians or hospitals is also covered when obtaining plan care is not reasonable because of distance and urgency.	Covered in full for around-the-clock emergency care by participating physicians and in participating hospitals. Emergency care by nonparticipating physicians or hospitals is also covered when obtaining plan care is not reasonable because of distance and urgency.
Ambulance service	Covered in full for local transportation after satisfying deductible	Covered in full	Covered in full

TABLE 11-1 (cont.)

	A Comparison: Insured Plan versus HMOs		
	Insured Comprehensive Major Medical Expense Plan	Group-Model HMO	Individual Practice Association HMO
Maternity Care			
Hospital	Covered in full after deductible	Covered in full	Covered in full
Physician	Covered at 80% after deductible	Covered in full	Covered in full
Mental Health Care			
Hospital	Covered as regular hospitalization, i.e., 365-day/lifetime limitation	Covered in full for 45 days per year	Covered in full for 30 days during 12-month period
Inpatient physician	Covered as regular inpatient physician care	Covered in full for 45 days per year	Covered in full for 30 days during 12-month period
Outpatient physician	Covered at 50% up to $30 per visit	Covered for 30 visits per year; first 3 visits covered in full, member pays $10 per visit for next 27 visits	Covered for 20 visits per period; first 3 visits covered in full, member pays 25% of regular fee for next 7 visits, member pays 50% of regular fee for next 10 visits
Alcohol and drug addiction	Covered like other mental health services	No special limits; covered as other medical and mental health services	After detoxification treatment, covered as for mental health problems

Dental Care			
Hospital	Covered for hospital costs when confinement is necessary for dental care	Covered for hospital costs when confinement is necessary for dental care	Covered for hospital costs when confinement is necessary for dental care
Dentist or dental surgeon	Covered for treatment of accidental injury to natural teeth	Covered for treatment of accidental injury to natural teeth and certain oral surgical procedures (e.g., impacted wisdom teeth)	Covered for treatment of diseases and injuries to the jaw and removal of impacted wisdom teeth
Outpatient Medication			
Prescription drugs	Covered at 80% after deductible, if related to treatment of nonoccupational illness or injury	Not covered	Covered in full after $50 deductible per person per contract year
Injections	Covered at 80% after deductible, if related to treatment of nonoccupational illness or injury	Covered in full	Covered in full
Prescribed Home Health Services	Covered at 80% after deductible	Covered in full	Covered in full
Allergy Care	Covered at 80% after deductible	Covered in full	Covered in full
Eligibility	Spouse and unmarried dependent children to age 19 or age 23 if a full-time student	Spouse and unmarried dependent children to age 19 or 23 if a full-time student	Spouse and unmarried dependent children through age 19 or 23 if a full-time student
Conversion	Conversion to individual coverage available	Conversion to nongroup coverage available	Conversion to individual enrollment available at same benefit level

Cross–Blue Shield plan, or employer; rather, a choice can be made each time medical care is needed. However, employees are offered incentives to use the PPO, including lower or reduced deductibles and copayments as well as increased benefits such as preventive health care.

Employers were disappointed with some of the early PPOs. While discounts were received, they seemed to have little effect on benefit costs because discounts were from higher-than-average fees, or providers were more likely to perform diagnostic tests or prolong hospital stays to generate additional fees to compensate for the discounts. Needless to say, these PPOs seldom lasted long.

The successful PPOs today emphasize quality care and utilization review. In selecting physicians and hospitals, PPOs look not only at the type of care provided but also at the provider's cost-effectiveness. In this era of fierce competition among medical care providers, these physicians and hospitals are often willing to accept discounts in hopes of increasing patient volume. It is also important for a PPO to monitor and control utilization on an ongoing basis. In some cases bonuses are provided if the quantity of care (such as the number of visits to a physician and diagnostic tests performed) is below specified utilization targets. However, there is always the risk that a low quantity of care may also be associated with a low quality of care.

Over time PPOs, like HMOs, have continued to evolve. Some PPOs provide benefits on a prepaid basis, while others perform a gatekeeper function. If a specialist is not recommended by a subscriber's primary-care physician, benefits may be reduced. With these changes it is sometimes difficult to determine the exact form of a managed care organization. However, those that operate as traditional HMOs generally provide medical expense coverage at a slightly lower cost than those that operate as traditional PPOs, but there are wide variations among HMOs as well as among PPOs. Therefore a careful analysis of quality of care, cost, and financial stability is necessary before a particular HMO or PPO is selected.

Exclusive-Provider Organizations

A variation of the preferred-provider organization is the exclusive-provider organization, or EPO. The primary difference is that an EPO does not provide coverage outside the preferred-provider network, except in those infrequent cases where the network does not contain an appropriate specialist. This aspect of an EPO makes it very similar to an HMO.

Regulation

PPOs are subject to much less stringent regulation than HMOs. In fact, until recently, they were largely unregulated. As a result the NAIC passed the Preferred Provider Arrangements Model Act, which has now been adopted by more than half the states. The act is relatively brief and establishes only a minimal regulatory framework. The act requires PPOs to incorporate cost-containment mechanisms, such as utilization review, to determine whether a service is medically necessary. Covered persons must be given reasonable access to medical services The act also allows PPOs to provide incentives for persons to use the preferred-provider network and to place limitations on the number and types of providers with whom they will contract.

POINT-OF-SERVICE PLANS

A newer and fast-growing type of managed care arrangement is the point-of-service (POS) plan. It is estimated that 25 to 30 percent of managed care subscribers are covered under such plans. A POS plan is a hybrid arrangement that combines aspects of a traditional medical expense plan with an HMO or a PPO. With a POS plan, participants in the plan elect, at the time medical treatment is needed, whether to receive treatment within the plan's network or outside the network. Expenses received outside the network are reimbursed as if the subscriber was covered under a traditional indemnity plan. However, the deductibles and copayments tend to be higher. For example, one plan has a $500 annual deductible for out-of-network office visits, and only 70 percent of the costs above the deductible are reimbursed.

Employers that use point-of-service plans hope that these plans will encourage a greater number of older and illness-prone employees to leave more expensive traditional benefit plans and join HMOs or PPOs, which are viewed as being better able to control escalating medical costs. The early experience has shown this to be the case. One interesting result is that while new POS plan subscribers still have the security of occasionally seeing an outside specialist, most subscribers have confined their visits solely to physicians within the HMO or PPO.

There are two basic types of point-of-service plans—the open-ended HMO and the gatekeeper PPO. An open-ended HMO can take the basic form of any of the HMOs previously described. However, at any time a subscriber can elect to go outside the HMO network of medical care providers.

It can be argued that any PPO is actually a POS plan. However, the normal usage of the term *POS* implies a higher degree of managed care than is found in most PPOs. A gatekeeper PPO requires the PPO participant to elect a primary care physician in the manner of an HMO subscriber. This physician acts as a gatekeeper to control utilization and refer members to specialists within the PPO network. However, a subscriber can elect to go outside the network.

Under some POS plans a subscriber can go outside the plan's network without informing the plan of this fact. In other POS plans, the subscriber must notify the gatekeeper that such treatment will be sought. Even though the gatekeeper has no power to prevent the out-of-network treatment, the gatekeeper may be able to convince the subscriber that proper treatment is available within the network. Furthermore, the gatekeeper can better manage future medical care by being aware of all medical treatment that a subscriber is receiving.

MULTIPLE-OPTION PLANS

Until recently an employer who wanted to make an HMO option available to employees had to enter into a separate contractual arrangement with the HMO. Unless a PPO was sponsored by the insurance company or Blue Cross–Blue Shield plan of an employer, a similar contractual arrangement was also required. Several insurance companies and Blue Cross–Blue Shield plans are now providing all these options under a single medical expense contract. For example, one insurer is marketing a so-called triple-option plan that gives employees the choice of a traditional fee-for-service indemnity plan, an indemnity plan using a PPO, or an HMO. In most cases the HMOs and PPOs used in such arrangements have been formed or purchased by the insurance company or Blue Cross–Blue Shield plan, but occasionally a contractual relationship has been established with an existing HMO or PPO.

These plans offer certain advantages to the employer. First, administration is easier since all elements of the plan are purchased from a single provider. Second, costs may be lower since the entire plan, including the HMO, is normally subject to experience rating. Because federally qualified HMOs cannot fully use experience rating, only nonfederally qualified HMOs are typically used in multiple-option plans.

12

Group Medical Expense Benefits: Plan Provisions and Taxation

Chapter Outline

This chapter is devoted primarily to a discussion of many of the major provisions in medical expense plans. To a large extent these provisions are similar—if not identical—to those discussed in the earlier chapter on group term life insurance. However, certain provisions are either unique to medical expense plans or different from those found in other types of group benefits. These provisions pertain to eligibility, coordination of benefits, the effect of medicare, termination (including postretirement benefits), and claims. Several of the provisions have been affected by the passage of the Health Insurance Portability and Accountability Act in 1996.

The last portion of the chapter describes the tax treatment of medical expense benefits. One unusual characteristic of this tax treatment is the difference in the way that insured benefits and self-funded benefits are treated.

ELIGIBILITY

The eligibility requirements for medical expense coverage are essentially the same as those discussed earlier for group term insurance—an employee must usually be in a covered classification, must satisfy any probationary period, and must be full-time. Coverage is rarely made available to part-time employees. In addition, medical expense contracts often contain an actively-at-work provision. This may be waived for larger employers for whom adverse selection tends to be less of a problem than for smaller groups, since any adverse selection for a large group will be reflected in future premiums through the experience-rating process.

Eligibility requirements may vary somewhat if an employer changes insurance companies. Even though it has been adopted by only a few states, most insurance companies follow the procedures established by the NAIC Model Regulation on Group Coverage Discontinuance and Replacement for medical expense coverage (and possibly other group coverages). This regulation stipulates that coverage will be provided (but possibly limited) under a new plan to anyone who (1) was covered under the prior plan at the date it was discontinued and (2) is in an eligible classification of the new plan. Employees actively at work on the date coverage is transferred are automatically covered under the new plan and are exempt from any probationary periods. If the new plan contains a preexisting-conditions provision, benefits applicable to an individual's preexisting conditions are limited to the lesser of (1) the maximum benefits of the new plan (ignoring the preexisting conditions) or (2) the maximum benefits of the prior plan.

Employees who are not actively at work on the date coverage is discontinued under the old plan (such as an employee disabled by illness or injury or employees suffering temporary interruptions of employment) must be included in the new plan. However, their benefits can be limited to the old plan's level until they meet the new plan's actively-at-work requirement. Two other points should be made concerning the transfer of coverage. First, the new plan will not pay benefits for expenses covered by the old plan under an extension-of-benefits provision (discussed later), and second, when applying any deductibles or waiting periods under the new plan, credit is often given for the satisfaction (or partial satisfaction) of the same or similar provisions during the last 3 months of the old plan. For example, assume that coverage is transferred in the middle of a calendar year and the new plan contains the same $200-a-year calendar deductible as the old plan. If an employee has already satisfied the deductible under the old plan, no new deductible will be required for the remainder of the calendar year provided that (1) the expenses used to satisfy the deductible under the old plan will satisfy the deductible under the new plan, and (2) the expenses were incurred during the last 3 months of the old plan. If only $140 of the $200 was incurred during those last 3 months, an additional $60 deductible will be required under the new plan for the remainder of the calendar year.

Dependent Eligibility

Typically the same medical expense benefits that are provided for an eligible employee will also be available for that employee's dependents. Conversely, however, dependent coverage is rarely available unless the employee also has coverage. As long as any necessary payroll deductions have been authorized, dependent coverage is typically effective on the same date as the employee's coverage. If coverage under a contributory plan is not elected within 31 days after dependents are eligible, future coverage will be available only during an open enrollment period or when satisfactory evidence of insurability can be provided. However, if an employee was previously without dependents (and therefore had no dependent coverage), any newly acquired dependents (by birth, marriage, or adoption) will be eligible for coverage as of the date they gain dependent status.

The term *dependents* most commonly refers to an employee's spouse who is not legally separated from the employee and any unmarried dependent children (including stepchildren and adopted children) under the age of 19. However, coverage is usually provided for children to age 23 if they are full-time students. In addition, coverage may also continue (and is required to be continued in some states) for children who are incapable of earning their own living because of a physical or mental infirmity. Such children will be considered dependents as long as this condition exists, but periodic proof of the condition may be required by the insurance company. If an employee has dependent coverage, all newly acquired dependents (by birth, marriage, or adoption) are automatically covered.

Some persons that meet the definition of a dependent may be ineligible for coverage because they are in the armed forces or they are eligible for coverage under the same plan as employees themselves. This latter restriction, however, may not apply to a spouse unless the spouse is actually covered under the plan. Some plans also exclude coverage for any dependents residing outside the United States or Canada.

Most medical expense plans contain a "nonconfinement" provision for dependents, which is similar to the actively-at-work provision for employees. Under this provision a dependent is not covered if he or she is confined for medical care or treatment in a hospital or at home at the time of eligibility. Coverage, however, will become effective when the dependent is released from such confinement.

When coverage is transferred, dependents are treated the same as employees, except that any actively-at-work provision is usually replaced by a nonconfinement provision.

OBRA '93

Until the passage of the Omnibus Budget Reconciliation Act of 1993 (OBRA '93), provisions regarding eligibility were determined by the employer and/or any applicable state laws. OBRA '93 brought the federal government into the picture with a series of rules designed to better guarantee that benefits are available to children. Some of these rules pertain to eligibility.

Coverage for Adopted Children

One rule is in the form of an amendment to ERISA. If a work-related group medical expense plan provides coverage for dependent children of participants or beneficiaries, it must provide benefits for adopted children or children placed for adoption under the same terms and conditions that apply to natural children. For purposes of this change, a *child* is defined as a person under the age of 18 at the time of adoption or placement for adoption. Placement for adoption occurs at the time in the adoption process when the plan participant or beneficiary assumes and retains the legal duty for the total or partial support of a child to be adopted.

In addition to providing coverage, a plan cannot restrict benefits because of a preexisting condition at the time coverage is effective as long as the adoption or placement for adoption occurs while the parent is eligible for plan participation.

Medical Child Support Orders

Two other rules have as their goal the shifting of medicaid cost from the government to the private sector by requiring employer-provided benefit plans to pick up more of the cost of providing medical expense benefits to the children of divorced and separated parents. The first of these rules amended ERISA by requiring employer-sponsored medical expense plans to recognize qualified medical child support orders by providing benefits for a participant's children in accordance with the requirements of such an order.

The act defines a *medical child support order* as a court judgment, decree, or order that (1) provides for child support with respect to the child of a group plan participant or provides benefit coverage to such a child, is ordered under state domestic relations law, and relates to benefits under the plan or (2) enforces a state medical support law enacted under the new medicaid rules discussed below. The support order then becomes *qualified* if two additional requirements are met. First, the order must create or recognize the right of the child to receive benefits for which the plan participant or other beneficiary is entitled under a group plan. Second, the order must include such information as the name and last known mailing address of the plan participant and the child, a reasonable description of the coverage to be provided, the period for which coverage must be provided, and each plan to which the order applies. However, a qualified order cannot require a plan to offer any benefit that is not already available under the plan unless the benefits are necessary to meet the requirements of a state medical child support law established under the Social Security Act.

When a plan administrator receives a medical child support order, the administrator must promptly notify the participant and each child named under the order and inform them of the plan's procedure for determining if the order is a qualified medical child support order. Under the act, all group plans must establish reasonable written procedures for determining whether these orders are qualified.

Changes in Medicaid Rules

Under the final rule that will be discussed, states were encouraged (under threat of losing some medicaid reimbursement) to adopt a series of laws relating to medical child support. One of these laws prohibits plan administrators from denying enrollment of a child under a parent's insurance plan on the grounds that (1) the child was born out of wedlock, (2) the child is not claimed as a dependent on the parent's federal income tax return, or (3) the child does not reside with the parent or in the insurer's service area. In addition, a second law provides that if a court orders a parent to provide medical support, the parent's plan must enroll the child without regard to any enrollment restrictions. If the parent fails to enroll the child, enrollment can be made by the child's other parent or by the state medicaid agency. The employer is required to withhold from the parent's compensation any payments that the parent must make toward the cost of coverage.

Portability

Some of the most significant parts of the Health Insurance Portability and Accountability Act are the provisions dealing with "portability" of medical expense coverage. These provisions do not allow an employee to take specific insurance from one job to another. Rather, they put limitations on preexisting-conditions exclusions and allow an employee to use evidence of prior insurance coverage to reduce or eliminate the length of any preexisting-conditions exclusion when the employee moves to another medical expense plan. These provisions should minimize job lock for employees by eliminating the fear that medical expense coverage will be lost if an employee changes jobs.

The portability provisions apply to almost all group health insurance plans (either insured or self-funded) as long as they have at least two active participants on the first day of the plan year. Note that the same definition of *group health plan* mentioned in the initial discussion of the Health Insurance Portability and Accountability Act in chapter 9 applies to the portability provisions. These provisions are effective for plan years beginning on or after July, 1, 1997, if a plan is not subject to collective bargaining. Collectively bargained plans are subject to the provisions on the later of July 1, 1997, or the ending date of the last collective-bargaining agreement applying to a plan.

Limitations on Preexisting Conditions

Restrictions for preexisting conditions are limited to a maximum of 12 months (18 months for late enrollees). In addition, the period for preexisting conditions must be reduced for prior creditable coverage as defined below. It should be noted that there is nothing in the act that prohibits an employer from imposing a waiting period before a new employee is eligible to enroll in a medical expense plan. However, any waiting period must be applied uniformly without regard to the health status of potential plan participants or beneficiaries. In addition, the waiting period must run concurrently with any preexisting-conditions period. For example, an employee might be subject to a preexisting-conditions period of 7 months because of prior coverage. If the employer's plan had a 3-month waiting period for enrollment, the length of the preexisting-conditions period after enrollment could be only 4 months. An HMO is also permitted to have an affiliation period of up to 2 months (3 months for late enrollees) if the HMO does not impose a preexisting-conditions provision and if the affiliation period is applied without regard to health status-related factors.

Under the act, a *preexisting condition* is defined as a mental or physical condition for which medical advice, diagnosis, care, or treatment was recommended or received within the 6-month period ending on the enrollment date. No preexisting-conditions exclusions can apply to pregnancy or to newborn children or, if under age 18, to newly adopted children or children newly placed for adoption as long as they become covered for creditable coverage within 30 days of birth, adoption, or placement. In addition, the use of genetic information as a preexisting condition is prohibited unless there is a diagnosis of a preexisting medical condition related to the information.

The 12-month limitation for preexisting conditions applies if an employee enrolls when he or she is initially eligible for coverage. It also applies in the case of special enrollment periods (discussed in chapter 9) that are required by the act for employees and dependents who lose other coverage and for new dependents. Anyone who does not enroll in an employer's plan during the first period he or she is eligible or during a special enrollment period is a late enrollee and can be subject to a preexisting-conditions period of 18 months.

Creditable Coverage

The act defines creditable coverage as coverage under an individual policy, an employer-provided group plan (either insured or self-funded), an HMO, medicare, medicaid, or various public plans, regardless of whether the coverage is provided to a person as an individual, an employee, or a dependent. However, coverage is not creditable if there has been a break in coverage of 63 days or more.

In determining the length of a person's preexisting-conditions period, the period of prior creditable coverage must be subtracted. Assume, for example, that an employer's plan has a preexisting-conditions period of 12 months. If a new employee has 12 months or more of creditable coverage, the preexisting-conditions period will be satisfied. If the period of creditable coverage is only 7 months, then the preexisting-conditions period will run 5 more months. Note, however, that if the employee has been without coverage for at least 63 days between jobs, the full preexisting-conditions period will apply.

Employers have two ways in which they can apply creditable coverage: on a blanket basis to all categories of medical expense coverage or on a benefit-specific basis. For example, if an employee had prior coverage that excluded prescription drugs, this particular coverage could be subject to the full preexisting-conditions period, while the period for other benefits would be reduced because creditable coverage had applied to them. For administrative ease, an employer would probably pick the first method.

The act requires an employer to give persons losing group coverage a certificate that specifies the period of creditable coverage under the plan they are leaving, including any period of COBRA coverage.

State Options

The act's provisions on portability generally override state laws. However, state laws that provide greater portability are not overridden. For example, a look-back period of less than 6 months might be required, or the maximum preexisting-conditions period could be less than 12 months.

Benefits for Domestic Partners

In the mid-1980s, the plans of a few employers began to define the term *dependent* broadly enough to include unmarried domestic partners. For example, one plan covers unmarried couples as long as they live together, show financial interdependence and joint responsibility for each other's common welfare, and consider themselves life partners. This type of requirement is fairly typical, as is the additional requirement that the employee's relationship must have lasted some specified minimum period of time, such as 6 or 12 months. The employee must usually give the employer an affidavit that these requirements have been satisfied.

By the mid-1990s, an estimated 10 percent of employers provided medical expense benefits to domestic partners. Most plans provide benefits to domestic partners engaged in either heterosexual or homosexual relationships. Some plans provide benefits only to persons of the opposite sex of the employee, and a small number of plans limit benefits only to persons of the same sex. The rationale for the latter is that persons of opposite sexes can obtain benefits by marrying, whereas this option is not available to persons of the same sex.

The number of employees obtaining coverage for domestic partners has been relatively small, with many employers experiencing enrollment of less than one percent when only partners of the same sex are covered. Some employers have experienced enrollment of up to 4 percent if partners of either sex are covered.

(Enrollments of partners of the opposite sex are more than double the enrollments of partners of the same sex.) This low enrollment is due primarily to two factors. First, the domestic partner is probably also working and has medical expense coverage from his or her employer. Second, some employees are unwilling to make their living arrangement or sexual preference known in the workplace.

Despite predictions that domestic partners would have adverse claims experience (primarily due to AIDS), the claims experience has been good. As a group, domestic partners tend to be young and healthy, and maternity claims are minimal. Most, if not all, insurers that levied surcharges on premiums for domestic partners when the coverage was new have now dropped the surcharges.

COORDINATION OF BENEFITS

In recent years the percentage of individuals having duplicate group medical expense coverage has increased substantially and is estimated to be about 10 percent. Probably the most common situation is the one in which a husband and wife both work and have coverage under their respective employers' noncontributory plans. If the employer of either spouse also provides dependent coverage on a noncontributory basis, the other spouse (and other dependents if both employers provide such coverage) will be covered under both plans. If dependent coverage is contributory, it will be necessary for a couple with children to elect such coverage under one of their plans. However, because a spouse is considered a dependent, he or she will also have duplicate coverage when the election is made. Duplicate coverage may also arise when

- an employee has two jobs
- children are covered under both a parent's and a stepparent's plans
- an employee elects coverage under a contributory plan even though he or she is covered as a dependent under another plan. This could result from ignorance or from an attempt to collect double the amount if a claim should occur. In many cases this coverage is elected because it is broader, even though it still results in an element of duplicate coverage.

Duplicate coverage can also occur if an individual has coverage under a group plan that is not provided by an employer. A common example involves children whose parents have purchased accident coverage for them through their schools.

In the absence of any provisions to the contrary, group medical expense plans are obligated to provide benefits in cases of duplicate coverage as if no other coverage exists. However, to prevent individuals from receiving benefits that exceed their actual expenses, most group medical expense plans contain a *coordination-of-benefits (COB) provision,* under which priorities are established for the payment of benefits by each plan covering an individual.

Most COB provisions are based on the Model Group Coordination of Benefits Regulation promulgated by the National Association of Insurance Commissioners. This regulation is periodically revised, and all or portions of one of the versions have now been adopted by almost all states. As with all NAIC model legislation and regulations, some states have adopted the COB provisions with variations.

Although some flexibility is allowed, virtually all COB provisions apply when other coverage exists through the group insurance plans or group benefit arrangements (such as the Blues, HMOs, or self-funded plans) of another employer. They may also apply to no-fault automobile insurance benefits and to student coverage that is either sponsored or provided by educational institutions. However, these provisions virtually never apply (and cannot in most states) to any other coverages provided under contracts purchased on an individual basis outside of the employment relationship.

Determination of Primary Coverage

The usual COB provision stipulates that any other plan without the COB provision is primary and that any plan with it is secondary. If more than one plan has a COB provision, the following priorities are established:

- Coverage as an employee is usually primary to coverage as a dependent. The exception to this rule occurs if a retired person is covered (1) by medicare, (2) under a retiree plan of a former employer, and (3) as a dependent of a spouse who is an active employee. In this case coverage as a dependent is primary, medicare is secondary, and the retiree plan pays last.
- Coverage as an active employee (or as that person's dependent) is primary to coverage as a retired or laid-off employee (or as that person's dependent). However, this rule is ignored unless both plans contain the rule.
- Coverage as an active employee (or that person's dependent) is primary to a plan that provides COBRA continuation benefits. This rule is also ignored unless both plans contain the rule.
- If the specific rules of a court decree state that one parent must assume responsibility for his or her child's health care expenses, and the plan of that parent has actual knowledge of the terms of the court decree, then that plan is primary.
- If the parents of dependent children are married or are not separated (regardless of whether they have ever been married) or if a court awards joint custody without specifying that one parent has the responsibility to provide health care coverage, the plan of the parent whose birthday falls earlier in the calendar year is primary and the plan of the parent with the later birthday is secondary.

- If the parents of dependent children are not married, are separated (regardless of whether they have ever been married), or are divorced and if there is no court decree allocating responsibility for the child's health care expenses, the following priorities apply:

  - The plan of the parent with custody is primary.
  - The plan of the stepparent who is the spouse of the parent with custody is secondary.
  - The plan of the parent without custody is tertiary.
  - The plan of the stepparent who is the spouse of the parent without custody pays last.

- If none of the previous rules establishes a priority, the plan covering the person for the longest period of time is primary. However, if this rule also fails to determine the primary plan, then allowable expenses are shared equally among the plans.

Determination of Benefits Payable

The actual mechanics of the previously described COB provision are demonstrated in the following example, which assumes that a person has coverage under the plans of two employers:

Plan A has basic benefits with a maximum of (1) $300 per day for semiprivate hospital accommodations up to 31 days, (2) $1,000 for hospital extras, and (3) $1,500 for surgery. It has no deductibles or coinsurance.

Plan B has comprehensive major medical expense coverage with (1) a $200 calendar-year deductible, (2) 80 percent coinsurance, and (3) a $250,000 maximum. Hospital benefits are limited to the cost of semiprivate accommodations.

Assume also that this person incurs the following expenses:

Semiprivate room for 8 days at $500 per day	$4,000
Other hospital charges	1,200
Surgeon's fees	2,000
Total expenses	$7,200

If there were no COB provision in either plan, plan A would pay $4,900 ($2,400 for hospital room and board, $1,000 for hospital extras, and $1,500 for surgery), and plan B would pay $5,600 (assuming no portion of the deductible had previously been satisfied). This latter amount consists of 80 percent of covered expenses that exceed the $200 deductible. Consequently the person would collect benefits totaling $10,500, or $3,300 in excess of his or her actual expenses.

Before the COB provision is used, it must first be determined whether the provision applies to a given claim. It will apply only if the sum of the benefits under the plans involved (assuming there is no provision) exceeds an individual's allowable expenses. *Allowable expenses* are defined as any necessary, reasonable, and customary items of expense, all or a portion of which are covered under at least one of the plans that provides benefits to the person for whom the claim is made. However, under a primary plan the amount of any benefit reductions resulting from a covered person's failure to comply with the plan's provisions (such as second opinions or precertification) is not considered an allowable expense. In addition, the difference between the cost of a private hospital room and the cost of a semiprivate hospital room is not considered an allowable expense unless the patient's stay in a private room is medically necessary. When the allowable expenses are determined, any deductibles, coinsurance, and plan maximum are ignored.

In the previous example the entire $7,200 is considered allowable expenses. Because the sum of the benefits otherwise payable under the two plans ($10,500) exceeds this amount, the COB provision applies. If the sum of the benefits did not exceed the allowable expenses, the COB provision would not apply, and each plan would pay its benefits as if it was the only existing plan.

When the COB provision applies, a person receives benefits equal to 100 percent of his or her allowable expenses and no more. The primary plan pays its benefits as if no other coverage exists, and the secondary plan (or plans) pays the remaining benefits. If plan A in this example is primary, it will pay $4,900, and plan B will pay the remaining $2,300 of expenses. If plan B is primary, it will pay $5,600, and plan A will pay the remaining $1,600.

The Preservation of Deductibles and Coinsurance

The preservation of deductibles and coinsurance was acceptable under 1985 NAIC provisions. The major rationale for such a provision was that the traditional approach negated the cost-containment effects of deductibles and coinsurance, since most persons would be indemnified for 100 percent of their expenses even if both plans contained these cost-saving features. However, most states did not adopt this portion of the provisions, and the NAIC deleted it in 1987. However, a few states do allow the preservation of deductibles and coinsurance and permit one of two approaches to be used.

The first approach is similar to the traditional approach but allows the secondary plan to pay the difference between 80 percent (or more if the plan so provides) of total allowable expenses actually incurred less whatever the primary plan paid. In the example 80 percent of allowable expense is $5,760. If plan A is primary and pays $4,900, plan B will be required to pay only $860 if it uses the 80 percent figure.

The second approach for preserving deductibles and coinsurance does not use the concept of allowable expense. Rather, the secondary plan pays the difference, if any, between (1) the amount it would have paid if it had been primary and (2) the amount the primary plan paid. This approach maintains the benefit provisions of the secondary plan—deductibles, coinsurance, and any other policy limitations or exclusions. In the example, plan B would pay $5,600 if it had been primary. If plan A was actually primary, it would pay $4,900 and plan B would pay an additional $700.

When it is permissible to preserve deductibles and coinsurance, most states require a plan to comply with certain rules that were contained in the deleted portion of the NAIC provisions:

- Covered persons must be given prior notice that they will not receive 100 percent of their expenses if duplicate coverage exists. This gives them the opportunity to discontinue coverage under one of the plans if that is possible and is in their best interest.
- The plan must allow a person who is otherwise eligible for coverage under the plan but not enrolled in it to enroll if his or her coverage under another group plan terminates for any reason and cannot be replaced. The rationale for this provision is that the COB provision tends to encourage working families to drop duplicate coverage. This rule prevents a total loss of protection if coverage under the plan that was not dropped is later terminated.
- If a plan uses the second approach (the one without the concept of allowable expense), it cannot have a coinsurance factor of less than (1) 50 percent for mental or nervous disorders or alcohol and drug abuse treatments, (2) 50 percent for benefits if a covered person fails to obtain or follow cost-containment provisions, such as second surgical opinions or preadmission certification, and (3) 75 percent for other covered expenses. The latter restriction, however, does not apply to dental care, vision care, hearing care, or prescription drugs.

Always-Secondary Plans

In most states, insured medical expense plans (including the Blues, HMOs, and PPOs) are not required to use a coordination-of-benefits provision. However, when such a provision is used, it must comply with the appropriate state rules. Self-funded plans, on the other hand, are not bound by these rules and can use any type of coordination-of-benefits provision. As a rule a self-funded plan will use a provision that is identical or similar to that imposed on insured plans. Unfortunately some self-funded plans have been designed so that they are excess or "always secondary" to any other medical expense plan.

The most extreme situation occurs if a person is covered under two self-funded plans, each of which takes an always-secondary approach. Each plan will pay as if it was secondary. In the previous example this means that plan A will pay $1,600 and plan B will pay $2,300. This total of $3,900 is less than either plan would pay if it was primary. This issue has been the subject of several court cases, and some (but not all) courts have stated that the always-secondary position cannot prevail. While these courts have ordered an equitable payment of benefits to the covered person, that person has been forced to take the matter to court.

A similar situation exists if a person is covered under a self-funded plan that is always secondary (but would be primary if the state's rules applied) and an insured plan that is legitimately secondary because of the state's coordination-of-benefits rules. However, the results are usually somewhat different. In most states the insured plan must pay the covered person two amounts—the first, what the insured plan is obligated to pay as the secondary plan, and the second, the difference between what the self-funded plan pays on a secondary basis and what it would have paid if it had settled the claim as the primary payer of benefits. This second amount is considered an advance to the covered person, and the insured plan receives a right of subrogation. In other words, the insured plan has the right to take legal action to recover the amount of the advance from the self-funded plan. If the amount is recovered, the advance is in effect repaid. If there is no recovery, the covered person has no obligation to repay the insured plan.

THE RELATIONSHIP WITH MEDICARE

Since most employees and their dependents will be eligible for medicare upon reaching age 65 (and possibly under other circumstances), a provision that will eliminate any possible duplication of coverage is necessary. The simplest solution would be to exclude any person eligible for medicare from eligibility under the group contract. However, in most cases this approach would conflict with the Age Discrimination in Employment Act, which prohibits discrimination in welfare benefit plans for active employees.

Medicare Secondary Rules

As mentioned in the chapter on social security, employers with 20 or more employees must make coverage available under their medical expense plans to active employees aged 65 or older and to active employees' spouses who are eligible for medicare. Unless an employee elects otherwise, the employer's plan is primary and medicare is secondary. Except in plans that require large employee contributions, it is doubtful that employees will elect medicare to be primary since employers are prohibited from offering active employees or their spouses a medicare carve-out, a medicare supplement, or some other incentive not to enroll in the employer's plan.

Medicare is the secondary payer of benefits in two other situations. The first situation involves persons who are eligible for medicare benefits to treat end-stage renal disease with dialysis or kidney transplants. Medicare provides these benefits to any insured workers (either active or retired) and to their spouses and dependent children, but the employer's plan is primary during the first 18 months of treatment only; after that time medicare is primary and the employer's plan is secondary. It should be noted that the employer's plan could totally exclude dialysis and/or kidney transplants, in which case medicare would pay. However, the employer is prevented by law from excluding these benefits for the first 18 months if they are covered thereafter. This rule for renal disease applies to medical expense plans of all employers, not just those with 20 or more employees.

Medicare is also the secondary payer of benefits to disabled employees (or the disabled dependents of employees) under age 65 who are eligible for medicare and who are covered under the medical expense plan of large employers (defined as plans with 100 or more employees). Medicare, however, does not pay anything until a person has been eligible for social security disability income benefits for 2 years. The rule applies only if an employer continues medical expense coverage for disabled persons; there is no requirement for such a continuation.

Medicare Carve-Outs and Supplements

An employer's plan may cover certain persons aged 65 or older who are not covered by the provisions of the Age Discrimination in Employment Act—specifically retirees and active employees of firms with fewer than 20 employees. Although there is nothing to prevent an employer from terminating coverage for these persons, many employers provide them with either a medicare carve-out or medicare supplement.

With a *medicare carve-out*, plan benefits are reduced to the extent that benefits are payable under medicare for the same expenses. (Medicare may also pay for some expenses not covered by the group plan.) For example, if a person who incurs $1,000 of covered expenses is not eligible for medicare, $720 in benefits will be paid under a medical expense plan that has a $100 deductible and an 80 percent coinsurance provision. However, if the same person is eligible for medicare, and if medicare pays $650 for the same expenses, the employer's plan will pay only $70, for a total benefit of $720.

Some medical expense plans use a more liberal carve-out approach and reduce covered expenses (rather than benefits payable) by any amounts received under medicare. In the previous example the $650 paid by medicare would be subtracted from the $1,000 of covered expenses, which would leave $350. After the deductible and coinsurance are applied to this amount, the employer's plan would pay $200, so the covered person would receive a total of $850 in benefits, or $130 more than a person not eligible for medicare.

As an alternative to using a carve-out approach, some employers use a *medicare supplement* that provides benefits for certain specific expenses not covered under medicare. These include (1) the portion of expenses that is not paid by medicare because of deductibles, coinsurance, or copayments, and (2) certain expenses excluded by medicare, such as prescription drugs. Such a supplement may or may not provide benefits similar to those available under a carve-out plan.

TERMINATION OF COVERAGE

In the absence of any provisions for continuation or conversion, group medical expense coverage on an employee generally ceases on the earliest of the following:

- the date on which employment terminates. In some contracts, coverage ceases on the last day of the month in which employment terminates.
- the date on which the employee ceases to be eligible
- the date on which the master contract terminates
- the date on which the overall maximum benefit of major medical coverage is received
- the end of the last period for which the employee has made any required contribution

Coverage on any dependent usually ceases on the earliest of the following:

- the date on which he or she ceases to meet the definition of dependent
- the date on which the coverage of the employee ceases for any reason except the employee's receipt of the overall maximum benefit
- the date on which the dependent receives the overall maximum benefit of major medical coverage
- the end of the last period for which the employee has made any required contribution for dependent coverage

However, coverage often continues past these dates because of federal legislation or employer practices.

The Continuation of Coverage under COBRA

The Consolidated Omnibus Budget Reconciliation Act of 1985 (COBRA) requires that group health plans allow employees and certain beneficiaries to elect to have their current health insurance coverage extended at group rates for up to 36 months following a "qualifying event" that results in the loss of coverage for a "qualified beneficiary." The term *group health plan* as used in the act is broad enough to include medical expense plans, dental plans, vision care plans, and prescription drug plans, regardless of whether benefits are self-insured or provided through other entities such as insurance companies or HMOs. COBRA applies even if the cost of a plan is paid solely by employees as long as the plan would not be available at the same cost to an employee if he or she were not employed. However, there is one exception to this rule: voluntary benefit plans under which the employer's only involvement is to process payroll deductions are not subject to COBRA.

The act applies only to employers who had 20 or more employees on a typical business day during the preceding calendar year. (However, church and government plans are exempt from the act.) Failure to comply with the act will result in an excise tax of up to $100 per day for each person denied coverage. The tax can be levied on the employer as well as on the entity (such as an insurer or HMO) that provides or administers the benefits.

Since the passage of COBRA, a qualified beneficiary has been defined as any employee, or the spouse or dependent child of the employee, who on the day before a qualifying event was covered under the employee's group health plan. Effective 1997, the Health Insurance Portability and Accountability Act expanded the definition to include any child who is born to or placed for adoption with the employee during the period of COBRA coverage. This change gives automatic eligibility for COBRA coverage to the child as well as the right to have his or her own election rights if a second qualifying event occurs.

Under the act each of the following is a qualifying event if it results in the loss of coverage by a qualified beneficiary:

- the death of the covered employee
- the termination of the employee for any reason except gross misconduct. This includes quitting, retiring, or being fired for anything other than gross misconduct.
- a reduction of the employee's hours so that the employee or dependent is ineligible for coverage
- the divorce or legal separation of the covered employee and his or her spouse
- for spouses and children, the employee's eligibility for medicare
- a child's ceasing to be an eligible dependent under the plan

The act specifies that a qualified beneficiary is entitled to elect continued coverage without providing evidence of insurability. The beneficiary must be allowed to continue coverage identical to that provided to employees and dependents to whom a qualifying event has not occurred. If a medical expense plan includes such items as dental care or vision care as an integral part of the plan, the beneficiary must also be allowed to continue coverage without these benefits, even though such an option is not available to active employees or their dependents. Long-term care coverage is not subject to COBRA rules.

Coverage for persons electing continuation can be changed when changes are made to the plan covering active employees and their dependents. The continued coverage must extend from the date of the qualifying event to the earliest of the following:

- 18 months for employees and dependents when the employee's employment has terminated or coverage has been terminated because of a reduction in hours. This period is extended to 29 months for a qualified beneficiary if the Social Security Administration determines that the beneficiary was or became totally disabled at any time during the first 60 days of COBRA coverage.
- 36 months for other qualifying events
- the date the plan terminates for all employees
- the date the coverage ceases because of a qualified beneficiary's failure to make a timely payment of premium
- the date a qualified beneficiary becomes entitled to medicare or becomes covered (as either an employee or dependent) under another group health plan, provided the group health plan does not contain an exclusion or limitation with respect to any preexisting condition. If the new plan does not cover a preexisting condition, the COBRA coverage can be continued until the earlier of (1) the remainder of the 18- or 36-month period or (2) the time when the preexisting-conditions provision no longer applies.

If a second qualifying event (such as the death or divorce of a terminated employee) occurs during the period of continued coverage, the maximum period of continuation is 36 months. For example, if an employee terminates employment, the employee and family are eligible for 18 months of COBRA coverage. If the employee dies after 15 months, a second qualifying event has occurred for the employee's spouse and dependent children. The normal period of COBRA continuation resulting from the death of an employee is 36 months. However, because the spouse and children have already had COBRA coverage for 15 months, the second qualifying event extends coverage for an additional 21 months

At the termination of continued coverage, a qualified beneficiary must be offered the right to convert to an individual insurance policy if a conversion privilege is generally available to employees under the employer's plan.

Notification of the right to continue coverage must be made at two times by a plan's administrator. First, when a plan becomes subject to COBRA or when a person becomes covered under a plan subject to COBRA, notification must be given to an employee as well as to his or her spouse. Second, when a qualifying event occurs, the employer must notify the plan administrator, who then must notify all qualifying beneficiaries within 14 days. In general the employer has 30 days to notify the plan administrator. However, an employer may not know of a qualifying event if it involves divorce, legal separation, or a child's ceasing to be eligible for coverage. In these circumstances the employee or family member must notify the employer within 60 days of the event, or the right to elect COBRA coverage will be lost. The time period for the employer to notify the plan administrator begins when the employer is informed of the qualifying event as long as this occurs within the 60-day period.

The continuation of coverage is not automatic; it must be elected by a qualifying beneficiary. The election period starts on the date of the qualifying event and may end not earlier than 60 days after actual notice of the event to the qualifying beneficiary by the plan administrator. Once coverage is elected, the beneficiary has 45 days to pay the premium for the period of coverage prior to the election.

Under COBRA the cost of the continued coverage may be passed on to the qualifying beneficiary, but the cost cannot exceed 102 percent of the cost to the plan for the period of coverage for a similarly situated active employee to whom a qualifying event has not occurred. The extra 2 percent is supposed to cover the employer's extra administrative costs. The one exception to this rule occurs for months 19 through 29 if an employee is disabled, in which case the premium can then be as high as 150 percent. Qualifying beneficiaries must have the option of paying the premium in monthly installments. In addition, there must be a grace period of at least 30 days for each installment.

COBRA has resulted in significant extra costs for employers. Surveys indicate that coverage is elected by approximately 20 percent of those persons who are entitled to a COBRA continuation. The length of coverage averages almost one year for persons eligible for an 18-month extension and almost 2 years for persons eligible for a 36-month extension. While significant variations exist among employers, claim costs of persons with COBRA coverage generally run between 150 percent and 200 percent of claim costs for active employees and dependents. Moreover, administrative costs are estimated to be about $20 per month for each person with COBRA coverage.

The Continuation of Coverage in Addition to COBRA

Even before the passage of COBRA it was becoming increasingly common for employers (particularly large employers) to continue group insurance coverage for certain employees—and sometimes their dependents—beyond the usual termination dates. Obviously when coverage is continued now, at a minimum an employer must comply with COBRA. However, an employer can be more liberal than COBRA by paying all or a portion of the cost, providing continued coverage for additional categories of persons, or continuing coverage for a longer period of time. Some states have continuation laws for insured medical expense plans that might require coverage to be made available in situations not covered by COBRA. One example is coverage for employees of firms with fewer than 20 employees; another is coverage for periods longer than those required by COBRA.

Retired Employees

Even though not required to do so by the Age Discrimination in Employment Act, many employers continue coverage on retired employees. Although coverage can also be continued for retirees' dependents, it is often limited only to spouses. Retired employees under age 65 usually have the same coverage as the active employees have. However, coverage for employees aged 65 or older (if included under the same plan) may be provided under a carve-out plan that includes medicare or a medicare supplement. The lifetime maximum for persons eligible for medicare is often much lower (such as $5,000 or $10,000) than for active employees. Usually this maximum is not subject to any provision that restores benefits that have been paid.

The subject of retiree benefits has become a major concern to employers since the Financial Accounting Standards Board (FASB) issued a proposal in 1989 for the accounting for postretirement benefits other than pensions. Final rules were issued in 1990. Under the FASB rules, to be phased in between 1993 and 1997, employers are required to do the following:

- recognize the present value of future retiree medical expense benefits on the firm's balance sheet with other liabilities
- record the cost for postretirement medical benefits in the period when an employee performs services. This is comparable to the accounting for pension costs.
- amortize the present value of the future cost of benefits accrued prior to new rules

These new rules are in contrast to the long-used practice of paying retiree medical benefits or premiums out of current revenue and recognizing these costs as expenses when paid. Although the rules are probably logical from a financial accounting standpoint, the effect on employers has been significant. Employers who have elected to immediately recognize the liability have had to show reduced earnings and net worth. Firms that have elected to amortize the liability (often because immediate recognition would wipe out net worth) will be affected for years to come.

The new FASB rules have resulted in two major changes by employers. First, many employers have lowered or eliminated retiree benefits or are considering such a change. However, there are legal uncertainties as to whether benefits that have been promised to retirees can be eliminated or reduced. Many employers also feel that there is a moral obligation to continue these benefits. As a result most employers are not altering plans for current retirees or active employees who are eligible to retire. Rather the changes apply to future retirees only. These changes, which seem to be running the gamut, include the following:

- the elimination of benefits for future retirees
- the shifting of more of the cost burden to future retirees by reducing benefits. Such a reduction may be accomplished by providing lower benefit maximums, covering fewer types of expenses, or increasing copayments.
- adding or increasing retiree sharing of premium costs after retirement
- shifting to a defined-contribution approach to funding retiree benefits. For example, an employer might agree to pay $5 per month toward the cost of coverage after retirement for each year of service by an employee. Thus an employer would make a monthly contribution of $150 for an employee who retired with 30 years of service, but the employer would make a contribution of only $75 for an employee with 15 years of service. Many plans of this nature have been designed so that the employer's contribution increases with changes in the consumer price index, subject to maximum increases such as 5 percent per year.
- encouraging retirees to elect benefits from managed care plans. With this approach, retirees are required to pay a significant portion of the cost if coverage is continued through a traditional indemnity plan.

A second change is that employers will increasingly explore methods to prefund the benefits. However, there are no alternatives for prefunding that are as favorable as the alternatives for funding pension benefits. One alternative is the use of a 501(c)(9) trust (or VEBA). As discussed in the chapter on alternative funding methods, there are limitations on the deductibility of contributions to a 501(c)(9) trust. Furthermore, a 501(c)(9) trust can be used to fund retiree benefits only if it is currently being used to fund benefits for active employees.

Another alternative is to prefund medical benefits within a pension plan. Contributions are tax deductible, and earnings accumulate tax free. The IRS rules for qualified retirement plans permit the payment of benefits for medical expenses from a pension plan if certain requirements are satisfied:

- The medical benefits must be subordinate to the retirement benefits. This rule is met if the cost of the medical benefits provided does not exceed 25 percent of the employer's aggregate contribution to the pension plan. For many employers this figure is too low to allow the entire future liability to be prefunded.
- A separate account must be established and maintained for the monies allocated to medical benefits. This account can be an aggregate account for nonkey employees, but individual separate accounts must be maintained for key employees, and medical benefits attributable to a key employee (and his or her family members) can be made only from the key employee's account.
- The employer's contributions for medical benefits must be ascertainable and reasonable.

Although the rules for funding retiree medical benefits in a pension plan are restricted and administratively complex, they offer an employer the greatest opportunity to deduct the cost of prefunded benefits.

Surviving Dependents

Coverage can also be continued for the survivors of deceased active employees and/or deceased retired employees. However, coverage for the survivors of active employees is not commonly continued beyond the period required by COBRA, and coverage for the survivors of retired employees may be limited to surviving spouses. In both instances the continued coverage is usually identical to what was provided prior to the employee's death. It is also common for the employer to continue the same premium contribution level.

Laid-off Employees

Medical expense coverage can be continued for laid-off workers, and large employers frequently provide such coverage for a limited period. Few employers provide coverage beyond the period required by COBRA, but some employers continue to make the same premium contribution, at least for a limited period of time.

Disabled Employees

As with group term life insurance, medical expense coverage can be continued for an employee (and dependents) when he or she has a temporary interruption of employment, including one arising from illness or injury. Many employers also cover employees who have long-term disabilities or who have retired because of a disability. In most cases this continuation of coverage is contingent upon satisfaction of some definition of total (and possibly permanent) disability. When continuing coverage for disabled employees, an employer must determine the extent of employer contributions. For example, the employer may continue the same premium contribution as for active employees. However, there is nothing to prevent a different contribution rate—either lower or higher.

Extension of Benefits

When coverage is terminated rather than continued, most medical expense plans extend benefits for any covered employee or dependent who is totally disabled at the time of termination. However, the disability must have resulted from an illness or injury that occurred while the person was covered under the group contract. Generally the same level of benefits will be provided as before termination. Although some contracts will cover only expenses associated with the same cause of disability, other contracts will cover any expenses that would have been paid under the terminated coverage, regardless of cause.

Under basic medical expense contracts the extension of benefits generally ceases after 3 months, or when the individual is no longer totally or continuously disabled, whichever comes first. A similar provision is used in major medical contracts, but the time period is longer (generally 12 months or the end of the benefit period following the one in which termination took place).

Conversion

Except when termination results from the failure to pay any required premiums, medical expense contracts usually contain (and are often required to contain) a conversion provision, whereby most covered persons whose group coverage terminates are allowed to purchase individual medical expense coverage without evidence of insurability and without any limitation of benefits for preexisting conditions. Covered persons commonly have 31 days from the date of termination of the group coverage to exercise this conversion privilege, and coverage is then effective retroactively to the date of termination.

This conversion privilege is typically given to any employee who has been insured under the group contract (or under any group contract it replaced) for at least 3 months, and it permits the employee to convert his or her own coverage as well as any dependent coverage. In addition, a spouse or child whose dependent coverage ceases for any other reason may also be eligible for conversion (for example, a spouse who divorces or separates, and children who reach age 19).

A person who is eligible for both the conversion privilege and the right to continue the group insurance coverage under COBRA has two choices when eligibility for coverage terminates. He or she can either elect to convert under the provisions of the policy or elect to continue the group coverage. If the latter choice is made, the COBRA rules specify that the person must again be eligible to convert to an individual policy within the usual conversion period (31 days) after the maximum continuation-of-coverage period ceases. Policy provisions may also make the conversion privilege available to persons whose coverage terminates prior to the end of the maximum continuation period.

The insurance company has the right to refuse the issue of a "conversion" policy to anyone (1) who is covered by medicare or (2) whose benefits under the converted policy, together with similar benefits from other sources, would result in overinsurance according to the insurance company's standards. These similar benefits may be found in other coverages that the individual has (either group or individual coverage) or for which the individual is eligible under any group arrangement.

The use of the word *conversion* is often a misnomer. In actuality a person whose coverage terminates is only given the right to purchase a contract on an individual basis at individual rates. Most Blue Cross–Blue Shield plans and some HMO plans offer a conversion policy that is similar or identical to the terminated group coverage. However, most insurance companies offer a conversion policy (or a choice of policies) that contains a lower level of benefits than existed under the group coverage. Traditionally the conversion policy contained only basic hospital and surgical coverages even if major medical coverage was provided under the group contract. Now many insurance companies provide (and are required to provide in many states) a conversion policy that includes major medical benefits, which do not necessarily have to be as broad as those under the former group coverage.

Some plans offer a conversion policy that is written by another entity. For example, an HMO might enter into a contractual arrangement with an insurance company. In some cases the HMO and insurance company are commonly owned or have a parent-subsidiary relationship.

Self-funded plans, which are exempt from state laws that mandate a conversion policy, may still provide such a benefit. Rather than providing coverage directly to the terminated employee, an agreement is made with an insurance company to make a policy available. This agreement is typically part of a broader contract with the insurer to also provide administrative services and/or stop-loss protection. Because the availability of a conversion policy results in a charge (such as $0.65 per employee per month), most self-funded plans do not provide any continuation of coverage beyond what is required by COBRA.

Group-to-Individual Portability

The Health Insurance Portability and Accountability Act makes it easier for individuals who use group medical expense coverage to find alternative coverage in the individual marketplace. The purpose of the federal legislation seems to be to encourage states to adopt their own mechanisms to achieve this goal. The federal rules will apply in a state only if the state fails to have its plan in effect by either January 1, 1998, or July 1, 1998, depending on which provisions of the act apply in a specific state.

It is assumed that most states will adopt their own plans so that the federal rules will not become effective. The state alternative must do all the following:

- provide a choice of health insurance coverage to all eligible individuals
- not impose any preexisting-conditions restrictions
- include at least one policy form of coverage that is either comparable to comprehensive health coverage offered in the individual marketplace or comparable to or a standard option of coverage available under the group or individual laws of the state

In addition, the state must implement one of the following:

- one of the NAIC model laws on individual market reform
- a qualified high-risk pool
- certain other mechanisms specified in the act

If a state fails to adopt an alternative to federal regulation, then insurance companies, HMOs, and other health plan providers in the individual marketplace will be required to make coverage available on a guaranteed-issue basis to individuals with 18 or more months of creditable coverage and whose most recent coverage was under a group health plan. However, coverage does not have to be provided to an individual who has other health insurance or who is eligible for COBRA coverage, medicare, or medicaid. No preexisting-conditions exclusions can be imposed. Health insurers have three options for providing coverage to eligible individuals:

- They may offer every health insurance policy they offer in the state.
- They may offer their two most popular policies in the state, based on premium volume.
- They may offer a low-level and a high-level coverage as long as they contain benefits that are similar to other coverage offered by the insurer in the state.

Rules similar to those described in chapter 9 for group health insurance coverage require the renewal of individual coverage.

CLAIMS

Medical expense contracts that provide benefits on a service basis (such as HMOs and the Blues) generally do not require covered persons to file claim forms. Rather, the providers of services perform any necessary paperwork and are then reimbursed directly.

Medical expense contracts that provide benefits on an indemnity basis typically require that the insurance company (or other provider) be given a written proof of loss (that is, a claim form) concerning the occurrence, character, and extent of the loss for which a claim is made. This form usually contains portions that must be completed and signed by the employee, a representative of the employer, and the provider of medical services.

The period during which an employee must file a claim depends upon the provider of coverage and any applicable state requirements. An employee generally has at least 90 days (or as soon as is reasonably possible) after medical expenses are incurred to file. Some insurance companies require that they be notified within a shorter time (such as 20 days) about any illness or injury on which a claim may be based, even though they give a longer time period for the actual filing of the form itself.

Individuals have the right under medical expense plans to assign their benefits to the providers of medical services. Such an assignment, which authorizes the insurance company to make the benefit payment directly to the provider, may generally be made by completing the appropriate portion of the claim form. In addition, the insurance company has the right (as it does in disability income insurance) to examine any person for whom a claim is filed at its own expense and with the physician of its own choice.

Most self-funded plans contain subrogation provisions. If state law allows, they are also commonly contained in the group medical expense contracts of HMOs, the Blues, and insurance companies. A subrogation provision gives the plan (or the organization that provides plan benefits) the right to recover from a third party who is responsible through negligence or other wrongdoing for a covered person's injuries that result in claims being paid. If a covered person receives a settlement from the third party (or their liability insurance company) for medical expenses that the plan has already paid, the covered person must reimburse the plan. The plan also has the right to seek a recovery for benefits paid if legal action is not taken by the person who receives benefits.

FEDERAL TAXATION

In many respects the federal tax treatment of group medical expense premiums and benefits parallels that of other group coverage if they are provided through an insurance company, a Blue Cross–Blue Shield plan, a health maintenance organization, or a preferred-provider organization. Contributions by the employer for an employee's coverage or the coverage of the employee's dependents are tax deductible to the employer as long as the employee's overall compensation is reasonable. Employer contributions do not create any income tax liability for an employee. Moreover, benefits are not taxable to an employee except when they exceed any medical expenses incurred. The value of any employer-provided coverage for an employee's domestic partner, less any employee contributions, represents taxable income to the employee unless the partner qualifies under IRS rules as the employee's dependent.

One major difference between group medical expense coverage and other forms of group insurance is that a portion of an employee's contribution for coverage may be tax deductible as a medical expense if that individual itemizes his or her income tax deductions. Under the Internal Revenue Code individuals are allowed to deduct certain medical care expenses (including dental expenses) for which no reimbursement was received. This deduction is limited to expenses (including amounts paid for insurance) that exceed 7.5 percent of the person's adjusted gross income.

If a sole proprietorship or partnership pays the cost of medical expense coverage for a proprietor or partner or family members, this amount constitutes taxable income to the proprietor or partner. However, the proprietor or partner may be entitled to an income tax deduction for a percentage of this amount. As a result of the Health Insurance Portability and Accountability Act, this percentage is 40 in 1997, 45 from 1998 through 2002, 50 in 2003, 60 in 2004, 70 in 2005, and 80 thereafter. The deduction cannot exceed the individual's earned income from the proprietorship or partnership that provides the medical expense plan, and the deduction is available only if the proprietor or partner is not eligible to participate in any subsidized medical expense plan of another employer of the proprietor, partner, or the proprietor's or partner's spouse. It is important to recognize that this is not an itemized deduction, but rather it is a deduction in arriving at adjusted gross income. The remainder of the cost of the medical expense coverage can be deducted as an itemized expense to the extent that it and other medical expenses exceed the 7.5 percent threshold that was previously described.

The tax situation may be different if an employer provides medical expense benefits through a self-funded plan (referred to in the Internal Revenue Code as a self-insured medical reimbursement plan), under which employers either (1) pay the providers of medical care directly or (2) reimburse employees for their medical expenses. If a self-funded plan meets certain nondiscrimination requirements for highly compensated employees, the employer can deduct benefit payments as they are made, and the employee will have no taxable income. If a plan is discriminatory, the employer will still receive an income tax deduction. However, all or a portion of the benefits received by "highly compensated individuals," but not by other employees, will be treated as taxable income. A highly compensated individual of a company is (1) one of the five highest-paid officers of the firm, (2) a shareholder who owns more than 10 percent of the firm's stock, or (3) one of the highest-paid 25 percent of all the firm's employees. There are no nondiscrimination rules if a plan is not self-funded and provides benefits through an insurance contract, a Blue Cross–Blue Shield plan, an HMO, or a PPO.

To be considered nondiscriminatory a self-funded plan must meet certain requirements regarding eligibility and benefits. The plan must provide benefits (1) for 70 percent or more of "all employees," or (2) for 80 percent or more of all eligible employees if 70 percent or more of all employees are eligible. The following can be excluded from the all-employees category without affecting the plan's nondiscriminatory status:

- employees who have not completed 3 years of service
- employees who have not attained age 25
- part-time employees. Anyone who works fewer than 25 hours per week is automatically considered a part-time employee. Persons who work 25 or more hours, but fewer than 35 hours per week, may also be counted as part-time as long as other employees in similar work for the employer have substantially more hours.
- seasonal employees. Anyone who works fewer than 7 months of the year is automatically considered a seasonal employee. Persons who work between 7 and 9 months of the year may also be considered seasonal as long as other employees have substantially more months of employment.
- employees who are covered by a collective-bargaining agreement if accident-and-health benefits were a subject of collective bargaining

Even if a plan fails to meet the percentage requirements regarding eligibility, it can still qualify as nondiscriminatory as long as the IRS is satisfied that the plan benefits a classification of employees in a manner that does not discriminate in favor of highly compensated employees. This determination is made on a case-by-case basis.

To satisfy the nondiscrimination requirements for benefits, the same type and amount of benefits must be provided for all employees covered under the plan, regardless of their compensation. In addition, the dependents of other employees cannot be treated less favorably than the dependents of highly compensated employees. However, because diagnostic procedures are not considered part of a self-funded plan for purposes of the nondiscrimination rule, a higher level of this type of benefit is permissible for highly compensated employees.

If a plan is discriminatory in either benefits or eligibility, highly compensated employees must include the amount of any "excess reimbursement" in their gross income for income tax purposes. If highly compensated employees receive any benefits that are not available to all employees covered under the plan, these benefits are considered an excess reimbursement. For example, if a plan pays 80 percent of covered expenses for employees in general, but 100 percent for highly compensated employees, the extra 20 percent of benefits constitutes taxable income.

If a self-funded plan discriminates in the way it determines eligibility, highly compensated employees will have excess reimbursements for any amounts they receive. The amount of this excess reimbursement is determined by a percentage that is calculated by dividing the total amount of benefits highly compensated employees receive (exclusive of any other excess reimbursements) by the total amount of benefits paid to all employees (exclusive of any other excess reimbursements). Using the previous example, assume a highly compensated employee receives $2,000 in benefits during a certain year. If other employees receive only 80 percent of this amount (or $1,600), the highly compensated employee will have received an excess reimbursement of $400. If the plan also discriminates in the area of eligibility, the highly compensated employee will incur additional excess reimbursement. For example, if 60 percent of the benefits (ignoring any benefits already considered excess reimbursement) are given to highly compensated employees, 60 percent of the remaining $1,600 ($2,000 − $400), or $960, will be added to the $400, for a total excess reimbursement of $1,360.

If a plan provides benefits only for highly compensated employees, all benefits received will be considered an excess reimbursement, since the percentage is 100 percent.

13

Group Dental Insurance and Other Group Insurance Benefits

Chapter Outline

Previous chapters have considered the three traditional types of group insurance: life insurance, disability income insurance, and medical expense insurance. This chapter focuses on three of the newer and/or less common types of group insurance coverage: group dental insurance, group long-term care insurance, and group legal expense insurance. It also covers voluntary benefit plans, which may be either group or individual insurance. Finally, there is a brief discussion of property and liability insurance as a group benefit.

GROUP DENTAL INSURANCE

Since the early 1970s group dental insurance has been one of the fastest-growing employee benefits. It has been estimated that in the last 25 years the percentage of employees who have dental coverage has grown from about 5 percent to over 60 percent. Over 90 percent of firms with 500 or more employees make coverage available. Many employee benefit consultants feel that by the early part of the next century most employees, except for those who work for very small employers, will have dental coverage.

To a great extent, group dental insurance contracts have been patterned after group medical expense contracts, and they contain many similar, if not identical, provisions. Like group medical expense insurance, however, group dental insurance has many variations. Dental plans may be limited to specific types of expenses or they may be broad enough to cover virtually all dental expenses. In addition, coverage can be obtained from various types of providers, and benefits can be in the form of either services or cash payments.

The concept of managed care has had a significant role in the evolvement of group dental insurance plans. However, this evolvement has been somewhat different than that of medical expense plans. Group dental plans are more likely than medical expense plans to provide benefits on a traditional fee-for-service basis. However, these traditional plans are also more likely to take a managed care approach to providing benefits. The most common example of this is the emphasis on providing a higher level of benefits for preventive care. It is interesting to note that as group dental plans have become more prevalent, the percentage of persons receiving preventive care has continued to increase. As a result, the percentage of persons needing care for more serious dental problems has continued to decrease.

One other difference between group medical expense plans and group dental plans is that providers of managed dental care arrangements have been more likely to offer coverage to very small groups.

Providers of Dental Coverage

Group dental benefits may be offered by insurance companies, dental service plans, the Blues, and managed care plans. Like medical expense coverage, a significant portion of dental coverage is also self-funded. An employer may either self-administer the plan or use the services of a third-party administrator. In either case, the plan may use a preferred-provider network to provide dental services.

Insurance Companies

Insurance companies are a major provider of dental coverage, often on an indemnity basis. Coverage is usually offered independently of other group insurance coverages, but it may be incorporated into a major medical contract.

However, if it is part of a major medical contract, the coverage is often referred to as an *integrated dental plan,* and the benefits are frequently subject to the same provisions and limitations as benefits that are available under a separate dental plan.

Dental Service Plans

Most states have dental service plans, often called *Delta Plans* or *Delta Dental Plans,* that write approximately one-quarter of the dental coverage along with the Blues. However, the extent of their use varies widely by state, and western states generally have larger and more successful plans than states in other parts of the country. The majority of these plans are nonprofit organizations that are sponsored by state dental associations. In addition, they are patterned after Blue Shield plans, and dentists provide service benefits on a contractual basis. Also like Blue Shield, state Delta Plans are coordinated by a national board, Delta Dental Plans, Inc.

Blue Cross–Blue Shield

Many Blue Cross–Blue Shield plans also provide dental coverage. In some cases the Blues have contractual arrangements that are similar to those that dental service plans have with dentists; in other cases benefits are paid on an indemnity basis just as if an insurance company were involved. Finally, a few of the Blues market dental coverage through Delta Plans in conjunction with their own medical expense plans.

Managed Care Plans

A significant and growing amount of dental coverage is provided through managed care plans, often sponsored by insurance companies or the Blues. However, the majority of dental benefits are provided through traditional fee-for-service plans. Because dental expenses are more predictable than medical expenses, the emphasis on preventive care by managed care plans provides a real potential to hold down future costs.

Coverage can be obtained from dental health maintenance organizations (DHMOs), which operate like health maintenance organizations but provide dental care only. Like HMOs, DHMOs can take the form of closed-panel plans or individual practice associations. Estimates are that about one-quarter of employers offer a DHMO option to employees but usually as an alternative to a fee-for-service plan.

Coverage can also be obtained from PPOs, which have enjoyed rapid growth in recent years. Point-of-service plans have also become increasingly common for providing dental coverage.

Self-Funded Plans

For several years it has been common for large employers to self-fund dental benefits, and recently the concept has spread to smaller employers. Under the technique, often called direct reimbursement, the employee visits the dentist, pays the bill, and then submits the bill to the employer or a third-party administrator for reimbursement. This process often generates significant savings for the employer, largely because of a significant savings in administrative costs. The claims process is relatively simple since most reimbursements are small in size, and large claims do not exist because of the caps on benefit amounts. The number of claims is also fairly stable from year to year. One problem that often occurs in the self-funding of benefits is the lack of control over utilization. However, this has been a minimal problem in dental treatment since employees seem to have a natural reluctance to visit the dentist unless it is absolutely necessary.

Contractual Provisions

Although group dental insurance contracts have been patterned after group medical expense contracts, some of their provisions are different, and others are unique to dental coverage. These provisions pertain to eligibility, benefits, exclusions, benefit limitations, predetermination of benefits, and termination.

Eligibility

In contributory plans most employers use the same eligibility requirements for dental coverage as they use for medical expense coverage. However, some employers have different probationary periods for the two coverages. Probationary periods are used because members of a group who previously had no dental insurance usually have a large number of untreated dental problems. In addition, because many dental care expenditures are postponable, an employee who anticipates coverage under a dental plan in the future will be inclined to postpone treatment that is not crucial. Depending on the group's characteristics, the number of first-year claims for a new plan or for new employees and their dependents under an existing dental plan can be expected to run between 20 and 50 percent more than long-run annual claims. Therefore to counter this higher-than-average number of claims, some employers use a longer probationary period for dental benefits than for medical expense benefits. Other employers may have the same probationary period for both types of coverage but will impose waiting periods before certain types of dental expenses will be covered (such as 12 months for orthodontics).

Longer-than-usual probationary periods or waiting periods will initially minimize claims, but unless an organization has a high turnover rate, the result may be false economy. Many persons who do not have coverage will merely postpone treatment until they do have coverage. This postponement may actually lead to increased claims, because existing dental conditions will only become more severe and will then require more expensive treatment. For this reason some benefit consultants feel that dental plans should at most contain relatively short probationary and waiting periods.

Another method of countering high first-year claims is to require evidence of insurability. For example, an insurance company might require any person who desires coverage from the dental plan to undergo a dental examination. If major dental problems are disclosed, the person must have them corrected before insurance coverage will become effective.

Since dental expenditures are postponable and somewhat predictable, the problem of adverse selection under contributory plans is more severe for dental insurance than for many other types of group insurance. To counter this adverse selection, insurance companies impose more stringent underwriting (including eligibility) requirements on contributory dental plans than they do on other types of group insurance. In addition, most insurance companies insist on a high percentage of participation (such as 80 or 85 percent), and a few will actually not write contributory coverage. Many insurance companies will also insist on having other business besides dental coverage from the employer.

The problem of adverse selection is particularly severe when persons desire coverage after the date on which they were initially eligible to participate. These persons most likely want coverage because they or someone in their family needs dental treatment. Dental insurance contracts contain several provisions that try to minimize this problem, including one or a combination of the following:

- reducing benefits (usually by 50 percent) for a period of time (such as one year) following the late enrollment
- reducing the maximum benefit to a low amount (such as $100 or $200) for the year following the late enrollment
- excluding some benefits for a certain period (such as one or 2 years) following the late enrollment period. This exclusion may apply to all dental expenses except those that result from an accident, or it may apply only to a limited array of benefits (such as orthodontics and prosthetics).

Benefits

Most dental insurance plans pay for almost all types of dental expenses, but a particular plan may provide more limited coverage. One characteristic of dental insurance that is seldom found in medical expense plans is the inclusion of benefits for both routine diagnostic procedures (including oral examinations and X rays) and preventive dental treatment (including teeth cleaning and fluoride treatment). In fact, a few dental plans actually require periodic oral examinations as a condition for continuing eligibility. There is clear evidence that the cost of providing these benefits will be more than offset by the avoidance of the expensive dental procedures that are required when a condition is not discovered early or when a preventive treatment has not been given.

In addition to benefits for diagnostic and preventive treatment, benefits for dental expenses may be provided for the following categories of dental treatment:

- restoration (including fillings, crowns, and other procedures used to restore the functional use of natural teeth)
- oral surgery (including the extraction of teeth as well as other surgical treatment of diseases, injuries, and defects of the jaw)
- endodontics (treatment for diseases of the dental pulp within teeth, such as root canals)
- periodontics (treatment of diseases of the surrounding and supporting tissues of the teeth)
- prosthodontics (the replacement of missing teeth and structures by artificial devices, such as bridgework and dentures)
- orthodontics (the prevention and correction of dental and oral anomalies through the use of corrective devices, such as braces and retainers)

Most dental plans will usually cover any expenses that arise from the first five categories listed above, and they may include benefits for orthodontics. Whatever benefits are provided may be on a scheduled basis, on a nonscheduled basis, or on some combination of the two.

Scheduled Plans. A scheduled dental plan is similar to a surgical expense plan in which benefits are paid up to the amount specified in the fee schedule. Table 13-1 is an excerpt from one such dental schedule.

Most scheduled dental plans provide benefits on a first-dollar basis and contain no deductibles or specified coinsurance percentage. However, benefit maximums are often lower than usual-and-customary charges, thereby forcing employees to bear a portion of the costs of their dental services. For example, if a schedule is designed to provide maximum benefits that are equal to approximately 80 percent of the usual-and-customary charges, employees are in effect subject to an 80 percent coinsurance provision. In order to encourage diagnostic and preventive services, some dental schedules are designed so that the fees for these services are almost completely covered, while benefits for other dental services are paid at a lower level.

Unlike a surgical schedule, which lists only the more common surgical procedures, a dental schedule is essentially an all-inclusive list of the covered dental services. If a service is not on the list, most contracts will cover it, but only if the schedule contains what could be considered a suitable substitute. In addition, any benefits paid will be limited to the amount specified for the substitute service.

TABLE 13-1	
Dental Services	**Maximum Benefit**
Diagnostic	
Initial oral examination	$ 15.00
Periodic oral examination	10.00
Preventive	
Prophylaxis (14 years of age or older)	30.00
Prophylaxis (under 14 years of age)	20.00
Prosthodontics	
Complete upper denture	400.00

Although once common, scheduled dental plans are now used less frequently than either nonscheduled plans or combination plans.

Nonscheduled Plans. Nonscheduled dental plans, often called comprehensive dental plans, are the most common type of dental coverage. They resemble major medical expense contracts because dental expenses are paid on a reasonable-and-customary basis, subject to any exclusions, limitations, or copayments in the contract. The use of the term *nonscheduled* is something of a misnomer, since many nonscheduled plans actually do contain a schedule of the covered dental services, but they do not list specific benefit amounts for individual services.

Nonscheduled dental plans usually have both deductibles and coinsurance provisions. Although a single deductible and a single coinsurance percentage may apply to all dental services, the more common practice is to treat different classes of dental services in different ways. The typical nonscheduled dental plan breaks dental services into three broad categories: diagnostic and preventive services, basic services (such as fillings, oral surgery, periodontics, and endodontics), and major services (such as inlays, crowns, dentures, and orthodontics).

Diagnostic and preventive services are typically covered in full and are not subject to a deductible or coinsurance. (They are, however, subject to any other contract limitations.) The other two categories, however, are generally subject to an annual deductible (usually between $50 and $100 per person). In addition to the deductible, the cost of basic services may be reimbursed at a higher percentage (most often 80 percent), while major services are subject to a lower percentage (most often 50 percent).

While significant variations exist among DHMOs, these plans are likely to have no deductibles or lower deductibles than fee-for-service plans. They are also much more likely to cover basic services in full and provide a higher level of reimbursement for major services other than orthodontics.

Combination Plans. Combination plans contain features of both scheduled and nonscheduled plans. The typical combination plan covers diagnostic and preventive services on a usual-and-customary basis but uses a fee schedule for other dental services.

Exclusions

Exclusions are found in all dental plans, but their number and type vary. Some of the more common exclusions are charges for the following:

- services that are purely cosmetic, unless necessitated by an accidental bodily injury while a person is covered under the plan. (Orthodontics, although often used for cosmetic reasons, can usually also be justified as necessary to correct abnormal dental conditions.)
- replacement of lost, missing, or stolen dentures, or other prosthetic devices
- duplicate dentures or other prosthetic devices
- oral hygiene instruction or other training in preventive dental care
- services that do not have uniform professional endorsement
- occupational injuries to the extent that benefits are provided by workers' compensation laws or similar legislation
- services furnished by or on behalf of government agencies, unless there is a requirement to pay
- certain services that began prior to the date that coverage for an individual became effective (for example, a crown for which a tooth was prepared prior to coverage)

Limitations

Dental insurance plans also contain numerous limitations that are designed to control claim costs and to eliminate unnecessary dental care. In addition to deductibles and coinsurance, virtually all dental plans have overall benefit maximums. Except for DHMOs, which usually do not have a calendar-year limit, most plans contain a calendar-year maximum (varying from $500 to $2,000) but no lifetime maximum. However, some plans have only a lifetime maximum (such as $1,000 or $5,000), and a few plans contain both a calendar-year maximum and a large lifetime maximum. These maximums may apply to all dental expenses, or they may be limited to all expenses except those that arise from orthodontics (and occasionally periodontics). In the latter case, benefits for orthodontics will be subject to a separate, lower lifetime maximum, typically between $500 and $2,000.

Most dental plans limit the frequency with which some benefits will be paid. Routine oral examinations and teeth cleaning are usually limited to once every 6 months, and full mouth X rays to once every 24 or 36 months. The replacement of dentures may also be limited to one time in some specified period (such as 5 years).

The typical dental plan also limits benefits to the least expensive type of accepted dental treatment for a given dental condition. For example, if either a gold or silver filling can be used, benefit payments will be limited to the cost of a silver filling, even if a gold filling is inserted.

Predetermination of Benefits

The majority of dental contracts provide for a pretreatment review of certain dental services by the insurance company. Although this procedure is usually not mandatory, it does allow both the dentist and the patient to know just how much will be paid under the plan before the treatment is performed. In addition, it enables the insurance company (or other provider of benefits) to have some control over the performance of unnecessary or more-costly-than-necessary procedures, by giving patients an opportunity to seek less costly care (possibly from another dentist) if they learn that benefits will be limited.

In general, the predetermination-of-benefits provision (which goes by several names, such as precertification or prior authorization) applies only in nonemergency situations and when a dentist's charge for a course of treatment exceeds a specified amount (varying from $100 to $300). The dentist in effect files a claim form (and X rays if applicable) with the insurance company just as if the treatment had already been performed. The insurance company reviews the form and returns it to the dentist. The form specifies the services that will be covered and the amount of reimbursement. If and when the services are actually performed, payment is made to the dentist by the insurance company after the claim form has been returned with the appropriate signatures and the date of completion.

When the predetermination-of-benefits provision has not been followed, benefits will still be paid. However, neither the dentist nor the covered person will know in advance what services will be covered by the insurance company or how much the insurance company will pay for these services.

Termination

Coverage under dental insurance plans typically terminates for the same reasons it terminates under medical expense coverage (described in chapter 12). Rarely is there any type of conversion privilege for dental benefits, even when the coverage is written as part of a major medical contract. However, dental coverage is subject to the continuation rules of COBRA.

Benefits for a dental service received after termination may still be covered as long as (1) the charge for the service was "incurred" prior to the termination date, and (2) treatment is completed within 60 or 90 days after termination. For example, the charge for a crown or bridgework is incurred once the preparation of the tooth (or teeth) has begun, even though the actual installation of the crown or bridgework (and the billing) does not take place until after the coverage terminates. Similarly charges for dentures are incurred on the date the impressions for the dentures are taken, and charges for root canal therapy are incurred on the date the root canal is opened.

GROUP LONG-TERM CARE INSURANCE

In the 1980s insurance companies started to market long-term care insurance policies to individuals. Many of the earlier policies had limited benefits and expensive premiums. As the products have evolved, benefits have improved while premiums have remained stable or decreased. As with universal life insurance, success in the individual marketplace led to interest in group long-term care insurance as an employee benefit. The first group long-term plan was written in 1987, and a small but growing number of employers, mostly large ones, now make coverage available. The number of insurance companies writing coverage has also grown, but the number still remains relatively small and is primarily limited to the largest group insurance carriers.

At best the growth of group long-term care insurance can be described as slow and cautious for several reasons. First, the individual long-term care insurance market is still in an evolving state, due partially to the lack of adequate actuarial data to design and price coverage. The situation is not unlike the early days of disability income insurance. Second, the tax status of group long-term care coverage has been uncertain, with most tax experts feeling that employer-provided benefits, unlike medical expense benefits, would result in taxation to employees. To the extent that employers want to spend additional benefit dollars, they want to spend them on benefits for which employees receive favorable tax benefits. As a result almost all group long-term care plans have been financed solely by employee contributions. However, the Health Insurance Portability and Accountability Act now provides favorable tax treatment for long-term care insurance. The effect of this act is discussed later in this chapter. Third, there has been uncertainty about whether long-term care can be included in a cafeteria plan on a tax-favored basis. This issue has also been addressed by the Health Insurance Portability and Accountability Act (which states that long-term care can't be included). Finally, participation in group plans has been modest because older employees who feel they have a need for the coverage often find it too expensive. A surprise, however, with many of the early plans has been the higher-than-expected participation by employees in the 40-to-50 age bracket.

Before a description of the existing plans is undertaken, it is important to discuss the need for long-term care protection and the sources already available to meet this need.

The Need for Long-term Care

The need for long-term care arises from the following factors:

- an aging population
- increasing costs
- the inability of families to provide full care
- the inadequacy of insurance protection

An Aging Population

Long-term care has traditionally been thought of as a problem primarily for the older population. The population aged 65 or over is the fastest-growing age group; today it represents about 11 percent of the population, a figure that is expected to increase to between 20 and 25 percent over the next 50 years. The segment of the population aged 85 and over is growing at an even faster rate. While less than 10 percent of the over-65 group is over 85 today, this percentage is expected to double over the next two generations.

An aging society presents changing problems. Those who needed long-term care in the past were most likely to have suffered from strokes or other acute diseases. With longer life spans, a larger portion of the elderly will be incapacitated by chronic conditions such as Alzheimer's disease, arthritis, osteoporosis, and lung and heart disease—conditions that often require continuing assistance with day-to-day needs. The likelihood that a nursing home will be needed increases dramatically with age. One percent of persons between the ages of 65 and 74 reside in nursing homes, and the percentage increases to 6 percent between the ages of 75 and 84. At age 85 and over, the figure rises to approximately 25 percent.

It should be noted that the elderly are not the only group of persons who need long-term care. Many younger persons are unable to care for themselves because of handicaps resulting from birth defects, mental conditions, illnesses, or accidents.

Increasing Costs

Nearly $50 billion is spent each year on nursing home care. This cost is increasing faster than inflation because of the growing demand for nursing home beds and the shortage of skilled medical personnel. The cost of complete long-term care for an individual can also be astronomical, with annual nursing home costs of $30,000 to $50,000 not being unusual.

The Inability of Families to Provide Full Care

Traditionally long-term care has been provided by family members, often at considerable personal sacrifice and great personal stress. However, it is becoming more difficult for families to provide long-term care for the following reasons:

- the geographic dispersion of family members

- increased participation in the paid work force by women and children
- fewer children in the family
- more childless families
- higher divorce rates
- the inability of family members to provide care because they themselves are growing old

The Inadequacy of Insurance Protection

Private medical expense insurance policies (both group and individual) almost always have an exclusion for convalescent, custodial, or rest care. Some policies, particularly group policies, do provide coverage for extended-care facilities and for home health care. In both cases the purpose is to provide care in a manner that is cheaper than care in a hospital. However, coverage is provided only if a person also needs medical care; benefits are not provided if a person is merely "old" and needs someone to care for him or her.

Medicare is also inadequate because it does not cover custodial care unless this care is needed along with the medical or rehabilitative treatment provided in skilled nursing facilities or under home health care benefits.

Sources of Long-term Care

There are several sources other than insurance that are available for providing long-term care. However, there are drawbacks associated with each source.

One source is to rely on personal savings. Unless a person has substantial resources, however, this approach may force an individual and his or her dependents into poverty. It may also mean that the financial objective of leaving assets to heirs will not be met.

A second source is to rely on welfare. The medicaid program in most states will provide benefits, which usually include nursing home care, to the "medically needy." However, a person is not eligible unless he or she is either poor or has exhausted most other assets (including those of a spouse). There is also often a social stigma associated with the acceptance of welfare.

Life-care facilities are growing in popularity as a source of meeting long-term care needs. With a life-care facility, residents pay an "entrance fee" that allows them to occupy a dwelling unit but usually does not give them actual ownership rights. The entrance fee may or may not be refundable if the resident leaves the facility voluntarily or dies. As a general rule, the greater the refund is, the higher the entrance fee will be. Residents pay a monthly fee that includes meals, some housecleaning services, and varying degrees of health care. If a person needs long-term care, he or she must give up the independent living unit and move to the assisted-living or nursing home portion of the facility, but the monthly fee normally remains the same. The disadvantages of this option are that the cost of a life-care facility is beyond the reach of many persons, and a resident must be in reasonably good health and able to live independently at the time the facility is entered. Therefore the decision to use a life-care facility must be made in advance of the need for long-term care. Once such care is needed or is imminent, this approach is no longer viable.

A few insurers now include long-term care benefits in some cash value life insurance policies. Essentially an insured can begin to use this accelerated benefit while still living. For example, if the insured is in a nursing home, he or she might receive a benefit equal to 25 or 50 percent of the policy face. However, any benefit reduces the future death benefit payable to heirs.

Group Long-term Care Policies

Most of the early group long-term care policies were designed for specific large employers, and much variation existed. For the last few years, most insurance companies have had a standard group long-term care product, which in virtually all cases is consistent with the provisions in the Long-Term Care Insurance Model Act of the National Association of Insurance Commissioners. The result is that group policies tended to be comparable to the broadest policies sold in the individual marketplace. However, the nature of long-term policies is likely to change as a result of the Health Insurance Portability and Accountability Act.

Effect of Health Insurance Portability and Accountability Act

The tax treatment of long-term care insurance was finally clarified by the Health Insurance Portability and Accountability Act. Because favorable tax treatment is only given if long-term care insurance policies meet prescribed standards, the nature of long-term coverage is also likely to change. In most cases, the imposition of federal standards results in broader coverage for consumers. However, Congress seems to have been concerned with the revenue loss associated with this tax legislation. As a result, policies that are modified to comply with the federal standards may actually provide more limited coverage than has been previously required in several states, posing a dilemma for the states. Unless they approve the sale of more restrictive policies, state residents will not obtain the new tax benefits. However, the approval of these policies may make it more difficult for an insured to qualify for benefits. Consumers who want to purchase long-term care insurance may also be faced with a difficult and confusing decision unless a state adopts the federal standards for all policies: Should the choice of policy be based on the potential long-term care benefits or on tax advantages?

It should be emphasized that the long-term care changes in the act are primarily changes in the income tax code. States still have the authority to regulate long-term care insurance contracts. They have no obligations to bring state rules and regulations into conformity with these tax changes. However, failure to do so will result in new policies issued in a state not meeting the definition of qualified long-term care insurance, thus preventing the state's residents from obtaining the tax advantages the act provides.

Eligibility for Favorable Tax Treatment. The act provides favorable tax treatment to a *qualified long-term care insurance contract.* This is defined as any insurance contract that meets all the following requirements:

- The only insurance protection provided under the contract is for *qualified long-term care services.*
- The contract cannot pay for expenses that are reimbursable under medicare.
- The contract must be guaranteed renewable.
- The contract does not provide for a cash surrender value or other money that can be borrowed or paid, assigned, or pledged as collateral for a loan.
- All refunds of premiums and policyholder dividends must be applied as future reductions in premiums or to increase future benefits.
- The policy must comply with various consumer protection provisions. For the most part, these are the same provisions contained in the NAIC model act and already adopted by most states. However, the new federal act requires the issuer of any level-premium contract to offer a nonforfeiture benefit that can take the form of one of the following: paid-up insurance, extended term insurance, a shortened benefit period, or any similar benefit allowed by regulations that might be issued.

The act defines q*ualified long-term care services* as necessary diagnostic, preventive, therapeutic, curing, treating, and rehabilitative services, and maintenance or personal care services that are required by a chronically ill individual and are provided by a plan of care prescribed by a licensed health care practitioner.

A *chronically ill person* is one who has been certified as meeting one of the following requirements:

- The person is expected to be unable to perform, without substantial assistance from another person, at least two activities of daily living for a period of at least 90 days due to a loss of functional capacity. The act allows six activities of daily living, and a qualified long-term care policy must contain at least five of the six. (The secretary of health and human services is permitted to prescribe regulations so that a person having a level of disability similar to the level of disability of a person who cannot perform two activities of daily living would also be considered chronically ill.)

- Substantial services are required to protect the individual from threats to health and safety due to substantial cognitive impairment.

The act also provides that any contract issued before January 1, 1997, that met the long-term care requirements in the state where the policy was issued will be considered a qualified long-term care contract. However, at the time this book is being revised, it is unclear whether a person who becomes newly covered after January 1, 1997, under a group contract that was in effect prior to that time will be eligible for favorable tax treatment.

Federal Income Tax Provisions. Beginning in 1997, a qualified long-term care insurance contract is treated as accident and health insurance. Therefore any employer contributions are deductible to the employer and do not result in any taxable income to an employee. Benefits received under a group plan are received tax free by an employee with one possible exception. Under contracts written on a per diem basis, proceeds are excludible from income up to $175 per day. (This figure is indexed annually after 1997.) Amounts in excess of $175 are also excludible to the extent that they represent actual costs for long-term care services.

Coverage cannot be offered through a cafeteria plan on a tax-favored basis. In addition, if an employee has a flexible spending account for unreimbursed medical expenses, any reimbursements for long-term care services must be included in the employee's income.

With some exceptions, expenses for long-term care services, including insurance premiums, are treated like other medical expenses. That is, self-employed persons may deduct a portion of premiums paid, and persons who itemize deductions can include the cost of long-term care services, including insurance premiums, for purposes of deducting medical expenses in excess of 7.5 percent of adjusted gross income. However, there is a cap on the amount of personally paid long-term care insurance premiums that can be claimed as medical expenses. These limits, based upon a covered individual's age and subject to cost-of-living adjustments after 1997, are shown in table 13-2.

TABLE 13-2	
Age	**Annual Deductible Limit per Covered Individual**
40 or younger	$ 200
41–50	375
51–60	700
61–70	2,000
older than 70	2,500

In addition, deductions cannot be taken for payments made to a spouse or relative who is not a licensed professional with respect to such services.

Policy Characteristics

Eligibility for Coverage. The typical eligibility rules (that is, full time, actively at work, and so on) apply to group long-term care policies. At a minimum, coverage can be purchased for an active employee and/or spouse. Some policies also provide coverage to retirees and to other family members such as children, parents, parents-in-law, and possibly adult children. There is a maximum age for eligibility, but it may be as high as 80.

Cost. As previously mentioned, the cost of group long-term care coverage is almost always borne by the employee. Initial premiums are usually in 5-year age brackets and increase significantly with age. For example, one plan has an annual premium of $200 for persons aged 40–44 and $850 for persons aged 60–65. Once coverage is elected, premiums remain level and do not increase when a person enters another age bracket. Coverage is guaranteed renewable, so premiums can be increased by class.

Under some plans, premiums are payable for life. Under other plans premiums are higher but cease at retirement age. Such a plan is analogous to a life insurance policy that is paid up at age 65. Virtually all plans contain a waiver-of-premium provision that becomes effective when a covered person starts to receive benefits.

Levels of Care. There are several levels of care that long-term care policies can provide:

- *skilled-nursing care,* which consists of daily nursing and rehabilitative care that can be performed only by, or under the supervision of, skilled medical personnel and must be based on a doctor's orders
- *intermediate care,* which involves occasional nursing and rehabilitative care that must be based on a doctor's orders and can be performed only by, or under the supervision of, skilled medical personnel
- *custodial care,* which is primarily to handle personal needs such as walking, bathing, dressing, eating, or taking medicine and can usually be provided by someone without professional medical skills or training
- *home health care,* which is received at home and includes part-time skilled nursing care, speech therapy, physical or occupational therapy, part-time services from home health aides, and help from homemakers or chore workers
- *adult day care,* which is received at centers specifically designed for the elderly who live at home, but whose spouses or families are not available to stay home during the day. The level of care received is

similar to that provided for home health care. Most adult day-care centers also provide transportation to and from the center.

Most policies cover at least the first three levels of care, and many cover all five. Unlike some individual long-term care policies, group contracts do not make the receipt of one level of benefits contingent upon having received a prior higher level of long-term care.

Some policies also provide benefits for respite care, which allows occasional full-time care at home for a person who is receiving home health care. Respite-care benefits enable family members (or other persons) who are providing much of the home care to take a needed break.

It is becoming increasingly common for policies to contain a bed reservation benefit. This benefit continues payments to a long-term care facility for a limited time (such as 20 days) if a patient must temporarily leave because of hospitalization. Without a continuation of payments, the bed may be rented to someone else and unavailable upon the patient's release from the hospital.

Some newer policies provide assisted-living benefits for facilities that provide care for the frail elderly who are no longer able to care for themselves but do not need the level of care provided in a nursing home.

Benefits. Benefits are usually limited to a specific dollar amount per day, with $50 to $100 being common. A few plans allow participants to select varying benefit levels (for example, $50, $75, or $100 per day) when coverage is initially elected. Benefits may vary by level of care, with the highest benefits being provided for skilled nursing care and the lowest level for home health care and/or adult day care if they are covered. For example, home health care benefits are often paid at one-half the level of custodial care benefits. Annual respite care benefits are usually limited to some multiple, such as 20, of the maximum daily benefit. Most states require insurance companies to offer protection against inflation, usually in the form of benefits increasing periodically with some index like the consumer price index. However, inflation increases are often capped at some annual maximum, such as 3 percent.

While a few group long-term care plans provide benefits for an unlimited duration, most limit benefits to a period of time, ranging from 3 to 7 years, or to some equivalent dollar maximum. It should be noted that most persons who enter nursing homes either are discharged or die within 2 years. However, it is not unusual for stays to last 7 years or longer. As in the case of disability income insurance, benefits are often subject to a waiting period, which may vary from 10 to 150 days with 90 days being most common.

Eligibility for Benefits. Until recently most group long-term care policies required a prior hospitalization in order to qualify for benefits. Almost all insurance companies now use a new criterion, which specifies several so-called activities of daily living (ADLs). While variations exist, the six ADLs that can be in a qualified long-term care insurance contract include eating, bathing, dressing, transferring from bed to chair, using the toilet, and maintaining continence. In order to receive benefits, there must be independent certification that a person is totally dependent on others to perform a certain number of these activities. For example, one insurer lists seven activities and requires total dependence for any three of them; another insurer requires dependence for two out of a list of six. Note that a policy with seven criteria cannot be a qualified long-term care contract, nor can a policy that allows the inability to perform only one ADL to trigger benefits.

Newer policies contain a second criterion (which a qualified long-term care contract must contain) that, if satisfied, will result in the payment of benefits even if the activities of daily living can be performed. This criterion is based on cognitive impairment, which can be caused by Alzheimer's disease, strokes, or other brain damage. Cognitive impairment is generally measured through tests performed by trained medical personnel. Because eligibility for benefits often depends on subjective evaluations, most insurance companies use some form of case management. Case management may be mandatory, with the case manager determining eligibility, working with the physician and family to decide on an appropriate type of care, and periodically reassessing the case. Case management may also be voluntary, with the case manager making recommendations about the type of care needed and providing information about the sources for care.

Preexisting Conditions. Almost all group long-term care policies have a preexisting-conditions provision. Benefits typically are not paid during the first 6 months of plan participation for care needed for a condition that was treated within 6 months prior to participation.

Exclusions. Several exclusions are found in group long-term care policies:

- war
- institutional care received outside the United States
- treatment for drug or alcohol abuse
- intentionally self-inflicted injury
- attempted suicide
- confinement or care for which benefits are payable under workers' compensation or similar laws
- confinement or care for which the insured or the insured's estate is not required to pay

In contrast to many older individual policies, group contracts have not been written to exclude organic-based mental diseases such as Alzheimer's.

Renewability and Portability. Group long-term care plans are guaranteed renewable. If a participant leaves, the group coverage can usually be continued on a direct-payment basis, under either the group contract or an individual contract.

GROUP LEGAL EXPENSE INSURANCE

Plans that cover the legal expenses of employees have been a common benefit in several European countries for many years. However, until the mid-1970s the concept was not widely used in the United States. The plans that did exist were almost always established by unions and were financed from general union funds. Usually the legal services were provided by attorneys who were employed by the unions, and the only legal services covered were those limited to job-related difficulties, such as suspensions or workers' compensation disputes.

The limited extent of legal expense plans was due to the existence of several obstacles, all of which have been substantially reduced or eliminated in recent years. Prior to 1971 all states had laws that made it illegal for insurance companies (or other organizations) to market group legal insurance plans under which contributions were paid in advance by the covered persons or by anyone else on their behalf. (However, self-funded plans, whose benefits were paid from the general revenues of unions or employers as reimbursement for legal expenses, did not usually come under these limitations.)   In 1971 the U.S. Supreme Court declared that these laws were unconstitutional, and the states have replaced them with laws that allow group legal benefits to be provided (subject to some restrictions) by a plan that is funded in advance.

The Supreme Court ruling actually did little to encourage the growth of legal expense plans, since federal tax laws did not give favorable treatment to legal expense benefits, and the Taft-Hartley Act did not allow legal expense benefits to be a subject of collective bargaining. However, in 1973 the Taft-Hartley Act was amended to make legal expense benefits a new subject of collective bargaining, and the Tax Reform Act of 1976 gave favorable tax treatment to certain legal expense plans by providing that neither the premiums paid by employers nor the benefits received under the plans constitute taxable income to employees. As a result of these changes the number of legal expense plans grew considerably, and several thousand employers now provide these benefits to their employees. However, most of these employers offer group legal benefits only to union employees (as a result of collective bargaining) through negotiated trusteeships that provide the benefits on an uninsured basis. Some employers have established voluntary plans under which an employee can elect to participate if he or she desires. In some cases this is part of a cafeteria plan, and the employee pays the full cost of the coverage on an after-tax basis. It is also becoming increasingly common for employers to offer some legal expense benefits under employee-assistance plans.

It is unlikely that group legal expense plans will continue to grow at a rate as rapid as in the past. Under provisions of the 1976 tax act, Sec. 120 of the Internal Revenue Code was established. This code section allowed an employer to pay annual premiums to a "prepaid legal services plan" of up to $70 for each employee without the employee incurring any taxable income. In order to qualify as a prepaid legal services plan, a group legal expense plan had to meet specific requirements regarding funding and nondiscrimination. Sec. 120 was always subject to a sunset provision, but the date of expiration was extended several times. However, the section was allowed to expire at the end of 1992. Unless Sec. 120 is revived at some future date (and periodically there are bills in Congress to do this), any premiums paid by the employer for group legal expenses coverage will be treated as taxable income for employees. Benefits will be taxable if a plan is self-funded. If Sec. 120 is revived, favorable tax treatment could also be provided to group legal expense benefits provided (within limits) under a cafeteria plan.

Types of Plans

The types of group legal expense plans vary significantly in the ways they provide legal services. When an employer or negotiated trusteeship establishes a group legal expense plan, benefits can be self-funded or purchased from another organization. These other organizations include prepaid plans that are sponsored by state bar associations, groups of attorneys, or other organizations (either profit or nonprofit) formed for this purpose. Although some insurance companies market group plans that provide legal expense benefits, few plans of this type actually exist.

Benefits can be provided on a closed-panel basis, on an open-panel basis, or on some combination of these two. By far the most common are closed-panel plans, under which covered persons must obtain legal services from lawyers who are selected by the provider of benefits. These may be lawyers who are full-time employees of the plan or lawyers who provide benefits for plan members but who also have other clients. Under an open-panel plan, covered persons may be able to choose their own lawyer, or they may have to select one from a limited list of lawyers who have agreed to the terms and conditions of the plan (such as agreeing to charge no more than the plan's suggested fee schedule). When these two types of plans are combined, the plan that results will usually have its own lawyers provide routine legal services on a closed-panel basis, but it will use an open-panel approach when covered persons are faced with more serious legal problems.

Like medical or dental expense benefits, legal expense benefits can be provided either as services or as reimbursements for actual expenses. Virtually all closed-panel plans use a service approach and provide full benefits without requiring any copayments by the covered persons. Open-panel plans may also provide benefits on a service basis, primarily when eligible lawyers agree to the fee structure paid by the plan. When benefits are paid on the basis of actual charges incurred by a covered person, deductibles and coinsurance are sometimes used.

Benefit Schedules

Benefits under legal expense plans can be provided on either a scheduled basis or on a comprehensive basis. *Scheduled legal expense plans* list the specific types of legal expenses for which benefits will be paid. While significant variations exist among plans, most at least cover the following:

- consultation and advice on any legal matter
- preparation of legal documents, such as deeds, wills, and powers-of-attorney
- adoption
- personal bankruptcy
- defense of civil suits
- juvenile delinquency proceedings
- domestic problems, such as separation, divorce, or annulment
- criminal defense

When benefits are provided on an indemnity basis, the maximum benefit for each covered legal service is usually limited to a flat amount or to a maximum hourly fee. In addition, there may be an overall maximum annual benefit (such as $1,000). Whether it provides benefits on a service or an indemnity basis, a scheduled legal expense plan may also limit the frequency with which benefits will be paid for each covered service. Under some plans the participating lawyers also agree to provide discounted services that are not otherwise included in the plan.

Comprehensive legal expense plans are like major medical expense plans in that all legal expenses are covered except for those that are specifically excluded. Common exclusions include legal expenses that arise from the following:

- business activities or transactions
- class action suits
- cases that have contingent fees
- actions against the legal expense plan
- actions against the employer
- actions against the union
- IRS audits

In addition, these plans generally exclude expenses that are not charged by a lawyer (such as court costs and fines). These plans usually provide benefits on a closed-panel basis and have no overall benefit maximums or internal dollar limitations.

VOLUNTARY BENEFITS

A major area of growth for insurance companies in recent years has been through the marketing of voluntary benefits for employees, some of which have already been discussed in this book These products—which can be either group insurance or individual insurance—vary considerably among insurance companies. Even the names used to describe these products are not uniform, with terminology like *payroll deduction plans* and *worksite marketing* often being used. For purposes of this book, *voluntary benefits* will be defined as products provided by the employer that the employee purchases and for which he or she pays 100 percent of the premium.

It is difficult to measure the extent of voluntary benefits because statistics are often included with other group or individual products sold by a company. However, most estimates of the percentage of employers offering at least one voluntary benefit fall into the 50 to 70 percent range.

Reasons for Increase in Popularity

Voluntary benefits have increased in popularity in recent years, primarily because of employers' attempts to contain the rising costs of employee benefits. For example, an employer may determine that it cannot afford to institute a new group insurance program and pay any portion of the cost of coverage. Even though employees would naturally like to have the employer share in the cost, the ease of payroll deduction and more liberal underwriting still make a payroll deduction plan attractive to them. In addition, the portability of the coverage is often appealing.

Voluntary benefits have also grown in popularity as a method of providing individual insurance coverage to supplement the benefits provided under a group plan financed by the employer. For example, an employer may pay for a group disability income plan that provides benefits equal to 50 percent of salary. Voluntary benefits then allow employees to purchase additional protection.

Changes in demographics make it increasingly difficult for employers to offer an overall benefit plan that meets the needs of all employees. One alternative is to offer a cafeteria plan. Another option is to provide a basic core of benefits that all employees want. Additional benefits can be offered on a voluntary basis.

Another reason for the increase in the popularity of voluntary benefits is the increased availability of products. More insurance companies have entered the market to obtain additional revenue at a time when revenue from other sources has been decreasing. As is often the case, this has sometimes resulted in lower costs and more liberal underwriting. However, before entering the voluntary benefits market, agents should be sure they are dealing with a stable company whose market line will stay current with the changing demands of the marketplace.

Market Characteristics

The voluntary market is very diverse. The remainder of this section briefly describes some of the variations.

Insurance Company Involvement

It is estimated that between 150 and 200 insurance companies offer voluntary benefits, with the number of companies offering individual products being about double the number of companies offering group products and with some companies offering both individual and group products. For a few companies, 50 to 100 percent of their premium income is from voluntary products. For the majority of companies, the figure is under 10 percent.

As a general rule, individual carriers tend to target employers with 250 or fewer employees, while group carriers target somewhat larger markets. However, many insurance companies will provide coverage for the employees of almost any size employer, with the least interest being shown in very small (under 25) and large (2,500 or more) employees. Most companies target employees in the $20,000 to $50,000 income range.

Types of Products Available

The major goal of most insurance companies in the voluntary market is to sell life insurance to employees and their dependents. Individual carriers are heavily concentrated in this market. Life insurance is also the most popular product of group carriers, but they are more likely to also offer health insurance products.

Life insurance products run the gamut from basic term insurance to variable universal life insurance. The most prevalent health insurance products are short-term and long-term disability income. Major medical coverage is seldom offered, but some insurance companies sell dread-disease policies and hospital-indemnity coverage. Dental insurance, prescription drug coverage, and vision coverage are also found, usually in the group insurance market. A newer and increasingly common product is long-term care insurance. A few companies also write property and liability insurance.

Depending on the size of the employer, group products can be tailored to the employer's needs. In the individual marketplace, some providers of voluntary products sell the standard products that are listed in their rate books. Other carriers have specialized products for this market. This is common for universal life insurance and among companies that specialize in voluntary benefits.

Underwriting

Surveys of both employers and employees indicate that the success of a voluntary benefit plan is affected by insurance company underwriting. Although some voluntary benefits are individually underwritten, most plans are responsive to market demands and use either simplified underwriting or guaranteed issues, with group coverage being more likely than individual coverage to have the latter. As a general rule, employers want guaranteed-issue coverage unless simplified underwriting will result in significant cost savings to employees. Several factors affect the underwriting policy of an insurance company, including size, participation level, and issue limits. For example, an insurance company might use simplified underwriting for its universal life product if there is a minimum 8 percent participation rate among employers with 500 employees and the issue limit is $100,000. For a group of 50 employees, the percentage might be 15 and the issue limit, $85,000. For guaranteed issue, the figures might be 35 percent and $80,000 for employers with 500 employees and 55 percent and $50,000 for employers with 50 employees.

Cost

It is estimated that voluntary benefits are about 10 percent less expensive than coverage purchased in the individual marketplace outside the employment relationship. However, significant variations exist. Even when there is no cost differential, the ease of payroll deduction is appealing to employees.

Since both employers and employees have considerable interest in voluntary products being offered on a tax-favored basis, benefits may be provided under a cafeteria plan. However, the use of a cafeteria plan may pose problems, and some benefit consultants feel that voluntary benefits should be kept separate from a firm's cafeteria plan. The issue arises over regulation by ERISA. Most voluntary plans, being employee pay all, are exempt from ERISA rules, which is a definite plus from the employer's perspective. Any benefits purchased under a cafeteria plan are technically purchased with employer funds, even if made with voluntary salary reductions. It is argued that this would bring a voluntary benefit plan under ERISA rules. In 1996 the Pension and Welfare Benefits Administration issued an advisory opinion that ERISA did not apply to premium-conversion plans (also called premium-only plans) used to allow before-tax salary reductions for medical expense benefits. However, the government has not addressed the issue of other voluntary benefits.

Methods of Premium Payment

The vast majority of voluntary benefits use payroll deduction (also referred to as *salary allotment* or *salary reduction*) as the method for premium payments, with the employer remitting the premiums to the insurance company. However, some insurance companies will bill employees directly if an employer is unwilling to participate in a payroll deduction arrangement. Payroll deduction is very popular with employees, and direct billing will probably have an adverse effect on plan participation. However, it may also reduce the rate at which coverage lapses when employment terminates.

Premiums are usually determined by the benefits purchased and the frequency of payroll deductions. However, life insurance is often sold on a money-purchase basis. The term *money purchase* comes from the fact that amounts of coverage are sold on the basis of what can be purchased with a given premium, such as $1, $2, or $5 per week (or other period). Since the amount of coverage is a function of the employee's attained age, larger amounts of coverage are available to younger employees than to older employees.

Some insurance companies sell universal life insurance on a money-purchase basis, but other companies take a different approach. Rather than selecting the desired premium, employees choose the amount of pure death protection. Several options—such as $10,000, $25,000, and $50,000—may be offered, and the available options may vary by salary level or position. A minimum periodic premium will then be specified for each option and a given employee's age. The premium will be sufficient to generate a cash value at retirement age if the insurer's current interest assumptions are met. Employees, however, can elect to pay higher premiums so that a larger cash value will develop. Some insurers set the initial premium at a multiple (such as twice) of the pure insurance cost; others make it an amount that will generate a cash value equal to a percentage (such as 50 percent) of the original amount of insurance. After the policy has been in force for some time period, employees typically have flexibility in premium levels similar to what is available to persons purchasing universal life insurance outside the employment relationship.

Portability

Individual products are automatically portable when an employee terminates employment. However, there are several possibilities with group coverage. In a few cases, coverage ceases; in some cases, the employee must convert to an individual policy. In most cases, the employee can continue the group coverage on a direct-bill basis.

Premiums often remain the same after termination of employment, but they may have to be paid less frequently. For example, instead of paying a monthly periodic deduction, an individual may be billed quarterly. Under some plans, an extra administrative charge is made for the cost of direct billing.

Enrollment

Enrollment in voluntary plans can take many forms, and most insurance companies use more than one method. For individual policies, the agent or broker is usually involved in the enrollment process. Group plans also frequently use group sales representatives. Some insurance companies use professional enrollers, and occasionally direct mail enrollment is undertaken.

Numerous methods are also employed to encourage plan enrollment. Printed materials are often provided to employees in the workplace and may even be sent to the employees' homes. Meetings are frequently held with employees, usually on a group basis. Other methods of communicating the plan include the use of videotapes and toll-free telephone numbers.

PROPERTY AND LIABILITY INSURANCE

In the mid-1960s it was thought that property and liability insurance, especially automobile insurance, would be the next major employee benefit. However, by the late 1970s most of the insurance companies that had entered this market were no longer willing to write property and liability coverage as an employee benefit. In fact, many began to dismiss this benefit as an idea whose time might never come. The current status of property and liability insurance as an employee benefit is that for several years it has been offered by a few large employers. Detailed statistics from the insurance industry are difficult to obtain since most coverage is actually mass-marketed individual insurance and is not reported as a group benefit. However, estimates indicate that no more than about one percent of personal property and liability insurance is provided as the result of an employer-arranged plan.

Reasons for Slow Growth

The slow growth of group property and liability plans can be traced to several factors, namely unfavorable tax treatment, a low potential for cost savings, a lack of employer enthusiasm, and regulatory restrictions.

Unfavorable Tax Treatment

The Internal Revenue Code specifically exempts employer contributions for certain employee benefits from inclusion in employees' taxable income. This exemption does not apply to property and liability insurance. Although the employer is allowed an income tax deduction, an employee must report as taxable income any contributions made in his or her behalf for property and liability coverage. Note, however, that the portion of any premium that applies to medical or no-fault benefits is treated as health insurance and is not included in income.

In general, employers, unions, and employees prefer that employer dollars be used to provide nontaxable benefits. Therefore without employer contributions it is often difficult to offer employees property and liability insurance at a substantial enough saving to encourage significant participation.

Lower Potential for Cost Savings

The potential for savings under group property and liability insurance plans is typically less than it is under group insurance plans that provide life insurance, disability income, or medical expense benefits. Under these latter plans there is a substantial reduction in agents' commissions when compared to commissions received on individual coverage. Such savings do not occur in property and liability insurance, because commissions scales for individual insurance are lower as a percentage of premium. The main reason for this lower scale is that a less intense marketing effort is required by agents, since consumers are more likely to seek out property and liability coverage on their own, rather than be solicited by agents. Therefore a higher portion of commissions are for services that are performed for the client, rather than for the agents' marketing efforts. These services (for example, financial responsibility filings, automobile changes, and certificates of insurance for mortgagees) must still be performed for coverage that is provided on a group basis.

A second source of savings under most types of group insurance coverage results from the reduction or elimination of individual underwriting, which, together with other savings, more than offsets the cost of covering poor risks at group rates. However, this is not the case in property and liability insurance, particularly in automobile insurance. Not only are savings lower, but there are proportionately many more substandard drivers who must pay surcharged premiums in the individual property and liability insurance marketplace than there are persons with poor health in the individual life and health insurance marketplace. The lack of individual underwriting in property and liability insurance will usually mean that the average rate for the group members is higher than some persons would pay in the individual marketplace. Consequently to avoid getting only the poor risks, group property and liability insurance plans generally use individual—but possibly liberalized—underwriting. As a result poorer risks are charged a higher premium or are ineligible for coverage in some cases.

Under the most successful group property and liability plans, savings have averaged only between 5 and 15 percent when compared with the same insurance company's rates for individual coverage. However, property and liability rates vary widely among insurance companies, and this group rate may still be higher than what many employees are paying for their individual coverage. Without a significant cost advantage there is little incentive for an employee to switch to a group property and liability plan, except perhaps for the simplicity of paying premiums on a payroll-deduction basis. This is particularly true when the employee has an established relationship with his or her current property and liability insurance company or agent. Consequently it may be difficult to enroll the minimum percentage (usually 30 or more) of employees required by the insurance company.

Lack of Employer Enthusiasm

In addition to the unfavorable tax treatment of employer contributions to the employee, many employers feel that group property and liability plans will place a strain on their relationship with employees. While the magnitude of the problem varies among employers that offer group property and liability plans, it is an undisputed fact that dissatisfaction with the plan and the employer does occur when employees (1) are ineligible for coverage because of underwriting considerations, (2) find the coverage more expensive than their current individual coverage, or (3) have disputes over claims. In spite of this dissatisfaction, however, some employers view property and liability insurance as a desirable benefit because of high visibility.

Regulatory Restrictions

Once common in almost all states, some type of regulation or statute that hinders the marketing of group property and liability insurance still exists in several states. These *fictitious group insurance statutes,* or similar regulations, prohibit the grouping of individual risks in order to give them favorable treatment in underwriting, coverage, or rates, with the possible exception of rate reductions that are the result of savings in expenses. In effect, what is done for group life insurance, medical expense, and disability coverages cannot be done for property and liability insurance. These laws apply only to true group insurance products; payroll deduction plans are not affected. In addition, the laws of some states effectively prohibit true group insurance products because there is no specific statute that allows these products to be written.

Many states also have regulations that prohibit any person who is not a licensed insurance agent from advising in the sale of property and liability insurance. This prevents the employer from performing any other functions besides those of a purely administrative nature, such as accepting applications or deducting premiums from payroll.

Federal regulatory restrictions are another reason for lack of union interest, since the Federal Labor Code prohibits a negotiated trusteeship from providing property and liability coverage. However, the benefit can still be bargained for and provided under a plan established by the employer.

Types of Plans

Most employer-provided property and liability insurance plans are not true group insurance but are payroll deduction plans of individual insurance similar to the salary allotment plans described earlier in this chapter. The cost of these plans is usually borne entirely by the participating employees. Besides handling the payroll deductions, the employer has little, if any, responsibility for plan administration. Employees are solicited by representatives of the insurance company, usually by mail or phone. Some insurance companies may actually have agents on or near the employer's premises, but most insurance companies give group members toll-free numbers to contact their representatives.

Payroll deduction property and liability insurance plans are usually not experience rated but are offered at a slight discount because of the administrative savings associated with mass marketing. Premiums for employees vary because they are based on the same factors as individual property and liability insurance (such as age, driving record, or value of the home), which also means that some employees may be ineligible for coverage. Most plans offer automobile insurance, and a few also offer other coverages, such as homeowners insurance and umbrella liability insurance. Employees usually have the same choices regarding the amount and type of coverage that they would have in the individual marketplace, and the contracts offered are usually identical. However, modifications that attempt to decrease the cost of the payroll deduction coverage are sometimes made. These include larger deductibles and provisions in the automobile insurance policy that eliminate coverage for medical expenses to the extent that they are paid under the employer's medical expense plan.

A few companies offer property and liability insurance on a true group basis and use both a master contract and experience rating for the group. All employees are usually eligible. The coverages offered to the employees are usually the same as those offered under payroll deduction plans, but the rating structure tends to be less refined, particularly for automobile insurance. Instead of having several dozen classifications that are based on factors such as age, sex, and driving record, there may only be three or four classifications based solely on driving record. In virtually all cases when true group property and liability plans are made available, the insurance company will insist on employer contributions of between 25 and 50 percent of the cost of the coverage and on participation by a large percentage of employees, possibly as high as 75 percent.

14

Employee Benefit Marketing

Chapter Outline

The marketing of employee benefits is a complex and specialized process that is subject to frequent changes as a result of the influences of employers, organized labor, and federal and state regulations. Competition is intense, and the buyer often uses competitive bidding. Many employers continually review benefit plans for ways to contain cost increases and to improve the services received from insurance companies or from other providers of benefits or services. Therefore it is essential for agents, brokers, consultants, third-party administrators, and insurance companies to maintain a high level of technical competence and to provide continuous service.

In this chapter group insurance marketing is described with respect to (1) the types of buyers, (2) the types of sellers and their representatives, and (3) the marketing process.

THE BUYERS

The buyers of group benefits can be categorized by both the type and the size of their group. The buyers of coverage for employees consist primarily of employers, trustees, and associations. (These and other types of eligible groups are discussed in an earlier chapter.) While it is difficult to precisely categorize the group benefit market by the size of groups, certain generalizations can be made.

Approximately one-half of all employee benefit plans are established for groups of fewer than 25 employees. However, these groups account for only between 10 and 15 percent of the total dollar volume of employee benefits. In most cases the person making group insurance decisions for these small groups (unless the decisions are dictated by collective bargaining) is the owner or chief executive officer of the organization.

The next largest segment of the market (25 to 30 percent of all groups) consists of groups from organizations that have 25 to 100 employees. These groups also represent only between 10 and 15 percent of the total employee benefit premium volume. Again, the person making group insurance decisions tends to be the organization's owner or chief executive.

Groups of 100 to 500 employees account for only about 10 percent of group benefit plans, but they represent approximately 25 percent of the total dollars spent on employee benefits. Because of the greater flexibility available in plan design (including the consideration of alternative funding methods) and the various ways in which the plan can be administered, there is a need to devote more time to group insurance matters than the owner or chief executive of an organization can afford to spend. Therefore while possibly retaining the final decision-making authority, this person usually delegates the actual task of benefit planning to some employee in the organization—frequently the personnel director but sometimes an administrative or financial vice president.

Groups of more than 500 employees account for only a small percentage of the group benefit plans in existence, but these plans represent approximately half of the benefit dollars spent by employers. Firms of this size usually have one or more persons who devote their full time to group insurance matters. These persons may be in a separate "insurance" or "benefit" department, or they may be part of a personnel, financial, or administrative department.

THE SELLERS

The sellers of employee benefit products and services consist primarily of insurance companies, the Blues, HMOs, PPOs, and third-party administrators. Just as certain generalizations were made about who makes employee benefit decisions within an organization, some generalizations can be made about where products and services are purchased. However, the breakdown by size is different.

Employers with fewer than 10 employees, who have more limited choices than larger employers, usually purchase coverage from MEWAs or the Blues. However, there are significant geographic differences with respect to the purchase of medical expense coverage. In some areas the Blues, because of large discounts and community rating, have a significant cost advantage and are the primary providers of coverage. In other areas the Blues are minor players and provide little coverage to such small employers. In still other areas a very competitive marketplace exists.

The choice of products and services increases for employers with 10 to 25 employees. Not only is coverage available from MEWAs and the Blues, but it can also frequently be obtained from HMOs and PPOs. For this size group, insurance companies also have products that are sold directly to employers rather than through MEWAs.

If an employer has more than 25 employees, the possibility of self-funding of benefits, particularly medical expense benefits, becomes very real. In this marketplace there is a significant demand for the purchase of administrative services from insurance companies and third-party administrators.

The functions and methods of compensation for each of the participants in the group benefit sales process are discussed below.

Agents

Insurance company agents play a major role in marketing group insurance, particularly to groups that have fewer than 100 employees. Agents usually locate the prospective group insurance cases, but the extent of their further involvement in the sales process varies depending on the size of the group. For very small groups virtually all sales activities are conducted by the agent. For larger groups the agent is likely to call on the group representative of the insurance company for assistance in selling, installing, and servicing the case. To many agents the selling of group insurance is not a specialty but is rather the selling of just another product in the portfolio of their insurance company. While some agents limit their activities to group insurance sales, most specialists in this area need to sell the products of more than one company and therefore operate as brokers.

Agents are compensated in the form of commission payments from the insurance company. When compared with the commission rates for individual insurance, the commission rates for group insurance are considerably lower. In general, this reflects the fact that the premium on a group insurance contract is usually much larger than the premium on an average-sized individual policy. In addition, for all but the smallest cases the agent typically relies on a group representative of the insurance company to perform many of the sales and service activities pertaining to the case.

For multiple-employer trusts the commission rate is normally 10 percent of the initial annual premium, and this rate usually remains the same in renewal years, although it may drop slightly.

For other groups two approaches are used. The larger the group, the more common it is for commissions to be determined by negotiation between the policyowner, the agent, and the insurance company. However, commissions are also frequently determined by one of two basic types of commission schedules. The *standard (or regular) schedule* has high first-year commission rates and lower rates in renewal years. The *level schedule* has the same commission rates for both the first year and any renewal years. These two schedules are typically designed so that over some period of time (often 10 years) the same overall commission will be paid for a given amount of premium, regardless of which schedule is used. An example of each type of schedule is shown in table 14-1.

TABLE 14-1

Annual Premium		Standard Schedule		Level Schedule
		First Year	Renewal Years	
First	$ 1,000	20.0%	5.00%	6.50%
Next	4,000	20.0	3.00	4.70
"	5,000	15.0	1.50	2.85
"	10,000	12.5	1.50	2.60
"	10,000	10.0	1.50	2.35
"	20,000	5.0	1.50	1.85
"	200,000	2.5	1.00	1.15
"	250,000	1.0	0.50	0.55
"	2,000,000	0.5	0.25	0.25
Over	2,500,000	0.1	0.10	0.10

It is important to note that these are sliding (or graded) scales based on additional increments of premium volume, not on the total premium volume. For example, using the regular scale, the first-year commission on a group case with an annual premium volume of $40,000 is calculated as follows:

$$
\begin{array}{rcrcl}
\$ \ 1,000 & \times & 20.0\% & = & \$ \ \ 200 \\
4,000 & \times & 20.0 & = & 800 \\
5,000 & \times & 15.0 & = & 750 \\
10,000 & \times & 12.5 & = & 1,250 \\
10,000 & \times & 10.0 & = & 1,000 \\
\underline{10,000} & \times & \underline{\ \ 5.0} & = & \underline{\ \ \ 500} \\
\$40,000 & & & & \$4,500 \ \text{(or } 11.25\% \text{ of the total}
\end{array}
$$

premium)

After the first year the commission under either of these schedules may be further subdivided into selling commissions and service commissions, with the agent who sold the case receiving the latter only if he or she continues to service the case. An agent may voluntarily terminate his or her relationship with the case. In addition, most insurance companies allow the client to request a change in the servicing agent.

In many cases the agent may choose either commission schedule. The standard schedule obviously produces a higher income for the agent in early years and will generate a larger total income if the case is cancelled after a short period of time. However, the level schedule should be more beneficial if substantial increases in premium volume are expected in a case's renewal years. Insurance companies are concerned about using the standard commission schedule when there is a high probability that a group insurance case will either change insurers or lapse. Consequently many insurers require that the level schedule be used for transferred business, reinstated cases, fully contributory plans, or groups below a certain size. In addition, the level schedule may also be mandatory for very large groups when competitive bidding requires that expenses be held to a minimum and be recoverable in the early years of a contract.

Brokers and Consultants

The majority of large group insurance buyers retain a broker or employee benefit consultant to provide professional advice on group insurance matters and to aid them in dealing with insurance companies. Brokers and consultants are agents of the buyers and owe their allegiance to the buyers rather than to the insurance companies through which they place their clients' coverages. Traditionally the major distinction between brokers and consultants was that brokers were compensated on a commission basis for the coverages they placed in behalf of clients, while consultants were compensated by fees charged to the clients. From a practical standpoint, the distinction between brokers and consultants has become blurred and is more semantic than real. Generally those persons or organizations that call themselves brokers operate on a commission basis, but they also charge fees for advice and services that do not result in the sale of a product. While some consulting firms still operate solely on a fee basis, many receive commissions from insurance companies for business they have placed for their clients. This may be their sole compensation for placing the coverage (with fees charged for other services), or it may offset the higher fee that a client is charged for this service. The commission schedules insurance companies use for brokers and benefit consultants are usually the same as those used for agents. However, for large cases it is common for the commission to be a negotiated amount. Over the last few years, many insurance companies have lowered the commission rates that they pay. As a result, brokers and consultants are more likely than in the past to do one or both of the following: charge fees for services that were previously performed at no additional cost or increase the fee levels already being charged for services.

Some group insurance business is placed by brokers who specialize in other types of insurance. For example, a broker who handles a client's property and liability insurance may also have the opportunity to place group insurance coverages. However, the majority of brokers and consultants who become involved in group sales—ranging from individuals or small local firms to very large national and international firms (or departments or divisions of these firms)—are specialists in the area of group insurance. These large firms, which often also handle their clients' property and liability insurance needs, account for the majority of premium volume that is placed through brokers and consultants, and they are well suited to serving the needs of clients whose organizations are geographically widespread. Many of the employees of these firms are former group representatives.

Group Representatives

The group representative is an employee of the insurance company who is generally located outside the home office and specializes in the selling and servicing of his or her company's group insurance products. The group representative's sales activities are conducted through the agents, brokers, and consultants whom the group representative educates and motivates to place group insurance business with his or her company. In addition, the group representative aids the agents, brokers, or consultants in prospecting, securing necessary underwriting data, designing plans, and preparing and presenting group insurance proposals. After a plan is sold, the group representative is frequently involved in the enrolling of eligible employees, the administrative procedures of installing the case, and the providing of services necessary to keep the case in force. Group representatives almost always receive a salary, and most are eligible for bonuses based on performance. Significant variations exist among companies, and some pay a low salary but offer the potential for a bonus that exceeds the salary, while others pay a much higher salary and give a much smaller bonus. The bonus is frequently a function of the commissions paid the agents, brokers, or consultants with whom the group representative has dealt. In addition, it may also be a function of the persistency and profitability of the group insurance cases with which the group representative has been involved.

Service Plans

Intense competition exists among insurance companies, the Blues, and HMOs for the sale of medical expense coverage. With rare exceptions the Blues and HMOs have traditionally marketed their products and services through employees who receive a salary (and possibly a bonus) rather than through agents, brokers, and consultants who are paid a commission. One competitive advantage enjoyed by these organizations is that the compensation paid to their salespersons is usually lower than the commissions that are paid by insurance companies to agents, brokers, or consultants who produce a comparable volume of business. However, in recent years many Blue Cross–Blue Shield plans have started marketing their products through insurance agents as well as through their own salaried employees. The Blues, like the group representatives of insurance companies, have also developed close working relationships with the larger brokerage or employee benefit consulting firms in order to encourage their consideration of the Blues as a source for placing their clients' coverages. If coverage is placed with the Blues, brokers or consultants will charge their clients fees, except in those instances when the Blues pay commissions

Third-Party Administrators

Third-party administrators are persons or organizations who are hired to provide certain administrative services to group benefit plans. Traditionally their primary role has been to administer plans that are written for associations or negotiated trusteeships. The functions of these administrators include receiving employee reports and contributions, keeping track of employee eligibility, preparing any reports required by state and federal laws, and handling complaints and grievances. In addition, the administrator will be involved in certain aspects of the claims process. At a minimum this will probably involve the certification of eligibility and the processing of claims forms for submission to an insurance company, but it may also include paying claims from the trust's funds. Besides professional administrators, third-party administrators may be banks and insurance companies.

Many multiple-employer welfare arrangements, including those of insurance companies, are administered by third-party administrators. The functions that are performed by the administrator vary and are subject to negotiations between the administrator and the sponsor of the trust.

The increasing use of alternative funding methods, including total self-funding, has resulted in the need for employers to provide many of the services (such as claims handling) that are performed by an insurance company when traditional fully insured contracts are purchased. When employers have been unable to provide these services themselves in a cost-effective manner, they have often turned to third-party administrators. In some cases these third-party administrators are professionals who specialize solely in these tasks; in other cases they are brokers, consultants, or insurance companies that market these services to their clients as additional products. Over the last decade the use of third-party administrators has increased dramatically, particularly for medical expense benefits.

THE MARKETING PROCESS

While the main goal of employee benefit marketing is to "close the sale," the process can be divided into two broad categories of activities: those that precede the sale and those that follow the sale. Presale activities include prospecting and the development and presentation of the group insurance proposal; postsale activities include the enrollment of employees and the actual installation, servicing, and renewal of the group insurance plan.

Prospecting

Prospecting is the first step in the marketing process. It involves persuading the employer (or the employer's broker or consultant) to accept a group insurance proposal from the insurance company (or Blue Cross–Blue Shield plan, HMO, PPO, or other provider of benefits or services). To be successful in actually presenting a proposal, prospecting also involves convincing the employer to provide the information necessary for the preparation of the proposal.

The process of prospecting tends to vary for different segments of the group insurance market. For very small groups (under 10 or 15 employees), the plans marketed are usually provided through multiple-employer welfare arrangements rather than through the traditional group insurance arrangements of insurance companies. Some of the sales activities in this segment are conducted by agents who specialize in group insurance, but a large portion of the sales activities is conducted by agents or brokers whose primary sales activities take place in the individual marketplace. (In fact, the multiple-employer trusts of many insurance companies are actually considered for marketing purposes to be part of the product line of the individual insurance department rather than part of the group insurance department.) In many cases the agent or broker will have had previous contacts with the employer in regard to his or her personal or business insurance. However, it is also in the marketing to small groups that prospecting without known contacts (cold canvasing) is most likely to take place. Because of the modest premiums that these small groups generate, all the sales activities (not just prospecting) are usually carried out by the agent or broker with little direct involvement by representatives from the insurance company. Because of the limited and relative inflexibility of products available for these small groups, training of agents or brokers in this market is often oriented toward what products are available rather than toward group insurance planning in general.

As the size of groups increases, the chance of successful prospecting diminishes rapidly unless the agent or broker (1) has a known contact who is a key person in an organization's decision-making process for group insurance matters and (2) has a more sophisticated understanding of group insurance. In these segments of the group insurance market, group representatives spend considerable time training agents or brokers in the intricacies of group insurance and motivating them to develop prospects. For medium-size groups the agent or broker may do the actual prospecting alone or with the group representative, or he or she may give qualified leads to the group representative who will perform this function.

For large groups the situation is usually different since most large firms retain brokers or employee benefit consultants to advise them on employee benefit programs and to aid them in the implementation of any decisions that are made, including the placing of insurance coverages. Therefore in this segment of the employee benefit market, prospecting can be viewed as a two-part process. On one hand there is intense competition among brokers and consultants to obtain the large firms as clients. On the other hand, since the clients are seldom successfully approached except through the broker or consultant, the prospecting consists of group representatives (and representatives of the Blues and third-party administrators) who develop a close working relationship with the brokers or consultants to encourage the consideration of the group representatives' organization as a provider of group insurance or other employee benefit products or services.

Developing the Proposal

In the broadest sense the development of a benefit plan proposal involves designing the benefit plan, calculating the premium rate or rates, and putting the proposal in its final form for presentation.

It is at this stage of the marketing process that the majority of the under-writing will be done for a case that is ultimately written. In effect, most insurance companies are saying that the benefit plan presented to the employer will probably be acceptable to the company at the rates specified if the proposal leads to an application for coverage. However, most insurance companies "hedge" their positions and will not make an absolute commitment to write the coverage at this stage, except possibly for very large groups that have already been reviewed by the senior underwriting personnel. In many cases the preliminary underwriting is done in field offices and the proposal specifies that home office approval will be necessary. In addition, the proposal will include any assumptions made in the preliminary underwriting that must be verified before the case is finally accepted. Finally, any underwriting conditions that must be met before coverage will be written (such as a certain percentage participation) are listed in the proposal. Obtaining the necessary information for underwriting is often difficult for insurance companies, particularly when the agent or broker primarily sells individual insurance. In the individual marketplace the agent or broker is accustomed to obtaining much of the necessary underwriting information from the client at the time an application is written rather than prior to the sales presentation. Furthermore, the small employers that are approached by these agents or brokers tend to be less sophisticated in group insurance matters than large employers, and they often fail to see the necessity for providing detailed information at this point in the sales process. Consequently for the sales process to continue past the prospecting stage, it is necessary that agents and brokers recognize the importance of obtaining underwriting information and that they be willing and able to convey this importance to the employer.

The premium rates presented in the group insurance proposal are based on the employee census that is provided prior to the development of the proposal, and thus they are usually only tentative rates, a fact that is clearly stated in the proposal. The final premium rates will usually be determined at the time a group insurance plan is installed and will be based on the census of employees covered under the plan at its inception.

While variations exist among insurance companies and the amount of detail tends to increase as the size of the group insurance case becomes larger, most proposals contain at least the following information:

- a description of each coverage included in the plan
- a schedule of the tentative premium rates and the total premium for each coverage
- a description of the persons eligible for coverage under the plan
- any underwriting assumptions or conditions
- details for servicing the plan, such as the procedures and facilities for administering claims
- general information about the insurance company, including its size, financial strength, and products and services

For large group insurance cases, detailed information will usually be provided concerning the insurance company's retention and how premium rates and reserves are calculated.

As with prospecting, the process of developing a proposal differs depending on whether coverage is written for a small group, a large client that is controlled by a broker or benefit consultant, or a group that falls somewhere between these two extremes. For small groups that are written through multiple-employer welfare arrangements, the preparation of a proposal is usually a relatively simple matter. Since little or no flexibility is available for the coverages offered, the plan design consists primarily of an agent or broker describing the available options and determining the employer's preferences. The preliminary underwriting is typically carried out by the agent or broker in the sense that it is his or her responsibility to determine whether the employer meets the trust's relatively rigid underwriting criteria. Since the rate structure is fairly simplified, the agent or broker will also usually determine the tentative premium based on the census data provided by the employer. The proposal typically consists of (1) a standard brochure or packet of information that describes the trust and its benefits and (2) a brief premium-calculation presentation that contains a list of the employees to be covered and the tentative premium to be paid by the employer for the initial period of coverage.

Under some multiple-employer welfare arrangements, particularly when they are being used to write coverage for groups larger than 10 or 15 employees, the underwriting, premium calculations, and preparation of the proposal are carried out by the insurance company or the administrator of the trust. Furthermore, as the size of the group written through the trust increases, additional underwriting information (such as past claims history) may also be requested.

The situation is quite different for large groups. For group insurance cases that are not controlled by large brokers or benefit consultants, the group representative will play a major role in the development of the proposal. It is usually the group representative, possibly along with the agent or broker, who will meet with the employer. Depending on the relationship between the employer and the agent or broker, the group representative may have to put considerable effort into convincing the employer that it is worth the time to proceed with the proposal. This will include countering any of the employer's objections and convincing the employer that the insurance company can provide the products and services necessary to meet his or her needs. It is also at this time that the group representative must determine whether the employer is a serious prospect (that is, whether there is some possibility that the employer will add coverages or change insurers). In addition, the group representative must assess whether the employer is likely to meet the underwriting standards of the insurance company. For example, an insurance company may be unwilling to prepare a proposal for an employer that has a history of frequently changing insurers.

If the development of the proposal proceeds beyond the initial contact stage, the group representative must (1) determine the employer's objectives, (2) aid the employer in designing the benefit plan for which the proposal will be made, and (3) obtain the information required to complete the development of the proposal. The data from the employer will then be provided to the insurance company, usually through a field office. The rating and actual design of the proposal will normally be conducted at the field office, but except for small cases the underwriting function is likely to be performed at the home office or at a regional office in the case of large insurance companies. However, for very large cases it is common for the entire process, not just the underwriting, to be completed at some level higher than the field office.

To complete the proposal, the insurance company obviously needs a description of the benefit plan desired and a census of covered employees containing any information that will affect underwriting or premium calculations. At a minimum this information will probably include age and sex, but it may also include marital status, geographic location, income, and an indication of whether there are dependents. This census may have an actual list of employees by name or it may consist of aggregate data. In addition, most insurance companies will commonly request the following information from the prospect or the prospect's agent, broker, or consultant:

- the reason for transferring (unless it is a new case)
- the nature of the employer's industry
- a history of changes in the number of employees
- a statement indicating whether the plan is contributory and, if so, the amount of the employer's contribution
- the length of time with the current insurer
- premiums, rates, and claims experience with the current insurer for each line of coverage (usually for the prior 3 years)
- a statement indicating whether collective bargaining is involved
- copies of information on the current plan (such as benefit booklets or certificates of insurance)
- the most recent premium statement from the current insurer

- any renewal information from the current insurer

When a large broker or benefit consultant controls a group insurance case, the broker or consultant will design the benefit plan in conjunction with the employer. In some cases the business will be placed with the existing insurance company or with a company that is either wanted by the employer or recommended by the broker or consultant. In other cases bids will be requested from several sources based on specifications prepared by the broker or consultant. In general, the bidding process is not open to every insurance company (or other provider of benefits) but is done on an invitation basis. The decision about which insurance companies are invited to bid may be made at the discretion of the consultant or may be determined by the employer. For example, some employers may want bids only from companies headquartered in the same state.

The bidding specifications are accompanied by a cover letter that invites the insurance company to bid and states the last date on which bids may be received or postmarked. This date is usually from 45 to 90 days prior to the date coverage will become effective. The specifications typically consist of a description of the plan desired, a census of employees, and any information the insurance company will need to properly underwrite and rate the case (see the previous list). Based on this data the insurance company is asked to present a bid in the form of monthly and annual premiums for the coverage desired. In addition, a "net cost illustration" or "retention exhibit" will usually be requested for a 2- to 5-year period. This illustration must show the projected premiums, incurred claims, retention, and dividends for each year, and it is often required to be based on assumptions listed in the specifications.

The insurance company is typically confronted with a rigid set of specifications on which it must bid. However, some specifications are flexible and allow an insurance company to suggest changes in the specifications and to present a bid based on these suggestions. Furthermore, the specifications will ask numerous questions about the insurance company's practices and ability to service the case. The following are only a few of the many questions that are commonly asked:

- How are incurred claims defined?
- How is retention defined?
- How is the level of reserves determined?
- What is the interest rate credited to reserves?
- How are catastrophic losses handled in the experience-rating process?
- What charges are levied against the group's experience when coverage is converted?
- For what period of time are rates guaranteed?
- How much notice of rate changes is given at renewal?
- What is the procedure for handling claims?

- What services are provided in the area of cost containment?
- If you are selected to provide coverage, on what date will the master contract and certificates of insurance be delivered?

Presenting the Proposal

The successful presentation of a proposal will lead to a sale that is closed when the employer submits a signed application and the first periodic premium. For small groups the agent or broker will make the presentation of the proposal directly to the employer. In general there is little room for negotiations, and the employer will either accept or reject the initial proposal.

For large groups when the employer is dealt with directly, the agent or broker may also present the proposal. However, because of the technical expertise necessary, the group representative will probably be involved, and will either present the proposal or assist the agent or broker. It is at this point that further negotiation on plan design and revision of the proposal are most likely to take place.

When a group insurance case is put out to bid by a large broker or benefit consultant, there is usually no direct contact between the insurance company and the employer in the initial stages of the presentation. Rather, the presentation is made, usually by the group representative, to the broker or consultant, who then evaluates the proposals and makes a recommendation to the employer. This recommendation may be for the employer to select a specific proposal, but it often consists of presenting an employer with two or three proposals that best meet the employer's objectives. In this latter instance, the group representatives of the insurance companies involved are typically asked to meet with both the broker or consultant and the employer to further discuss the proposals. At this stage of the process it is not unusual to give each company in contention a copy of the proposals that their competitors have submitted.

Enrollment

The first step in the postsale activities of group marketing involves the enrollment of employees in the plan. If the plan is noncontributory, the employer must provide the insurance company with enrollment cards or a list of all employees to be covered and a certification that they have met all eligibility requirements, such as being actively at work or having satisfied a probationary period. If a plan is contributory, it must be properly marketed to the employees in order to encourage the maximum enrollment. In fact, unless the solicitation of employees is effective, the actual installation of the plan may never occur because of insufficient enrollment. Usually the insurance company prepares the solicitation materials, such as letters or benefit booklets. For small employers these may be standardized materials, but for large employers they will be custom designed. If a group is large enough, the insurance company may even prepare audiovisual presentations. Although the actual solicitation will always involve the employer, it may consist only of the employer's providing these materials to the employees. However, it is common for the employer to allow group meetings (during normal working hours) in which the agent, broker, or group representative can explain the plan to the employees and answer their questions.

The actual enrollment of employees either shortly follows or takes place simultaneously with the solicitation process. It consists of requesting the employees to complete enrollment forms supplied by the insurance company. These enrollment forms are usually brief, but they will be more detailed if the plan involves any individual underwriting of employees in addition to the usual group underwriting. Although the agent, broker, or group representative may conduct the actual enrollment, it is common for the employer's supervisory personnel to carry out this activity.

While proper marketing of a contributory plan to employees is crucial, a noncontributory plan must also be properly presented to employees if they are to fully understand and appreciate its provisions. In many cases this means that the plan will be presented to employees in virtually the same manner as if it was contributory.

Installation

When the enrollment procedure is completed, the insurance company calculates the final premium rates and prepares the master contract (or joinder agreement in the case of a multiple-employer trust) and any other administrative materials for the employer as well as the certificates of insurance for the employees. The agent or broker usually delivers these materials to small employers, but in larger cases the task is most often performed by the group representative, who is accompanied by the agent or broker. At this point the agent, broker, or group representative thoroughly reviews the plan with the employer and explains its administrative aspects, such as premium billings, claims procedures, and the enrollment and termination of employees. The importance of this meeting with the employer should not be ignored since the future success of a group insurance case is often a function of how well these administrative procedures are explained and thus understood by the employer.

Servicing the Case

Similarly the importance of properly servicing a group insurance case cannot be overlooked. Good service will not only increase the employer's satisfaction, but it will also minimize the possibility that the case will be transferred to another insurance company at the time of renewal. In addition, it may also lead to other business for the insurance company or the agent or broker when the employer adds a new coverage or renews an existing coverage.

The process of servicing a case begins when the initial sale is made and continues throughout its life. Except for small groups, the group representative usually conducts the servicing. However, some insurance companies have trained personnel whose sole function is to service group insurance cases, which allows the group representative to devote more of his or her time to sales activities. Most requests for service relate to routine administrative matters that involve billing, claims, or enrollment procedures. As previously mentioned, these requests will be minimized if a case is properly installed. To discover whether there is any difficulty with a group insurance case at its earliest stage, the group representative must develop a close working relationship with other functional departments of the insurance company. For example, correspondence between the employer and claims personnel may be the first indication of any potential dissatisfaction.

Even when no specific problems exist, the group representative will schedule periodic visits with the employer to discuss such items as the administration of the plan, claim trends, and new federal or state regulations that affect the plan. These visits may lead to suggestions that changes be made in the plan so that it will better meet the employer's desires and needs.

One of the most important and possibly most difficult aspects of servicing a group insurance case will occur at the time of renewal, particularly if a rate increase is proposed. Because the shock of a large rate increase may be a catalyst that encourages an employer to seek out another insurance company, it is important for the group representative to keep the employer periodically informed of the group's experience and current trends so that the size of the increase will not be unexpected. It is also at renewal time that the group representative, often accompanied by the agent or broker, should thoroughly review the group insurance case to determine whether it is appropriate to make any changes. If the employer is considering changing insurance companies, the group representative should emphasize any potential limitations of such an action. For example, additional administrative costs will undoubtedly be incurred with the installation of a new plan. Furthermore, there may be the potential for some employees to lose benefits in the transfer because of differing provisions of the new insurance company's plan, the application of a preexisting-conditions provision, or the inability of an employee to immediately meet an actively-at-work requirement.

15
Alternative Funding Methods

Chapter Outline

In recent years employers have increasingly considered—and often adopted—benefit funding methods that are alternatives to the traditional fully insured group insurance contract. Under the traditional group insurance contract the employer pays premiums in advance to the insurance company, which then has the financial responsibility both for paying claims (if and when they occur) and for assuming the administrative expenses associated with the contract. In addition, the insurance company bears the risk that claims will be larger than anticipated.

REASONS FOR ALTERNATIVE FUNDING

The increasing interest in alternatives to the traditional fully insured group arrangement has focused on two factors: cost savings and improved cash flow. To a large extent this interest has grown in response to the rising cost of medical care that has resulted in an increase in the cost of providing medical expense benefits. Even though alternative funding methods are most commonly used for providing medical expense benefits, many of the methods described here are also appropriate for other types of benefits.

Cost Savings

Savings can result to the extent that either claims or the insurance company's retention can be reduced. Retention—the portion of the insurance company's premium over and above the incurred claims and dividends—includes such items as commissions, premium taxes, risk charges, and profit. Traditionally, alternative funding methods have not focused on reducing claims, since the same benefits will normally be provided (and therefore the same claims will be paid) regardless of which funding method is used. However, this focus has changed as state laws and regulations increasingly mandate the types and levels of benefits that must be contained in medical expense contracts. To the extent that these laws and regulations apply only to benefits that are included in insurance contracts, employers can avoid providing these mandated benefits by using alternative funding methods that do not involve insurance contracts.

Modifications of fully insured contracts are usually designed either to lower or eliminate premium taxes or to reduce the insurance company's risk and consequently the risk charge. Alternative funding methods that involve a degree of self-funding may be designed to also reduce other aspects of retention and to reduce claims by excluding mandated benefits.

Improved Cash Flow

Under a fully insured contract an employer has the ability to improve cash flow because premiums are collected before the funds will actually be needed to pay claims. The employer will generally be credited with interest while these funds are held in reserves. Alternative funding arrangements that are intended to improve cash flow are designed either to postpone the payment of premiums to the insurance company or to keep the funds that would otherwise be held in reserves in the employer's hands until the insurance company needs them. Such an arrangement is particularly advantageous to the employer when these funds can be invested at a higher rate of interest than that credited by the insurance company to reserves. It must be remembered, however, that earnings on funds invested by the employer are generally subject to income taxation, while interest credited to reserves by the insurance company is tax free.

METHODS OF ALTERNATIVE FUNDING

Totally self-funded (or self-insured) employee benefit plans are the opposite of traditional fully insured group insurance plans. Under totally self-funded plans the employer is responsible for paying claims, administering the plan, and bearing the risk that actual claims will exceed those expected. However, very few employee benefit plans that use alternative methods of funding have actually turned to total self-funding. Rather, the methods used typically fall somewhere between the two extremes.

The methods of alternative funding can be divided into two general categories: those that primarily modify traditional fully insured group insurance contracts and those that have some self-funding (either partial or total). The first category includes

- premium-delay arrangements
- reserve-reduction arrangements
- minimum-premium plans
- cost-plus arrangements
- retrospective-rating arrangements

These alternative funding methods are regarded as modifications of traditional fully insured plans because the insurance company has the ultimate responsibility for paying all benefits promised under the contract. Most insurance companies will allow only large employers to use these modifications, and although practices differ among insurance companies, generally a group insurance plan must generate between $150,000 and $250,000 in claims before these funding methods will be available to the employer.

The second category of alternative funding methods includes

- total self-funding from current revenue and self-administration
- self-funding with stop-loss coverage and/or ASO arrangements
- funding through a 501(c)(9) trust

In contrast to the first category of alternative funding methods, some of these alternatives can be used by small employers.

Premium-Delay Arrangements

Premium-delay arrangements allow the employer to defer payment of monthly premiums for some time beyond the usual 30-day grace period. In fact, these arrangements lengthen the grace period, most commonly by 60 or 90 days. The practical effect of premium-delay arrangements is that they enable the employer to have continuous use of the portion of the annual premium that is approximately equal to the claim reserve. For example, a 90-day premium delay allows the employer to use 3 months (or 25 percent) of the annual premium for other purposes. This amount roughly corresponds to what is usually in the claim reserve for medical expense coverage. Generally the larger this reserve is on a percentage basis, the longer the premium payment can be delayed. Because the insurance company still has a statutory obligation to maintain the claim reserve, it must use other assets besides the employer's premiums for this purpose. In most cases these assets come from the insurance company's surplus.

A premium-delay arrangement has a financial advantage to the extent that an employer can earn a higher return by investing the delayed premiums than by accruing interest on the claim reserve. In actual practice, interest is still credited to the reserve, but this credit is offset by either an interest charge on the delayed premiums or an increase in the insurance company's retention.

Upon termination of an insurance contract with a premium-delay arrangement, the employer is responsible for paying any deferred premiums. However, the insurance company is legally responsible for paying all claims incurred prior to termination, even if the employer fails to pay the deferred premiums. Consequently most insurance companies are concerned about the employer's financial position and credit rating. For many insurance companies the final decision of whether to enter into a premium-delay arrangement, or any other alternative funding arrangement that leaves funds in the hands of the employer, is made by the insurer's financial experts after a thorough analysis of the employer. In some cases this may mean that the employer will be required to submit a letter of credit or some other form of security.

Reserve-Reduction Arrangements

A reserve-reduction arrangement is similar to a premium-delay arrangement. Under the usual reserve-reduction arrangement the employer is allowed (at any given time) to retain an amount of the annual premium that is equal to the claim reserve. Generally such an arrangement is allowed only after the contract's first year, when the pattern of claims and the appropriate amount of the reserve can be more accurately estimated. In succeeding years if the contract is renewed, the amount retained will be adjusted according to changes in the size of the reserve. As with a premium-delay arrangement the monies retained by the employer must be paid to the insurance company upon termination of the contract. Again, the advantage of this approach lies in the employer's ability to earn more on these funds than it would earn under the traditional insurance arrangement.

A few insurance companies offer another type of reserve-reduction arrangement for long-term disability income coverage. Under a so-called limited-liability arrangement the employer purchases from the insurance company a one-year contract in which the insurer agrees to pay claims only for that year, even though the employer's "plan" provides benefits to employees for longer periods. Consequently enough reserves are maintained by the insurance company to pay benefits only for the duration of the one-year contract. At renewal the insurance company agrees to continue paying the existing claims as well as any new claims. In effect, the employer pays the insurance company each year for existing claims as the benefits are paid to employees, rather than when disabilities occur. A problem for employees under this type of arrangement is the lack of security for future benefits. For example, if the employer goes bankrupt and the insurance contract is not renewed, the insurance company has no responsibility to continue benefit payments. For this reason several states will not allow this type of arrangement.

The limited-liability arrangement contrasts with the usual group contract in which the insurance company is responsible for paying disability income claims to an employee for the length of the benefit period (as long as the employee remains disabled). On average each disability claim will result in the establishment of a reserve equal to approximately five times the employee's annual benefit.

Minimum-Premium Plans

Minimum-premium plans were designed primarily to reduce state premium taxes. However, many minimum-premium plans also improve the employer's cash flow.

Under the typical minimum-premium plan the employer assumes the financial responsibility for paying claims up to a specified level, usually from 80 to 95 percent of estimated claims (with 90 percent most common). The specified level may be determined on either a monthly or an annual basis. The funds necessary to pay these claims are deposited into a bank account that belongs to the employer. However, the actual payment of claims is made from this account by the insurance company, which acts as an agent of the employer. When claims exceed the specified level, the balance is paid from the insurance company's own funds. No premium tax is levied by the states on the amounts the employer deposits into such an account, as it would have been if these deposits had been paid directly to the insurance company. In effect, for premium-tax purposes the insurance company is only considered to be the administrator of these funds and not a provider of insurance. Unfortunately the IRS considers these funds to belong to the employer, and death benefits represent taxable income to beneficiaries. Consequently minimum-premium plans are used to insure disability income and medical expense benefits rather than life insurance benefits.

Under a minimum-premium plan the employer pays a substantially reduced premium, subject to premium taxation, to the insurance company for administering the entire plan and for bearing the cost of claims above the specified level. Because such a plan may be slightly more burdensome for an insurance company to administer than would a traditional group arrangement, the retention charge may also be slightly higher. Under a minimum-premium arrangement the insurance company is ultimately responsible for seeing that all claims are paid, and it must maintain the same reserves that would have been required if the plan had been funded under a traditional group insurance arrangement. Consequently the premium will include a charge for the establishment of these reserves, unless some type of reserve-reduction arrangement has also been negotiated.

Some insurance regulatory officials view the minimum-premium plan primarily as a loophole used by employers to avoid paying premium taxes. In several states there have been attempts to seek court rulings or legislation that would require premium taxes to be paid either on the funds deposited in the bank account or on claims paid from these funds. Most of these attempts have been unsuccessful, but court rulings in California require the employer to pay premium taxes on the funds deposited in the bank account. If similar attempts are successful in the future, the main advantage of minimum-premium plans will be lost.

Cost-Plus Arrangements

Cost-plus arrangements (often referred to by other names such as flexible funding) are frequently used by large employers to provide life insurance benefits. Under such an arrangement the employer's monthly premium is based on the claims paid by the insurance company during the preceding month, plus a specified retention charge that is uniform throughout the policy period. To the extent that an employer's loss experience is less than that assumed in a traditional premium arrangement, the employer's cash flow is improved. However, an employer with worse-than-expected experience, either during the early part of the policy period or during the entire policy period, could also have a more unfavorable cash flow than if a traditional insurance arrangement were used. To prevent this from occurring, many insurance companies place a maximum limit on the employer's monthly premium so that the aggregate monthly premiums paid at any time during the policy period do not exceed the aggregate monthly premiums that would have been paid if the cost-plus arrangement had not been used.

Retrospective-Rating Arrangements

Under retrospective-rating arrangements the insurance company charges the employer an initial premium that is less than what would be justified by the expected claims for the year. In general this reduction will be between 5 and 10 percent of the premium for a traditional group insurance arrangement. However, if claims plus the insurance company's retention exceed the initial premium, the employer will be called upon to pay an additional amount at the end of the policy year. Because an employer will usually have to pay this additional premium, one advantage of a retrospective-rating arrangement is the employer's ability to use these funds during the year.

This potential additional premium is subject to a maximum amount based on some percentage of expected claims. For example, assume that a retrospective-rating arrangement bases the initial premium on the fact that claims will be 93 percent of those actually expected for the year. If claims in fact are below this level, the employer will receive an experience refund. If they exceed 93 percent, the retrospective-rating arrangement will be "triggered," and the employer will have to reimburse the insurance company for any additional claims paid, up to some percentage of those expected, such as 112 percent. The insurance company bears claims in excess of 112 percent, so some of the risk associated with claims fluctuations is passed on to the employer. This will reduce both the insurance company's risk charge and any reserve for claims fluctuations. The amount of these reductions will depend on the actual percentage specified in the contract, above which the insurance company will be responsible for claims. This percentage and the one that triggers the retrospective-rating arrangement are subject to negotiations between the insurance company and the employer. In general the lower the percentage that triggers the retrospective arrangement is, the higher will be the percentage above which the insurance company is fully responsible for claims. In addition, the better the cash-flow advantage the employer has, the greater will be the risk of claims fluctuations.

In all other respects a retrospective-rating arrangement is identical to the traditional group insurance contract.

Total Self-Funding and Self-Administration

The purest form of a self-funded benefit plan is one in which the employer pays benefits from current revenue (rather than from a trust), administers all aspects of the plan, and bears the risk that benefit payments will exceed those expected. In addition to eliminating state premium taxes, avoiding state-mandated benefits, and improving cash flow, the employer has the potential to reduce its operating expenses to the extent that the plan can be administered at a lower cost than the insurance company's retention (other than premium taxes). A decision to use this kind of self-funding plan is generally considered most desirable when all the following conditions are present:

- predictable claims. Budgeting is an integral part of the operation of any organization, and it is necessary to budget for benefit payments that will have to be paid in the future. This can best be done when a specific type of benefit plan has a claim pattern that is either stable or shows a steady trend. Such a pattern is most likely to occur in those types of benefit plans that have a relatively high frequency of low-severity claims. Although a self-funded plan may still be appropriate when the level of future benefit payments is difficult to predict, the plan will generally be designed to include stop-loss coverage (discussed later in this chapter).

- a noncontributory plan. Several difficulties arise if a self-funded benefit plan is contributory. Some employees may resent paying "their" money to the employer for benefits that are contingent on the firm's future financial ability to pay claims. If claims are denied, employees under a contributory plan are more likely to be bitter toward the employer than they would be if the benefit plan were noncontributory. Finally, ERISA requires that a trust must be established to hold the employees' contributions until the plan uses the funds. Both the establishment and maintenance of the trust will result in increased administrative costs to the employer.

- a nonunion situation. Self-funding of benefits for union employees may not be feasible if a firm is subject to collective bargaining. Self-funding (at least by the employer) clearly cannot be used if benefits are provided through a negotiated trusteeship. Even when collective bargaining results in benefits being provided through an individual employer plan, unions often insist that benefits be insured in order to guarantee that union members will actually receive them. An employer's decision about whether to use self-funding is most likely motivated by the potential to save money. When unions approve of self-funding, they also frequently insist that some of these savings be passed on to union members through additional or increased benefits.

- the ability to effectively and efficiently handle claims. One reason that many employers do not use totally self-funded and self-administered benefit plans is the difficulty in handling claims as efficiently and effectively as an insurance company or other benefit-plan administrator would handle them. Unless an employer is extremely large, only one person or a few persons will be needed to handle claims. Who in the organization can properly train and supervise these people? Can they be replaced if they should leave? Will anyone have the expertise to properly handle the unusual or complex claims that might occur? Many employers want some insulation from their employees in the handling of claims. If employees are unhappy with claim payments under a self-administered plan, dissatisfaction (and possibly legal actions) will be directed toward the employer rather than toward the insurance company. The employer's inability to handle claims, or its lack of interest in wanting to handle them, does not completely rule out the use of self-funding. As will be discussed later, employers can have claims handled by another party through an administrative-services-only contract.

- the ability to provide other administrative services. In addition to claims, the employer must determine whether the other administrative services normally included in an insured arrangement can be provided in a cost-effective manner. These services are associated with plan design, actuarial calculations, statistical reports, communication with employees, compliance with government regulations, and the preparation of government reports. Many of these costs are relatively fixed, regardless of the size of the employer, and unless the employer can spread them out over a large number of employees, self-administration will not be economically feasible. As with claims administration, an employer can purchase needed services from other sources.

- the ability to obtain discounts from medical care providers if medical expense benefits are self-funded. In order to obtain much of the cost savings associated with managed care plans, the employer must be able to secure discounts from the providers of medical care. Large employers whose employees live in a relatively concentrated geographic region may be able to enter into contracts with local providers. Other employers may use the services of third-party administrators who have either established or entered into contracts with preferred-provider networks.

The extent of total self-funding and self-administration differs significantly among the different types of group benefit plans. Plans that provide life insurance or accidental death and dismemberment benefits do not usually lend themselves to self-funding because of infrequent and large claims that are difficult to predict. Only very large employers can expect stable and predictable claims on an annual basis. In addition, federal income tax laws impede the use of self-funding for death benefits, since any payments to beneficiaries are considered taxable income to the beneficiaries. Such a limitation does not exist if the plan is insured.

The most widespread use of self-funding and self-administration occurs in short-term disability income plans, particularly those in which the maximum duration of benefits is limited to 6 months or less. For employers of most any size, the number and average length of short-term absences from work are relatively predictable. In addition, the payment of claims is relatively simple, since benefits can be (and usually are) made through the usual payroll system of the employer.

Long-term disability income benefits are occasionally self-funded by large employers. Like death claims, long-term disability income claims are difficult to predict for small employers because of their infrequent occurrence and potentially large size. In addition, because small employers receive only a few claims of this type, it becomes economically unjustifiable to self-administer such claims.

The larger the employer is, the more likely that its medical expense plan will be self-funded. The major problem with a self-funded medical expense plan is not the prediction of claims frequency but rather the prediction of the average severity of claims. Although infrequent, claims of $300,000 to $500,000 or more do occasionally occur. Most small and medium-size employers are unwilling to assume the risk that they might have to pay such a large claim. Only employers with several thousand employees are large enough to anticipate that such claims will regularly occur and to have the resources that will be necessary to pay any unexpectedly large claims. This does not mean that smaller employers cannot self-fund medical benefits. To avoid the uncertainty of catastrophic claims, these employers often self-fund basic medical expense benefits and insure major medical expense benefits or self-fund their entire coverage but purchase stop-loss protection.

It is not unusual to use self-funding and self-administration in other types of benefit plans, such as those providing coverage for dental care, vision care, prescription drugs, or legal expenses. Initially it may be difficult to predict the extent to which these plans will be utilized. However, once the plans have "matured," the level of claims tends to be fairly stable. Furthermore, these plans are commonly subject to maximums so that the employer has little or no risk of catastrophic claims. Although larger employers may be able to economically administer the plans themselves, smaller employers commonly purchase administrative services.

Self-Funding with Stop-Loss Coverage and/or ASO Arrangements

Two of the problems associated with self-funding and self-administration are the risk of catastrophic claims and the employer's inability to provide administrative services in a cost-effective manner. For each of these problems, however, solutions have evolved—namely stop-loss coverage and administrative-services-only (ASO) contracts—that still allow an employer to use elements of self-funding. Although an ASO contract and stop-loss coverage can be provided separately, they are commonly written together. In fact, most insurance companies require an employer with stop-loss coverage to have a self-funded plan administered under an ASO arrangement, either by the insurance company or by a third-party administrator.

Until recently stop-loss coverage and ASO contracts were generally provided by insurance companies and were available only to employers with at least several hundred employees. However, these arrangements are increasingly becoming available to small employers, and in many cases the administrative services are now being purchased from third-party administrators who operate independently from insurance companies.

Stop-Loss Coverage

Aggregate stop-loss coverage is one form of protection for employers against an unexpectedly high level of claims. If total claims exceed some specified dollar limit, the insurance company assumes the financial responsibility for those claims that are over the limit, subject to the maximum reimbursement specified in the contract. The limit is usually applied on an annual basis and is expressed as some percentage of expected claims (typically between 115 percent and 135 percent). This arrangement can be thought of as a form of reinsurance and is treated as such by some regulatory officials. It is interesting to note that the employer is responsible for the paying of all claims to employees, including any payments that are received from the insurance company under the stop-loss coverage. In fact, since the insurance company has no responsibility to the employees, no reserve for claims must be established.

Aggregate stop-loss coverage results in (1) an improved cash flow for the employer and (2) a minimization of premium taxes, since they must be paid only on the stop-loss coverage. However, these advantages will be partially (and perhaps totally) offset by the cost of the coverage. In addition, many insurance companies will insist that the employer purchase other insurance coverages or administrative services in order to obtain aggregate stop-loss coverage.

Stop-loss plans may also be written on a "specific" basis, similar to the way an insured plan with a deductible is written. In fact, this arrangement (most commonly used with medical expense plans) is often referred to as a *big-deductible plan* or as *shared funding*. The deductible amount may vary from $1,000 to $250,000 but is most commonly in the range of $10,000 to $20,000. It is usually applied on an annual basis and pertains to each person insured under the contract. Although in the past stop-loss coverage was written primarily for large employers, more recently it has been written for employers with as few as 25 employees. These plans have particular appeal for small employers who have had better-than-average claims experience but who are too small to qualify for experience rating and the accompanying premium savings.

The deductible specified in the stop-loss coverage is the amount the employer must assume before the stop-loss carrier is responsible for claims and is different from the deductible that an employee must satisfy under the medical expense plan. For example, employees may be given a medical expense plan that has a $200 annual deductible and an 80 percent coinsurance provision. If stop-loss coverage with a $5,000 stop-loss limit has been purchased, an employee will have to assume the first $200 in annual medical expenses, and the plan will then pay 80 percent of any additional expenses until it has paid a total of $5,000. At that time the stop-loss carrier will reimburse the plan for any additional amounts that the plan must pay to the employee. The stop-loss carrier has no responsibility to pay the employer's share of claims under any circumstances, and most insurance companies require that employees be made aware of this fact.

Misunderstandings often arise over two variations in specific stop-loss contracts. Most contracts settle claims on a *paid* basis, which means that only those claims paid during the stop-loss period under a benefit plan are taken into consideration in determining the liability of the stop-loss carrier. Some stop-loss contracts, however, settle claims on an *incurred* basis. In these cases the stop-loss carrier's liability is determined on the basis of the date a loss took place rather than when the benefit plan actually made payment. For example, assume an employee was hospitalized last December, but the claim was not paid until this year. This is an incurred claim for last year, but a paid claim for this year.

A second variation has an impact on an employer's cash flow. Assume an employer has a medical expense plan with a $20,000 stop-loss limit and that an employee has a claim of $38,000. If the stop-loss contract is written on a *reimbursement* basis, the employer's plan must pay the $38,000 claim before the plan's administrator can submit an $18,000 claim to the stop-loss carrier. If the stop-loss contract is written on an *advance-funding* basis, the employer's plan does not actually have to pay the employee before seeking reimbursement.

Most insurance companies that provide stop-loss coverage for medical expense plans will also agree to provide a conversion contract to employees whose coverage terminates. However, the employer must pay an additional monthly charge to have this benefit for employees.

ASO Contracts

Under an administrative-services-only contract the employer purchases specific administrative services from an insurance company or from an independent third-party administrator. These services will usually include the administration of claims, but they may also include a broad array of other services. In effect, the employer has the option to purchase services for those administrative functions that can be handled more cost effectively by another party. Under ASO contracts, the administration of claims is performed in much the same way as it is under a minimum-premium plan; that is, the administrator has the authority to pay claims from a bank account that belongs to the employer or from segregated funds in the administrator's hands. However, the administrator is not responsible for paying claims from its own assets if the employer's account is insufficient.

In addition to listing the services that will be provided, an ASO contract also stipulates the administrator's authority and responsibility, the length of the contract, the provisions for terminating and amending the contract, and the manner in which disputes between the employer and the administrator will be settled. The charges for the services provided under the contract may be stated in one or some combination of the following ways:

- a percentage of the amount of claims paid
- a flat amount per processed claim
- a flat charge per employee
- a flat charge for the employer

Payments for ASO contracts are regarded as fees for services performed, and they are therefore not subject to state premium taxes. However, one similarity to a traditional insurance arrangement may be present: The administrator may agree to continue paying any unsettled claims after the contract's termination but only with funds provided by the employer.

Funding through a 501(c)(9) Trust

Sec. 501(c)(9) of the Internal Revenue Code provides for the establishment of *voluntary employees' beneficiary associations* (commonly called either *501(c)(9) trusts* or *VEBAs*), which are funding vehicles for the employee benefits that are offered to members. The trusts have been allowed for many years, but until the passage of the 1969 Tax Reform Act, they were primarily used by negotiated trusteeships and association groups. The liberalized tax treatment of the funds accumulated by these trusts resulted in their increased use by employers as a method of self-funding employee benefit plans. However, the Tax Reform Act of 1984 imposed more restrictive provisions on 501(c)(9) trusts, and their use has diminished somewhat, particularly by smaller employers who previously had overfunded their trusts primarily as a method to shelter income from taxation.

Advantages

The use of a 501(c)(9) trust offers the employer some advantages over a benefit plan that is self-funded from current revenue. Contributions can be made to the trust and can be deducted for federal income tax purposes at that time, just as if the trust were an insurance company. Appreciation in the value of the trust assets or investment income earned on the trust assets is also free of taxation. The trust is best suited for an employer who wishes to establish either a fund for claims that have been incurred but not paid or a fund for possible claims fluctuations. If the employer does not use a 501(c)(9) trust in establishing these funds, contributions cannot be deducted until they are paid in the form of benefits to employees. In addition, earnings on the funds will be subject to taxation.

Although the Internal Revenue Code requires that certain fiduciary standards be maintained regarding the investment of the trust assets, the employer does have some latitude and does have the potential for earning a return on the trust assets that is higher than what is earned on the reserves held by insurance companies. A 501(c)(9) trust also lends itself to use by a contributory self-funded plan, since ERISA requires that under a self-funded benefit plan a trust must be established to hold the contributions of employees until they are used to pay benefits.

There is also flexibility regarding contributions to the trust. Although the Internal Revenue Service will not permit a tax deduction for "overfunding" a trust, there is no requirement that the trust must maintain enough assets to pay claims that have been incurred but not yet paid. Consequently an employer can "underfund" the trust in bad times and make up for this underfunding in good times with larger-than-normal contributions. However, any underfunding must be shown as a contingent liability on the employer's balance sheet.

Disadvantages

The use of a 501(c)(9) trust is not without its drawbacks. The cost of establishing and maintaining the trust may be prohibitive, especially for small employers. In addition, the employer must be concerned about the administrative aspects of the plan and the fact that claims might deplete the trust's assets. However, as long as the trust is properly funded, ASO contracts and stop-loss coverage can be purchased.

Requirements for Establishment

In order to qualify under Sec. 501(c)(9), a trust must meet certain requirements, some of which may hinder its establishment. These requirements include the following:

- Membership in the trust must be objectively restricted to those persons who share a common employment-related bond. Internal Revenue Service regulations interpret this broadly to include active employees and their dependents, surviving dependents, and employees who are retired, laid off, or disabled. Except for plans maintained pursuant to collective-bargaining agreements, benefits must be provided under a classification of employees that the IRS does not find to be discriminatory in favor of highly compensated individuals. It is permissible for life insurance, disability, severance pay, and supplemental unemployment compensation benefits to be based on a uniform percentage of compensation. In addition, the following persons may be excluded in determining whether the discrimination rule has been satisfied: (1) employees who have not completed 3 years of service, (2) employees under age 21, (3) seasonal or less-than-half-time employees, and (4) employees covered by a collective-bargaining agreement if the class of benefits was subject to good-faith bargaining.

- With two exceptions membership in the trust must be voluntary on the part of employees. Members can be required to participate (1) as a result of collective bargaining or (2) when participation is not detrimental to them. In general, participation is not regarded as detrimental if the employee is not required to make any contributions.

- The trust must provide only eligible benefits. The list of eligible coverages is broad enough that a trust can provide benefits because of death, medical expenses, disability, and unemployment. Retirement benefits, deferred compensation, and group property and liability insurance cannot be provided.

- The sole purpose of the trust must be to provide benefits to its members or their beneficiaries. Trust assets can be used to pay the administrative expenses of the trust, but they cannot revert to the employer. If the trust is terminated, any assets that remain after all existing liabilities have been satisfied must either be used to provide other benefits or be distributed to members of the trust.

- The trust must be controlled by (1) its membership, (2) independent trustees (such as a bank), or (3) trustees or other fiduciaries, at least some of whom are designated by or on behalf of the members. Most 501(c)(9) trusts are controlled by independent trustees selected by the employer.

Limitation on Contributions

The contributions to a 501(c)(9) trust (except collectively bargained plans for which Treasury regulations prescribe separate rules) are limited to the sum of (1) the qualified direct cost of the benefits provided for the taxable year and (2) any permissible additions to a reserve (called a qualified asset account). The qualified direct cost of benefits is the amount that would have been deductible for the year if the employer had paid benefits from current revenue.

The permissible additions may be made only for disability, medical, supplemental unemployment, severance pay, and life insurance benefits. In general the amount of the permissible additions includes (1) any sums that are reasonably and actuarially necessary to pay claims that have been incurred but remain unpaid at the close of the tax year and (2) any administration costs with respect to these claims. If medical or life insurance benefits are provided to retirees, deductions are also allowed for funding these benefits on a level basis over the working lives of the covered employees. However, for retirees' medical benefits, current medical costs must be used rather than costs based on projected inflation. In addition, a separate account must be established for postretirement benefits provided to key employees. Contributions to these accounts are treated as annual additions for purposes of applying the limitations that exist for contributions and benefits under qualified retirement plans.

The amount of certain benefits for which deductions will be allowed is limited. Life insurance benefits for retired employees cannot exceed amounts that are tax free under Sec. 79. Annual disability benefits cannot exceed the lesser of (1) 75 percent of a disabled person's average compensation for the highest 3 years or (2) $90,000. Supplemental unemployment compensation benefits and severance benefits cannot exceed 75 percent of average benefits paid plus administrative costs during any 2 of the immediately preceding 7 years. In determining this limit, annual benefits in excess of $45,000 cannot be taken into account.

In general it is required that the amount of any permissible additions be actuarially certified. However, deductible contributions can be made to reserves without such certification as long as certain safe-harbor limits on the size of the reserve are not exceeded. The safe-harbor limits for supplemental unemployment compensation benefits and severance benefits are the same as the amounts previously mentioned. For short-term disability benefits, the limit is equal to 17.5 percent of benefit costs (other than insurance premiums for the current year), plus administrative costs for the prior year. For medical benefits, the percentage is 35. The Internal Revenue Code provides that the limits for life insurance benefits and long-term disability income benefits will be those prescribed by regulations. However, no regulations have been issued.

Employer deductions cannot exceed the limits as previously described. However, any excess contributions may be deducted in future years to the extent that contributions for those years are below the permissible limits.

There are several potential adverse tax consequences if a 501(c)(9) trust does not meet prescribed standards. If reserves are above permitted levels, additional contributions to the reserves are not deductible and earnings on the excess reserves are subject to tax as unrelated business income. (This effectively negates any possible advantage of using a 501(c)(9) trust to prefund postretirement medical benefits.) In addition, an excise tax is imposed on employers maintaining a trust that provides disqualified benefits. The tax is equal to 100 percent of the disqualified benefits, which include (1) medical and life insurance benefits provided to key employees outside the separate accounts that must be established, (2) discriminatory medical or life insurance benefits for retirees, and (3) any portion of the trust's assets that revert to the employer.

16

Group Insurance Pricing

One of the least understood aspects of group insurance is the pricing process. In the simplest sense group insurance pricing is no different from pricing in other industries. The insurance company must generate enough revenue to cover its costs (claims and expenses) and to contribute to the net worth of the company. However, this similarity is often overlooked because of the unique terminology that is associated with insurance pricing and because the price of a group insurance product is initially determined on the basis of expected, but uncertain, future events rather than on current tangible cost estimates. In addition, a group insurance plan may be subject to experience rating so that the final price to the consumer can be determined only after the coverage period has ended.

The purpose of this chapter is not to make readers experts in the actuarial intricacies of group insurance pricing, commonly referred to as *rate making,* but rather to provide an understanding of basic principles and concepts. Rate making consists of two distinct steps: (1) the determination of a unit price, referred to as a *rate* or *premium rate,* for each unit of benefit (such as each $1,000 of life insurance); and (2) the determination of the total price, or premium, that the policyowner will pay for the entire amount of coverage purchased. The mechanics of rate making differ, depending upon whether a particular group is subject to manual rating or experience rating. When *manual rating* is used, the premium rate is determined independently of a particular group's claims; when *experience rating* is used, the past claims experience of a group is considered in determining future premiums for the group and/or in adjusting past premiums after a policy period has ended.

The major objective of rate making for all types of group insurance is to develop premium rates that are both adequate and equitable. Adequate rates must be sufficient to cover both incurred claims and expenses and to generate the desired profit or contribution to the insurance company's surplus. Obviously the success and solvency of any group insurance operation is contingent on the long-run adequacy of premium rates. Therefore several states, concerned about the solvency of insurance companies, have laws and regulations regarding the adequacy of rates. The most significant of these is the New York law that prohibits any insurance company doing business in that state from issuing in any state a group health insurance contract (either medical expense or disability income) that does not appear to be self-supporting on the basis of reasonable assumptions concerning expected claims and expenses. New York also specifies the minimum group term life insurance rates that these companies may charge for any group that has not previously been insured for life insurance.

Equitable rates require each group to pay a premium that reflects the cost of providing coverage to that group. Again, practical considerations and state regulations act to encourage equity. The overpricing of group coverage for some segments of the market will result in lost business; the underpricing for other segments will attract unprofitable business. Most states also have laws and regulations that try to encourage equity by prohibiting unfair discrimination in insurance rates. The objective of equity has resulted in group insurance rates that differ because of such factors as the age, sex, and income distribution of a group's members and the size of a group, its geographic location, its occupational hazards, and its claims experience. As is discussed later, the factors that are considered vary with the type of group insurance coverage.

MANUAL RATING

In the manual-rating process, premium rates are established only for broad classes of group insurance business, and the insurance company does not consider the past claims experience of a particular group when determining that group's rates. However, claims experience is not entirely ignored since the aggregate claims experience for a class of business is used to determine the premium rates for that class.

Manual rating is used with small groups for which no credible individual loss experience is available. This lack of credibility exists because the group's size makes it impossible to determine whether other-than-average loss experience is due to random chance or is truly reflective of the group. Manual rating is also frequently used to determine the initial premiums for groups that are subject to experience rating, particularly when a group's past experience is unobtainable or when a group is being written for the first time. In addition, experience rating typically uses a weighting of manual rates and the actual experience of a group to determine the premium. (Rates for very large groups may be based solely on a group's own experience.)

Rating Basis

Prior to the actual calculation of manual premium rates, it is necessary to develop a basis on which the rates will be determined. This involves a decision regarding (1) what benefit unit to use, (2) the extent to which rates will be refined by factors affecting claims, and (3) the frequency with which premiums will be paid.

Benefit Unit

Subject to certain adjustments, the premium for a group is calculated by multiplying the premium rate by the number of benefit units provided. While variations do occasionally exist, the benefit units predominantly used for the most common types of group insurance are shown in table 16-1.

TABLE 16-1	
Type of Group Insurance	**Benefit Unit**
Term life (including accidental death and dismemberment)	Each $1,000 of death benefit
Short-term disability income	Each $10, $50, or $100 of weekly income
Long-term disability income	Each $100 of monthly income
Medical expense (including dental)	Each employee and each category of dependents

Factors Affecting Claims

As previously mentioned, equity requires that rates reflect those factors that result in different claims experience for different groups. Although there are variations among insurance companies, the following discussion indicates the factors used by most insurance companies to determine rates for life, disability income, medical expense, and dental insurance:

Sex. The sex of insured persons is taken into account for determining rates for all the types of insurance mentioned in the previous paragraph.

Age. Age is also used as a rating factor for life insurance, disability income, and medical expense insurance. However, dental insurance rates usually do not take age into consideration.

Geographic Location. At one time geographic location was a rating factor for medical expense insurance and dental insurance only. However, an increasing number of insurance companies are using geographic variations for determining life insurance and disability income insurance rates. For these latter types of insurance, rates may not be determined separately for a wide variety of locations. Rather the insurance company may have only two or three rate schedules, with each schedule applying to several different geographic locations on the basis of past experience.

Occupation. Occupation is virtually always reflected in both group term insurance rates and accidental death and dismemberment rates. It may also be reflected in disability income, medical expense, and dental insurance rates, but the number of groups for which it is of concern is relatively small. Consequently some companies ignore it as a rating factor but may not write such coverages when certain occupations are involved.

Income. At one time the income level of group members was commonly used as a factor in establishing disability income, medical expense, and dental insurance rates. Currently income level is still a factor in determining dental insurance premiums, but it is more likely to be an underwriting consideration only in disability income and medical expense insurance.

Size. The size of a group will also affect rates since the proportion of the premium needed for expenses will decrease as the size of a group increases. All manual premium rates are based on an assumption that the size of a group falls within a certain range. If the size of a group varies from this range, an appropriate rate adjustment is made to reflect this differential.

Time. A final factor considered in the calculation of rates is the length of time for which the rates will be used. This is a concern primarily for coverages that involve medical and dental claims, which over time will be expected to increase in severity because of inflation. In inflationary times, monthly rates that are guaranteed for three months can be lower than those guaranteed for one year.

Frequency of Premium Payment Period

Because group insurance premiums are usually paid monthly, this is the period for which rates are generally determined. When premiums can be paid less frequently (such as annually), they are usually slightly lower than the sum of the monthly premiums for the same period of coverage.

Calculation of Manual Rates

Manual rating involves the calculation of the *manual premium rates* (also called tabular rates) that are quoted in an insurance company's rate book. These manual rates are applied to a specific group insurance case in order to determine a *final premium rate* (sometimes called an average premium rate) that will then be multiplied by the number of benefit units to obtain a premium for the group.

There are three manual-rating methods. However, if identical assumptions are used, each method should result in approximately the same premium for any given group. The first method determines separate manual rates for groups with certain characteristics that an insurance company feels will affect claims experience. A second approach establishes a single "standard manual rate" that is adjusted in the premium-calculation process to compensate for any characteristics that deviate from those of the standard group. A third method merely combines the first two approaches and considers some factors in determining the manual rate and other factors in determining the final premium rate.

The first step in the calculation of manual premium rates is the determination of the *net premium rate,* which is the amount necessary to support the cost of expected claims. For any given classification the net premium rate is calculated by multiplying the probability (frequency) of a claim's occurring by the expected amount (severity) of the claim. For example, if the probability that an employee aged 50 will die in the next month is .0005, then the net monthly premium for each $1,000 of coverage will be .0005 x $1,000, or $.50. Since premiums are collected before the claims will be paid, the insurance company will adjust this figure downward for anticipated interest earnings on these funds.

In general, insurance companies that write a large volume of any given type of group insurance will rely on their own experience in determining the frequency and severity of future claims. Insurance companies that do not have enough past data for reliable future projections can turn to many sources for useful statistics. Probably the major source is the Society of Actuaries, which regularly collects and publishes aggregate data on the group insurance business that is written by a number of large group insurance companies. Other sources of information are industry trade organizations and various agencies of the federal government.

The second and final step in the calculation of manual premium rates is the adjustment of the net premium rates for expenses, a risk charge, and a contribution to surplus. Expenses include commissions, premium taxes, claims settlement costs, and other costs associated with the acquisition and servicing of group insurance business. The risk charge represents a contribution to the insurance company's contingency reserve as a cushion against unanticipated and catastrophic amounts of claims. The contribution to surplus or net worth represents the profit margin of the insurance company. While mutual companies are legally nonprofit, they, like stock insurance companies, require a contribution to net worth that is a source of financing for future growth.

From the standpoint of equity, the adjustment of the net premium rate is complex. Some factors such as premium taxes and commissions vary with the premium charge. However, the premium tax rate is not affected by the size of a group, whereas the commission rate decreases as the size of a group increases. To a large degree the expenses of settling claims vary with the number, and not the size, of claims. It costs just as much administratively to pay a $10,000 claim under a group life insurance plan as it does to pay a $100,000 claim. Certain other costs also tend to be fixed regardless of the size of a group. For simplicity some insurance companies adjust or load their net premium rates by a constant percentage. However, other insurance companies consider the different patterns of expenses by using a percentage plus a constant charge. For example, if the net premium rate is $.60, this might be increased by 20 percent plus $.10 to arrive at a manual premium rate of $.82 (that is, $.60 x 1.2 + $.10). Because neither approach adequately accounts for the difference in expenses as a result of a group's size, another adjustment based on the size of the group will be made in the calculation of the final premium rate.

Calculation of Premiums

Probably the best way to explain the actual calculation of group insurance premiums is to discuss some examples. The following analysis focuses primarily on group term life insurance, with some emphasis on how the structure of manual premium rates and the premium calculation process differ for certain other types of group insurance.

Group Term Life Insurance

The mechanics of calculating a final premium rate and the premium for a particular group will vary among insurance companies because of the differences in methods of preparing manual premium rates and the process by which adjustments are made to these rates. The usual approach taken for all but the smallest groups parallels that used in the 1961 Standard Group Life Insurance Premium Rates. These rates, based on the 1960 Commissioners Standard Group Mortality Table, were jointly promulgated by the insurance commissioners of several states and were required to be used as minimum initial rates for new group insurance business, including groups that had previously been written by other insurance companies. The rationale for setting these minimum rates was to prevent insurance companies from adversely affecting existing policyowners by writing new business at a loss, with the hope of recovering that loss through rate increases in future years. In effect an insurance company could not charge lower rates than these minimum rates during the first year it had a group insurance case on the books. However, the minimum rates did not apply upon renewal. Since New York applied these rates on an extraterritorial basis, any company licensed in New York had to use these rates in any state where it did business. (Note, however, that the majority of life insurers are not licensed in New York.) Companies licensed in New York are still subject to the 1961 minimum rates but only on group insurance cases that have not been previously written; the rates no longer apply to transferred business. A few other states also have minimum rate laws, but their effect is primarily to apply the minimum rates to companies that do business in these states but are not licensed in New York.

The following example is based on the 1961 minimum rates. It should be pointed out, however, that the manual premium rates of most insurance companies (except when the minimum rates apply) are significantly below these rates.

The 1961 minimum rates consist of a table of manual premium rates for males (with female rates being 60 percent of male rates) for each age from 15 to 95. Table 16-2 is an abbreviated version of these rates on a monthly basis per $1,000 of coverage at selected ages. As with most rate tables the ages are those at a person's attained age (nearest birthday).

TABLE 16-2

Age at Nearest Birthday	Male Rate	Female Rate
20	$0.23	$0.14
25	0.25	0.15
30	0.27	0.16
35	0.32	0.19
40	0.45	0.27
45	0.68	0.41
50	1.06	0.64
55	1.65	0.99
60	2.51	1.51
65	3.78	2.27
70	5.81	3.49

These rates assume that the coverage contains both a waiver-of-premium provision on disabled lives and a conversion privilege. Consequently they are higher than if neither of these additional benefits was included. When an employee converts coverage to an individual policy, a charge is assessed against the group insurance business of an insurance company to reflect the increased mortality that results from the adverse selection on conversions. The amount of this assessment (commonly $50 to $75 per $1,000 of converted insurance) is transferred to the individual insurance department of the company to compensate it for having to write the converted business at too low a rate.

TABLE 16-3

Age	Males	Females
25	20	30
30	0	30
35	10	30
40	30	10
45	30	10
50	20	10

The premium-calculation process starts with the determination of an "unadjusted cost," based on a census of the covered employees and the manual rates. For example, assume a firm has 230 employees. For the sake of simplicity also assume that each of these employees has $10,000 of life insurance and that the group has the age distribution shown in table 16-3.

The unadjusted cost is then calculated as shown in table 16-4.

TABLE 16-4

Age	Sex	Number of Employees		Amount of Coverage (in Thousands)		Unadjusted Rate (per Thousand)		Unadjusted Cost
25	M	20	x	10	x	$0.25	=	$ 50.00
35	M	10	x	10	x	0.32	=	32.00
40	M	30	x	10	x	0.45	=	135.00
45	M	30	x	10	x	0.68	=	204.00
50	M	20	x	10	x	1.06	=	212.00
25	F	30	x	10	x	0.15	=	45.00
30	F	30	x	10	x	0.16	=	48.00
35	F	30	x	10	x	0.19	=	57.00
40	F	10	x	10	x	0.27	=	27.00
45	F	10	x	10	x	0.41	=	41.00
50	F	10	x	10	x	0.64	=	64.00

Total unadjusted cost = $915.00

The unadjusted cost is then "adjusted" for expenses in a procedure consisting of two steps. First, an expense charge equal to the lesser of (1) $.20 per $1,000 of insurance provided or (2) $8.00 is added to the unadjusted cost. In this example, the $8.00 is added because $.20 x 2,300 (based on the providing of $2,300,000 of insurance) is $460. For all practical purposes this charge can be treated as an $8.00 expense constant since virtually no groups exist that provide less than the $40,000 of coverage necessary for a lower charge.

The second step is to reduce the sum of the unadjusted cost and the expense charge calculated above by a percentage based on the volume of a group insurance case as determined by its monthly premium. The reductions shown in table 16-5 (for selected premiums) and adopted in 1971 are used with the 1961 minimum rates.

Thus the initial monthly premium for the group in this example is

Unadjusted cost	$915.00
Plus lesser of $.20 per $1,000 or $8.00	8.00
Monthly premium before expense reduction	$923.00
Less expense reduction (14 percent)	129.22
Adjusted monthly premium	$793.78

TABLE 16-5	
Monthly Premium before Reduction	**Percentage Expense Reduction**
Under $200	0
200–224	1
225–249	2
250–299	3
.	.
.	.
.	.
800–899	13
900–999	14
1,000–1,199	15
.	.
.	.
.	.
45,000–59,999	33
60,000–79,999	34
80,000 and over	35

The initial monthly premium is also used to calculate the final monthly premium rate per $1,000 of protection for the group:

$$\text{Monthly premium rate per thousand} = \frac{\text{Adjusted monthly premium}}{\text{Total volume (in thousands)}}$$

$$= \frac{\$793.78}{\$2,300} = \$0.345$$

This final monthly premium rate (usually rounded to either the nearest cent or one-tenth of a cent) is used throughout the first policy year and is multiplied each month by the amount of insurance in force to calculate the monthly premium due. Adjustments to the final monthly premium rate as a result of changes in the makeup of employees by age or sex are not made until the beginning of the next policy year, when a new rate per $1,000 of coverage is determined as part of the renewal process. Thus the initial rate is guaranteed for one year, assuming no change in the benefit structure of the plan.

It is possible to make one other adjustment to the 1961 minimum premium rates. Although the rates are designed so that most industries can be written at the manual rates, employers in industries that are considered hazardous can be charged a higher rate. This increased rate is in the form of a surcharge per $1,000 of coverage and is added to the sum of the unadjusted cost and the expense charge before the expense reduction percentage is applied. The industry ratings used with the 1961 rates are expressed as +1, +2, and so forth. For example, an industry with a +1 rating can be expected to have about one death claim per year per 1,000 employees in excess of those assumed in the manual rates. The charge for this excess mortality is $.08 per $1,000 of coverage per month for each unit of extra rating. In the previous example a +1 rating would have resulted in an increased charge of $184 (that is, 2,300 x $.08) before the expense reduction was made. Therefore the adjusted monthly premium would have been calculated as follows:

Unadjusted cost	$ 915.00
Plus lesser of $.20 per $1,000 or $8.00	8.00
Plus industry surcharge	184.00
Total cost before expense reduction	$1,107.00
Less expense reduction (15 percent)	166.05
Adjusted monthly premium	$ 940.95

Similarly a +2 rating reflects the expectation of two extra death claims per year, resulting in an added premium of $.16 per $1,000 per month of $368.

Variations for Large Groups. Insurance companies use the premium-calculation process discussed above for most groups over a certain size, usually from 10 or more to 50 or more lives, but variations do exist. For example, some insurance companies do not incorporate a charge for a waiver of premium into their manual rates. Rather an extra charge, which usually differs by industry, is added for this coverage. Also a few companies use manual rates that vary by age but not sex. These unisex rate tables are based on assumptions about the ratio of males to females in the group. However, an adjustment is usually made in the premium-calculation process if the actual group ratio differs from this assumption.

TABLE 16-6	
Monthly Premium before Adjustment	**Percentage Adjustment**
Under $200	+ 25
200–249	+ 22
250–299	+ 18
.	.
.	.
.	.
600–699	+ 2
700–799	+ 1
800–999	0
1,000–1,099	− 1
1,100–1,200	− 2
.	.
.	.
.	.
50,000–74,999	−14
75,000 and over	−15

Insurance companies may have a constant expense charge similar to the $8.00 previously described. Some companies incorporate a level of expenses into their manual rate so that there is no expense reduction for a certain-size group. In the final premium-calculation process an adjustment will be made, and larger groups will receive an expense reduction while smaller groups will receive an expense surcharge. Table 16-6 is one such table of adjustments.

Variations for Small Groups. The manual-rating process for small groups, including those written by multiple-employer trusts, differs from that of large groups in several ways. In general, the manual rates are banded by age, typically in 5-year intervals. Table 16-7 is an example of one such monthly rate table for each $1,000 of coverage.

TABLE 16-7

Age at Nearest Birthday	Male Rate	Female Rate
Under 30	.25	.19
30–34	.30	.23
35–39	.35	.27
40–44	.50	.38
45–49	.80	.60
50–54	1.20	.90
55–59	1.70	1.25
60–64	2.50	1.90
65–69	3.70	2.75
70–74	5.50	4.00
75 and over	9.00	6.75

An unadjusted cost is developed based on a census of the employees by age and sex. Since the manual rates are loaded for most expenses, and since the groups written tend to be reasonably close in size, typically no adjustment for size is made. However, to compensate for the expenses of periodic billings, most insurance companies apply a flat fee to all groups, commonly between $10 and $20 per billing. Some companies do not levy this charge if the premium is paid annually. To reflect the administrative costs associated with record keeping, some insurance companies also levy a modest one-time expense charge when coverage is added for a new employee.

In the past it was common for short-term disability income rates to be expressed on the basis of each $10 of weekly benefit. This is probably still the norm, but many insurance companies are now expressing their rates in terms of a higher weekly benefit, such as $50 or $100.

In contrast to large groups for which the initial monthly premium is used to determine a monthly premium rate that will apply for a specified period of time, the monthly premium rate for small groups will be recalculated each month based not only on the volume of insurance, but also on changes in the makeup of employees by age and sex, just as if the group was being newly written. However, most insurance companies do guarantee that the manual rates that were used when the group was initially written (and any future manual rates applicable to the group) will remain applicable for some period of time. This period may vary from 60 days to one year, but 6 months is the most common period.

Accidental Death and Dismemberment Insurance

Accidental death and dismemberment insurance is usually not written as a separate coverage, but rather it is added by an endorsement to a group term insurance contract. A single manual rate typically applies to all employees regardless of age or sex, but it will vary depending on whether coverage is written (1) for nonoccupational accidents or (2) on a 24-hour basis for both nonoccupational and occupational accidents. The rate for nonoccupational coverage generally does not vary by industry and ranges from $.04 to $.06 per $1,000 of principal sum per month. However, the rate for coverage on a 24-hour basis does vary by industry, and although it falls within this same range for low-risk industries, it may be several times higher for hazardous industries. Some companies calculate a separate cost for the accidental death and dismemberment coverage and add it to the charge for the group term life insurance. However, since most employers purchase accidental death and dismemberment coverage, many insurance companies incorporate the cost into the manual rates for group term life insurance, making the principal sum equal to the amount of life insurance protection purchased, and an additional charge will be levied only if a higher level of accidental death and dismemberment coverage is desired.

Dependent Life Insurance

Dependent life insurance is typically added as additional coverage to a group life insurance contract that provides life insurance protection for employees. Because dependent life insurance coverage is usually a modest fixed amount (such as $2,000 on the spouse and $1,000 on each child) that generates a relatively small additional premium, a very simplified rate structure tends to be used. However, several variations do exist. Some insurance companies have a single flat rate, independent of the type or number of dependents, for each employee who has dependent coverage. Other companies have two separate flat rates: one for the spouse's coverage and the other for children's coverage. The rate for the children's coverage is a family rate regardless of the number of children, and it is based upon an average-sized family.

Flat rates are based on the assumption that the group has an average age mix of employees. If the group of employees is older than average, the flat rate for dependent coverage may be adjusted (particularly when it applies to spouses) to reflect the likelihood that the dependents are also above average in age when compared to the dependents of most other groups. A flat rate is commonly used when the cost of dependent coverage is paid entirely by the employees. The uniform charge is easy to communicate to employees, and it simplifies the payroll-deduction process for the employer.

Some insurance companies also use a rate for dependent coverage that varies with the employee's age, thereby assuming that older employees have older dependents. Basing the rate on the employee's age may seem illogical, but it is administratively simpler and less expensive than having to determine the ages of dependents. A single variable rate may apply to the total family coverage for the spouse and all children, or it may apply only to the spouse. In this latter case a flat rate is generally used if coverage for children is also provided.

Short-term Disability Income Insurance

In addition to varying by age, by sex, and possibly by geographic location, manual rates for disability income insurance also differ according to (1) the maximum benefit period, (2) the length of the waiting period, and (3) the writing of coverage either on a 24-hour basis or only for nonoccupational disabilities.

Some insurance companies (particularly insurance companies for small groups) have only a single standard short-term disability income plan that they will sell, and therefore they only need a single manual rate table. On the other hand some companies allow the employer to exercise a degree of flexibility in designing the plan that will be purchased, and rather than make adjustments to a single rate table, these companies will usually have several rate tables that vary by such factors as maximum benefit period (such as 13 or 26 weeks) and waiting period (such as 7 days for all disabilities or 7 days for illnesses and no waiting period for injuries). If any other variations are allowed, appropriate adjustments will be made.

An adjustment may be made for the nature of the industry the group represents. Ignoring the occupational injuries and diseases that are covered under workers' compensation, a few occupations are still characterized by higher-than-average disability income claims. As an alternative to a rate adjustment, some insurance companies have underwriting standards that prohibit the writing of coverage for these groups.

Until the passage of amendments to the Civil Rights Act pertaining to pregnancy, it was common for insurance companies to have one manual rate for plans that did not provide benefits for pregnancy-related disabilities and another for plans that did provide such benefits. Since most employers can no longer exclude pregnancy as a cause of disability, rates for coverage without this benefit are usually not published, except for the employers of small groups that still have an option regarding this benefit.

In contrast to group life insurance for which the rates for females are lower than the rates for males, disability income rates are higher for females. Ignoring pregnancy-related disabilities, the claims of females at younger ages still somewhat exceed those of males. However, because male and female claims are comparable at older ages, the rates for later years seldom vary. Table 16-8, which illustrates one insurance company's monthly manual rates per $10 of weekly benefit, shows how this rate differential is even more pronounced at younger ages if maternity coverage is included.

In the past it was common for short-term disability income rates to be expressed on the basis of each $10 of weekly benefit. This is probably still the norm, but many insurance companies are now expressing their rates in terms of a higher weekly benefit, such as $50 or $100.

TABLE 16-8		
Age	**Male**	**Female**
Under 30	$0.27	$0.91
30–34	0.42	0.91
35–39	0.48	0.91
40–44	0.63	0.91
45–49	0.71	1.03
50–54	1.12	1.12
55–59	1.26	1.26
60–64	1.62	1.62
65–69	2.27	2.27

Long-term Disability Income Insurance

Like short-term disability income rates, the manual rates for long-term coverage vary by age, sex, the length of the benefit period, the length of the waiting period, and possibly geographic location. In addition, the manual rates reflect the fact that benefits will be integrated with social security and certain other disability income benefits for which an employee might be eligible. To the extent that variations are allowed in the integration provision that was assumed in developing the manual rates, an adjustment will be made in the premium-calculation process. As is also the case with short-term rates, an adjustment might be made for certain occupations.

Unlike short-term disability income rates that are commonly expressed on the basis of a weekly benefit, long-term rates are typically expressed on the basis of a monthly benefit, usually per $100. In contrast to the coverages previously discussed, long-term disability claims fluctuate with general economic conditions. Consequently insurance companies review and possibly revise their manual rates (and/or their underwriting standards) as economic conditions change.

Medical Expense Insurance

In many ways the manual rates for medical expense insurance (and also dental insurance) are similar to those for disability income insurance because variations exist by age, sex, and the provisions of the plan, including the size of the deductible, the coinsurance percentage, and the level of benefits. Most insurance companies have manual rates for the few standard plans that will be sold, and only large employers are given the flexibility to deviate from these plans. Any such deviation will then be reflected in adjustments to the manual rates. Adjustments may also be made to the manual rates if the employer is in an industry that is characterized by higher-than-average claims.

One other factor, geographic location, is always a variable in the manual rates because of the significant differences in medical costs across the country. Depending on group size, an adjustment for location may be made in one of two ways. For large groups the rating process usually starts with a manual rate that does not consider the location of employees. Each county (or other geographic subdivision) where coverage will be written is then assigned a factor that is based on the cost of health care in that location as compared with the "average" cost that is assumed in the manual rates. For example, if Seattle were 20 percent higher than average, it would have a factor of 1.2. If all a firm's employees were there, the manual rates for that group would be multiplied by a location factor of 1.2 in the process of determining the group's premium. If employees were in several locations, a composite factor would be calculated as shown in table 16-9.

TABLE 16-9					
	Number of Employees		**Location Factor**		**Product**
Seattle	100	x	1.2	=	120
Kansas City	70	x	1.0	=	70
Birmingham	30	x	0.7	=	21
	200				211

$$\text{Location Factor} = \frac{\text{Total product}}{\text{Total number of employees}} = \frac{211}{200} = 1.055$$

Consequently the manual rate for this group would be increased by 5.5 percent because of the employees' location.

A slightly different approach is used for small groups. Because employees are usually in one location, most companies have manual rate tables for between 10 and 15 rating territories, and each county in which employees are located is assigned a specific territorial rating. The following territorial classifications are from the rating manual of one insurance company for counties in three of the states where it writes business:

California
  Los Angeles   10
  Alameda, Contra Costa, Marin, Orange, Riverside,
      San Bernardino, San Francisco, San Mateo, Santa Clara,
      Solano   9
  Imperial, Kern, San Diego, San Luis Obispo, Santa Barbara,
      Ventura   8
  All other counties   7

Georgia
  Clayton, Cobb, DeKalb, Fulton   6
  Catoosa, Chatham, Gwinnett, Walker   4
  All other counties   3

Maine
  Entire state   2

Table 16-10, an excerpt from the manual rate tables of the same company, shows how the monthly cost for coverage under a plan written through one of their multiple-employer trusts varies by geographic area.

TABLE 16-10					
Age	**Class of Coverage**	**Area 2**	**Area 4**	**Area 7**	**Area 10**
Under 30	Male	$ 70.00	$ 82.10	$102.90	$112.90
Under 30	Female	76.00	90.00	115.20	150.90
Under 30	Male and dependents	204.80	244.50	318.50	418.30
Under 30	Female and dependents	199.10	239.00	310.50	412.70
30–44	Male	104.90	122.00	153.50	196.50
30–44	Female	112.10	133.00	169.80	222.30
30–44	Male and dependents	274.80	327.10	421.60	557.30
30–44	Female and dependents	265.90	318.50	412.60	548.30

The previous example lists manual rates for dependent coverage that are applied regardless of the number of dependents, the relationship of the dependents to the employee, or the ages of the dependents. For any size group, this is one of the three common methods for pricing dependent coverage. Under all three methods, the rate for dependent coverage is usually a function of the employee's age rather than of the dependents' ages. However, the other two methods do take the number of dependents and their relationship to the insured into consideration. One method uses a certain rate for dependent coverage if there is only one dependent and another rate if there are two or more dependents. However, the other approach has three rates: one for coverage that is elected only for a spouse, another for coverage that is elected only for children, and a third for coverage that is elected for both a spouse and children.

Because medical expense claims are continually increasing as a result of inflation, a trend factor must be applied to past claims experience when manual rates are developed. This is a complex and often perplexing task for most insurance companies. Not only has the overall cost of medical care increased faster than the general cost of living (as measured by the consumer price index), but the increases have been erratic from year to year and virtually impossible to predict with any degree of accuracy. In addition, because these increases vary significantly for each category of medical expenses, different trend factors must be applied to different categories of claims.

At one time insurance companies guaranteed group insurance premium rates for at least 12 months and possibly for as long as 2 or 3 years. However, to protect themselves against unexpected increases in claims due to increases in the cost of medical care, many insurance companies will now guarantee medical expense rates for no more than 6 months. In fact, a number of multiple-employer trusts have only 3-month guarantees, or they contain provisions whereby rates can be increased at any time, provided notice of the rate increase is given 30 or 60 days in advance. Some companies allow an employer to select the length of the rate guarantee, such as 6 months or one year. However, the longer the rate guarantee, the higher the rate.

Dental Insurance

Although the rating of dental insurance is similar in many ways to the rating of medical expense insurance, there are some significant differences. Most insurance companies do not vary their manual rates by the ages of group members. Rather, an adjustment is usually made for the income levels of employees, since higher-paid persons are much more likely to obtain dental care. This adjustment is usually in the form of a percentage based on the extent to which the portion of employees with incomes higher than some figure (such as $30,000) exceeds the proportion of such employees that is assumed in the manual rates. An adjustment is also made for certain occupations (such as salespeople or teachers) that use dental services more frequently than average. Finally, the manual rates will usually be increased when a plan is new (or expands benefits) if the employees have been informed beforehand. Under these circumstances there is a tendency to postpone needed dental care until the plan is installed.

EXPERIENCE RATING

With experience rating, an insurance company considers a group's claims experience, either at the issue date or at the end of a policy period, when determining the premium rate for that group. When applied prospectively (that is, to future periods), experience rating is used to determine (1) adjustments in renewal premiums (either upward or downward) for those groups whose claims experience has deviated from what was expected and (2) initial premiums for large groups that change insurance carriers.

In addition to determining the premium rate for the next policy period (usually 12 months), experience rating is also used to compute the refund for those groups that had better claims experience than anticipated. This refund is commonly referred to as a *dividend* by mutual insurance companies and a *retrospective rate credit* or *premium refund* by stock insurance companies. (Since the majority of group insurance business is written by mutual companies, the term *dividend* will be used here.)   Under some experience-rating arrangements the premium at the end of a policy period may also be retroactively adjusted upward if a group's claims experience has been worse than anticipated, and an additional premium will be charged. These arrangements are not very common and are discussed in the chapter on alternative funding methods.

Rationale for Experience Rating

One argument in favor of experience rating is that it achieves the ultimate degree of premium equity among policyowners. Even though manual rating also results in equity because it considers the obvious factors that affect claims, it is impossible to measure and make adjustments in the manual rates for such factors as lifestyle, working conditions, and morale, all of which contribute to the level of claims experience. Experience rating is also the most cost-effective way to reflect the general health of a group in the premium that is charged.

Probably the major reason for using experience rating is the competition that exists in the group insurance marketplace. If an insurance company were to use identical rates for all groups regardless of their experience, the employers with good experience would soon seek out insurance companies that offered lower rates, or they would turn to self-funding as a way to reduce costs. The insurance company that did not consider claims experience would therefore be left with only the poor risks. This is exactly the situation that led most of the Blues to abandon community rating for group insurance cases above a certain size. Experience rating allows an insurance company to acquire and retain the better cases (from a claims-experience standpoint) and to determine an appropriate premium for the groups that have worse-than-average claims experience.

Dividend Calculation

It is perhaps putting the cart before the horse to explain experience rating for dividend purposes (which occurs at the end of a policy period) before discussing its use to determine premiums (which occurs at the beginning of that period). However, calculating dividends tends to be more complicated and is easier to discuss first. An explanation follows of how the experience-rating process is different for determining premiums on a prospective basis.

TABLE 16-11
Illustrative Dividend Calculation

1. Premiums paid		$100,000
2. Incurred claims [a + (c − b) + d + e]		$ 79,800
a. Paid death claims	$70,000	
b. Beginning reserve for death claims	$14,000	
c. Ending reserve for death claims	$15,000	
d. Charge for approved disability claims	$ 7,500	
e. Conversion charges	$ 1,300	
3. Stop-loss limit (120% of premium paid)		$120,000
4. Incurred claims subject to experience rating (lesser of 2 or 3)		$ 79,800
5. Expected claims		$ 84,000
6. Credibility factor		0.8
7. Claims charge [(0.8 x 4) + (0.2 x 5)]		$ 80,640
8. Retention charge (f + g + h + i + j −k)		$ 9,800
f. Charge for stop-loss coverage	$ 2,500	
g. Commissions	$ 2,000	
h. Premium taxes	$ 2,000	
I. Administration	$ 1,500	
j. Contingency reserve (risk charge) and surplus contribution	$ 3,000	
k. Interest on reserves	$ 1,200	
9. Dividend earned [1 − (7 + 8)]		$ 9,560
10. Deficit carried forward from prior periods		$ 3,000
11. Deficit to be carried forward to future periods (9 − 10) if less than 0 OR Dividend payable (9 − 10) if greater than 0		− $ 6,560

At first glance the process of using experience rating to determine dividends appears complex. However, the actual mechanics are relatively simple, and much of the confusion stems from the fact that the process is lengthy. In addition, both the format and the terminology vary somewhat among insurance companies. This discussion focuses on the illustration in table 16-11 and explains the steps used to calculate the dividend for a group term life insurance case. Although this illustration can be considered a typical example of a dividend calculation, variations could have been (and often are) used in several steps. Therefore the more commonly used and significant variations are described for group term life insurance as well as for other types of group insurance.

Premiums Paid

Step 1 shows the total amount of premiums that the policyowner actually paid during the experience-rating period (usually one year) before any adjustment was made to reflect the actual experience of the group. In most instances this will be the sum of 12 monthly premiums. The premiums paid may have been based on manual rates or on the group's past experience.

Incurred Claims

Step 2 involves the determination of incurred claims, which are those claims attributable to the recently ended period of coverage that was subject to experience rating (that is, the *experience period*). It may seem as if the incurred claims are those claims that were paid during the experience period. Unfortunately it is not that simple. Some of the claims that were paid during the experience period may actually be attributable to prior periods and must be subtracted from the incurred claims. In addition, other claims that are attributable to the experience period may not have been reported or may be in the course of settlement. However, their value must be estimated. Therefore an appropriate determination of incurred claims is as follows:

incurred claims = claims paid during the experience period
 − claims paid during the experience period but incurred during prior periods
 + estimate of claims incurred during the experience period but to be paid in future periods

In actual practice incurred claims are usually expressed as follows:

incurred claims = paid claims
 + ending claim reserve
 − beginning claim reserve
 or
incurred claims = paid claims
 + change in claim reserve

This *claim reserve,* which is often referred to as the *open-and-unreported claim reserve,* represents an estimate by the insurance company for (1) claims that have been approved but not yet paid, (2) claims that are in the course of settlement, and (3) claims that have been incurred but not yet reported. In addition, when disability income coverage or medical expense coverage is experience rated, an additional amount must be added to this estimate for any claims that have been incurred, reported, and approved but are not yet payable. Essentially these claims arise from disabilities or current medical claims that will continue beyond the experience period.

Based on past experience, most insurance companies can closely estimate the percentage of claims that will be paid after the close of the experience period for a given type of coverage. While this estimate reflects companywide experience and may not reflect the experience of a particular policyowner, it is usually applied to each group insurance case rather than determining the claim reserve on a case-by-case basis. In general the claim reserve is based either on a percentage of the annual premium (before experience rating) or on a percentage of claims paid. The first approach is most common for small groups, and the latter approach tends to be used for large groups. This percentage varies considerably by type of coverage, with the claim reserve for group term life insurance usually ranging between 10 to 15 percent of the annual premium (and up to 25 percent if a waiver of premium for disability is included), and the claim reserve for medical expense coverage often ranging from 20 to 65 percent, depending on what benefits are involved.

Two other factors enter into the incurred claims amount for group term life insurance: disability claims and conversion charges. In addition to death claims, there may be disability claims if a group insurance contract contains a waiver-of-premium provision or another type of disability provision. Once a waiver-of-premium claim has been approved, a charge is made for future death claims, since no future premiums will be received for the disabled employee. This charge is based on the probability that the disabled employee will die prior to recovery or termination of coverage (for example, at age 65). On the average the charge will be about $750 for each $1,000 of coverage. If the insurance contract continues, an additional $250 per $1,000 of coverage will be charged if a death claim is paid. If the employee recovers or coverage terminates prior to death, the $750 charge will be credited back to the policyowner.

As mentioned earlier in this chapter, a conversion charge is levied against the group insurance department of an insurance company to reflect the increased mortality on converted coverage. In the experience-rating procedure this charge is transferred to the group policyowner as a charge per $1,000 of coverage converted (commonly $50 to $75).

Stop-Loss Limit

Step 3 specifies the stop-loss limit—the maximum amount of claims that will be charged to the group in step 4 of the experience-rating calculation. Its purpose is to minimize the effect of any chance fluctuations that might occur from year to year, including catastrophic losses within the group, such as an accident that kills several employees. These chance fluctuations tend to become relatively smaller as the size of a group increases, and a stop-loss limit may not be used for very large groups.

The stop-loss limit is usually expressed as a percentage of the premiums paid, and the actual percentage is subject to negotiation between the policyowner and the insurance company. In this illustration 120 percent is used, so the amount of incurred claims that enters into the experience-rating calculation is limited to a maximum of $120,000. Since this exceeds the actual amount of incurred claims, the latter amount is used in step 4.

Obviously a charge must be made somewhere for incorporating a stop-loss provision into an experience-rating contract, since the insurance company is obligated to pay any excess amount over the stop-loss limit. The charge in this illustration is shown in step 8. In practice this charge is the same for all similar-sized groups that use the same stop-loss percentage. The charge is a percentage of premiums paid, and it becomes smaller as either the size of the group or the stop-loss percentage increases. In effect this charge for stop-loss coverage can be viewed as a manual rate charge for losses in excess of some limit, with only those losses below the limit subject to experience rating.

Expected Claims

The amount of expected claims in step 5 represents the portion of the premiums paid that the insurance company has anticipated would be necessary to pay claims during the experience period. This amount may have been derived either from average experience as in manual rating or from the past experience of the particular group.

Credibility

The credibility factor (step 6), which can vary from zero to one, is a statistical measure of the reliability of the group's past experience. In other words, it is a measure of the probability that the group's actual experience is a true reflection of the group and is not the result of chance occurrences. The credibility factor varies by the size of the group and the type of coverage. In general, the larger the group is, the greater the reliability of estimates (because of the law of large numbers) will be. In addition, actual experience tends to deviate less from the estimates of expected claims (on a relative basis) as the frequency of claims rises. Therefore a greater degree of credibility can be attributed to a group's medical expense claims than to its life insurance claims.

In actual practice, credibility factors are usually based on the size of a group as determined by the number of persons (lives) who are insured. However, some insurance companies base their credibility factors on the annual premium of a group. The factors vary somewhat among insurance companies, but the excerpt in table 16-12 from the rate manual of one insurance company is a typical example of the first approach.

TABLE 16-12		
Size of Group (Lives)	Life Insurance and Long-term Disability Income Insurance	Medical Expense Insurance and Short-term Disability Income Insurance
100	0.0	0.2
200	0.2	0.5
400	0.4	0.8
600	0.7	1.0
800	0.9	1.0
1,000 or more	1.0	1.0

Adjustments in these factors may be made to reflect any characteristics of either the group or the insurance contract that are not the norm. For example, an older group of employees might be assigned a higher credibility factor than a younger group whose claims are more likely to be due to random fluctuations. In addition, the level of any stop-loss limit may have an effect. As the stop-loss charge is increased (meaning the stop-loss limit is lowered), the credibility that can be assigned to the remaining claims below the stop-loss limit also increases.

Similarly the size of the credibility factor may be influenced by the amount of the risk charge levied on the group for establishing a contingency reserve. If an insurance company has an adequate contingency reserve for a group insurance case, it is more likely to allow the use of a higher credibility factor than can be statistically justified. This practice will result in reduced claims charges for years when the employer has good experience and increased claims charges for years when it has bad experience. Although it is desired by employers with a history of better-than-average claims experience, a higher-than-justified credibility factor will lead to a larger-than-usual deficit for a group with bad experience. It will also increase the probability that the employer will terminate the contract before the deficit is eliminated. A larger contingency reserve can balance the financial consequences of this possibility.

Claims Charge

Once the credibility factor is determined, the process of calculating what claims will be charged against the group in the experience period is relatively simple and can be expressed by the following formula:

claims charge = (z) (incurred claims subject to experience rating)
    + (1 − z) (expected claims)
where z is the credibility factor

In effect the claims charge is a weighted average of (1) the incurred claims that are subject to experience rating and (2) the expected claims, with the incurred claims being assigned a weight equal to the credibility factor and the expected claims being assigned a weight equal to one minus the credibility factor. In step 7 of table 16-11 the claims charge is calculated as follows:

$$
\begin{aligned}
\text{claims charge} \quad &= \quad .08\ (\$79{,}800) + (1 - 0.8)\ (\$84{,}000) \\
&= \quad 0.8\ (\$79{,}800) + 0.2\ (\$84{,}000) \\
&= \quad \$63{,}840 + \$16{,}800 \\
&= \quad \$80{,}640
\end{aligned}
$$

If a credibility factor of 1.0 is used, the claims charge will be equal to the incurred claims that are subject to experience rating, and the expected claims will not be taken into consideration.

Large Amounts of Coverage

In many group term life insurance contracts there is considerable disparity in the amounts of coverage, and top executives often have much greater coverage than the lowest-paid employees. Claims that arise from the deaths of employees who have large amounts of coverage can have a significant impact on a group's experience for the years in which they occur. Consequently several methods have been used to exclude these claims (or at least a portion of them) from the process of determining the claims charge in experience rating. One of these methods is the stop-loss limit that was previously mentioned. However, its primary purpose is to limit the claims charge because of a higher-than-anticipated frequency of claims, rather than because of a few high-severity claims. Some of the other methods used to handle these large claims are

- excess-amounts pooling. This approach limits the amount of insurance that is subject to experience rating on any one person. Amounts over the limit are not experience rated but are subject to manual rates based on the ages of the individuals involved. This results in a "pooling" or an "insurance" charge that is added to either the claims charge or the retention charge, depending on the insurance company's practice. These excess amounts may also be subject to evidence of insurability.
- a lower credibility factor. Under this method the credibility factor normally used for a certain-size group is reduced if there is a significant difference between the smallest and largest amounts of coverage. This results in more weight being placed on the group's expected claims than on their incurred claims.
- an extra contingency reserve. Under this approach the excess of claims above a certain limit is ignored in the experience-rating process for

dividend purposes but is charged against a contingency reserve that has been established (with an appropriate annual charge) for this reason.

Retention

The *retention* (step 8) in a group insurance contract is usually defined as the excess of premiums paid over claims payments and dividends. It consists of charges for (1) the stop-loss coverage, (2) expenses (commissions, premium taxes, and administrative expenses), (3) a risk charge, and (4) a contribution to the insurance company's surplus. In this particular illustration the sum of these charges is reduced by the interest that is credited to certain reserves—the claim reserve and any contingency reserves—that the insurance company holds in order to pay future claims attributable to this contract. However, some insurance companies do not subtract this interest when determining retention, but rather they treat it as an additional premium paid.

For large groups each item in the retention is calculated separately, based on the group's actual experience. For small groups a formula is usually applied that is based on insurance company averages. This formula varies by the size of a group and the type of coverage involved, and most often it is either a percentage of the claims charge or a flat charge plus a percentage of the claims charge.

Dividend Earned

The dividend earned (step 9) is computed by adding the retention to the claims charge and then subtracting this sum from the premiums paid. This is the dividend amount attributable to the group insurance case for the current experience period.

Prior Deficits

Under most experience-rated group insurance plans, any deficits from past periods must be made up before any future dividends will be paid. Whenever the sum of the claims charge and the retention charge for any experience period exceeds the premiums paid and results in a negative dividend earned, there is a deficit. In step 10 of table 16-11 a $3,000 deficit from prior periods exists. Interestingly the insurance company will have no opportunity to recover this deficit if the insurance contract is not renewed. However, the fact that there is always a chance of nonrenewal is one of the reasons why a risk charge is levied.

As additional protection against the nonrenewal of insurance contracts that have a deficit, some insurance companies require that part of any dividend earned be placed in a *claims fluctuation reserve* when experience is favorable. Monies are drawn from the reserve to indemnify the insurance company for the years in which there is a deficit. Since this reserve lessens the possibility that the insurance company will lose money on a group insurance case, it is usually accomplished by a lower risk charge.

Dividend Payable

The final step in the dividend-calculation process (step 11) is to establish whether a dividend is payable. This is determined by subtracting any deficit that has been carried forward (or placed in a claims fluctuation reserve) from the dividend earned for the experience period. If this figure is positive, it is the amount of the dividend; if the figure is negative, it is the amount of the cumulative deficit that is to be carried forward.

In this illustration, only one type of coverage is experience rated. However, when an employer has more than one type of coverage that is experience rated with the same insurance company, a single dividend is usually determined for the combined package. This typically involves the determination of a separate claims charge for each coverage and a single retention charge for the entire package. Because "losses" for one type of coverage will often be offset by "gains" for other types of coverage, the relative fluctuation in the overall experience will tend to be less than the fluctuations in the experience of some or all of the individual coverages. Therefore the overall premium can often be reduced (or the dividend increased) because the insurance company will levy a lower risk charge and/or require a lower contingency reserve.

Renewal Rating

Experience rating is also often used to develop future premiums for group insurance cases based on the past experience of the group. For the most part the procedure is similar to that for determining dividends, and in fact the two procedures are usually done at the same time. However, there are some differences. In most cases the experience-rating period will be 3 to 5 years instead of a single year, and thus cumulative premiums and charges for this period will be used. In addition, a more conservative (that is, lower) credibility factor will normally be applied. For example, an insurance company that uses a credibility factor of 0.8 for dividend purposes for a particular case might use a factor of 0.6 for renewal-rating purposes. Furthermore, since a premium is being developed for the future, it is also necessary to adjust past claims and the retention, not only to reflect current cost levels but also to include expected trends for the next year. Adjustments must also be made to account for any changes in the coverage. Once a renewal premium expected to be sufficient to cover claims and retention is calculated, an additional amount is added for future dividends. This amount in effect becomes a safety margin for the insurance company should both claims and retention be higher than anticipated; otherwise it is returned as an experience dividend to the policyowner.

Experience rating may also be used to develop the initial premiums for any transferred business, requiring the insurance company to obtain past data from the policyowner regarding its experience with the previous carrier. A policyowner may be reluctant to provide this information because poor experience (and the resulting rate increase) is often the reason for changing insurance companies. However, the existence of the poor claims experience is exactly the information the insurance company needs. In fact, some insurance companies actually refuse to write transferred coverage, particularly for large groups, unless verifiable prior claims experience is provided.

If possible the past data are used to determine what the premiums and charges would have been if the new contract had been written by the new carrier in previous years. If this can be accomplished, the procedure is a simplified application of the principles previously described. If it cannot be accomplished, manual rating may be used for small groups, but judgment may play a large role in determining the premiums for large groups.

17

Other Group Benefits

Chapter Outline

In the first chapter employee benefits were divided into five categories:

- legally required social insurance payments
- payments for private insurance and retirement plans
- payments for time not worked

- extra payments to employees
- services to employees

There are variations among employers, but typically about one-quarter of the sum spent on employee benefits is devoted to payments for legally required social insurance programs. Somewhat more than one-third is spent on employee benefits devoted to payments for retirement plans and group insurance. Often overlooked is the significance of all the remaining types of benefits that may be provided to employees, which as a group account for about one-third of the employee benefit dollars employers spend. Since the list is extensive, not every possible benefit will be described. Rather, the discussion is devoted to the following list of more commonly provided "other" benefits:

- vacations
- holidays
- personal time off with pay
- personal time off without pay (family leave)
- supplemental unemployment benefit plans
- educational assistance
- moving-expense reimbursement
- suggestion awards
- service awards
- productivity and safety achievement awards
- holiday bonuses and gifts
- no-additional-cost services
- employee discounts
- dependent-care assistance
- adoption assistance
- wellness programs
- employee-assistance programs
- financial planning programs for executives
- preretirement-counseling programs
- transportation/free parking
- company cars
- subsidized eating facilities

Some of these benefits, such as holidays and vacations, are provided by most employers; other benefits, such as financial planning, are provided by relatively few employers. There are many reasons one employer may provide a certain array of benefits: to satisfy specific needs of its employees, for competitive reasons, or because of traditions within its locality or industry. Collective bargaining, the personal whims of the employer, and state laws may also play a role.

With rare exceptions the cost of providing these benefits is tax deductible to the employer. However, the tax treatment of employees receiving benefits varies, and the treatment of each benefit is described separately.

MEANING OF HIGHLY COMPENSATED EMPLOYEE

Several of the benefits discussed in this chapter are subject to nondiscrimination rules. Specifically these benefits are educational assistance, service awards, safety achievement and productivity awards, no-additional-cost services, employee discounts, dependent-care assistance, adoption assistance, and employee-assistance programs. In each case, there are rules designed to prevent or discourage the benefit plan from discriminating in favor of highly compensated employees.

The consequences of a plan's being discriminatory vary. In some cases, no employees can receive benefits on a tax-favored basis; in other cases, this penalty applies to highly compensated employees only.

As used in this chapter, a highly compensated employee is one who meets the definition in Sec. 414(q) of the Internal Revenue Code. This definition is also used for the nondiscrimination rules that apply to qualified retirement plans. A *highly compensated employee* is an employee who meets one of the following criteria:

- is a 5 percent owner of the firm during the current year or was a 5 percent owner during the previous year
- had compensation from the employer in excess of $80,000 during the previous year. However, the employer can elect to define this category of employees as only those whose compensation puts them in the top 20 percent of the organization's employees. The $80,000 figure is subject to indexing after 1997.

This definition is from the 1996 Small Business Job Protection Act and replaces a more administratively complex definition that was used for several years.

It is interesting to note that this definition of highly compensated employee is not the same as the one used with the nondiscrimination rules for self-insured medical reimbursement plans or the one used for cafeteria plans.

PAYMENTS FOR TIME NOT WORKED

Vacations

In terms of employer cost the most significant benefit mentioned in this chapter is paid vacations. In 1996 the U.S. Chamber of Commerce estimated that the cost to employers of providing vacations to employees was equal to 5.4

percent of base pay.[1] The number of vacation days given to employees increased steadily from World War II until the adverse economic times of the late 1970s. During the last few years this trend has leveled off, and few companies have increased the number of vacation days provided.

While the specifics of vacation plans vary widely, most plans are based on length of service, and the number of vacation days given to any particular employee normally increases over time. There is usually a short waiting period (3 to 6 months) during which employees are ineligible for vacations, but for competitive reasons there is often no waiting period for management employees. Table 17-1 is one employer's benefit schedule for its vacation plan.

TABLE 17-1	
Length of Service	**Vacation Days**
First 6 months After 6 months 1–5 years 6–15 years 16 years or more	0 1 for each month in the remaining calendar year (max. of 10) 10 15 20

Some firms have different schedules for different classes of employees, with higher-paid employees tending to have more vacation time, particularly in the earlier years of service. In contrast to many types of benefits, vacation benefits are often given to part-time employees.

In recent years many employers have adopted cafeteria plans in which employees have some choice in designing their own benefit plans. Although most companies with cafeteria plans have a basic vacation schedule that is outside the cafeteria plan, employees may have the option of using their benefit dollars to purchase extra vacation days, often subject to approval of their supervisor and usually subject to a maximum additional number of days.

Several major issues must be addressed in properly designing a vacation plan. One is the treatment of unused vacation days. Some employers require that any unused vacation days be forfeited; others allow them to be carried over to the next year, subject to certain limitations. A few businesses compensate employees for unused vacation days. Another issue is the question of when employees can take their vacations. In general, supervisory approval is necessary, and vacations may not be allowed during busy work times. Junior employees may also have to schedule their vacations around those of senior employees so that the number of people away from work at the same time is minimized. Other issues that must be addressed are those of how unused vacation days will be treated upon termination of employment and whether sicknesses and holidays occurring during vacation periods will be treated as vacation days.

The compensation employees receive during periods of vacation is treated the same as compensation for time worked and is taxed accordingly.

Holidays

Employers normally pay employees for certain holidays. At a minimum employees usually receive pay for

- New Year's Day
- Memorial Day
- the Fourth of July
- Labor Day
- Thanksgiving
- Christmas

Most employees receive at least 3 and sometimes as many as 9 or 10 additional holidays, which may include

- Martin Luther King's Birthday
- Washington's Birthday
- Lincoln's Birthday
- Presidents' Day
- Good Friday
- Columbus Day
- the Friday after Thanksgiving
- Veterans Day
- Christmas Eve
- New Year's Eve
- the employee's birthday
- various state holidays

For some institutions, such as banks, holidays are prescribed by law. However, for most companies, management decides which holidays to give, subject to collective bargaining if applicable.

When a scheduled holiday falls on a Saturday, employees who normally do not work on that day are given the preceding Friday off. When a holiday falls on Sunday, it is normally observed on Monday. Restaurants and retail establishments are increasingly open for business on holidays. When this occurs, employees who work are usually paid at least time and a half and sometimes as much as triple time.

Some companies, realizing that not all employees want to take the same holidays, try to satisfy these needs by adopting holiday plans that include a minimum number of *scheduled holidays* coupled with a specific number of *floating holidays* to be taken at an employee's option. Usually there is no requirement that the days taken actually be holidays, so in effect they become additional vacation days in lieu of holidays.

Like vacation pay, holiday pay is taxed as regular income.

Personal Time Off with Pay

Since personal situations that require an employee to be away from work occasionally arise, many employers allow employees to take time off with pay for certain reasons, the more common of which are the following:

- reserve/National Guard duty. Laws sometimes require that employees get time off for reserve or National Guard duty, but there is no stipulation that pay continue during this period. However, most employers pay their employees the difference between their regular pay and any compensation received for reserve or National Guard duty.
- voting time. Many states require that employees get time off to vote, but most do not require the employee to be compensated for this time. However, the time period is short, usually no more than two hours, and most employers who grant such time off continue regular pay. Since polls are typically open 12 hours or more, it is questionable whether this benefit is necessary in the absence of state law.
- jury duty. Most employers grant (and may be required to grant) time off for jury duty. Since employees are usually compensated for jury duty, some employers pay only the difference between this amount and an employee's regular pay. However, the amount paid for jury duty is small and often just barely covers an employee's extra expenses. Therefore many employers continue regular compensation with no deduction.
- a death in the family. Employers often allow up to 5 days off with pay for the death of family members. At a minimum this usually includes the death of a parent, child, spouse, or other relative residing in the household. Some employers allow a shorter period of time, such as a day or a half day, to attend funerals of other relatives and sometimes even persons other than relatives.
- sabbatical leaves. Sabbatical leaves are well established as employee benefits at educational institutions. Typically faculty members are permitted an extended leave of a semester or a year after a specified period of service, such as 7 years. During the sabbatical leave the faculty member receives full or partial pay while performing no services for the employer. However, the faculty member is often required to complete a research project or some similar activity as a condition of the sabbatical. Noneducational employers, particularly those having employees with professional degrees, sometimes provide similar

benefits to professional employees to give them an opportunity to engage in research or study that is not directly job related.

Some less common reasons that employers may allow time off with pay include the employee's marriage and serving as a witness in a court proceeding. Since other personal reasons for needing time off may arise, employers may grant 2 or 3 days of personal leave that can be taken at an employee's discretion.

Personal Time Off without Pay (Family Leave)

For many years most industrialized countries have had legislation that enables employees to be away from work for extended periods without jeopardizing their jobs. The reasons for such leave vary among countries, as does the extent to which the employer must continue to provide pay and benefits to an employee on leave.

Over the last two decades an increasing number of American employers have voluntarily begun to allow employees to take time off without pay. Reasons for such leave may include active military duty, extended vacations, honeymoons, education, the birth or adoption of a child, and the illness of a family member. Usually such time off has been subject to the approval of the employer. Family leave is becoming more and more common as many states and the federal government adopt family-leave legislation.

State Laws

In recent years the legislatures of almost every state have considered family-leave legislation, and more than half the states have enacted such legislation. As a general rule these laws allow an employee to take an unpaid leave of absence for reasons such as the birth or adoption of a child and the illness of a family member. The length of leave allowed varies considerably among states, but it usually ranges from 3 to 6 months. When the family leave is completed, the employer is required to allow the employee to return to the same or a comparable job.

Almost all family-leave laws apply to public employers, and about half of the laws apply to private employers with more than a minimum number of employees, usually in the range of 25 to 100. In all states, employers are allowed to limit family leave to employees who have met certain eligibility requirements. While these requirements vary, the most common requirement is at least one year of full-time employment. At a minimum most family-leave laws allow an employee to continue medical expense coverage at his or her own cost. Some laws require all employee benefits to be made available.

Federal Law

In 1993, the first federal family-leave legislation—the Family and Medical Leave Act—became effective. Unlike some federal legislation, it applies not only to private employers but also to nonprofit organizations and government entities, including Congress. The provisions of this legislation cover only a small percentage of the nation's employers but approximately two-thirds of all employees.

Despite concerns by employers that the act would increase costs and lower productivity, the actual effect seems to have been minimal, partly because many large employers already had leave policies similar to the act's provisions. A report issued in May 1996 by the Bipartisan Commission on Family and Medical Leave reported the following:

- Approximately 90 percent of employers reported that there was no noticeable effect on productivity, profitability, and growth as a result of the act.
- Only about 16 percent of the persons eligible for leave actually took it. The vast majority of persons who did not take leave for which they were eligible said they could not afford the resulting wage loss.
- The median length of leave time is 10 days.
- The group most likely to take leave is employees between the ages of 25 and 34.

The legislation applies only to employers who have more than 50 employees within a 75-mile radius. To comply with the 50-employee requirement, an employer needs only to have that many employees during each workday of 20 or more calendar weeks during the current or preceding calendar year. Part-time employees and employees on unpaid leaves of absence are included in the calculation. The 50-employee requirement is based on "joint employment," which means that two or more related companies can be treated as a single employer on the basis of factors such as common management, interrelations between operations, centralized control of labor relations, and the degree of common ownership or management. The 75-mile radius is based on the shortest route that can be taken on either public roads or public transportation.

With some exceptions, a worker must be allowed to take up to 12 weeks of unpaid leave in any 12-month period for the birth or adoption of a child; to care for a child, spouse, or parent with a serious health condition; or for the worker's own serious health condition that makes it impossible to perform a job. An employer may use any one of the following four methods to determine the 12-month period to which the family leave applies:

- the calendar year
- any fixed 12-month period
- the 12-month period beginning with any employee's first leave
- a rolling 12-month period measured backward from the date leave is used

With one exception, the method chosen must apply uniformly to all employees. The exception occurs if a multistate employer operates in one or more states with family leave legislation that mandates a method different from the one chosen. In that case the employer is permitted to comply with the state's requirement for employees located in that state but must use the chosen method for employees in other states.

A serious health condition is defined as one that requires continuing treatment from a health care provider. The regulations implementing the act generally define this as meaning that the condition will require absence from work, school, or regular daily activities for more than 3 calendar days. However, the regulations also include treatment for pregnancy and certain chronic conditions, such as diabetes and asthma, as being serious health conditions even though treatment at any time may last less than 3 days. In addition, the definition includes health problems that are not ordinarily incapacitating on a day-to-day basis, but for which a person is undergoing a series of multiple treatments. Examples in the regulations include chemotherapy or radiation for cancer, kidney dialysis, and physical therapy for severe arthritis. The regulations specifically exclude the following from the definition of a serious health condition: common colds, flu, upset stomach, and routine dental problems. Stress is also excluded, but mental illness arising from stress can qualify.

The act applies to both full-time and part-time employees. The latter must be allowed to take leave on a basis that is proportional to that given to full-time employees. However, leave can be denied to anyone who has not worked for the employer for at least one year and worked at least 1,250 hours during that period.

In most cases, the rules allow employees to take leave intermittently or by working a reduced week, but only with the employer's approval. The exception is that leave because of a person's or family member's serious health condition may be taken whenever medically necessary.

An employer is allowed to substitute an employee's accrued paid leave for any part of the 12-week period of family leave. In addition, an employer can deny leave to a salaried employee within the highest-paid 10 percent of its workforce if the leave would create a substantial and grievous injury to the organization's operations.

An employee is required to provide 30 days' notice for foreseeable leaves for birth, adoption, or planned medical treatment. The employer can require an employee to provide a doctor's certification of a serious illness. An employer can also require a second opinion but must pay for the cost.

During the period of leave an employer has no obligation to continue an employee's pay or most benefits, and the employee is ineligible for unemployment compensation. However, an employer must continue to provide health care benefits during the leave as if the worker was still employed. The employee must continue to pay any required plan contributions and must be given a 30-day grace period for such payments. The employer is also required to send the employee a notice no later than 15 days before the grace period expires stating that coverage will be terminated if the premium is not paid. The employer is allowed to recover the cost of the health care benefits paid during the leave if the employee does not return to work.

Upon returning from leave, an employee must be given his or her former job or one that is equivalent. The employee must also be permitted to regain any benefits that he or she enjoyed prior to the leave without having to meet any requalification requirements. With respect to retirement plans, any period of leave must be treated as continued service for purposes of vesting and eligibility to participate.

Employers must comply with the new federal law as well as with any applicable state laws. Since most existing state laws have at least one provision that is broader than the federal legislation, an employer must have a broad understanding of both laws.

An employer should have a clear, written family-leave policy that is consistently enforced. In establishing this policy the employer should address such issues as

- eligibility requirements
- employee certification of need for leave
- employee rights upon returning from leave
- employer rights if employee terminates at end of leave

The federal law requires an employer to post a notice explaining the Family and Medical Leave Act, a sample of which is contained in material from the Labor Department, which administers the law. An employer must also include a copy of its leave policies with this notice or provide written guidance whenever an employee requests leave under the act.

Supplemental Unemployment Benefit Plans

Collective-bargaining agreements may require employers to contribute to a supplemental unemployment benefit (SUB) plan that is designed to supplement state unemployment insurance benefits for workers who are unemployed. These plans rarely exist for nonunion employees. Benefits are often payable for at least a year and with regular unemployment benefits may be as high as 95 percent of what the worker was earning while employed.

SUB plans typically require employers to contribute to a SUB fund on the basis of the compensation of currently active employees, and employee contributions may also be required. The fund is usually maintained by trustees selected by the collective bargaining agent, and it is frequently a common fund maintained for several employers. Employer contributions to the fund are income tax deductible, and if the fund is properly designed, earnings on fund assets may also be exempt from income taxation. Benefit payments to employees are fully taxable.

EXTRA PAYMENTS TO EMPLOYEES

Educational Assistance

For several years the Internal Revenue Code has provided favorable tax treatment to employees who receive benefits from their employers for educational assistance. At the time this book was being revised, Sec. 127 of the Code, which allows employees to receive annually the first $5,250 of these benefits on a tax-free basis, was scheduled to expire for courses beginning after June 30, 1997. (However, the date has been extended several times before and will probably be extended again, or the Code section may be made permanent.) In order for benefits to be tax free, the employer's plan cannot discriminate with respect to eligibility in favor of officers, shareholders, highly compensated employees, or their dependents. In addition, no more than 5 percent of the benefits may be paid out to shareholders or owners (or their dependents) who are more-than-5-percent owners of the firm.

Eligible benefits include tuition, fees, and books. The costs of supplies and equipment are also included as long as they are not retained after completion of the course. Meals, lodging, and transportation associated with educational expenses cannot be received tax free, nor can tax-free educational assistance be provided for graduate-level courses beginning after June 30, 1996. For purposes of Sec. 127, a graduate-level course is defined as any course taken by an employee who has a bachelor's degree or is receiving credit toward a more advanced degree, if the particular course can be taken for credit by any individual in a program leading to a law, business, medical, or other advanced academic or professional degree. Courses involving sports, games, or hobbies are also ineligible for favorable tax treatment. Although an employer's plan can pay for any of these types of courses, an employee will be taxed on the value of the employer's contribution to their cost.

If Congress fails to extend the favorable tax treatment for a broadly defined educational assistance program, employees will still be allowed to deduct any educational expenses that are incurred (1) to maintain or improve a skill required in employment or (2) to meet the express requirements of the employer as a condition for retaining employment. To the extent that these benefits are paid for by the employer, they will be treated as taxable compensation. However, the corresponding deduction effectively makes them a tax-free benefit. Other types of educational expenses, such as costs incurred to qualify the employee for a new trade or business, are not deductible.

Moving-Expense Reimbursement

In order to attract new employees and to encourage current employees to move to suit the employer's needs, many businesses provide reimbursement for moving expenses. Such reimbursement is includible in an employee's income, but the employee is allowed certain offsetting income tax deductions if specified rules are satisfied. To receive the deductions, the employee must have moved because of a change in job location. In addition, the employee must satisfy both a distance test and a time test. The distance test requires that the employee's new workplace be at least 50 miles farther from the employee's old residence than the employee's old workplace (or old residence if the employee was previously unemployed). The time test requires the employee to work full time in the general location of the new residence for at least 39 weeks during the 12 months following the move. An employee may take the applicable deductions in anticipation of satisfying the time test, but additional taxes will be payable if the time test is not ultimately met.

If all the preceding rules are satisfied, an employee may deduct the following expenses:

- transportation expenses in moving household goods and personal effects
- travel, meals, and lodging expenses in moving to the new residence

An employer may pay for other expenses, such as expenses to sell an old residence or temporary living costs at the new location. Because these reimbursements will be taxable income without a corresponding deduction, the employer may give the employee a bonus to offset the increased tax.

Suggestion Awards

Some employers, particularly those in manufacturing industries, give awards to employees who make suggestions that will improve the operating efficiency of the firm if implemented. The awards are often a percentage of the firm's estimated savings over some specified future period of time but may be subject to a maximum dollar amount. If a suggestion plan is properly administered, the benefits of the plan may far exceed its costs while at the same time increasing the motivation and involvement of employees.

Suggestion awards are included in an employee's gross income for tax purposes.

Service Awards

Many employers provide awards to employees for length of service. These awards are often nominal for short periods of service (5 or 10 years) and may consist of such items as key chains, flowers, or pens. Awards typically increase in value for longer periods of service, and employees may actually be given some choice in the award received.

If the value of a service award is *de minimis,* it is not included in an employee's income. To be *de minimis* the value of the benefit must be so minimal that accounting for the cost of the benefit would be unreasonable or administratively impractical. Service awards of higher value may also be excludible from an employee's income if they are considered *qualified plan awards*. However, the total amount excludible from an employee's income for qualified plan awards (which also include awards for safety) cannot exceed $1,600 per year. Qualified plan awards must be provided under a permanent written program that does not discriminate in favor of officers, shareholders, or highly compensated employees. In addition, the average annual cost of all awards under the plan cannot exceed $400.

Productivity and Safety Achievement Awards

Some employers provide awards for productivity and safety achievement. Productivity awards are fully treated as compensation. However, while awards for safety achievement given to professional, administrative, managerial, or clerical employees are fully taxable, such awards are treated as qualified plan awards for other employees and are included in the $1,600 figure mentioned previously under service awards.

Holiday Bonuses and Gifts

Many employers give gifts or bonuses to employees, particularly at Christmastime. Since the value of such gifts is typically small, some employees tend to resent gifts of money. Therefore gifts such as liquor or a ham are often given.

As with service awards, a holiday gift does not result in taxation for an employee as long as the market value of the gift is small.

SERVICES TO EMPLOYEES

No-Additional-Cost Services

Employers in many service industries provide their employees with free or discounted services. Examples include telephone service to employees of phone companies and airline tickets to employees of airlines. As long as the following rules are satisfied, the cost of these services is not includible in an employee's gross income for tax purposes:

- The services cannot be provided on a basis that discriminates in favor of highly compensated employees.
- The employer must not incur any significant additional cost or lost revenue in providing the services. For example, giving a standby ticket to an airline employee if there were unsold seats on a flight would satisfy this requirement, but giving an airline ticket to an employee when potential paying customers were denied seats would not.

- The services must be those that are provided in the employer's line of
  business in which the employee actually works. Therefore if a business
  owns both an airline and a chain of hotels, an employee of the hotels can
  be given a room as a tax-free benefit but not an airline ticket. However,
  unrelated employers in the same line of business, such as airlines, may
  enter into reciprocal arrangements under which employees of any party
  to the arrangement may obtain services from the other parties.

Employee Discounts

Just as no-additional-cost services are an important employee benefit in
certain service industries, discounts on the merchandise sold by manufacturers
and retailers are an important benefit to employees in these industries. Discounts
may also be provided on services sold by other types of businesses, such as the
commission charged by a brokerage house or insurance company.

Rules similar to those discussed for no-additional-cost services apply to
discounts. Employees have no taxable income as long as the discounts are made
available on a nondiscriminatory basis and are provided on goods or services
ordinarily sold to nonemployees in the employer's line of business in which the
employee works. However, there are some additional rules. Discounts received
on real estate or on personal property normally held as an investment (for
example, gold coins or securities) are not received tax free. Furthermore, there is
a limit on the size of a discount that can be received tax free. For merchandise
the discount cannot exceed the gross profit percentage of the price at which the
merchandise is offered for sale to customers. For example, if an employer had a
gross profit margin of 40 percent on a particular product and an employee
purchased the merchandise at a 50 percent discount, the extra 10 percent would
be taxable income to the employee. In the case of services, including insurance
policies, the tax-free discount cannot exceed 20 percent of the price at which the
service is offered to nonemployee customers in the normal course of the
employer's business. The type of service that cannot be received tax free
involves loans that financial institutions give to employees at a discounted rate of
interest.

Dependent-Care Assistance

Changes in society and the workforce often create changing needs for both
employers and employees. When the workforce was largely male and most
families had two parents, caring for children and older parents frequently was the
female spouse's responsibility. As the number of families headed by two wage
earners or by single parents has increased, so has the need for dependent care.
This change in demographics has also created problems for employers. Caring
for family members can lead to increased absenteeism, tardiness, turnover, and
time taken as family leave. Workplace morale can also suffer if the employer is
viewed as insensitive to employee responsibilities.

The nature of employee benefit plans has changed as employers have increasingly responded to the need for dependent care. Child-care benefits are increasingly common, and a small but growing number of firms also make eldercare benefits available. Firms that have dependent-care assistance plans generally feel that such plans alleviate the problems cited in the previous paragraph. Furthermore, the availability of the benefit often makes it easier to hire new employees.

In addition to a formal dependent-care assistance plan, there are other ways in which employers can respond to employee needs to care for family members. These include flexible work schedules, part-time employment, job sharing, salary reduction options under cafeteria plans, and family-leave policies that are more liberal than those required by federal and state laws.

Child-Care Plans

Several alternative types of benefits can be provided under child-care plans. A few employers maintain on-site day-care centers, and the number is growing. On the other hand, some employers have closed on-site centers and provide alternative forms of assistance because of the following problems encountered with on-site centers:

- difficulty in obtaining qualified child-care providers
- difficulty in obtaining liability insurance
- difficulty, time, and expense associated with obtaining necessary zoning variances and child-care licenses
- distractions caused by parents and children being so close together
- underutilization. While this type of facility would be expected to be popular, many employees prefer other alternatives. A site close to home is often more appealing than a location that may involve a long commute for parent and child. An on-site location may be less convenient if both parents share in child-care activities. Employees may also prefer a different type of child-care arrangement.

Some employers provide benefits by supporting a limited number of off-site child-care centers. The employer may make arrangements to reserve spaces for employees' children at these centers and/or arrange for corporate discounts for employees.

Probably the most common approach is to provide reimbursements to employees who make their own arrangements for child care, either at child-care centers or in their own home or the home of a caregiver. Reimbursement is sometimes tied to pay levels, with lower-paid workers receiving higher reimbursements.

When employees are required to make their own arrangements under a child-care plan, employers may provide information and referral services—often through a contract with community or private referral services. In addition to providing assistance in locating a quality child-care center, these services can provide help in finding drop-in facilities when the usual child-care arrangement has fallen through or when school is closed for a day. They may also maintain a list of persons who will care for temporarily ill children at home or for children after school hours. Such services may also be a source of information about facilities that can be used during summer and other school vacations.

Eldercare Benefits

While benefits to care for elderly dependents are much less prevalent than benefits for child care, the need for these benefits continues to grow as parents live longer. In addition, as many couples have delayed having children until later in life, they have become part of what is often referred to as the sandwich generation. They must care for elderly parents at the same time they are raising their own children.

Although eldercare benefits may take a variety of forms, frequently they are much like those provided under child-care plans. Within limits, the employer may pay for costs associated with home care for elderly dependents or care at day-care facilities for the elderly. One interesting development in this area is the establishment of centers that care for both children and the elderly, with the elderly assisting in such activities as the feeding and teaching of the children. Studies have shown that the two groups are very compatible. Children, particularly those without grandparents nearby, can benefit from the attention and knowledge they receive from the elderly, while the elderly can have a feeling of usefulness.

Other employer activities with respect to eldercare may include the following:

- seminars on issues affecting the elderly
- information on services available to provide eldercare and how to use the services
- employer-sponsored support groups where employees can share experiences and learn from others
- expansion of employee-assistance plans to include eldercare
- making long-term care insurance available to employees, and including parents as an eligible group for coverage

Taxation of Benefits

Under the Internal Revenue Code, dependent care is a tax-free benefit to employees up to statutory limits as long as certain requirements are met. The amount of benefits that can be received tax free is limited to $5,000 for single persons and married persons who file jointly and to $2,500 for married persons who file separately. The benefits must be for care to a qualifying individual—a child under age 13 for whom the employee is allowed a dependency deduction on his or her income tax return and a taxpayer's spouse or other dependent who is mentally or physically incapable of caring for himself or herself. Although benefits must generally be for dependent care only, educational expenses at the kindergarten or preschool level can also be paid.

Dependent-care benefits are subject to a series of rules. If the rules are not met, highly compensated employees are taxed on the amount of benefits received. However, the benefits for other employees still retain their tax-free status. The following rules must be met:

- Eligibility, contributions, and benefits under the plan cannot discriminate in favor of highly compensated employees or their dependents.
- No more than 25 percent of the benefits may be provided to the class composed of persons who own more than a 5 percent interest in the firm.
- Reasonable notification of the availability of benefits and the terms of the plan must be provided to eligible employees.
- By January 31 of the following year each employee must receive an annual statement that indicates the amounts paid or expenses incurred by the employer to provide benefits.
- The average benefit provided to nonhighly compensated employees must be at least 55 percent of the average benefit provided to highly compensated employees.

In meeting the 55 percent benefit test, an employer can exclude employees earning under $25,000 if benefits are provided through a salary reduction agreement. For both the 55 percent benefit test and the nondiscrimination rule for eligibility, an employer can exclude employees who (1) are under age 21, (2) have not completed 1 year of service, or (3) are covered under a collective bargaining unit that has bargained over dependent-care benefits.

Even if an employer does not provide assistance for dependent care, other tax-saving options may be available to employees. Under the Code a tax credit (subject to limits) is available for child-care expenses. In addition, the employer may have the opportunity to make before-tax contributions to a cafeteria plan that includes dependent care as an option.

Adoption Assistance

While many types of benefits have long been available to natural parents because of the birth of a child, comparable benefits historically have not been available to adoptive parents. Over the last few years this disparity has begun to change. Even before the passage of family-leave legislation, many employers had established comparable leave policies for natural parents and adoptive parents. For example, if an employer allowed maternity leave (either paid or unpaid) for a new mother, no distinction was made between natural mothers and adoptive mothers. Leave may also be available for time involved in qualifying for the adoption and taking possession of the child.

A smaller number of employers provide reimbursement for some or all of the following expenses associated with adoption:

- legal fees
- adoption agencies' fees
- the birth mother's medical expenses
- the adoptive parents' medical expenses for physical examinations required by the adoption source
- the child's uninsured medical expenses
- foster care charges for the child prior to placement with the adoptive family
- transportation expenses associated with taking custody of the child
- extra expenses associated with foreign adoptions

Reimbursements are generally available only to employees who have satisfied some minimum service requirement, most commonly one year. Amounts typically range from $1,000 to $3,000 per adoption, but higher amounts may be paid for adoptions involving handicapped children or children from a foreign country. There may also be a lifetime cap, such as $6,000.

Prior to 1997, adoption assistance for costs other than medical expenses generally represented taxable income to an employee. Beginning in 1997, employer payments of up to $5,000 per child for qualified adoption expenses can be excluded from an employee's gross income if an employer has an adoption-assistance program that satisfies IRS requirements. The amount is increased to $6,000 for certain children with special needs.

The adoption-assistance program must be a separate written plan, and employees must have reasonable notification of the availability of the program and its benefits. The program cannot discriminate in favor of highly compensated employees or their dependents, and no more than 5 percent of the benefits under the plan can be paid to shareholders or owners (or their dependents) who are more-than-5-percent owners of the firm.

Qualified adoption expenses include reasonable and necessary adoption fees, court costs, attorney's fees, travel expenses, and other expenses directly related to the legal adoption of an eligible child, defined as a child who is under age 18 or who is incapable of caring for himself or herself. Expenses incurred in adopting a spouse's child or carrying out a surrogate parenting arrangement are not qualified adoption expenses, nor are expenses that are reimbursed from other sources. In addition, expenses to adopt a foreign child are not qualified adoption expenses unless the adoption becomes final.

The $5,000 (or $6,000) exclusion from gross income is available to employees with an adjusted gross income of $75,000 or less, and married couples must file joint returns to obtain the exclusion. For employee with higher adjusted gross incomes, the exclusion is gradually phased out until it is eliminated when adjusted gross income reaches $115,000.

An employee can claim both the exclusion from income and a similar tax credit that is available to all taxpayers for adoption expenses. However, claiming both the exclusion and the tax credit for the same adoption expense is not permitted. In addition, the credit is not available for expenses that were paid by employer-provided adoption assistance regardless of whether the employer paid the expenses through an adoption-assistance program.

Wellness Programs

Traditional benefit programs have been designed to provide benefits (1) to employees for their medical expenses and disabilities or (2) to their dependents if the employee should die prematurely. In the last few years there has been an increasing trend among employers, particularly large corporations, to initiate programs that are designed to promote the well-being of employees (and possibly their dependents). Some of these programs have been aimed at the discovery and treatment of medical conditions before they become severe and result in large medical expenses, disabilities, or death. Other programs have focused on changing employees' lifestyles in order to eliminate the possible causes of future medical problems. A few programs, such as making flu shots available to employees, actually provide medical treatment. Recent studies have shown that the costs of establishing and maintaining many of these programs are more than offset by the lower amounts paid for medical expense, disability, and death benefits. In addition, if long-term disabilities and premature deaths can be eliminated, the expenses associated with training new employees can be minimized. Many firms also feel these programs increase productivity by improving the employees' sense of well-being, their work attitudes, and their family relationships.

Medical Screening Programs

The use of a medical screening program to discover existing medical conditions is not new, but it has often covered the costs (frequently up to some dollar limit) of routine physical examinations only for selected groups of management employees. Although this benefit may be highly valued by these employees, and its use as an executive benefit has been increasing somewhat, there are doubts—even among the medical profession—as to its cost effectiveness, particularly when it is provided on an annual basis. Certain medical conditions will undoubtedly be discovered during a complete physical, but most of them could also be diagnosed by less frequent and less costly forms of medical examinations.

In recent years there has been a significant increase in the number of employers that sponsor periodic medical screening programs that detect specific medical problems, such as hypertension (high blood pressure), high cholesterol levels, breast cancer, prostate cancer, and colorectal cancer. Generally such screenings are conducted at the employment site during regular working hours. Sometimes a screening will be conducted by a physician, but it is usually performed by lower-paid medical professionals. In addition, screenings can sometimes be obtained at little or no cost through such organizations as the American Red Cross, the American Heart Association, or the American Cancer Association.

Lifestyle-Management Programs

Lifestyle-management programs are primarily designed to encourage employees and often their dependents to modify their behavior so that they will lead healthier lives. Most of these programs strive to discover and eliminate conditions that increase the likelihood of cardiovascular problems (the source of a significant percentage of medical expenses and premature deaths). Some of these conditions (such as obesity and smoking) are obvious, but medical screening can also detect less obvious conditions like hypertension, high cholesterol levels, and the degree of an employee's physical fitness. The types of programs often instituted to promote cardiovascular health include

- smoking-cessation programs
- fitness programs. These may consist of formal exercise programs or only exercise facilities (such as swimming pools, exercise rooms, or jogging tracks). Some employee benefit consultants question whether facilities for competitive sports (such as racquetball courts) can be cost justified because their availability is limited, and they are often a source of injuries.
- weight-reduction programs
- nutrition programs. These are often established in conjunction with weight-reduction programs, but they can also teach methods of cholesterol reduction even if there is no weight problem.
- stress-management programs

These programs may be available to any employees who express an interest in them, or they may be limited only to those employees who have been evaluated and found to be in a high-risk category for cardiovascular disease. This evaluation may consist of questionnaires regarding health history, blood pressure reading, blood chemistry analyses, and fitness tests. Generally these evaluations and meetings to describe the programs and their value are conducted during regular working hours. However, the programs themselves are usually conducted during nonworking hours, possibly at lunchtime or just after work.

Many wellness programs are designed to include employees, their spouses, and sometimes other family members. In many instances it will not be possible to change an employee's lifestyle unless the lifestyle of his or her entire family also changes. For example, it is not very probable that an employee will stop smoking if his or her spouse also smokes and is making no attempt to stop. Similarly a weight-reduction or nutrition program will probably be more effective if all family members alter their eating habits.

Programs designed to eliminate alcohol or drug abuse are another example of lifestyle management. Participation may be voluntary or it can be mandatory for employees who are known to have alcohol or drug problems and who want to keep their jobs. When these programs have been successful, many employers have found a decrease in employee absenteeism.

The employer may either conduct these wellness activities on the premises or use the resources of other organizations. For example, overweight employees might be sent to Weight Watchers, employees with alcohol problems might be encouraged to attend Alcoholics Anonymous, and employees with back problems might be enrolled in programs at a local YMCA.

Some employers have also instituted programs that seek to minimize back problems—the reason for a large percentage of employee absenteeism and disability claims. These programs are generally intended for employees who have a history of back trouble, and they consist of exercises as well as education in how to modify or avoid activities that can aggravate existing back conditions.

More recently many employers have become concerned with the spread of AIDS and its effect on the cost of benefit plans. As a result they have instituted educational programs aimed at encouraging employees to avoid activities that may result in the transmission of AIDS.

Employers in increasing numbers are subscribing to wellness newsletters and distributing them to employees. To encourage wellness for the entire family, these newsletters are often mailed to employees' homes.

Taxation of Benefits

Since medical screening programs are treated as medical expenses for tax purposes, employees have no taxable income as a result of participating in these programs. Unless the cost of providing lifestyle-management programs is *de minimis,* participation will probably result in taxation to employees. The costs of programs that promote general health, such as smoking cessation or weight control, are not considered medical expenses. While the cost of providing these programs to employees is deductible by the employer, an employee will incur taxable income unless the purpose of the program is to alleviate a specific medical problem. However, there is one exception to this general rule. Employees incur no taxable income as a result of being provided with or using athletic facilities that are located on the employer's premises.

Employee-Assistance Programs

As the trend toward fostering wellness in the workplace continues, an increasing number of employers are establishing employee-assistance programs. These programs are designed to help employees with certain personal problems through a plan that provides

- treatment for alcohol or drug abuse
- counseling for mental problems and stress
- counseling for family and marital problems
- financial, legal, and tax advice
- referrals for child care or eldercare
- crisis intervention

Numerous studies have shown that proper treatment of these problems is very cost effective and leads to reduced sick days, hospital costs, disability, and absenteeism. It is also argued that employee morale and productivity are increased as a result of the concern shown for employees' personal problems.

Traditionally employee-assistance programs have used job performance as the basis for employer concern. Essentially an employee is told that his or her work is substandard and asked if a problem exists that he or she would like to discuss with someone. If the employee says yes, referral is made to an appropriate counselor or agency. No attempt is made by the employee's supervisor to diagnose the specific problem. Newer employee-assistance programs go beyond this approach by allowing employees who have problems to go directly to the program and seek help. Dependents can usually use the employee asistance program and can often seek help without the employee's knowledge.

Another recent trend in employee-assistance programs is to coordinate them more closely with the employer's medical expense plan. For example, several employee-assistance programs act as the gatekeeper for mental health and substance abuse services. An employee must go through the employee-assistance program before benefits can be received under his or her medical expense coverage. The objective of this approach is to establish a course of treatment that will have maximum effectiveness for the costs incurred.

Access to an employee-assistance program is through a counselor who may be a company employee, but most often an employer establishes the plan through a professional organization that specializes in such programs. Information provided to the counselor by the employee is kept confidential. Many problems can be solved by discussion between the counselor and the employee, and most plans have 24-hour counseling available, through either a telephone hotline or on-duty personnel. If the counselor cannot solve an employee's problem, it is the counselor's responsibility to make a preliminary determination about the type of professional help the employee should receive. In many cases this treatment can be provided under existing medical expense or legal expense plans or through community agencies. The costs of other types of treatment are usually paid totally or in part by the employer. As long as the treatment is for the purpose of alleviating medical conditions, including mental illness, an employee has no taxable income. If the treatment is for a nonmedical condition, the employee will have taxable income as the result of employer payments.

Financial Planning Programs for Executives

Employers are increasingly providing financial planning as a benefit to employees. Although traditionally this benefit was limited to a small number of top executives, many firms are now expanding their programs to include members of middle management. In addition, financial planning education and advice are now offered to many employees as part of a broader preretirement-counseling program. Any program in overall financial planning must take into consideration the benefits that are provided or that are potentially available under group insurance plans, under social insurance programs, and through the individual efforts of employees.

The concept of providing financial planning for a limited number of top executives has been widely practiced for many years, particularly in large corporations. However, within the last few years a significant number of corporations have expanded these programs to include middle management employees in the $50,000 to $100,000 annual salary range. Businesses have deemed this financial planning benefit as necessary for top executives, who have limited time for their own financial affairs, so that they can be free to devote their full talents to important business decisions. A company may also find it easier to attract and retain executives who look upon the financial planning program as a way to make existing compensation more valuable (for example, by providing a larger spendable income through tax planning or a greater accumulation of wealth through investment planning).

Although group meetings are sometimes used (for example, to explain certain types of investments or changes in the tax laws), most financial planning programs provide for individual counseling of employees to suit their own particular circumstances and needs.

Types of Planning

Financial planning is composed of many separate but interrelated segments:

- compensation planning, including the explanation of employee benefits and an analysis of any available compensation options
- preparation of tax returns
- estate planning, including the preparation of wills and planning to both minimize estate taxes and maintain proper estate liquidity

- investment planning, including both investment advice and investment management
- insurance planning, including information on how to meet life insurance, medical expense, disability, and property and liability needs

A financial planning program may be designed to provide either selected services from the list above or a comprehensive array of services. Comprehensive financial planning can be thought of as a series of interrelated and continuing activities that begin with the collection and analysis of personal and financial information, including the risk attitudes of an employee. This information is used (1) to establish the priorities and time horizons for attaining personal objectives and (2) to develop the financial plan that will meet these objectives. Once the plan is formulated, the next critical step is the actual implementation of the plan. A proper financial planning program should also include a process for measuring the performance of any plan so that, if unacceptable, either the plan can be changed or the employee's objectives revised.

Sources of Financial Planning

A few firms provide financial planning services using the organization's own employees. Most firms purchase the services either from outside specialists (such as lawyers, accountants, insurance agents, or stockbrokers) or from companies or individuals that do comprehensive financial planning.

Significant differences exist among financial planning firms. Some operate solely on a fee basis and give only advice and counseling, in which case it is the employee's responsibility to have his or her own attorney, insurance agent, or other financial professional implement any decisions. These financial planning firms often work closely with the other professionals in handling the employee's affairs. The cost of using a fee-only financial planning firm varies, depending upon what services it provides, but initial fees of $5,000 per employee and annual charges of $1,000 to $2,000 are not uncommon.

Other financial planning firms operate on a product-oriented basis and sell products (usually insurance or investments) in addition to other financial planning services. The fact that these firms receive commissions from the products they sell may eliminate or reduce any fees paid by the employer. Unfortunately the insurance or investment advice of these firms may be slanted in favor of the products they sell. Therefore employers must make sure that the advice of outside specialists will be unbiased and will be presented in a professional manner.

Taxation

Fees paid for financial planning are tax deductible by the employer as long as the total compensation paid to an employee is reasonable. The amount of any fees paid to a financial planning firm or other professional in behalf of an individual employee becomes taxable income to the employee. However, an employee may be able to take miscellaneous itemized deductions for certain services relating to tax matters and investment advice. Services the employer provides to executives on an individual basis also result in taxable income.

Preretirement-Counseling Programs

Businesses, aware of the pitfalls that await unprepared retired employees, have increasingly begun to offer preretirement counseling. It has been estimated that this benefit is offered by approximately 75 percent of companies with 20,000 or more employees. For companies with under 1,000 employees, the figure is closer to 15 or 20 percent. Most of these companies have made this benefit available to all employees over a specific age (such as 50 or 55), but an increasing number of organizations allow employees of any age to participate. Retired employees may also be invited to take advantage of any program benefits that are of interest to them.

Preretirement-counseling programs differ from financial planning programs for executives in that there is very little individual counseling. Rather, employees meet in groups to listen to media presentations and speakers, and they are given the opportunity to ask questions and discuss their concerns. This counseling may take place during nonwork hours, but there is an increasing trend to have it provided during work hours, often in a concentrated one- or two-day period. Most companies encourage spouses to participate. Often one program is developed for all employees, although some organizations vary their programs for different classifications of employees (such as management employees and blue-collar workers).

When these programs are successful, the fears that many employees have about retirement can be alleviated. They will learn that with proper planning retirement can be not only financially comfortable but also a meaningful period in their lives.

Financial Planning

Some preretirement-counseling programs devote at least half their time to the financial aspects of retirement. Because proper financial planning for retirement must begin many years prior to actual retirement, the amount of time devoted to this subject will be greatest in programs that encourage employees to begin participation at younger ages.

Some financial planning meetings help employees identify and determine what their financial needs will be after retirement and what resources will be available to meet those needs from the company's benefit plans and from social security. If retirement needs will not be met by these sources, employees are informed about how their individual efforts can supplement retirement income through savings or investments. They are also told about the specific advantages and risks associated with each method of saving or investment. In addition, issues such as the need for wills and estate planning may be discussed. Such preretirement financial planning is conducted on a group basis; the programs are unlikely to provide investment advice on an individual basis or through an investment management service, as described in the previous section on financial planning programs for executives. However, some employers do give employees financial planning reports that are prepared through a computerized financial planning system. These reports, which may vary in length from 20 to 60 pages, are generated from the data on a questionnaire completed by the employee. They may offer advice on such topics as the additional amount of money that should be saved for retirement or compare the cost of working with the cost of retiring.

Many employers now make computer software available to employees so they can enter basic personal and financial data for varying scenarios related to retirement, education funding, and the like. The major advantage of these computer programs is that an employee can quickly evaluate alternative assumptions about factors such as retirement dates and savings rates. One potential drawback to the use of computer programs is the lack of employee understanding about the assumptions and reasoning that lie behind the input into the program and about the output that results. Therefore it is important that computer programs be accompanied by proper training in their purpose, use, and interpretation.

Other Aspects of Preretirement Counseling

Preretirement counseling focuses on other aspects of retirement besides financial needs. The following are some of the questions that must also be faced by most retired workers and that are often addressed in preretirement-counseling programs:

- living arrangements. What are the pros and cons of selling a house and moving into an apartment or condominium? Is relocation in the Sunbelt away from family members and friends advisable?
- health. Can changes in lifestyle lead to healthier retirement years?
- free time. How can the time that was previously devoted to work be used? What opportunities are available for volunteer work, part-time employment, or continuing education? What leisure activities or community activities can be adopted that will continue into retirement? (Studies have shown that alcoholism, divorce, and suicide tend to increase among the retired. Much of this increase has been attributed to the lack of activities to fill free time and to the problems encountered by husbands and wives who are constantly together for the first time in their lives.)

Sources of Preretirement Counseling

An organization may establish and maintain its own program of preretirement counseling. However, many organizations (such as benefit-counseling firms and the American Association of Retired Persons) have developed packaged programs that are sold to other organizations. These programs typically consist of media presentations and information regarding the types of speakers that should be used in counseling sessions. Generally these packaged programs are flexible enough to be used with almost any type of employee group. Most firms actually conduct preretirement-counseling programs with a combination of their own employees and outside speakers or organizations. It is becoming common to see the use of an organization's own retirees in the counseling process.

Taxation

As long as no specific services are provided to employees on an individual basis, they do not have taxable income to report as a result of participating in preretirement counseling programs.

Transportation/Free Parking

Some employers have long provided transportation benefits to employees as a fringe benefit. These benefits have been in the form of various types of reimbursement for commuting expenses, the use of company-owned vehicles for vanpooling, and free parking. However, except for free parking, employees have usually had taxable income as a result of these benefits. In order to increase the use of public transportation and decrease the reliance on the use of private passenger automobiles, the Comprehensive National Energy Policy Act of 1992 changed the tax rules governing transportation benefits. As a result of the act, the Internal Revenue Code provides favorable taxation to transportation benefits that meet the definition of a *qualified transportation fringe,* which includes the following:

- transportation in a commuter highway vehicle if such transportation is in connection with travel between the employee's residence and place of employment. The commuter vehicle must have a capacity of at least six adults other than the driver. In addition, at least 80 percent of the mileage use of the vehicle must reasonably be expected to be for transporting employees to and from work and occur when at least one-half of the seating capacity of the vehicle is filled. Traditional vanpools, in which one employee usually has possession of an employer-provided vehicle to drive other employees to work, come under this definition as long as these criteria are satisfied.

- transit passes. These include any pass, token, fare card, voucher, or similar item entitling a person to transportation as long as such transportation is on a mass transit facility or in a commuter highway vehicle as previously described.
- qualified parking. This includes parking provided on or near the business premises of the employer or near a location from which the employee commutes to work by using a mass transit facility or a commuter highway vehicle. Qualified parking does not include any parking on or near a premises used by the employee for residential purposes.

As long as a qualified transportation fringe is provided in addition to (and not in lieu of) any compensation otherwise payable to an employee, the value of the benefit is excluded from gross compensation up to the following amounts, which are subject to cost-of-living adjustments:

- $65 per month in the aggregate for any transit passes and transportation in a commuter highway vehicle
- $170 per month for qualified parking

Amounts in excess of the above and the value of employer transportation benefits that do not meet the definition of a qualified transportation fringe are fully taxable to employees.

Two additional points should be made about qualified benefits. First, they can be provided on a discriminatory basis. Second, the employer can either provide the benefits directly or give a cash reimbursement to the employee with one exception: cash reimbursement for a transit pass is not acceptable if such a pass is available for direct distribution by the employer to the employee.

Company Cars

Employers often provide employees with company cars (or other types of vehicles). In addition to using a vehicle for business purposes, an employee may also be allowed to use the car for commuting to and from work and for other personal purposes. However, an employee who drives a company car for personal use must include the value of this use in his or her taxable income.

The method for valuing the use of a car is determined by the employer, and several choices are available. The most common method for valuing the car is for the employer to report an annual cost that is a percentage of the car's annual lease value. This value is determined by a table prepared by the IRS and is based on a car's fair market value unless an employer can clearly justify a lower value. Under this table a car with a fair market value of $20,000 to $20,999 has an annual lease value of $5,600. This figure is then multiplied by the ratio of personal-use miles to total miles. For example, if 20 percent of the miles driven are personal miles, the employer must report $1,120 of income for the employee. Additional income must also be reported if the employer pays for gas.

A second alternative is for the employer to annually report the entire lease value of the car as taxable income. If the employer uses this alternative, the employee can claim an income tax deduction for any business use of the vehicle if the employee itemizes his or her deduction. However, the deduction is subject to the 2 percent floor requirement for miscellaneous deductions. This alternative is less favorable to the employee but administratively less burdensome to the employer.

A third alternative is to report a value that is based solely on the employee's use of the vehicle. Under IRS regulations a flat mileage rate may be used for each personal mile driven. The mileage rate, which is adjusted annually, is 31.5 cents in 1997. This alternative is available only if a car's fair market value does not exceed a specified value ($15,700 in 1997) and one of the following criteria is satisfied: (1) more than 50 percent of the car's use is for business, (2) the car is used each day in an employer-sponsored commuting pool, or (3) the car is driven at least 10,000 miles per year and is used primarily by employees.

The final alternative is available if the employer has a written policy that the employee must commute in the vehicle and cannot use the vehicle for other than minimal personal use. In this case the value of the car's use is $1.50 times the number of one-way commutes or $3 times the number of round-trip commutes.

Subsidized Eating Facilities

Employers often provide fully or partially subsidized eating facilities for employees. While lunch is the most commonly served meal, breakfast and dinner may also be served. Such facilities offer a place for employees to discuss common issues and may minimize the chance that employees will take prolonged lunch periods at off-site restaurants. The popularity of these facilities will tend to vary with the price of meals, the convenience of alternative places to eat, and the quality of the food served.

The subsidized value of meals served to employees is excluded from taxable income as long as the meals are (1) provided on the business premises and (2) furnished for the convenience of the employer. In general, meals are considered to be furnished for the employer's convenience if there are inadequate facilities in the area for employees to obtain meals within a reasonable period of time. If the requirements regarding the business premises and/or the convenience of the employer are not satisfied, the subsidized value of any meals consumed by employees is included in taxable income.

Employees are not allowed to deduct any portion of the cost they pay for individual meals. However, if an employee is required to have a fixed periodic charge for meals deducted from wages or salary (such as $15 per week), this amount is excluded from taxable income.

NOTE

1   United States Chamber of Commerce, *Employee Benefits*, 1996.

18

Group Benefit Plan Design and Administration

Chapter Outline

If either a single type of group insurance plan or an overall employee benefit plan is to be properly designed and managed, many questions must be answered. For example, should the plan reflect the wants of employees or the needs of employees as perceived by the employer? Should it have a probationary period for eligibility? Under what circumstances should the plan be self-insured? These questions are only subparts of six much broader issues:

- What are the employer's objectives?
- What types of benefits should be provided in the plan?
- What provisions for controlling costs should be contained in the plan?

- How should the plan be communicated to employees?
- How should the plan be funded?
- To what extent should administrative functions be outsourced?

The last question was discussed in the chapter on alternative funding methods and will not be discussed further. Most of the remaining questions have been touched upon throughout this book, but a more detailed discussion follows.

Unfortunately for those who like precise answers, plan design and management is an art rather than a science. However, decisions must be made. In some cases the advantages and disadvantages of the various answers to these questions must be weighed; in other cases compromises must be made when the answers to two or more questions conflict.

Too often the proper design of a group benefit plan is viewed as a one-time decision rather than as an evolving process. However, benefit plans that were appropriate for yesterday's workforce may not meet the needs of tomorrow's workforce. As times and organizations change, employers' answers to the questions raised in this chapter may also have to change. For this reason these issues must frequently be restudied to determine whether a group benefit plan is continuing to meet its desired purpose.

EMPLOYER'S OBJECTIVES

No benefit plan is properly designed unless it meets the employer's objectives. Although these objectives may be unclear or nonexistent, particularly in small firms, most large corporations have (and all firms should have) specific written objectives that have been approved by the board of directors (or by the owners of the firm). These objectives will vary for each individual organization, depending on such factors as size, location, industry, the results of collective bargaining, and the employer's philosophy. Without such objectives it is difficult for the agent, broker, benefit consultant, or third-party administrator to make recommendations or for the firm's benefit specialist to make decisions.

Types of Objectives

Objectives for benefit plans can be general and part of a firm's overall compensation objective (that is, cash and fringe benefits in the aggregate) in order to achieve a compensation package that is competitive within the firm's geographic area or industry. Such an "average" objective usually means that the firm wants both its wages and salaries and its fringe benefits to be similar to what the competition is offering its employees. There is usually little room for creativity in the design of a group benefit plan, unless the plans of the competition are quite diverse.

Some firms have separate objectives for cash compensation and employee benefits. For example, a growing firm may want its cash compensation to be competitive, but it may want its overall employee benefit plan to be above average in order to attract new employees. A difficulty for the plan designer with this type of objective is determining whether the firm wants all aspects of the employee benefit plan to be better than average, or whether it would be willing to accept, for example, an average program of group insurance benefits but a better-than-average pension plan and more vacation time for its employees. It should be noted that most objectives, even when they are much more detailed, tend to apply to employee benefits in the aggregate rather than to specific types of benefits.

It has become increasingly common for firms, particularly large ones, to maintain a lengthy and often detailed list of objectives for their employee benefit programs. The following are the objectives of one such firm:

- to establish and maintain an employee benefit program that is based primarily on the employees' needs for leisure time and protection against the risks of old age, loss of health, and loss of life
- to establish and maintain an employee benefit program that complements the efforts of employees in their own behalf
- to evaluate the employee benefit plan annually for its effect on employee morale and productivity, giving consideration to turnover, unfilled positions, attendance, employee complaints, and employee opinions
- to compare the employee benefit plan annually with that of other leading companies in the same field and to maintain a benefit plan with an overall level of benefits (based on cost per employee) that falls within the second quintile of these companies
- to maintain a level of benefits for nonunion employees that represents the same level of expenditures per employee as for union employees
- to determine annually the cost of new, changed, and existing programs as a percentage of salaries and wages; and to maintain this percentage as much as possible
- to self-fund benefits to the extent that long-run cost savings can be expected for the firm and catastrophic losses can be avoided
- to coordinate all benefits with social insurance programs to which the company makes payments
- to provide benefits on a noncontributory basis, except benefits for dependent coverage, for which employees should pay a portion of the cost
- to maintain continual communications with all employees concerning benefit programs

Most lists of objectives contain few, if any, specific details regarding what provisions or what types of benefits should be contained in an employee benefit plan. Rather, they establish guidelines—instead of specific performance goals—within which management must operate. For example, the objectives listed above indicate that this firm wants a plan that is understood and appreciated by employees and that is designed with employee opinion in mind. No mention, however, is made of how this is to be done. As will be seen later in this chapter, there may be alternative ways for this firm to achieve its objectives. Similarly the objectives establish guidelines for the cost of providing benefits. Although the firm wants to have a better-than-average plan, it does not want to be a leader. There is a very specific objective about what the relationship between the cost of benefits for union and nonunion employees should be. However, nothing is mentioned to indicate that the benefits for the two groups must also be identical. If the two groups have different needs, different types and levels of benefits may be desirable.

One additional point about employer objectives should be made. Often a firm's primary (and possibly only) objective is to establish an overall employee benefit plan that channels as large a portion of the benefits as possible to the owner or owners. Although this is a poor objective for an overall plan, it is a reality that must be recognized, most commonly in small firms or in firms that have few owners. Large, publicly held corporations sometimes wish to provide better benefits for their executives than for other employees. However, these extra benefits are likely to be provided under separate executive compensation plans, rather than under the benefit plan that applies to all employees.

Who Should Receive Benefits?

As part of establishing its objectives, an employer must determine its responsibilities to various categories of persons who might be eligible for coverage under the firm's overall benefit program. The list is much longer than one might initially think. It includes

- active full-time employees
- dependents of active full-time employees
- retired employees
- dependents of retired employees
- part-time employees
- dependents of part-time employees
- disabled employees
- dependents of disabled employees
- survivors of deceased employees
- employees who have terminated employment
- dependents of employees who have terminated employment
- employees who are temporarily separated from employment (for example, employees on family leave)
- dependents of employees who are temporarily separated from employment

Obviously most benefits are given to employees and some benefits are given to their dependents, such as medical expense coverage. Whether other groups on the list receive any benefits is a result of several factors. These include the attitude of the employer and the degree to which protection is available under other programs, such as social security. In addition, federal and state laws play a role. For example, some benefits must be continued because of family leave legislation. In addition, medical expense coverage must be continued in many cases as a result of COBRA. The extent to which benefits might be provided to each of these categories of persons has been touched upon throughout this book.

TYPES OF BENEFITS A PLAN SHOULD PROVIDE

A major decision for any employer is what types and levels of benefits to include in an overall employee benefit plan. For those few firms that do not have an employee benefit program, this decision involves choosing which benefits to offer initially. However, in most cases the decision is ongoing and involves either the offering of new or improved benefits or the redesigning of all or a major portion of the benefit plan. An objective of most employee benefit plans is to meet the "needs" of employees. But what are these needs? If they vary for different groups of employees, should different benefit plans be established? Or should a single plan be designed in which employees are allowed to choose from alternative benefits?

Determining Needs

Every employer wants its employees to appreciate the benefits that are provided. However, employers are becoming increasingly aware that employee benefit programs are failing to achieve this desired level of appreciation. To some extent this is due to the fact that as employee benefit plans have grown more comprehensive, employees have begun to take the benefits for granted. In addition, the growing consensus seems to be that the traditional methods of determining what types and levels of benefits to offer have lost much of their effectiveness. These include basing benefits on the following factors:

- the employer's perception of the employees' needs. This perception is largely based on the opinions of a firm's top management employees, whose compensation is much higher than that of the average employee. Therefore it is not surprising that many recent studies have shown that management's perception of employees' needs often differs from what the employees themselves feel they need.
- what competitors are doing. Too often the emphasis is placed on having an employee benefit package that is virtually identical to that of the competition, even though the makeup of the workforce may be different and the employees may have different needs.

- collectively bargained benefits. Many employers pattern their benefit plans for salaried employees after their negotiated plans for union employees. Again, the needs of salaried employees may be substantially different and may call for a totally different plan.
- tax laws and regulations. Benefit plans are often designed to include those benefits that are best suited to the high tax brackets of top executives. The average employee who is in a modest tax bracket may actually have a preference for certain benefits even though they will result in currently taxable income.

In the last few years, two trends have taken place. First, employers have increasingly taken a marketing-research approach to employee benefit planning. The employees' preferences for benefits are determined similarly to the way that consumers' demands for products are determined. For the most part this approach has been used only for nonunion employees, since benefits for union employees are decided by collective bargaining. However, some employers and some unions use this procedure as a guide in their negotiations over benefits for union employees. Second, employers have increasingly turned to a life-cycle approach to benefit planning.

The Use of Marketing Research

A marketing-research approach can be used for different purposes. Most often it is selected as a way to determine (1) how funds should be allocated to new types of benefits or (2) how funds should be used to improve current benefits. This can be for a one-time change in a firm's benefit plan or for changes that are implemented over time. In addition, a marketing-research approach can also help an employer to determine what alternative provisions employees would prefer regarding a specific type of benefit. For example, a firm that allocates additional funds to a long-term disability plan could determine whether employees would prefer a shorter waiting period or an increase in the size of the monthly benefit.

Marketing-research techniques must be used with caution. They can have a negative effect on employee morale unless the employer is committed to using the results of marketing research in benefit decision making. Therefore this approach should not be undertaken unless the employer intends to base expenditures for benefits on satisfying what employees perceive as their needs. In addition, employees must be made aware that changes in the employer's overall benefit program will be subject to financial constraints and possibly to trade-offs among benefits.

Although a variety of marketing-research techniques can be used in benefit planning, the techniques that employers most commonly choose fall into three major categories: personal interviews, simplified questionnaires, and sophisticated research methods.

Personal Interviews. Personal interviews with employees (either alone or in small groups) are probably the most effective marketing-research technique for a small firm or for a benefit program that is limited to a small number of employees. On this scale it is also usually the least expensive technique. An advantage of personal interviewing is that it can be used to collect the same type of information as both simplified questionnaires and sophisticated research techniques. Since it is important in personal interviewing for the employees to feel they can speak candidly, it may be desirable to have the interviews conducted by someone outside the firm and to hold group interviews without the supervisor's presence.

Simplified Questionnaires. A simplified questionnaire often has two major parts: one determines benefit preferences; the other determines demographic data (such as age, sex, marital status, years of service, and salary range). The questionnaire is called "simplified" because employees are basically asked only to indicate and/or rank their preferences. However, the actual analysis of the data that are gathered may be a complex task, and unless a firm is small, the analysis will probably require the use of a computer. It is important to use a clear, brief questionnaire that is not annoying to employees, so it is best that the questionnaire be initially given to a few employees in order to determine their reactions.

Figure 18-1 shows a sample of a part of a simplified questionnaire on benefit preferences. The example is typical of most questionnaires because it applies to a broad range of benefits and not just to group insurance. It should be noted that the questionnaire is essentially a structured one and is not open-ended. Employees are requested only to rank their preferences, and they are not given the opportunity to state whether each benefit is important or whether it should be improved. They are also required to make their preferences known regarding possible trade-offs between benefits and pay. Even though the questionnaire is structured, employees are still given the opportunity to make general comments. Such a feature should be incorporated into any questionnaire as a way of letting employees know that their opinions will be heard. It may also result in useful and sometimes surprising information for the employer

Sophisticated Research Methods. One difficulty with simplified question-naires, and to some extent personal interviews, is that they fail to measure the intensity of employees' preferences. Consequently some firms have used more sophisticated marketing-research techniques in an attempt to measure the degree of importance that employees place on various benefit alternatives. These more sophisticated research techniques are typically used only when specific alternatives have been formulated by the employer. Therefore they are often used as a follow-up to personal interviews and simplified questionnaires, and they frequently involve additional interviews and/or questionnaires.

FIGURE 18-1

Employee Benefit Questionnaire

1. In the right-hand column below rank the benefits from 1 to 7 in their importance to you and your family. Use 1 for the most important, 2 for the next most important, etc.

Benefit	Importance
Pension Plan	_____
Life Insurance	_____
Sick Pay	_____
Long-term Disability Income	_____
Medical Insurance	_____
Holidays	_____
Vacations	_____

2. To the list of benefits below add the two benefits you would most like to see added by this company. In the right-hand column rank the benefits listed according to their need for improvement or adoption. Use 1 for the benefit you feel should have the highest priority for improvement or adoption, 2 for the next highest, etc.

Benefit	Need for Improvement or Adoption
Pension Plan	_____
Life Insurance	_____
Sick Pay	_____
Long-term Disability income	_____
Medical Expense Insurance	_____
Holidays	_____
Vacations	_____
_____	_____
_____	_____

3. How would you prefer that additional funds for benefits be used? (check one)
   _____Improve or add benefit programs.
   _____Reduce currently required employee contributions.

4. Which of the following statements reflects your opinion? (check one)
   _____More emphasis should be placed on improving wages and salaries and less on improving benefits.
   _____More emphasis should be placed on improving benefits and less on improving wages and salaries.
   _____The same emphasis as in the past should be placed on improving both benefits and wages and salaries.

5. Please use the back of this form to make any additional comments you feel will be of use to the company in its desire to improve the employee benefit programs.

Figure 18-2 illustrates one example of how preferences might be measured with a questionnaire.

FIGURE 18-2

Employee Benefit Questionnaire

The following benefit changes are being considered for adoption by this company in the next fiscal year. Although the company is committed to making improvements in its benefit package, financial considerations dictate that only some of these proposed changes can be adopted at that time. The first item on the list has been given a "value" of 100. Please rank the other items in their relative importance to you. For example, if item 2 is 3 times as important, it should be given a value of 300. If it is only half as important, it should be given a value of 50.

Proposed Change	*Value*
1. Increase lifetime major medical maximum from $500,000 to $1 million.	100
2. Eliminate employee contributions to long-term disability coverage.	_____
3. Increase life insurance coverage from 1 1/2 to 2 times base earnings.	_____
4. Add Columbus Day to list of holidays.	_____
5. Increase the annual number of sick days from 10 to 12.	_____

Once the information is gathered, the firm must decide which benefits to adopt, based on employees' preferences and other cost and administrative considerations. For example, assume that the firm using the questionnaire is willing to spend up to $400 annually per employee to improve its benefit package. Also assume that the figures in table 18-1 represent the average importance of each proposed benefit to employees, as well as the expected annual cost per employee of providing each benefit.

It is clear that the employees feel the second proposed change (which has an annual cost of $200 per employee) is most important by a substantial margin, so it will most likely be adopted. However, it is difficult to determine what other benefit or benefits will be offered. The last proposed change will definitely not be made because only $200 per employee remains for additional benefit changes. The firm is therefore faced with two alternatives—either add Columbus Day as a holiday or increase both the life insurance coverage and the major medical lifetime maximum. Because the average importance of each alternative to employees is 240, and only one can be made within the cost constraint, the

TABLE 18-1		
Change	Average Value	Annual Cost per Employee
1	100	$100
2	310	200
3	140	100
4	240	200
5	190	250

deciding factor will hinge on other considerations. The firm may look at the administrative aspects of each change or the effect of inflation on long-range costs. The firm may also analyze the data in terms of the demographic characteristics of employees. For example, long-time employees may have a slight preference for the insurance benefits, while younger employees would like the extra holiday. If the firm wishes to favor the older employees, it will change the insurance benefits; if morale is low among younger employees, it might decide to add the holiday instead.

These other considerations may also be the deciding factor for employers even when employee preferences are clear. However, if employees are led to believe that their preferences will be the primary consideration, other considerations should be weighed only when there are modest differences in employee preferences.

Life-Cycle Benefits

The design of employee benefit plans traditionally focused solely on providing active employees with protection against the financial consequences of illness, disability, retirement, and death. Over time other types of benefits began to be offered, but plan design tended to focus on the employee's being part of a traditional family. Over the last two decades, the demographic makeup of the workforce has changed dramatically. As a result, many employers are frequently taking a life-cycle approach to benefit planning. While the traditional benefits are still part of the core of most overall employee benefit plans, employers are increasingly designing benefit plans with the realization that benefit needs may differ for males and females, and may differ when employees are single, when they have and raise children, when they care for elderly parents, and when they retire.

Intuition would lead one to believe that a life-cycle benefit plan would increase costs because it would tend to provide benefits that would be used by all categories of employees. To some extent this may be true. However, many employers who have taken this approach feel that additional costs are minimal and/or result in offsetting cost savings. For example, flexible work schedules that allow employees to better take care of dependents may cost little or nothing. Other benefits may result in significant cost savings due to less absenteeism and lower employee turnover. In addition, an employer may pass the majority of the cost of some benefits on to the employees who use them. For example, an employer may establish a day care center but charge a fee for its use to offset some of its operating costs. An employer may also make a voluntary long-term care insurance plan available on a payroll-deduction basis. Finally, employees may not automatically have all benefits; they might have to elect the benefits they want with a predetermined amount of employer funds under a cafeteria plan.

Many of the benefits employees want at various stages in their lives are probably fairly obvious. However, many employers use questionnaires and personal interviews to determine these varying needs. One employer, in designing its life-cycle benefit plan, used the life-cycle stages shown in table 18-2 and found the benefits indicated to be some of those of particular value to persons in that category.

TABLE 18-2

Life-Cycle Stage	Desired Benefit
Young, unmarried workers	Extra vacation Fitness programs
Newlyweds	Marriage leave
Employees in childbearing years	Prenatal courses Parental leave Adoption assistance
Workers during child-rearing years	Day care centers Flexible work schedules
Employees dealing with divorce	Legal assistance
Workers in eldercare years	Long-term care insurance Support groups
Retirees	Medicare supplements Retiree job banks Preretirement counseling
Employees facing death	Grief counseling Funeral leave

Different Plans

From an administrative standpoint it is easiest for a firm to have a single employee benefit plan that applies to all employees. Nevertheless, some firms have different plans for different groups of employees, especially when the benefits for union employees are determined by collective bargaining. If the benefits for the union employees are provided through a negotiated trusteeship, a separate plan must be designed for the nonunion employees. The employer must then decide whether to play "follow the leader" and provide identical benefits to the nonunion employees or to design a plan that reflects their different needs. When benefits are provided through a negotiated trusteeship, the employer is more likely to develop a "different" plan for nonunion employees than when the employer is required to provide benefits to union employees through group insurance contracts that are purchased by the employer. Under these circumstances employers often find it simpler administratively to purchase a single contract that covers all employees.

Even when unions are not involved, an employer may still decide to have different plans for different groups of employees. Usually one plan will be limited to hourly employees, another to salaried employees. In addition, a plan that offers supplemental benefits to top management may also be provided (but it will often be publicized only to those employees who are eligible for these benefits). Some firms that have employees in different parts of the country have also found it desirable to provide somewhat different benefits at some or all locations in order to remain locally competitive. Different plans also typically exist for retired employees and other categories of persons who are not active full-time employees or their dependents.

Having different plans for different groups of employees is not without its disadvantages. Administrative costs are usually increased, communications with employees become more difficult, and resentment can occur if one group of employees feels its benefit plan is inferior to that of another group. To minimize this latter possibility, some firms have designed their plans so that an overall comparison is difficult. Each plan will have its own positive and negative features when examined next to the plans for other groups of employees.

Different plans can also result by giving choices to employees. For example, one group of employees may elect an HMO or PPO option, while another group may elect coverage under a traditional medical expense plan. A trend in recent years has been the growth of cafeteria plans. Because of their popularity and complexity, a separate chapter is devoted to them.

PLAN PROVISIONS FOR CONTROLLING COSTS

Employers have always been concerned about the costs of providing employee benefits. Traditionally this concern has led to plan provisions that transfer these costs to employees rather than reduce them. These provisions include probationary periods, benefit limitations, and contributory financing.

Many recent attempts to control costs have been directed primarily toward the rapidly increasing costs of medical care, and for the most part these cost-containment provisions have been designed to reduce administrative and claim costs without transferring them to employees. Since methods for controlling the costs of medical expenses are discussed throughout earlier chapters, they will not be discussed here. Rather, the focus is on provisions and activities that can be used with all types of benefit plans.

Probationary Periods

Probationary periods reduce costs to employers because any claims that employees incur during this time must be borne by the employees themselves. In addition, probationary periods reduce the adverse selection that would most likely exist without their use. Administrative costs are also minimized for employees who terminate employment shortly after being hired. However, probationary periods do impose hardship on newer employees who incur claims but find themselves without benefits. (Employees can minimize these hardships by proper use of COBRA and temporary medical expense policies.) Primarily for competitive reasons in attracting employees, the use and length of probationary periods, particularly in medical expense plans, have been decreasing except in high turnover situations.

Benefit Limitations

Benefit limitations in the form of deductibles, coinsurance, maximum benefits, and exclusions for certain types of expenses are common in medical expense insurance. However, some of these techniques can also be used in other types of insurance, as in the following examples:

- the limiting of benefits to a maximum percentage of income in disability income plans. In addition to reducing the amount of the benefits paid by the employer, a maximum percentage also minimizes the possibility of feigned and unnecessarily prolonged disabilities.
- the setting of maximum benefits under dental plans for expenses such as orthodontics. There is little doubt that the availability of benefits will encourage treatment of orthodontic conditions, particularly when the treatment is primarily sought for cosmetic reasons. There is also the feeling that dentists will encourage the treatment of relatively minor conditions if a patient has coverage for orthodontics.

Contributory Financing

Many benefit plans require each employee to pay a portion of the premium costs for his or her own coverage. This may lower the employer's costs and/or may enable the employer to use these saved dollars to provide additional or improved benefits. There are several arguments both for and against contributory financing, but in many instances it is a moot point, since the decision is determined by collective bargaining or competition.

When contributory financing is used for benefits other than pension plans, employees are generally able to voluntarily elect or decline coverage. To the extent that some employees decline coverage, the costs to the employer will be further lowered. However, this savings may be offset by the adverse selection that can result because of those who did elect coverage. Furthermore, having the option to decline coverage could mean that employees or their dependents will be without coverage should a loss occur. Finally, there tend to be greater administrative costs associated with a contributory plan than with a noncontributory plan.

Advocates of contributory plans feel that sharing in the cost will increase the employees' awareness and appreciation of both the plan and the contribution the employer is making. However, this opinion can be countered by the argument that payroll deductions for benefits are a source of employee dissatisfaction since they may view the employer as "cheap" for not paying the entire cost of the plan.

Although there are no empirical studies to support the contention, it has been argued that employees are less likely to misuse medical and dental benefits under a contributory plan, because they realize that such misuse will probably lead to an increase in their future contributions.

Contributory financing can be used to encourage desired employee behavior. Employees who elect a managed care plan in lieu of a traditional medical expense plan often have a smaller contribution toward the cost of their coverage or possibly no contribution at all. In many cases, this lower contribution is determined by the cost savings to the employer. For example, if the cost of coverage to an employer for an unmarried employee is $150 under an HMO and $200 under an indemnity plan, the employee who elects the indemnity plan will be required to pay $50 more per month than an employee who elects the HMO. This alone will encourage many employees to elect the managed care plan. However, employers who want to encourage managed care because it tends to have lower annual cost increases might actually make the differential larger, perhaps $75.

Cost Containment

Recent attempts to control benefit costs have concentrated on either reducing the size of claims or minimizing the administrative costs associated with benefit plans. Rather than transfer the costs to employees, these techniques try to lower costs, or to at least lower the rate at which costs are increasing. Although employers are concerned primarily with their own costs, some of the advantages of this cost containment will affect the employees in the form of increased benefits or a lower rate of increase for the employees' own out-of-pocket expenses.

Other than provisions or practices associated solely with medical expense plans, the following is a list of some of the more common cost-containment techniques that employers are currently using:

- alternative funding methods that lower administrative costs and improve cash flow
- competitive bidding among insurance companies and third-party administrators that lowers administrative costs
- wellness programs and employee-assistance plans that reduce future claims

BENEFIT PLAN COMMUNICATION

Traditionally employers have placed a low priority on the communication of their benefit plans to employees. They have taken the attitude that employees appreciated any benefits given to them. The little information that was made available tended to be only the literature that the insurance companies providing the coverage had prepared.

Over the last few years this situation has changed dramatically. Federal law requires employers to disclose a substantial amount of information to employees about their benefit plans. In addition, employers have come to realize that many employees take their benefits for granted, that they fail to realize the value of these benefits to themselves and their families, and that they are unaware of the employer's dollar outlay.

Not only will effective communication solve this problem, it may also minimize the dissatisfaction that arises from misunderstandings about the benefit program, and it may reduce turnover to the extent that employees realize the true value of their benefits. Employers have also learned that effective communication is necessary to obtain employee support if cost-containment efforts are to be successful.

Finally, benefit communication is increasingly important as employees are given more choice with regard to their own benefits. This is occurring as more employees have alternative medical expense plans, cafeteria plans, and retirement plans allowing investment choices.

Most benefit consultants feel that an effective communication program should have four primary objectives:

- to create an awareness and appreciation of the way current benefits improve employees' financial security
- to provide a high level of understanding about available benefits
- to encourage the wise use of benefits
- to comply with legal requirements

Effective Communication

Employees will obtain information about benefits in some manner. Without an effective communications program, an employee is likely to rely on the grapevine, which often provides incomplete and inaccurate information. Good communication rarely just happens. Rather, it requires the employer to have objectives in a manner similar to that used for benefit plan design. While any list of objectives is likely to include the clear and concise dissemination of information about current benefits, other objectives may change over time. For example, an employer may want to encourage employees to switch to a managed care plan.

Depending on the circumstance, communication may be ongoing or on a one-time basis. In either case, benefit consultants feel that it is important for employers to design communication materials so that employees are told that they and their needs are important to the firm, that the employer cares what employees think about benefits, and that the employer wants employees to understand their benefits. A successful long-run communication program also has a method for obtaining feedback so that the employer can determine the effectiveness of its communication. Steps can be taken to rectify inadequate information, and past experience can be of value in designing future communications.

Several factors can complicate the communication process. For example, an employer may have different plans for different groups of employees and therefore may have to design alternative communication strategies. While it may be possible to have the strategies be somewhat similar, the sophistication levels of the employee groups may call for an entirely different approach. A similar problem may occur if an employer has multiple locations. In addition, employers must take the needs of non-English-speaking employees into consideration.

Whatever form a communication plan may take, communication specialists recommend that several basic factors be present:

- The communication should be written in a style that is clear and understandable. Legalese and benefit jargon should be avoided.
- The communication should make it clear what a benefit means to an employee. For example, if an employer is trying to encourage enrollment in a managed care plan, the lack of any deductibles and copayments should be emphasized.
- The communication should explain why changes are being made. The effectiveness of the communication is likely to be lessened if an employer is not open and honest. Too many employers fail to realize that employees are smart enough to read between the lines of communication that is less than forthright.
- The communication should make use of graphics and examples. Too often communication that lacks these features is boring and therefore less effective.

Methods of Communication

The communication of benefit plans to employees is now regarded as a highly sophisticated task. No single method of communication is likely to accomplish all the desired objectives, so several methods must be combined. To meet these objectives, many employers hire communications experts who generally report to the person responsible for employee benefits. Other employers use the services of benefit-consulting firms, many of which have developed specialized units for advising their clients in this particular area. Benefit plans can be communicated to employees in audiovisual presentations, in face-to-face meetings, through printed materials, and more recently with interactive communication through telephones and computers.

Audiovisual Presentations

Audiovisual presentations are a very effective way to communicate benefit plans to new employees or to explain significant changes in existing benefit plans to current employees. It is much easier to require employees to view audiovisual presentations than to read printed materials. In addition, if properly done, audiovisual presentations can convey the employer's concern for the well-being of its employees, and they can explain proper benefit use more effectively than printed materials. In the past many audiovisual presentations have been dull and sometimes uninformative. Recently, however, many employers have adopted more sophisticated communications methods, and they view these presentations, if not their entire communication program, as a way of "advertising" their employee benefit plans. In fact, some employers have actually hired advertising firms to design not only their audiovisual programs but other aspects of their communication program as well.

Meetings with Employees

Face-to-face meetings with employees can also be an effective way to explain employee benefit plans and to answer employee questions. For small employers this technique is generally used to present benefit plans to new employees or to explain the changes in existing plans. Large employers often combine meetings with audiovisual presentations. It is obvious that whoever conducts these meetings (be it the employer, agent, broker, consultant, or group representative) must be truly knowledgeable about the plan. In addition, it is just as important that he or she be able to effectively communicate this knowledge to the employees.

The number of employees who attend a meeting may determine its effectiveness. A large meeting may be satisfactory if its purpose is primarily to present information. However, a series of small meetings may be more manageable and appropriate if employee opinions or questions are being solicited. These smaller-sized meetings can be used in lieu of a large meeting or as follow-up meetings to a large group presentation. When employees must make decisions regarding their benefit plans, meetings with individual employees may also be necessary.

Group meetings can be used for other purposes besides explaining new or changed benefit plans. They can be held periodically to reexplain benefits, to answer employee questions, or to listen to employee concerns and suggestions. However, every employer should also have a procedure by which employees can have ready access to a "knowledgeable" person when they have any problems to discuss or questions to ask. Although this can often be accomplished by telephone, face-to-face meetings should be used when necessary.

The employer's attitude toward a group meeting can influence its effectiveness. Employers should not regard these meetings as necessary formalities, but rather they should view them as a way to communicate their concern about the security of their employees and the benefits with which they are provided. The success of face-to-face meetings may also depend to some degree on their time and location. To achieve maximum employee interest and attention, the facilities should be comfortable and not overcrowded. In addition, meetings should be held during normal working hours, not at the end of the working day, when many employees may be concerned about whether the meeting will end on time.

Printed Materials

Virtually every employer provides employees with some printed materials about their employee benefit plans. At a minimum this material consists of group insurance certificates and the information that is required to be distributed under the disclosure provisions of ERISA. The next most commonly provided source of information is the benefit handbook. If there is a typical benefit handbook, it can best be described as a reference book that summarizes the benefit plans that are available to all employees. In addition to describing group insurance benefits, it will include information about an organization's retirement plan, vacation policy, and possibly other benefits (such as educational assistance). Each plan will be described in terms of eligibility, benefits, and what employee contributions are required.

Traditionally these benefit handbooks merely described each benefit plan separately; they did not discuss the relationship between the various benefit plans or the availability of certain social insurance benefits. Newer benefit handbooks are more likely to focus on the potential causes of lost income to an employee or his or her family. For example, rather than discuss short-term and long-term disability income plans separately, they will include a single section on disability income that describes how a short-term disability plan will initially pay benefits and at what point it will be replaced by the long-term disability plan and social security.

Because of the general nature of benefit handbooks, many employers also give each employee a *personalized benefit statement,* usually on an annual basis.

Some employers feel that employees will better appreciate the value of their benefits if they are aware of the magnitude of the cost to the employer. Figure 18-3 is an example of one form that is used for reporting this information. However, the most common form of personalized benefit statement specifies the plans for which the employee is eligible and what benefits are available to that particular employee (or his or her family) under each of these plans. Figure 18-4 shows a portion of one such statement.

FIGURE 18-3

BENEFIT STATEMENT REVIEW FOR

_____

Many of us forget that there is more to our paycheck than the amount we take home. The following are the "extras" that were provided in 19___ and their value as determined by the cost to your employer.

		Annual Value	Value per Hour
(1)	Social Security (employer's contribution)	$_____	$_____
(2)	Workers' Compensation Insurance Premium	_____	_____
(3)	State Unemployment Insurance Premium	_____	_____
(4)	Paid Holidays	_____	_____
(5)	Vacation Days	_____	_____
(6)	Pension	_____	_____
(7)	Salary Continuation	_____	_____
(8)	Long-term Disability Income Insurance	_____	_____
(9)	Life Insurance	_____	_____
(10)	Medical Expense Insurance (employer's contribution)	_____	_____
(11)	Others		
	_____	_____	_____
	_____	_____	_____

The $_____ value of those sometimes forgotten benefits is equal to _____% of the $_____ you received as salary or wages in 19___. These benefits are provided to protect you and your family from certain financial risks and to help provide for your future retirement.

FIGURE 18-4

PERSONAL STATEMENT OF BENEFITS

This Personal Statement of Benefits lists the benefits that both protect you and your family now and provide security for your future. We know you will find this statement informative, and we hope it will be useful in your personal planning.

Health Care Benefits

You have elected coverage for
☐ yourself   ☐ your family   ☐ You have not elected coverage

The highlights of your Comprehensive Medical Plan are summarized in the following table. See your employee handbook for further details.

In-Hospital Benefits	Out-of-Hospital Benefits	Special Benefits
$100 deductible per person each calendar year (3-deductible maximum per family)		100% of outpatient emergency treatment of accidental injury (no deductible)
100% of covered expenses, including maternity care, after the deductible is met	80% of first $3,000 of covered expenses, then 100% of remaining covered expenses	
	50% of psychiatric treatment ($30-a-visit maximum benefit)	100% of diagnostic X-ray and laboratory tests (deductible applies)

Overall Plan Maximum: $1,000,000 per Person

Disability Income Benefits

Salary Continuation Plan
- Your full salary continues for _____ weeks, then 3/4 of your salary continues for _____ weeks.

Long-term Disability Income Plan
- If disabled over 26 weeks, you will receive _____ a month. This is 60 percent of your base pay and includes benefits under the corporation's plan and any social security benefits, other than family benefits, for which you are eligible.
- If you have eligible dependents you can receive additional family benefits under social security up to _____ a month.

If total long-term disability income from the above sources exceeds 80 percent of your base pay, disability benefits under the corporation's plan will be reduced to bring the total to the 70 percent level.

Other types of printed information (such as company newsletters, personal letters to employees at home, or notices in pay envelopes) may also be of value. This may be the simplest and least expensive way of announcing benefit changes that need little explanation (such as an increase in the daily hospital room-and-board benefit). They are also an effective way to advertise or remind employees about the wellness programs that are available or what cost-containment provisions are included in their medical expense coverage. Experience has shown that without occasional reminders, the use of these programs and provisions by employees will decrease.

Vendors of employee benefit products and services may also make printed materials available for distribution to employees.

Interactive Voice-Response Systems

Employers are increasingly turning to newer technologies to communicate and manage benefit plans. One of these technologies is the telephone and the use of interactive voice-response systems. At one extreme, a telephone system can be as simple as merely giving information to all employees about such matters as times for employee meetings, enrollment deadlines, and plan changes. However, this use of the telephone requires all employees to have either a telephone or some alternative method to receive the information. From this point, telephone systems can get increasingly complex. At the next level, the system can allow employees, through a menu of options, to request general information and materials such as enrollment forms. Carried even further, the system can enable employees to obtain specific information about their own benefits, such as the amount of life insurance they have or the balance in their 401(k) account. Of course, if personal information is available, employees will need to be given a personal identification number to access the information. At the most complex extreme, telephones can be used to allow employees to make benefit elections and changes. For example, an employee may be able to change investment options for a 401(k) plan or to change from one medical expense plan to another during open enrollment periods.

There are both advantages and disadvantages to the use of telephone systems for benefit communication. Among the advantages are

- They can be designed to allow employee access on a 24-hour basis.
- They enable employees to get quick and accurate responses.
- They make it possible for employees to maintain a degree of anonymity without having to disclose information to in-house personnel.
- They allow human resources personnel to spend more time on issues other than routine phone inquiries.

However, there are also drawbacks and limitations, some of which can be overcome with proper planning and design:

- There is a lack of human interaction. This by itself will turn off some employees to using the telephone system if they can obtain the same information and perform the same transactions by calling someone personally. If the telephone system is the only way that employees can request certain information or initiate certain transactions, it is important that a new system be well publicized and possibly established in small increments. A well-designed system will be simple to use and not leave employees in an endless maze of pushing buttons. It will also give employees a method to reach a real person when they feel it is necessary to speak to one.
- Telephone systems can become increasingly expensive as they are expanded to allow employees a wider range of options. For some firms, the cost may outweigh the benefits.
- To the extent employees can make benefit changes and elections by merely pushing a button, there is the possibility of mistakes being made. Therefore it is necessary for the telephone response system to confirm all transactions over the phone and allow employees to enter needed corrections. In addition, a written confirmation should be sent to employees, possibly requiring the return of a signed copy of the confirmation.
- Telephone systems are not conducive to inputting data such as the name of a new dependent for purposes of obtaining medical expense coverage.

Computers

While telephone systems can be used effectively for obtaining information and simple benefit plan enrollments, computers enable employers to use technology to a much greater extent. Computerized benefit systems can either be on employees' personal computers at their work stations or on computer terminals located at centralized stations. By pressing the appropriate key an employee can get a general description of the company's various plans. By inputting appropriate data (including an identification number) an employee may also be able to obtain information about his or her own particular situation. For example, an employee could determine his or her potential disability income or retirement benefit. An employee may also be able to obtain the answers to "what if" questions. For example, if I contribute $100 per month to a 401(k) plan that is expected to earn 7 percent annually, how much will I have at age 65? Or if I elect these options under a cafeteria plan, will any additional employer dollars remain for other benefits, or will I have to make an additional contribution through a payroll deduction?

As the last question indicates, the use of computers can facilitate the administration of a cafeteria plan. In fact, some employers are actually using the computer to make benefit selections. To have some verification in writing, a form is either printed on the spot for an employee to sign and return or generated in the personnel office, reviewed, and sent to the employee for signing.

Computers also facilitate data input, such as the name of a new beneficiary for life insurance coverage or the name of a new spouse who is being added to an employee's medical expense coverage.

Computers can be used to educate employees as well as provide benefit information. For example, employees can be given information comparing the pros and cons of a managed care plan to a traditional indemnity plan. Employees can also be given information to help them in their overall personal financial planning. With the capabilities to use sound and graphics, computers can be used to provide education that is not only informative but also fun to use.

Finally, employers are beginning to use computers to disseminate legally required information, such as summary plan descriptions.

Many of the same advantages and disadvantages of using telephone systems also apply to the use of computers. The major drawback to a computerized benefit system is cost in relation to return on investment. Moreover, the success of such a system requires a high level of technical competence at the human resources and management information systems levels.

BENEFIT OUTSOURCING

Historically, most organizations have fully administered their benefit programs with their own employees. However, it has not been unusual for an organization to outsource some administrative functions to other parties. For example, third-party administrators have been used to administer self-funded medical expense plans, and actuaries have been used to perform some of the compliance functions for qualified retirement plans.

More recently there has been a significant increase in the outsourcing of employee benefit administration, with estimates indicating that between 40 and 50 percent of all employers currently use outsourcing to some degree. Surveys also indicate that another 15 to 20 percent of employers are actively exploring the use of outsourcing. In the last portion of this chapter, the reasons for outsourcing are identified. In addition, the types of functions commonly outsourced and the types of vendors used for outsourcing are described. Finally, the factors that must be considered when entering into a contract for outsourcing are discussed.

Reasons for Outsourcing

There are many reasons why an employer might decide to outsource benefit administration. The most common reason is that the organization lacks the technical and regulatory expertise to perform many of the necessary functions. For example, few employers have a staff with the expertise to perform actuarial calculations or utilization reviews. Functions of this nature are best left to firms that have a staff of specialists in these areas. Closely correlated with this reason is the desire of firms to seek more value for the dollars spent on benefits. While outsourcing costs money, it is often cheaper than performing the same functions in house. Some of this savings is because of the high cost of the hardware and software that is increasingly needed. An outside vendor can spread this cost over many customers.

Better service to employees is also an often cited reason for outsourcing. Vendors frequently have 800 numbers and a staff that specializes in specific benefit functions. Persons who answer telephones are typically trained to have the ability to handle 90 percent or more of the inquiries they receive. But more important, they have the ability to transfer the more complex calls to the appropriate person to handle the issue.

Another cited reason for outsourcing is that the organization should focus its attention on the firm's core activities. Outsourcing enables a firm to lower the size of the staff that administers its benefits or at least have the staff remain stable or grow more slowly in an era when benefit administration is becoming increasingly complex.

Functions Outsourced

Significant variations exist with respect to the benefit functions that are outsourced. Systems, staff, or both can be outsourced. Systems outsourcing refers to the use of an outsourcing organization's computer and other systems while retaining an in-house staff to perform administrative functions. Staff outsourcing refers to the outsourcing of people but the continued use of the organization's systems.

Outsourcing can also be classified as either partial or full. With partial outsourcing, an employer uses an outsourcing organization's personnel and/or staff for some benefit functions but continues other functions in house. The term *full outsourcing* refers to those situations where most benefit functions are outsourced. Even with full outsourcing, some functions, such as financial management of benefit plans and benefit plan design, remain the responsibility of senior personnel at the firm.

Most employers use partial outsourcing. Among the most common functions to be outsourced are

- COBRA administration
- administration of medical and dental claims
- utilization review
- vision care programs
- record keeping of defined-benefit pension plans
- record keeping and administration of defined-contribution retirement plans
- record keeping and administration of flexible spending accounts

- preretirement planning
- benefit communication

Vendors Used for Outsourcing

Many types of organizations operate as vendors for outsourcing. In addition, employers who outsource may use several vendors because vendors often specialize in a limited number of activities. In fact, some vendors are very specialized. For example, some vendors may specialize in only one type of benefit such as vision care.

The major providers of outsourcing services include benefit consulting firms, insurance companies, stock brokerage firms, mutual funds, and third-party administrators. Stock brokerage firms and mutual funds tend to be involved almost solely in functions relating to retirement plans. While the other vendors often engage in a wide variety of activities, they may also specialize in a limited number of outsourcing services. For example, benefit consulting firms frequently focus their activities on regulatory compliance, eligibility determination, and enrollment.

Recently a small number of large organizations have been marketing themselves as having the ability to provide complete outsourcing for an employer. The number of firms that do all their outsourcing with only one vendor is still very small but likely to grow.

The Decision to Outsource

The decision to outsource is not a simple task. An organization must determine what functions should be outsourced and what functions can best be performed in house. Consideration also needs to be given to the firm's personnel. Outsourcing often involves working with computers and other systems. It is important that people with expertise in these areas be involved. In addition, the help of the internal benefit staff is vital. However, their assistance may be affected by the fact—either real or perceived—that outsourcing may result in the loss of their jobs.

Once a vendor has been selected to provide an outsourcing service, the process of changing vendors can be complex and expensive. Therefore a high degree of care should go into the vendor-selection process. There should also be contingency plans for changing vendors if that need arises.

A formal outsourcing process begins with a request for proposal (RFP) in which vendors are asked to bid to provide services. The RFP should clearly spell out the goals of outsourcing and identify the major responsibilities of the potential parties to an outsourcing contract.

The outsourcing contract itself needs to clearly establish responsibilities of both the vendor and the employer but yet be flexible enough to address situations that may arise in the future. Proper planning must be done with respect to data to make sure data important to the employer are not destroyed by the vendor—for example, while converting the data to the vendor's systems. It is also important for the employer to be able to retrieve data if the contract with the vendor terminates.

A good outsourcing contract (at least from the employer's standpoint) will contain performance guarantees. These guarantees may relate to factors such as timeliness, accuracy, productivity improvements, and employee complaints.

Since the primary purpose of outsourcing is to save money in the long run, it is also very important to address vendor compensation. The contract should not be so open-ended that unforeseen costs are automatically passed on to the employer. Even fixed-price contracts may prove to be expensive if a firm downsizes, but the vendor gets the same compensation for servicing a smaller number of employers.

Some other issues that must be addressed include confidentiality and security of data, vendor responsibility for systems upgrades and employer responsibility to pay for them, insurance and/or bonding requirements, and procedures for resolving disputes among the parties.

19

Cafeteria Plans

Chapter Outline

For several years some organizations have had benefit plans that give a limited number of key executives some choice in the selection of types and levels of employee benefits that will be provided with employer contributions. Although many organizations have benefit programs in which optional or supplemental benefits may be elected by all (or many) employees, the cost of these benefits must normally be borne by the employees on an aftertax, payroll-deduction basis. With the possible exception of an HMO option, employees have no choice about how employer dollars will be spent.

In the past few years, many organizations have established benefit programs in which all (or almost all) the employees can design their own benefit packages by purchasing benefits with a prespecified amount of employer dollars from a number of available options. Generally these *cafeteria plans* (often referred to as flexible benefit plans or cafeteria compensation plans) also allow additional benefits to be purchased on a payroll-deduction basis. Today it is estimated that more than 25 percent of employers with more than 500 employees have a full-fledged cafeteria plan. Most of these employers and many smaller employers offer premium-conversion plans and/or flexible spending accounts.

THE RATIONALE FOR CAFETERIA PLANS

The growth in employee benefits has caused two problems. First, some employers feel that many employees do not recognize and appreciate the magnitude of their employee benefits because, as benefits increase, employee appreciation often seems to decrease. Advocates of cafeteria plans argue that by giving employees a stated dollar amount with which they must select their own benefits (from a list of options), employees will become more aware of the actual cost of these benefits and will be more likely to appreciate the benefits they choose.

A second problem is that the inflexible benefit structure of conventional employee benefit plans does not adequately meet the various benefit needs of all employees, often leading to employee dissatisfaction. For example, single employees often resent the medical coverage that married employees receive for their families, since the single employees receive no benefit of corresponding value. Similarly employees who have no dependents often see little value in life insurance and would prefer other benefits. Those who favor the concept of cafeteria plans feel that such dissatisfaction can be minimized if employees have the option to select their own benefits. Advocates of cafeteria plans hope that this increased employee satisfaction will result in a better employee-retention record and in greater ability to attract new employees.

Some employers see the cafeteria approach to benefit planning as an opportunity to control the escalating benefit costs associated with inflation and with the new requirements of recently enacted federal and state legislation. Since a cafeteria plan is essentially a defined-contribution plan rather than a defined-benefit plan, it provides a number of opportunities for controlling increases in costs. For example, it may encourage employees to choose medical expense options that have larger deductibles or a greater degree of managed care so they can more efficiently use the fixed number of dollars allotted to them under the plan. A cafeteria plan may also enable the employer to pass on to the employees any increased benefit costs that result from having to comply with legislation that mandates additional benefits. In addition, since increases in employer contributions for optional benefits are not directly related to increases in benefit costs, the employer can grant percentage increases in the amounts available for benefits that are less than the actual overall increase in employee benefit costs.

It should be noted that early cafeteria plans were designed primarily to meet the varying needs of employees. In contrast, newer plans are much more likely to be instituted as a cost-saving technique.

THE NATURE OF CAFETERIA PLANS

In its purest sense a cafeteria plan can be defined as any employee benefit plan that allows an employee to have some choice in designing his or her own benefit package by selecting different types or levels of benefits that are funded with employer dollars. At this extreme a benefit plan that allows an employee to select an HMO as an option to an insured medical expense plan can be classified as a cafeteria plan. However, the more common use of the term *cafeteria plan* denotes something much broader—a plan in which choices can be made among several different types of benefits and possibly cash.

Prior to the addition of Sec. 125 to the Internal Revenue Code in 1978, the use of cafeteria plans had potentially adverse tax consequences for an employee. If an employee had a choice among benefits that were normally nontaxable (such as medical expense insurance or disability income insurance) and benefits that were normally taxable (such as life insurance in excess of $50,000 or cash), then the doctrine of constructive receipt would result in an employee's being taxed as if he or she had elected the maximum taxable benefits that could have been obtained under the plan. Therefore if an employee could elect cash in lieu of being covered under the employer's medical expense plan, an employee who elected to remain in the medical expense plan would have taxable income merely because cash could have been elected. Obviously this tax environment was not conducive to the use of cafeteria plans unless the only benefits they offered were normally of a nontaxable nature.

Permissible Benefits

Currently Sec. 125 of the Code defines a cafeteria plan as a written plan under which all participants are employees and under which all participants may choose between two or more benefits consisting of (1) *qualified benefits* and (2) cash. Qualified benefits essentially include any welfare benefits excluded from taxation under the Internal Revenue Code except scholarships and fellowships, transportation benefits, educational assistance, no-additional-cost services, employee discounts, and *de minimis* fringe benefits. The latter include dependent life insurance coverage in amounts of $2,000 or less. The Health Insurance Portability and Accountability Act expanded this list of exceptions to include any product that is advertised, marketed, or offered as long-term care insurance. Thus medical expense benefits (other than long-term care insurance), disability benefits, accidental death and dismemberment benefits, vacations, and dependent-care assistance (such as day-care centers) can be included in a cafeteria plan. The Code also allows group term life insurance to be included, even in amounts exceeding $50,000. In general a cafeteria plan cannot include benefits that defer compensation except for a qualified Sec. 401(k) or similar plan.

The prohibition of benefits that defer compensation has an important impact on vacation benefits. If an employee elects vacation benefits for the plan year of a cafeteria plan, the vacation days cannot be carried over into the following plan year because this would be a deferral of compensation. (Note: Regular vacation days are considered to have been taken before the additional days elected under the cafeteria plan.) However, an employee can elect to exchange these days for cash as long as the election is made and the cash is actually received prior to the end of the plan year. If this is not done, the days are forfeited and their value is lost.

The term *cash* is actually broader than it would otherwise appear. In addition to the actual receipt of dollars, a benefit is treated as cash as long as (1) it is not a benefit specifically prohibited by Sec. 125 as cash and (2) it is provided on a taxable basis. This latter provision means that either (1) the cost of the benefit is paid by the employee with aftertax dollars on a payroll-deduction basis or (2) employer dollars are used to obtain the benefit, but the employer reports the cost of the benefit as taxable income for the employee. This rule would allow the inclusion of group automobile insurance or long-term care insurance in a cafeteria plan but not on a tax-favored basis. It also allows long-term disability coverage to be provided on an aftertax basis, so that disability income benefits can be received tax free.

The list of benefits that Sec. 125 specifically prohibits from being treated as cash includes any benefits provided under Sec. 117 (scholarships and tuition expenses) and Sec. 132 (various fringe benefits such as discounts and transportation benefits) of the Internal Revenue Code.

As long as a benefit plan offering choice meets the definition of a cafeteria plan, the issue of constructive receipt does not apply. Employees will have taxable income only to the extent that normally taxable benefits—group term life insurance in excess of $50,000 and cash—are elected. An employer can have a benefit plan that offers choice but does not meet the statutory definition of a cafeteria plan. In such a case the issue of constructive receipt will come into play if the plan contains any benefits that normally result in taxable income.

Choice of Medical Expense Plans

Employers often allow employees a choice of medical expense plans for themselves or their employees. However, there is often confusion over whether this choice constitutes a cafeteria plan. If it does, the employer will need to comply with the rules of Sec. 125 or be subject to the statutory penalties for noncompliance.

Assume an employer has a noncontributory medical expense plan that allows employees to elect among two or more managed care plans. If this is the only choice offered to employees, it is not a cafeteria plan because there is no cash option. It is only a choice among qualified benefits.

Now assume that an employer gives employees the option of electing either a noncontributory managed care plan or an indemnity plan for which the employee must make a monetary contribution on an aftertax basis. Again, by itself this is not a cafeteria plan because there is no option of electing cash.

However, if employees are allowed to pay their share of the premiums for the indemnity plan on a before-tax basis through a premium-conversion plan (discussed later in this chapter), a cafeteria plan has been created under Sec. 125. Because salary reductions technically become employer dollars, the employees who elect salary reductions are considered to be choosing between cash and a qualified benefit.

Some employers allow an employee to elect out of medical expense coverage and receive cash. For example, some employees may feel that they do not need coverage under the employer's plan because they are adequately covered under their spouse's plans. If the cost to provide coverage to employees is $2,000 per year, the employer might feel financially justified in offering these employees $1,000 to waive coverage. Since these employees have a choice between the medical expense coverage and cash, a cafeteria plan has been created.

Benefit Election

Sec. 125 requires that benefit elections under a cafeteria plan be made prior to the beginning of a plan year. These elections cannot be changed during the plan year except under certain specified circumstances if the plan allows such changes. While there is no requirement that these changes be included in a plan, some or all of them are included in most plans.

Changes in benefit elections are permitted under the following circumstances:

- changes in family status. IRS regulations do not specifically define what is meant by changes in family status. However, the regulations include examples of the following:
  - an employee's marriage or divorce
  - the death of an employee's spouse or a dependent
  - the birth or adoption of a child
  - the commencement or termination of employment by the employee's spouse
  - a change from part-time to full-time employment status or vice versa by the employee or the employee's spouse
  - an unpaid leave of absence taken by either the employee or the employee's spouse
  - a significant change in an employee's or spouse's health coverage that is attributable to the spouse's employment
- separation from service. An employee who separates from service during a period of coverage may revoke existing benefit elections and terminate the receipt of benefits. However, the plan must prohibit the employee from making new benefit elections for the remainder of the plan year if he or she returns to service for the employer. An employee

must be allowed to continue health insurance coverage under COBRA upon separation from service.

- cessation of required contributions. A cafeteria plan can terminate coverage if an employee fails to make the required premium payments for the benefits elected. The employee is then prohibited from making new elections for the remainder of the plan year.

- plan cost changes. A cafeteria plan can allow for an automatic adjustment of employee contributions if the cost of a health plan is increased or decreased by an insurance company or other independent third-party provider of benefits. Such an adjustment is not allowed because of changes in self-insured health plans. Regulations also allow the revocation of previous elections and the selection of another health plan with *similar* coverage if costs are increased *significantly*. IRS regulations do not define either of the italicized terms.

- plan coverage changes. An employee may also change to a *similar* health plan if a third-party provider of health benefits *significantly* curtails or ceases to provide health coverage during a plan year. This provision is particularly helpful in situations involving the insolvency of a provider of health benefits. An employee can also change elections if an employer adds an entirely new benefit (for example, dental insurance) to a health plan in the middle of the plan year of the cafeteria plan.

Payroll Deductions and Salary Reductions

Under some cafeteria plans, employees are allowed to allocate only a predetermined employer contribution for benefits. Other cafeteria plans are designed so that employees can obtain additional benefits with optional payroll deductions or salary reductions.

Many cafeteria plans that provide a wide array of benefits allow an employee to elect an aftertax payroll deduction to obtain additional benefits. For example, under a cafeteria plan an employee might be given $200 per month with which to select varying types and levels of benefits. If the benefits the employee chooses cost $240, the employee has two options—either to decrease the benefits selected or to authorize a $40 payroll deduction. Even though the payroll deduction is on an aftertax basis, the employee will gain to the extent that the additional benefits can be selected at a lower cost through a group arrangement than in the individual marketplace.

Sec. 125 also allows employees to purchase certain benefits on a before-tax basis through the use of a premium-conversion plan or a flexible spending account (FSA). Premium-conversion plans or FSAs, which are technically cafeteria plans, can be used by themselves or incorporated into a more comprehensive cafeteria plan. They are most commonly used alone by small employers who are unwilling to establish a broader plan, primarily for cost reasons. The cafeteria plans of most large employers contain one or both of these arrangements as an integral part of the plan.

Before-tax salary reductions reduce taxable income for federal income tax purposes. In most (but not all) states, they also reduce the income subject to state tax.

Premium-Conversion Plans

A premium-conversion plan (also called a premium-only plan, or POP) allows an employee to elect a before-tax salary reduction to pay his or her premium contribution to any employer-sponsored health or other welfare benefit plan. For example, an employer might provide medical expense coverage to employees at no cost but make a monthly charge for dependent coverage. Under a premium-conversion plan the employee can pay for the dependent coverage with a before-tax salary reduction.

As a rule premium-conversion plans are established for medical and dental expenses only. If such plans are used for group term life insurance, the cost of coverage in excess of $50,000 must be reported as income, which defeats the purpose of the salary reduction. If these plans are used for disability income coverage, benefits will be taxable as noncontributory employer-provided coverage because the amount of any salary reduction is considered to be the employer's money

Flexible Spending Accounts

An FSA allows an employee to fund certain benefits on a before-tax basis by electing to take a salary reduction, which can then be used to fund the cost of any qualified benefits included in the plan. However, FSAs are used almost exclusively for medical and dental expenses not covered by the employer's plan and for dependent-care expenses.

The amount of any salary reduction is, in effect, credited to an employee's reimbursement account, and benefits are paid from this account when an employee properly files for such reimbursement. Reimbursements are typically made on a monthly or quarterly basis. The amount of the salary reduction must be determined prior to the beginning of the plan year. Once the amount is set, changes are allowed only under the specified circumstances previously mentioned for benefit elections. A separate election must be made for each benefit, and the funds are accounted for separately. Monies from a salary reduction for one type of expense cannot be used as reimbursement for another type of expense.

If the monies in the FSA are not used during the plan year, they are forfeited and belong to the employer. Although some employers keep the forfeited money and use it to offset the cost of administering the FSA program, almost anything can be done with the money, except for giving it back only to the persons who have forfeited it. Some employers give the money to charity; others credit it on a pro rata basis to the amounts of all participants in the FSA program for the following year or use it to reduce future benefit costs (such as contributions to a medical expense plan) for all employees.

An election to participate in an FSA program not only reduces salary for federal income tax purposes but also lowers the wages on which social security taxes are levied. Therefore those employees who are below the wage-base limit after the reduction will pay less in social security taxes, and their future income benefits under social security may also be smaller. However, the reduction in benefits will be small in most cases unless the salary reduction is large. It should be noted that the employer's share of social security tax payments will also decrease. In some cases, the employer's savings may actually be large enough to fully offset the cost of administering the FSA program.

One issue employers have faced over the years has been whether to limit benefit payments to the amount of an account balance or to allow an employee at any time during the year to receive benefits equal to his or her annual salary reduction. For example, an employee might contribute $100 per month to an FSA to provide benefits for the cost of unreimbursed medical expenses. During the first month of the plan the employee makes only $100 of the $1,200 annual contribution. If the employee incurs $300 of unreimbursed medical expenses during the month, should he or she be allowed to withdraw $100 or the full $300? The objection to allowing a $300 withdrawal is that the employer will lose $200 if the employee terminates employment before making any further contribution. IRS regulations do not give the employer any choice with respect to health benefits (that is, medical and dental expenses). FSAs must allow an amount equal to the full annual contribution to be taken as benefits any time during the year. Therefore the employee will be entitled to a benefit of $300 after the first month. However, the IRS regulations do allow a choice in reimbursement policies for other types of benefits, such as dependent-care expenses. For these benefits, most plans limit aggregate benefits to the total contributions made until the time benefits are received.

TYPES OF PLANS

Core-Plus Plans

Probably the most common type of full-fledged cafeteria plan is one that offers a basic core of benefits to all employees, plus a second layer of optional benefits that permits an employee to choose which benefits he or she will add to the basic benefits. These optional benefits can be "purchased" with dollars, or credits, that are given to the employee as part of the benefit package. If these credits are inadequate to purchase the desired benefits, an employee can make additional purchases with aftertax contributions or with before-tax reductions under a premium-conversion plan and/or a flexible spending account.

Perhaps the best way to demonstrate how cafeteria plans operate is to include a brief description of some existing plans.

EXAMPLE 1: The first example is the core-plus plan of an educational organization with 3,000 employees. While this type of plan is common, it should be noted that the list of optional benefits in this example is more extensive than what is found in most cafeteria plans.

All employees receive a minimum level of benefits, called *basic benefits,* as follows:

- term life insurance equal to one-half of salary
- travel accident insurance (when on the employer's business)
- disability income insurance
- 2 to 4 weeks' vacation

Employees are also given *flexible credits,* equal to between 3 and 6 percent of salary (depending on length of service, with the maximum reached after 10 years), which can be used to purchase additional or "optional" benefits. There is a new election of benefits each year, and no carryover of any unused credits is allowed. The optional benefits are the following:

- an array of medical expense options. Although there is no charge for HMO coverage, a charge is made for coverage under an indemnity plan, and additional flexible credits are given if a person elects no medical expense coverage.
- additional life insurance up to 4 1/2 times salary
- accidental death insurance when the basic travel accident insurance does not apply
- dental insurance for the employee and dependents
- up to 2 weeks' additional vacation time
- cash

If an employee does not have enough flexible credits to purchase the desired optional benefits, additional amounts may be contributed on a payroll-deduction basis for all but more vacation time. In addition, a salary reduction may be elected for contributions to a flexible spending account that provides dependent-care-assistance benefits.

A variation of the core-plus approach is to have the core plan be an "average" plan for which the employee makes no contribution. If certain benefits are reduced, the employee may then receive credits that can be used either to increase other benefits or, if the plan allows, to increase cash compensation.

Additional benefits can typically be obtained through employee payroll deductions.

EXAMPLE 2: This plan covers 15,000 nonunion employees in one division of a major industrial conglomerate. Employees may elect to reduce certain benefits and receive credits that can be either used to purchase additional benefits, taken in cash, or contributed to the company's 401(k) plan. Additional benefits may be purchased on a payroll-deduction basis.

The plan applies to four types of benefits:

- medical expense insurance
- employee life insurance
- accidental death and dismemberment insurance
- dependent life insurance

Several medical expense insurance options are available. The standard coverage, for which there is neither a charge nor a credit, is a point-of-service plan. Employees may elect a traditional indemnity plan, but this option results in a charge. Several HMO options are also available, all of which result in credits.

There are several employee life insurance options that range from 1/2 to 5 times salary. The standard coverage for which there is no credit or charge is 1 1/2 times salary.

Although several supplemental accidental death and dismemberment options and a single dependent life insurance option are available, they result in a charge to the employee. So in effect there is no basic benefit in these areas.

Modular Plans

Another type of cafeteria plan is one in which an employee has a choice among several predesigned benefit packages. Typically at least one of the packages can be selected without any employee cost. If an employee selects a more expensive package, he or she will be required to contribute to the cost of the package. Some employers may also include a bare-bones benefit package, which results in cash being paid to an employee who selects it.

Under some cafeteria plans using this approach (often referred to as a modular approach), the predesigned packages may have significant differences. A comparison of two packages may show one to be better than others in certain cases but inferior in others. Other employers using this approach have virtually identical packages, with the major difference being in the option selected for the medical expense coverage. For example, the plan of one large bank offers three traditional insured plans, two HMOs, and a preferred-provider organization.

Modular plans are growing in popularity for two reasons. First, adverse selection can be more easily controlled under modular plans than under core-plus plans. Second, modular plans are easier to administer and communicate. For both these reasons, small employers who have full-fledged cafeteria plans are most likely to take a modular approach.

EXAMPLE 3: The third example is a large financial institution's cafeteria plan that covers almost 20,000 employees. There are seven predesigned benefit packages that can be chosen, with each package designed for a specific segment of the employee population. Each package has one of three medical expense plans and varying amounts of group term life insurance. The packages contain differing combinations of dental insurance, vision coverage, and dependent care benefits. All offer the same level of disability income coverage.

A "cost" is associated with each package. Some packages cost an employee nothing, other packages require an employee contribution, and at least one option has a negative cost, meaning that an employee who selects it gets additional cash compensation. The cost of each package can vary for two reasons. First, an employee can elect whether to have medical expense coverage for dependents. Second, HMO and PPO choices are available in many of the employee locations.

Salary-Reduction-Only Plans

The final example is a cafeteria plan that consists solely of the two types of salary reductions that can be used in a cafeteria plan—a premium-conversion option and a flexible spending account.

EXAMPLE 4: The final example is the plan of a small nonprofit organization. Employees are allowed to elect salary reductions for each of the following:

- the employee's share of the cost of medical and dental insurance premiums for dependents. (Under this plan the employer pays the full cost of the employee's coverage.)
- qualifying medical care expenses. These are any medical expenses normally deductible on Schedule A of an employee's federal income tax return (without regard to any gross income limitations). Note that these deductible expenses must not have been reimbursed by insurance.
- eligible dependent-care expenses. These are expenses for the types of benefits that could be provided in a qualified dependent-care-assistance

program. The maximum annual salary reduction for this category of benefits is limited to $5,000 to prevent the plan from being discriminatory because too large a portion of the benefits would be provided to highly compensated employees.

Employees can request reimbursements at the end of each month and must file an appropriate form accompanied by documentation (bills and receipts) to support their request. For administrative purposes reimbursement requests must be for at least $50 except in the last quarter of the year.

The maximum reimbursement at any time for dependent-care expenses is the accumulated amount in an employee's account. Unused amounts in reimbursement accounts at the end of the year are donated to the United Way.

OBSTACLES TO CAFETERIA PLANS

Certain obstacles must be overcome before a cafeteria plan can be successfully implemented. Recent changes in federal tax laws and proper plan design would seem sufficient to overcome many of these obstacles. However, it must be realized that any organization that adopts a cafeteria plan other than a simple flexible spending account will face a complex, costly, and time-consuming project.

The Legislative Environment

Undoubtedly the largest obstacle to cafeteria plans for several years was the unsettled federal income tax picture. This picture was finally clarified in 1984 by the passage of the Tax Reform Act and the IRS issuance of regulations governing cafeteria plans. Since then the number of cafeteria plans has grown significantly, particularly among large firms. However, almost every year either a federal tax bill alters Sec. 125 in some way, new IRS regulations are issued, or proposals for change are made by elected officials. The benefits that can be included in a cafeteria plan are changed, the nondiscrimination rules are altered, or the rules for flexible spending accounts are "clarified." This continuing uncertainty has caused many employers to take a wait-and-see attitude toward cafeteria plans.

Meeting Nondiscrimination Rules

Sec. 125 imposes complex nondiscrimination tests on cafeteria plans, causing many employees to view cafeteria plans unfavorably. If these tests are not met, adverse tax consequences for key employees and/or highly compensated employees may actually result in higher taxable income for these employees than if no cafeteria plan existed. From a practical standpoint the test will usually be met if an employer has a full-fledged cafeteria plan that applies to all employees. However, care must be exercised in designing a plan that either covers only a segment of the employees or has only a small percentage of employees participating. The latter situation often occurs with flexible spending accounts.

As is often the case, the nondiscrimination tests are not applicable if a plan is maintained under provisions of a collective-bargaining agreement.

The Concentration Test

Under the concentration test no more than 25 percent of the tax-favored benefits provided under the plan can go to *key employees* (as defined for the Sec. 79 nondiscrimination rules). This test is a particular problem if an employer has a large percentage of key employees and if key employees, being higher paid, contribute large amounts to a flexible spending account.

If a plan fails the concentration test, key employees must include in gross income the maximum taxable benefits that could have been elected under the plan. In effect these employees are subject to the doctrine of constructive receipt.

The Eligibility Test

Cafeteria plans are subject to a two-part eligibility test, both parts of which must be satisfied. The first part of the test stipulates that no employee be required to complete more than 3 years of employment as a condition for participation and that the employment requirement for each employee be the same. In addition, any employee who satisfies the employment requirement and is otherwise entitled to participate must do so no later than the first day of the plan year following completion of the employment requirement unless the employee has separated from service in the interim.

The second part of the test requires that eligibility for participation must not be discriminatory in favor of highly compensated employees, who are defined as any of the following:

- officers
- shareholders who own more than 5 percent of the voting power or value of all classes of the firm's stock
- employees who are highly compensated based on all facts and circumstances
- spouses or dependents of any of the above

The eligibility test uses table 19-1, which is found in IRS regulations and can best be explained with the following example.

An employer has 1,000 employees—800 nonhighly compensated and 200 highly compensated. The percentage of nonhighly compensated employees is 80 percent (800/1000), for which the table shows a safe harbor percentage of 35. This means that if the percentage of nonhighly compensated employees eligible for the plan is equal to at least 35 percent of the percentage of highly

Nonhighly Compensated Employee Concentration Percentage	Safe Harbor Percentage	Unsafe Harbor Percentage
0–60	50	40
61	49.25	39.25
62	48.50	38.50
63	47.75	37.75
64	47	37
65	46.25	36.25
66	45.50	35.50
67	44.75	34.75
68	44	34
69	43.25	33.25
70	42.50	32.50
71	41.75	31.75
72	41	31
73	40.25	30.25
74	39.50	29.50
75	38.75	28.75
76	38	28
77	37.25	27.25
78	36.50	26.50
79	35.75	25.75
80	35	25
81	34.25	24.25
82	33.50	23.50
83	32.75	22.75
84	32	22
85	31.25	21.25
86	30.50	20.50
87	29.75	20
88	29	20
89	28.25	20
90	27.50	20
91	26.75	20
92	26	20
93	25.25	20
94	24.50	20
95	23.75	20
96	23	20
97	22.25	20
98	21.50	20
99	20.75	20

TABLE 19-1

compensated employees eligible, the plan satisfies the eligibility test. Assume that 160 people, or 80 percent of the highly compensated employees, are eligible.

Then at least 28 percent, or 224, of the nonhighly compensated employees must be eligible for the plan (calculations: .80 x .35 = .28 and .28 x 800 = 224).

The table also shows an unsafe harbor percentage of 25 percent. Using this figure instead of 35 percent yields 160 employees. If fewer than this number of nonhighly compensated employees are eligible, the eligibility test is failed.

If the number of eligible nonhighly compensated employees falls between the numbers determined by the two percentages (from 160 to 223 employees in this example), IRS regulations impose a facts-and-circumstances test to determine whether the eligibility test is passed or failed. According to the regulations, the following factors will be considered: (1) the underlying business reason for the eligibility classification, (2) the percentage of employees eligible, (3) the percentage of eligible employees in each salary range, and (4) the extent to which the eligibility classification is close to satisfying the safe harbor rule. However, the regulations also state that none of these factors alone is determinative, and other facts and circumstances may be relevant.

If a plan fails the eligibility test, highly compensated employees must include in gross income the maximum taxable benefits that could have been elected under the plan.

Nondiscriminatory Contributions and Benefits

Cafeteria plans cannot discriminate in favor of highly compensated participants with respect to contributions or benefits. Sec. 125 states that a cafeteria plan is not discriminatory if the plan's nontaxable benefits and total benefits (or the employer contributions allocable to each) do not discriminate in favor of highly compensated employees. In addition, a cafeteria plan providing health benefits is not discriminatory if contributions under the plan for each participant include an amount equal to one of the following:

- 100 percent of the health benefit cost for the majority of similarly situated (that is, family or single coverage) highly compensated employees
- at least 75 percent of the health benefit cost for the similarly situated participant with the best health benefit coverage

Contributions exceeding either of these amounts are nondiscriminatory if they bear a uniform relationship to an employee's compensation.

The Employer's Obligation

Under the most liberal cafeteria plan each employee has an unrestricted choice of the benefits his or her employer provides. Some critics of this concept argue that both the motivational and the security aspects of a cafeteria plan may be damaged by unwise employee selection because many employees may not have the expertise to select the proper benefits. In addition, there is concern about the organization's moral and perhaps legal obligation to prevent employees from financial injury through faulty decisions. These concerns have been incorporated into the design of most plans presently in existence. Employees are given both certain basic benefits that provide a minimum level of security and a series of optional benefits on top of the basic ones.

Negative Attitudes

Some negative attitudes toward cafeteria plans have been expressed by employees, insurers, and unions. No cafeteria plan can be truly successful without the support of the employees involved. In order to win the employees' initial support and to overcome any potential negative attitudes, companies that contemplate the development of such programs must spend a considerable amount of time and resources in making sure that employees are adequately informed about (1) the reasons for the proposed program, (2) its advantages and disadvantages, and (3) its future implications. For best results the opinions of employees should be solicited and weighed, and employees should be involved in various aspects of the decision-making process.

Some insurers have been reluctant to participate in cafeteria plans. A few seem unwilling to try anything new; others are concerned about the problem of adverse selection as a result of employee choice. However, as explained below, the problem of adverse selection can be minimized.

Unions have also had a negative attitude. Union management often feels that bargaining for a cafeteria plan is contrary to the practice of bargaining for the best benefit program for all employees. There is also a concern that a cafeteria plan will be used primarily as a cost-containment technique to pass on the cost of future benefit increases to union members. Consequently the existing programs often apply only to nonunion employees.

Adverse Selection

When employees are allowed a choice in selecting benefits, the problem of adverse selection arises. This means that employees who are likely to have claims will tend to pick the benefits that will minimize their out-of-pocket costs. For example, an employee who previously selected a medical expense option with a high deductible might switch to a plan with a lower deductible if medical expenses are ongoing. An employee who previously rejected dental insurance is likely to elect this benefit if dental care is anticipated in the near future.

It should be noted that adverse selection is a problem whether a plan is insured or self-funded. The problem even exists outside of cafeteria plans if choice is allowed. However, the degree of choice within a cafeteria plan tends to make the potential costs more severe unless actions are taken to combat the problem.

Several techniques are used to control adverse selection in cafeteria plans. Benefit limitations and restrictions on coverage can be included if a person wishes to add or change coverage at a date later than initial eligibility. This technique has been common in contributory benefit plans for many years. Another technique is to price the options accordingly. If an option is likely to encourage adverse selection, the cost to the employee for that option should be higher than what would have been charged if the option had been the only one available. Such pricing has been difficult in the past, but it is becoming easier and more accurate as more experience with cafeteria plans develops. The control of adverse selection is also one reason for the use of predesigned package plans. If, for example, the medical expense plan in one option is likely to encourage adverse selection, the option may not include other benefits for which adverse selection is also a concern (such as dental benefits). To further counter increased costs from the medical expense plan, the option may also offer minimal coverage for other types of benefits.

Cost

It is an accepted fact that an organization that adopts a cafeteria plan will incur initial development and administrative costs that are over and above those of a more traditional benefit program. Some of this extra cost is the value of the employee hours that must be spent in preparing the program for implementation. Another sizable portion must be paid for the reprogramming of the organization's computer system to include necessary information and to accept the employees' benefit elections. ERISA also requires the annual filing of Form 5500.

Until recently the cost of a cafeteria plan was beyond the means of all but large employers. However, package plans developed by many insurers now make this approach financially available to employers with only a few hundred employees.

Continuing costs will depend on such factors as the benefits included in the plan, the number of options available with each benefit, the frequency with which employees may change benefit elections, and the number of employees covered by the plan. The firms with cafeteria plans have incurred increased costs because of the need for additional employees to administer the program and additional computer time to process employee choices. However, the costs have been regarded as small in relation to the total cost of providing employee benefits. In addition, as cafeteria plans have grown in popularity, many vendors have developed software packages that can be used to provide administrative functions more cost effectively.

ISSUES IN PLAN DESIGN

Before committing itself to the establishment of a cafeteria program, an employer must be sure a valid reason exists for converting the company's traditional benefit program to a cafeteria approach. For example, if there is strong employee dissatisfaction with the current benefit program, the solution may lie in clearly identifying the sources of dissatisfaction and making appropriate adjustments in the existing benefit program, rather than making a shift to a cafeteria plan. However, if employee dissatisfaction arises from widely differing benefit needs, conversion to a cafeteria plan may be quite appropriate. Beyond having a clearly defined purpose for converting from a traditional benefit program to a cafeteria program and being willing to bear the additional administrative costs associated with a cafeteria approach, the employer must face a number of considerations in designing the plan.

The Type and Amount of Benefits to Include

Probably the most fundamental decision that must be made in designing a cafeteria plan is determining what benefits should be included. An employer who wants the plan to be viewed as meeting the differing needs of employees must receive employee input concerning the types of benefits perceived as most desirable. An open dialogue with employees will undoubtedly lead to suggestions that every possible employee benefit be made available. The enthusiasm of many employees for a cafeteria plan will then be dampened when the employer rejects some—and possibly many—of these suggestions for cost, administrative, or psychological reasons. Consequently it is important that certain ground rules be established regarding the benefits that are acceptable to the employer.

The employer must decide whether the plan should be limited to the types of benefits provided through traditional group insurance arrangements or be expanded to include other benefits. At a minimum it is important to ensure that an overall employee benefit program provide employees with protection against all major areas of personal risk. This suggests a benefit program with at least *some* provision for life insurance, disability income protection, medical expense protection, and retirement benefits, but it is not necessary that *all* these benefits be included in a cafeteria plan. For example, most employers have a retirement plan separate from their cafeteria plan because of Sec. 125 requirements. Other employers make a 401(k) plan one of the available cafeteria options.

In some respects a cafeteria plan may be an ideal vehicle for providing less traditional types of benefits. Two examples are extra vacation time and child care. Some plans allow an employee to use flexible credits to purchase additional days of vacation. When available, this option has proven a popular benefit, particularly among single employees. A problem may arise, however, if the work of vacationing employees must be assumed by nonvacationing employees in addition to their own regularly assigned work. Those not electing extra vacation time may resent doing the work of someone else who is away longer than the normal vacation period. In recent years employers have been under increasing pressure to provide care for employees' children, which represents an additional cost if added to a traditional benefit program. Employees who include child-care benefits in a cafeteria plan can pay for the cost of such benefits, possibly with dollars from an FSA. However, lower-paid employees may be better off financially by paying for child care with out-of-pocket dollars and electing the income tax credit available for dependent-care expenses.

One question that may arise is whether dependent life insurance should be included in a cafeteria plan. As mentioned before, amounts of $2,000 or less do not fit the definition of a qualified benefit and cannot be included. If the amount of coverage available exceeds $2,000, the benefit can be provided as long as it is treated as a cash benefit. An employee electing coverage with employer-provided dollars will have taxable income as determined by Table I. Since this amount will exceed the actual cost of the coverage in some cases, dependent life insurance is often made available outside a cafeteria plan. When it is included in a cafeteria plan, there is frequently a requirement that it be purchased with aftertax salary reductions.

Cost is an important consideration in a cafeteria plan. The greater the number of benefits, particularly optional benefits, the greater the administrative costs. A wide array of options may also be confusing to many employees and require extra personnel to counsel employees or to answer their questions.

Level of Employer Contributions

An employer has considerable latitude in determining the amount of dollars that will be available to employees to purchase benefits under a cafeteria plan. These dollars may be a function of one or more of the following factors: salary, age, family status, and length of service.

The major difficulty arises in situations in which the installation of a cafeteria plan is not accompanied by an overall increase in the amount of the employer's contributions to the employee benefit plan. It is generally felt that each employee should be provided with enough dollars so that he or she can purchase optional benefits that, together with basic benefits, are at least equivalent to the benefits provided by the older plan.

Including a Premium-Conversion or FSA Option

A premium-conversion or FSA option under a cafeteria plan enables employees to lower taxes and increase spendable income. Ignoring administrative costs, there is probably no reason not to offer employees this option for benefits such as dependent care or for health insurance premiums. However, salary reductions for unreimbursed medical expenses pose a dilemma. While such deductions save taxes for an employee, they may also result in nearly 100 percent reimbursement for medical expenses, which may negate many cost-containment features in the employer's medical expense plan.

Change of Benefits

Because employees' needs change over time, a provision regarding their ability to change their benefit options must be incorporated in a cafeteria plan.

As a rule, changes are allowed prior to the beginning of the plan year. Additional changes may be allowed as long as they are permissible under Sec. 125 regulations.

Two situations may complicate the issue of the frequency with which benefits may be changed. First, the charges to employees for optional benefits must be adjusted periodically to reflect experience under the plan. If the charges for benefits rise between dates on which employees may change benefit selections, the employer must either absorb these charges or pass them on to the employees, probably through increased payroll deductions. Consequently most cafeteria plans allow benefit changes on annual dates that are the same as the dates when charges for benefits are recalculated as well as the date on which any insurance contracts providing benefits under the plan are renewed.

The second situation arises when the amount of the employer's contribution is based on compensation. If an employee receives a pay increase between selection periods, should he or she be granted more dollars to purchase additional benefits at that time? Under most cafeteria plans the dollars available to all employees are calculated only once a year, usually before the date by which any annual benefit changes must be made. Any changes in the employee's status during the year will have no effect on the employer's contribution until the date on which a recalculation is made in the following year.

Appendix A

Federal Tax Laws
Affecting Group Benefit Plans

The following citations are for students who wish to research further the tax laws pertaining to group benefits that are provided by employer contributions. Federal tax laws treat employee contributions for group insurance like payments for individual insurance, and therefore they are not deductible to employees, except for certain medical and dental costs if an employee itemizes deductions. In addition, benefits attributable to employee contributions are treated like benefits from individual insurance and are generally free of income taxation. All references are to sections (§) of the Internal Revenue Code or to regulations (Reg.) under the Code.

GROUP TERM LIFE INSURANCE

Deductibility of Employer Contributions

- deductibles as ordinary-and-necessary business expense   §162
- exception if employer is beneficiary   §264

Income Tax Liability to Employees

- first $50,000 generally tax free   §79
- determination of cost on amounts in excess of $50,000   Reg. 1.79-3(d)
- special rules for groups of fewer than 10   Reg. 1.79-1(d)

Taxation of Proceeds

- free of income tax   §101
- subject to estate tax unless incidents of ownership assigned   §2042

RETIRED LIVES RESERVE

Deductibility of Employer Contributions

- deductible as business expense   §162

Income Tax Liability to Employees

- no taxation from contribution to reserve   §83

GROUP DISABILITY INCOME INSURANCE

Deductibility of Employer Contributions

- deductible as business expense   §162

Income Tax Liability to Employees

- no taxation from employer contributions   §106

Taxation of Benefits

- generally taxable, possibly subject to tax credit   §22

GROUP MEDICAL AND DENTAL INSURANCE

Deductibility of Employer Contributions

- deductible as business expense   §162

Income Tax Liability to Employees

- no taxation from employer contributions   §106

Taxation of Benefits

- tax free in general   §105
- exception for discriminatory self-insured medical reimbursement plans §105

GROUP LONG-TERM CARE INSURANCE

Deductibility of Employer Contributions

- deductible as business expense   §162

Income Tax Liability to Employees

- no taxation from employer contributions to qualified contract   §106

Taxation of Benefits

- no taxation under qualified contract except for high per diem benefits   §105

GROUP LEGAL EXPENSE PLANS

Deductibility of Employer Contributions

- deductible as business expense   §162

Income Tax Liability to Employees

- no taxation from employer contributions   §120

Taxation of Benefits

- none if "prepaid"   §120
- taxable if not "prepaid"   §61

GROUP PROPERTY AND LIABILITY INSURANCE

Deductibility of Employer Contributions

- deductible as business expense   §162

Income Tax Liability to Employees

- employer contributions represent taxable income   §61

Taxation of Benefits

- free of taxation   §165

CAFETERIA PLANS

Avoidance of Constructive Receipt

- constructive receipt avoided if plan properly designed   §125

Before-Tax Contributions

- before-tax contributions allowed   §125

OTHER GROUP BENEFITS

Vacations

- taxed as compensation   §61

Holidays

- taxed as compensation   §61

Supplemental Unemployment Benefits

- benefits taxed as compensation   §85
- tax-free growth of earnings on fund to provide benefits   §501

Educational Assistance

- tax-free receipt of first $5,250 of benefits under nondiscriminatory plan   §127

Moving Expenses

- reportable as income   §61
- allowal of offsetting deductions for certain expenses   §217

Awards

- suggestion awards included in income   §74
- qualified plan awards tax free within limits   §§74, 274
- any awards tax free if *de minimis*   §132

Holiday Bonuses and Gifts

- tax free only if *de minimis*   §132

No-Additional-Cost Services

- tax free with satisfaction of certain rules   §132

Employee Discounts

- tax free with satisfaction of certain rules   §132

Dependent-Care Assistance

- tax free up to $5,000 ($2,500 for marrieds filing separately) with satisfaction of certain rules   §129

Adoption Assistance

- tax free up to $5,000 per child ($6,000 for a child with special needs) with satisfaction of certain rules   §137

Wellness Programs

- tax free to extent considered medical expenses   §105
- most other benefits result in taxable income unless *de minimis*   §132

Employee-Assistance Plans

- benefits tax free if purpose is to alleviate medical conditions   §105

Financial Planning Programs

- fees to outside professionals represent taxable income   §61
- offsetting deductions allowed for certain expenses   §212

Transportation/Free Parking

- tax free within limits if provided as a qualified transportation fringe   §132

Subsidized Eating Facilities

- tax free if furnished for employer's convenience   §119

Appendix B

Employee Benefit Acronyms

AHP	approved health plan or accountable health plan
ADA	Americans with Disabilities Act
ADEA	Age Discrimination in Employment Act
AIME	average indexed monthly earnings
ASO	administrative-services-only
COB	coordination of benefits
COBRA	Consolidated Omnibus Budget Reconciliation Act
COLA	cost-of-living adjustment
CPI	consumer price index
DHMO	dental health maintenance organization
DI	disability income or disability insurance
EEOC	Equal Employment Opportunity Commission
EPO	exclusive-provider organization
ERISA	Employee Retirement Income Security Act
FASB	Financial Accounting Standards Board
FSA	flexible spending account
GULP	group universal life insurance plan

HIPAA	Health Insurance Portability and Accountability Act
HIPC	health insurance purchasing cooperative
HMO	health maintenance organization
IPA	individual practice organization
JCAHO	Joint Committee on Accreditation of Healthcare Organizations
IRS	Internal Revenue Service
MET	multiple-employer trust
MEWA	multiple-employee welfare arrangement
MSA	medical spending account
NAIC	National Association of Insurance Commissioners
NCQA	National Committee for Quality Assurance
OASDHI	old-age, survivors, disability, and health insurance
OASDI	old-age, survivors, and disability insurance
OBRA '93	Omnibus Budget Reconciliation Act of 1993
PIA	primary insurance amount plan
POP	premium-only plan
POS	point-of-service
PPO	preferred-provider organization
RC	reasonable and customary
RLR	retired lives reserve
SUB	supplemental unemployment benefit
UI	unemployment insurance

UL   universal life insurance

UR   utilization review

URC   usual, reasonable, and customary

VEBA   Voluntary Employees' Beneficiary Association

Glossary

accelerated benefits • a provision in a group life insurance contract that allows an insured to receive a portion of his or her death benefit while still living if one or more of the following events occur: (1) a terminal illness that is expected to result in death within 6 or 12 months, (2) a specified catastrophic illness, and (3) the incurring of nursing home and possibly other long-term care expenses

accidental death and dismemberment insurance • insurance that gives additional benefits if an employee dies accidentally or suffers certain types of injuries. Coverage is commonly provided as a rider to a group life insurance contract but may also be provided through a separate group insurance contract.

accumulation period • the time period within which expenses used to satisfy a per-cause deductible must be incurred for each illness or accident

actively-at-work provision • an eligibility provision for group benefit coverage, whereby an employee is not eligible for coverage if absent from work because of sickness, injury, or other reasons on the otherwise effective date of his or her coverage

administrative-services-only contract • *See* ASO contract.

adoption assistance • a benefit plan designed to provide benefits for legal, medical, and other expenses associated with the adoption of a child

adult day care • day care at centers specifically designed for the elderly who live at home, but whose spouses or families cannot stay home to care for them during the day

adverse selection • the tendency of those who are most likely to have claims to also be those who are the most likely to seek insurance

Age Discrimination in Employment Act • a 1967 law that prohibits age discrimination for most working persons. The act, which applies only to employers with 20 or more employees, prohibits discrimination with respect to employee benefits for employees aged 40 and older.

agent • an employee of an insurance company who acts as a representative of the insurance company in the sale of the company's products, including employee benefits

aggregate stop-loss coverage • stop-loss coverage under which the insurance company is responsible if total claims under a self-funded plan exceed some specified dollar limit during a set time period

AHP • *See* approved (accountable) health plan.

all-causes deductible • a deductible that must be satisfied only once during any given time period, regardless of the number of causes from which medical expenses arise

ambulatory care center • a facility, separate from a hospital, that is operated primarily to perform surgical procedures. It has continuous physicians' services and professional nursing services but does not provide overnight accommodations for patients.

American Accreditation HealthCare Commission, Inc. (formerly Utilization Review Accreditation Commission) • an organization that accredits external organizations that perform utilization review. The commission now also accredits managed care organizations.

Americans with Disabilities Act • a federal law designed to make it possible for disabled persons to join the mainstream of everyday life. Among other provisions, the act makes it unlawful to discriminate on the basis of disability against a qualified individual with respect to any term, condition, or privilege of employment. This includes payments for private insurance and retirement plans, legally required payments for government programs such as social security, payments for time not worked, extra cash payments to employees, and the cost of services to employees, such as wellness programs and retirement counseling.

annual return/report (Form 5500) • an annual report that ERISA requires plan administrators to file with the Internal Revenue Service within 210 days after the end of the plan year. The return includes financial information about the plan and must be given to plan participants upon written request.

"any willing provider" law • a state law requiring HMOs and other networks of medical care providers to accept any provider who is willing to accept the medical expense plan's basic terms and fees

approved (accountable) health plan (AHP) • the medical providers that can deal with a health insurance purchasing cooperative

ASO contract • a contractual arrangement under which an employer purchases specific administrative services from an insurance company or an independent third-party administrator. These services usually include the administration of claims, but they may also include a wide variety of other services.

assignment • a provision in a group benefit plan under which a covered person may transfer any or all rights under the contract (including benefit payments) to another party

assisted-living benefits • long-term care benefits for facilities that provide care for the frail elderly who are no longer able to care for themselves but who do not need the level of care provided in a nursing home

assumption-of-risk doctrine • a common-law defense available to employers under which a worker cannot recover damages for an injury if he or she knowingly assumed the risks inherent in the job

average indexed monthly earnings (AIME) • the basis on which a worker's primary insurance amount (PIA) is determined under social security. It is based on an average of the wages on which social security taxes have been paid after these amounts have been adjusted for changes in wage levels and, if applicable, after certain years have been excluded.

bed reservation benefit • a benefit under a long-term care insurance policy that continues to pay a long-term care facility for a limited time if a patient must temporarily leave because of hospitalization. Without a continuation of benefits, the bed might be rented to someone else and unavailable upon the patient's release from the hospital.

beneficiary • a person designated by a group benefit plan participant, or by the terms of the plan, who is or who may be entitled to a benefit under the plan

benefit handbook • an employee reference book that summarizes the benefit plans available to all employees

benefit outsourcing • *See* outsourcing.

benefit period • the period of time benefits will be paid prior to which a new deductible for benefits must be satisfied

benefit schedule • a schedule that classifies employees who are eligible for coverage under a benefit plan and specifies the amount of coverage that is provided to the members of each class

benefit statement • a personalized statement that specifies the benefit plans for which an employee is eligible and what benefits are available to that particular employee and his or her family. It is usually given to employees on an annual basis.

big-deductible plan • *See* specific stop-loss coverage.

birthing center • a facility, separate from a hospital, designed to provide a homelike atmosphere for the delivery of babies. Deliveries are performed by nurse-midwives, and mothers and babies are released shortly after birth.

Blue Cross and Blue Shield Association • the national organization that sets standards for Blue Cross and Blue Shield plans

Blue Cross and Blue Shield plans • nonprofit organizations formed for the purpose of prepaying subscribers' medical care expenses. Blue Cross plans provide coverage primarily for hospital expenses, and Blue Shield plans provide coverage primarily for physicians' services.

broker • a representative of the buyer of insurance who owes his or her allegiance to the buyer rather than to the organization through which coverage is placed. Brokers have traditionally been compensated on the basis of commissions for the coverages they have placed in behalf of clients, but fees may also be charged.

buy-up plan • a benefit plan under which a covered person can purchase additional coverage at his or her own expense

cafeteria plan • a benefit program in which employees can design their own benefit packages by purchasing benefits with a prescribed amount of employer dollars from a number of available options

calendar-year deductible • an all-causes deductible that applies to medical expenses incurred within a calendar year. A new deductible must be satisfied in a subsequent calendar year.

carryover provision • a provision in a medical expense plan that allows any expenses applied to the deductible and incurred during the last 3 months of the year to be applied to the deductible for the following year

carve-out • the practice of excluding certain classes or employees from a benefit plan and providing benefits to them under an alternative arrangement. Carve-outs are generally used to contain employee costs or provide broader or tax-favored benefits to key employees and executives.

case management • *See* utilization review.

certificate of insurance • a description of the coverage provided to employees. Although it is given to the employees, it is not part of the master contract.

Civil Rights Act (pregnancy provision) • a federal law requiring that women affected by pregnancy, childbirth, or related medical conditions be treated the same for employment-related purposes as other persons who are not so affected but who are similar in their ability to work

claim reserve • an estimate by the insurance company for claims that have been approved but not yet paid, claims that are in the course of settlement, and claims that have been incurred but not yet reported

claims charge • the amount included in the experience rating formula for claims that will be charged against a group. It is equal to (1) the incurred claims subject to experience rating multiplied by the credibility factor plus (2) expected claims multiplied by one minus the credibility factor.

claims fluctuation reserve • a reserve into which insurance companies require that part of a dividend earned be placed. Monies are drawn from the reserve to indemnify the insurance company for the years in which a group insurance case has a deficit.

closed-panel plan • a benefit plan under which covered persons must obtain services from practitioners selected by the provider of benefits

coalition • a group of employers, unions, providers of health care, insurance companies, and regulators whose purpose is to control costs and improve the quality of health care. They may act as a catalyst for health care legislation or as a purchasing group to negotiate lower-cost coverage for members.

COBRA • a provision of the Consolidated Omnibus Budget Reconciliation Act of 1985 that requires group health plans to allow employees and certain beneficiaries to elect that their current health insurance coverage be extended at group rates for up to 36 months following a qualifying event that results in the loss of coverage. The provision applies only to employers with 20 or more employees. In addition, a person electing COBRA continuation can be required to pay a premium equal to as much as 102 percent of the cost to the employee benefit plan for the period of coverage for a similarly situated active employee to whom a qualifying event has not occurred.

coinsurance • the percentage of covered expenses under a major medical plan that will be paid once a deductible is satisfied. The most common coinsurance is 80 percent.

COLA • *See* cost-of-living adjustments.

combination dental plan • a dental plan under which diagnostic and preventive services are covered on a usual-and-customary basis but other dental services are covered on the basis of a fee schedule

common accident provision • a provision in a major medical expense contract whereby if two or more members of the same family are injured in the same accident, the covered medical expenses for all family members will at most be subject to a single deductible, usually equal to the individual deductible amount

community rating • the practice of using the same rate structure for all subscribers to a medical expense plan, regardless of their past or potential loss experience and regardless of whether coverage is written on an individual or a group basis

competitive bidding • the process of preparing specifications for a benefit plan and inviting several providers of coverage or third-party administrators to present a document detailing the cost at which they are willing to provide desired benefits or services

comprehensive legal expense plan • a legal expense plan that covers all legal expenses except those that are specifically excluded

comprehensive major medical plan • a major medical plan that is designed to stand alone without any accompanying basic medical expense coverages

concurrent utilization review • the process of monitoring the length of a hospital stay and determining whether other alternatives to hospitals can be used. The process is usually carried out by a registered nurse and typically begins with precertification of a hospital stay.

consultants • representatives of the buyers of insurance and employee benefits who owe allegiance to the buyers rather than to the organizations through which they place their clients' coverage. Traditionally consultants have been compensated on the basis of fees charged to clients.

contributory negligence doctrine • a common-law defense available to employers, under which a worker cannot collect if his or her negligence contributed in any way to an injury

contributory plan • an employee benefit plan under which participants pay a portion, or possibly all, of the cost of their own coverage

conversion • a provision in a group benefit plan that gives an employee whose coverage ceases the right to convert to an individual insurance policy without providing evidence of insurability. The conversion policy may or may not be identical to the prior group coverage.

conversion charge • a charge levied against a group term life insurance plan in the experience rating process that reflects the increased mortality associated with coverage that has been converted to an individual policy

coordination of benefits provision • a provision in most group medical expense plans under which priorities are established for the payment of benefits if an individual is covered under more than one plan. Coverage as an employee is generally primary to coverage as a dependent. When parents are divorced, the plan of the parent with custody is primary, the plan of the spouse of the parent with custody is secondary, and the plan of the parent without custody pays last. Other rules apply to specific situations.

copayment • *See* percentage participation.

core-plus plan • a cafeteria plan with a basic core of benefits for all employees and a second layer of optional benefits that an employee can choose with employer-provided monies. An employee can typically purchase further benefits with aftertax contributions or with before-tax reductions under a premium-conversion plan and/or a flexible spending account.

corridor deductible • a deductible in a major medical plan under which an individual will receive no benefits until he or she has incurred a specific amount of covered expenses above those paid by his or her basic coverages

cost containment • the attempt to control benefit costs by reducing the size of claims or minimizing administrative costs associated with benefit plans. This approach is in contrast to cost shifting, which transfers costs to employees.

cost-of-living adjustments (COLA) • increases in benefit levels because of changes in some index, such as the CPI. These increases apply to social security income benefits and sometimes to benefits under private insurance and retirement programs.

cost-plus arrangement • an alternative funding arrangement frequently used by large employers to provide life insurance benefits. Under this arrangement, the employer's monthly premium is based on the claims paid by the insurance company during the preceding month, plus a specified retention charge that is uniform throughout the policy period.

cost shifting • the attempt by employers to control benefit costs by shifting these costs to employees. Examples include the requiring of larger employee contributions and increased deductibles.

covered classification • one of the classifications in a group benefit schedule. In order to have coverage, an employee must fall into one of the covered classifications. No employee may be in more than one classification, and it is the employer's responsibility to determine the appropriate classification for each employee.

credibility • a statistical measure of the reliability of a group's past claims experience

creditor-debtor group • an eligible group for purposes of providing insurance. The debtors are the insureds, but the creditor is the policyowner and beneficiary of the coverage.

currently insured • an insured status under OASDI that requires a person to have credit for at least 6 quarters of coverage out of the 13-quarter period ending with the quarter in which death occurs

current revenue funding • the practice of funding benefits out of a firm's current revenue. This is in contrast to prefunding certain benefits such as retirement income or postretirement life insurance.

custodial care • care given to help with personal needs such as walking, bathing, dressing, eating, or taking medicine. Such care can usually be provided by someone without professional medical skills or training.

death-benefit-only plan • a benefit plan under which the employee agrees to pay a death benefit to the employee's beneficiary out of corporate assets. Death benefits in excess of $5,000 result in taxable income to the beneficiary.

deductible • the initial amount of medical expenses an individual must pay before he or she will receive benefits under a medical expense plan

Delta Plans • service plans sponsored by state dental associations for the purpose of providing dental benefits. They are also called Delta Dental Plans.

de minimis • the value of a benefit that is so minimal that accounting for its cost would be unreasonable or administratively impractical. Some employee benefits, that would otherwise be taxable can be given to employees on a tax-free basis for this reason.

dental health maintenance organization (DHMO) • an HMO that provides dental care only

dependent • most commonly defined under a group medical expense plan to include an employee's spouse who is not legally separated from the employee and any other unmarried dependent children (including stepchildren and adopted children) under age 19 or, if full-time students, age 23

dependent-care assistance • employer-provided benefits, often in the form of reimbursements of day-care expenses for children. However, dependent-care assistance can be provided for elderly parents and may also include flexible work schedules, part-time job sharing, and family leave policies.

dependent life insurance • group life insurance on the lives of eligible dependents of persons covered under the plan. Amounts of coverage are usually limited, and the employee is automatically the beneficiary.

diagnostic X-ray and laboratory expense benefits • medical expense benefits for the cost of diagnostic X-ray and laboratory expenses when performed on an out-patient basis and when not otherwise covered under other portions of a basic medical expense plan

direct reimbursement • a self-funded dental insurance plan under which the employee selects the provider of dental services, pays any charges incurred, and submits the bills to the employer for reimbursement

disability insured • the insured status under OASDI necessary to receive disability benefits. It requires that a worker (1) be fully insured and (2) have had a minimum amount of work under social security within a recent period.

dividend • the refund given by mutual insurance companies to groups that are experience rated and have had better claims experience than anticipated

dividend earned • the dividend attributable to a group insurance case for the current experience period. It is computed by adding the retention to the claims charge and then subtracting this sum from the premiums paid.

dividend payable • the dividend earned for an experience period reduced by any deficit that has been carried forward or placed in a claims fluctuation reserve

doctrine of comity • the practice by which states recognize within their own territory the laws of other states. Under this doctrine, it is generally accepted that the state in which a group insurance contract is delivered has governing jurisdiction.

doctrine of constructive receipt • the principle under which an employee who is given a choice of benefits is taxed as if he or she had elected the maximum taxable benefit that could have been obtained under the plan even if the actual election had been a benefit that is normally nontaxable. The issue of constructive receipt when choice is given can be overcome by using a cafeteria plan.

Earnings and Benefit Estimate Statement • a statement issued by the Social Security Administration that enables an employee to verify his or her contributions to the OASDHI program. The statement also contains an estimate of benefits that will be available because of retirement, disability, or death.

earnings schedule • a benefit schedule under which benefits are a function of each employee's earnings

earnings test • the process for determining whether income benefits of social security beneficiaries under age 70 should be reduced because of wages that exceed a specified level. One portion of the test applies to social security beneficiaries aged 65 through 69, and another portion applies to beneficiaries under age 65. The earnings threshold at which benefits are reduced changes annually on the basis of changes in national wage levels.

educational assistance • a benefit plan designed to compensate employees for costs associated with education. If provided in accordance with specific IRS rules, benefits can be received on a tax-free basis.

eldercare benefits • dependent-care assistance for elderly dependents. It may include costs associated with home care for elderly dependents or care at day-care facilities for the elderly. Other employer activities related to eldercare may include seminars on issues affecting the elderly, referral services for information, employer-sponsored support groups, and making parents an eligible group for coverage under the employer's long-term care insurance plan.

elimination period • *See* waiting period.

employee-assistance program • an employer-provided program to help employees with certain personal problems. Benefits may include treatment for alcohol or drug abuse, counseling for mental and marital problems, referrals for child care or eldercare, and crisis intervention.

employee benefit planning • the process of establishing, reviewing, and modifying an overall benefit plan. Steps include determining needs, analyzing costs, implementing the plan, communicating the plan to employees, and monitoring the plan's performance.

employee benefits • all benefits and services, other than wages for time worked, that employers provide to employees in whole or in part. Narrower definitions include only employer-provided benefits for situations involving death, accident, sickness, retirement, or unemployment.

Employee Retirement Income Security Act • *See* ERISA.

employee welfare benefit plan • those group benefits, other than retirement benefits, to which ERISA applies. While most employee benefits fall under the definition, there are some exceptions. Specifically excluded are government plans, church plans, plans to comply with workers' compensation, unemployment compensation, and disability insurance laws. Compensation for absences from work because of sickness, vacation, holidays, etc., are also excluded to the extent that such compensation is paid out of the employer's general assets. Payroll-deduction plans are also generally excluded as long as no contribution is made by the employer and participation is completely voluntary for employees.

employer mandate • an approach to national health insurance that requires virtually all employers to make medical expense coverage available to employees and their dependents and to pay a portion of the cost

entire contract clause • a provision in a group insurance contract stating that the insurance policy, the policyowner's application that is attached to the policy, and any individual applications of any insured person constitute the entire insurance contract. The insurance company cannot use any other statements made by the policyowner or by any insured as the basis for contesting coverage.

ERISA • a federal act to protect the interests of participants in employee benefit plans and participants' beneficiaries. Sections of the act affecting group benefits are those dealing with fiduciary responsibility and reporting and disclosure.

excess-amounts pooling • the process by which the amount of insurance that is subject to experience rating on any one person is limited. Amounts in excess of the limit are not experience rated but are subject to manual rates based on the ages of the individuals involved.

exclusive-provider organization (EPO) • a variation of a preferred-provider organization in which coverage is not provided outside the preferred-provider network, except in those infrequent cases where the network does not have an appropriate specialist

expected claims • the portion of premiums paid that the insurance company has anticipated will be necessary to pay claims during the experience period

experience period • the period subject to experience rating

experience rating • the practice by which the actual experience of a particular group is a factor in determining the premium the policyowner is charged

extended care facility • a health care facility for a person who no longer requires the full level of medical care provided by a hospital but does need a period of convalescence under supervised medical care

extension of benefits • a provision in a medical expense plan under which benefits are extended for any covered employee or dependent who is totally disabled at the time coverage would otherwise terminate. The disability must have resulted from an injury or illness that occurred while the person was covered under the group contract. The length of the extension generally ranges from 3 to 12 months.

facility-of-payment provision • a provision in a group life insurance contract under which the insurance company can pay a small specified amount to any person who incurred funeral or other expenses relating to the last illness or death of the person insured • a provision in a group life insurance contract under which the insurance company can pay periodic monthly proceeds to any person or institution who appears to have assumed the responsibility for the care, custody, or support of a minor beneficiary. This provision is only in effect until a claim is made by the beneficiary's guardian.

Family and Medical Leave Act • a federal law that requires employers with more than 50 employees within a 75-mile radius to allow employees to take up to 12 weeks of unpaid leave in any 12-month period, for the birth or adoption of a child; to care for a child, spouse, or parent with a serious health condition; or for the worker's own serious health condition that makes it impossible to perform a job. The employee must be allowed to return to an equivalent job, and health care benefits, but not pay or other employee benefits, must be continued during the period of the leave.

family deductible • a provision in a major medical plan that waives future deductibles for all family members once a specified aggregate dollar amount of medical expenses has been incurred or after a specified number of family members have satisfied their individual deductibles

family leave • an employer practice under which employees, within limits, may take personal time off without pay for reasons such as active military duty, extended vacations, honeymoons, education, the birth or adoption of a child, and the illness of the employee or a family member

Federal Employer's Liability Act • a federal law that provides workers' compensation benefits to railroad employees and employees aboard ships

Federal Employees Compensation Act • federal law that provides workers' compensation benefits to employees of the federal government and the District of Columbia

fee schedule • a list of covered benefits and the maximum fee that will be paid to the provider of benefits. Such a schedule is found in many surgical expense policies, dental policies, vision care plans, and group legal expense plans.

fellow-servant doctrine • a common-law defense available to employers under which a worker cannot collect if an injury resulted from a fellow worker's negligence

fictitious group insurance statute • a state regulation that prohibits the grouping of individual property and liability insurance risks in order to give them favorable treatment in underwriting, coverage, or rates

fiduciary • a person who exercises discretionary authority or control over an employee benefit plan's management and provides investment advice to the plan for compensation or has discretionary authority or responsibility in the plan's administration. ERISA requires that a fiduciary discharge his or her duties regarding the plan solely in the interest of the participants and their beneficiaries.

final premium rate • a manual rate after it has been applied to a specific group insurance case. It is then multiplied by the number of benefit units to obtain a premium for the group.

financial planning program • an employer-provided plan, traditionally limited to a small number of topics, to offer financial planning as a benefit to employees. Some firms provide benefits to members of middle management. Benefits include services or reimbursement for preparation of tax returns, estate planning, investment planning, and insurance planning.

first-dollar coverage • coverage for benefits without a deductible or coinsurance

501(c)(9) trust (VEBA) • a funding arrangement under which an employer can establish a trust to provide a benefit to employees because of death, medical expenses, disability, and unemployment. If the trust is properly designed in light of stringent IRS rules, the employer, within limits, can deduct contributions to the trust at the time they are made.

flat-benefits schedule • a benefit schedule under which the same amount of coverage is provided for all employees regardless of salary or position

flexible benefit plan • *See* cafeteria plan.

flexible funding • *See* cost-plus arrangement.

flexible spending account • a provision in a cafeteria plan that allows an employee to fund certain benefits on a before-tax basis by electing to take a salary reduction, which can then be used to fund the cost of any qualified benefits included in the plan. Benefits are paid from an employee's account as expenses are incurred, but monies in the account are forfeited if they are not used by the end of the plan year.

floating holiday • a holiday that can be taken at an employee's option. It is usually more like an additional vacation day since there is usually no requirement that it be taken on an actual holiday.

formulary • a list of preferred medicines for a specific medical condition

fully insured • an insured status under OASDI. This status requires one of the following: (1) 40 quarters of coverage or (2) credit for at least as many quarters (but a minimum of 6) of coverage as there are years elapsing after 1950 (or after the year in which age 21 is reached, if later) and before the year in which a person dies, becomes disabled, or reaches age 62, whichever occurs first.

gatekeeper PPO • a preferred-provider organization that requires a participant to select a primary care physician in the manner of an HMO subscriber. However, at the time medical service is needed, the participant can elect to go outside the PPO network.

grace period • a period specified in a group insurance contract (usually 31 days) during which a policyowner may pay any overdue premium without interest

group insurance • a method of providing employee benefits, characterized by a group contract, experience rating of large groups, and group underwriting

group-model HMO • a closed-panel HMO under which physicians and other medical personnel are employees of another legal entity that has a contractual relationship with the HMO to provide medical services for its subscribers

group representative • an employee of an insurance company who specializes in the selling and servicing of his or her company's group insurance products

group term carve-out • a practice by which coverage for certain employees under a group term life insurance plan is limited to the $50,000 that can be provided income tax free. Coverage in excess of $50,000 is then provided under some alternative arrangement, often a form of cash value life insurance.

group universal life insurance • a flexible-premium group life insurance policy that divides the pure protection and cash value accumulation into separate and distinct components. The interest rate credited to cash value accumulations can vary, but there is a minimum guarantee.

group variable universal life insurance • a group universal life insurance contract under which certificate holders can allocate net premiums to one or more of several investment accounts. The investment risk is borne by the certificate holders.

Health Insurance Portability and Accountability Act • federal legislation, passed in 1996, that reforms the health care system through numerous provisions. The act's primary purpose is to make insurance more available, particularly when an employed person changes jobs or becomes unemployed.

health insurance purchasing cooperative (HIPC) • an entity that acts as a broker between the purchasers and the providers of medical expense coverage

health maintenance organization (HMO) • a managed system of health care that provides a comprehensive array of medical services on a prepaid basis to voluntarily enrolled persons living within a specific geographic region. HMOs both finance health care and deliver health services. There is an emphasis on preventive care as well as cost control.

Health Maintenance Organization Act • a federal act in 1973 that introduced the concept of the federally qualified HMO. The act provided grants and loans to HMOs and also required many employers to offer the HMO as a dual option to its employees.

highly compensated employee • a class of employee against whom discrimination is prohibited if an employee benefit plan is to receive the most favorable income tax treatment. The term is defined differently in sections of the Internal Revenue Code that apply to different types of employee benefits. One definition applies to self-insured medical reimbursement plans, another definition applies to cafeteria plans, and a third definition in Sec. 414 applies to qualified retirement plans and numerous other types of benefits such as dependent-care assistance, no-additional-cost services, and educational assistance. *See* references in the index to specific definitions.

HIPAA • *See* Health Insurance Portability and Accountability Act.

HIPC • *See* health insurance purchasing cooperative.

HMO • *See* health maintenance organization.

home health care • care that is received at home and includes part-time skilled nursing care, speech therapy, physical or occupational therapy, part-time services from home health aides, and help from homemakers or chore workers

home health care benefits • benefits provided in a patient's home following hospitalization when a physician has ordered necessary part-time nursing care. Benefits are often provided for (1) nursing care; (2) physical, occupational, and speech therapy; and (3) medical supplies and equipment.

hospice • a health care facility or service providing benefits to terminally ill persons. The emphasis is on easing the physical and psychological pain associated with death rather than on curing a medical condition.

hospital expense benefits • benefits provided under a medical expense plan for hospital charges incurred. Benefits are for room and board and other charges for certain services and supplies ordered by a physician during a person's hospital confinement.

incontestability provision • a provision in a group insurance contract stating that, except for the nonpayment of premiums, the validity of the contract cannot be contested after it has been in force for a specified period, usually either one or 2 years

incurred claims • those claims attributable to the recently ended period of coverage that was subject to experience rating equal to (1) claims paid during the experience period, less (2) claims paid during the experience period but incurred during the prior period, plus (3) an estimate of claims incurred during the experience period but to be paid in future periods

indemnity benefits • benefits expressed in terms of dollar maximums

individual employer group • the most common type of eligible group for group insurance purposes. The employer is the policyowner and may be a corporation, a partnership, or a sole proprietorship.

individual equity • the principle under which benefits for any individual are actuarially related to contributions made by that individual

individual practice association • an HMO under which participating physicians practice individually or in small groups in their own offices. In many cases these physicians also accept non-HMO patients on a traditional fee-for-service basis.

initial deductible • a deductible that must be satisfied before any benefits are paid under a medical expense plan

integrated deductible • a relatively large deductible under a major medical plan, with any amounts paid under basic coverages available to satisfy the deductible

integrated dental plan • a dental insurance plan incorporated into a major medical contract

interactive voice-response system • a telephone system for administering employee benefits that allows employees to obtain information about benefit plans and possibly to make benefit changes and elections

intermediate care • care involving occasional nursing and rehabilitative care that must be based on a doctor's orders and can be performed only by or under the supervision of skilled medical personnel

JCAHO • *See* Joint Commission on Accreditation of Healthcare Organizations.

joinder agreement • a contract between a multiple-employer welfare arrangement and an employer that spells out the relationship between the MEWA and the employer and specifies the coverages to which the employer has subscribed

Joint Commission on Accreditation of Healthcare Organizations (JCAHO) • the primary organization that accredits hospitals and other types of medical care facilities. JCAHO is also starting to accredit managed care organizations.

key employee • a participant in an employee benefit plan who, at any time during the plan year or the preceding 4 plan years, is or has been any of the following: (1) an officer who earns more than 50 percent of the Internal Revenue Code limit on the amount of the benefits payable by a defined-benefit plan, (2) one of the 10 employees owning the largest interest in a firm and having an annual compensation from the firm of more than $30,000, (3) a more-than-5-percent owner of a firm, or (4) a more-than-one-percent owner of a firm who earns over $150,000 per year.

labor union group • an eligible group for purposes of providing benefits to members. The policyowner is the labor union. Because of federal prohibitions, premiums come either solely from union funds or partially from union funds and members' contributions.

length-of-service schedule • a benefit schedule under which the amount of coverage is a function of an employee's length of service

level commission schedule • a commission schedule that has the same commission rates for both the first year and any renewal years

life-cycle benefits • a benefit plan that takes into account the fact that different persons have different benefit needs and that these needs will change over the course of a person's life

lifestyle management program • a wellness program primarily designed to encourage employees and often their dependents to modify behavior so that they will lead healthier lives. Examples include programs for smoking cessation, weight reduction, and stress management.

limited-liability arrangement • a reserve-reduction arrangement for long-term disability income insurance. The employer purchases a one-year contract in which the insurer agrees to pay claims for that year only, even for employees who are already disabled.

major medical insurance • a medical insurance plan designed to provide substantial protection against catastrophic medical expenses. There are few exclusions and limitations, but deductibles and coinsurance are commonly used.

managed care • a process to deliver cost-effective health care without sacrificing quality or access. Common characteristics include controlled access to providers, comprehensive case management, preventive care, risk sharing, and high-quality care.

managed competition plan • a philosophy for national health insurance based on the idea that competition for medical expense insurance should be based on price rather than on the risk characteristics of those needing coverage

mandated benefits • benefits that states require be included in group insurance contracts issued in the state

manual rating • the process of determining a premium rate on the basis of broad classes of group insurance business, rather than on a particular group's claims

manual premium rate • the rate that is quoted in an insurance company's rate book

mass-marketed individual insurance • *See* voluntary benefits.

master contract • a contract issued to someone other than the persons insured that provides benefits to a group of individuals who have a specific relationship to the policyowner

maternity management • a cost-containment technique that identifies high-risk pregnancies and provides proper medical treatment

maturity value benefit • a provision in a group term life insurance plan under which the face amount of a totally disabled employee's life insurance benefit will be paid to the employee in a lump sum or in monthly installments

McCarran-Ferguson Act (Public Law 15) • a federal law that exempts insurance from certain federal regulations to the extent that individual states actually regulate insurance. It also provides that most other federal laws are not applicable to insurance unless they are specifically related to the business of insurance.

medicaid • a federal/state program to provide medical expense benefits for certain classes of low-income individuals and families

medical child support order • a court judgment, decree, or order that (1) provides for child support for the child of a group plan participant or provides benefit coverage to such a child, is ordered under state domestic relations law, and relates to benefits under a plan or (2) enforces a state medical support law enacted under medicaid rules

medical savings account • an alternative to first-dollar coverage under a medical expense plan. An employee is given medical expense coverage that has a high deductible, and money is deposited into the medical spending account so that the employee can pay for expenses below the deductible amount. Any monies not used at the end of the year are paid to the employee.

medical screening program • a wellness program designed to discover and treat medical conditions before they become severe and result in large medical expense, disability, or death claims. Common examples are screening for cholesterol, high blood pressure, and breast cancer.

medicare • the health insurance portion of the social security program that is available to persons aged 65 or older and limited categories of persons under age 65

medicare carve-out • an employer-provided medical expense plan for persons over age 65 under which benefits are reduced to the extent that they are payable under medicare for the same expense

medicare cost plan • an HMO under which medicare participants can receive care from the HMO or go outside the HMO network for services as desired

medicare health care prepayment plan • an HMO that gives medicare participants limited services, usually those available under part B of medicare. Participants must go outside of the HMO network for other services.

medicare risk plan • an HMO under which medicare recipients can elect coverage in lieu of the regular medicare program

medicare secondary rules • regulations that specify when medicare will be secondary to an employer's medical expense plan for disabled employees and active employees aged 65 or older

medicare select policy • a private insurance policy available to medicare participants under an experimental program in some states. The policy provides benefits that are comparable to those available to a participant under medicare, supplemented by a medigap policy.

medicare supplement • an employer-provided medical expense plan for employees aged 65 or older under which benefits are provided for certain specific expenses not covered under medicare. These may include a portion of expenses not paid by medicare because of deductibles, coinsurance, or copayments and certain expenses excluded by medicare, such as prescription drugs.

Mental Health Parity Act • federal legislation that requires annual and lifetime dollar limits on mental health benefits to be on par with limits that apply to other medical conditions. The act applies to employers with more than 50 employees.

MET • *See* multiple-employer trust.

MEWA • *See* multiple-employer welfare arrangement.

minimum-premium plan • an alternative funding arrangement under which the employer assumes the financial responsibility for paying claims up to a specified level, such as 90 percent of estimated claims. The actual payment of claims is made with employer funds by the insurance company, which acts as an agent of the employer. When claims exceed the specified level, the balance is paid from the insurance company's own funds.

misstatement-of-age provision • a provision in a group life insurance policy stating that the premium will be adjusted to reflect the true age of the individual if the age has been misstated. Unlike individual life insurance, there is no adjustment in the benefits that will be paid.

mixed-model HMO • an HMO that has characteristics of two or more of the basic HMO forms. It occurs most often when one HMO purchases a different type of HMO or when an HMO expands its capacity or geographic region by adding additional medical care providers under a different type of arrangement.

model laws • sample legislation promulgated by the NAIC that individual states at their discretion can adopt either as written or with changes

modular plan • a type of cafeteria plan in which an employee has a choice among several predesigned benefit packages. The employee cannot pick and choose specific benefits.

money-purchase plan • a payroll deduction plan under which the amounts of coverage are sold on the basis of what can be purchased with a given premium

morbidity • the sickness and disability rates of a group of persons covered under an employee benefit plan

mortality • the death rate of a group of persons covered under a benefit plan

multiple-employer trust (MET) • a fully insured multiple-employer welfare arrangement

multiple-employer welfare arrangement (MEWA) • an eligible group for purposes of providing benefits to participants. It is a legal entity in the form of a trust, which is the policyowner, and may be sponsored by an insurance company or some other person or organization.

multiple-option plan • a single medical expense contract that combines two or more of the following: a traditional medical expense plan, an HMO, or a PPO. Such arrangements simplify administration and allow the entire plan to be subject to experience rating.

NAIC • *See* National Association of Insurance Commissioners.

National Association of Insurance Commissioners (NAIC) • an association composed of state insurance regulatory officials that has as its goal the promotion of uniformity in legislation and administrative rules affecting insurance

National Committee for Quality Assurance (NCQA) • an independent nonprofit organization that represents managed care organizations and the purchasers of managed care. It accredits managed care organizations and has established a quality measurement program to help consumers evaluate the quality of care provided by managed care plans.

NCQA • *See* National Committee for Quality Assurance.

negotiated trusteeship • an eligible group for group insurance purposes. It is formed as a result of collective bargaining over benefits between a union and the employers of the union members. The policyowner is a trust with an equal number of trustees from the employers and the union.

net premium rate • the amount necessary to support the cost of expected claims

network-model HMO • an HMO that contracts with two or more independent groups of physicians to provide medical services to its subscribers

Newborns' and Mothers' Health Protection Act • federal legislation that establishes minimum hospital stays for maternity that must be covered by insurance carriers

no-additional-cost service • a service an employer can provide to an employee without any adverse income tax consequences. The service must normally be provided in the employer's line of business in which the employee actually works, and the employer must not incur any significant additional cost or revenue in providing the service.

no-gag rule • legislation that prevents managed care organizations from including provisions in contracts with doctors that prevent them from discussing with patients treatment options that may not be covered under their plans or from referring extremely ill patients for specialized care outside their plans

no-loss no-gain legislation • a state law that prohibits a new insurance company from denying (by using a preexisting-conditions clause) the continuing claims of persons that were covered under a prior group insurance plan if these claims would otherwise be covered under the new contract

noncontributory plan • an employee benefit plan under which the employer pays the entire cost of the coverage

nondiscrimination rules • rules that deny favorable treatment to employee benefit plans that do not provide equitable benefits to a large cross section of employees. Not all plans are subject to nondiscrimination rules, and different rules may apply to different types of benefits.

nonoccupational disability laws • *See* temporary disability laws.

nonscheduled dental plan • a dental plan under which benefits are paid on the basis of reasonable-and-customary charges. However, there may be a schedule of covered dental services.

OASDHI • the old age, survivors, disability, and heath insurance program of the federal government, commonly referred to as social security

OASDI • the old-age, survivors, and disability insurance portion of the social security program

open-ended HMO • an HMO that allows a subscriber to go outside the HMO network of medical care providers

open-panel plan • a benefit plan under which covered persons may obtain services from any practitioner or may have to select one from a limited list of practitioners who have agreed to the plan's terms and conditions

outsourcing • the process of contracting with third parties to perform functions associated with employee benefit administration

party-in-interest • a person who is subject to the prohibited-transactions provisions of ERISA. A party-in-interest includes any plan fiduciary, any counsel or employee of the plan, any person providing services to the plan, any employer of employees covered under the plan, and any relative of a party-in-interest.

payroll deduction plan • *See* voluntary benefits.

pension schedule • a benefit schedule found in group life insurance plans under which the amount of coverage is a function of an employee's projected pension at retirement

per-cause deductible • a deductible amount that must be satisfied for each separate accident or illness before major medical benefits are paid

percentage participation • the percentage of covered medical expenses that will not be paid by a medical expense plan and that must be paid by a person receiving benefits

per diem reimbursement • the practice of reimbursing hospitals on the basis of a set amount for every day a patient is hospitalized, regardless of what the actual charges might be

persistency • the length of time a group insurance contract will remain on the insurance company's books

pharmacy benefit manager • an organization that administers prescription drug plans on behalf of self-funded employers, third-party administrators, HMOs, PPOs, insurance companies, and other providers of prescription drug benefits

physician-hospital organization (PHO) • a legal entity, formed by one or more physicians' groups and hospitals, that negotiates, markets, and contracts the services of the physicians and hospitals

physicians' visits expense benefits • benefits for fees of attending physicians other than surgeons. Benefits may be provided for hospital visits only but may also be provided for home and office visits.

PIA • *See* primary insurance amount.

point-of-service plan • a hybrid arrangement that combines aspects of a traditional medical expense plan with an HMO or a PPO. At the time of medical treatment, a participant can elect whether to receive treatment within the plan's network or outside the network.

position schedule • a benefit schedule under which the amount of coverage is based on an employee's position within a firm

PPO • *See* preferred-provider organization.

preadmission certification • a requirement under many medical expense plans that a covered person or his or her physician obtain prior authorization for any nonemergency hospitalization

preadmission testing • the practice of performing diagnostic tests and X rays on an outpatient basis prior to hospitalization

predetermination-of-benefits provision • a provision in a dental insurance contract under which there is a requirement for a pretreatment review of certain dental services, generally when they exceed some specified dollar amount

preexisting-conditions provision • a provision that excludes coverage, but possibly only for a limited period of time, for a physical and/or mental condition for which a covered person in a benefit plan received treatment or medical advice within a specified time period prior to becoming eligible for coverage

preferred-provider organization (PPO) • groups of health care providers that contract with employers, insurance companies, union trust funds, third-party administrators, or others to provide medical care services at a reduced fee. PPOs may be organized by the providers themselves or by organizations such as insurance companies, the Blues, or groups of employers.

Pregnancy Discrimination Act • *See* the Civil Rights Act (pregnancy provision).

premium • the total price that a group insurance policyowner will pay for the entire amount of coverage purchased

premium-conversion plan • a provision in a cafeteria plan under which an employee can elect a before-tax salary reduction to pay his or her premium contribution to an employer-sponsored health or other welfare benefit plan

premium-delay arrangement • an alternative funding method that allows the employer to defer payment of monthly premiums for some time period beyond the usual 30-day grace period

premium-only plan • *See* premium-conversion plan.

premium rate • the price for each unit of group insurance benefit, such as each $1,000 of life insurance

preretirement-counseling program • an employer-provided benefit to make employees aware of the pitfalls that can result if they are unprepared for retirement. Benefits are usually in the form of group meetings that focus on such issues as financial planning, living arrangements after retirement, health issues for retirees, and use of free time after retirement.

prescription drug expense benefits • basic medical expense benefits for the cost of prescription drugs. These benefits are often separate from other medical expense coverage because of techniques that can be used to contain costs.

primary insurance amount (PIA) • the amount a worker will receive under social security if he or she retires at age 65 or becomes disabled. It is also the amount on which all other social security income benefits are based.

probationary period • a period of time that must be satisfied before an employee is eligible for coverage under a group benefit plan

prohibited transaction • an activity specified in ERISA that may not be engaged in by a party-in-interest to a benefit plan. Prohibited transactions include the selling or leasing of property; the lending of money; the furnishing of goods, services, or facilities; and the transfer of any asset to or for the use of a party-in-interest.

prospecting • the first step in the process of marketing employee benefits. It involves persuading the employer or the employer's representative to accept a proposal from the provider of employee benefit products or services.

prospective utilization review • the process of analyzing a case to see what type of medical treatment is necessary. Preadmission authorization, second surgical opinions, and predetermination of dental benefits are examples.

qualified benefits • benefits (other than cash) that can be provided under a cafeteria plan. They include any welfare benefits excluded from taxation under the Internal Revenue Code except scholarships and fellowships, transportation benefits, educational assistance, no-additional-cost services, employee discounts and *de minimis* fringe benefits.

qualified long-term care insurance contract • a long-term care contract that meets specified standards and qualifies for favorable tax treatment under the Health Insurance Portability and Accountability Act.

qualified plan award • an award for service, productivity, or safety achievement that can be excludible from an employee's income. However, the total amount excludible cannot exceed $1,600 per year for any employee, and the awards must be provided under a permanent written plan that does not discriminate in favor of officers, shareholders, or highly compensated employees.

qualified transportation fringe • employer-provided benefit for transportation to work and parking. Employees may receive this benefit tax free, within limits, as long as certain rules are adhered to.

quarters of coverage • the basis on which eligibility for benefits under the OASDI portion of social security is determined. Credit for up to 4 quarters of coverage may be earned in any calendar year.

radiation therapy expense benefits • benefits to cover the cost of radiation therapy when it is administered on an outpatient basis. Benefits are provided for the administration of the therapy, the use of facilities, and any materials used in preparation for therapy.

rate making • the process of pricing group insurance and employee benefit products

rating basis • the basis on which group insurance rates will be determined, involving decisions on the benefit unit to use, the extent to which rates will be refined by factors affecting claims, and the frequency with which premiums will be paid

reasonable-and-customary charge • a charge that falls within the range of fees normally charged for a given procedure by physicians with similar training and experience in a geographic region. It is usually based on some percentile of the range of charges for specific medical procedures.

rehabilitation benefit • a benefit under workers' compensation laws or disability income plans that provides rehabilitative services for disabled workers. Benefits may be given for medical rehabilitation and for vocational rehabilitation, including training, counseling, and job placement.

relative-value schedule • a variation of a fee schedule in surgical expense plans. The value of each surgical procedure is expressed in unit values that are relative to each other. The relative value is multiplied by a dollar-conversion factor to determine the maximum benefit that will be paid.

reserve-reduction arrangement • an alternative funding method under which the employer is allowed at any given time to retain an amount of the annual premium equal to the claim reserve

respite-care benefits • benefits under long-term care insurance that provide reimbursement for occasional full-time care at home for a person who is receiving home health care. These benefits enable family members (or other persons) who are providing much of the home care to take a needed break.

retention • the excess of premiums paid over claims payments and dividends

retired lives reserve • a fund established during employees' working years to pay all or a part of the cost of group term insurance after retirement

retrospective rate credit • a refund given by stock insurance companies to groups that are experience rated and have had better claims experience than anticipated

retrospective-rating arrangement • an alternative funding method under which the employer pays an initial premium that is less than what would be justified by the expected claims for the year. However, if claims plus the insurance company's retention exceed the initial premium, the employer will be called upon to pay an additional amount at the end of the policy year. There is a cap put on the employer's additional payment, above which the insurance company assumes the risk.

retrospective utilization review • an analysis of a case after the fact to see if the medical treatment performed was appropriate. It may lead to the denial of claims, but its main purpose is to monitor trends so that future actions can be taken in high-cost situations.

risk charge • a factor in the calculation of rates for group insurance benefits. It represents a contribution to an insurance company's contingency reserve as a cushion against unanticipated and catastrophic amounts of claims.

salary continuation plan • an uninsured arrangement to replace lost income for a limited period of time, usually starting on the first day of disability

salary-reduction-only plan • a cafeteria plan that consists solely of one or both types of before-tax salary reductions that can be used in a cafeteria plan—a premium-conversion plan or a flexible spending account

scheduled dental plan • a dental plan under which benefits are paid up to the amount specified in a fee schedule

scheduled legal expense plan • a legal expense plan that specifies types of legal expenses for which benefits will be paid

second-injury fund • a state fund whose purpose is to encourage employers to hire workers with a permanent physical impairment from a prior work-related injury. If the employee suffers a subsequent work-related injury, the employer is only responsible for providing benefits equal to those that would have been provided to a worker who had not suffered the first injury. Any remaining benefits are provided by the second-injury fund.

second surgical opinion • a cost-containment strategy under which covered persons are encouraged or required to obtain the opinion of another physician after certain categories of surgery have been recommended. If a second opinion is mandatory, benefits are reduced if the second opinion is not obtained. Benefits are usually provided for the cost of a third opinion if the opinions of the first two physicians are in disagreement.

Section 79 • the Internal Revenue Code provision that provides favorable tax treatment to employer contributions for life insurance that qualifies as group term insurance

self-funding • a method by which an employer can finance the cost of an employee benefit plan. In the method's purest sense, the employer pays benefits from current revenue, administers all aspects of the plan, and bears the risk that benefit payments will exceed those expected.

self-insurance • *See* self-funding.

service benefits • medical expense benefits expressed in terms of services that will be provided by hospitals or physicians rather than in terms of dollar maximums

settlement option • the methods by which proceeds from a group life insurance contract can be received. In general, proceeds are payable in a lump sum unless the insured or the beneficiary has selected an optional form of settlement.

shared funding • *See* specific stop-loss coverage.

sick-leave plan • *See* salary continuation plan.

single-payer plan • an approach to national health insurance under which everyone is automatically covered by a single program run by the government

skilled-nursing care • daily nursing and rehabilitative care that can be performed only by or under the supervision of skilled medical personnel and that must be based on doctors' orders

skilled-nursing facility • *See* extended care facility.

Small Employer Health Insurance Availability Model Act • an NAIC-model act designed to promote medical expense coverage for small employers. Most states have adopted some form of the act.

social adequacy • a basic principle of social insurance programs under which benefits are designed to provide a minimum floor of income to all beneficiaries regardless of their economic status

social insurance • government-run or -regulated insurance programs designed primarily to solve major social problems that affect a large portion of society. Distinguishing characteristics are compulsory employment-related coverage, partial or total employer financing, benefits prescribed by law, benefits as a matter of right, and emphasis on social adequacy.

social security • the term commonly used to identify the old-age, survivors, disability, and health insurance (OASDHI) program of the federal government.

specific stop-loss coverage • a stop-loss arrangement under which the insurance company reimburses the employer to the extent that claims for any person exceed a specified dollar amount during a given time period

staff-model HMO • an HMO that owns its own facilities and hires its own physicians. It may also own hospitals, laboratories, or pharmacies, or it may contract for these services.

standard commission schedule • a commission schedule that has high first-year commission rates and lower rates in renewal years

stop-loss coverage • protection for employers who self-fund benefits. Under this arrangement, an insurance company provides coverage if claims exceed some specified limit during a set period of time. It may apply to aggregate claims or claims on each individual employee.

successive beneficiary provision • a provision found in group term insurance contracts for the payment of proceeds if no beneficiary has been named or if all the beneficiaries have died before the insured. This provision gives the insurance company the right to pay the proceeds at their option to any one or more of the following survivors of the insured person: spouse, children, parents, brothers and sisters, or executor of the employee's estate.

summary annual report • a brief description of a plan's annual return/report (Form 5500) that must be automatically provided to each plan participant within 9 months after the end of a plan year.

summary of material modification • a document required by ERISA that must be automatically provided to plan participants and the Department of Labor within 210 days after the end of a plan year in which a material change was made to the plan

summary plan description • a detailed report about an employee benefit plan that ERISA requires a plan administrator to give plan participants and the Department of Labor within 120 days after the plan's adoption

supplemental accident expense benefits • benefits in some medical expense plans to cover expenses associated with accidents to the extent that these expenses are not otherwise covered

supplemental unemployment benefit plan • a plan established in collective bargaining agreements under which employers are required to supplement state unemployment insurance benefits for unemployed workers

supplemental life insurance • additional life insurance that all or certain classes of employees may purchase. Coverage is generally contributory and may be either incorporated into a basic group life insurance contract or contained in a separate contract.

supplemental major medical plan • a major medical plan that is coordinated with various basic medical expense coverages

surgical expense benefits • medical expense benefits for physicians' charges associated with surgical procedures

survivor income benefit insurance • a group life insurance plan designed to relate benefits to the actual needs of each employee's survivors. Benefits are paid in the form of periodic income to specific dependents who survive the employee, and no death benefits are paid unless an employee has qualified survivors.

Table I • *See* Uniform Premium Table I.

temporary disability laws • programs in a few states that require employers to provide short-term disability income benefits to employees for non-work-related disabilities. These laws are often referred to as nonoccupational disability laws.

terminal report • a report that ERISA requires be filed with the Internal Revenue Service for an employee welfare benefit plan that has been terminated. This report must be given to plan participants upon request.

third-party administrator • a person or organization hired to provide certain administrative services to employee benefit plans

trade association group • an eligible group for purposes of providing benefits to employees. It usually consists of employers in the same industry or type of business. The master contract may be issued directly to the trade association or to a trust that has been established.

24-hour coverage • a single benefit plan that responds to injuries whether they occur on or off the job. In effect, this arrangement combines medical expense coverage, disability income coverage, and workers' compensation benefits into a single plan.

underwriting • the process by which an insurance applicant is evaluated, decisions are made on the applicant's acceptability for insurance, and a rating basis is established

unemployment insurance • joint federal and state programs to provide income benefits to unemployed workers who meet the specific program requirements. In most states these programs are financed entirely by employer contributions.

Uniform Premium Table I • a table incorporated into IRS regulations for Section 79 that is used to determine imputed income for group term insurance in excess of $50,000

United States Longshoremen's and Harbor Workers' Act • a federal law that provides workers' compensation benefits for stevedores, longshoremen, and workers who repair ships

universal access • the availability of medical expense coverage to all persons, even though they may not actually purchase coverage

universal coverage • a goal of many national health insurance programs whose purpose is to see that all persons have coverage for medical expenses

utilization review • the process of reviewing the appropriateness and quality of care provided to patients. It may be conducted on a prospective, concurrent, or retroactive basis.

Utilization Review Accreditation Commission • *See* American Accreditiation HealthCare Commission, Inc.

VEBA • *See* 501(c) (9) trust.

vision care expense benefits • benefits for vision care expenses that are not usually covered under other medical expense plans. Benefits are provided for the cost of eye examinations and eyeglasses or contact lenses.

voluntary benefits • a plan offered to employees under which they may purchase individual insurance coverage with premiums paid through payroll deductions by the employer

voluntary employees' beneficiary association (VEBA) • *See* 501(c)(9) trust.

waiting period • a period of time that an employee must be disabled before benefits commence under certain employee benefit plans, such as disability income insurance, social security, and workers' compensation insurance. Waiting periods for disabilities resulting from accidents may differ from waiting periods for disabilities resulting from sickness.

waiver-of-premium provision • a provision in group insurance plans under which coverage is continued without the payment of premiums as long as an employee is totally disabled

welfare benefit • the term used to describe employee benefits other than retirement benefits

wellness program • an employer-provided program to promote the well-being of employees and sometimes their dependents. A program may be designed to discover and treat medical conditions before they become severe and/or change employees' lifestyles to eliminate possible causes of future medical problems.

workers' compensation laws • laws enacted in all states under which employers are required to provide benefits to employees for losses resulting from work-related accidents or diseases. Benefits include medical care, disability income, income for survivors, and rehabilitative services.

Index